中国教育统计年鉴

EDUCATIONAL STATISTICS YEARBOOK OF CHINA

2013

中华人民共和国
教育部发展规划司

DEPARTMENT OF DEVELOPMENT & PLANNING
MINISTRY OF EDUCATION
THE PEOPLE'S REPUBLIC OF CHINA

图书在版编目(CIP)数据

中国教育统计年鉴. 2013/中华人民共和国教育部发展规划司编. —北京：人民教育出版社，2014. 9
ISBN 978-7-107-29149-4

Ⅰ.①中… Ⅱ.①中… Ⅲ.①教育统计—统计资料—中国—2013—年鉴 Ⅳ. ①G526. 6 - 54

中国版本图书馆 CIP 数据核字(2014)第 222560 号

人民教育出版社出版发行
网址：http://www.pep.com.cn
山东临沂新华印刷物流集团有限责任公司印装 全国新华书店经销
2014 年 9 月第 1 版 2014 年 9 月第 1 次印刷
开本：787 毫米×1 092 毫米 1/16 印张：45. 75
字数：960 千字 印数：0 001 ~1 200 册
定价：96. 00 元

《中国教育统计年鉴》编辑委员会名单

说　明

《中国教育统计年鉴》（2013）是一本全面反映中华人民共和国教育事业发展情况的资料性年鉴，是由教育部发展规划司根据全国各省、自治区、直辖市教育委员会、教育厅填报的学校基层报表数字整理汇编而成的。教育部教育管理信息中心承担了数据的计算机处理汇总工作。

本年鉴包括以下部分：综合部分、高等教育、中等教育、初等教育、幼儿教育、特殊教育、全国各级各类学校的分布情况、办学条件、科学研究等。

本年鉴是各有关部门研究教育改革和发展的必备资料工具书，是教育界各机关、学校指导部门制定教育计划、指导教育改革必不可少的依据。

本年鉴所列资料，暂缺教育经费2012年数字；未含台湾省、香港特别行政区和澳门特别行政区的数字；凡未注明年份的均为2013年的数字。

Notes from the Compiler

The Educational Statistics Yearbook of China for 2013 is an informational yearbook com- prehensively reflecting the development of the educational undertaking of the People's Republic of China, and it was compiled by the Department of Development and Planning of Ministry of Education, based on the synthetic statistical returns relating to schools of various types and levels completed by the Educational Commissions (or the Bureaus of Education) of the provincial governments and the goverments of various autonomous regions and municipalities directly under the State Council All data were processed and calculated using Computers by the Educational Management Information Center of Ministry of Education.

The yearbook is composed of the following parts: summary tables, higher education, secondary education, primary education, pre-primary education, special education, geographical distribution of schools by type and level, Physical Facilities, Scientific Research Activities.

The yearbook is a requisite reference for all departments concerned with the study of educational reform and development, and provides indispensable factual information to the educational community (circles), the state organs, and all supervisory bodies of education (schools) engaged in curricular development and the guidance of educational reform.

The yearbook lacks the data of Education Expenditure, Taiwan Province. Hong Kong Special Administrative Region and Macao Special Administrative Region. Data in tables are for 2013, unless otherwise notified.

备　注

自2011年起，我部对教育事业统计报表进行了全面改革，贯彻实施了国家统计局首次颁布的《统计用城乡划分代码》。新的城乡划分标准，将原来的城市、县镇、农村的三个分类调整为三大类七小类，即城区（含主城区、城乡结合区）、镇区（含镇中心区、镇乡结合区、特殊区域）、乡村（含乡中心区、村庄）。

2013年全国教育事业发展统计公报[1]

中华人民共和国教育部

2014年5月

2013年，在党中央国务院坚强领导下，教育优先发展战略地位进一步落实，教育系统全面贯彻落实教育规划纲要，努力推进教育事业健康持续发展，着力促进教育公平、调整教育结构、提高教育质量，在培养优秀人才、服务经济社会发展等方面取得了新成绩，为经济社会发展提供了有力的人才保障和智力支持。

一、学前教育

全国共有幼儿园19.86万所，比上年增加1.73万所，在园幼儿（包括附设班）3894.69万人，比上年增加208.93万人。幼儿园园长和教师共188.51万人，比上年增加20.76万人。学前教育毛入园率[2]达到67.5%，比上年提高3个百分点。

二、义务教育

全国共有义务教育阶段学校26.63万所，比上年减少1.55万所。全国义务教育阶段共招生3191.44万人；在校生1.38亿人；专任教师906.56万人；九年义务教育巩固率[3]92.3%。

1. 小学

全国共有小学21.35万所，比上年减少1.51万所；招生1695.36万人，比上年减少19.31万人；在校生9360.55万人，比上年减少335.35万人；毕业生1581.06万人，比上年减少60.50万人。小学学龄儿童净入学率[4]达到99.71%；其中，男女童净入学率分别为99.70%和99.72%，女童高于男童0.02个百分点。

小学教职工[5]549.49万人，比上年减少4.36万人；专任教师558.46万人，比上年减少823人。专任教师学历合格率[6]99.83%，比上年提高0.02个百分点。生师比16.76:1，与上年的17.36:1有所改善。

普通小学（含教学点）校舍建筑面积62064.85万平方米，比上年增长3002.92万平方米。设施设备配备达标的学校比例[7]情况分别为：体育运动场（馆）面积达标学校比例51.44%，体育器械配备达标学校比例52.13%，音乐器械配备达标学校比例50.13%，美术器械配备达标学校比例50.09%，数学自然实验仪器达标学校比例54.19%。

2. 初中

全国共有初中学校5.28万所（其中职业初中40所），比上年减少412所。招生1496.09万人，比上年减少74.68万人；在校生4440.12万人，比上年减少322.94万人；毕业生1561.55万人，比上年减少99.23万人。初中阶段毛入学率104.1%，比上年提升2.0个百分点。初中毕业生升学率91.2%，比上年提高2.8个百分点。

初中教职工392.88万人，比上年减少1.03万人；专任教师348.10万人，比上年减少2.34万人。初中专任教师学历合格率99.28%，比上年提高0.16个百分点。生师比12.76∶1，比上年的13.59∶1有所改善。

初中校舍建筑面积50079.41万平方米，比上年增长2497.35万平方米。设施设备配备达标的学校比例情况分别为：体育运动场（馆）面积达标学校比例69.68%，体育器械配备达标学校比例72.84%，音乐器械配备达标学校比例70.34%，美术器械配备达标学校比例70.04%，理科实验仪器达标学校比例77.57%。

3. 进城务工人员随迁子女和农村留守儿童

全国义务教育阶段在校生中进城务工人员随迁子女[8]共1277.17万人。其中，在小学就读930.85万人，在初中就读346.31万人。

全国义务教育阶段在校生中农村留守儿童[9]共2126.75万人。其中，在小学就读1440.47万人，在初中就读686.28万人。

三、特殊教育

全国共有特殊教育学校1933所，比上年增加80所；特殊教育学校共有专任教师4.57万人。全国共招收特殊教育学生6.60万人，比上年增加278人；在校生36.81万人，比上年减少1.06万人。其中，视力残疾学生4.01万人，听力残疾学生8.92万人，智力残疾学生18.50万人，其他残疾学生5.38万人。特殊教育毕业生5.07万人，比上年增加0.21万人。

普通小学、初中随班就读和附设特教班招收的学生3.50万人，在校生19.08万人，分别占特殊教育招生总数和在校生总数的53.12%和51.84%。

四、高中阶段教育

全国高中阶段教育[10]共有学校2.62万所，比上年减少643所；招生1497.45万人，比上年减少101.29万人；在校学生4369.92万人，比上年减少225.36万人。高中阶段毛入学率86.0%，比上年提高1.0个百分点。

1. 普通高中

全国普通高中1.34万所，比上年减少157所；招生822.70万人，比上年减少21.91万人，降低2.59%；在校生2435.88万人，比上年减少31.29万人，降低1.27%；毕业生798.98万人，比上年增加7.47万人，增长0.94%。

普通高中教职工247.36万人，比上年增加1.10万人；专任教师162.90万人，比上年增加3.40万人，生师比14.95∶1，比上年的15.47∶1有所改善；专任教师学历合格率96.80%，比上年提高 0.36 个百分点。

普通高中共有校舍建筑面积 43560.14 万平方米，比上年增长 1313.49 万平方米。普通高中设施设备配备达标的学校比例情况分别为：体育运动场（馆）面积达标学校比例 82.86 %，体育器械配备达标学校比例 84.67%，音乐器械配备达标学校比例 82.52%，美术器械配备达标学校比例 82.94%，理科实验仪器达标学校比例 86.02%。

2. 成人高中

全国成人高中 611 所，比上年减少 85 所；在校生 11.07 万人，比上年减少 3.35 万人；毕业生 10.40 万人，比上年减少 1.23 万人。成人高中教职工 6061 人，比上年减少 1282 人；专任教师 4618 人，比上年减少 1183 人。

3. 中等职业教育

全国中等职业教育[11]共有学校 1.23 万所，比上年减少 401 所。其中，普通中等专业学校 3577 所，比上年减少 104 所；职业高中 4267 所，比上年减少 250 所；技工学校 2882 所，比上年减少 19 所；成人中等专业学校 1536 所，比上年减少 28 所。

中等职业教育招生 674.76 万人，比上年减少 79.38 万人，占高中阶段教育招生总数的 45.06%。其中，普通中专招生 271.47 万人，比上年减少 5.89 万人；职业高中招生 183.53 万人，比上年减少 30.37 万人；技工学校招生 133.50 万人，比上年减少 23.56 万人；成人中专招生 86.26 万人，比上年减少 19.55 万人。

中等职业教育在校生 1922.97 万人，比上年减少 190.72 万人，占高中阶段教育在校生总数的 44.00%。其中，普通中专在校生 772.18 万人，比上年减少 40.38 万人；职业高中在校生 534.22 万人，比上年减少 88.83 万人；技工学校在校生 386.59 万人，比上年减少 37.22 万人；成人中专在校生 229.98 万人，比上年减少 24.29 万人。

中等职业教育毕业生 674.44 万人，比上年减少 4550 人。其中，普通中专毕业生 265.21 万人，比上年减少 1053 人；职业高中毕业生 204.52 万人，比上年减少 12.92 万人；技工学校毕业生 116.88 万人，比上年减少 3.63 万人；成人中专毕业生 87.83 万人，比上年增加 16.20 万人。

中等职业教育学校共有教职工 115.34 万人，比上年减少 3.60 万人。其中，普通中等专业学校教职工 41.93 万人，比上年减少 1.13 万人；职业高中教职工 37.54 万人，比上年减少 1.89 万人；技工学校教职工 26.94 万人，比上年增加 1337 人；成人中等专业学校教职工 7.27 万人，比上年减少 4767 人。

中等职业教育学校共有专任教师 86.79 万人，比上年减少 1.30 万人，生师比[12]22.97:1，比上年的 24.19:1 有所改善。其中，普通中等专业学校专任教师 30.36 万人，比上年减少 1979 人；职业高中专任教师 30.14 万人，比上年减少 1.03 万人；技工学校专任教师 19.92 万人，比上年增加 2298 人；成人中等专业学校专任教师 5.20 万人，比上年减少 2186 人。

五、高等教育

全国各类高等教育在学总规模达到 3460 万人，高等教育毛入学率达到 34.5%。全国共有普通高等学校和成人高等学校 2788 所，比上年减少 2 所。其中，普通高等学校 2491 所（含独立学院 292 所），比上年增加 49 所；成人高等学校 297 所，比上年减少 51 所。普通高校中本科院校

1170 所，比上年增加 25 所；高职（专科）院校 1321 所，比上年增加 24 所。全国共有培养研究生单位 830 个，其中普通高校 548 个，科研机构 282 个。

研究生招生 61.14 万人，比上年增加 2.17 万人，增长 3.68%，其中，博士生招生 7.05 万人，硕士生招生 54.09 万人。在学研究生 179.40 万人，比上年增加 7.41 万人，增长 4.31%，其中，在学博士生 29.83 万人，在学硕士生 149.57 万人。毕业研究生 51.36 万人，比上年增加 2.72 万人，增长 5.59%，其中，毕业博士生 5.31 万人，毕业硕士生 46.05 万人。

普通高等教育本专科共招生 699.83 万人，比上年增加 11.00 万人，增长 1.60%；在校生 2468.07 万人，比上年增加 76.76 万人，增长 3.21%；毕业生 638.72 万人，比上年增加 13.99 万人，增长 2.24%。

成人高等教育本专科共招生 256.49 万人，比上年增加 12.54 万人；在校生 626.41 万人，比上年增加 43.30 万人；毕业生 199.77 万人，比上年增加 4.34 万人。

全国高等教育自学考试学历教育报考 766.30 万人次，取得毕业证书 73.42 万人；非学历教育报考 958.7 万人次。

普通高等学校本科、高职（专科）全日制在校生平均规模 9814 人，其中，本科学校 14261 人，高职（专科）学校 5876 人。

普通高等学校教职工 229.63 万人，比上年增加 4.19 万人；专任教师 149.69 万人，比上年增加 5.66 万人。普通高校生师比为 17.53∶1。成人高等学校教职工 5.64 万人，比上年减少 9195 人；专任教师 3.36 万人，比上年减少 5746 人。

普通高等学校校舍总建筑面积[13] 84154.95 万平方米，比上年增加 3094.53 万平方米；教学科研仪器设备总值[14] 3309.58 亿元，比上年增加 374.21 亿元。

六、成人培训与扫盲教育

全国接受各种非学历高等教育的学生 678.56 万人次，当年已结业 933.77 万人次；接受各种非学历中等教育的学生达 4914.65 万人次，当年已结业 5340.34 万人次。

全国职业技术培训机构 11.23 万所，比上年减少 1.15 万所；教职工 48.22 万人；专任教师 27.43 万人。

全国有成人小学 2.18 万所，在校生 124.26 万人，教职工 4.36 万人，其中，专任教师 2.26 万人；成人初中 1768 所，在校生 48.23 万人，教职工 7281 人，其中，专任教师 5833 人。

全国共扫除文盲 50.59 万人，比上年减少 7.99 万人；另有 61.92 万人正在参加扫盲学习，比上年减少 6.98 万人。扫盲教育教职工 3.27 万人，比上年减少 5607 人；专任教师 1.54 万人，比上年减少 2402 人。

七、民办教育

全国共有各级各类民办学校（教育机构）14.90 万所，比上年增加 9057 所；招生 1494.52 万人，比上年增加 44.49 万人；各类教育在校生达 4078.31 万人，比上年增加 167.29 万人。其中：

民办幼儿园 13.35 万所，比上年增加 8813 所；入园儿童 907.96 万人，比上年增加 42.34 万人；在园儿童 1990.25 万人，比上年增加 137.51 万人。

民办普通小学 5407 所，比上年增加 194 所；招生 111.28 万人，比上年增加 6.85 万人；在校生 628.60 万人，比上年增加 30.75 万人。

民办普通初中 4535 所，比上年增加 202 所；招生 162.11 万人，比上年增加 4.31 万人；在校生 462.35 万人，比上年增加 10.94 万人。

民办普通高中 2375 所，比上年增加 4 所；招生 79.82 万人，比上年减少 2.31 万人；在校生 231.64 万人，与上年减少 3.31 万人。

民办中等职业学校 2482 所，比上年减少 167 所；招生 73.16 万人，比上年减少 10.60 万人；在校生 207.94 万人，比上年减少 32.94 万人。另有非学历教育学生 30.23 万人。

民办高校 718 所（含独立学院 292 所），比上年增加 11 所；招生 160.19 万人，比上年减少 949 人；在校生 557.52 万人，比上年增加 24.34 万人。其中，硕士研究生在校生 335 人，本科在校生 361.64 万人，专科在校生 195.85 万人；另有自考助学班学生、预科生、进修及培训学生 25.84 万人。民办的非学历高等教育机构 802 所，各类注册学生 87.99 万人。

另外，还有其他民办培训机构 2.01 万所，943.56 万人次接受了培训。

注释：

[1] 各项统计数据均未包括香港特别行政区、澳门特别行政区和台湾省。部分数据因四舍五入的原因，存在着与分项合计不等的情况。

[2] 毛入学率，是指某一级教育不分年龄的在校学生总数占该级教育国家规定年龄组人口数的百分比。含学前教育、初中阶段、高中阶段和高等教育。

[3] 九年义务教育巩固率，是指初中毕业班学生数占该年级入小学一年级时学生数的百分比。

[4] 小学学龄儿童净入学率，是指小学教育在校学龄人口数占小学教育国家规定年龄组人口总数的百分比，是按各地不同入学年龄和学制分别计算的。

[5] 因九年一贯制学校的教职工数计入初中阶段教育，十二年一贯制学校的教职工数计入高中阶段教育，而专任教师是按照教育层次进行归类，存在小学教职工数据小于专任教师数据的情况。

[6] 学历合格专任教师比例，是指某一级教育具有国家规定的最低学历要求的专任教师数占该级教育专任教师总数的百分比。各级教育教师的最低学历要求，参照《中华人民共和国教师法》中的相关规定。取得小学教师资格，应当具备中等师范学校毕业及其以上学历；取得初级中学教师、初级职业学校文化、专业课教师资格，应当具备高等师范专科学校或者其他大学专科毕业及其以上学历；取得高级中学教师资格和中等专业学校、技工学校、职业高中文化课、专业课教师资格，应当具备高等师范院校本科或者其他大学本科毕业及其以上学历。

[7] 设施设备配备达标的学校，是指体育运动场（馆）面积、体育器械配备达到《教育部卫生部财政部关于印发国家学校体育卫生条件试行基本标准的通知》（教体艺［2008］5 号）的相关标准；音乐器材配备、美术器材配备、数学自然实验仪器、理科实验仪器等达到各省、自治区、直辖市规定的仪器配备相关标准。含普通小学、初中和普通高中。

[8] 进城务工人员随迁子女，是指户籍登记在外省（区、市）、本省外县（区）的乡村，随务工父母到输入地的城区、镇区（同住）并接受义务教育的适龄儿童少年。

[9] 农村留守儿童，是指外出务工连续三个月以上的农民托留在户籍所在地家乡，由父、母单方或其他亲属监护接受义务教育的适龄儿童少年。

［10］高中阶段包括普通高中、成人高中、中等职业学校。

［11］中等职业教育包括普通中等专业学校、职业高中、技工学校和成人中等专业学校。

［12］中等职业教育生师比不含技工学校数据。

［13］［14］包括学校产权和非产权独立使用。

资料来源：本公报中技工学校数据来自人力资源和社会保障部；高等教育自学考试数据来自教育部考试中心；其他数据均来自教育部发展规划司。

目　　录

第一部分　教育事业发展

一、综合部分

各级各类学校校数、教职工、专任教师情况 …… 2
各级各类学历教育学生情况 …… 3
各级各类非学历教育学生情况 …… 4
各级各类民办教育基本情况 …… 4
各级各类学校女学生数 …… 5
各级各类学校女教师、女教职工数 …… 6
各级各类学校少数民族学生数 …… 7
各级各类学校少数民族教师、教职工数 …… 8
各级各类学校校数 …… 9
各级各类学历教育学生数 …… 10
各级各类学历教育招生数 …… 11
各级各类学校教职工数 …… 12
各级各类学校专任教师数 …… 13
高中阶段学生数的构成 …… 14
教育规模 …… 14
小学学龄儿童净入学率 …… 15
各级教育毛入学率 …… 15
各级普通学校毕业生升学率 …… 16
每十万人口各级学校平均在校生数 …… 16
各级普通学校生师比 …… 17
普通高等学校校均规模 …… 17
各级自学考试基本情况 …… 18

二、高等教育

高等教育学校（机构）数 …… 20
普通高等学校校数 …… 21
普通高等学校在校生规模 …… 21
普通高等学校设置（研究生、本科）专业数 …… 22
普通高等学校设置（高职（专科））专业数 …… 22
高等教育学校（机构）学生数 …… 23
分部门、分计划研究生数（总计） …… 24
分部门、分计划研究生数（普通高校） …… 24
分部门、分计划研究生数（科研机构） …… 26
分学科研究生数（总计） …… 26

分学科研究生数(普通高校) …… 28
分学科研究生数(科研机构) …… 28
在职人员攻读硕士学位分学科学生数 …… 30
普通高等学校工科分大类本科学生数 …… 31
普通、成人本、专科分举办者学生数 …… 32
普通本、专科分性质类别学生数 …… 32
成人本、专科分性质类别学生数 …… 34
普通本科分学科学生数 …… 34
普通专科分专业大类学生数 …… 35
成人本科分学科学生数 …… 36
成人专科分学科学生数 …… 37
网络本科分学科学生数 …… 38
高等教育学生数变动情况 …… 38
网络专科分学科学生数 …… 39
高等教育非学历教育学生情况 …… 40
高等教育学生中其他情况 …… 41
外国留学生情况 …… 42
高等教育学校(机构)教职工情况(总计) …… 44
高等教育学校(机构)教职工情况(普通高校) …… 44
高等教育学校(机构)教职工情况(成人高校) …… 46
研究生指导教师情况(总计) …… 48
研究生指导教师情况(普通高校) …… 48
分学科专任教师数(总计) …… 50
分学科专任教师数(普通高校) …… 51
分学科专任教师数(成人高校) …… 52
分学科专任教师数(民办的其他高等教育机构) …… 53
专任教师、聘请校外教师学历情况(总计) …… 54
专任教师、聘请校外教师学历情况(普通高校) …… 54
专任教师、聘请校外教师学历情况(成人高校) …… 55
专任教师、聘请校外教师学历情况(民办的其他高等教育机构) …… 55
专任教师年龄情况(总计) …… 56
专任教师年龄情况(普通高校) …… 56
专任教师年龄情况(成人高校) …… 57
专任教师年龄情况(民办的其他高等教育机构) …… 57
专任教师、聘请校外教师岗位分类情况(总计) …… 58
专任教师、聘请校外教师岗位分类情况(民办的其他高等教育机构) …… 58
专任教师变动情况(总计) …… 60
专任教师变动情况(民办的其他高等教育机构) …… 60
资产情况(总计) …… 62
资产情况(民办的其他高等教育机构) …… 62
校舍情况(总计) …… 64
校舍情况(普通高校) …… 65
校舍情况(成人高校) …… 66

校舍情况（民办的其他高等教育机构） …… 67

三、中等教育

（一）高中阶段教育

普通高中校数、班数 …… 69
普通高中班额情况 …… 70
普通高中学生数 …… 71
中学学校教职工数（初级中学、九年一贯制学校、职业初中、完全中学、高级中学、十二年一贯制学校） …… 72
普通高中分课程专任教师学历情况 …… 74
普通高中专任教师专业技术职称、年龄结构情况 …… 74
普通高中专任教师变动情况 …… 76
普通高中学生、专任教师政治面貌及其他 …… 76
普通高中办学条件（一） …… 78
普通高中办学条件（二） …… 78
普通高中办学条件（三） …… 80
成人高中基本情况 …… 80
中等职业学校（机构）数 …… 81
中等职业学校分办学类型及举办者的中职学生及教职工情况 …… 82
中等职业学校（机构）各类学生数 …… 84
中等职业学校（机构）各类女学生数 …… 84
中等职业学校（机构）学生分科类情况（总计） …… 86
中等职业学校（机构）学生分科类情况（全日制学生） …… 87
中等职业学校（机构）学生分科类情况（普通中专） …… 88
中等职业学校（机构）学生分科类情况（成人中专） …… 89
中等职业学校（机构）学生分科类情况（职业高中） …… 90
中等职业学校（机构）分年龄学生数 …… 91
中等职业学校（机构）分年龄女学生数 …… 91
中等职业学校（机构）学生变动情况 …… 92
中等职业学校（机构）女学生变动情况 …… 92
中等职业学校（机构）学生其他情况 …… 94
中等职业学校（机构）培训学生情况 …… 94
中等职业学校（机构）外国留学生情况 …… 95
中等职业学校（机构）教职工数（总计） …… 96
中等职业学校（机构）教职工数（普通中专） …… 96
中等职业学校（机构）教职工数（成人中专） …… 98
中等职业学校（机构）教职工数（职业高中） …… 98
中等职业学校（机构）教职工数（其他机构） …… 100
中等职业学校（机构）分科专任教师数（总计） …… 102
中等职业学校（机构）分科专任教师数（普通中专学校） …… 103
中等职业学校（机构）分科专任教师数（成人中专学校） …… 104
中等职业学校（机构）分科专任教师数（职业高中学校） …… 105
中等职业学校（机构）分科专任教师数（其他机构） …… 106
中等职业学校（机构）专任教师、聘请校外教师学历情况（合计） …… 107

中等职业学校(机构)专任教师、聘请校外教师学历情况(普通中专学校) …… 108
中等职业学校(机构)专任教师、聘请校外教师学历情况(成人中专学校) …… 109
中等职业学校(机构)专任教师、聘请校外教师学历情况(职业高中) …… 110
中等职业学校(机构)专任教师、聘请校外教师学历情况(其他机构) …… 111
中等职业学校(机构)专任教师分年龄情况 …… 112
中等职业学校(机构)专任教师、聘请校外教师岗位分类情况 …… 114
中等职业学校(机构)专任教师变动情况 …… 116
中等职业学校(机构)资产情况 …… 118
中等职业学校(机构)教职工其他情况 …… 120
中等职业学校(机构)校舍情况 …… 121
中等职业学校(机构)校舍情况(普通中专学校) …… 122
中等职业学校(机构)校舍情况(成人中专学校) …… 123
中等职业学校(机构)校舍情况(职业高中学校) …… 124
中等职业学校(机构)校舍情况(其他机构) …… 125
职业技术培训机构基本情况 …… 126
职业技术培训机构资产情况 …… 128

(二)初中阶段教育

初中阶段校数、班数 …… 130
初中班额情况 …… 131
初中学生数 …… 132
初中学龄人口及在校学生情况 …… 134
初中分课程专任教师学历情况 …… 136
初中专任教师专业技术职称、年龄结构情况 …… 138
初中专任教师变动情况 …… 140
初中学生、专任教师政治面貌及其他 …… 142
初中办学条件(一) …… 143
初中办学条件(二) …… 144
初中办学条件(三) …… 144
成人初中基本情况 …… 146

四、初等教育(小学)

小学校数、教学点数及班数 …… 148
小学班额情况 …… 149
小学学生数 …… 150
小学学龄人口入学及在校生情况 …… 152
小学教职工数 …… 156
小学分课程专任教师学历情况 …… 158
小学专任教师专业技术职称、年龄结构情况 …… 158
小学专任教师变动情况 …… 160
小学学生、教职工政治面貌及其他 …… 160
小学办学条件(一) …… 162
小学办学条件(二) …… 164
小学办学条件(三) …… 164

成人小学基本情况…………………………………………………………………………………… 165

五、工读学校

工读学校基本情况…………………………………………………………………………………… 168

六、特殊教育

特殊教育基本情况…………………………………………………………………………………… 170
特殊教育学校教职工数……………………………………………………………………………… 172
特殊教育学校专任教师学历、职称情况 ………………………………………………………… 172
特殊教育专任教师变动情况………………………………………………………………………… 172
特殊教育学校办学条件(一) ……………………………………………………………………… 174
特殊教育学校办学条件(二) ……………………………………………………………………… 174

七、幼儿教育

幼儿园园数、班数 …………………………………………………………………………………… 176
幼儿教育分年龄学生数……………………………………………………………………………… 178
幼儿教育分年龄学生数(城区) …………………………………………………………………… 179
幼儿教育分年龄学生数(城乡结合区) …………………………………………………………… 180
幼儿教育分年龄学生数(镇区) …………………………………………………………………… 181
幼儿教育分年龄学生数(镇乡结合区) …………………………………………………………… 182
幼儿教育分年龄学生数(乡村) …………………………………………………………………… 183
幼儿园教职工数……………………………………………………………………………………… 184
幼儿园园长、专任教师学历、职称情况…………………………………………………………… 186
幼儿园教职工、专任教师政治面貌及其他 ……………………………………………………… 188
幼儿园办学条件(一) ……………………………………………………………………………… 190
幼儿园办学条件(二) ……………………………………………………………………………… 190

八、各级各类学校分布情况

高等教育学校(机构)数 …………………………………………………………………………… 192
高等学校(机构)研究生数 ………………………………………………………………………… 194
普通高校研究生数…………………………………………………………………………………… 196
科研机构研究生数…………………………………………………………………………………… 198
高等教育本、专科学生数 …………………………………………………………………………… 200
高等教育普通本、专科学生数 ……………………………………………………………………… 202
高等教育成人本、专科学生数 ……………………………………………………………………… 204
高等教育网络本科、专科生学生数 ………………………………………………………………… 206
综合大学本科、专科生学生数 ……………………………………………………………………… 208
高等理工院校本科、专科生学生数 ………………………………………………………………… 210
高等农业院校本科、专科生学生数 ………………………………………………………………… 212
高等林业院校本科、专科生学生数 ………………………………………………………………… 214
高等医药院校本科、专科生学生数 ………………………………………………………………… 216
高等师范院校本科、专科生学生数 ………………………………………………………………… 218
高等语文院校本科、专科生学生数 ………………………………………………………………… 220

高等财经院校本科、专科生学生数 …… 222
高等政法院校本科、专科生学生数 …… 224
高等体育院校本科、专科生学生数 …… 226
高等艺术院校本科、专科生学生数 …… 228
高等民族院校本科、专科生学生数 …… 230
高等职业学校本科、专科生学生数 …… 232
广播电视大学本、专科学生数 …… 234
职工高等学校本、专科学生数 …… 236
教育学院本、专科学生数 …… 238
管理干部学院本、专科学生数 …… 240
其他机构本、专科学生数 …… 242
普通高等学校举办函授、业余、脱产分本专科学生数 …… 244
在职人员攻读硕士学位学生数 …… 246
高等教育非学历教育学生情况(总计) …… 248
高等教育非学历教育学生情况(普通高校) …… 250
高等教育非学历教育学生情况(成人高校) …… 252
高等教育非学历教育学生情况(科研机构) …… 254
高等教育非学历教育学生情况(民办的其他高等教育机构) …… 256
外国留学生情况 …… 258
高等教育学校(机构)教职工情况(总计) …… 260
高等教育学校(机构)女教职工情况(总计) …… 262
高等教育学校(机构)教职工情况(普通高校) …… 264
高等教育学校(机构)女教职工情况(普通高校) …… 266
高等教育学校(机构)教职工情况(成人高校) …… 268
高等教育学校(机构)女教职工情况(成人高校) …… 270
高等教育学校(机构)教职工情况(民办的其他高等教育机构) …… 272
高等教育学校(机构)女教职工情况(民办的其他高等教育机构) …… 274
专任教师学历、职称情况(总计) …… 276
专任教师学历、职称情况(普通高校) …… 277
专任教师学历、职称情况(成人高校) …… 278
专任教师学历、职称情况(民办的其他高等教育机构) …… 279
聘请校外教师学历情况(总计) …… 280
聘请校外教师学历情况(普通高校) …… 281
聘请校外教师学历情况(成人高校) …… 282
聘请校外教师学历情况(民办的其他高等教育机构) …… 283
资产情况(学校产权)(总计) …… 284
资产情况(学校产权)(普通高校) …… 286
资产情况(学校产权)(成人高校) …… 288
资产情况(学校产权)(民办的其他高等教育机构) …… 290
资产情况(非学校产权独立使用) …… 292
资产情况(非学校产权独立使用)(普通高校) …… 294
资产情况(非学校产权独立使用)(成人高校) …… 296
资产情况(非学校产权独立使用)(民办的其他高等教育机构) …… 298

校舍情况(总计) …… 300
校舍情况(普通高校) …… 301
校舍情况(成人高校) …… 302
校舍情况(民办的其他高等教育机构) …… 303
普通高中校数、班数(总计) …… 304
普通高中校数、班数(城区) …… 305
普通高中校数、班数(城乡结合区) …… 306
普通高中校数、班数(镇区) …… 307
普通高中校数、班数(镇乡结合区) …… 308
普通高中校数、班数(乡村) …… 309
普通高中学生数(总计) …… 310
普通高中学生数(城区) …… 311
普通高中学生数(城乡结合区) …… 312
普通高中学生数(镇区) …… 313
普通高中学生数(镇乡结合区) …… 314
普通高中学生数(乡村) …… 315
普通高中女学生数 …… 316
普通中学教职工数(总计) …… 317
普通中学教职工数(城区) …… 318
普通中学教职工数(城乡结合区) …… 319
普通中学教职工数(镇区) …… 320
普通中学教职工数(镇乡结合区) …… 321
普通中学教职工数(乡村) …… 322
普通中学女教职工数 …… 323
普通中学教职工总数中民办教职工数 …… 324
普通高中专任教师学历、职称情况(总计) …… 326
普通高中专任教师学历、职称情况(城区) …… 328
普通高中专任教师学历、职称情况(城乡结合区) …… 330
普通高中专任教师学历、职称情况(镇区) …… 332
普通高中专任教师学历、职称情况(镇乡结合区) …… 334
普通高中专任教师学历、职称情况(乡村) …… 336
普通高中办学条件(一)(总计) …… 338
普通高中办学条件(一)(城区) …… 340
普通高中办学条件(一)(城乡结合区) …… 342
普通高中办学条件(一)(镇区) …… 344
普通高中办学条件(一)(镇乡结合区) …… 346
普通高中办学条件(一)(乡村) …… 348
普通高中办学条件(二)(总计) …… 350
普通高中办学条件(二)(城区) …… 352
普通高中办学条件(二)(城乡结合区) …… 354
普通高中办学条件(二)(镇区) …… 356
普通高中办学条件(二)(镇乡结合区) …… 358
普通高中办学条件(二)(乡村) …… 360

中等职业学校(机构)数 …… 362
中等职业学校(机构)学生数 …… 364
中等职业学校(机构)女学生数 …… 366
普通中等专业学生数 …… 368
普通中等专业学校女学生数 …… 370
成人中等专业学生数 …… 372
成人中等专业女学生数 …… 374
职业高中学生数 …… 376
职业高中女学生数 …… 378
中等职业学校(机构)分年龄学生数 …… 380
中等职业学校(机构)分年龄女学生数 …… 382
中等职业学校(机构)培训结业学生情况 …… 384
中等职业学校(机构)培训注册学生情况 …… 386
中等职业学校(机构)学生数变动情况 …… 388
中等职业学校(机构)女学生数变动情况 …… 390
中等职业学校(机构)外国留学生情况 …… 392
中等职业学校(机构)教职工数 …… 394
中等职业学校(机构)女教职工数 …… 396
普通中等专业学校(机构)教职工数 …… 398
普通中等专业学校(机构)女教职工数 …… 400
成人中等专业学校教职工数 …… 402
成人中等专业学校女教职工数 …… 404
职业高中学校教职工数 …… 406
职业高中学校女教职工数 …… 408
其他机构教职工数 …… 410
其他机构女教职工数 …… 412
中等职业学校(机构)专任教师职称、学历情况 …… 414
普通中等专业学校专任教师职称、学历情况 …… 416
成人中等专业学校专任教师职称、学历情况 …… 418
职业高中学校专任教师职称、学历情况 …… 420
其他机构专任教师职称、学历情况 …… 422
中等职业学校(机构)资产情况(学校产权) …… 424
中等职业学校(机构)资产情况(非学校产权中独立使用) …… 426
普通中专学校资产情况(学校产权) …… 428
普通中专学校资产情况(非学校产权中独立使用) …… 430
成人中专学校资产情况(学校产权) …… 432
成人中专学校资产情况(非学校产权中独立使用) …… 434
职业高中学校资产情况(学校产权) …… 436
职业高中学校资产情况(非学校产权中独立使用) …… 438
其他机构资产情况(学校产权) …… 440
其他机构资产情况(非学校产权中独立使用) …… 442
中等职业学校(机构)校舍情况(总计) …… 444
普通中专学校校舍情况 …… 445

成人中专学校校舍情况…………………………………………………………………… 446
职业高中学校校舍情况…………………………………………………………………… 447
其他机构校舍情况………………………………………………………………………… 448
职业技术培训机构基本情况（总计） …………………………………………………… 450
职工技术培训学校基本情况……………………………………………………………… 452
农村成人文化技术培训学校基本情况…………………………………………………… 454
其他培训机构基本情况…………………………………………………………………… 456
职业技术培训机构资产情况……………………………………………………………… 458
职工技术培训学校资产情况……………………………………………………………… 460
农村成人文化技术培训学校资产情况…………………………………………………… 462
其他培训机构资产情况…………………………………………………………………… 464
初中校数、班数（总计） ………………………………………………………………… 466
初中校数、班数（城区） ………………………………………………………………… 468
初中校数、班数（城乡结合区） ………………………………………………………… 469
初中校数、班数（镇区） ………………………………………………………………… 470
初中校数、班数（镇乡结合区） ………………………………………………………… 471
初中校数、班数（乡村） ………………………………………………………………… 472
初中学生数（总计） ……………………………………………………………………… 473
初中学生数（城区） ……………………………………………………………………… 474
初中学生数（城乡结合区） ……………………………………………………………… 475
初中学生数（镇区） ……………………………………………………………………… 476
初中学生数（镇乡结合区） ……………………………………………………………… 477
初中学生数（乡村） ……………………………………………………………………… 478
初中女学生数……………………………………………………………………………… 479
初中专任教师学历、职称情况（总计） ………………………………………………… 480
初中专任教师学历、职称情况（城区） ………………………………………………… 482
初中专任教师学历、职称情况（城乡结合区） ………………………………………… 484
初中专任教师学历、职称情况（镇区） ………………………………………………… 486
初中专任教师学历、职称情况（镇乡结合区） ………………………………………… 488
初中专任教师学历、职称情况（乡村） ………………………………………………… 490
初中办学条件（一）（总计） …………………………………………………………… 492
初中办学条件（一）（城区） …………………………………………………………… 494
初中办学条件（一）（城乡结合区） …………………………………………………… 496
初中办学条件（一）（镇区） …………………………………………………………… 498
初中办学条件（一）（镇乡结合区） …………………………………………………… 500
初中办学条件（一）（乡村） …………………………………………………………… 502
初中办学条件（二）（总计） …………………………………………………………… 504
初中办学条件（二）（城区） …………………………………………………………… 506
初中办学条件（二）（城乡结合区） …………………………………………………… 508
初中办学条件（二）（镇区） …………………………………………………………… 510
初中办学条件（二）（镇乡结合区） …………………………………………………… 512
初中办学条件（二）（乡村） …………………………………………………………… 514
小学校数、教学点数及班数（总计） …………………………………………………… 516

小学校数、教学点数及班数(城区) …… 518
小学校数、教学点数及班数(城乡结合区) …… 520
小学校数、教学点数及班数(镇区) …… 522
小学校数、教学点数及班数(镇乡结合区) …… 524
小学校数、教学点数及班数(农村) …… 526
小学学生数(总计) …… 528
小学学生数(城区) …… 530
小学学生数(城乡结合区) …… 532
小学学生数(镇区) …… 534
小学学生数(镇乡结合区) …… 536
小学学生数(乡村) …… 538
五年制小学学生数…… 540
小学女学生数…… 542
小学教职工数(总计) …… 544
小学教职工数(城区) …… 546
小学教职工数(城乡结合区) …… 548
小学教职工数(镇区) …… 550
小学教职工数(镇乡结合区) …… 552
小学教职工数(乡村) …… 554
小学教职工总数中民办教职工数…… 556
小学女教职工数…… 558
小学专任教师学历、职称情况(总计) …… 560
小学专任教师学历、职称情况(城区) …… 562
小学专任教师学历、职称情况(城乡结合区) …… 564
小学专任教师学历、职称情况(镇区) …… 566
小学专任教师学历、职称情况(镇乡结合区) …… 568
小学专任教师学历、职称情况(乡村) …… 570
小学办学条件(一)(总计) …… 572
小学办学条件(一)(城区) …… 574
小学办学条件(一)(城乡结合区) …… 576
小学办学条件(一)(镇区) …… 578
小学办学条件(一)(镇乡结合区) …… 580
小学办学条件(一)(乡村) …… 582
小学办学条件(二)(总计) …… 584
小学办学条件(二)(城区) …… 586
小学办学条件(二)(城乡结合区) …… 588
小学办学条件(二)(镇区) …… 590
小学办学条件(二)(镇乡结合区) …… 592
小学办学条件(二)(乡村) …… 594
工读学校基本情况…… 596
特殊教育基本情况(总计) …… 598
特殊教育基本情况(城区) …… 600
特殊教育基本情况(城乡结合区) …… 602

特殊教育基本情况(镇区) …… 604
特殊教育基本情况(镇乡结合区) …… 606
特殊教育基本情况(乡村) …… 608
特殊教育女学生数 …… 610
特殊教育学校教职工数(总计) …… 612
特殊教育学校女教职工数 …… 613
特殊教育学校专任教师学历、职称情况 …… 614
特殊教育学校办学条件(一) …… 616
特殊教育学校办学条件(二) …… 618
幼儿园基本情况(总计) …… 619
幼儿园基本情况(城区) …… 620
幼儿园基本情况(城乡结合区) …… 621
幼儿园基本情况(镇区) …… 622
幼儿园基本情况(镇乡结合区) …… 623
幼儿园基本情况(乡村) …… 624
幼儿教育中女儿童数 …… 625
幼儿园教职工数(总计) …… 626
幼儿园教职工数(城区) …… 627
幼儿园教职工数(城乡结合区) …… 628
幼儿园教职工数(镇区) …… 629
幼儿园教职工数(镇乡结合区) …… 630
幼儿园教职工数(乡村) …… 631
幼儿园女教职工数 …… 632
幼儿园园长、专任教师学历、职称情况(总计) …… 634
幼儿园园长、专任教师学历、职称情况(城区) …… 636
幼儿园园长、专任教师学历、职称情况(城乡结合区) …… 638
幼儿园园长、专任教师学历、职称情况(镇区) …… 640
幼儿园园长、专任教师学历、职称情况(镇乡结合区) …… 642
幼儿园园长、专任教师学历、职称情况(乡村) …… 644
幼儿园校舍及其他情况(总计)(一) …… 646
幼儿园校舍及其他情况(城区)(一) …… 648
幼儿园校舍及其他情况(城乡结合区)(一) …… 650
幼儿园校舍及其他情况(镇区)(一) …… 652
幼儿园校舍及其他情况(镇乡结合区)(一) …… 654
幼儿园校舍及其他情况(乡村)(一) …… 656
幼儿园办学条件(总计)(二) …… 658
幼儿园办学条件(城区)(二) …… 659
幼儿园办学条件(城乡结合区)(二) …… 660
幼儿园办学条件(镇区)(二) …… 661
幼儿园办学条件(镇乡结合区)(二) …… 662
幼儿园办学条件(乡村)(二) …… 663

第二部分　办学条件

教育基本建设投资

教育基本建设投资完成情况(总计) …… 666
地方所属各级学校投资完成情况 …… 668

第三部分　科学研究活动及其他

一、自然科学与技术

普通高等学校科技人力情况 …… 672
普通高等学校科技经费情况 …… 674
普通高等学校研究与发展课题、成果情况 …… 676

二、社会科学

普通高等学校人文、社会科学人力情况 …… 680
普通高等学校人文、社会科学研究与发展经费情况 …… 682
普通高等学校人文、社会科学研究与发展课题、成果情况 …… 684

附表:

国内生产总值 …… 687
各地区国内生产总值(2012 年) …… 688
国家财政收支总额及增长速度 …… 689
中央财政和地方财政收支总额 …… 690
人口数及构成 …… 691
各地区按性别分的 15 岁及以上文盲人口 …… 692
各地区按性别和受教育程度分的人口 …… 693

CONTENTS

Part Ⅰ

THE DEVELOPMENT OF THE EDUCTIONAL UNDERTAKING

Summary Tables

Number of Schools, Educational Personnel and Full-time Teachers by Type and Level 2
Number of Students of Formal Education by Type and Level 3
Number of Students of Non-formal Education by Type and Level 4
Number of Non-government Schools by Type and Level 4
Number of Female Students of Schools by Type and Level 5
Number of Female Educational Personnel and Full-time Teachers of Schools by Type and Level 6
Number of Minority Students of Schools by Type and Level 7
Number of Minority Educational Personnel and Full-time Teachers of Schools by Type and Level 8
Number of Schools by Type and Level 9
Number of Students of Formal Education by Type and Level 10
Number of Entrants of Formal Education by Type and Level 11
Number of Educational Personnel of Schools by Type and Level 12
Number of Full-time Teachers of Schools by Type and Level 13
Composition of Students in Senior Secondary Education 14
Size of Education 14
Net Enrolment Ratio of School-age Children in Primary Schools 15
Gross Enrolment Ratio of Education by Level 15
Promotion Rate of Graduates of Regular Schools by Level 16
Number of Enrolment of Per 100, 000 Inhabitants by Level 16
Pupil-Teacher Ratio of Regular Schools by Level 17
Average Size of Regular Higher Educational Institutions 17
Basic Statistics of State-administered Examination for Self-learners by Level 18

Higher Education

Number of Higher Education Institutions 20
Number of Regular Higher Educational Institutions 21
Size of Enrolment of Regular Higher Educational Institutions 21
Number of Specialities and Educational Programs Offered by Regular Higher Educational Institutions 22
Number of Specialities and Number of Educational Programs Offered by Regular Higher Educational Institutions ... 22
Number of Students in Higher Education Institutions 23
Number of Postgraduate Students by Sector and Program (Total) 24
Number of Postgraduate Students by Sector and Program (Regular HEIs) 24
Number of Postgraduate Students by Sector and Program (Research Institutes) 26

Number of Postgraduate Students by Academic Field (Total) 26
Number of PostgraduateStudents by Academic Field (Regular HEIs) 28
Number of Postgraduate Students by Academic Field (Research Institutes) 28
Number of On-the-job Students Studying for Master's Degree by Discipline 30
Number of Engineering Students for Normal Courses by Subfield of Study in Regular HEIs 31
Number of Students for Regular and Adult Programs by Providers in HEIs 32
Number of Students for Regular Programs by Type of Schools in HEIs 32
Number of Students for Adult Programs by Type of Schools in HEIs 34
Number of Regular Students for Normal Courses in HEIs by Discipline 34
Number of Reqular Students for Short-cycle Courses in HEIs by Discipline 35
Number of Adult Students for Normal Courses in HEIs by Discipline 36
Number of Adult Students for Short-cycle Courses in HEIs by Discipline 37
Number of Web-based Students for Normal Courses in HEIs by Discipline 38
Changes in Enrolment of Higher Educations 38
Number of Web-based Students for Short-cycle Courses in HEIs by Discipline 39
Number of Students of Non-formal Education of Higher Education 40
Other Circumstances of Students in Higher Education 41
Information on International Students 42
Number of Educational Personnel in HEIs (Total) 44
Number of Educational Personnel in HEIs (Regular HEIs) 44
Number of Educational Personnel in HEIs (Adult HEIs) 46
Number of Supervisors of Postgraduate Programs (Total) 48
Number of Supervisors of Postgraduate Programs (Regular HEIs) 48
Number of Full-time Teachers by Field of Study (Total) 50
Number of Full-time Teachers by Field of Study (Regular HEIs) 51
Number of Full-time Teachers by Field of Study (Adult HEIs) 52
Number of Full-time Teachers by Field of Study (Other Non-government HEIs) 53
Number of Academic Qualifications of Full-time and Part-time Teachers in HEIs (Total) 54
Number of Academic Qualifications of Full-time and Part-time Teachers in HEIs (Regular HEIs) 54
Number of Academic Qualifications of Full-time and Part-time Teachers in HEIs (Adult HEIs) 55
Number of Academic Qualifications of Full-time and Part-time Teachers in HEIs (Other Non-government HEIs) 55
Number of Full-time Teachers by Age (Total) 56
Number of Full-time Teachers by Age (Regular HEIs) 56
Number of Full-time Teachers by Age (Adult HEIs) 57
Number of Full-time Teachers by Age (Other Non-government HEIs) 57
Number of Full-time and Part-time Teachers Classified by Teaching Content in HEIs (Total) 58
Number of Full-time and Part-time Teachers Classified by Teaching Content in HEIs (Other Non-government HEIs) 58
Changes of Full-time Teachers in HEIs (Total) 60
Changes of Full-time Teachers in HEIs (Other Non-government HEIs) 60
Condition of Fixed Assets and Teaching Resources (Total) 62
Condition of Fixed Assets and Teaching Resources (Other Non-government HEIs) 62
Condition of School Buildings (Total) 64
Condition of School Buildings (Regular HEIs) 65
Condition of School Buildings (Adult HEIs) 66
Condition of School Buildings (Other Non-government HEIs) 67

Secondary Education

Senior Secondary Education

Number of Regular Senior Secondary Schools and Classes ······ 69
Size of Class in Regular Senior Secondary Schools ······ 70
Number of Students in Regular Senior Secondary Schools ······ 71
Number of Educational Personnel in General Secondary Schools ······ 72
Number of Full-time Teachers in Regular Senior Secondary Schools by Subject Taught & Academic Qualifications ······ 74
Number of Full-time Teachers in Regular Senior Secondary Schools by Rank and Age ······ 74
Changes of Full-time Teachers in Regular Senior Secondary Schools ······ 76
Supplementary Information on Students and Full-time Teachers of Regular Senior Secondary Schools ······ 76
Condition of School Buildings in Regular Senior Secondary Schools (1) ······ 78
Condition of School Buildings in Regular Senior Secondary Schools (2) ······ 78
Condition of School Buildings in Regular Senior Secondary Schools (3) ······ 80
Basic Statistics of Adult High Schools ······ 80
Number of Secondary Vocational Schools (Institutions) ······ 81
Number of Students and Educational Personnel of Secondary Vocational Schools by Types and Providers ······ 82
Number of students in Secondary Vocational Schools (Institutions) ······ 84
Number of Female students in Secondary Vocational Schools (Institutions) ······ 84
Number of Students by Field of Education in Secondary Vocational Schools (Institutions) (Total) ······ 86
Number of Students by Field of Education in Secondary Vocational Schools (Institutions) (Full-time Students) ······ 87
Number of Students by Field of Education in Secondary Vocational Schools (Institutions) (Regular SSSs) ······ 88
Number of Students by Field of Education in Secondary Vocational Schools (Institutions) (Adult SSSs) ······ 89
Number of Students by Field of Education in Secondary Vocational Schools (Institutions) (Vocational High Schools) ······ 90
Number of Students by Age in Secondary Vocational Schools (Institutions) ······ 91
Number of Female Students by Age in Secondary Vocational Schools (Institutions) ······ 91
Changes in Enrolment of Secondary Vocational Schools (Institutions) ······ 92
Changes in Female Enrolment of Secondary Vocational Schools (Institutions) ······ 92
Supplementary Information on Students in Secondary Vocational Schools (Institutions) ······ 94
Number of Trainees in Secondary Vocational Schools (Institutions) ······ 94
Number of Foreign Students in Secondary Voactional Schools (Institutions) ······ 95
Number of Educational Personnel in Secondary Vocational Schools (Total) ······ 96
Number of Educational Personnel in Secondary Vocational Schools (Institutions) (Regular SSSs) ······ 96
Number of Educational Personnel in Secondary Vocational Schools (Institutions) (Adult SSSs) ······ 98
Number of Educational Personnel in Secondary Vocational Schools (Institutions) (Vocational High Schools) ······ 98
Number of Educational Personnel in Secondary Vocational Schools (Institutions) (Other Institutions) ······ 100
Number of Full-time Teachers by Field of Education in Secondary Vocational Schools (Institutions) (Total) ······ 102
Number of Full-time Teachers by Field of Education in Secondary Vocational Schools (Institutions) (Regular SSSs) ······ 103
Number of Full-time Teachers by Field of Education in Secondary Vocational Schools (Institutions) (Adult SSSs) ······ 104
Number of Full-time Teachers by Field of Education in Secondary Vocational Schools (Institutions) (Vocational High Schools) ······ 105
Number of Full-time Teachers by Field of Education in Secondary Vocational Schools (Institutions) (Other Institutions) ······ 106

Number of Full-time and Part-time Teachers by Academic Qualifications in Secondary Vocational Schools (Institutions) (Total) ········ 107
Number of Full-time and Part-time Teachers by Academic Qualifications in Secondary Vocational Schools (Institutions) (Regular SSSs) ········ 108
Number of Full-time and Part-time Teachers by Academic Qualifications in Secondary Vocational Schools (Institutions) (Adult SSSs) ········ 109
Number of Full-time and Part-time Teachers by Academic Qualifications in Secondary Vocational Schools (Institutions) (Vocational High Schools) ········ 110
Number of Full-time and Part-time Teachers by Academic Qualifications in Secondary Vocational Schools (Institutions) (Other Institutions) ········ 111
Number of Full-time Teachers by Age in Secondary Vocational Schools (Institutions) ········ 112
Number of Full-time and Part-time Teachers by Teaching Course in Secondary Vocational Schools (Institutions) ······ 114
Changes of Full-time Teachers in Secondary Vocational Schools (Institutions) ········ 116
Condition of Fixed Assets and Teaching Resources in Secondary Vocational Schools (Institutions) ········ 118
Supplementary Information on Educational Personnel in Secondary Vocational Schools (Institutions) ········ 120
Condition of School Buildings in Secondary Vocational Schools (Institutions) (Total) ········ 121
Condition of School Buildings in Secondary Vocational Schools (Institutions) (Regular SSSs) ········ 122
Condition of School Buildings in Secondary Vocational Schools (Institutions) (Adult SSSs) ········ 123
Condition of School Buildings in Secondary Vocational Schools (Institutions) (Vocational High Schools) ········ 124
Condition of School Buildings in Secondary Vocational Schools (Institutions) (Other Institutions) ········ 125
Basic Statistics of Vocational Technical Training Institutions ········ 126
Condition of Fixed Assets and Teaching Resources in Vocational-Technical Training Institutions ········ 128

Junior Secondary Education

Number of Schools, Classes of Junior Secondary Education ········ 130
Size of Junior Secondary Schools Education Classes ········ 131
Number of Students in Junior Secondary Schools ········ 132
Number of School-age Population and Enrolment of Junior Secondary Schools ········ 134
Number of Full-time Teachers in Junior Secondary Schools by Subject Taught & Academic Qualification ········ 136
Number of Full-time Teachers in Junior Secondary Schools by Prefessional Rank and Age ········ 138
Changes of Full-time Teachers in Junior Secondary Schools ········ 140
Supplementary Information on Students and Full-time Teachers of Junior Secondary Schools ········ 142
Condition of School Buildings in Junior Secondary Schools (1) ········ 143
Condition of School Buildings in Junior Secondary Schools (2) ········ 144
Condition of School Buildings in Junior Secondary Schools (3) ········ 144
Basic Statistics of Adult Junior Secondary Schools ········ 146

Primary Education (Primary Schools)

Number of Schools, External Teaching Sites & Classes in Primary Schools ········ 148
Size of Primary Classes ········ 149
Number of Students in Primary Schools ········ 150
Number of Schools-age Population of Primary Schools ········ 152
Number of Educational Personnel in Primary Schools ········ 156
Number of Full-time Teachers in Primary School by Subject Taught and Academic Qualification ········ 158
Number of Full-time Teachers in Primary Schools by Professional Rank and Age ········ 158
Changes of Full-time Teachers in Primary Schools ········ 160

Supplementary Information on Students and Educational Personnel of Primary Schools ······ 160
Condition of School Buildings in Primary Schools (1) ······ 162
Condition of School Buildings in Primary Schools (2) ······ 164
Condition of School Buildings in Primary Schools (3) ······ 164
Basic Statistics of Adult Primary Schools by Province ······ 165

Correctional Work-Study Schools

Basic Statistics of Correctional Work-study Schools ······ 168

Special Education

Basic Statistics of Special Education ······ 170
Number of Educational Personnel in Special Education Schools ······ 172
Number of Full-time Teachers in Special Education Schools by Academic Qualification and Professional Rank ··· 172
Changes of Full-time Teachers in Special Education Schools ······ 172
Condition of School Buildings in Special Education Schools (1) ······ 174
Condition of School Buildings in Special Education Schools (2) ······ 174

Pre-Primary Education

Number of Kindergartens, Classes in Pre-Primary Education ······ 176
Number of Students in Pre-school Education by Age ······ 178
Number of Students in Pre-school Education by Age (Urban Area) ······ 179
Number of Students in Pre-school Education by Age (Urban-rural Transitional Area) ······ 180
Number of Students in Pre-school Education by Age (Counties & Towns Area) ······ 181
Number of Students in Pre-school Education by Age (County-town Transitional Area) ······ 182
Number of Students in Pre-school Education by Age (Rural Area) ······ 183
Number of Educational Personnel in Kindergarten ······ 184
Number of Kindergarten Heads, Full-time Teachers by Academic Qualification and Professional Rank ······ 186
Supplementary Information on Educational Personnel, Full-time Teachers of Kindergarten ······ 188
Condition of Kindergarten Buildings (1) ······ 190
Condition of Kindergarten Buildings (2) ······ 190

Geographical Distribution of Schools by Type and Level

Number of Higher Education Institutions ······ 192
Number of Postgraduate Students in Higher Education Institutions ······ 194
Number of Postgraduate Students in Regular Higher Education Institutions ······ 196
Number of Postgraduate Students in Research Institutes ······ 198
Number of Students Enrolled in Normal and Short-cycle Courses in Higher Education ······ 200
Number of Regular Students Enrolled in Normal and Short-cycle Courses in Higher Education ······ 202
Number of Adult Students Enrolled in Normal and Short-cycle Courses in Higher Education ······ 204
Number of Web-based Students Enrolled in Normal and Short-cycle Courses in Higher Education ······ 206

Number of Students of Comprehensive Universities ········· 208
Number of Students of Institutions of Science & Technology ········· 210
Number of Students of Institutions of Agriculture ········· 212
Number of Students of Institutions of Forestry ········· 214
Number of Students of Institutions of Medicine & Pharmacy ········· 216
Number of Students of Institutions of Teachers ········· 218
Number of Students of Institutions of Languages & Literatures ········· 220
Number of Students of Institutions of Finance & Economies ········· 222
Number of Students of Institutions of Political Science & Law ········· 224
Number of Students of Institutions of Physical Culture ········· 226
Number of Students of Institutions of Art ········· 228
Number of Students of Nationalities Institutions ········· 230
Number of Students of Higher Vocational Colleges ········· 232
Number of Students in Radio/TV Universities ········· 234
Number of Students in Workers' Colleges ········· 236
Number of Students in Educational Colleges ········· 238
Number of Students in Institutes for Administration ········· 240
Number of Students in Other Insitutes ········· 242
Number of Students in Correspondence divisions, Sparetime Schools & Short-cycle Courses for Adults run by Regular HEIs ········· 244
Number of On-the-job Students Studying for Master's Degree ········· 246
Number of Students in Non-formal Education of HEIs (Total) ········· 248
Number of Students in Non-formal Education of Regular HEIs ········· 250
Number of Students in Non-formal Education of Adults HEIs ········· 252
Number of Students in Non-formal Education of Research Institutes ········· 254
Number of Students in Non-formal Education of Other Non-government HEIs ········· 256
Information on Foreign Students ········· 258
Number of Educational Personnel in HEIs (Total) ········· 260
Number of Female Educational Personnel in HEIs (Total) ········· 262
Number of Educational Personnel in Regular HEIs ········· 264
Number of Female Educational Personnel in Regular HEIs ········· 266
Number of Educational Personnel in Adults HEIs ········· 268
Number of Female Educational Personnel in Adult HEIs ········· 270
Number of Educational Personnel in Other Non-government HEIs ········· 272
Number of Female Educational Personnel in Other Non-government HEIs ········· 274
Number of Full-time Teacher by Academic Qualification and Professional Rank (Total) ········· 276
Number of Full-time Teacher by Academic Qualification and Professional Rank (Regular HEIs) ········· 277
Number of Full-time Teacher by Academic Qualification and Professional Rank (Adult HEIs) ········· 278
Number of Full-time Teacher by Academic Qualification and Professional Rank (Other Non-government HEIs) ········· 279
Number of Part-timeTeacher by Academic Qualification (Total) ········· 280
Number of Part-timeTeacher by Academic Qualification (Regular HEIs) ········· 281
Number of Part-timeTeacher by Academic Qualification (Adults HEIs) ········· 282
Number of Part-timeTeacher by Academic Qualification (Other Non-government HEIs) ········· 283
Condition of Fixed Assets and Teaching Resources (Owned by HEIs) (Total) ········· 284
Condition of Fixed Assets and Teaching Resources (Owned by HEIs) (Regular HEIs) ········· 286
Condition of Fixed Assets and Teaching Resources (Owned by HEIs) (Adult HEIs) ········· 288

Condition of Fixed Assets and Teaching Resources (Owned by HEIs) (Other Non-government HEIs) ………… 290
Condition of Fixed Assets and Teaching Resources (Not Owned by HEIs) (Total) ………… 292
Condition of Fixed Assets and Teaching Resources (Not Owned by HEIs) (Regular HEIs) ………… 294
Condition of Fixed Assets and Teaching Resources (Not Owned by HEIs) (Adult HEIs) ………… 296
Condition of Fixed Assets and Teaching Resources (Not Owned by HEIs) (Other Non-government HEIs) ………… 298
Condition of School Buidings (Total) ………… 300
Condition of School Buidings (Regular HEIs) ………… 301
Condition of School Buidings (Adult HEIs) ………… 302
Condition of School Buidings (Other Non-government HEIs) ………… 303
Number of Schools and Classes in Regular Senior Secondary Schools (Total) ………… 304
Number of Schools and Classes in Regular Senior Secondary Schools (Urban Area) ………… 305
Number of Schools and Classes in Regular Senior Secondary Schools (Urban-rural Transitional Area) ………… 306
Number of Schools and Classes in Regular Senior Secondary Schools (Counties & Towns Area) ………… 307
Number of Schools and Classes in Regular Senior Secondary Schools (County-town Transitional Area) ………… 308
Number of Schools and Classes in Regular Senior Secondary Schools (Rural Area) ………… 309
Number of Students in Regular Senior Secondary Schools (Total) ………… 310
Number of Students in Regular Senior Secondary Schools (Urban Area) ………… 311
Number of Students in Regular Senior Secondary Schools (Urban-rural Transitional Area) ………… 312
Number of Students in Regular Senior Secondary Schools (Counties & Towns Area) ………… 313
Number of Students in Regular Senior Secondary Schools (County-town Transitional Area) ………… 314
Number of Students in Regular Senior Secondary Schools (Rural Area) ………… 315
Number of Female Students in Regular Senior Secondary Schools ………… 316
Number of Educational Personnel in General Secondary Schools (Total) ………… 317
Number of Educational Personnel in General Secondary Schools (Urban Area) ………… 318
Number of Educational Personnel in General Secondary Schools (Urban-rural Transitional Area) ………… 319
Number of Educational Personnel in General Secondary Schools (Counties & Towns Area) ………… 320
Number of Educational Personnel in General Secondary Schools (County-town Transitional Area) ………… 321
Number of Educational Personnel in General Secondary Schools (Rural Area) ………… 322
Number of Female Educational Personnel in General Secondary Schools ………… 323
Number of General Secondary Schools Educational Personnel Maintained by the Communties ………… 324
Number of Full-time Teachers in Regular Senior Secondary Schools by Academic Qualification and Professional Rank (Total) ………… 326
Number of Full-time Teachers in Regular Senior Secondary Schools by Academic Qualification and Professional Rank (Urban Area) ………… 328
Number of Full-time Teachers in Regular Senior Secondary Schools by Academic Qualification and Professional Rank (Urban-rural Transitional Area) ………… 330
Number of Full-time Teachers in Regular Senior Secondary Schools by Academic Qualification and Professional Rank (Counties & Towns Area) ………… 332
Number of Full-time Teachers in Regular Senior Secondary Schools by Academic Qualification and Professional Rank (County-town Transitional Area) ………… 334
Number of Full-time Teachers in Regular Senior Secondary Schools by Academic Qualification and Professional Rank (Rural Area) ………… 336
Condition of School Buildings in Regular Senior Secondary Schools (1) (Total) ………… 338
Condition of School Buildings in Regular Senior Secondary Schools (1) (Urban Area) ………… 340
Condition of School Buildings in Regular Senior Secondary Schools (1) (Urban-rural Transitional Area) ………… 342
Condition of School Buildings in Regular Senior Secondary Schools (1) (Counties & Towns Area) ………… 344

Condition of School Buildings in Regular Senior Secondary Schools (1) (County-town Transitional Area) ········ 346
Condition of School Buildings in Regular Senior Secondary Schools (1) (Rural Area) ········ 348
Condition of School Buildings in Regular Senior Secondary Schools (2) (Total) ········ 350
Condition of School Buildings in Regular Senior Secondary Schools (2) (Urban Area) ········ 352
Condition of School Buildings in Regular Senior Secondary Schools (2) (Urban-rural Transitional Area) ········ 354
Condition of School Buildings in Regular Senior Secondary Schools (2) (Counties & Towns Area) ········ 356
Condition of School Buildings in Regular Senior Secondary Schools (2) (County-town Transitional Area) ········ 358
Condition of School Buildings in Regular Senior Secondary Schools (2) (Rural Area) ········ 360
Number of Secondary Vocational Schools (Institutions) ········ 362
Number of students in Secondary Vocational Schools (Institutions) ········ 364
Number of Female students in Secondary Vocational Schools (Institutions) ········ 366
Number of Students in Reg. Specialized Sec. Schools ········ 368
Number of Female Students in Reg. Specialized Sec. Schools ········ 370
Number of Students in Adult Specialized Sec. Schools ········ 372
Number of Female Students in Adult Specialized Sec. Schools ········ 374
Number of Students in Vocational High Schools ········ 376
Number of Female Students in Vocational High Schools ········ 378
Number of Students by Age in Secondary Vocational Schools (Institutions) ········ 380
Number of Female Students by Age in Secondary Vocational Schools (Institutions) ········ 382
Number of Graduates in Secondary Vocational Schools (Institutions) ········ 384
Number of Enrolment in Secondary Vocational Schools (Institutions) ········ 386
Changes of Enrolment in Secondary Vocational Schools (Institutions) ········ 388
Changes of Female Enrolment in Secondary Vocational Schools (Institutions) ········ 390
Number of Foreign Students in Secondary Vocational Schools (Institutions) ········ 392
Number of Educational Personnel in Secondary Vocational Schools (Institutions) ········ 394
Number of Female Educational Personnel in Secondary Vocational Schools (Institutions) ········ 396
Number of Educational Personnel in Regular Specialized Secondary Vocational Schools (Institutions) ········ 398
Number of Female Educational Personnel in Regular Specialized Secondary Schools (Institutions) ········ 400
Number of Educational Personnel in Adult Specialized Sec. Schools ········ 402
Number of Female Educational Personnel in Adult Specialized Sec. Schools ········ 404
Number of Educational Personnel in Vocational High Schools ········ 406
Number of Female Educational Personnel in Vocational High Schools ········ 408
Number of Educational Personnel in Other Institutions ········ 410
Number of Female Educational Personnel in Other Institutions ········ 412
Number of Full-time Teachers By Professional Rank and Academic Qualifications in Secondary Vocational Schools (Institutions) ········ 414
Number of Full-time Teachers By Professional Rank and Academic Qualifications in Reg. Specialized Sec. Schools ········ 416
Number of Full-time Teachers By Professional Rank and Academic Qualifications in Adult Specialized Sec. Schools ········ 418
Number of Full-time Teachers By Professional Rank and Academic Qualifications in Vocational High Schools ··· 420
Number of Full-time Teachers By Professional Rank and Academic Qualifications in Other Institutions ········ 422
Condition of Fixed Assets and Teaching Resources in Secondary Vocational Schools (Institutions) (Owned by SVSs) ········ 424
Condition of Fixed Assets and Teaching Resources in Secondary Vocational Schools (Institutions) (Not Owned by SVSs) ········ 426

Condition of Fixed Assets and Teaching Resources in Regular SSSs (Owned by Regular SSSs) ………… 428
Condition of Fixed Assets and Teaching Resources in Regular SSSs (Not Owned by Regular SSSs) ………… 430
Condition of Fixed Assets and Teaching Resources in Adult SSSs (Owned by Adult SSSs) ………… 432
Condition of Fixed Assets and Teaching Resources in Adult SSSs (Not Owned by Adult SSSs) ………… 434
Condition of Fixed Assets and Teaching Resources in Vocational High Schools (Owned by VHSs) ………… 436
Condition of Fixed Assets and Teaching Resources in Vocational High Schools (Not Owned by VHSs) ………… 438
Condition of Fixed Assets and Teaching Resources in Other Institutions (Owned by SVSs) ………… 440
Condition of Fixed Assets and Teaching Resources in Other Institutions (Not Owned by SVSs) ………… 442
Condition of School Buidings in Secondary Vocational Schools (Institutions) (Total) ………… 444
Condition of School Buidings in Regular Specialized Sec. Schools ………… 445
Condition of School Buidings in Adult Specialized Sec. Schools ………… 446
Condition of School Buidings in Vocational High Schools ………… 447
Condition of School Buidings in Vocational High Schools ………… 448
Basic Statistics of Vocational Technical Training Institutions (Total) ………… 450
Basic Statistics of Vocational Technical Training Schools ………… 452
Basic Statistics of Technical Training Schools for Peasants ………… 454
Basic Statistics of Others ………… 456
Condition of Fixed Assets and Teaching Resources in Vocational Technical Training Institutions ………… 458
Condition of Fixed Assets and Teaching Resources in Technical Training Schools ………… 460
Condition of Fixed Assets and Teaching Resources in Technical Training Schools for Peasants ………… 462
Condition of Fixed Assets and Teaching Resources in Others ………… 464
Number of Schools, Classes of Junior Secondary Schools (Total) ………… 466
Number of Schools, Classes of Junior Secondary Schools (Urban Area) ………… 468
Number of Schools, Classes of Junior Secondary Schools (Urban-rural Transitional Area) ………… 469
Number of Schools, Classes of Junior Secondary Schools (Counties & Towns Area) ………… 470
Number of Schools, Classes of Junior Secondary Schools (County-town Transitional Area) ………… 471
Number of Schools, Classes of Junior Secondary Schools (Rural Area) ………… 472
Number of Students in Junior Secondary Schools (Total) ………… 473
Number of Students in Junior Secondary Schools (Urban Area) ………… 474
Number of Students in Junior Secondary Schools (Urban-rural Transitional Area) ………… 475
Number of Students in Junior Secondary Schools (Counties & Towns Area) ………… 476
Number of Students in Junior Secondary Schools (County-town Transitional Area) ………… 477
Number of Students in Junior Secondary Schools (Rural Area) ………… 478
Number of Female Students in Junior Secondary Schools ………… 479
Number of Full-time Teachers in Junior Secondary Schools by Academic Qualifications and Professional Rank (Total) ………… 480
Number of Full-time Teachers in Junior Secondary Schools by Academic Qualifications and Professional Rank (Urban Area) ………… 482
Number of Full-time Teachers in Junior Secondary Schools by Academic Qualifications and Professional Rank (Urban-rural Transitional Area) ………… 484
Number of Full-time Teachers in Junior Secondary Schools by Academic Qualifications and Professional Rank (Counties & Towns Area) ………… 486
Number of Full-time Teachers in Junior Secondary Schools by Academic Qualifications and Professional Rank (County-town Transitional Area) ………… 488
Number of Full-time Teachers in Junior Secondary Schools by Academic Qualifications and Professional Rank (Rural Area) ………… 490

Condition of School Buildings in Junior Secondary Schools (1) (Total) 492
Condition of School Buildings in Junior Secondary Schools (1) (Urban Area) 494
Condition of School Buildings in Junior Secondary Schools (1) (Urban-rural Transitional Area) 496
Condition of School Buildings in Junior Secondary Schools (1) (Counties & Towns Area) 498
Condition of School Buildings in Junior Secondary Schools (1) (County-town Transitional Area) 500
Condition of School Buildings in Junior Secondary Schools (1) (Rural Area) 502
Condition of School Buildings in Junior Secondary Schools (2) (Total) 504
Condition of School Buildings in Junior Secondary Schools (2) (Urban Area) 506
Condition of School Buildings in Junior Secondary Schools (2) (Urban-rural Transitional Area) 508
Condition of School Buildings in Junior Secondary Schools (2) (Counties & Towns Area) 510
Condition of School Buildings in Junior Secondary Schools (2) (County-town Transitional Area) 512
Condition of School Buildings in Junior Secondary Schools (2) (Rural Area) 514
Number of Schools, External Teaching Sites & Classes in Primary Schools (Total) 516
Number of Schools, External Teaching Sites & Classes in Primary Schools (Urban Area) 518
Number of Schools, External Teaching Sites & Classes in Primary Schools (Urban-rural Transitional Area) 520
Number of Schools, External Teaching Sites & Classes in Primary Schools (Counties & Towns Area) 522
Number of Schools, External Teaching Sites & Classes in Primary Schools (County-town Transitional Area) 524
Number of Schools, External Teaching Sites & Classes in Primary Schools (Rural Area) 526
Number of Students in Primary Schools (Total) 528
Number of Students in Primary Schools (Urban Area) 530
Number of Students in Primary Schools (Urban-rural Transitional Area) 532
Number of Students in Primary Schools (Counties & Towns Area) 534
Number of Students in Primary Schools (County-town Transitional Area) 536
Number of Students in Primary Schools (Rural Area) 538
Number of Students in 5-year Primary Schools 540
Number of Female Students in Primary Schools 542
Number of Educational Personnel in Primary Schools (Total) 544
Number of Educational Personnel in Primary Schools (Urban Area) 546
Number of Educational Personnel in Primary Schools (Urban-rural Transitional Area) 548
Number of Educational Personnel in Primary Schools (Counties & Towns Area) 550
Number of Educational Personnel in Primary Schools (County-town Transitional Area) 552
Number of Educational Personnel in Primary Schools (Rural Area) 554
Number of Primary Schools Educational Personnel Maintained by Communities 556
Number of Female Educational Personnel in Primary Schools 558
Number of Full-time Teacher in Primary Schools by Academic Qualification and Professin Rank (Total) 560
Number of Full-time Teacher in Primary Schools by Academic Qualification and Professin Rank (Urban Area) 562
Number of Full-time Teacher in Primary Schools by Academic Qualification and Professin Rank (Urban-rural Transitional Area) 564
Number of Full-time Teacher in Primary Schools by Academic Qualification and Professin Rank (Counties & Towns Area) 566
Number of Full-time Teacher in Primary Schools by Academic Qualification and Professin Rank (County-town Transitional Area) 568
Number of Full-time Teacher in Primary Schools by Academic Qualification and Professin Rank (Rural Area) 570
Condition of School Buildings in Primary Schools (1) (Total) 572

Condition of School Buildings in Primary Schools (1) (Urban Area) 574
Condition of School Buildings in Primary Schools (1) (Urban-rural Transitional Area 576
Condition of School Buildings in Primary Schools (1) (Counties & Towns Area) 578
Condition of School Buildings in Primary Schools (1) (County-town Transitional Area) 580
Condition of School Buildings in Primary Schools (1) (Rural Area) 582
Condition of School Buildings in Primary Schools (2) (Total) 584
Condition of School Buildings in Primary Schools (2) (Urban Area) 586
Condition of School Buildings in Primary Schools (2) (Urban-rural Transitional Area) 588
Condition of School Buildings in Primary Schools (2) (Counties & Towns Area) 590
Condition of School Buildings in Primary Schools (2) (County-town Transitional Area) 592
Condition of School Buildings in Primary Schools (2) (Rural Area) 594
Basic Statistics of Correctional Work-study Schools 596
Basic Statistics of Special Education (Total) 598
Basic Statistics of Special Education (Urban Area) 600
Basic Statistics of Special Education (Urban-rural Transitional Area) 602
Basic Statistics of Special Education (Counties & Towns Area) 604
Basic Statistics of Special Education (County-town Transitional Area) 606
Basic Statistics of Special Education (Rural Area) 608
Number of Female Students in Special Education 610
Number of Educational Personnel in Special Education Schools (Total) 612
Number of Female Educational Personnel in Special Education Schools 613
Number of Full-time Teachers in Special Education Schools by Academic Qualification and Professional Rank ... 614
Condition of School Buildings in Special Education Schools (1) 616
Condition of School Buildings in Special Education Schools (2) 618
Basic Statistics of Kindergartens (Total) 619
Basic Statistics of Kindergartens (Urban Area) 620
Basic Statistics of Kindergartens (Urban-rural Transitional Area) 621
Basic Statistics of Kindergartens (Counties & Towns Area) 622
Basic Statistics of Kindergartens (County-town Transitional Area) 623
Basic Statistics of Kindergartens (Rural Area) 624
Number of Female Children in Kindergartens 625
Number of Educational Personnel in Kindergarten (Total) 626
Number of Educational Personnel in Kindergarten (Urban Area) 627
Number of Educational Personnel in Kindergarten (Urban-rural Transitional Area) 628
Number of Educational Personnel in Kindergarten (Counties & Towns Area) 629
Number of Educational Personnel in Kindergarten (County-town Transitional Area) 630
Number of Educational Personnel in Kindergarten (Rural Area) 631
Number of Female Educational Personnel in Kindergarten 632
Number of Kindergarten Heads, Full-time Teachers by Academic Qualification and Professional Rank (Total) 634
Number of Kindergarten Heads, Full-time Teachers by Academic Qualification and Professional Rank (Urban Area) 636
Number of Kindergarten Heads, Full-time Teachers by Academic Qualification and Professional Rank (Urban-rural Transitional Area) 638
Number of Kindergarten Heads, Full-time Teachers by Academic Qualification and Professional Rank (Counties & Towns Area) 640

Number of Kindergarten Heads, Full-time Teachers by Academic Qualification and Professional Rank (County-town Transitional Area) ········ 642
Number of Kindergarten Heads, Full-time Teachers by Academic Qualification and Professional Rank (Rural Area) ········ 644
Statistics of Kindergarten Buildings and Others (Total) (1) ········ 646
Statistics of Kindergarten Buildings and Others (Urban Area) (1) ········ 648
Statistics of Kindergarten Buildings and Others (Urban-rural Transitional Area) (1) ········ 650
Statistics of Kindergarten Buildings and Others (Counties & Towns Area) (1) ········ 652
Statistics of Kindergarten Buildings and Others (County-town Transitional Area) (1) ········ 654
Statistics of Kindergarten Buildings and Others (Rural Area) (1) ········ 656
Statistics of Kindergarten Buildings and Others (Total) (2) ········ 658
Statistics of Kindergarten Buildings and Others (Urban Area) (2) ········ 659
Statistics of Kindergarten Buildings and Others (Urban-rural Transitional Area) (2) ········ 660
Statistics of Kindergarten Buildings and Others (Counties & Towns Area) (2) ········ 661
Statistics of Kindergarten Buildings and Others (County-town Transitional Area) (2) ········ 662
Statistics of Kindergarten Buildings and Others (Rural Area) (2) ········ 663

Part Ⅱ

PHYSICAL FACILITIES

Capital Construction Investment in the Educational Sector

Data on the Completion of Capital Construction Investment in the Educational Sector (Total) ········ 666
Data on the Completion of Capital Construction Investment in the Educational Sector ········ 668

Part Ⅲ

SCIENTIFIC RESEARCH ACTIVITES & OTHER

Natural Science and Technology

Scientific and Technical Manpower in Regular HEIs ········ 672
S & T Expenditure in Regular HEIs ········ 674
Statistics of R & D Projects and Achievements in Regular HEIs ········ 676

Social Science

Professional Manpower in Regular HEIs in the Fields of the Humanities and Social Science ········ 680
Humanities and Social Sciences R & D Expenditure in Regular HEIs ········ 682
Basic Statistics of Humunities and Social Sciences R & D and Achievements in Regular HEIs ········ 684

Appendixes

Gross Domestic Product ········ 687

Gross Domestic Product by Region (2012) ······ 688
Total Government Revernue and Expenditures and Their Increase Rate ······ 689
Total Revenue and Expenditures of Central and Local Governments ······ 690
Population and Its Composition ······ 691
Illterate Population Aged 15 and Over by Sex and Region ······ 692
Population by Sex, Educational Level and Region ······ 693

第一部分
Part I

教育事业发展
THE DEVELOPMENT OF THE EDUCATIONAL UNDERTAKING

一、综合部分
Summary Tables

各级各类学校校数、教职工、专任教师情况

Number of Schools, Educational Personnel and Full-time Teachers by Type and Level

	学校数(所) Schools	教职工数(人) Educational Personnel	专任教师(人) Full-time Teachers
一、高等教育 Higher Education			
(一)研究生培养机构(不计校数) Institutions Providing Postgraduate Programs	(830)		
1. 普通高校 Regular HEIs	(548)		
2. 科研机构 Research Institutes	(282)		
(二)普通高等学校 Regular HEIs	2491	2296262	1496865
1. 本科院校 HEIs Offering Degree Programs	1170	1657517	1055036
其中:独立学院 of Which:Independent Institutions	292	186262	138815
2. 高职(专科)院校 Higher Vocational Colleges	1321	630044	436561
3. 其他机构(点)(不计校数) Other Institutions	(33)	8701	5268
(三)成人高等学校 Adult HEIs	297	56417	33647
(四)民办的其他高等教育机构 Other Non-government HEIs	(802)	28394	13350
二、中等教育 Secondary Education	80797	7569100	5988381
(一)高中阶段教育 Senior Secondary Education	26225	3633057	2501569
1. 高中 Senior Secondary Schools	13963	2479655	1633626
普通高中 Regular Senior Secondary Schools	13352	2473594	1629008
完全中学 Combined Secondary Schools	5861	1061968	521094
高级中学 Regular High Schools	6591	1243624	1065888
十二年一贯制学校 12-year Schools	900	168002	42026
成人高中 Adult High Schools	611	6061	4618
2. 中等职业教育 Secondary Vocational Education	12262	1153402	867943
普通中专 Regular Specialized Secondary Schools	3577	419315	303585
成人中专 Adult Specialized Secondary Schools	1536	72715	52021
职业高中 Vocational High Schools	4267	375370	301440
技工学校 Skilled Workers Schools	2882	269443	199189
其他机构(教学点)(不计校数) Other Institutions	(451)	16559	11708
(二)初中阶段教育 Junior Secondary Education	54572	3936043	3486812
1. 初中 Junior Secondary Schools	52804	3928762	3480979
初级中学 Regular Junior Secondary Schools	38747	2894926	2587399
九年一贯制学校 9-year Schools	14017	1032777	449797
十二年一贯制学校 12-year Schools			42848
完全中学 Combined Secondary Schools			399952
职业初中 Vocational Junior Secondary Schools	40	1059	983
2. 成人初中 Adult Junior Secondary Schools	1768	7281	5833
三、初等教育 Primary Education	235369	5538480	5607283
(一)普通小学 Regular Primary Schools	213529	5494877	5584644
小学 Primary Schools	213529	5494877	5096634
九年一贯制学校 9-year Schools			449126
十二年一贯制学校 12-year Schools			38884
(二)成人小学 Adult Primary Schools	21840	43603	22639
其中:扫盲班 of Which: Literacy Classes	15104	32658	15399
四、工读学校 Correctional Work-Study Schools	78	2687	1851
五、特殊教育 Special Education Schools	1933	55096	45653
六、学前教育 Pre-school Education Institutions	198553	2826753	1663487

注:1. 完全中学的学校数和教职工数计入高中阶段教育,九年一贯制学校的校数和教职工数计入初中阶段教育,十二年一贯制学校的校数和教职工数计入高中阶段教育。专任教师是按照教育层次划分归类。

2. "( )"内数据为不计校数。

Note: 1. The numbers of Complete Secondary Schools and their educational personnel are calculated into the number of Senior Secondary education, the numbers of Combined Primary and Lower Secondary Schools and their educational personnel are calculated into the Junior Secondary education, and the numbers of the Combined Primary and Secondary Schools and their educational personnel are calculated into Senior Secondary education. The fulltime teachers are classified by educational level.

2. The data within "( )" are not calculated as the number of schools.

各级各类学历教育学生情况

Number of Students of Formal Education by Type and Level

单位：人

unit:person

	毕业生数 Graduates	招生数 Entrants	在校生数 Enrolment
一、高等教育 Higher Education			
（一）研究生 Postgraduates	513626	611381	1793953
博　士 Doctor's Degree	53139	70462	298283
硕　士 Master's Degree	460487	540919	1495670
（二）普通本专科 Undergraduates in Regular HEIs	6387210	6998330	24680726
本　科 Normal Courses	3199716	3814331	14944353
专　科 Short-cycle Courses	3187494	3183999	9736373
（三）成人本专科 Undergraduates in Adult HEIs	1997729	2564934	6264145
本　科 Normal Courses	811159	1038158	2654596
专　科 Short-cycle Courses	1186570	1526776	3609549
（四）其他各类高等学历教育 Students Enrolled in Other Formal Programs			
1. 在职人员攻读硕士学位 Master's Degree Programs for On-the-job Personnel		167576	558730
2. 网络本专科生 Web-based Undergraduates	1560762	2200729	6146406
本　科 Normal Courses	536702	804378	2175100
专　科 Short-cycle Courses	1024060	1396351	3971306
二、中等教育 Secondary Education	30887540	29935409	88582754
（一）高中阶段教育 Senior Secondary Education	14838197	14974542	43699228
1. 高中 Senior Secondary Schools	8093801	8226961	24469522
普通高中 Regular Senior Secondary Schools	7989789	8226961	24358817
完全中学 Combined Secondary Schools	2551466	2689932	7914286
高级中学 Regular High Schools	5242878	5308309	15814322
十二年一贯制学校 12-year Schools	195445	228720	630209
成人高中 Adult High Schools	104012		110705
2. 中等职业教育 Secondary Vocational Education	6744396	6747581	19229706
普通中专 Regular Specialized Secondary Schools	2652082	2714716	7721842
成人中专 Adult Specialized Secondary Schools	878323	862591	2299806
职业高中 Vocational High Schools	2045182	1835317	5342194
技工学校 Skilled Workers Schools	1168809	1334957	3865864
（二）初中阶段教育 Junior Secondary Education	16049343	14960867	44883526
1. 初中 Junior Secondary Schools	15615452	14960867	44401248
初级中学 Regular Junior Secondary Schools	11559429	10863869	32340393
九年一贯制学校 9-year Schools	1760777	1804465	5256281
十二年一贯制学校 12-year Schools	206450	231841	666538
完全中学 Combined Secondary Schools	2081587	2057158	6127520
职业初中 Vocational Junior Secondary Schools	7209	3534	10516
2. 成人初中 Adult Junior Secondary Schools	433891		482278
三、初等教育 Primary Education	16988501	16953556	94848050
（一）普通小学 Regular Primary Schools	15810583	16953556	93605487
小学 Primary Schools	14315683	15451429	84998824
九年一贯制学校 9-year Schools	1372707	1381950	7920436
十二年一贯制学校 12-year Schools	122193	120177	686227
（二）成人小学 Adult Primary Schools	1177918		1242563
其中：扫盲班 of Which: Literacy Classes	505877		619228
四、工读学校 Correctional Work-Study Schools	3596	3891	9307
五、特殊教育 Special Education Schools	50739	65977	368103
六、学前教育 Pre-school Education Institutions	14917314	19700271	38946903

注：1. 完全中学、九年一贯制学校和十二年一贯制学校的学生数按教育层次分别计入对应教育阶段的学生数中。

2. 特殊教育学生数中包括义务教育阶段随班就读的学生、其他学校附设特教班。

Note: 1. Number of the students in Combined Secondary Schools, 9 - year Schools, 12 - year Schools are classified by educational level.

2. Number of the Students Followed in the Regular Primary and Middle School in the Special Education.

各级各类非学历教育学生情况

Number of Students of Non-formal Education by Type and Level

单位：人

unit:person

	结业生数 Completers	注册学生数 Enrolment
总 计 Total	**62741102**	**55932104**
一、高等教育 Higher Education	9337748	6785562
(一)研究生课程进修班 Postgraduate Courses	48329	69321
(二)自考助学班 Classes run by Non-government HEIs for Students Preparing for Self-directed State-administered Examinations	194882	405329
(三)普通预科生 College-preparatory Classes		42514
(四)进修及培训 In-service Training	9094537	6268398
其中:资格证书培训 of Which:For Certificates of Vocational Qualifications	2351305	1979966
岗位证书培训 For Certificates of Job-related Qualifications	2504684	1713103
二、中等职业教育 Secondary Vocational Education	53403354	49146542
其中:资格证书培训 of Which:For Certificates of Vocational Qualifications	8693004	8028370
岗位证书培训 For Certificates of Job-related Qualifications	12781963	11670337
(一)中等职业学校 Secondary Vocational Schools	6247386	3986943
其中:资格证书培训 of Which:For Certificates of Vocational Qualifications	2467512	1757692
岗位证书培训 For Certificates of Job-related Qualifications	2048427	1182845
(二)职业技术培训机构 Other Vocational-technical Training Institutions	47155968	45159599
其中:资格证书培训 of Which:For Certificates of Vocational Qualifications	6225492	6270678
岗位证书培训 For Certificates of Job-related Qualifications	10733536	10487492

各级各类民办教育基本情况

Number of Non-government Schools by Type and Level

单位：人

unit:person

	学校数(所) Schools	毕业生数 Graduates	招生数 Entrants	在校生数 Enrolment	教职工数 Educational Personnel	专任教师 Full-time Teachers	另有其他学生数 Other Students
一、民办高等教育 Non-government Higher Education							
(一)民办高校 Non-government HEIs	718	1332720	1601879	5575218	398400	281415	258426
硕 士 Master's Degree			181	335			
本科学生 Normal Courses		719535	921391	3616363			
专科学生 Short-cycle Courses		613185	680307	1958520			
其中:独立学院 of Which:Independent Institutions	292	593397	688917	2758465	186262	138815	28956
本科学生 Normal Courses		543697	641025	2608259			
专科学生 Short-cycle Courses		49700	47892	150206			
(二)民办其他高等教育机构 Other Non-government HEIs	(802)				28394	13350	879922
二、民办中等教育 Non-government Secondary Education							
(一)高中阶段教育 Senior Secondary Education	4857	1538303	1529785	4395853	446456	318307	
1. 民办普通高中 Regular Senior Secondary Schools	2375	747589	798192	2316445	328642	240426	
2. 民办中等职业教育 Secondary Vocational Education	2482	790714	731593	2079408	117814	77881	302303
(二)初中阶段教育 Junior Secondary Education	4535	1384917	1621113	4623482	337166	258662	
1. 民办普通初中 Regular Junior Secondary Schools	4535	1384917	1621113	4623482	337166	258662	
三、民办普通小学 Non-government Regular Primary Schools	5407	1008291	1112846	6286015	204861	151800	
四、民办幼儿园 Non-government Pre-school Education	133451	6347047	9079575	19902536	1848754	1020215	
另有:民办培训机构(不计校数) Other Vocational-technical Training Institutions	(20104)				229537	129634	9435604

注:1. “另有其他学生数”包括:自考助学班学生、预科生、进修及培训学生数。
2. 民办中等职业教育数据中未含技工学校数据。
3. “( )”内数据为不计校数。

Note: 1. Number of the other Students Followed in the Classes runby Non-government HEIs for Students Preparing for State-administered Examinatims for Self-directed Leamers, College-preparatory Classes, In-service Traning.
2. Data on non-government secondary vocational education does not include those of skilled workers schools.
3. The numbers within “( )” are not included.

各级各类学校女学生数

Number of Female Students of Schools by Type and Level

单位：人

unit：person

	总计 Total	男 Male	女学生 Female Students 人数 Number	占学生总数的比重(%) Percentage
一、高等教育 Higher Education				
(一)研究生 Postgraduates	1793953	915469	878484	48.97
博　士 Doctor's Degree	298283	188207	110076	36.90
硕　士 Master's Degree	1495670	727262	768408	51.38
(二)普通本专科 Undergraduate in Regular HEIs	24680726	11911527	12769199	51.74
本　科 Normal Courses	14944353	7206309	7738044	51.78
专　科 Short-cycle Courses	9736373	4705218	5031155	51.67
(三)成人本专科 Undergraduate in Adult HEIs	6264145	2801387	3462758	55.28
本　科 Normal Courses	2654596	1159003	1495593	56.34
专　科 Short-cycle Courses	3609549	1642384	1967165	54.50
(四)其他各类高等学历教育 Students Enrolled in Other Formal Programs				
1. 在职人员攻读硕士学位 Master's Degree Programs for On-the-job Personnel	558730	379343	179387	32.11
2. 网络本专科生 Web-based Undergraduates	6146406	3130417	3015989	49.07
本　科 Normal Courses	2175100	1035577	1139523	52.39
专　科 Short-cycle Courses	3971306	2094840	1876466	47.25
二、中等教育 Secondary Education	88582754	46625481	41957273	47.37
(一)高中阶段教育 Senior Secondary Education	43699228	22800059	20899169	47.83
1. 高中 Senior Secondary Schools	24469522	12295090	12174432	49.75
普通高中 Regular Senior Secondary Schools	24358817	12239917	12118900	49.75
完全中学 Combined Secondary Schools	7914286	3997003	3917283	49.50
高级中学 Regular High Schools	15814322	7893981	7920341	50.08
十二年一贯制学校 12-year Schools	630209	348933	281276	44.63
成人高中 Adult High Schools	110705	55173	55532	50.16
2. 中等职业教育 Secondary Vocational Education	19229706	10504969	8724737	45.37
普通中专 Regular Specialized Secondary Schools	7721842	3584853	4136989	53.58
成人中专 Adult Specialized Secondary Schools	2299806	1263725	1036081	45.05
职业高中 Vocational High Schools	5342194	2868899	2473295	46.30
技工学校 Skilled Workers Schools	3865864	2787492	1078372	27.89
(二)初中阶段教育 Junior Secondary Education	44883526	23825422	21058104	46.92
1. 初中 Junior Secondary Schools	44401248	23564942	20836306	46.93
初级中学 Regular Junior Secondary Schools	32340393	17028783	15311610	47.35
九年一贯制学校 9-year Schools	5256281	2880110	2376171	45.21
十二年一贯制学校 12-year Schools	666538	392980	273558	41.04
完全中学 Combined Secondary Schools	6127520	3257526	2869994	46.84
职业初中 Vocational Junior Secondary Schools	10516	5543	4973	47.29
2. 成人初中 Adult Junior Secondary Schools	482278	260480	221798	45.99
三、初等教育 Primary Education	94848050	50868566	43979484	46.37
(一)普通小学 Regular Primary Schools	93605487	50292799	43312688	46.27
小学 Primary Schools	84998824	45521537	39477287	46.44
九年一贯制学校 9-year Schools	7920436	4366870	3553566	44.87
十二年一贯制学校 12-year Schools	686227	404392	281835	41.07
(二)成人小学 Adult Primary Schools	1242563	575767	666796	53.66
其中：扫盲班 of Which：Literacy Classes	619228	286616	332612	53.71
四、工读学校 Correctional Work-Study Schools	9307	8042	1265	13.59
五、特殊教育 Special Education Schools	368026	235536	132490	36.00
六、学前教育 Pre-school Education Institutions	38946903	20964619	17982284	46.17

各级各类学校女教师、女教职工数

Number of Female Educational Personnel and Full-time Teachers of Schools by Type and Level

单位：人

unit：person

	教职工 Educational Personnel	其中：女教职工 of Which Female Educational Personnel		专任教师 Full-time Teachers	其中：女专任教师 of Which Female Full-time Teachers	
		人数 Number	占教职工总数的比重（%） Percentage		人数 Number	占专任教师总数的比重（%） Percentage
一、高等教育 Higher Education						
（一）研究生培养机构（不计校数） Institutions Providing Postgraduate Programs						
1. 普通高校 Regular HEIs						
2. 科研机构 Research Institutes						
（二）普通高等学校 Regular HEIs	2296262	1070126	46.60	1496865	714450	47.73
1. 本科院校 HEIs Offering Degree Programs	1657517	757592	45.71	1055036	487868	46.24
其中：独立学院 of Which：Independent Institutions	186262	93880	50.40	138815	69391	49.99
2. 高职（专科）院校 Higher Vocational Colleges	630044	308885	49.03	436561	224345	51.39
3. 其他机构（点）（不计校数） Other Institutions	8701	3649	41.94	5268	2237	42.46
（三）成人高等学校 Adult HEIs	56417	27364	48.50	33647	17769	52.81
（四）民办的其他高等教育机构 Other Non-government HEIs	28394	14936	52.60	13350	6777	50.76
二、中等教育 Secondary Education	7569100	3771599	49.83	5988381		
（一）高中阶段教育 Senior Secondary Education	3633057	1787985	49.21	2501569		
1. 高中 Senior Secondary Schools	2479655	1251277	50.46	1633626	813921	49.82
普通高中 Regular Senior Secondary Schools	2473594	1248709	50.48	1629008	811941	49.84
完全中学 Combined Secondary Schools	1061968	544547	51.28	521094	255322	49.00
高级中学 Regular High Schools	1243624	602307	48.43	1065888	536685	50.35
十二年一贯制学校 12-year Schools	168002	101855	60.63	42026	19934	47.43
成人高中 Adult High Schools	6061	2568	42.37	4618	1980	42.88
2. 中等职业教育 Secondary Vocational Education	1153402	536708	46.53	867943		
普通中专 Regular Specialized Secondary Schools	419315	199873	47.67	303585	154955	51.04
成人中专 Adult Specialized Secondary Schools	72715	33973	46.72	52021	26292	50.54
职业高中 Vocational High Schools	375370	179125	47.72	301440	152069	50.45
技工学校 Skilled Workers Schools	269443	116194	43.12	199189		
其他机构（教学点）（不计校数） Other Institutions	16559	7543	45.55	11708	5860	50.05
（二）初中阶段教育 Junior Secondary Education	3936043	1983614	50.40	3486812	1801497	51.67
1. 初中 Junior Secondary Schools	3928762	1981096	50.43	3480979	1799565	51.70
初级中学 Regular Junior Secondary Schools	2894926	1407484	48.62	2587399	1316213	50.87
九年一贯制学校 9-year Schools	1032777	573175	55.50	449797	226333	50.32
十二年一贯制学校 12-year Schools				42848	25538	59.60
完全中学 Combined Secondary Schools				399952	231061	57.77
职业初中 Vocational Junior Secondary Schools	1059	437	41.27	983	420	42.73
2. 成人初中 Adult Junior Secondary Schools	7281	2518	34.58	5833	1932	33.12
三、初等教育 Primary Education	5538480	3228192	58.29	5607283	3399257	60.62
（一）普通小学 Regular Primary Schools	5494877	3209818	58.41	5584644	3388375	60.67
小学 Primary Schools	5494877	3209818	58.41	5096634	3066446	60.17
九年一贯制学校 9-year Schools				449126	291347	64.87
十二年一贯制学校 12-year Schools				38884	30582	78.65
（二）成人小学 Adult Primary Schools	43603	18374	42.14	22639	10882	48.07
其中：扫盲班 of Which：Literacy Classes	32658	13902	42.57	15399	7538	48.95
四、工读学校 Correctional Work-study Schools	2687	971	36.14	1851	711	38.41
五、特殊教育 Special Education Schools	55096	37685	68.40	45653	33079	72.46
六、学前教育 Pre-school Education Institutions	2826753	2591701	91.68	1663487	1630288	98.00

注：普通高中的教职工数中包含普通初中的教职工数。

Note：Data on Educational Personnel in Junior Secondary Education Schools are included in Regular Senior Secondary Education Schools.

各级各类学校少数民族学生数
Number of Minority Students of Schools by Type and Level

单位：人
unit：person

	总计 Total	少数民族学生 Minority Students	
		人数 Number	占学生总数的比重(%) Percentage
一、高等教育 Higher Education			
(一)研究生 Postgraduates	1793953	107392	5.99
博　士 Doctor's Degree	298283	17333	5.81
硕　士 Master's Degree	1495670	90059	6.02
(二)普通本专科 Undergraduate in Regular HEIs	24680726	1844503	7.47
本　科 Normal Courses	14944353	1167597	7.81
专　科 Short-cycle Courses	9736373	676906	6.95
(三)成人本专科 Undergraduate in Adult HEIs	6264145	502741	8.03
本　科 Normal Courses	2654596	218624	8.24
专　科 Short-cycle Courses	3609549	284117	7.87
(四)其他各类高等学历教育 Students Enrolled in Other Formal Programs			
1. 在职人员攻读硕士学位 Master's Degree Programs for On-the-job Personnel	558730		
2. 网络本专科生 Web-based Undergraduates	6146406	371979	6.05
本　科 Normal Courses	2175100	129788	5.97
专　科 Short-cycle Courses	3971306	242191	6.10
二、中等教育 Secondary Education			
(一)高中阶段教育 Senior Secondary Education			
1. 高中 Senior Secondary Schools			
普通高中 Regular Senior Secondary Schools	24358817	2109133	8.66
完全中学 Combined Secondary Schools	7914286	661098	8.35
高中级学 Regular High Schools	15814322	1415457	8.95
十二年一贯制学校 12-year Schools	630209	32578	5.17
成人高中 Adult High Schools	592983	36007	6.07
2. 中等职业教育 Secondary Vocational Education			
普通中专 Regular Specialized Secondary Schools	7721842	648968	8.40
成人中专 Adult Specialized Secondary Schools	2299806	191944	8.35
职业高中 Vocational High Schools	5342194	373246	6.99
技工学校 Skilled Workers Schools			
(二)初中阶段教育 Junior Secondary Education			
1. 初中 Junior Secondary Schools	44401248	4710203	10.61
初级中学 Regular Junior Secondary Schools	32340393	3555055	10.99
九年一贯制学校 9-year Schools	5256281	515925	9.82
十二年一贯制学校 12-year Schools	666538	33850	5.08
完全中学 Combined Secondary Schools	6127520	601916	9.82
职业初中 Vocational Junior Secondary Schools	10516	3457	32.87
2. 成人初中 Adult Junior Secondary Schools			
三、初等教育 Primary Education			
(一)普通小学 Regular Primary Schools	93605487	10409488	11.12
小学 Primary Schools	84998824	9580668	11.27
九年一贯制学校 9-year Schools	7920436	789653	9.97
十二年一贯制学校 12-year Schools	686227	39167	5.71
(二)成人小学 Adult Primary Schools	1242563	132102	10.63
其中:扫盲班 of Which: Literacy Classes			
四、工读学校 Correctional Work-Study Schools			
五、特殊教育 Special Education Schools	368026	28534	7.75
六、学前教育 Pre-school Education Institutions	38946903	3155937	8.10

注：成人高中数据包括成人初中数据。
Note: Data on Minority Students of Adult Junior Secondary Schools are included in the data of Adult High Schools.

各级各类学校少数民族教师、教职工数

Number of Minority Educational Personnel and Full-time Teachers of Schools by Type and Level

单位：人

unit：person

	教职工 Educational Personnel	少数民族教职工 Minority Educational Personnel		专任教师 Full-time Teachers	少数民族专任教师 Minority Full-time Teachers	
		人数 Number	占教职工总数的比重(％) Percentage		人数 Number	占专任教师总数的比重(％) Percentage
一、高等教育 Higher Education						
(一)研究生培养机构(不计校数) Institutions Providing Postgraduate Programs						
1. 普通高校 Regular HEIs						
2. 科研机构 Research Institutes						
(二)普通高等学校 Regular HEIs	2296262	122644	5.34	1496865	79439	5.31
1. 本科院校 HEIs Offering Degree Programs	1657517	90272	5.45	1055036	57539	5.45
其中：独立学院 of Which：Independent Institutions	186262	6842	3.67	138815	4680	3.37
2. 高职(专科)院校 Higher Vocational Colleges	630044	31948	5.07	436561	21668	4.96
3. 其他机构(点)(不计校数) Other Institutions	8701	424	4.87	5268	232	4.40
(三)成人高等学校 Adult HEIs	56417	3161	5.60	33647	1826	5.43
(四)民办的其他高等教育机构 Other Non-government HEIs	28394	252	0.89	13350	136	1.02
二、中等教育 Secondary Education						
(一)高中阶段教育 Senior Secondary Education						
1. 高中 Senior Secondary Schools	2486936	184345	7.41	1639459	121459	7.41
普通高中 Regular Senior Secondary Schools	2473594	183921	7.44	1629008	121170	7.44
完全中学 Combined Secondary Schools	1061968	83280	7.84	521094	38484	7.39
高级中学 Regular High Schools	1243624	92187	7.41	1065888	80345	7.54
十二年一贯制学校 12-year Schools	168002	8454	5.03	42026	2341	5.57
成人高中 Adult High Schools	13342	424	3.18	10451	289	2.77
2. 中等职业教育 Secondary Vocational Education						
普通中专 Regular Specialized Secondary Schools	419315	25523	6.09	303585	18487	6.09
成人中专 Adult Specialized Secondary Schools	72715	3973	5.46	52021	3002	5.77
职业高中 Vocational High Schools	375370	18447	4.91	301440	14310	4.75
技工学校 Skilled Workers Schools						
其他机构(教学点)(不计校数) Other Institutions	16559	386	2.33	11708	265	2.26
(二)初中阶段教育 Junior Secondary Education						
1. 初中 Junior Secondary Schools	3928762	353776	9.00	3480979	311437	8.95
初级中学 Regular Junior Secondary Schools	2894926	259125	8.95	2587399	233306	9.02
九年一贯制学校 9-year Schools	1032777	94373	9.14	449797	40747	9.06
十二年一贯制学校 12-year Schools				42848	2400	5.60
完全中学 Combined Secondary Schools				399952	34727	8.68
职业初中 Vocational Junior Secondary Schools	1059	278	26.25	983	257	26.14
2. 成人初中 Adult Junior Secondary Schools						
三、初等教育 Primary Education						
(一)普通小学 Regular Primary Schools	5494877	588411	10.71	5584644	589984	10.56
小学 Primary Schools	5494877	588411	10.71	5096634	543760	10.67
九年一贯制学校 9-year Schools				449126	43732	9.74
十二年一贯制学校 12-year Schools				38884	2492	6.41
(二)成人小学 Adult Primary Schools	43603	3544	8.13	22639	1175	5.19
其中：扫盲班 of Which：Literacy Classes						
四、工读学校 Correctional Work-study Schools						
五、特殊教育 Special Education Schools	55096	4070	7.39	45653	3356	7.35
六、学前教育 Pre-school Education Institutions	2826753	158839	5.62	1663487	102672	6.17

注：成人高中少数民族教职工数和专任教师数包括成人初中少数民族教职工数和专任教师数。

Note：The number of Minority Educational Personnel and Full – time teachers employed by Adult Junior High Schools is included in that employed by Adult High Schools.

各级各类学校校数

Number of Schools by Type and Level

单位：所

unit：institution

	1949	1965	1978	1980	1985	2000	2005	2010	2012	2013
一、高等教育 Higher Education										
（一）研究生培养机构（不计校数） Institutions Providing Postgraduate Programs						738	766	797	811	830
1. 普通高校 Regular HEIs						415	450	481	534	548
2. 科研机构 Research Institutes						323	316	316	277	282
（二）普通高等学校 Regular HEIs	205	434	598	675	1016	1041	1792	2358	2442	2491
1. 本科院校 HEIs Offering Degree Programs						599	701	1112	1145	1170
2. 高职（专科）院校 Higher Vocational Colleges						442	1091	1246	1297	1321
3. 其他机构（点）（不计校数） Other Institutions							428	56	36	33
（三）成人高等学校 Adult HEIs	1	964	10395	2775	1216	772	481	365	348	297
（四）民办的其他高等教育机构 Other Non-government HEIs							1077	836	823	802
二、中等教育 Secondary Education							96082	85063	81662	80797
（一）高中阶段教育 Senior Secondary Education							31532	28584	26868	26225
1. 高中 Senior Secondary Schools							17066	14712	14205	13963
普通高中 Regular Senior Secondary Schools	1597	4112	49215	31300	17318	14564	16092	14058	13509	13352
成人高中 Adult High Schools						1939	974	654	696	611
2. 中等职业教育 Secondary Vocational Education							14466	13872	12663	12262
普通中专 Regular Specialized Secondary Schools	1171	1265	2760	3069	3557	3646	3207	3938	3681	3577
成人中专 Adult Specialized Secondary Schools						4634	2582	1720	1564	1536
职业高中 Vocational High Schools						7655	5822	5206	4517	4267
技工学校 Skilled Workers Schools	3	281	2013	3305	3548	3792	2855	3008	2901	2882
其他机构（教学点）（不计校数） Other Institutions							2386	2012	509	451
（二）初中阶段教育 Junior Secondary Education							64550	56479	54794	54572
1. 普通初中 Regular Junior Secondary Schools	2448	13990	113130	87077	75903	62704	61885	54823	53167	52764
2. 职业初中 Vocational Junior Secondary Schools						1194	601	67	49	40
3. 成人初中 Adult Junior Secondary Schools						2001	2064	1589	1578	1768
三、初等教育 Primary Education							427697	290597	255400	235369
（一）普通小学 Regular Primary Schools	346769	1681939	949323	917316	832309	553622	366213	257410	228585	213529
（二）成人小学 Adult Primary Schools					100337	156839	61484	33187	26815	21840
其中：扫盲班 of Which: Literacy Classes					176076	104863	43572	22227	18092	15104
四、工读学校 Correctional Work-Study Schools					98	74	77	77	79	78
五、特殊教育 Special Education Schools		266	292	292	375	1539	1593	1706	1853	1933
六、学前教育 Pre-school Education Institutions		19226	163952	170419	172262	175836	124402	150420	181251	198553

各级各类学历教育学生数

Number of Students of Formal Education by Type and Level

单位：万人

unit：10 thousand persons

	1949	1965	1978	1980	1985	2000	2005	2010	2012	2013
一、高等教育 Higher Education										
（一）研究生（人） Postgraduates（person）	629	4546	10934	21604	87331	301239	978610	1538416	1719818	1793953
（二）普通本专科 Undergraduates in Regular HEIs	11.65	67.44	85.63	114.37	170.31	556.09	1561.78	2231.79	2391.32	2468.07
（三）成人本专科 Undergraduates in Adult HEIs	0.01	41.30	140.80	155.40	172.50	353.64	436.07	536.04	583.11	626.41
（四）其他各类高等学历教育 Students Enrolled in Other Formal Programs										
1. 在职人员攻读硕士学位 Master's Degree Programs for On-the-job Personnel							25.47	42.03	48.99	55.87
2. 网络本专科生 Web-based Undergraduates							265.27	453.14	570.41	614.64
二、中等教育 Secondary Education							10297.15	10019.66	9421.42	8858.28
（一）高中阶段教育 Senior Secondary Education							4030.94	4677.33	4595.28	4369.92
1. 高中 Senior Secondary Schools							2430.90	2438.83	2481.59	2446.95
普通高中 Regular Senior Secondary Schools	20.72	130.82	1553.08	969.79	741.13	1201.26	2409.09	2427.34	2467.17	2435.88
成人高中 Adult High Schools				75.12	138.98	32.40	21.81	11.50	14.42	11.07
2. 中等职业教育 Secondary Vocational Education							1600.04	2238.50	2113.69	1922.97
普通中专 Regular Specialized Secondary Schools	22.88	54.74	88.92	124.34	157.11	489.52	629.77	877.71	812.56	772.18
成人中专 Adult Specialized Secondary Schools	0.01	351.80	123.90	449.40		169.26	112.55	212.40	254.27	229.98
职业高中 Vocational High Schools		77.50		31.92	184.34	414.56	582.43	726.33	623.05	534.22
技工学校 Skilled Workers Schools	0.27	10.10	38.20	70.04	74.17	140.10	275.30	422.05	423.81	386.59
（二）初中阶段教育 Junior Secondary Education							6266.21	5342.33	4826.14	4488.35
1. 普通初中 Regular Junior Secondary Schools	83.18	802.97	4995.17	4538.29	3964.83	6167.65	6171.81	5275.91	4761.18	4439.07
2. 职业初中 Vocational Junior Secondary Schools		365.84		13.45	45.23	88.64	43.14	3.42	1.88	1.05
3. 成人初中 Adult Junior Secondary Schools				302.57	273.30	18.77	51.27	63.00	63.08	48.23
三、初等教育 Primary Education							11171.83	10135.36	9860.23	9484.81
（一）普通小学 Regular Primary Schools	2439.10	11620.90	14624.00	14627.00	13370.20	13013.25	10864.07	9940.70	9695.90	9360.55
（二）成人小学 Adult Primary Schools	1326.80	823.70	6467.20	1646.10	303.23	480.88	307.76	194.66	164.33	124.26
其中：扫盲班 of Which：Literacy Classes	1326.80		1806.70	1220.90	518.98	249.32	192.44	108.08	68.91	61.92
四、工读学校 Correctional Work-Study Schools					0.65	0.77	0.84	1.07	1.06	0.93
五、特殊教育 Special Education Schools		2.29	3.09	3.31	4.17	37.76	36.44	42.56	37.88	36.81
六、学前教育 Pre-school Education Institutions		171.30	787.70	1150.80	1479.70	2244.18	2179.03	2976.67	3685.76	3894.69

各级各类学历教育招生数

Number of Entrants of Formal Education by Type and Level

单位：万人

unit：10 thousand persons

	1949	1965	1978	1980	1985	2000	2005	2010	2012	2013
一、高等教育 Higher Education										
（一）研究生（人）Postgraduates（person）	242	1456	10708	3616	46871	128484	364831	538177	589673	611381
（二）普通本专科 Undergraduates in Regular HEIs	3.06	16.42	40.15	28.12	61.92	220.61	504.46	661.76	688.83	699.83
（三）成人本专科 Undergraduates in Adult HEIs					78.78	156.15	193.03	208.43	243.96	256.49
（四）其他各类高等学历教育 Students Enrolled in Other Formal Programs										
1. 在职人员攻读硕士学位 Master's Degree Programs for On-the-job Personnel							10.17	12.49	14.06	16.76
2. 网络本专科生 Web-based Undergraduates							89.10	166.37	196.45	220.07
二、中等教育 Secondary Education							3520.98	3423.24	3169.51	2993.54
（一）高中阶段教育 Senior Secondary Education							1533.39	1706.66	1598.74	1497.45
1. 高中 Senior Secondary Schools							877.73	836.24	844.61	822.70
普通高中 Regular Senior Secondary Schools	7.11	45.89	692.91	383.40	257.51	472.69	877.73	836.24	844.61	822.70
成人高中 Adult High Schools				50.05	107.61	30.47				
2. 中等职业教育 Secondary Vocational Education							655.66	870.42	754.13	674.76
普通中专 Regular Specialized Secondary Schools	9.74	20.85	44.70	46.76	66.83	132.59	241.13	316.61	277.36	271.47
成人中专 Adult Specialized Secondary Schools				152.22		53.39	47.95	116.11	105.81	86.26
职业高中 Vocational High Schools		55.67		24.06	98.49	150.39	248.21	278.67	213.90	183.53
技工学校 Skilled Workers Schools			25.70	33.13	35.54	50.38	118.37	159.02	157.06	133.50
（二）初中阶段教育 Junior Secondary Education							1987.58	1716.58	1570.77	1496.09
1. 普通初中 Regular Junior Secondary Schools	34.12	299.89	2005.98	1550.91	1349.40	2263.30	1976.52	1715.49	1570.24	1495.73
2. 职业初中 Vocational Junior Secondary Schools		250.81		6.66	17.61	32.27	11.06	1.09	0.53	0.35
3. 成人初中 Adult Junior Secondary Schools				194.81	237.02	14.67				
三、初等教育 Primary Education							1671.74	1691.70	1714.66	1695.36
（一）普通小学 Regular Primary Schools	680.00	3296.02	3315.36	2942.34	2298.17	1946.47	1671.74	1691.70	1714.66	1695.36
（二）成人小学 Adult Primary Schools				248.29	194.95	452.52				
其中：扫盲班 of Which：Literacy Classes				720.48	326.14	210.61				
四、工读学校 Correctional Work-Study Schools					0.32	0.44	0.35	0.40	0.45	0.39
五、特殊教育 Special Education Schools			0.59	0.59	0.92	5.29	4.93	6.49	6.57	6.60
六、学前教育 Pre-school Education Institutions						1531.11	1356.24	1700.39	1911.92	1970.03

各级各类学校教职工数

Number of Educational Personnel of Schools by Type and Level

单位：万人

unit:10 thousand persons

	1949	1965	1978	1980	1985	2000	2005	2010	2012	2013
一、高等教育 Higher Education										
(一)研究生培养机构(不计校数) Institutions Providing Postgraduate Programs										
1. 普通高校 Regular HEIs										
2. 科研机构 Research Institutes										
(二)普通高等学校 Regular HEIs	4.60	33.30	51.80	63.20	87.06	111.28	174.21	215.66	225.44	229.63
1. 本科院校 HEIs Offering Degree Programs						92.69	119.78	154.80	162.76	165.75
2. 高职(专科)院校 Higher Vocational Colleges						17.50	44.00	60.32	62.24	63.00
3. 其他机构(点)(不计校数) Other Institutions						1.08	10.43	0.54	0.43	0.87
(三)成人高等学校 Adult HEIs				6.45	14.34	18.70	14.89	7.71	6.56	5.64
(四)民办的其他高等教育机构 Other Non-government HEIs							4.81	3.81	3.19	2.84
二、中等教育 Secondary Education							685.77	709.63	760.79	756.91
(一)高中阶段教育 Senior Secondary Education							682.48	708.68	365.93	363.31
1. 高中 Senior Secondary Schools							573.16	586.39	246.99	247.97
普通高中 Regular Senior Secondary Schools	10.40	67.70	391.70	389.70	355.69	491.10	572.02	585.93	246.26	247.36
成人高中 Adult High Schools					5.65	2.17	1.13	0.47	0.73	0.61
2. 中等职业教育 Secondary Vocational Education							109.32	122.29	118.94	115.34
普通中专 Regular Specialized Secondary Schools	2.40	12.20	23.70	29.80	40.32	48.81	33.48	43.50	43.06	41.93
成人中专 Adult Specialized Secondary Schools				3.19		20.84	12.13	8.53	7.75	7.27
职业高中 Vocational High Schools		30.60		4.10	21.59	44.69	38.93	40.32	39.43	37.54
技工学校 Skilled Workers Schools			6.66	13.61	21.53	23.96	20.40	26.63	26.81	26.94
其他机构(教学点)(不计校数) Other Institutions							4.38	3.30	1.89	1.66
(二)初中阶段教育 Junior Secondary Education							3.29	0.94	394.86	393.60
1. 普通初中 Regular Junior Secondary Schools									393.74	392.77
2. 职业初中 Vocational Junior Secondary Schools							2.40	0.22	0.17	0.11
3. 成人初中 Adult Junior Secondary Schools					7.29	0.79	0.89	0.73	0.95	0.73
三、初等教育 Primary Education							624.82	617.56	559.58	553.85
(一)普通小学 Regular Primary Schools	84.90	407.50	562.00	605.40	602.10	645.49	613.22	610.98	553.85	549.49
(二)成人小学 Adult Primary Schools				2.02		16.24	11.61	6.58	5.73	4.36
其中:扫盲班 of Which: Literacy Classes				7.40		11.01	8.94	5.04	3.83	3.27
四、工读学校 Correctional Work-Study Schools					0.32	0.27	0.26	0.26	0.27	0.27
五、特殊教育 Special Education Schools		0.37	0.69	0.80	1.15	4.37	4.23	4.92	5.36	5.51
六、学前教育 Pre-school Education Institutions		16.20	46.90	61.00	79.80	114.43	115.20	184.93	249.00	282.68

各级各类学校专任教师数
Number of Full-time Teachers of Schools by Type and Level

单位：万人

unit:10 thousand persons

	1949	1965	1978	1980	1985	2000	2005	2010	2012	2013
一、高等教育 Higher Education										
(一)研究生培养机构(不计校数) Institutions Providing Postgraduate Programs										
1. 普通高校 Regular HEIs										
2. 科研机构 Research Institutes										
(二)普通高等学校 Regular HEIs	1.61	13.81	20.63	24.69	34.43	46.28	96.58	134.31	144.03	149.69
1. 本科院校 HEIs Offering Degree Programs						37.08	63.00	93.55	101.40	105.50
2. 高职(专科)院校 Higher Vocational Colleges						8.66	26.79	40.41	42.34	43.66
3. 其他机构(点)(不计校数) Other Institutions						0.53	6.80	0.35	0.30	0.53
(三)成人高等学校 Adult HEIs				3.32	6.93	9.34	8.43	4.59	3.94	3.36
(四)民办的其他高等教育机构 Other Non-government HEIs							2.25	1.78	1.49	1.34
二、中等教育 Secondary Education							555.36	592.30	599.38	598.84
(一)高中阶段教育 Senior Secondary Education							205.64	239.32	248.18	250.16
1. 高中 Senior Secondary Schools							130.66	152.17	160.08	163.36
普通高中 Regular Senior Secondary Schools	1.40	7.79	74.13	57.07	49.17	75.69	129.95	151.82	159.50	162.90
成人高中 Adult High Schools					3.23	1.35	0.71	0.35	0.58	0.46
2. 中等职业教育 Secondary Vocational Education							74.98	87.15	88.10	86.79
普通中专 Regular Specialized Secondary Schools	1.56	5.51	9.96	12.87	17.40	25.64	20.30	29.50	30.56	30.36
成人中专 Adult Specialized Secondary Schools				1.78		11.83	7.50	5.70	5.42	5.20
职业高中 Vocational High Schools		5.29		1.65	11.58	28.18	28.25	30.70	31.17	30.14
技工学校 Skilled Workers Schools			2.80	6.14	8.89	14.00	16.11	19.05	19.69	19.92
其他机构(教学点)(不计校数) Other Institutions							2.82	2.20	1.26	1.17
(二)初中阶段教育 Junior Secondary Education							349.72	352.97	351.20	348.68
1. 普通初中 Regular Junior Secondary Schools	5.26	37.92	244.07	244.90	215.99	324.86	347.18	352.34	350.28	348.00
2. 职业初中 Vocational Junior Secondary Schools		14.42		0.67	2.49	3.83	2.02	0.20	0.15	0.10
3. 成人初中 Adult Junior Secondary Schools					5.00	0.43	0.51	0.44	0.76	0.58
三、初等教育 Primary Education							563.71	564.58	561.58	560.73
(一)普通小学 Regular Primary Schools	83.60	385.71	522.55	549.94	537.68	586.03	559.25	561.71	558.55	558.46
(二)成人小学 Adult Primary Schools				1.65	2.87	4.76	4.47	2.87	3.03	2.26
其中:扫盲班 of Which: Literacy Classes				4.83	4.26	2.93	3.17	1.95	1.78	1.54
四、工读学校 Correctional Work-Study Schools					0.13	0.15	0.17	0.17	0.18	0.19
五、特殊教育 Special Education Schools		0.26	0.42	0.48	0.73	3.20	3.19	3.97	4.37	4.57
六、学前教育 Pre-school Education Institutions		6.18	27.75	41.07	54.99	85.65	72.16	114.42	147.92	166.35

高中阶段学生数的构成
Composition of Students in Senior Secondary Education

	合计 Total	普通高中 Regular Senior Secondary Schools	成人高中 Adult High Schools	中等职业教育 Secondary Vocational Education				
				小计 Subtotal	中等专业学校 Regular Specialized Secondary Schools	成人中专 Adult Specialized Secondary Schools	职业高中 Vocational High Schools	技工学校 Skilled Workers Schools
学生数(万人) No. of Students (10 thousand persons)								
1965	622.9	130.8		492.1	52.7	351.8	77.5	10.1
1980	1720.5	969.8	75.1	675.6	124.3	449.4	31.9	70.0
1985	1295.7	741.1	139.0	415.6	157.1		184.3	74.2
1990	1528.6	717.3	47.8	763.5	224.4	158.8	247.1	133.2
2000	2463.2	1201.3	32.4	1229.5	489.5	169.3	414.6	156.1
2001	2606.3	1405.0	31.0	1170.3	457.9	189.2	383.1	140.1
2002	2889.8	1683.8	33.5	1172.5	456.4	153.3	428.1	134.7
2003	3240.9	1964.8	21.5	1254.6	502.4	105.5	455.7	191.1
2004	3649.0	2220.4	19.4	1409.2	554.5	103.3	516.9	234.5
2005	4030.9	2409.1	21.8	1600.0	629.8	112.5	582.4	275.3
2006	4341.9	2514.5	17.5	1809.9	725.8	107.6	655.6	320.8
2007	4527.5	2522.4	18.1	1987.0	781.6	113.0	725.2	367.1
2008	4545.7	2476.3	12.7	2056.7	817.3	120.6	750.3	368.5
2009	4624.4	2434.3	11.5	2178.7	840.4	161.0	778.4	398.8
2010	4677.3	2427.3	11.5	2238.5	877.7	212.4	726.3	422.1
2012	4595.3	2467.2	14.4	2113.7	812.6	254.3	623.0	423.8
2013	4369.9	2435.9	11.1	1923.0	772.2	230.0	534.2	386.6
比重(%)Percentage								
1965	100	21.00		79.00	8.46	56.48	12.44	1.62
1980	100	56.37	4.37	39.27	7.22	26.12	1.85	4.07
1985	100	57.20	10.73	32.08	12.12		14.22	5.73
1990	100	46.93	3.13	49.95	14.68	10.39	16.17	8.71
2000	100	48.77	1.32	49.91	19.87	6.87	16.83	6.34
2001	100	53.91	1.19	44.90	17.57	7.26	14.70	5.38
2002	100	58.27	1.16	40.57	15.79	5.30	14.81	4.66
2003	100	60.63	0.66	38.71	15.50	3.25	14.06	5.90
2004	100	60.80	0.50	38.60	15.20	2.80	14.20	6.40
2005	100	59.80	0.54	39.69	15.60	2.79	14.40	6.83
2006	100	57.91	0.40	41.68	16.72	2.48	15.10	7.39
2007	100	55.71	0.40	43.89	17.26	2.50	16.02	8.11
2008	100	54.48	0.28	45.25	17.98	2.65	16.51	8.11
2009	100	52.64	0.25	47.11	18.17	3.48	16.83	8.62
2010	100	52.64	0.25	47.11	18.17	3.48	16.83	8.62
2012	100	53.69	0.31	46.00	17.68	5.53	13.56	9.22
2013	100	55.74	0.25	44.00	17.67	5.26	12.22	8.85

教育规模
Size of Education

单位：万人

unit:10 thousand persons

年　份 Year	学校数(万所) Schools (10 thousand)	在校生数 Enrolment	教职工数 Educational Personnel	教育人口 Educational Population	教育人口比重(%) Proportion of Education Population
1985	144	21753	1261	23014	22.0
1990	136	23654	1432	25086	22.2
1997	157	31076	1577	32653	26.7
1998	155	31809	1580	33389	27.0
1999	159	32672	1596	34268	27.5
2000	149	32093	1592	33685	26.8
2001	135	32135	1574	33709	26.6
2002	117	31873	1579	33452	26.2
2003	96	31989	1610	33599	26.2
2004	68	32558	1597	34155	26.4
2005	65	36904	1624	38528	29.6
2006	63	31860	1652	33512	25.6
2007	66	32187	1675	33862	25.8
2008	58	32099	1692	33791	25.6
2009	55	32098	1716	33814	25.5
2010	53	32217	1741	33958	25.4
2011	53	32756	1782	34538	25.9
2012	52	32143	1810	33953	25.3
2013	52	31813	1837	33650	25.1

小学学龄儿童净入学率

Net Enrolment Ratio of School-age Children in Primary Schools

单位：万人

unit:10 thousand persons

年　份 Year	学龄儿童净入学率 Net Enrolment Ratio of School-age Children		
	全国学龄儿童数 No. of School-age Children	已入学学龄儿童数 No. of School-age Childen Enrolled	净入学率(%) Net Enrolment Ratio
1965	11603.2	9829.1	84.7
1980	12219.6	11478.2	93.0
1985	10362.3	9942.8	95.9
1990	9740.7	9529.7	97.8
1999	12991.4	12872.8	99.1
2000	12445.3	12333.9	99.1
2001	11766.4	11561.2	99.1
2002	11310.4	11150.0	98.6
2003	10908.3	10761.6	98.7
2004	10548.1	10437.1	98.9
2005	10207.0	10120.3	99.2
2006	10075.5	10001.5	99.3
2007	9947.9	9896.8	99.5
2008	9772.0	9727.1	99.5
2009	9606.6	9548.6	99.4
2010	9501.5	9473.3	99.7
2011	9522.4	9502.5	99.8
2012	9296.8	9282.7	99.9
2013	8962.1	8935.7	99.7

注:1991 年以前的净入学率是按 7 - 11 周岁统一计算的;从 1991 年起净入学率是按各地不同入学年龄和学制分别计算的。

Note: Net Enrolment Ratio of school-age children before 1991 was calculated on the basis of primary school pupils aged 7 - 11 enroled. From 1991 onwards its calculation has taken account of the age of entry and the lenth of schooling prevailing.

各级教育毛入学率

Gross Enrolment Ratio of Education by Level

单位：%

unit:%

年　份 Year	小学 Primary Education 按各地相应学龄计算 According to Provincial Entrant Age Primary Schools Years	初中阶段 Junior Secondary Education 12 - 14 周岁 the Age of 12 - 14	高中阶段 Senior Secondary Education 15 - 17 周岁 the Age of 15 - 17		高等教育 Higher Education 18 - 22 周岁 the Age of 18 - 22
			职前 Pre. Job	全口径 Full Aperture	
1991	109.5	69.7	23.9		3.5
1992	109.4	71.8	22.6	26.0	3.9
1993	107.3	73.1	24.1	28.4	5.0
1994	108.7	73.8	26.2	30.7	6.0
1995	106.6	78.4	28.8	33.6	7.2
1996	105.7	82.4	31.4	38.0	8.3
1997	104.9	87.1	33.8	40.6	9.1
1998	104.3	87.3	34.4	40.7	9.8
1999	104.3	88.6	35.8	41.0	10.5
2000	104.6	88.6	38.2	42.8	12.5
2001	104.5	88.7	38.6	42.8	13.3
2002	107.5	90.0	38.4	42.8	15.0
2003	107.2	92.7	42.1	43.8	17.0
2004	106.6	94.1	46.5	48.1	19.0
2005	106.4	95.0	50.9	52.7	21.0
2006	106.3	97.0	57.7	59.8	22.0
2007	106.2	98.0		66.0	23.0
2008	105.7	98.5		74.0	23.3
2009	104.8	99.0		79.2	24.2
2010	104.6	100.1		82.5	26.5
2011	104.2	100.1		84.0	26.9
2012	104.3	102.1		85.0	30.0
2013	104.4	104.1		86.0	34.5

各级普通学校毕业生升学率

Promotion Rate of Graduates of Regular Schools by Level

单位：%

unit：%

年　份 Year	小学升初中 Promotion Rate of Primary Schools Graduates	初中升高级中学 Promotion Rate of Junior Secondary Schools Graduates	高中升高等教育 Promotion Rate of Senior Secondary Schools Graduates
1990	74.6	40.6	27.3
1991	77.7	42.6	28.7
1992	79.7	43.6	34.9
1993	81.8	44.1	43.3
1994	86.6	47.8	46.7
1995	90.8	50.3	49.9
1996	92.6	49.8	51.0
1997	93.7	51.5	48.6
1998	94.3	50.7	46.1
1999	94.4	50.0	63.8
2000	94.9	51.2	73.2
2001	95.5	52.9	78.8
2002	97.0	58.3	83.5
2003	97.9	59.6	83.4
2004	98.1	63.8	82.5
2005	98.4	69.7	76.3
2006	100.0	75.7	75.1
2007	99.9	80.5	70.3
2008	99.7	82.1	72.7
2009	99.1	85.6	77.6
2010	98.7	87.5	83.3
2011	98.3	88.9	86.5
2012	98.3	88.4	87.0
2013	98.3	91.2	87.6

注：高中升学率为普通高校招生数与普通高中毕业生数之比。

Note：Promotion Rate of Senior Secondary Schools Graduates is the Ratio of Total Number of New Entrants Admitted to HEIs to the Total Number of Graduates of Regular Senior Secondary Schools of the Current Year.

每十万人口各级学校平均在校生数

Number of Enrolment of Per 100,000 Inhabitants by Level

单位：人

unit：person

年　份 Year	高等教育 Higher Education	高中阶段 Senior Secondary Education	初中阶段 Junior Secondary Education	小学 Primary Education	学前教育 Pre-school Education
1991	304	1355	3465	10502	1907
1992	313	1365	3518	10413	2072
1993	376	1448	3599	10656	2190
1994	433	1293	3681	10819	2219
1995	457	1610	3945	11010	2262
1996	470	1780	4180	11273	2208
1997	482	1905	4289	11435	2058
1998	519	1978	4408	11287	1944
1999	594	2032	4656	10855	1864
2000	723	2000	4969	10335	1782
2001	931	2021	5161	9937	1602
2002	1146	2283	5240	9525	1595
2003	1298	2523	5209	9100	1560
2004	1420	2824	5058	8725	1617
2005	1613	3070	4781	8358	1676
2006	1816	3321	4557	8192	1731
2007	1924	3409	4364	8037	1787
2008	2042	3463	4227	7819	1873
2009	2128	3495	4097	7584	2001
2010	2189	3504	3955	7448	2230
2011	2253	3495	3779	7403	2554
2012	2335	3411	3535	7196	2736
2013	2418	3227	3279	6913	2876

各级普通学校生师比

Pupil-Teacher Ratio of Regular Schools by Level

年 份 Year	普通小学 Regular Primary Schools	初中 Junior Secondary Schools	普通高中 Regular Senior Secondary Schools	中等职业学校 Secondary Vocational Schools	普通高校 Regular HEIs		
					全国 Total	本科院校 HEIs Offering Degree Programs	高职(专科)院校 Higher Vocational Colleges
1993	22.37	15.65	14.96	13.42	8.00	7.82	8.61
1994	22.85	16.07	12.16	14.26	9.25	9.00	10.10
1995	23.30	16.73	12.95	15.98	9.83	9.71	10.16
1996	23.73	17.18	13.45	16.42	10.36	10.32	10.20
1997	24.16	17.33	14.05	16.92	10.87	10.80	10.85
1998	23.98	17.56	14.60	16.36	11.62	11.63	11.09
1999	23.12	18.17	15.16	15.68	13.37	13.67	12.23
2000	22.21	19.03	15.87	15.24	16.30	16.04	17.65
2001	21.64	19.24	16.73	15.04	18.22	18.47	17.15
2002	21.04	19.25	17.80	16.58	19.00	20.60	14.20
2003	20.50	19.13	18.35	17.63	17.00	21.07	14.75
2004	19.98	18.65	18.65	19.15	16.22	17.44	13.15
2005	19.43	17.80	18.54	21.34	16.85	17.75	14.78
2006	19.17	17.15	18.13	22.65	17.93	17.77	18.26
2007	18.82	16.52	17.48	23.13	17.28	17.31	17.20
2008	18.38	16.07	16.78	23.32	17.23	17.21	17.27
2009	17.88	15.47	16.30	25.27	17.27	17.23	17.35
2010	17.70	14.98	15.99	25.69	17.33	17.38	17.21
2011	17.71	14.38	15.77	24.97	17.42	17.48	17.28
2012	17.36	13.59	15.47	24.19	17.52	17.65	17.23
2013	16.76	12.76	14.95	22.97	17.53	17.71	17.11

普通高等学校校均规模

Average Size of Regular Higher Educational Institutions

单位:人

unit: person

	1994	1995	1996	1997	1998	1999	2000	2001	2002	2003	2004	2005	2006	2007	2008	2009	2010	2011	2012	2013
全 国 Total	2591	2758	2927	3112	3335	3815	5289	5870	6471	7143	7704	7666	8148	8571	8679	9086	9298	9446	9675	9814
本科院校 HEIs Offering Degree Programs	3418	3632	3857	4062	4418	5275	6916	8730	10454	11662	13561	13514	13937	14057	12097	12634	13100	13564	13999	14261
高职(专科)院校 Higher Vocational Colleges	1338	1405	1466	1594	1701	1975	2282	2337	2523	2893	3209	3909	4515	5095	5564	5903	5904	5813	5858	5876

各级自学考试基本情况

Basic Statistics of State-administered Examination for Self-learners by Level

单位：人，人次

unit：person

	2009		2010		2011		2012		2013	
	上半年 First half year	下半年 Second half year	上半年 First half year	下半年 Second half year	上半年 First half year	下半年 Second half year	上半年 First half year	下半年 Second half year	上半年 First half year	下半年 Second half year
毕业生人数 Graduates	309921	310476	345668	341650	370579	372220	373793	357395	403213	331020
本科 Normal Course	203559	199526	230802	230103	245765	265090	272829	263114	300028	244401
专科 Short-cycle Course	106362	110950	114866	111547	124814	107130	100964	94281	103185	86619
单科合格科次数 Passed Main-courses	5244892	4946679	4980013	4476856	4939058	4248183	4717831	4020534	4504154	3791344
本科 Normal Course	3499720	3416760	3428805	2977456	3662985	3246036	3633315	3162536	3575846	3048174
专科 Short-cycle Course	1745172	1529919	1551208	1499400	1276073	1002147	1084516	857998	928308	743170
报考人数 Applicants	5517385	4907514	5160123	4489937	4955069	4271640	4507361	4031649	4025917	3637105
本科 Normal Course	3426273	3144203	3325005	2784408	3407382	3008956	3244057	2945818	3015420	2746375
专科 Short-cycle Course	2091112	1763311	1835118	1705529	1547687	1262684	1263304	1085831	1010497	890730
首次报考人数 First Time	1268590	640676	983545	600171	916300	553999	895881	551496	808792	524943
本科 Normal Course	798761	432287	664099	388448	667822	395108	668477	386221	617437	385927
专科 Short-cycle Course	469829	208389	319446	211723	248478	158891	227404	165275	191355	139016
报考科次 Main-courses be Examined	12870134	11842415	12144181	10883416	11588813	10015717	10581826	9398641	9318675	8644834
本科 Normal Course	7584122	7605841	7813197	6892876	8021397	7187670	7739886	7020328	7114731	6645457
专科 Short-cycle Course	5286012	4236574	4330984	3990540	3567416	2828047	2841940	2378313	2203944	1999377
实考人数 Actual Examined	4318889	3754772	4026556	3460358	4218387	3695715	3576943	3122577	3328968	2840782
本科 Normal Course	2737622	2452057	2640442	2180587	2941630	2650905	2630548	2333736	2524541	2196518
专科 Short-cycle Course	1581267	1302715	1386114	1279771	1276757	1044810	946395	788841	804427	644264
实考科次 Actual Main-courses Examined	9781330	8761276	9122514	8074603	8850467	7455512	8012441	6881607	7356184	6331928
本科 Normal Course	6188572	5725407	5958059	5182160	6267730	5489553	6007967	5282901	5706255	5008220
专科 Short-cycle Course	3592758	3035869	3164455	2892443	2582737	1965959	2004474	1598706	1649929	1323708
在档考生人数 Exmainees with Study Record	31608711	31938911	32714917	32973438	33519159	33700938	34223026	34417127	34822706	35016629
本科 Normal Course	11774649	12007410	12440707	12599052	13021109	13151127	13546775	13669882	13987291	14128817
专科 Short-cycle Course	19834062	19931501	20136081	20236257	20359921	20411682	20538122	20609116	20697286	20749683
其中：新生数 of Which：Current Session	1268590	640676	983545	600171	916300	553999	895881	551496	808792	524943
本科 Normal Course	798761	432287	664099	388448	667822	395108	668477	386221	617437	385927
专科 Short-cycle Course	469829	208389	319446	211723	248478	158891	227404	165275	191355	139016

二、高等教育
Higher Education

高等教育学校(机构)数

Number of Higher Education Institutions

单位：所

unit：institution

	合计 Total	中央部门 HEIs under Central Ministries & Agencies			地方 HEIs under Local Auth.				民办 Non-government
		小计 Subtotal	教育部 HEIs under MOE	其他部门 HEIs under Other Central Agencies	小计 Subtotal	教育部门 HEIs under MOE	其他部门 Run by Non-ed. Dept.	地方企业 Local Enterprises	
(一)研究生培养机构(不计校数) Institutions Providing Postgraduate Programs	830	348	73	275	477	412	64	1	5
1. 普通高校 Regular HEIs	548	107	73	34	436	411	25		5
2. 科研机构 Research Institutes	282	241		241	41	1	39	1	
(二)普通高等学校 Regular HEIs	2491	113	73	40	1661	1015	598	48	717
1. 本科院校 HEIs Offering Degree Programs	1170	110	73	37	668	601	67		392
其中:独立学院 of Which:Independent Institutions	292								292
2. 高职(专科)院校 Higher Vocational Colleges	1321	3		3	993	414	531	48	325
(三)成人高等学校 Adult HEIs	297	13	1	12	283	96	146	41	1
(四)民办的其他高等教育机构 Other Non-government HEIs	802								802

普通高等学校校数

Number of Regular Higher Educational Institutions

单位:所

unit：institution

	合 计 Total	本科院校 HEIs Offering Degree Programs	高职(专科)院校 Higher Vocational Colleges	其中:高等职业技术学院 of Which：Tertiary Vocational-technical Colleges
总计 Total	**2491**	**1170**	**1321**	**1184**
综合大学 Comprehensive University	589	281	308	306
理工院校 Natural Sciences & Technology	883	337	546	531
农业院校 Agriculture	83	43	40	40
林业院校 Forestry	20	7	13	13
医药院校 Medicine & Pharmacy	185	102	83	37
师范院校 Teacher Training	211	151	60	5
语文院校 Language & Literature	54	29	25	24
财经院校 Finance & Economics	256	118	138	127
政法院校 Political Science & Law	71	32	39	33
体育院校 Physical Culture	32	16	16	15
艺术院校 Art	89	40	49	49
民族院校 Ethnic Nationality	18	14	4	4
总计中:民办高校 of the Total:Non-government HEIs	717	392	325	318

普通高等学校在校生规模
Size of Enrolment of Regular Higher Educational Institutions

单位:所

unit: institution

	学校数 Institutions	300 人及以下 300 and Under	301 – 500 人 301 to 500	501 – 1000 人 501 to 1000	1001 – 1500 人 1001 to 1500	1501 – 2000 人 1501 to 2000	2001 – 3000 人 2001 to 3000	3001 – 4000 人 3001 to 4000	4001 – 5000 人 4001 to 5000	5001 – 10000 人 5001 to 10000	10001 – 20000 人 10001 to 20000	20001 – 30000 人 20001 to 30000	30001 人及以上 30001 and Over
总 计 Total	**2491**	**45**	**22**	**62**	**73**	**72**	**120**	**159**	**152**	**834**	**702**	**206**	**44**
综合大学 Comprehensive University	589	9	4	7	13	12	20	43	34	193	166	65	23
理工院校 Natural Sciences & Technology	883	13	8	25	27	22	47	51	56	286	262	76	10
农业院校 Agriculture	83	2		1		2	4	5	3	26	27	9	4
林业院校 Forestry	20	1		1				1		11	5	1	
医药院校 Medicine & Pharmacy	185			3	3	7	7	12	11	89	48	5	
师范院校 Teacher Training	211	4	3	2	2	6	9	6	6	56	85	26	6
语文院校 Language & Literature	54	1		5	2	1	2	4	8	19	10	2	
财经院校 Finance & Economics	256	4	1	5	7	7	7	14	14	101	77	18	1
政法院校 Political Science & Law	71	2	2	3	4	4	8	11	11	19	7		
体育院校 Physical Culture	32	4	2	1	5	2	3	1	2	11	1		
艺术院校 Art	89	5	2	9	10	9	11	10	7	18	8		
民族院校 Ethnic Nationality	18						2	1		5	6	4	

普通高等学校设置(研究生、本科)专业数
Number of Specialities and Educational Programs Offered by Regular Higher Educational Institutions

	合计 Total	哲学 Philosophy	经济 Economics	法学 Law	教育 Education	文学 Literature	历史 History	理学 Science	工学 Engineering	农学 Agriculture	医学 Medicine	管理学 Administration	其他 other
博士 Doctor's Degree													
种数 No. of Sp.	464	9	18	38	20	24	9	63	149	35	64	19	3
点数 No. of Ed. Prog.	9280	204	479	623	218	473	239	1711	3114	539		472	4
硕士 Master's Degree													
种数 No. of Sp.	472	9	18	38	20	24	9	63	150	35	63	19	11
点数 No. of Ed. Prog.	28464	631	1648	2735	1132	1774	566	4293	8774	1053	3089	1994	17
普通本科 General Bachelor's Degree													
种数 No. of Sp.	576	5	20	37	19	66	7	47	196	33	52		
点数 No. of Ed. Prog.	46623	95	2255	1664	1778	4727	314	4716	15024	1016	1799		
成人本科 Adult Bachelor's Degree													
种数 No. of Sp.	364	2	17	17	15	29	4	28	123	20	34		
点数 No. of Ed. Prog.	12996	3	639	690	867	1082	138	1053	3491	341	886		

普通高等学校设置(高职(专科))专业数

Number of Specialities and Number of Educational Programs Offered by Regular Higher Educational Institutions

	普通专科 General Associate Bachelor's Degrees		成人专科 Adult Associate Bachelor's Degrees	
	种数 No. of Sp.	点数 No. of Ed. Prog.	种数 No. of Sp.	点数 No. of Ed. Prog.
总　计 Total	**1108**	**47347**	**698**	**23425**
农林牧渔大类 Agriculture, Forestry,Husbandry and Fishing	85	1260	48	615
交通运输大类 Transportation and Communication	98	1823	54	640
生化与药品大类 Biochemistry and Medicine	39	1434	29	500
资源开发与测绘大类 Resources Development and Survey	64	845	54	535
材料与能源大类 Material and Energy	63	827	30	385
土建大类 Civil Engineering	55	4208	36	1704
水利大类 Water Resources	26	184	15	129
制造大类 Manufacturing	96	5999	53	2782
电子信息大类 Electronic Information	89	6597	56	2532
环保、气象与安全大类 Environment Protection,Meteorology and Safety	25	371	13	134
轻纺食品大类 Light,Textile and Food	69	1226	45	334
财经大类 Finance	64	7690	44	5301
医药卫生大类 Medical and Health	43	1968	31	1315
旅游大类 Tourism	23	2253	15	861
公共事业大类 Public Service	42	840	21	822
文化教育大类 Culture and Education	87	5471	67	3091
艺术设计传媒大类 Artistic Design and Mass Media	90	3706	61	1227
公安大类 Public Security	23	138	16	34
法律大类 Law	27	507	10	484

高等教育学校(机构)学生数

Number of Students in Higher Education Institutions

单位：人

unit: person

	毕(结)业生数 Graduates	授予学位数 Degree Awarded	招生数 Entrants				在校生数 Enrolment	预计毕业生数 Estimated Graduates for Next Year
			合计 Total	其中 of Which				
				应届生 Autumn Session	春季招生 Spring Session	预科生转入 Preparatory Students Enrolled		
研究生 Postgraduates	513626	509520	611381	409567			1793953	665984
博　士 Doctor's Degree	53139	51714	70462	30252			298283	146941
硕　士 Master's Degree	460487	457806	540919	379315			1495670	519043
普通本专科 Undergraduates in Regular HEIs	6387210	3130415	6998330	6469438	7670	36349	24680726	6737474
本　科 Normal Courses	3199716	3130415	3814331	3413912	5884	34441	14944353	3497450
专　科 Short-cycle Courses	3187494		3183999	3055526	1786	1908	9736373	3240024
成人本专科 Undergraduates in Adult HEIs	1997729	126057	2564934				6264145	2362194
本　科 Normal Courses	811159	126057	1038158				2654596	940037
专　科 Short-cycle Courses	1186570		1526776				3609549	1422157
网络本专科生 Web-based Undergraduates	1560762	40267	2200729		1134022		6146406	
本　科 Normal Courses	536702	40267	804378		413513		2175100	
专　科 Short-cycle Courses	1024060		1396351		720509		3971306	
在职人员攻读硕士学位 Master's Degree Programs for On-the-job Personnel		103468	167576				558730	
自考助学班 Class run by Non-government HEIs for Students Preparing for Self-directed State-administered Examination	194882						405329	
普通预科生 College-preparatory Classes							42514	
研究生课程进修班 Postgraduate Courses	48329						69321	
进修及培训 In-service Training	9094537						6268398	
留学生 Foreign Students	91251	19025	106448		31008		174806	

分部门、分计划
Number of Postgraduate Students

	学校(机构)数(所)(Schools)	毕业生数 Graduates			招生数 Entrants		
		合计 Total	博 士 Doctor's Degree	硕 士 Master's Degree	合计 Total	博 士 Doctor's Degree	硕 士 Master's Degree
总 计 Total	**830**	**513626**	**53139**	**460487**	**611381**	**70462**	**540919**
国家任务 State-planned Programs		368733	40776	327957	463076	58174	404902
委托培养 Contractual Programs		25001	8779	16222	29865	8966	20899
自筹经费 Self-financed Programs		119892	3584	116308	118440	3322	115118
一、中央部门所属 Under Central Ministries& Agencies	**348**	**268419**	**42794**	**225625**	**317258**	**56257**	**261001**
1. 教育部 Under MOE	73	217176	31830	185346	254179	42188	211991
2. 其他部门 Under Other Central Agencies	275	51243	10964	40279	63079	14069	49010
二、地方所属 Under Local Auth.	**482**	**245207**	**10345**	**234862**	**294123**	**14205**	**279918**
1. 教育部门 Run by Edu. Dept.	412	238158	10167	227991	285085	13928	271157
2. 其他部门 Run by Non-ed. Dept.	64	7045	178	6867	8857	277	8580
3. 地方企业 Run by Local Enterprises	1	4		4			
4. 民办 Non-government	5				181		181

分部门、分计划
Number of Postgraduate Students

	学校(机构)数(所)(Schools)	毕业生数 Graduates			招生数 Entrants		
		合计 Total	博 士 Doctor's Degree	硕 士 Master's Degree	合计 Total	博 士 Doctor's Degree	硕 士 Master's Degree
总 计 Total	**548**	**502426**	**49405**	**453021**	**596368**	**65785**	**530583**
国家任务 State-planned Programs		357935	37203	320732	448901	53684	395217
委托培养 Contractual Programs		24815	8634	16181	29511	8780	20731
自筹经费 Self-financed Programs		119676	3568	116108	117956	3321	114635
一、中央部门所属 Under Central Ministries& Agencies	**107**	**258085**	**39110**	**218975**	**303275**	**51641**	**251634**
1. 教育部 Under MOE	73	217176	31830	185346	254179	42188	211991
2. 其他部门 Under Other Central Agencies	34	40909	7280	33629	49096	9453	39643
二、地方所属 Under Local Auth.	**441**	**244341**	**10295**	**234046**	**293093**	**14144**	**278949**
1. 教育部门 Run by Edu. Dept.	411	238149	10167	227982	285069	13928	271141
2. 其他部门 Run by Non-ed. Dept.	25	6192	128	6064	7843	216	7627
3. 地方企业 Run by Local Enterprises							
4. 民办 Non-government	5				181		181

研究生数(总计)

by Sector and Program (Total)

单位:人
unit:person

在校生数 Enrolment			预计毕业生数 Estimated Graduates for Next Year		
合计 Total	博 士 Doctor's Degree	硕 士 Master's Degree	合计 Total	博 士 Doctor's Degree	硕 士 Master's Degree
1793953	**298283**	**1495670**	**665984**	**146941**	**519043**
1328978	224270	1104708	461438	100474	360964
118121	57171	60950	60195	36634	23561
346854	16842	330012	144351	9833	134518
960507	**240528**	**719979**	**372729**	**118239**	**254490**
773966	186937	587029	303342	94130	209212
186541	53591	132950	69387	24109	45278
833446	**57755**	**775691**	**293255**	**28702**	**264553**
808903	56861	752042	285331	28367	256964
24208	894	23314	7818	335	7483
335		335	106		106

研究生数(普通高校)

by Sector and Program (Regular HEIs)

单位:人
unit:person

在校生数 Enrolment			预计毕业生数 Estimated Graduates for Next Year		
合计 Total	博 士 Doctor's Degree	硕 士 Master's Degree	合计 Total	博 士 Doctor's Degree	硕 士 Master's Degree
1749864	**281959**	**1467905**	**650683**	**139957**	**510726**
1287226	208758	1078468	447039	93916	353123
116947	56377	60570	59740	36223	23517
345691	16824	328867	143904	9818	134086
919485	**224449**	**695036**	**358414**	**111356**	**247058**
773966	186937	587029	303342	94130	209212
145519	37512	108007	55072	17226	37846
830379	**57510**	**772869**	**292269**	**28601**	**263668**
808855	56861	751994	285315	28367	256948
21189	649	20540	6848	234	6614
335		335	106		106

分部门、分计划
Number of Postgraduate Students

	学校(机构)数(所) Institutions	毕业生数 Graduates			招生数 Entrants		
		合计 Total	博 士 Doctor's Degree	硕 士 Master's Degree	合计 Total	博 士 Doctor's Degree	硕 士 Master's Degree
总 计 Total	**282**	**11200**	**3734**	**7466**	**15013**	**4677**	**10336**
国家任务 State-planned Programs		10798	3573	7225	14175	4490	9685
委托培养 Contractual Programs		186	145	41	354	186	168
自筹经费 Self-financed Programs		216	16	200	484	1	483
一、中央部门所属 Under Central Ministries& Agencies	**241**	**10334**	**3684**	**6650**	**13983**	**4616**	**9367**
1. 教育部 Under MOE							
2. 其他部门 Under Other Central Agencies	241	10334	3684	6650	13983	4616	9367
二、地方所属 Under Local Auth.	**41**	**866**	**50**	**816**	**1030**	**61**	**969**
1. 教育部门 Run by Edu. Dept.	1	9		9	16		16
2. 其他部门 Run by Non-ed. Dept.	39	853	50	803	1014	61	953
3. 地方企业 Run by Local Enterprises	1	4		4			
4. 民办 Non-government							

分学科研
Number of Postgraduate

	毕业生数 Graduates			招生数 Entrants		
	合计 Total	博 士 Doctor's Degree	硕 士 Master's Degree	合计 Total	博 士 Doctor's Degree	硕 士 Master's Degree
总 计 Total	**513626**	**53139**	**460487**	**611381**	**70462**	**540919**
其中:女 of Which: Female	257314	19980	237334	305184	26896	278288
学术型学位 Academic Degree	381854	51248	330606	384803	68743	316060
专业学位 Professional Degree	131772	1891	129881	226578	1719	224859
哲学 Philosophy	4523	708	3815	4402	894	3508
经济学 Economics	23226	2328	20898	28007	2919	25088
法学 Law	40375	2828	37547	41723	3604	38119
教育学 Education	24890	938	23952	32594	1353	31241
文学 Literature	31581	1952	29629	31623	2415	29208
历史学 History	5273	822	4451	5642	957	4685
理学 Science	49992	10396	39596	60202	14158	46044
工学 Engineering	176436	18331	158105	217338	26588	190750
农学 Agriculture	17464	2435	15029	23388	3092	20296
医学 Medicine	58550	8228	50322	66525	9090	57435
军事学 Military Science	226	16	210	246	34	212
管理学 Administrators	65791	3698	62093	81313	4701	76612
艺术学 Art	15299	459	14840	18378	657	17721

研究生数(科研机构)
by Sector and Program (Research Institutes)

单位：人
unit:person

在校生数 Enrolment			预计毕业生数 Estimated Graduates for Next Year		
合计 Total	博士 Doctor's Degree	硕士 Master's Degree	合计 Total	博士 Doctor's Degree	硕士 Master's Degree
44089	**16324**	**27765**	**15301**	**6984**	**8317**
41752	15512	26240	14399	6558	7841
1174	794	380	455	411	44
1163	18	1145	447	15	432
41022	**16079**	**24943**	**14315**	**6883**	**7432**
41022	16079	24943	14315	6883	7432
3067	**245**	**2822**	**986**	**101**	**885**
48		48	16		16
3019	245	2774	970	101	869

究生数(总计)
Students by Academic Field (Total)

单位：人
unit:person

在校生数 Enrolment			预计毕业生数 Estimated Graduates for Next Year		
合计 Total	博士 Doctor's Degree	硕士 Master's Degree	合计 Total	博士 Doctor's Degree	硕士 Master's Degree
1793953	**298283**	**1495670**	**665984**	**146941**	**519043**
878484	110076	768408	312590	52527	260063
1247567	291123	956444	478914	143938	334976
546386	7160	539226	187070	3003	184067
14669	3790	10879	5837	1909	3928
77548	12612	64936	29548	6325	23223
121414	15416	105998	45641	7646	37995
85246	5455	79791	32642	2681	29961
93482	10258	83224	35887	5248	30639
17805	4100	13705	6940	2119	4821
183997	52683	131314	65316	23356	41960
648218	122475	525743	237534	63036	174498
63778	12570	51208	25103	6362	18741
196621	32422	164199	67091	13412	53679
888	178	710	356	100	256
238834	23982	214852	97330	13741	83589
51453	2342	49111	16759	1006	15753

分学科研

Number of Postgraduate Students

	毕业生数 Graduates			招生数 Entrants		
	合计 Total	博士 Doctor's Degree	硕士 Master's Degree	合计 Total	博士 Doctor's Degree	硕士 Master's Degree
总计 Total	**502426**	**49405**	**453021**	**596368**	**65785**	**530583**
其中:女 of Which: Female	253132	18739	234393	299371	25280	274091
学术型学位 Academic Degree	371817	47514	324303	372211	64073	308138
专业学位 Professional Degree	130609	1891	128718	224157	1712	222445
哲学 Philosophy	4401	677	3724	4277	854	3423
经济学 Economics	22790	2124	20666	27280	2668	24612
法学 Law	39571	2685	36886	40823	3447	37376
教育学 Education	24890	938	23952	32594	1353	31241
文学 Literature	31484	1918	29566	31535	2381	29154
历史学 History	5193	797	4396	5514	927	4587
理学 Science	47020	8855	38165	55965	12233	43732
工学 Engineering	171966	17162	154804	211562	25044	186518
农学 Agriculture	16625	2195	14430	22380	2809	19571
医学 Medicine	57798	8006	49792	65573	8829	56744
军事学 Military Science	222	16	206	242	34	208
管理学 Administrators	65337	3626	61711	80422	4606	75816
艺术学 Art	15129	406	14723	18201	600	17601

分学科研

Number of Postgraduate Students

	毕业生数 Graduates			招生数 Entrants		
	合计 Total	博士 Doctor's Degree	硕士 Master's Degree	合计 Total	博士 Doctor's Degree	硕士 Master's Degree
总计 Total	**11200**	**3734**	**7466**	**15013**	**4677**	**10336**
其中:女 of Which: Female	4182	1241	2941	5813	1616	4197
学术型学位 Academic Degree	10037	3734	6303	12592	4670	7922
专业学位 Professional Degree	1163		1163	2421	7	2414
哲学 Philosophy	122	31	91	125	40	85
经济学 Economics	436	204	232	727	251	476
法学 Law	804	143	661	900	157	743
教育学 Education						
文学 Literature	97	34	63	88	34	54
历史学 History	80	25	55	128	30	98
理学 Science	2972	1541	1431	4237	1925	2312
工学 Engineering	4470	1169	3301	5776	1544	4232
农学 Agriculture	839	240	599	1008	283	725
医学 Medicine	752	222	530	952	261	691
军事学 Military Science	4		4	4		4
管理学 Administrators	454	72	382	891	95	796
艺术学 Art	170	53	117	177	57	120

究生数(普通高校)
by Academic Field (Regular HEIs)

单位：人
unit: person

在校生数 Enrolment			预计毕业生数 Estimated Graduates for Next Year		
合计 Total	博士 Doctor's Degree	硕士 Master's Degree	合计 Total	博士 Doctor's Degree	硕士 Master's Degree
1749864	**281959**	**1467905**	**650683**	**139957**	**510726**
861561	104522	757039	306740	50202	256538
1209306	274808	934498	465589	136954	328635
540558	7151	533407	185094	3003	182091
14266	3650	10616	5690	1850	3840
75437	11740	63697	28686	5945	22741
118904	14912	103992	44685	7451	37234
85246	5455	79791	32642	2681	29961
93157	10118	83039	35782	5198	30584
17491	4033	13458	6807	2090	4717
171310	45999	125311	60865	20375	40490
630803	116804	513999	231692	60617	171075
60758	11606	49152	24037	5962	18075
193878	31615	162263	66218	13124	53094
876	178	698	352	100	252
236827	23694	213133	96660	13634	83026
50911	2155	48756	16567	930	15637

究生数(科研机构)
by Academic Field (Research Institutes)

单位：人
unit: persons

在校生数 Enrolment			预计毕业生数 Estimated Graduates for Next Year		
合计 Total	博士 Doctor's Degree	硕士 Master's Degree	合计 Total	博士 Doctor's Degree	硕士 Master's Degree
44089	**16324**	**27765**	**15301**	**6984**	**8317**
16923	5554	11369	5850	2325	3525
38261	16315	21946	13325	6984	6341
5828	9	5819	1976		1976
403	140	263	147	59	88
2111	872	1239	862	380	482
2510	504	2006	956	195	761
325	140	185	105	50	55
314	67	247	133	29	104
12687	6684	6003	4451	2981	1470
17415	5671	11744	5842	2419	3423
3020	964	2056	1066	400	666
2743	807	1936	873	288	585
12		12	4		4
2007	288	1719	670	107	563
542	187	355	192	76	116

在职人员攻读硕士学位分学科学生数

Number of On-the-job Students Studying for Master's Degree by Discipline

单位：人

unit：person

	授予学位数 Degree Awarded	招生数 Entrants	在校生数 Enrolment
总　计 Total	**103468**	**167576**	**558730**
其中：女 of Which：Female	37850	56398	179387
学术型学位 Academic Degree	7741	7677	30363
专业学位 Professional Degree	95727	159899	528367
哲学 Philosophy	37	3	36
经济学 Economics	535	287	901
法学 Law	6856	7013	21367
教育学 Education	11866	21475	53798
文学 Literature	937	428	1868
历史学 History	26	4	54
理学 Science	401	106	721
工学 Engineering	51636	98496	337701
农学 Agriculture	7907	12830	46367
医学 Medicine	3092	5245	18796
军事学 Military Science	1		
管理学 Administrators	18500	19546	72040
艺术学 Art	1674	2143	5081

普通高等学校工科分大类本科学生数

Number of Engineering Students for Normal Courses by Subfield of Study in Regular HEIs

单位：人

unit: person

	毕业生数 Graduates	招生数 Entrants	在校生数 Enrolment
总　计 Total	**1058768**	**1274915**	**4953334**
地矿类 Applied Geology	4153	5470	19417
材料类 Materials Science	166632	192694	770773
机械类 Mechanical Engineering	18236	19290	78179
仪器仪表类 Instrument & Meter	53070	67204	254572
能源动力类 Thermal & Nuclear Energy	18103	23678	89270
电气信息类 Electronics & Information	66867	85166	333078
土建类 Civil Engineering & Architcture	153371	169416	669709
水利类 Hydraulics	42227	45712	180759
测绘类 Sruvey & Measure	166609	207793	773439
环境与安全类 Environment and Safety	104161	129974	517237
化工与制药类 Chemical Engineering & Pharmaceutics	10656	13062	52334
交通运输类 Transportation	8564	10863	40308
海洋工程类 Oceanic	42518	53022	200305
轻工纺织食品类 Light Industry, Textile and Food	11312	13386	52303
航空航天类 Aeronautics & Astronautics	15657	16348	69161
武器类 Weaponry	10857	11588	49617
工程力学类 Engineering Mechanics	8115	8958	35409
生物工程类 Biotechnology	24739	31433	117953
农业工程类 Agriculture Engineering	2882	3288	12883
林业工程类 Forestry Engineering	5191	6703	25524
公安技术类 Public Security Technology	3043	3360	13124

普通、成人本、专科

Number of Students for Regular and Adult

	毕业生数 Graduates			招生数 Entrants	
	合计 Total	本科 Normal Courses	专科 Short-cycle Courses	合计 Total	本科 Normal Courses
一、普通本、专科总计 Undergraduate in Regular HEIs Total	**6387210**	**3199716**	**3187494**	**6998330**	**3814331**
1. 中央部门所属院校 Under Central Ministries & Agencies	425715	407845	17870	462692	445289
其中：教育部所属院校 of Which: Under MOE	322540	318156	4384	340675	337090
2. 地方所属学校 Under Local Auth.	4664441	2073816	2590625	4977401	2450669
其中：民办 of Which: Non-government	1297054	718055	578999	1558237	918373
二、成人本、专科总计 Undergraduate in Adult HEIs Total	**1997729**	**811159**	**1186570**	**2564934**	**1038158**
1. 中央部门所属院校 Inst. Under SEDC	274168	155233	118935	304780	175405
其中：教育部所属院校 of Which: Under MOE	226931	131101	95830	254285	147756
2. 地方所属学校 Under Local Auth.	1687895	654446	1033449	2216693	859735
其中：民办 of Which: Non-government	35666	1480	34186	43461	3018

普通本、专科分

Number of Students for Regular

	毕业生数 Graduates			招生数 Entrants	
	合计 Total	本科 Normal Courses	专科 Short-cycle Courses	合计 Total	本科 Normal Courses
总　计 Total	**6387210**	**3199716**	**3187494**	**6998330**	**3814331**
其中：女 of Which: Female	3274056	1623403	1650653	3843225	2090027
一、普通高等学校 Regular HEIs	**6346827**	**3199716**	**3147111**	**6965343**	**3814331**
本科院校 HEIs Offering Degree Programs	3896194	3164020	732174	4332254	3791273
其中：独立学院 of Which: Independent Institutions	591872	543196	48676	687234	640713
高职(专科)院校 Higher Vocational Colleges	2406749	745	2406004	2608385	860
其他机构(点)(不计校数) Other Institutions	43884	34951	8933	24704	22198
综合大学 Comprehensive Universities	1724029	899984	824045	1870525	1045126
理工院校 Natural Sciences & Tech.	2338763	1010016	1328747	2547398	1194961
农业院校 Agriculture	257382	151718	105664	281988	177141
林业院校 Forestry	47391	26631	20760	54824	30064
医药院校 Medicine & Pharmacy	361848	174004	187844	408283	214059
师范院校 Teacher Training	655598	457456	198142	698142	536202
语文院校 Language & Literature	97632	46420	51212	116439	65523
财经院校 Finance & Economics	614251	283487	330764	689307	360720
政法院校 Political Science & Law	84052	34005	50047	101261	49506
体育院校 Physical Culture	28531	21933	6598	30907	25960
艺术院校 Art	86190	48623	37567	104287	59399
民族院校 Ethnic Minorities	51160	45439	5721	61982	55670
二、成人高等学校 Adult HEIs	**40383**		**40383**	**32987**	

分举办者学生数
Programs by Providers in HEIs

单位:人
unit: person

	在校生数 Enrolment			预计毕业生数 Estimated Graduates for Next Year		
专科 Short-cycle Courses	合计 Total	本科 Normal Courses	专科 Short-cycle Courses	合计 Total	本科 Normal Courses	专科 Short-cycle Courses
3183999	**24680726**	**14944353**	**9736373**	**6737474**	**3497450**	**3240024**
17403	1809180	1757100	52080	446670	429234	17436
3585	1357187	1345126	12061	334969	330465	4504
2526732	17402457	9578736	7823721	4880370	2254416	2625954
639864	5469089	3608517	1860572	1410434	813800	596634
1526776	6264145	2654596	3609549	2362194	940037	1422157
129375	784047	471583	312464	313721	176313	137408
106529	651784	397604	254180	256554	145526	111028
1356958	5374304	2175167	3199137	2014526	761335	1253191
40443	105794	7846	97948	33947	2389	31558

性质类别学生数
Programs by Type of Schools in HEIs

单位: 人
unit: person

	在校生数 Enrolment			预计毕业生数 Estimated Graduates for Next Year		
专科 Short-cycle Courses	合计 Total	本科 Normal Courses	专科 Short-cycle Courses	合计 Total	本科 Normal Courses	专科 Short-cycle Courses
3183999	**24680726**	**14944353**	**9736373**	**6737474**	**3497450**	**3240024**
1753198	12769199	7738044	5031155	3288432	1710277	1578155
3151012	**24580211**	**14944353**	**9635858**	**6703145**	**3497450**	**3205695**
540981	16685593	14823313	1862280	4156153	3461636	694517
46521	2753416	2607168	146248	660974	612293	48681
2607525	7756258	3493	7752765	2502904	909	2501995
2506	138360	117547	20813	44088	34905	9183
825399	6661910	4132844	2529066	1808603	977727	830876
1352437	8760295	4654955	4105340	2475999	1107807	1368192
104847	1002655	682505	320150	268104	161638	106466
24760	187360	117504	69856	50781	28461	22320
194224	1529433	929868	599565	384103	189011	195092
161940	2635628	2086949	548679	695863	498837	197026
50916	387639	236941	150698	102514	50640	51874
328587	2375104	1386859	988245	643789	317477	326312
51755	335717	179996	155721	95705	41855	53850
4947	117749	98929	18820	29757	22867	6890
44888	354619	225575	129044	92596	52113	40483
6312	232102	211428	20674	55331	49017	6314
32987	**100515**		**100515**	**34329**		**34329**

成人本、专科分

Number of Students for Adult

	毕业生数 Graduates			招生数 Entrants	
	合计 Total	本科 Normal Courses	专科 Short-cycle Courses	合计 Total	本科 Normal Courses
总　计 Total	**1997729**	**811159**	**1186570**	**2564934**	**1038158**
其中:女 of Which:Female	1080234	456202	624032	1433919	591686
一、成人高等学校 Adult HEIs	**154136**	**13897**	**140239**	**192358**	**14323**
其中:全脱产 of Which:Full-time	78024	5191	72833	108091	6409
职工高等学校 Workers' Colleges	60623	3402	57221	67458	2021
农民高等学校 Peasants' Colleges	540		540	657	
管理干部学院 Institutes for Administration	17757	2771	14986	20775	3770
教育学院 Educational Colleges	20149	6580	13569	35166	7011
独立函授学院 Independent Correspondence Colleges					
广播电视大学 Radio/TV Universities	54894	1144	53750	68296	1521
其他机构 Other Institutions	173		173	6	
二、普通高等学校 Regular HEIs	**1843593**	**797262**	**1046331**	**2372576**	**1023835**
函授 Correspondence	1077304	480168	597136	1400573	615906
业余 Spare time Schools	759351	315045	444306	960086	403832
脱产 Full-time Courses for Adults	6938	2049	4889	11917	4097

普通本科分学科学生数

Number of Regular Students for Normal Courses in HEIs by Discipline

单位:人

unit: person

	毕业生数 Graduates	招生数 Entrants	在校生数 Enrolment	预计毕业生数 Estimated Graduates for Next Year
总　计 Total	**3199716**	**3814331**	**14944353**	**3497450**
其中: 女 of Which: Female	1623403	2090027	7738044	1710277
哲学 Philosophy	2034	2930	9205	2104
经济学 Economics	193530	223473	882890	210209
法学 Law	122676	138050	535423	132181
教育学 Education	104691	139887	517344	115184
文学 Literature	355662	366416	1479974	366583
其中:外语 of Which:Foreign Language	200312	199856	813777	202609
历史学 History	15773	18370	70836	17129
理学 Science	248790	277254	1076027	263721
工学 Engineering	1058768	1274915	4953334	1171858
农学 Agriculture	58752	68658	259837	61125
医学 Medicine	192344	238919	1064363	211467
管理学 Administrators	575152	697484	2750404	645874
艺术学 Art	271544	367975	1344716	300015
总计中:师范生 of the Total:Students Enrolled in Teacher Training Institutions	342076	351062	1436507	358307

性质类别学生数
Programs by Type of Schools in HEIs

单位：人
unit：person

专科 Short-cycle Courses	在校生数 Enrolment			预计毕业生数 Estimated Graduates for Next Year		
	合计 Total	本科 Normal Courses	专科 Short-cycle Courses	合计 Total	本科 Normal Courses	专科 Short-cycle Courses
1526776	**6264145**	**2654596**	**3609549**	**2362194**	**940037**	**1422157**
842233	3462758	1495593	1967165	1219367	489118	730249
178035	**447712**	**37283**	**410429**	**186473**	**16107**	**170366**
101682	233053	15989	217064	98088	6990	91098
65437	156032	6941	149091	67896	4161	63735
657	1168		1168	511		511
17005	46044	8033	38011	18695	2637	16058
28155	80504	18534	61970	30058	7594	22464
66775	163761	3775	159986	69122	1715	67407
6	203		203	191		191
1348741	**5816433**	**2617313**	**3199120**	**2175721**	**923930**	**1251791**
784667	3385061	1533904	1851157	1313767	560911	752856
556254	2406842	1074416	1332426	851779	359435	492344
7820	24530	8993	15537	10175	3584	6591

普通专科分专业大类学生数
Number of Regular Students for Short-cycle Courses in HEIs by Discipline

单位：人
unit：person

	毕业生数 Graduates	招生数 Entrants	在校生数 Enrolment	预计毕业生数 Estimated Graduates for Next Year
总　计 Total	**3187494**	**3183999**	**9736373**	**3240024**
其中：女 of Which：Female	1650653	1753198	5031155	1578155
农林牧渔大类 Agriculture，Forestry，Husbandry and Fishing	56295	55578	169938	56624
交通运输大类 Transportation and Communication	137055	160095	466262	146030
生化与药品大类 Biochemistry and Medicine	78844	68115	217477	76659
资源开发与测绘大类 Resources Development and Survey	48329	45210	145409	49821
材料与能源大类 Material and Energy	45039	39379	125455	44049
土建大类 Civil Engineering	313035	398400	1138612	364240
水利大类 Water Resources	12388	14678	42744	13879
制造大类 Manufacturing	422106	403256	1242864	416867
电子信息大类 Electronic Information	325817	290916	892212	303281
环保、气象与安全大类 Environment Protection，Meteorology and Safety	15114	14778	44913	15508
轻纺食品大类 Light，Textile and Food	57604	51005	159004	55774
财经大类 Finance	668469	676475	2078204	688711
医药卫生大类 Medical and Health	308106	324759	995420	319456
旅游大类 Tourism	104287	107128	320920	104995
公共事业大类 Public Service	32218	32966	96907	31477
文化教育大类 Culture and Education	358222	297318	992417	348263
艺术设计传媒大类 Artistic Design and Mass Media	154159	156091	457030	151469
公安大类 Public Security	9514	11259	34675	12871
法律大类 Law	40893	36593	115910	40050
总计中：师范生 of the Total：Students Enrolled in Teacher Training Institutions	176354	151276	521576	183392

成人本科分学科学生数

Number of Adult Students for Normal Courses in HEIs by Discipline

单位:人

unit:person

	毕业生数 Graduates	招生数 Entrants	在校学生数 Enrolment	预计毕业生数 Estimated Graduates for Next Year
总　计 Total	**811159**	**1038158**	**2654596**	**940037**
其中:女 of Which:Female	456202	591686	1495593	489118
哲学 Philosophy	54	66	100	1
经济学 Economics	27596	29128	86284	32831
法学 Law	48444	48182	125062	51175
教育学 Education	43508	60957	147477	57629
文学 Literature	100780	83162	236314	99187
其中:外语 of Which:Foreign Language	30754	24519	73552	30667
历史学 History	1851	1613	4465	1780
理学 Science	23938	21199	55288	23324
工学 Engineering	186133	253886	659393	227075
农学 Agriculture	13162	16774	40527	14641
医学 Medicine	153016	225261	544416	173409
管理学 Administrators	197677	280424	700896	241429
艺术学 Art	15000	17506	54374	17556
总计中:师范生 of the Total:Students Enrolled in Teacher Training Institutions	107107	108195	272166	111467

成人专科分学科学生数

Number of Adult Students for Short-cycle Courses in HEIs by Discipline

单位:人

unit:person

	毕业生数 Graduates	招生数 Entrants	在校学生数 Enrolment	预计毕业生数 Estimated Graduates for Next Year
总　计 Total	**1186570**	**1526776**	**3609549**	**1422157**
其中:女 of Which: Female	624032	842233	1967165	730249
农林牧渔大类 Agriculture, Forestry, Husbandry and Fishing	24920	26878	60889	24961
交通运输大类 Transportation and Communication	39018	48229	121102	48858
生化与药品大类 Biochemistry and Medicine	15572	12257	34645	14415
资源开发与测绘大类 Resources Development and Survey	31401	43451	110888	41786
材料与能源大类 Material and Energy	13954	11163	33688	14989
土建大类 Civil Engineering	79967	120555	274092	104217
水利大类 Water Resources	6100	6061	14134	6181
制造大类 Manufacturing	151477	175476	420650	172139
电子信息大类 Electronic Information	93990	94988	229481	99186
环保、气象与安全大类 Environment Protection, Meteorology and Safety	2434	2281	5670	2419
轻纺食品大类 Light, Textile and Food	6920	7067	18008	7518
财经大类 Finance	330069	388347	904179	375361
医药卫生大类 Medical and Health	166766	233817	594172	189028
旅游大类 Tourism	21521	26447	58665	24281
公共事业大类 Public Service	36162	55051	117725	44977
文化教育大类 Culture and Education	120689	219231	478814	193228
艺术设计传媒大类 Artistic Design and Mass Media	29488	37372	88520	39732
公安大类 Public Security	1646	1492	5662	2418
法律大类 Law	14476	16613	38565	16463
总计中:师范生 of the Total: Students Enrolled in Teacher Training Institutions	65798	136518	286098	115583

网络本科分学科学生数

Number of Web-based Students for Normal Courses in HEIs by Discipline

单位:人

unit:person

	毕业生数 Graduates	招生数 Entrants	在校生数 Enrolment
总　计 Total	**536702**	**804378**	**2175100**
其中:女 of Which:Female	297952	425359	1139523
哲学 Philosophy			
经济学 Economics	29375	35464	109499
法学 Law	58168	72513	225293
教育学 Education	20553	31570	72766
文学 Literature	47233	44643	152240
其中:外语 of Which:Foreign Language	9744	7977	37766
历史学 History	538	544	1079
理学 Science	7124	6838	17208
工学 Engineering	92626	180650	418498
农学 Agriculture	3493	6936	13698
医学 Medicine	44579	67680	160369
管理学 Administrators	231162	354393	993794
艺术学 Art	1851	3147	10656
总计中:师范生 of the Total:Students Enrolled in Teacher Training Institutions	21112	23171	53200

高等教育学生

Changes in Enrolment of

	上学年初报表在校学生数 Enrolment at Beginning of Previous Academic Year	增加学生数 Factors of Increase					
		合计 Total	招生 No. of Students Admitted	复学 Students Resuming Studies	转入 Transfers from Other Inst.	其他 Others	合计 Total
博士生 Doctor's Degrees	283810	74920	70462	1182	286	2990	60447
硕士生 Master's Degrees	1436008	548653	540919	3190	1744	2800	488991
普通本科生 Students Enrolled in Normal Courses	14270888	4028120	3965793	28734	15665	17928	3354655
普通专科生 Students Enrolled in Short-cycle Courses	9642267	3512262	3402232	13233	81056	15741	3418156
成人本科生 Students Enrolled in Normal Courses Provided by Adult HEIs	2475495	1079312	1038158	7150	14020	19984	900211
成人专科生 Students Enrolled in Short-cycle Courses Provided by Adult HEIs	3355628	1584528	1526776	7023	20975	29754	1330607
网络本科生 Students Enroned in Normal Courses Provided by Web-based Programs	2002698	822335	804378	5498	3811	8648	649933
网络专科生 Students Enroned in Short-cycle Courses Provided by Web-based Programs	3701414	1423194	1396351	2792	3221	20830	1153302

网络专科分专业大类学生数

Number of Web-based Students for Short-cycle Courses in HEIs by Discipline

单位:人

unit:person

	毕业生数 Graduates	招生数 Entrants	在校生数 Enrolment
总　计 Total	**1024060**	**1396351**	**3971306**
其中:女 of Which: Female	501241	656091	1876466
农林牧渔大类 Agriculture, Forestry, Husbandry and Fishing	57671	61434	213440
交通运输大类 Transportation and Communication	22114	37035	84336
生化与药品大类 Biochemistry and Medicine	3381	4638	11543
资源开发与测绘大类 Resources Development and Survey	10773	20426	39718
材料与能源大类 Material and Energy	5254	5718	10287
土建大类 Civil Engineering	83221	150051	355818
水利大类 Water Resources	4910	6646	20089
制造大类 Manufacturing	45993	77157	190592
电子信息大类 Electronic Information	43146	53304	172766
环保、气象与安全大类 Environment Protection, Meteorology and Safety	1908	3331	8222
轻纺食品大类 Light, Textile and Food	877	1305	3646
财经大类 Finance	315424	403331	1215227
医药卫生大类 Medical and Health	49849	62550	163984
旅游大类 Tourism	4049	6566	21322
公共事业大类 Public Service	193084	281682	785008
文化教育大类 Culture and Education	101149	134603	388541
艺术设计传媒大类 Artistic Design and Mass Media	5203	6759	31034
公安大类 Public Security	848	935	2036
法律大类 Law	75206	78880	253697
总计中:师范生 of the Total: Students Enrolled in Teacher Training Institutions	16450	20392	40480

数变动情况

Higher Educations

单位: 人

unit: person

减少学生数 Factors of Decrease								本学年初报表在校学生数 Enrolment at Beginning of Current Academic Year
毕业 Graduates	结业 Completers of Courses without Formal Diplomas	休学 Suspended	退学 Quitting	开除 Expelled	死亡 Death	转出 Transfers to Other Inst.	其他 Others	
53139	628	1379	2201	22	27	178	2873	298283
460487	507	3903	5234	79	103	2306	16372	1495670
3199716	32813	47143	37275	1530	1142	16812	18224	14944353
3187494	28783	38362	59408	2539	586	73657	27327	9736373
811159	7027	9222	26690	188	26	15651	30248	2654596
1186570	10812	17038	47447	445	37	20541	47717	3609549
536702	5093	16689	43179	170	44	2308	45748	2175100
1024060	3409	40892	49987	252	37	2001	32664	3971306

高等教育非学历教育学生情况

Number of Students of Non-formal Education of Higher Education

单位：人

unit：person

	结业生数 Graduates		注册学生数 Enrolment	
	合计 Total	其中:女 of Which:Female	合计 Total	其中:女 of Which:Female
研究生课程进修班 Postgraduate Courses	48329	25652	69321	36182
自考助学班 Classes run by Non – government HEIs for Students Preparing for Self-directed State – administered Examinations	130839	70729	253164	121959
普通预科生 College – preparatory Classes			42514	22913
进修及培训 In – service Training	8350709	3395053	5540641	2414888
一个月以内 1 Month Under	5552781	1971213	3529331	1486116
一个月至三个月以内 1 Month to 3 Months Under	1832541	975386	1043841	480052
三个月至半年以内 3 Months to 6 Months Under	380664	194921	334787	168094
半年至一年以内 6 Months to 1 Year Under	378625	170185	393582	181448
一年及以上 1 Year and over	206098	83348	239100	99178
总计中:资格证书培训 of the Total: For Certificates of Vocational Qualifications	2216069	992959	1876552	853340
岗位证书培训 For Certificates of Job – related Qualifications	2387566	1096607	1641632	693962
第一产业类培训 Training for first industry	387774	134882	253769	90476
第二产业类培训 Training for Second Industry	1108198	312011	946395	277165
第三产业类培训 Training for Third Industry	6854737	2948160	4340477	2047247

高等教育学生中其他情况

Other Circumstances of Students in Higher Education

单位:人

unit: person

	共产党员 Member of C. P. A	共青团员 Member of C. Y. L	华侨 Overseas Chinese	港澳台 From HK, Macao and Taiwan	少数民族 Minorities	残疾人 Disabled
总计 Total	3407049	26616427	4808	30607	2826615	24308
研究生 Postgraduates	790141	749315	124	7020	107392	283
博士 Doctor's Degree	651391	685789	97	4091	90059	244
硕士 Master's Degree	138750	63526	27	2929	17333	39
普通本专科 Undergraduates in Regular HEIs	1599702	20938574	1917	19861	1844503	16079
本科 Normal Courses	286267	8344670	493	150	676906	8441
专科 Short-cycle Courses	1313435	12593904	1424	19711	1167597	7638
成人本专科 Undergraduates in Adult HEIs	474124	2610660	2767	2732	502741	1356
本科 Normal Courses	178385	1624171	1306	1012	284117	998
专科 Short-cycle Courses	295739	986489	1461	1720	218624	358
网络本专科生 Web-based Undergraduates	543082	2317878		994	371979	6590
本科 Normal Courses	276354	1551952		709	242191	2268
专科 Short-cycle Courses	266728	765926		285	129788	4322

	毕(结)业生数 Graduates	授予学位数 Degrees Awarded	招生数 Entrants	
			合计 Total	其中:春季招生 of Which: Spring Term
总　计 Total	**91251**	**19025**	**106448**	**31008**
其中:女 of Which:Female	43274	8324	52119	15858
按层次分 by Level of Training	21577	19025	34819	3723
博士研究生 Doctor's Degrees	1079	1054	2689	162
硕士研究生 Master's Degrees	5931	5541	9641	515
本科 Normal Courses	14132	12430	21743	2931
专科 Short-cycle Courses	435		746	115
培训 In-service Training	69674		71629	27285
分大洲 by Continent				
亚洲 Asia	53321	14041	62350	18089
非洲 Africa	7200	2206	9797	2312
欧洲 Europe	18356	1717	21185	5916
北美洲 North America	9580	645	9586	3939
南美洲 South America	1392	212	2046	377
大洋洲 Australia	1402	204	1484	375
分经费来源 by Sources of Support				
国际组织资助 Aided by IGOs	98	11	114	78
中国政府资助 Aided by Chinese Government	15965	5574	20915	2514
本国政府资助 Aided by Home Government	1168	324	986	181
学校间交换 Aided by Inter-institutional Exchanges	11163	659	13172	4954
自费 Self-supporting	62857	12457	71261	23281

生 情 况

International Students

单位：人、人次

unit：person

在校生数 Enrolment					
合计 Total	第一年 1st Year	第二年 2nd Year	第三年 3rd Year	第四年 4th Year	第五年及以上 5th Year and Over
174806	**92412**	**34990**	**22473**	**15217**	**9714**
77518	44175	14525	9217	6161	3440
108218	34386	28555	21133	14788	9356
8368	2715	2146	1744	945	818
22935	9598	7644	4149	1118	426
75860	21310	18523	15196	12723	8108
1055	763	242	44	2	4
66588	58026	6435	1340	429	358
113859	54234	24181	16295	11521	7628
20746	9440	4954	3127	2025	1200
24886	18054	3689	1845	928	370
10789	7597	1523	817	483	369
2574	1793	351	204	156	70
1952	1294	292	185	104	77
199	175	7	12	5	
36842	18786	8380	5403	3034	1239
2396	851	692	387	274	192
13492	11069	1265	653	259	246
121877	61531	24646	16018	11645	8037

高等教育学校(机构)
Number of Educational

	合计 Total	校本部 Educational Personnel			
		小计 Subtotal	专任教师		
			小计 Subtotal	正高级 Senior	副高级 Sub-senior
总　计 Total	**2352679**	**2235200**	**1530512**	**182982**	**442685**
其中:女 of Which: Female	1097490	1047550	732219	53118	195330
普通高校 Regular HEIs	2296262	2179314	1496865	181501	432356
成人高校 Adult HEIs	56417	55886	33647	1481	10329

高等教育学校(机构)
Number of Educational

	合计 Total	校本部 Educational Personnel			
		小计 Subtotal	专任教师		
			小计 Subtotal	正高级 Senior	副高级 Sub-senior
总　计 Total	**2296262**	**2179314**	**1496865**	**181501**	**432356**
其中:女 of Which: Female	1070126	1020402	714450	52494	190283
分类型:本科院校	1657517	1555626	1055036	162388	321169
by Type: HEIs Offering Degree Programs					
其中:独立学院 of Which: Independent Institutions	186262	185309	138815	15146	36018
高职(专科)院校 Higher Vocational Colleges	630044	615993	436561	18276	109543
其他机构 Other Institutions	8701	7695	5268	837	1644
分举办者:1. 中央部门所属	379181	324143	190097	50179	67734
by Providers: Central Ministries & Agencies					
教育部 Under MOE	292990	250812	146227	38728	53137
其他部门 Other Central Agencies	86191	73331	43870	11451	14597
2. 地方所属 Local Authorities	1518681	1460192	1025353	104303	298356
教育部门 Ed. Dept.	1188305	1136521	798147	93141	237562
其他部门 Non-Ed. Dept.	310417	304249	214438	10925	56830
地方企业 Local Enterprises	19959	19422	12768	237	3964
3. 民办 Non-government	398400	394979	281415	27019	66266

教职工情况(总计)
Personnel in HEIs (Total)

单位：人
unit：person

教职工数 Educational Personnel								
教职工 in Main Campus						科研机构人员 Personnel in Affiliated Research Org.	校办企业职工 Employees in School-run Factories & Farms	其他附设机构人员 Personnel in Others Subsidiary Units
Full-time Teachers			行政人员 Adm. Personnel	教辅人员 Supporting Staff	工勤人员 Workers			
中级 Middle	初级 Junior	未定职级 No-ranking						
611226	**209963**	**83656**	**323388**	**211969**	**169331**	**29918**	**31076**	**56485**
320996	118270	44505	149109	115630	50592	11166	9163	29611
596954	203713	82341	312606	205280	164563	29789	30864	56295
14272	6250	1315	10782	6689	4768	129	212	190

教职工情况(普通高校)
Personnel in HEIs (Regular HEIs)

单位：人
unit：person

教职工数 Educational Personnel								
教职工 in Main Campus						科研机构人员 Personnel in Affiliated Research Org.	校办企业职工 Employees in School-run Factories & Farms	其他附设机构人员 Personnel in Others Subsidiary Units
Full-time Teachers			行政人员 Adm. Personnel	教辅人员 Supporting Staff	工勤人员 Workers			
中级 Middle	初级 Junior	未定职级 No-ranking						
596954	**203713**	**82341**	**312606**	**205280**	**164563**	**29789**	**30864**	**56295**
313104	114819	43750	144446	112138	49368	11096	9091	29537
419806	106914	44759	226233	155480	118877	28153	24940	48798
54629	23362	9660	22907	11133	12454	84	428	441
174894	96425	37423	85147	49083	45202	1340	5411	7300
2254	374	159	1226	717	484	296	513	197
61986	6080	4118	57384	46396	30266	19971	12048	23019
47615	3901	2846	45250	35193	24142	15624	10952	15602
14371	2179	1272	12134	11203	6124	4347	1096	7417
431435	141172	50087	201057	130596	103186	9284	16923	32282
337699	94235	35510	155073	103543	79758	8497	14402	28885
88371	44452	13860	43166	25362	21283	673	2329	3166
5365	2485	717	2818	1691	2145	114	192	231
103533	56461	28136	54165	28288	31111	534	1893	994

高等教育学校(机构)
Number of Educational

	合计 Total	校本部 Educational Personnel			
		小计 Subtotal	专任教师		
			小计 Subtotal	正高级 Senior	副高级 Sub-senior
总　计 Total	**56417**	**55886**	**33647**	**1481**	**10329**
其中:女 of Which: Female	27364	27148	17769	624	5047
分类型:职工高等学校 by Type: Workers' Colleges	20890	20684	12812	335	3967
农民高等学校 Peasants' College	130	130	89		14
管理干部学院 Institutes for Administration	8555	8463	5044	478	1703
教育学院 Educational College	7708	7637	5329	239	1867
独立函授学院 Independent Correspondence Colleges					
广播电视大学 Radio/TV Universities	18384	18222	9929	427	2664
其他机构 Other Institutions	750	750	444	2	114
分举办者:1. 中央部门所属	1177	1167	501	53	211
by Provider: Under Central Ministries & Agencies					
教育部 Under MOE	513	503	151	19	70
其他部门 Other Central Agencies	664	664	350	34	141
2. 地方所属 Local Auth.	55240	54719	33146	1428	10118
教育部门 Ed. Dept.	27973	27746	16732	708	4992
其他部门 Non – ed. Dept.	23101	22845	14010	687	4301
地方企业 Local Enterprises	4166	4128	2404	33	825
3. 民办 Non – government					

教职工情况(成人高校)
Personnel in HEIs (Adult HEIs)

单位：人
unit：person

教职工数
Educational Personnel

教职工 in Main Campus						科研机构人员 Personnel in Affiliated Research Org.	校办企业职工 Employees in School-run	其他附设机构人员 Personnel in Others Subsidiary Units
Full-time Teachers			行政人员 Adm. Personnel	教辅人员 Supporting Staff	工勤人员 Workers			
中级 Middle	初级 Junior	未定职级 No-ranking						
14272	**6250**	**1315**	**10782**	**6689**	**4768**	**129**	**212**	**190**
7892	3451	755	4663	3492	1224	70	72	74
5740	2338	432	3557	2214	2101	9	111	86
40	35		20	14	7			
1985	688	190	1627	948	844	54	4	34
2076	997	150	1142	661	505	20		51
4232	2065	541	4256	2776	1261	46	97	19
199	127	2	180	76	50			
205	27	5	505	60	101	10		
51	7	4	311	12	29	10		
154	20	1	194	48	72			
14067	6223	1310	10277	6629	4667	119	212	190
7158	3186	688	5534	3584	1896	52	100	75
5844	2630	548	4012	2542	2281	67	76	113
1065	407	74	731	503	490		36	2

研究生指导

Number of Supervisors

	合计 Total	29 岁及以下 29 and Under	30—34 岁 30 to 34	35—39 岁 35 to 39
总　计 Total	**315815**	**1456**	**24808**	**52398**
其中:女 of Which: Female	90872	444	7825	18009
分职称:正高级 by Rank:Senior	154515	52	1714	8432
副高级 Sub-senior	146731	592	16346	39633
中级 Middle	14569	812	6748	4333
分指导关系:博士导师	18280	3	264	1135
by Level of Programs Supervised: Supervisors of Doctoral Programs				
其中:女 of Which: Female	2675		34	192
硕士导师 Supervisors of Master's Degree Programs	241200	1407	22978	46257
其中:女 of Which: Female	78448	434	7525	16836
博士、硕士导师	56335	46	1566	5006
Supervisors of Doc. & Mas. Degree Programs				
其中:女 of Which: Female	9749	10	266	981

研究生指导教

Number of Supervisors of

	合计 Total	29 岁及以下 29 and Under	30—34 岁 30 to 34	35—39 岁 35 to 39
总　计 Total	**295858**	**1393**	**23676**	**49430**
其中:女 of Which: Female	87326	438	7578	17312
分职称:正高级 by Rank:Senior	140419	44	1549	7440
副高级 Sub-senior	140971	569	15410	37685
中级 Middle	14468	780	6717	4305
分指导关系:博士导师	15123	3	230	958
by Level of Programs Supervised: Supervisors of Doctoral Programs				
其中:女 of Which: Female	2305		31	172
硕士导师 Supervisors of Master's Degree Programs	228784	1344	22002	43988
其中:女 of Which: Female	75958	428	7308	16284
博士、硕士导师	51951	46	1444	4484
Supervisors of Doc. & Mas. Degree Programs				
其中:女 of Which: Female	9063	10	239	856

教师情况(总计)

of Postgraduate Programs (Total)

单位：人

unit：person

40—44 岁 40 to 44	45—49 岁 44 to 49	50—59 岁 50 to 54	55—59 岁 55 to 59	60—64 岁 60 to 64	65 岁及以上 65 and Over
65994	**77822**	**50099**	**29752**	**7501**	**5985**
22274	22163	12091	6167	1195	704
23959	47877	36554	23872	6596	5459
40409	29309	13294	5779	870	499
1626	636	251	101	35	27
2370	4756	3863	2745	1293	1851
467	768	497	390	170	157
54510	57115	34322	19191	3739	1681
19895	18468	9742	4567	711	270
9114	15951	11914	7816	2469	2453
1912	2927	1852	1210	314	277

师情况(普通高校)

Postgraduate Programs (Regular HEIs)

单位：人

unit：person

40—44 岁 40 to 44	45—49 岁 45 to 49	50—54 岁 50 to 54	55—59 岁 55 to 59	60—64 岁 60 to 64	65 岁及以上 66 and Over
61854	**72618**	**46589**	**27825**	**7017**	**5456**
21472	21299	11548	5867	1142	670
21311	43516	33398	22100	6130	4931
38922	28468	12941	5625	852	499
1621	634	250	100	35	26
1960	3946	3171	2229	1081	1545
409	665	425	317	151	135
51637	53996	32396	18239	3573	1609
19325	17885	9389	4390	686	263
8257	14676	11022	7357	2363	2302
1738	2749	1734	1160	305	272

分学科专任教师数(总计)
Number of Full-time Teachers by Field of Study(Total)

单位：人
unit：person

	合计 Total	正高级 Senior	副高级 Sub-Senior	中级 Middle	初级 Junior	未定职级 No-ranking
总计 Total	**1530512**	**182982**	**442685**	**611226**	**209963**	**83656**
其中:女 of Which：Female	732219	53118	195330	320996	118270	44505
哲学 Philosophy	42514	5557	12767	16231	5653	2306
经济学 Economics	89649	10423	26548	35467	12048	5163
法学 Law	71293	7968	19966	29662	9792	3905
教育学 Education	129178	9836	36366	52361	22224	8391
其中:体育 of Which:Sport	62115	4389	19086	25506	10219	2915
文学 Literature	233489	18095	59459	105403	37232	13300
其中:外语 of Which:Foreign Language	131436	7296	30856	65416	21243	6625
历史学 History	18300	3214	5750	6697	1874	765
理学 Science	177933	28817	57890	65989	17744	7493
工学 Engineering	411187	52941	125670	163340	48797	20439
其中:计算机 of Which:Computer	96866	7488	25735	45222	14291	4130
农学 Agriculture	37474	6643	12084	13010	3858	1879
其中:林学 of Which:Forestry	6658	984	2079	2509	827	259
医学 Medicine	112337	19915	34592	37290	15022	5518
管理学 Administrators	121848	12785	33715	49169	18002	8177
艺术学 Art	85310	6788	17878	36607	17717	6320

分学科专任教师数(普通高校)

Number of Full-time Teachers by Field of Study (Regular HEIs)

单位：人

unit：person

	合计 Total	正高级 Senior	副高级 Sub-Senior	中 级 Middle	初 级 Junior	未定职级 No-ranking
总 计 Total	**1496865**	**181501**	**432356**	**596954**	**203713**	**82341**
其中:女 of Which: Female	714450	52494	190283	313104	114819	43750
哲学 Philosophy	41151	5455	12270	15694	5477	2255
经济学 Economics	86561	10180	25507	34191	11612	5071
法学 Law	69003	7818	19268	28691	9426	3800
教育学 Education	125714	9696	35325	50984	21488	8221
其中:体育 of Which:Sport	60997	4368	18794	25068	9917	2850
文学 Literature	227829	17882	57825	102906	36126	13090
其中:外语 of Which:Foreign Language	129078	7230	30212	64298	20789	6549
历史学 History	17702	3176	5497	6479	1800	750
理学 Science	174389	28692	56621	64513	17161	7402
工学 Engineering	402946	52749	123281	159724	47120	20072
其中:计算机 of Which:Computer	93870	7415	24967	43810	13639	4039
农学 Agriculture	36999	6635	11980	12810	3714	1860
其中:林学 of Which:Forestry	6607	982	2066	2487	813	259
医学 Medicine	111179	19830	34212	36820	14845	5472
管理学 Administrators	118874	12617	32822	47895	17481	8059
艺术学 Art	84518	6771	17748	36247	17463	6289

分学科专任教师数(成人高校)

Number of Full-time Teachers by Field of Study(Adult HEIs)

单位：人
unit: person

	合计 Total	正高级 Senior	副高级 Sub-Senior	中级 Middle	初级 Junior	未定职级 No-ranking
总计 Total	**33647**	**1481**	**10329**	**14272**	**6250**	**1315**
其中:女 of Which: Female	17769	624	5047	7892	3451	755
哲学 Philosophy	1363	102	497	537	176	51
经济学 Economics	3088	243	1041	1276	436	92
法学 Law	2290	150	698	971	366	105
教育学 Education	3464	140	1041	1377	736	170
其中:体育 of Which:Sport	1118	21	292	438	302	65
文学 Literature	5660	213	1634	2497	1106	210
其中:外语 of Which:Foreign Language	2358	66	644	1118	454	76
历史学 History	598	38	253	218	74	15
理学 Science	3544	125	1269	1476	583	91
工学 Engineering	8241	192	2389	3616	1677	367
其中:计算机 of Which:Computer	2996	73	768	1412	652	91
农学 Agriculture	475	8	104	200	144	19
其中:林学 of Which:Forestry	51	2	13	22	14	
医学 Medicine	1158	85	380	470	177	46
管理学 Administrators	2974	168	893	1274	521	118
艺术学 Art	792	17	130	360	254	31

分学科专任教师数(民办的其他高等教育机构)
Number of Full-time Teachers by Field of Study (Other Non-government HEIs)

单位：人
unit：person

	合计 Total	正高级 Senior	副高级 Sub-Senior	中级 Middle	初级 Junior	未定职级 No-ranking
总计 Total	**13350**	**1203**	**2524**	**4244**	**1961**	**3418**
其中:女 of Which: Female	6777	396	1133	2107	1139	2002
哲学 Philosophy	536	92	149	185	75	35
经济学 Economics	1106	142	327	368	140	129
法学 Law	486	51	147	160	81	47
教育学 Education	1022	71	201	347	207	196
其中:体育 of Which:Sport	344	10	34	106	88	106
文学 Literature	3882	208	515	1204	515	1440
其中:外语 of Which:Foreign Language	1820	71	214	659	273	603
历史学 History	194	17	61	58	36	22
理学 Science	876	111	197	285	144	139
工学 Engineering	2876	208	431	1013	416	808
其中:计算机 of Which:Computer	1694	84	209	572	208	621
农学 Agriculture	71	7	26	19	12	7
其中:林学 of Which:Forestry	23	1	5	7	5	5
医学 Medicine	556	104	127	152	64	109
管理学 Administrators	1163	118	256	360	211	218
艺术学 Art	582	74	87	93	60	268

专任教师、聘请校外教师学历情况(总计)

Number of Academic Qualifications of Full-time and Part-time Teachers in HEIs (Total)

单位：人

unit: person

	合计 Total	博　士 Doctor's Degrees	硕　士 Master's Degrees	本　科 Normal Courses	专科及以下 Short-cycle Courses and Under
1. 专任教师 Full-time Teachers	1530512	286148	542792	678793	22779
其中:女 of Which: Female	732219	96773	296439	330925	8082
正高级 Senior	182982	85298	35096	61017	1571
副高级 Sub-senior	442685	108988	107193	221028	5476
中　级 Middle	611226	81587	269027	252289	8323
初　级 Junior	209963	1772	91864	112219	4108
未定职级 No-ranking	83656	8503	39612	32240	3301
2. 聘请校外教师 Part-time Teachers	442176	62778	143739	212387	23272
其中:女 of Which: Female	170703	16123	60605	86454	7521
外籍教师 Foreign Teachers	14945	5812	4296	4745	92
其他高校教师 Other HEI Teachers	123654	25164	50908	45737	1845
正高级 Senior	78108	31324	23169	22542	1073
副高级 Sub-senior	135871	17881	43530	69789	4671
中　级 Middle	144400	10271	49926	75790	8413
初　级 Junior	39411	817	13955	21786	2853
未定职级 No-ranking	44386	2485	13159	22480	6262

注:不包含民办的其他高等教育机构数据。

Note: Data of Non-government HEIs are not included.

专任教师、聘请校外教师学历情况(普通高校)

Number of Academic Qualifications of Full-time and Part-time Teachers in HEIs (Regular HEIs)

单位：人

unit: person

	合计 Total	博　士 Doctor's Degrees	硕　士 Master's Degrees	本　科 Normal Courses	专科及以下 Short-cycle Courses and Under
1. 专任教师 Full-time Teachers	1496865	285353	535784	654660	21068
其中:女 of Which: Female	714450	96432	292464	318083	7471
正高级 Senior	181501	85098	34696	60144	1563
副高级 Sub-senior	432356	108636	105290	213169	5261
中　级 Middle	596954	81371	265857	242243	7483
初　级 Junior	203713	1765	90690	107658	3600
未定职级 No-ranking	82341	8483	39251	31446	3161
2. 聘请校外教师 Part-time Teachers	403330	62086	136231	183065	21948
其中:女 of Which: Female	153137	15908	57143	73074	7012
外籍教师 Foreign Teachers	14802	5812	4281	4617	92
其他高校教师 Other HEI Teachers	116892	24924	49020	41286	1662
正高级 Senior	76595	31145	22616	21775	1059
副高级 Sub-senior	123936	17572	40946	60915	4503
中　级 Middle	126304	10106	46823	61565	7810
初　级 Junior	33715	798	13063	17339	2515
未定职级 No-ranking	42780	2465	12783	21471	6061

专任教师、聘请校外教师学历情况(成人高校)

Number of Academic Qualifications of Full-time and Part-time Teachers in HEIs (Adult HEIs)

单位：人
unit：person

	合计 Total	博　士 Doctor's Degrees	硕　士 Master's Degrees	本　科 Normal Courses	专科及以下 Short-cycle Courses and Under
1. 专任教师 Full-time Teachers	33647	795	7008	24133	1711
其中:女 of Which: Female	17769	341	3975	12842	611
正高级 Senior	1481	200	400	873	8
副高级 Sub-senior	10329	352	1903	7859	215
中　级 Middle	14272	216	3170	10046	840
初　级 Junior	6250	7	1174	4561	508
未定职级 No-ranking	1315	20	361	794	140
2. 聘请校外教师 Part-time Teachers	38846	692	7508	29322	1324
其中:女 of Which: Female	17566	215	3462	13380	509
外籍教师 Foreign Teachers	143		15	128	
其他高校教师 Other HEI Teachers	6762	240	1888	4451	183
正高级 Senior	1513	179	553	767	14
副高级 Sub-senior	11935	309	2584	8874	168
中　级 Middle	18096	165	3103	14225	603
初　级 Junior	5696	19	892	4447	338
未定职级 No-ranking	1606	20	376	1009	201

专任教师、聘请校外教师学历情况(民办的其他高等教育机构)

Number of Academic Qualifications of Full-time and Part-time Teachers in HEIs (Other Non-government HEIs)

单位：人
unit：person

	合计 Total	博　士 Doctor's Degrees	硕　士 Master's Degrees	本　科 Normal Courses	专科及以下 Short-cycle Courses and Under
1. 专任教师 Full-time Teachers	13350	427	2606	9341	976
其中:女 of Which: Female	6777	128	1309	4881	459
正高级 Senior	1203	167	327	680	29
副高级 Sub-senior	2524	120	582	1704	118
中　级 Middle	4244	79	915	2983	267
初　级 Junior	1961	8	303	1467	183
未定职级 No-ranking	3418	53	479	2507	379
2. 聘请校外教师 Part-time Teachers	13327	1360	4114	7231	622
其中:女 of Which: Female	5689	407	1849	3172	261
外籍教师 Foreign Teachers	42	2	19	18	3
其他高校教师 Other HEI Teachers	2906	402	1218	1263	23
正高级 Senior	1958	506	679	721	52
副高级 Sub-senior	3946	563	1347	1971	65
中　级 Middle	4786	240	1455	2870	221
初　级 Junior	1466	22	331	936	177
未定职级 No-ranking	1171	29	302	733	107

专任教师年龄情况(总计)
Number of Full-time Teachers by Age (Total)

单位：人
unit：person

	合计 Total	29岁及以下 29 and Under	30—34岁 30 to 34	35—39岁 35 to 39	40—44岁 40 to 44	45—49岁 45 to 49	50—54岁 50 to 54	55—59岁 55 to 59	60—64岁 60 to 64	65岁及以上 65 and Over
总　计 Total	**1530512**	**241669**	**371099**	**272111**	**223718**	**200389**	**123541**	**70470**	**16983**	**10532**
其中:女 of Which：Female	732219	144204	204341	134114	100939	82214	44100	16768	3979	1560
正高级 Senior	182982	47	1307	8274	27332	55502	44064	31459	9061	5936
副高级 Sub-senior	442685	1258	31387	91584	114678	103778	59366	29962	6476	4196
中　级 Middle	611226	64401	255778	152945	73925	37121	17844	7600	1257	355
初　级 Junior	209963	117593	65929	15304	5873	2864	1538	807	46	9
未定职级 No-ranking	83656	58370	16698	4004	1910	1124	729	642	143	36

注:不含民办的其他高等教育机构数据。

Note：Data of Non-government HEIs are not included.

专任教师年龄情况(普通高校)
Number of Full-time Teachers by Age (Regular HEIs)

单位：人
unit：person

	合计 Total	29岁及以下 29 and Under	30—34岁 30 to 34	35—39岁 35 to 39	40—44岁 40 to 44	45—49岁 45 to 49	50—54岁 50 to 54	55—59岁 55 to 59	60—64岁 60 to 64	65岁及以上 65 and Over
总　计 Total	**1496865**	**236347**	**364180**	**266353**	**218156**	**195191**	**120305**	**68890**	**16920**	**10523**
其中:女 of Which：Female	714450	140835	200291	131045	97934	79609	42697	16507	3972	1560
正高级 Senior	181501	47	1307	8243	27071	55041	43651	31169	9039	5933
副高级 Sub-senior	432356	1247	31000	89978	112025	100787	57556	29129	6444	4190
中　级 Middle	596954	63090	251292	149587	71608	35594	16951	7229	1248	355
初　级 Junior	203713	114537	64064	14611	5591	2681	1441	733	46	9
未定职级 No-ranking	82341	57426	16517	3934	1861	1088	706	630	143	36

专任教师年龄情况（成人高校）
Number of Full-time Teachers by Age（Adult HEIs）

单位：人
unit：person

	合计 Total	29岁及以下 29 and Under	30—34岁 30 to 34	35—39岁 35 to 39	40—44岁 40 to 44	45—49岁 45 to 49	50—54岁 50 to 54	55—59岁 55 to 59	60—64岁 60 to 64	65岁及以上 65 and Over
总　计 Total	**33647**	**5322**	**6919**	**5758**	**5562**	**5198**	**3236**	**1580**	**63**	**9**
其中：女 of Which：Female	17769	3369	4050	3069	3005	2605	1403	261	7	
正高级 Senior	1481			31	261	461	413	290	22	3
副高级 Sub-senior	10329	11	387	1606	2653	2991	1810	833	32	6
中　级 Middle	14272	1311	4486	3358	2317	1527	893	371	9	
初　级 Junior	6250	3056	1865	693	282	183	97	74		
未定职级 No-ranking	1315	944	181	70	49	36	23	12		

专任教师年龄情况（民办的其他高等教育机构）
Number of Full-time Teachers by Age（Other Non-government HEIs）

单位：人
unit：person

	合计 Total	29岁及以下 29 and Under	30—34岁 30 to 34	35—39岁 35 to 39	40—44岁 40 to 44	45—49岁 45 to 49	50—54岁 50 to 54	55—59岁 55 to 59	60—64岁 60 to 64	65岁及以上 65 and Over
总　计 Total	**13350**	**3341**	**2933**	**1978**	**1785**	**1007**	**827**	**649**	**480**	**350**
其中：女 of Which：Female	6777	2127	1558	1019	812	460	355	248	135	63
正高级 Senior	1203	1	24	52	134	189	209	211	198	185
副高级 Sub-senior	2524	8	153	393	491	448	399	305	199	128
中　级 Middle	4244	657	1175	947	839	267	171	94	67	27
初　级 Junior	1961	968	571	231	111	38	23	16	3	
未定职级 No-ranking	3418	1707	1010	355	210	65	25	23	13	10

专任教师、聘请校外教

Number of Full-time and Part-time Teachers

	专任教师中按授课内容分 Full-time Teachers Classified by Teaching Content			
	合计 Total	公共课基础课 Common Required Course	专业课 Special Subjects	
			小计 Subtotal	其中:双师型 of Which: Double-teacher Type
总　计 Total	**1479071**	**398434**	**1080637**	**217994**
其中:女 of Which: Female	709345	209430	499915	106168
正高级 Senior	177313	33194	144119	18806
副高级 Sub-senior	428980	109608	319372	83124
中级 Middle	590317	167690	422627	116064
初级 Junior	202992	64042	138950	
未定职级 No-ranking	79469	23900	55569	
普通高校 Regular HEIs	**1446373**	**389051**	**1057322**	**211891**
其中:女 of Which: Female	692061	204209	487852	103005
正高级 Senior	175889	32880	143009	18368
副高级 Sub-senior	418943	106781	312162	80593
中级 Middle	576450	163716	412734	112930
初级 Junior	196912	62127	134785	
未定职级 No-ranking	78179	23547	54632	
成人高校 Adult HEIs	**32698**	**9383**	**23315**	**6103**
其中:女 of Which: Female	17284	5221	12063	3163
正高级 Senior	1424	314	1110	438
副高级 Sub-senior	10037	2827	7210	2531
中级 Middle	13867	3974	9893	3134
初级 Junior	6080	1915	4165	
未定职级 No-ranking	1290	353	937	

注:不含民办的其他高等教育机构数据。

Note: Data of Non-government HEIs are not included.

专任教师、聘请校外教

Number of Full-time and Part-time Teachers

	专任教师中按授课内容分 Full-time Teachers Classified by Teaching Content			
	合计 Total	公共课基础课 Common Required Course	专业课 Special Subjects	
			小计 Subtotal	其中:双师型 of Which: Double-teacher Type
总　　计 Total	**12940**	**4353**	**8587**	**1228**
其中:女 of Which: Female	6603	2175	4428	580
正高级 Senior	1169	378	791	174
副高级 Sub-senior	2448	871	1577	410
中级 Middle	4154	1607	2547	644
初级 Junior	1879	715	1164	
未定职级 No-ranking	3290	782	2508	

师岗位分类情况(总计)

Classified by Teaching Content in HEIs (Total)

单位：人
unit: person

聘请校外教师按授课内容分 Part-time Teachers Classfied by Teaching Content				专任教师中不任课人数 Full-time Teachers by Non-teaching				
合计 Total	公共课基础课 Common Required Course	专业课 Special Subjects		合计 Total	进修 In-service	科研 Research	病休 Sick Leave	其他 Others
		小计 Subtotal	其中：双师型 of Which: Double-teacher Type					
442176	**90389**	**351787**	**69795**	**51441**	**23760**	**8418**	**1952**	**17311**
170703	39303	131400	25588	22874	10706	2945	1157	8066
78108	11958	66150	9724	5669	1797	1929	98	1845
135871	26214	109657	28181	13705	6809	2821	402	3673
144400	31393	113007	31890	20909	11229	2781	946	5953
39411	10727	28684		6971	3080	547	434	2910
44386	10097	34289		4187	845	340	72	2930
403330	**78017**	**325313**	**65645**	**50492**	**23706**	**8083**	**1914**	**16789**
153137	34310	118827	24016	22389	10673	2757	1137	7822
76595	11584	65011	9410	5612	1797	1890	97	1828
123936	23107	100829	26377	13413	6794	2700	397	3522
126304	25488	100816	29858	20504	11204	2634	931	5735
33715	8299	25416		6801	3067	520	417	2797
42780	9539	33241		4162	844	339	72	2907
38846	**12372**	**26474**	**4150**	**949**	**54**	**335**	**38**	**522**
17566	4993	12573	1572	485	33	188	20	244
1513	374	1139	314	57		39	1	17
11935	3107	8828	1804	292	15	121	5	151
18096	5905	12191	2032	405	25	147	15	218
5696	2428	3268		170	13	27	17	113
1606	558	1048		25	1	1		23

师岗位分类情况(民办的其他高等教育机构)

Classified by Teaching Content in HEIs (Other Non-government HEIs)

单位：人
unit: person

聘请校外教师按授课内容分 Part-time Teachers Classfied by Teaching Content				专任教师中不任课人数 Full-time Teachers by Non-teaching				
合计 Total	公共课基础课 Common Required Course	专业课 Special Subjects		合计 Total	进修 In-service	科研 Research	病休 Sick Leave	其他 Others
		小计 Subtotal	其中：双师型 of Which: Double-teacher Type					
13327	**4010**	**9317**	**1185**	**410**	**69**	**41**	**12**	**288**
5689	1934	3755	437	174	37	8	8	121
1958	653	1305	210	34	4	2		28
3946	1251	2695	464	76	13	5	1	57
4786	1390	3396	511	90	11	10	6	63
1466	444	1022		82	7	18	2	55
1171	272	899		128	34	6	3	85

专任教师

Changes of Full-time

	上学年初报表专任教师数 Number of Full-time Teachers at Beginning of Previous Academic Year	增加专任 Factors of			
		合计 Total	录用毕业生 New Recruits from Current Year Graduates		
			小计 Subtotal	其中 of Which:	
				研究生 Completing Doc. & Mas. Deg.	本科 Completing Normal Courses
总　计 Total	**1479685**	**117133**	**55189**	**45478**	**4363**
其中:女 of Which: Female	701609	58595	30327	25093	2015
普通高校 Regular HEIs	**1440734**	**115851**	**54653**	**45205**	**4363**
其中:女 of Which: Female	681247	57841	29949	24899	2015
成人高校 Adult HEIs	**38951**	**1282**	**536**	**273**	
其中:女 of Which: Female	20362	754	378	194	

注:不含民办的其他高等教育机构数据。

Note: Data of Non-government HEIs are not included.

专任教师

Changes of Full-time Teachers in HEIs

	上学年初报表专任教师数 Number of Full-time Teachers at Beginning of Previous Academic Year	增加专任 Factors of			
		合计 Total	录用毕业生 New Recruits from Current Year Graduates		
			小计 Subtotal	其中 of Which:	
				研究生 Completing Doc. & Mas. Deg.	本科 Completing Normal Courses
总　计 Total	**14512**	**1976**	**535**	**254**	**5**
其中:女 of Which: Female	7266	1122	361	180	3

变动情况（总计）
Teachers in HEIs (Total)

单位：人
unit: person

教师数 Increase				减少专任教师数 Factors of Decrease				本学年初报表专任教师数 Number of Full-time Teachers at Beginning of Current Academic Year
外单位教师调入 Teachers Recruited from Other Units		校内、外非教师调入 Non-teaching Personnel Changed into Teachers						
小计 Subtotal	其中：高校调入 of Which: from Reg. HEIs	小计 Subtotal	其中：本校调整 of Which: with Change of Status in Their Own Institutions	合计 Total	自然减员 Retired from their Posts during Previous Academic Year	调离教师岗位 Transferred from Teaching to Non-teaching Posts	其他 Others	
32200	**16823**	**29744**	**17196**	**66306**	**22270**	**13252**	**30784**	**1530512**
15453	7897	12815	6819	27985	9496	5200	13289	732219
31786	**16689**	**29412**	**16967**	**59720**	**21569**	**12873**	**25278**	**1496865**
15240	7825	12652	6692	24638	9156	5031	10451	714450
414	**134**	**332**	**229**	**6586**	**701**	**379**	**5506**	**33647**
213	72	163	127	3347	340	169	2838	17769

变动情况（民办的其他高等教育机构）
(Other Non-government HEIs)

单位：人
unit: person

教师数 Increase				减少专任教师数 Factors of Decrease				本学年初报表专任教师数 Number of Full-time Teachers at Beginning of Current Academic Year
外单位教师调入 Teachers Recruited from Other Units		校内、外非教师调入 Non-teaching Personnel Changed into Teachers						
小计 Subtotal	其中：高校调入 of Which: from Reg. HEIs	小计 Subtotal	其中：本校调整 of Which: with Change of Status in Their Own Institutions	合计 Total	自然减员 Retired from their Posts during Previous Academic Year	调离教师岗位 Transferred from Teaching to Non-teaching Posts	其他 Others	
1156	**511**	**285**	**54**	**3138**	**707**	**248**	**2183**	**13350**
632	352	129	33	1611	373	112	1126	6777

资产
Condition of Fixed Assets

	占地面积(平方米) Area of School sites (m^2)			图书音像资料情况 Audio-visual ed. Resources	
				图书(万册) Books & Magazines in Libraries (10,000 volume)	
	合计 Total	其中:绿化用地面积 of Which: Green Areas	其中:运动场地面积 of Which: Sports Areas	合计 Total	当年新增 New Added in Current Year
学校产权 Owned by HEIs	**1699129270**	**521398682**	**127870363**	**225394.17**	**12100.87**
非学校产权中独立使用 Not Owned by HEIs	214403118	47280419	14578461	5660.61	165.21
普通高校 Regular HEIs					
学校产权 Owned by HEIs	**1670982872**	**514972205**	**124993256**	**221300.86**	**12000.96**
非学校产权中独立使用 Not Owned by HEIs	188357322	41031564	11210157	2291.65	94.31
成人高校 Adult HEIs					
学校产权 Owned by HEIs	**28146398**	**6426477**	**2877107**	**4093.31**	**99.91**
非学校产权中独立使用 Not Owned by HEIs	26045796	6248855	3368304	3368.96	70.90

注:不含民办的其他高等教育机构数据。

Note: Data of Non-government HEIs are not included.

资产情况
Condition of Fixed Assets

	占地面积(平方米) Area of School sites (m^2)			图书音像资料情况 Audio-visual ed. Resources	
				图书(万册) Books & Magazines in Libraries (10,000 volume)	
	合计 Total	其中:绿化用地面积 of Which: Green Areas	其中:运动场地面积 of Which: Sports Areas	合计 Total	当年新增 New Added in Current Year
学校产权 Owned by HEIs	**6288591**	**1386442**	**616512**	**1269.56**	**70.46**
非学校产权中独立使用 Not Owned by HEIs	7540177	1794857	1034781	62237.64	507.69

情况(总计)
and Teaching Resources (Total)

计算机数(台) No. of Computers			教室(间) Classroom(room)		固定资产值(万元) Fixed Assets (10,000 yuan)				
合计 Total	其中:教学用计算机 No. of Computers Used for Instruction		合计 Total	其中:网络多媒体教室 of Which: Network Multimedia Classroom	合计 Total	其中:信息化设备资产值 of Which: Assets of Information Facilities		其中:教学、科研仪器设备资产 of Which: Teaching Equipment & Instruments	
	小计 Subtotal	其中:平板电脑 of Which: Tablet PC				小计 Subtotal	当年新增 New Added in Current Year	小计 Subtotal	其中:软件 of Which: Software
9720437	**7400120**	**45816**	**592115**	**268851**	**151608742.67**	**32830625.18**	**3935309.70**	**9196778.12**	**1305119.28**
351634	234498	4394	51272	24489	8679861.83	1035565.76	73235.13		
9515032	**7247088**	**44777**	**561191**	**256364**	**149637264.76**	**32411012.86**	**3904708.65**	**9029793.45**	**1290660.78**
79693	62536	143	31829	14615	7257796.21	684801.25	53851.30		
205405	**153032**	**1039**	**30924**	**12487**	**1971477.91**	**419612.32**	**30601.05**	**166984.67**	**14458.50**
271941	171962	4251	19443	9874	1422065.62	350764.51	19383.83		

(民办的其他高等教育机构)
and Teaching Resources (Other Non-government HEIs)

计算机数(台) No. of Computers			教室(间) Classroom(room)		固定资产值(万元) Fixed Assets (10,000 yuan)				
合计 Total	其中:教学用计算机 No. of Computers Used for Instruction		合计 Total	其中:网络多媒体教室 of Which: Network Multimedia Classroom	合计 Total	其中:教学、科研仪器设备资产 of Which: Teaching Equipment & Instruments		其中:信息化设备资产值 of Which: Assets of Information Facilities	
	小计 Subtotal	其中:平板电脑 of Which: Tablet PC				小计 Subtotal	当年新增 New Added in Current Year	小计 Subtotal	其中:软件 of Which: Software
79993	**65957**	**971**	**6910**	**1582**	**478510.78**	**93881.92**	**7481.76**	**29814.87**	**4901.01**
16985	12404	97	5391	1101	205045.16	28802.12	5435.63		

校舍情况(总计)

Condition of School Buildings (Total)

单位：平方米
unit：m^2

	学校产权建筑面积 Floor Area of School Building Owned by HEIs				正在施工面积 Floor Area Under Construction	独立使用非学校产权建筑面积 Floor Area of School Building Not Owned by HEIs
	合计 Total	其中:危房 of Which: Dilapidated Buildings	其中:当年新增校舍 of Which: New Added in Current Year	其中:被外单位借用 of Which: Floor Space Hired by Other Schools or Units		
总　计 Total	**768812285**	**1242170**	**29077842**	**527849**	**55544866**	**100332587**
一、教学及辅助用房 Buildings for Instraction and Ancillary Uses	**343452463**	**433443**	**14714427**	**154350**	**27254604**	**43699568**
教室 Classroom	133855768	192574	5067082	68411	7405457	20826470
图书馆 Library	41517302	35257	1747606	8371	4966991	4513488
实验室、实习场所 Lab. And Practice Facilities	124926632	163319	5634647	65476	9675182	13970742
专用科研用房 Office Special for Research	14123825	16657	759934	7248	2358007	477147
体育馆 Gymnasium	21844304	3387	1185198	4044	2033521	2806064
会堂 Hall	7184632	22249	319960	800	815446	1105657
二、行政办公用房 Administrative	**45609027**	**99978**	**1504826**	**29557**	**3179433**	**5580063**
三、生活用房 Residential Buildings	**279386947**	**416981**	**10755492**	**250828**	**16677347**	**49492279**
学生宿舍(公寓)Students Dormitories	209761381	219456	8143463	150827	10446677	39535264
学生食堂 Students Dining Halls	30548209	23674	1186424	15004	1620864	4833513
教工宿舍(公寓) Apartments for Single	11833261	82794	663729	11389	2978878	2360274
教工食堂 Dining Halls for Teachers, Staff and Workers	1722786	896	66577	300	142549	294318
生活福利及附属用房 Residential, Welfare and Anxiliary Buildings	25521310	90161	695299	73308	1488379	2468910
四、教工住宅 Residential Quarters for Teachers &Workers	**88589493**	**263652**	**1446376**	**25256**	**6709497**	
五、其他用房 Other	**11774355**	**28116**	**656721**	**67858**	**1723985**	**1560677**

注:不包含民办的其他高等教育机构数据。

Note: Data of Non-government HEIs are not included.

校舍情况(普通高校)

Condition of School Buildings (Regular HEIs)

单位：平方米

unit：m²

	学校产权建筑面积 Floor Area of School Building Owned by HEIs				正在施工面积 Floor Area Under Construction	独立使用非学校产权建筑面积 Floor Area of School Building Not Owned by HEIs
	合计 Total	其中:危房 of Which: Dilapidated Buildings	其中:当年新增校舍 of Which: New Added in Current Year	其中:被外单位借用 of Which: Floor Space Hired by Other Schools or Units		
总　计 Total	**753806412**	**1184374**	**28819559**	**498713**	**54600804**	**87743134**
一、教学及辅助用房 Buildings for Instraction and Ancillary Uses	**336670661**	**422753**	**14564879**	**141385**	**26923139**	**36855965**
教室 Classroom	130201888	186438	5023520	60806	7200163	16854730
图书馆 Library	40857303	33530	1730575	7951	4946287	3986287
实验室、实习场所 Lab. And Practice Facilities	123253692	161859	5552113	64836	9606305	12206765
专用科研用房 Office Special for Research	14096904	16657	756934	7248	2343118	464281
体育馆 Gymnasium	21326722	3387	1181777	544	2018983	2476387
会堂 Hall	6934152	20882	319960		808283	867515
二、行政办公用房 Administrative	**44017278**	**96380**	**1499283**	**29407**	**2812781**	**4344494**
三、生活用房 Residential Buildings	**274534013**	**382964**	**10652613**	**236024**	**16459457**	**45036762**
学生宿舍(公寓) Students Dormitories	206453330	190720	8050624	143387	10325707	36429286
学生食堂 Students Dining Halls	29889876	23674	1177866	13504	1595190	4214798
教工宿舍(公寓) Apartments for Single	11720796	82609	662422	11389	2914032	2154634
教工食堂 Dining Halls for Teachers, Staff and Workers	1628515	896	66577		136649	214173
生活福利及附属用房 Residential, Welfare and Anxiliary Buildings	24841496	85065	695124	67744	1487879	2023871
四、教工住宅 Residential Quarters for Teachers &Workers	**86956982**	**254161**	**1446376**	**25256**	**6709497**	
五、其他用房 Other	**11627478**	**28116**	**656408**	**66641**	**1695930**	**1505913**

校舍情况(成人高校)
Condition of School Buildings (Adult HEIs)

单位：平方米
unit：m^2

	学校产权建筑面积 Floor Area of School Building Owned by HEIs				正在施工面积 Floor Area Under Construction	独立使用非学校产权建筑面积 Floor Area of School Building Not Owned by HEIs
	合计 Total	其中：危房 of Which：Dilapidated Buildings	其中：当年新增校舍 of Which：New Added in Current Year	其中：被外单位借用 of Which：Floor Space Hired by Other Schools or Units		
总　计 Total	**15005873**	**57796**	**258283**	**29136**	**944062**	**12589453**
一、教学及辅助用房 Buildings for Instraction and Ancillary Uses	**6781802**	**10690**	**149548**	**12965**	**331465**	**6843603**
教室 Classroom	3653880	6136	43562	7605	205294	3971740
图书馆 Library	659999	1727	17031	420	20704	527201
实验室、实习场所 Lab. And Practice Facilities	1672940	1460	82534	640	68877	1763977
专用科研用房 Office Special for Research	26921		3000		14889	12866
体育馆 Gymnasium	517582		3421	3500	14538	329677
会堂 Hall	250480	1367		800	7163	238142
二、行政办公用房 Administrative	**1591749**	**3598**	**5543**	**150**	**366652**	**1235569**
三、生活用房 Residential Buildings	**4852934**	**34017**	**102879**	**14804**	**217890**	**4455517**
学生宿舍(公寓) Students Dormitories	3308051	28736	92839	7440	120970	3105978
学生食堂 Students Dining Halls	658333		8558	1500	25674	618715
教工宿舍(公寓) Apartments for Single	112465	185	1307		64846	205640
教工食堂 Dining Halls for Teachers, Staff and Workers	94271			300	5900	80145
生活福利及附属用房 Residential, Welfare and Anxiliary Buildings	679814	5096	175	5564	500	445039
四、教工住宅 Residential Quarters for Teachers &Workers	**1632511**	**9491**				
五、其他用房 Other	**146877**		**313**	**1217**	**28055**	**54764**

校舍情况(民办的其他高等教育机构)
Condition of School Buildings (Other Non-government HEIs)

单位：平方米
unit：m^2

	学校产权建筑面积 Floor Area of School Building Owned by HEIs				正在施工面积 Floor Area Under Construction	独立使用非学校产权建筑面积 Floor Area of School Building Not Owned by HEIs
	合计 Total	其中：危房 of Which：Dilapidated Buildings	其中：当年新增校舍 of Which：New Added in Current Year	其中：被外单位借用 of Which：Floor Space Hired by Other Schools or Units		
总　计 Total	**2940264**		**173729**	**1000**	**263097**	**4509597**
一、教学及辅助用房 Buildings for Instraction and Ancillary Uses	**1400887**		**70096**	**1000**	**127432**	**2140482**
教室 Classroom	954385		46208	1000	88932	1279866
图书馆 Library	92949		1868		18804	234544
实验室、实习场所 Lab. And Practice Facilities	216363		19036		5654	349385
专用科研用房 Office Special for Research	4350		2000		54	15741
体育馆 Gymnasium	79519				10800	194480
会堂 Hall	53321		984		3188	66466
二、行政办公用房 Administrative	**211280**		**7410**		**23560**	**305567**
三、生活用房 Residential Buildings	**1210368**		**96223**		**103789**	**2013699**
学生宿舍(公寓)Students'Dormitories	861482		75659		74892	1547115
学生食堂 Students Dining Halls	169180		12604		16303	245889
教工宿舍(公寓) Apartments for Single	95572		6720		9516	96136
教工食堂 Dining Halls for Teachers, Staff and Workers	16505		1240		450	16404
生活福利及附属用房 Residential, Welfare and Anxiliary Buildings	67629				2628	108155
四、教工住宅 Residential Quarters for Teachers &Workers	**91473**				**8316**	
五、其他用房 Other	**26256**					**49849**

三、中等教育
Secondary Education

(一)高中阶段教育
Senior Secondary Education

普通高中校数、班数
Number of Regular Senior Secondary Schools and Classes

	学校数(所) Schools				班数(个) Classes
	合计 Total	完全中学 Combined Secondary Schools	高级中学 Regular High Schools	十二年一贯制学校 12 - year Schools	
总　计 Total	**13352**	**5861**	**6591**	**900**	**443170**
教育部门办 Run by Ed. Dept.	10788	4834	5736	218	395096
其他部门办 Run by Non-ed. Dept.	176	65	70	41	3415
地方企业办 Run by Local Enterprises	13	6	3	4	201
民办 Non-government	2375	956	782	637	44458
城区 Urban Area	6348	2774	3026	548	211249
教育部门办 Run by Ed. Dept.	4851	2178	2526	147	185399
其他部门办 Run by Non-ed. Dept.	85	32	32	21	1615
地方企业办 Run by Local Enterprises	7	4	3		96
民办 Non-government	1405	560	465	380	24139
其中:城乡结合区 of Which: Urban-rural Transitional Area	917	333	457	127	32056
教育部门办 Run by Ed. Dept.	617	235	370	12	26713
其他部门办 Run by Non-ed. Dept.	8	1	4	3	96
地方企业办 Run by Local Enterprises	2	1	1		24
民办 Non-government	290	96	82	112	5223
镇区 Counties & Towns Area	6296	2722	3294	280	216618
教育部门办 Run by Ed. Dept.	5404	2369	2982	53	197469
其他部门办 Run by Non-ed. Dept.	85	30	38	17	1710
地方企业办 Run by Local Enterprises	6	2		4	105
民办 Non-government	801	321	274	206	17334
其中:镇乡结合区 of Which: County-town Transitional Area	1592	592	903	97	55663
教育部门办 Run by Ed. Dept.	1301	484	806	11	49351
其他部门办 Run by Non-ed. Dept.	2		1	1	47
地方企业办 Run by Local Enterprises	1			1	9
民办 Non-government	288	108	96	84	6256
乡村 Rural Area	708	365	271	72	15303
教育部门办 Run by Ed. Dept.	533	287	228	18	12228
其他部门办 Run by Non-ed. Dept.	6	3		3	90
地方企业办 Run by Local Enterprises					
民办 Non-government	169	75	43	51	2985
总计中:其他学校附设班 of the Total: Classes Attached to Other Schools					2015
独立设置少数民族学校 Inde. Sec. Schools for Minorities	474	284	158	32	10921

普通高中班额情况
Size of Class in Regular Senior Secondary Schools

单位：个
unit：class

	合计 Total	一年级 Grade 1	二年级 Grade 2	三年级 Grade 3
总　计 Total	**443170**	**148513**	**146820**	**147837**
城区 Urban Area				
25 人及以下 Under 25 Persons	4487	1269	1470	1748
26－35 人 Between 26－35	12613	3750	4324	4539
36－45 人 Between 36－45	32217	10973	10699	10545
46－55 人 Between 46－55	80682	27588	26692	26402
56－65 人 Between 56－65	55995	18250	18721	19024
66 人及以上 Over 66 Persons	25255	8919	8270	8066
其中：城乡结合区 of Which：Urban-rural Transitional Area				
25 人及以下 Under 25 Persons	560	161	182	217
26－35 人 Between 26－35	1153	322	428	403
36－45 人 Between 36－45	4227	1442	1345	1440
46－55 人 Between 46－55	13769	4688	4607	4474
56－65 人 Between 56－65	7883	2620	2610	2653
66 人及以上 Over 66 Persons	4464	1691	1412	1361
镇区 Counties & Towns Area				
25 人及以下 Under 25 Persons	2073	565	593	915
26－35 人 Between 26－35	5315	1461	1713	2141
36－45 人 Between 36－45	22262	6933	7173	8156
46－55 人 Between 46－55	74361	24189	24670	25502
56－65 人 Between 56－65	68518	22606	23220	22692
66 人及以上 Over 66 Persons	44089	16813	14173	13103
其中：镇乡结合区 of Which：County-town Transitional Area				
25 人及以下 Under 25 Persons	510	130	159	221
26－35 人 Between 26－35	1203	378	364	461
36－45 人 Between 36－45	5144	1615	1647	1882
46－55 人 Between 46－55	21141	6852	7069	7220
56－65 人 Between 56－65	17669	5942	5975	5752
66 人及以上 Over 66 Persons	9996	3874	3162	2960
乡村 Rural Area				
25 人及以下 Under 25 Persons	314	66	119	129
26－35 人 Between 26－35	698	218	225	255
36－45 人 Between 36－45	2298	756	778	764
46－55 人 Between 46－55	5797	1908	1926	1963
56－65 人 Between 56－65	4310	1467	1453	1390
66 人及以上 Over 66 Persons	1886	782	601	503

普通高中学生数
Number of Students in Regular Senior Secondary Schools

单位：人
unit：person

	毕业生数 Graduates	招生数 Entrants	在校生数 Enrolment 合计 Total	其中:女 of Which: Female	一年级 Grade 1	二年级 Grade 2	三年级 Grade 3	预计毕业生数 Estimated Graduates for Next Year
总　计 Total	**7989789**	**8226961**	**24358817**	**12118900**	**8233790**	**8084933**	**8040094**	**8040094**
其中:女 of Which: Female	3946201	4086357	12118900		4089303	4028315	4001282	4001282
少数民族学生 Minority Students	611849	767125	2109133	1082289	768895	689903	650335	650335
十二年一贯制学校 12-year Schools	195445	228720	630209	281276	228952	208254	193003	193003
完全中学 Complete Schools	2551466	2689932	7914286	3917283	2691231	2630460	2592595	2592595
附设普通高中班 Regular Senior School Classes Attached	34864	30104	94950	46424	30152	31580	33218	33218
独立设置少数民族学校 Independent Schools for Minority	167668	218688	576045	301806	219551	183972	172522	172522
残疾人 Schools for Handicapped	3786	4364	14783	5751	4613	4962	5208	5208
随迁子女 Migrant Children	116231	255498	684722	310774	258692	223630	202400	195105
其中:外省迁入 of Which: from Other Province	26624	69331	159771	73203	70581	50417	38773	37970
本省外县迁入 From Other County	89607	186167	524951	237571	188111	173213	163627	157135
教育部门 Run by Ed. Dept.	7179766	7367953	21860183	10985456	7372878	7258507	7228798	7228798
其他部门 Run by Non – ed. Dept.	59269	57748	172592	88599	57775	56739	58078	58078
地方企业办 Run by Local Enterprises	3165	3068	9597	4838	3072	3382	3143	3143
民办 Non – government	747589	798192	2316445	1040007	800065	766305	750075	750075
城区 Urban Area	3661366	3735274	11144953	5599740	3739333	3707881	3697739	3697739
教育部门办 Run by Ed. Dept.	3246042	3294548	9865215	5016512	3297815	3283151	3284249	3284249
其他部门办 Run by Non-ed. Dept.	27954	27806	83390	41764	27833	27735	27822	27822
地方企业办 Run by Local Enterprises	1650	1465	4695	2371	1468	1671	1556	1556
民办 Non-government	385720	411455	1191653	539093	412217	395324	384112	384112
其中:城乡结合区 of Which: Urban-rural Transitional Area	559728	593986	1738362	857742	594093	577471	566798	566798
教育部门办 Run by Ed. Dept.	472327	499758	1475726	741837	499852	492098	483776	483776
其他部门办 Run by Non-ed. Dept.	1560	1331	4476	1908	1331	1677	1468	1468
地方企业办 Run by Local Enterprises	473	328	1185	592	328	383	474	474
民办 Non – government	85368	92569	256975	113405	92582	83313	81080	81080
镇区 Counties & Towns Area	4068002	4210455	12398955	6120642	4213158	4105850	4079947	4079947
教育部门办 Run by Ed. Dept.	3719066	3846043	11334432	5636226	3847656	3756190	3730586	3730586
其他部门办 Run by Non-ed. Dept.	29920	28367	84567	44509	28367	27463	28737	28737
地方企业办 Run by Local Enterprises	1515	1603	4902	2467	1604	1711	1587	1587
民办 Non – government	317501	334442	975054	437440	335531	320486	319037	319037
其中:镇乡结合区 of Which: County-town Transitional Area	1033340	1076048	3154717	1557127	1077586	1044035	1033096	1033096
教育部门办 Run by Ed. Dept.	920369	957805	2810471	1403646	958272	931236	920963	920963
其他部门办 Run by Non-ed. Dept.	1455	1250	3779	1918	1250	1282	1247	1247
地方企业办 Run by Local Enterprises	74	87	289	133	87	97	105	105
民办 Non-government	111442	116906	340178	151430	117977	111420	110781	110781
乡村 Rural Area	260421	281232	814909	398518	281299	271202	262408	262408
教育部门办 Run by Ed. Dept.	214658	227362	660536	332718	227407	219166	213963	213963
其他部门办 Run by Non-ed. Dept.	1395	1575	4635	2326	1575	1541	1519	1519
地方企业办 Run by Local Enterprises								
民办 Non-government	44368	52295	149738	63474	52317	50495	46926	46926

中学学校教职工数（初级中学、九年一贯制学校、
Number of Educational Personnel in

	教职工数 Educational Personnel			
	合计 Total	专任教师 Full-time Teachers	行政人员 Adm. Personnel	教辅人员 Supporting Staff
总　计 Total	**6402356**	**5597997**	**231675**	**270626**
其中：女 of Which：Female	3229805	2933435	56442	127010
少数民族 Minority	537697	478831	17126	19802
教育部门 Run by Ed. Dept.	5665009	5041100	192696	236855
其他部门 Run by Non-ed. Dept.	68052	54917	3913	2800
地方企业办 Run by Local Enterprises	3487	2892	176	167
民办 Non-government	665808	499088	34890	30804
城区 Urban Area	2327960	1993435	105457	112720
教育部门办 Run by Ed. Dept.	1938616	1698010	83052	94005
其他部门办 Run by Non-ed. Dept.	19391	15954	1205	1129
地方企业办 Run by Local Enterprises	1669	1264	89	113
民办 Non-government	368284	278207	21111	17473
其中：城乡结合区 of Which：Urban-rural Transitional Area	394094	336734	15366	17157
教育部门办 Run by Ed. Dept.	294418	262152	10028	12880
其他部门办 Run by Non-ed. Dept.	2313	1911	116	72
地方企业办 Run by Local Enterprises	349	238	24	19
民办 Non-government	97014	72433	5198	4186
镇区 Counties & Towns Area	3052946	2680712	93677	131273
教育部门办 Run by Ed. Dept.	2767143	2464100	80388	119026
其他部门办 Run by Non-ed. Dept.	43545	34649	2459	1523
地方企业办 Run by Local Enterprises	1757	1569	85	54
民办 Non-government	240501	180394	10745	10670
其中：镇乡结合区 of Which：County-town Transitional Area	779219	682838	23882	32837
教育部门办 Run by Ed. Dept.	688194	614484	19548	29021
其他部门办 Run by Non-ed. Dept.	1153	966	50	76
地方企业办 Run by Local Enterprises	141	141		
民办 Non-government	89731	67247	4284	3740
乡村 Rural Area	1021450	923850	32541	26633
教育部门办 Run by Ed. Dept.	959250	878990	29256	23824
其他部门办 Run by Non-ed. Dept.	5116	4314	249	148
地方企业办 Run by Local Enterprises	61	59	2	
民办 Non-government	57023	40487	3034	2661

职业初中、完全中学、高级中学、十二年一贯制学校）
General Secondary Schools

单位：人
unit：person

工勤人员 Workers	校办企业职工 Employees in School-run Factories & Farms	代课教师 Substitute Teachers	兼任教师 Part-time Teachers
298012	**4046**	**81802**	**20900**
111368	1550	50189	10606
21811	127	4355	3428
192077	2281	57739	13245
6394	28	1248	277
252		41	4
99289	1737	22774	7374
114451	1897	33203	8384
62596	953	24400	4042
1098	5	292	198
203		12	4
50554	939	8499	4140
24547	290	4524	1387
9300	58	2944	358
214		8	5
68			2
14965	232	1572	1022
145500	1784	34789	8120
102454	1175	22844	5366
4904	10	904	50
49		13	
38093	599	11028	2704
38739	923	9751	2100
24440	701	6290	1144
61		20	33
		2	
14238	222	3439	923
38061	365	13810	4396
27027	153	10495	3837
392	13	52	29
		16	
10642	199	3247	530

普通高中分课程专

Number of Full-time Teachers in Regular Senior Secondary Schools

	合计 Total	其中:女 of Which: Female	思想品德(政治) Rirtue Education	语文 Language & Literature	数学 Mathematics	外语 Foreign Language				物理 Physics
						小计 Subtotal	英语 English	日语 Japanese	俄语 Russian	
总　计 Total	**1629008**	**811941**	**100623**	**255547**	**252657**	**245988**	**243456**	**572**	**552**	**142527**
其中:女 of Which: Female	811941		51739	147275	103519	178022	176305	443	405	44431
少数民族 Minorities	121170	61877	8115	19495	17657	15898	15467	188	67	10309
研究生毕业 Graduate	93703	56441	6921	15184	13932	14539	14331	66	44	7318
本科毕业 Under-graduate	1483256	738034	90796	233818	232423	225191	222971	480	497	131234
专科毕业 Associate Bachelor	50736	17111	2845	6412	6240	6201	6099	25	11	3923
高中阶段毕业 High School Graduate	1269	338	61	127	60	51	49	1		50
高中阶段以下毕业 Below High School Graduate	44	17		6	2	6	6			2
城区 Urban Area	773716	420577	46756	119991	119726	117792	116311	425	227	68195
其中:城乡结合区 of Which: Urban-rural Transitional Area	118346	60903	7329	18284	18110	17917	17780	48	15	10295
镇区 Counties & Towns Area	800126	365912	50388	126917	124443	120064	119062	141	310	69703
其中:镇乡结合区 of Which: County-town Transitional Area	208809	97302	13251	32969	32063	31098	30914	19	60	17971
乡村 Rural Area	55166	25452	3479	8639	8488	8132	8083	6	15	4629

普通高中专任教师专业技术

Number of Full-time Teachers in Regular

	合计 Total	其中:女 of Which: Female	24岁及以下 24 Years and Under	25－29 25 to 29	30－34 30 to 34
总　计 Total	**1629008**	**811941**	**74536**	**276075**	**389339**
其中:女 of Which: Female	811941		48394	175063	221178
少数民族 Minorities	121170	61877	6937	22495	26616
中学高级 Senior	430223	165447		39	4682
中学一级 1st Grade	588678	286236	379	23845	178336
中学二级 2nd Grade	483894	282226	25576	193800	193253
中学三级 3rd Grade	11925	6191	2622	5383	2440
未定职级 No-ranking	114288	71841	45959	53008	10628
城区 Urban Area	773716	420577	30797	120332	184066
其中:城乡结合区 of Which: Urban-rural Transitional Area	118346	60903	5322	21403	29230
镇区 Counties & Towns Area	800126	365912	40360	144351	191576
其中:镇乡结合区 of Which: County-town Transitional Area	208809	97302	11114	38415	51889
乡村 Rural Area	55166	25452	3379	11392	13697

任教师学历情况
by Subject Taught & Academic Qualifications

单位：人
unit：person

化学 Chemistry	生物 Biology	地理 Geography	历史 History	信息技术 Infor Technology	通用技术 General Technology	体育与健康 Physical Training and Healthy	艺术 Art	音乐 Music	美术 Fine Arts	综合实践活动 Composite Practice	其他 Others	当年不任课 No Teaching Load in Current Year
137056	**97676**	**85731**	**92601**	**39270**	**11906**	**78396**	**2701**	**28119**	**30294**	**2876**	**11151**	**13889**
64141	52416	40447	45631	17082	3567	15592	1461	19038	13953	1019	6358	6250
10073	7140	6499	7074	3098	698	5922	204	2296	2025	112	3091	1464
8284	8108	4662	7411	1606	324	2140	82	722	1083	83	836	468
125174	87198	78232	82651	36147	10763	71364	2408	25856	27562	2540	8640	11259
3552	2342	2806	2503	1491	798	4668	201	1506	1605	235	1448	1960
42	26	30	36	24	21	223	9	35	44	18	217	195
4	2	1		2		1	1				10	7
65438	46435	40651	43657	18586	5936	38009	1106	13532	14566	1256	4929	7155
9899	7181	6369	6824	2814	923	5654	202	2222	2418	244	667	994
67071	47936	42113	45791	19335	5530	37748	1467	13622	14711	1515	5599	6173
17113	12619	11196	12167	5158	1560	9773	412	3736	4200	456	1330	1737
4547	3305	2967	3153	1349	440	2639	128	965	1017	105	623	561

职称、年龄结构情况
Senior Secondary Schools by Rank and Age

单位：人
unit：person

35－39 35 to 39	40－44 40 to 44	45－49 45 to 49	50－54 50 to 54	55－59 55 to 59	60 岁及以上 60 Years and Over
298799	**258936**	**212354**	**85048**	**32233**	**1688**
148000	113496	79027	25621	849	313
21686	19904	15873	5800	1799	60
48076	125951	156082	68388	25574	1431
196519	118645	50797	14488	5496	173
51069	12952	4611	1754	859	20
806	302	189	122	54	7
2329	1086	675	296	250	57
138828	126371	109362	46638	16173	1149
21603	18057	14811	5668	2068	184
149220	124941	97720	36358	15145	455
40484	31575	23114	8295	3744	179
10751	7624	5272	2052	915	84

普通高中专任

Changes of Full-time Teachers in

	上学年初报表专任教师数 Total Number of Full-time Teachers at Beginning of Previous Academic Year	增加教师 Factors of Increase				
		合计 Total	录用毕业生 New Recruits from Current Year Graduates		调入 Teachers Recruited from Other Units	校内调整 of Which: with Change of Status in Their Own Institutions
			小计 Subtotal	其中:师范生 of Which:Students Enrolled in Teacher Training Institutions		
总　计 Total	**1595035**	**142527**	**52027**	**42869**	**55184**	**26567**
其中:女 of Which: Female	782301	78915	34512	28633	27368	12580
城区 Urban Area	755590	65040	22725	18769	24917	12321
其中:女 of Which: Female	405408	37766	15516	12907	13013	6430
其中:城乡结合区 of Which: Urban-rural Transitional Area	115205	11720	4113	3594	5130	1590
其中:女 of Which: Female	58416	6472	2771	2411	2485	775
镇区 Counties & Towns Area	786177	70849	26845	22041	27707	13256
其中:女 of Which: Female	352935	37552	17412	14391	13137	5728
其中:镇乡结合区 of Which: County-town Transitional Area	204590	18990	7015	5655	7131	3521
其中:女 of Which: Female	93653	9972	4570	3703	3338	1515
乡村 Rural Area	53268	6638	2457	2059	2560	990
其中:女 of Which: Female	23958	3597	1584	1335	1218	422

普通高中学生、专任

Supplementary Information on Students and Full-time

	在校学生中 of Total Students			
	共产党员 Member of C. P. C.	共青团员 Member of C. Y. L.	华侨 Overseas Chinese	港澳台 From H. K, Macao and Taiwan
总　计 Total	**12527**	**18329630**	**1139**	**9549**
其中:女 of Which: Female	5596	9378723	503	4499
城区 Urban Area	6200	8517390	781	6028
其中:女 of Which: Female	2915	4418374	341	2754
其中:城乡结合区 of Which: Urban-rural Transitional Area	593	1328491	116	1370
其中:女 of Which: Female	277	670965	52	586
镇区 Counties & Towns Area	6197	9227566	282	3191
其中:女 of Which: Female	2633	4662806	132	1571
其中:镇乡结合区 of Which: County-town Transitional Area	1525	2335222	114	89
其中:女 of Which: Female	632	1180277	55	38
乡村 Rural Area	130	584674	76	330
其中:女 of Which: Female	48	297543	30	174

教师变动情况
Regular Senior Secondary Schools

单位：人
unit：person

	减 少 教 师 Factors of Decrease					本学年初报表专任教师数 Total Number of Full-time Teachers at Beginning of Current Academic Year
其他 Others	合计 Total	自然减员 Retired from Their Posts during Previcus Academic Year	调出 Transferred from Teaching to Non-Teaching Posts	校内调整 with Change of Status in Their Own Institutions	其他 Others	
8749	108554	11069	56984	27618	12883	1629008
4455	49275	4603	26554	12145	5973	811941
5077	46914	6333	22206	12354	6021	773716
2807	22597	2799	10905	5900	2993	420577
887	8579	869	4644	1577	1489	118346
441	3985	343	2260	632	750	60903
3041	56900	4380	31909	14306	6305	800126
1275	24575	1632	14353	5866	2724	365912
1323	14771	962	8668	3391	1750	208809
549	6323	348	3805	1397	773	97302
631	4740	356	2869	958	557	55166
373	2103	172	1296	379	256	25452

教师政治面貌及其他
Teachers of Regular Senior Secondary Schools

单位：人
unit：person

专任教师中 of Total Full-time Teachers			
共产党员 Member of C. P. C.	共青团员 Member of C. Y. L.	民主党派 Member of Non-Communist Part	华侨 Overseas Chinese
532953	**119314**	**28486**	**91**
225660	70789	12648	49
284051	54768	23173	71
137343	34178	10925	36
39500	8315	1862	9
17501	4998	743	6
232687	59831	4683	19
82145	34071	1492	13
59062	16858	1169	4
20862	9478	394	3
16215	4715	630	1
6172	2540	231	

普通高中

Condition of School Buildings in

	合计 Total	城区 Urban Area	其中:城乡结合区 of Which: Urban-rural Transitional Area
总　计 Total	**435601377**	**217767962**	**38830159**
其中: 危房 of Which: Floor Space of Dilapidated Buildings	8972702	3011354	261086
当年新增校舍 New Floor Space Added in Current Year	14904471	6434854	919820
一、教学及辅助用房 Teaching & Assistant Buildings	170626465	88954031	14773180
教室 Classroom	107534129	53258200	9056985
实验室 Laboratory	27009096	14252434	2324065
图书室 Library	13564788	7551241	1218385
微机室 PC-room	6509647	3446803	534429
语音室 Linguistic	2622970	1298359	237697
体育馆 Gymnasium	13385835	9146994	1401619
二、行政办公用房 Administrative	36174459	19967044	3078417
其中:教师办公室 of Which: for Teachers	21965305	11758148	1833145
三、生活用房 Residential and Welfare	200756503	90875407	18292511
教工宿舍 Apartments for Single	39237741	14648870	3116315
其中:教师周转宿舍 Accommodation for Circulation of Teachers	6417595	2371715	560937
学生宿舍 Students' Dormitories	108763702	49318094	10077469
食堂 Dining Halls	33768838	16167201	3344355
厕所 Toilet	9645644	5317551	895915
其他 Others	9340578	5423691	858457
四、其他用房 Rooms for Other Purposes	28043950	17971480	2686051

普通高中

Condition of School Buildings in

	占地面积(平方米) Areas of School Sites (m^2)			图书(册) Books & Magazines in Libraries (volume)	计算机数(台) No. of Computers		
	合计 Total	其中 of Which			合计 Total	其中:教学用计算机 No. of Computers Used for Instruction	
		绿化用地面积 Green Areas	运动场地面积 Sports Areas			小计 Subtotal	其中:平板电脑 of Which: Tablet PC
总　计 Total	**940695586**	**238491391**	**209433965**	**738857314**	**4123799**	**3146203**	**158288**
城区 Urban Area	419516153	113552344	98693985	379950833	2447141	1802746	87882
其中:城乡结合区 of Which: Urban-rural Transitional Area	80743435	23586112	17417115	57634787	468886	250115	11068
镇区 Counties & Towns Area	470936164	112156286	100526974	331517837	1542931	1236058	64908
其中:镇乡结合区 of Which: County-town Transitional Area	128281205	31790510	26394927	84304699	402253	325078	19367
乡村 Rural Area	50243269	12782761	10213006	27388644	133727	107399	5498

办学条件(一)

Regular Senior Secondary Schools (1)

单位：平方米

unit：m^2

镇区 Counties & Towns Area	其中:镇乡结合区 of Which：County-town Transitional Area	乡村 Rural Area
198648220	**53452872**	**19185195**
5488150	1222133	473198
7550898	2141907	918719
74850311	19752780	6822123
49618454	13022807	4657475
11831405	3200277	925257
5547604	1447388	465943
2826094	718508	236750
1224565	312742	100046
3802189	1051058	436652
14941864	3941707	1265551
9432025	2523202	775132
100078821	27343488	9802275
22050915	5626271	2537956
3536647	954478	509233
54367490	15076447	5078118
16150803	4598377	1450834
3918925	1071213	409168
3590688	971180	326199
8777224	2414897	1295246

办学条件(二)

Regular Senior Secondary Schools (2)

教室中：Classroom		教室中:普通教室(间) of Which：General Classroom		固定资产总值(万元) Total Value of Fixed Asset (10,000 yuan)		
合计 Total	其中:网络多媒体教室 of Which：Network Multimedia Classroom	合计 Total	其中:网络多媒体教室 of Which：Network Multimedia Classroom	合计 Total	其中:教学仪器设备资产值 of Which：Total Value of Equip & Instru. 小计 Subtotal	其中:实验设备 for Profession
847051	**445296**	**686706**	**389986**	**55903115.75**	**5841188.02**	**2186292.82**
410631	255846	325901	221342	30698477.98	3655603.95	1212676.19
65663	37299	51837	33147	5439062.94	484097.67	186291.01
402572	174939	333792	156130	22899232.76	1995072.31	897609.79
106910	48552	82778	41113	6486324.65	525816.32	239967.13
33848	14511	27013	12514	2305405.01	190511.76	76006.84

普通高中办学条件(三)

Condition of School Buildings in Regular Senior Secondary Schools (3)

单位：所

unit：school

	体育运动场(馆)面积达标校数 Schools No.：Sprots Areas Reached Standard	体育器械配备达标校数 Schools No.：Sports Equip. Reached Standard	音乐器械配备达标校数 Schools No.：Musical Instru. Reached Standard	美术器械配备达标校数 Schools No.：Fine Arts Instru. Reached Standard	理科实验仪器达标校数 Schools No.：Equip. of Natural Sci. Reached Standard	建立校园网校数 Schools No.：Campus Networks Set	接入互联网校数 School No.：Campus Networks Set
总计 Total	**11064**	**11305**	**11018**	**11074**	**11485**	**10746**	**12853**
城区 Urban Area	5403	5635	5527	5562	5662	5561	6162
其中:城乡结合区 of Which:Urban-rural Transitional Area	800	819	786	788	803	772	883
镇区 Counties & Towns Area	5098	5107	4949	4964	5252	4704	6026
其中:镇乡结合区 of Which:County-town Transitional Area	1291	1299	1249	1263	1325	1187	1505
乡村 Rural Area	563	563	542	548	571	481	665

成人高中

Basic Statistics of

	学校数(所) Schools	教学班(点)(个) External Teaching Sites	毕(结)业生数 Graduates	
			合计 Total	其中:女 of Which：Female
总　计 Total	**611**	**1588**	**104012**	**49086**
职工高中 Senior Sec. Schools for Staff &workers	146	450	44646	20403
农民高中 Senior Sec. Shools for Peasants	465	1138	59366	28683

中等职业学校(机构)数
Number of Secondary Vocational Schools (Institutions)

单位：所
unit：institution

	合计 Total	中央部门 under Central Ministries & Agencies	地方 Under Local Authorities 小计 Subtotal	教育部门 Run by Ed. Dept.	其他部门 Run by other Dept.	地方企业 Run by Local Enterprises	民办 Non-government
中等职业学校 Secondary Vocational Schools	9380	23	6875	5378	1412	85	2482
其中:普通中等专业学校 of Which：Reg. Specialized Sec. chools	3577	18	2667	1655	981	31	892
成人中等专业学校 Adults Specialized Sec. Schools	1536	3	1384	1116	242	26	149
职业高中学校 Vocational High Schools	4267	2	2824	2607	189	28	1441
其他机构(教学点)(不计校数) Other Institutions	451	2	385	277	102	6	64
附设中职班(不计校数) Secondary Vocational Classes Attached	1160	3	939	588	334	17	218

注:未含技工学校数据(下同)。
Note：Data on Skilled Workers are not included(Same as the Followings).

基本情况
Adult High Schools

单位：人
unit：person

注册学生数 Enrolment		教职工数 Educational Personnel		专任教师 Full-time Teacher		聘请校外教师 Part-time Teachers
合计 Total	其中:女 of Which：Female	合计 Total	其中:女 of Which：Female	合计 Total	其中:女 of Which：Female	
110705	**55532**	**6061**	**2568**	**4618**	**1980**	**4111**
57552	27947	2047	983	1629	791	896
53153	27585	4014	1585	2989	1189	3215

中等职业学校分办学类型及

Number of Students and Educational Personnel of Secondary

	合计 Total			中职全日制学生 Full-time Students of SVSs		
	毕业生数 Graduates	招生数 Entrants	在校学生数 Enrolment	毕业生数 Graduates	招生数 Entrants	在校学生数 Enrolment
总　计 Total	**5575587**	**5412624**	**15363842**	**4889729**	**4671192**	**13469039**
其中:女 of Which: Female	2756207	2634661	7646365	2450345	2301954	6803133
分办学类型:普通中专学校 by Type: Reg. Specialized Sec. Schools	2655479	2561860	7504748	2277920	2212386	6431282
成人中等专业学校	258957	211085	560889	146200	100276	319148
Adults Specialized Sec. Schools						
职业高中学校 Vocational High Schools	2194420	2113022	5847451	2019330	1863144	5388586
其他机构 Other Institutions	112903	94483	286375	102576	73442	231540
附设中职班	353828	432174	1164379	343703	421944	1098483
Secondary Vocational Classes Attached						
分举办者:1. 中央部门 by Providers: Under Central Ministries & Agencies	6257	4985	15647	6257	4985	15647
2. 地方 Under Local Authorities	4778616	4676046	13268787	4180028	4020134	11596111
教育部门 Under Ed. Dept	3725487	3691811	10347871	3212721	3153000	8986123
其他部门 Run by Non-ed. Dept	1017058	955532	2841295	931789	839439	2531859
地方企业 Run by Local Enterprises	36071	28703	79621	35518	27695	78129
3. 民办 Non-government	790714	731593	2079408	703444	646073	1857281

举办者的中职学生及教职工情况

Vocational Schools by Types and Providers

单位：人
unit：person

中职非全日制学生 Part-time Students of SVSs			教职工数 Educational Personnel							聘请校外教师 Part-time Teachers
				其中：专任教师 of Which：Full-time Teachers						
毕业生数 Graduates	招生数 Entrants	在校学生数 Enrolment	合计 Total	小计 Subtotal	正高级 Senior	副高级 Sub-senior	中级 Middle	初级 Junior	未定职级 No-ranking	
685858	**741432**	**1894803**	**883959**	**668754**	**3383**	**155455**	**268628**	**182596**	**58692**	**96619**
305862	332707	843232	420514	339176	1295	70033	137307	98828	31713	39789
377559	349474	1073466	419315	303585	1909	74596	119116	79912	28052	42425
112757	110809	241741	72715	52021	375	14773	23547	10743	2583	22590
175090	249878	458865	375370	301440	1009	63049	120933	89214	27235	29634
10327	21041	54835	16559	11708	90	3037	5032	2727	822	1970
10125	10230	65896								
			2452	1343	10	350	608	280	95	547
598588	655912	1672676	763693	589530	1444	146227	242211	162192	37456	83151
512766	538811	1361748	599809	483886	706	117795	201438	134284	29663	47991
85269	116093	309436	155412	100703	678	27087	38987	26577	7374	34595
553	1008	1492	8472	4941	60	1345	1786	1331	419	565
87270	85520	222127	117814	77881	1929	8878	25809	20124	21141	12921

中等职业学校

Number of students in Secondary

	毕业生数 Graduates		招生数 Entrants		
	合计 Total	其中:获得职业资格证书 of Which: Recitpents of Vocational Qualifications	合计 Total	其中:应届毕业 of Which: Graduates of Current Year 小计 Subtotal	其中:初中毕业生 of Which: Junior Secondary School Graduates
一、中职学生总计 Students of SVSs Total	5575587	4336937	5412624	4631934	4446788
其中:中职全日制学生 of Which: Full-time Students of SVSs	4889729	3874625	4671192	4332415	4187378
中职非全日制学生 Part-time Students of SVSs	685858	462312	741432	299519	259410
1. 普通中专学生 Students of Regular SSSs	2652082	1982561	2714716	2501162	2397610
2. 成人中专学生 Students of Adult SSSs	878323	596059	862591	397783	352537
3. 职业高中学生 Students of Vocational High Schools	2045182	1758317	1835317	1732989	1696641
二、培训学生 Trainees	6247386				
三、外国留学生 Foreign Students	1423				

注:SSSs＝中等专业学校

Note: SSSs＝Specialized Secondary Schools

中等职业学校

Number of Female students in Secondary

	毕业生数 Graduates		招生数 Entrants		
	合计 Total	其中:获得职业资格证书 of Which: Recitpents of Vocational Qualifications	合计 Total	其中:应届毕业 of Which: Graduates of Current Year 小计 Subtotal	其中:初中毕业生 of Which: Junior Secondary School Graduates
一、中职学生总计 Students of SVSs Total	2756207	2105777	2634661	2278446	2195851
其中:中职全日制学生 of Which: Full-time Students of SVSs	2450345	1904999	2301954	2146193	2080454
中职非全日制学生 Part-time Students of SVSs	305862	200778	332707	132253	115397
1. 普通中专学生 Students of Regular SSSs	1403900	1022619	1417207	1314924	1266410
2. 成人中专学生 Students of Adult SSSs	394311	264098	390020	179731	160347
3. 职业高中学生 Students of Vocational High Schools	957996	819060	827434	783791	769094
二、培训学生 Trainees	2818212				
三、外国留学生 Foreign Students	820				

注:SSSs＝中等专业学校

Note: SSSs＝Specialized Secondary Schools

（机构）各类学生数
Vocational Schools (Institutions)

单位：人
unit: person

其中：五年制高职中职段 of Which: 5-year Secondary Vocational Education	在校学生数 Enrolment					预计毕业生数 Estimated Graduates for Next Year	
	合计 Total	一年级 Grade 1	二年级 Grade 2	三年级 Grade 3	四年级及以上 Over Grade 4	合计 Total	其中：五年制高职中职段 of Which: 5-year Secondary Vocational Education
371335	15363842	5418413	5028833	4817693	98903	5392971	254986
371238	13469039	4674917	4423092	4279772	91258	4518852	254100
97	1894803	743496	605741	537921	7645	874119	886
342770	7721842	2716550	2524646	2400163	80483	2537549	237489
2254	2299806	865279	757926	667977	8624	1031010	2449
26311	5342194	1836584	1746261	1749553	9796	1824412	15048
	3986943						
	1837						

（机构）各类女学生数
Vocational Schools (Institutions)

单位：人
unit: person

其中：五年制高职中职段 of Which: 5-year Secondary Vocational Education	在校学生数 Enrolment					预计毕业生数 Estimated Graduates for Next Year	
	合计 Total	一年级 Grade 1	二年级 Grade 2	三年级 Grade 3	四年级及以上 Over Grade 4	合计 Total	其中：五年制高职中职段 of Which: 5-year Secondary Vocational Education
204078	7646365	2636321	2514584	2437947	57513	2601593	148528
204078	6803133	2302163	2243984	2202498	54488	2205891	147727
	843232	334158	270600	235449	3025	395702	801
190268	4136989	1416994	1359554	1311406	49035	1302569	139978
1195	1036081	391867	341418	299243	3553	466448	1753
12615	2473295	827460	813612	827298	4925	832576	6797
	1889212						
	1027						

中等职业学校(机构)学生分科类情况(总计)
Number of Students by Field of Education in Secondary Vocational Schools (Institutions) (Total)

单位：人
unit：person

	毕业生数 Graduates		招生数 Entrants			在校学生数 Enrolment	预计毕业生数 Estimated Graduates for Next Year
				其中:应届毕业 of Which：Graduates of Current Year			
	合计 Total	其中:获得职业资格证书 of Which：Reciptents of Vocational Qualifications	合计 Total	小计 Subtotal	其中:初中毕业生 of Which：Junior Secondary School Graduates		
总　计 Total	**5575587**	**4336937**	**5412624**	**4631934**	**4446788**	**15363842**	**5392971**
其中:女 of Which：Female	2756207	2105777	2634661	2278446	2195851	7646365	2601593
农林牧渔类 Agriculture, Forestry, Husbandry & Fisheries	757877	544841	467279	296524	278289	1722323	728156
资源环境类 Resources & Environment	46648	35561	33843	24760	22623	90803	39219
能源与新能源类 Energy Resources & New ER	29177	23213	20704	18051	16610	68184	26279
土木水利类 Civil Engineering & Water Conservancy	181180	140428	240140	207203	197368	624010	213117
加工制造类 Manufacturing	903618	773784	791948	698053	674385	2306826	819663
石油化工 Petroleum & Chemical Industries	40030	31421	35046	31347	29373	107439	39630
轻纺食品 Light, Textile & Food Industries	67322	56777	58300	46849	45263	152038	61433
交通运输类 Communication & Transport	327376	273548	457839	406793	389459	1135676	339925
信息技术类 Information Technology	1030628	840227	926561	801138	769299	2590293	938807
医药卫生类 Medicine, Pharmaceuticals & Health Care	500063	309022	519612	461249	442876	1470917	463608
休闲保健类 Recreations Services & Make-up Artists	25532	20132	30861	27448	26271	81875	26619
财经商贸类 Finance, Economics, Commerce & Trade	634290	480596	596711	518802	499293	1673386	591422
旅游服务类 Tourist Services	227547	187459	261323	224617	216804	689918	218721
文化艺术类 Culture & Arts	247456	189396	260997	227955	218037	748355	246907
体育与健身 Sports & Body-building	37920	23140	44709	40681	39029	121871	34377
教育类 Educational Services	365377	295739	511258	470615	457289	1396498	462045
司法服务类 Legal Services	23814	15887	22697	18487	17049	62428	25960
公共管理与服务类 Public Administration & Services	69921	49224	69000	52835	50747	180621	72223
其他 Others	59811	46542	63796	58527	56724	140381	44860

中等职业学校(机构)学生分科类情况(全日制学生)
Number of Students by Field of Education in Secondary Vocational Schools (Institutions) (Full-time Students)

单位: 人
unit: person

	毕业生数 Graduates		招生数 Entrants			在校学生数 Enrolment	预计毕业生数 Estimated Graduates for Next Year
				其中:应届毕业 of Which: Graduates of Current Year			
	合计 Total	其中:获得职业资格证书 of Which: Recipients of Vocational Qualifications	合计 Total	小计 Subtotal	其中:初中毕业生 of Which: Junior Secondary School Graduates		
总 计 Total	**4889729**	**3874625**	**4671192**	**4332415**	**4187378**	**13469039**	**4518852**
其中:女 of Which: Female	2450345	1904999	2301954	2146193	2080454	6803133	2205891
农林牧渔类 Agriculture, Forestry, Husbandry & Fisheries	625831	458858	302848	242637	231073	1224319	509030
资源环境类 Resources & Environment	42540	31853	26716	20875	19192	80262	34660
能源与新能源类 Energy Resources & New ER	27963	22148	19506	17377	15957	64243	25535
土木水利类 Civil Engineering & WaterConservancy	169911	131476	224954	202110	193094	588208	195651
加工制造类 Manufacturing	806409	704321	676069	644439	629660	2027120	705536
石油化工 Petroleum & Chemical Industries	38838	30539	33023	30082	28128	100530	37409
轻纺食品 Light, Textile & Food Industries	58069	49784	45253	40275	39066	124787	47392
交通运输类 Communication & Transport	290155	245664	412207	391197	377237	1017594	292317
信息技术类 Information Technology	870800	731228	766759	726820	704547	2185464	745814
医药卫生类 Medicine, Pharmaceuticals & Health Care	487727	304885	502435	456660	438469	1437962	448690
休闲保健类 Recreations Services & Make-up Artists	24284	19104	28700	26509	25448	75783	23414
财经商贸类 Finance, Economics, Commerce & Trade	532963	415754	531393	500889	484272	1504320	496134
旅游服务类 Tourist Services	202540	170865	225410	211780	205642	608801	187022
文化艺术类 Culture & Arts	221510	170835	234550	218604	210691	677963	212523
体育与健身 Sports & Body-building	36768	21988	43694	40361	38711	120388	33243
教育类 Educational Services	335371	273502	477732	451699	439636	1320943	420295
司法服务类 Legal Services	20335	12976	19257	16246	14988	53654	20138
公共管理与服务类 Public Administration & Services	49523	38966	46805	42653	41470	131167	45153
其他 Others	48192	39879	53881	51202	50097	125531	38896

中等职业学校(机构)学生分科类情况(普通中专)

Number of Students by Field of Education in Secondary Vocational Schools (Institutions) (Regular SSSs)

单位:人

unit: person

	毕业生数 Graduates		招生数 Entrants			在校学生数 Enrolment	预计毕业生数 Estimated Graduates for Next Year
				其中:应届毕业 of Which: Graduates of Current Year			
	合计 Total	其中:获得职业资格证书 of Which: Reciptents of Vocational Qualifications	合计 Total	小计 Subtotal	其中:初中毕业生 of Which: Junior Secondary School Graduates		
总　计 Total	**2652082**	**1982561**	**2714716**	**2501162**	**2397610**	**7721842**	**2537549**
其中:女 of Which: Female	1403900	1022619	1417207	1314924	1266410	4136989	1302569
农林牧渔类 Agriculture, Forestry, Husbandry & Fisheries	245420	172195	121165	98816	94648	515162	222151
资源环境类 Resources & Environment	27202	18091	15450	11252	10027	49008	21827
能源与新能源类 Energy Resources & New ER	20766	16585	14452	13424	12109	50561	20152
土木水利类 Civil Engineering & Water Conservancy	117608	86435	159623	139566	131826	410777	134388
加工制造类 Manufacturing	397679	344845	344263	327696	318856	1016269	345435
石油化工 Petroleum & Chemical Industries	26227	18979	24536	21935	20520	72433	26760
轻纺食品 Light, Textile & Food Industries	22707	19671	16793	15498	14529	53135	21218
交通运输类 Communication & Transport	164007	133911	234305	219856	209908	577572	165301
信息技术类 Information Technology	372365	298987	352797	330136	315623	979815	328310
医药卫生类 Medicine, Pharmaceuticals & Health Care	435172	260525	437104	396608	379487	1276142	401584
休闲保健类 Recreations Services & Make-up Artists	9986	7645	15175	14352	13642	36852	11013
财经商贸类 Finance, Economics, Commerce & Trade	327917	242289	352969	328943	316046	958316	305131
旅游服务类 Tourist Services	88483	70853	103294	97746	94232	276366	81428
文化艺术类 Culture & Arts	100723	69942	118495	108512	102525	341987	101965
体育与健身 Sports & Body-building	24696	13308	29214	26770	25217	80422	21853
教育类 Educational Services	222685	175423	324809	304624	295451	891715	282648
司法服务类 Legal Services	10211	4565	10321	9411	8349	29389	10795
公共管理与服务类 Public Administration & Services	21663	15507	22040	19543	18741	58056	19409
其他 Others	16565	12805	17911	16474	15874	47865	16181

中等职业学校(机构)学生分科类情况(成人中专)

Number of Students by Field of Education in Secondary Vocational Schools (Institutions) (Adult SSSs)

单位:人
unit: person

	毕业生数 Graduates		招生数 Entrants			在校学生数 Enrolment	预计毕业生数 Estimated Graduates for Next Year
				其中:应届毕业 of Which: Graduates of Current Year			
	合计 Total	其中:获得职业资格证书 of Which: Recipients of Vocational Qualifications	合计 Total	小计 Subtotal	其中:初中毕业生 of Which: Junior Secondary School Graduates		
总　计 Total	**878323**	**596059**	**862591**	**397783**	**352537**	**2299806**	**1031010**
其中:女 of Which: Female	394311	264098	390020	179731	160347	1036081	466448
农林牧渔类 Agriculture, Forestry, Husbandry & Fisheries	188842	118331	183967	64101	56984	594906	264202
资源环境类 Resources & Environment	7907	6668	8740	4585	4130	15833	8188
能源与新能源类 Energy Resources & New ER	1536	1332	1230	704	683	4272	918
土木水利类 Civil Engineering & Water Conservancy	17871	13295	21868	11040	10007	54374	25460
加工制造类 Manufacturing	120279	86630	128609	65271	55347	326203	133628
石油化工 Petroleum & Chemical Industries	1286	961	2173	1337	1317	7525	2613
轻纺食品 Light, Textile & Food Industries	10575	8066	13249	6722	6345	28968	15096
交通运输类 Communication & Transport	50361	39064	59464	28614	24944	155614	57676
信息技术类 Information Technology	194007	132865	174362	86998	76532	461772	216536
医药卫生类 Medicine, Pharmaceuticals & Health Care	20983	11331	25881	10890	10546	54180	21064
休闲保健类 Recreations Services & Make-up Artists	1477	1106	2532	1201	1073	6824	3471
财经商贸类 Finance, Economics, Commerce & Trade	117895	76849	77146	28434	24698	207227	109347
旅游服务类 Tourist Services	29001	19605	40964	17091	15156	93843	35504
文化艺术类 Culture & Arts	31410	22148	30722	12981	10944	81691	37417
体育与健身 Sports & Body-building	3372	2252	6303	5198	5181	12656	3333
教育类 Educational Services	40418	30769	43953	28376	26349	107748	52643
司法服务类 Legal Services	4065	3310	4931	3215	3035	12543	7330
公共管理与服务类 Public Administration & Services	21642	11046	24850	12001	10951	55296	28931
其他 Others	15396	10431	11647	9024	8315	18331	7653

中等职业学校(机构)学生分科类情况(职业高中)
Number of Students by Field of Education in Secondary Vocational Schools (Institutions) (Vocational High Schools)

单位：人
unit: person

	毕业生数 Graduates		招生数 Entrants			在校学生数 Enrolment	预计毕业生数 Estimated Graduates for Next Year
				其中:应届毕业 of Which: Graduates of Current Year			
	合计 Total	其中:获得职业资格证书 of Which: Recipients of Vocational Qualifications	合计 Total	小计 Subtotal	其中:初中毕业生 of Which: Junior Secondary School Graduates		
总　计 Total	**2045182**	**1758317**	**1835317**	**1732989**	**1696641**	**5342194**	**1824412**
其中:女 of Which: Female	957996	819060	827434	783791	769094	2473295	832576
农林牧渔类 Agriculture, Forestry, Husbandry & Fisheries	323615	254315	162147	133607	126657	612255	241803
资源环境类 Resources & Environment	11539	10802	9653	8923	8466	25962	9204
能源与新能源类 Energy Resources & New ER	6875	5296	5022	3923	3818	13351	5209
土木水利类 Civil Engineering & Water Conservancy	45701	40698	58649	56597	55535	158859	53269
加工制造类 Manufacturing	385660	342309	319076	305086	300182	964354	340600
石油化工 Petroleum & Chemical Industries	12517	11481	8337	8075	7536	27481	10257
轻纺食品 Light, Textile & Food Industries	34040	29040	28258	24629	24389	69935	25119
交通运输类 Communication & Transport	113008	100573	164070	158323	154607	402490	116948
信息技术类 Information Technology	464256	408375	399402	384004	377144	1148706	393961
医药卫生类 Medicine, Pharmaceuticals & Health Care	43908	37166	56627	53751	52843	140595	40960
休闲保健类 Recreations Services & Make-up Artists	14069	11381	13154	11895	11556	38199	12135
财经商贸类 Finance, Economics, Commerce & Trade	188478	161458	166596	161425	158549	507843	176944
旅游服务类 Tourist Services	110063	97001	117065	109780	107416	319709	101789
文化艺术类 Culture & Arts	115323	97306	111780	106462	104568	324677	107525
体育与健身 Sports & Body-building	9852	7580	9192	8713	8631	28793	9191
教育类 Educational Services	102274	89547	142496	137615	135489	397035	126754
司法服务类 Legal Services	9538	8012	7445	5861	5665	20496	7835
公共管理与服务类 Public Administration & Services	26616	22671	22110	21291	21055	67269	23883
其他 Others	27850	23306	34238	33029	32535	74185	21026

中等职业学校(机构)分年龄学生数

Number of Students by Age in Secondary Vocational Schools (Institutions)

单位：人

unit: person

	合计 Total	14岁及以下 14 Years and Under	15岁 15 Years	16岁 16 Years	17岁 17 Years	18岁 18 Years	19岁 19 Years	20岁 20 Years	21岁 21 Years	22岁及以上 22 Years and Over
总　计 Total	**15363842**	**195634**	**1967604**	**3580388**	**3656138**	**2499463**	**1096035**	**525189**	**336162**	**1507229**
其中：中职全日制学生 of Which: Full-time Students of SVSs	13469039	192470	1897858	3455652	3505429	2312268	933245	370452	205989	595676
中职非全日制学生 Part-time Students of SVSs	1894803	3164	69746	124736	150709	187195	162790	154737	130173	911553
1. 普通中专学生 Students of Regular SSSs	7721842	125356	1057685	1959668	1994094	1349652	584383	241494	130383	279127
2. 成人中专学生 Students of Adult SSSs	2299806	7252	119174	205623	237089	243094	190525	170473	146743	979833
3. 职业高中学生 Students of Vocational High Schools	5342194	63026	790745	1415097	1424955	906717	321127	113222	59036	248269

中等职业学校(机构)分年龄女学生数

Number of Female Students by Age in Secondary Vocational Schools (Institutions)

单位：人

unit: person

	合计 Total	14岁及以下 14 Years and Under	15岁 15 Years	16岁 16 Years	17岁 17 Years	18岁 18 Years	19岁 19 Years	20岁 20 Years	21岁 21 Years	22岁及以上 22 Years and Over
总　计 Total	**7646365**	**105447**	**996560**	**1814447**	**1854051**	**1252549**	**536903**	**254212**	**156592**	**675604**
其中：中职全日制学生 of Which: Full-time Students of SVSs	6803133	104084	965866	1758002	1785264	1161674	460379	179890	97739	290235
中职非全日制学生 Part-time Students of SVSs	843232	1363	30694	56445	68787	90875	76524	74322	58853	385369
1. 普通中专学生 Students of Regular SSSs	4136989	72283	574753	1062560	1081583	719179	302596	121949	63521	138565
2. 成人中专学生 Students of Adult SSSs	1036081	3160	56174	95764	110171	116704	87902	81251	66149	418806
3. 职业高中学生 Students of Vocational High Schools	2473295	30004	365633	656123	662297	416666	146405	51012	26922	118233

中等职业学校(机构)

Changes in Enrolment of Secondary

	上学年初报表在校学生数 Enrolment at Beginning of Previous Academic Year	增加学生数 Factors of Increase				
		合计 Total	招生 No. of Students Admitted	复学 Students Resuming Studies	转入 Transfers from Other Inst.	其他 Others
总　计 Total	**16898275**	**6101899**	**5412624**	**11185**	**481354**	**196736**
其中:中职全日制学生 of Which: Full-time Students of SVSs	14896641	5248256	4671192	10291	410501	156272
中职非全日制学生 Part-time Students of SVSs	2001634	853643	741432	894	70853	40464
1. 普通中专学生 Students of Regular SSSs	8135386	3028139	2714716	5902	241173	66348
2. 成人中专学生 Students of Adult SSSs	2534544	1017399	862591	1076	101563	52169
3. 职业高中学生 Students of Vocational High Schools	6228345	2056361	1835317	4207	138618	78219

中等职业学校(机构)

Changes in Female Enrolment of

	上学年初报表在校学生数 Enrolment at Beginning of Previous Academic Year	增加学生数 Factors of Increase				
		合计 Total	招生 No. of Students Admitted	复学 Students Resuming Studies	转入 Transfers from Other Inst.	其他 Others
总　计 Total	**8411755**	**2949007**	**2634661**	**4172**	**221272**	**88902**
其中:中职全日制学生 of Which: Full-time Students of SVSs	7523134	2567790	2301954	3875	192610	69351
中职非全日制学生 Part-time Students of SVSs	888621	381217	332707	297	28662	19551
1. 普通中专学生 Students of Regular SSSs	4360683	1576712	1417207	2353	123721	33431
2. 成人中专学生 Students of Adult SSSs	1141194	452197	390020	425	38539	23213
3. 职业高中学生 Students of Vocational High Schools	2909878	920098	827434	1394	59012	32258

学生变动情况
Vocational Schools (Institutions)

单位：人
unit: person

减少学生数 Factors of Decrease									本学年初报表在校学生数 Total Enrolment at Beginning of Current Academic Year
合计 Total	毕业 Graduates	结业 Completers of Courses without Formal Awards	休学 Suspended	退学 Quitting	开除 Expelled	死亡 Dead	转出 Transfers to Other Inst.	其他 Others	
7636332	**5575587**	**195185**	**36595**	**529651**	**10722**	**359**	**817400**	**470833**	**15363842**
6675858	4889729	115244	32872	470294	10617	358	742077	414667	13469039
960474	685858	79941	3723	59357	105	1	75323	56166	1894803
3441683	2652082	37967	19661	231475	6274	215	314638	179371	7721842
1252137	878323	81939	4943	82607	144	8	117663	86510	2299806
2942512	2045182	75279	11991	215569	4304	136	385099	204952	5342194

女学生变动情况
Secondary Vocational Schools (Institutions)

单位：人
unit: person

减少学生数 Factors of Decrease									本学年初报表在校学生数 Total Enrolment at Beginning of Current Academic Year
合计 Total	毕业 Graduates	结业 Completers of Courses Without Formal Awards	休学 Suspended	退学 Quitting	开除 Expelled	死亡 Dead	转出 Transfers to Other Inst.	其他 Others	
3714397	**2756207**	**89480**	**17369**	**241480**	**3274**	**108**	**387711**	**218768**	**7646365**
3287791	2450345	55093	15604	214061	3218	108	352722	196640	6803133
426606	305862	34387	1765	27419	56		34989	22128	843232
1800406	1403900	18094	9261	108017	1896	80	161947	97211	4136989
557310	394311	35062	2422	37586	61	2	54132	33734	1036081
1356681	957996	36324	5686	95877	1317	26	171632	87823	2473295

中等职业学校(机构)学生其他情况
Supplementary Information on Students in Secondary Vocational Schools (Institutions)

单位：人
unit: person

	共产党员 Member of C. P. A	共青团员 Member of C. Y. L	华侨 Overseas Chinese	港澳台 From H. K, Macao and Taiwan	少数民族 Minorities	残疾人 Disabled
总　计 Total	**52602**	**9010814**	**175**	**1968**	**1214158**	**15874**
其中:女 of Which: Female	17391	4644945	53	668	587388	5714
中职全日制学生 Full-time Students of SVSs	25940	8604715	168	1548	1041058	15215
中职非全日制学生 Part-time Students of SVSs	26662	406099	7	420	173100	659
1. 普通中专学生 Students of Regular SSSs	14734	4770978	73	1209	648968	9226
2. 成人中专学生 Students of Adult SSSs	30140	599952	10	470	191944	931
3. 职业高中学生 Students of Vocational High Schools	7728	3639884	92	289	373246	5717

中等职业学校(机构)培训学生情况
Number of Trainees in Secondary Vocational Schools (Institutions)

单位：人次
unit: person

	结业生数 Graduates		注册学生数 Enrolment	
	合计 Total	其中:女 of Which: Female	合计 Total	其中:女 of Which: Female
总　计 Total	**6247386**	**2818212**	**3986943**	**1889212**
其中:少数民族 of Which: Minority	519980	226164	333145	145004
资格证书培训 for Certificates of Vocational Qualifications	2467512	1097382	1757692	786583
岗位证书培训 for Certificates of Job-related Qualifications	2048427	894680	1182845	564441
按产业结构分:第一产业类培训 by Industry: Training for First Industry	1442486	642194	971664	453947
第二产业类培训 Training for Second Industry	1373805	468700	933231	327563
第三产业类培训 Training for Third Industry	3431095	1707318	2082048	1107702
按培训时间分:一个月以内 by Length of Training: 1 Month Under	3668855	1645374	2034619	957340
一个月至三个月以内 1 Month to 3 Months Under	1176721	552459	810081	392252
三个月至半年以内 3 Months to 6 Months	540019	243369	391693	179867
半年至一年以内 6 Months to 1 Year	539712	231171	324267	158200
一年及以上 1 Year and Over	322079	145839	426283	201553

中等职业学校(机构)外国留学生情况

Number of Foreign Students in Secondary Vocational Schools (Institutions)

单位：人

unit：person

	结业生数 Graduates		注册学生数 Enrolment	
	合计 Total	其中:女 of Which: Female	合计 Total	其中:女 of Which: Female
总　计 Total	**1423**	**820**	**1837**	**1027**
按时间分 by Time				
一个月以内 1 Month Under	998	578	441	307
一个月至三个月以内 1 Month to 3 Months	56	14	22	14
三个月至半年以内 3 Months to 6 Months	16	7	29	17
半年至一年以内 6 Months to 1 Year	131	92	219	128
一年及以上 1 Year and Over	222	129	1126	561
按大洲分 by Continent				
亚洲 Asia	1152	703	1541	886
非洲 Africa	10	1	58	10
欧洲 Europe	219	102	209	113
北美洲 North America	23	8	11	4
南美洲 South America	13	2	11	9
大洋洲 Oceania	6	4	7	5

中等职业学校

Number of Educational Personnel in

	教职工数 Educational		
	合计 Total	校本部 Educational Personnel	
		小计 Subtotal	专任教师 Full-time Teachers
总　计	**883959**	**874171**	**668754**
其中:女 of Which: Female	420514	415993	339176
正高级 Senior	4862	4835	3383
副高级 Sub-senior	182792	182546	155455
中　级 Middle	313249	312266	268628
初　级 Junior	218642	217544	182596
未定职级 No-ranking	164414	156980	58692
总计中:聘任制 of the Total: Part-time	170078	168612	130724
其中:女 of Which: Female	80961	80136	64508
正高级 Senior	1262	1261	943
副高级 Sub-senior	29006	28987	25303
中　级 Middle	56813	56662	49927
初　级 Junior	45335	44858	38411
未定职级 No-ranking	37662	36844	16140

中等职业学校(机构)

Number of Educational Personnel in

	教职工数 Educational		
	合计 Total	校本部 Educational Personnel	
		小计 Subtotal	专任教师 Full-time Teachers
总　计	**419315**	**413803**	**303585**
其中:女 of Which: Female	199873	197459	154955
正高级 Senior	2707	2693	1909
副高级 Sub-senior	86742	86602	74596
中　级 Middle	141431	141023	119116
初　级 Junior	99959	99250	79912
未定职级 No-ranking	88476	84235	28052
总计中:聘任制 of the Total: Part-time	73865	72912	54333
其中:女 of Which: Female	35595	35018	27029
正高级 Senior	576	576	434
副高级 Sub-senior	11454	11443	10075
中　级 Middle	23080	23032	20242
初　级 Junior	20028	19621	16396
未定职级 No-ranking	18727	18240	7186

(机构)教职工数(总计)
Secondary Vocational Schools (Total)

单位：人
unit：person

Personnel 教　职　工 in Main Campus			校办企业职工 Employees in School-run Factories & Farms	其他附设机构人员 Personnel in Other Subsidiary Units	聘请校外教师 Part-time Teachers
行政人员 Adm. Personnel	教辅人员 Supporting Staff	工勤人员 Workers			
82651	**57700**	**65066**	**5378**	**4410**	**96619**
28775	27485	20557	2321	2200	39789
1236	181	35	8	19	3021
20866	5559	666	50	196	20639
22941	19044	1653	157	826	37918
14604	18489	1855	218	880	16248
23004	14427	60857	4945	2489	18793
14182	11079	12627	521	945	
5428	5397	4803	211	614	
271	46	1		1	
2743	859	82	3	16	
3525	2980	230	11	140	
2606	3480	361	26	451	
5037	3714	11953	481	337	

教职工数(普通中专)
Secondary Vocational Schools (Institutions) (Regular SSSs)

单位：人
unit：person

Personnel 教　职　工 in Main Campus			校办企业职工 Employees in School-run Factories & Farms	其他附设机构人员 Personnel in Others Subsidiary Units	聘请校外教师 Part-time Teachers
行政人员 Adm. Personnel	教辅人员 Supporting Staff	工勤人员 Workers			
46654	**28153**	**35411**	**2786**	**2726**	**42425**
17349	14158	10997	969	1445	19032
640	120	24	8	6	1479
9367	2246	393	44	96	9258
12280	8787	840	61	347	15453
9250	9130	958	91	618	7650
15117	7870	33196	2582	1659	8585
7069	5025	6485	283	670	
2888	2572	2529	116	461	
113	28	1			
1043	279	46	3	8	
1576	1115	99	9	39	
1465	1655	105	11	396	
2872	1948	6234	260	227	

中等职业学校(机构)

Number of Educational Personnel in Secondary

	教职工数 Educational		
	合计 Total	校本部 Educational Personnel	
		小计 Subtotal	专任教师 Full-time Teachers
总　计	**72715**	**71608**	**52021**
其中:女 of Which: Female	33973	33456	26292
正高级 Senior	502	502	375
副高级 Sub-senior	17882	17838	14773
中　级 Middle	28891	28819	23547
初　级 Junior	13962	13931	10743
未定职级 No-ranking	11478	10518	2583
总计中:聘任制 of the Total: Part-time	13428	13363	10149
其中:女 of Which: Female	6216	6183	4890
正高级 Senior	92	92	74
副高级 Sub-senior	2971	2971	2568
中　级 Middle	5163	5163	4345
初　级 Junior	2862	2862	2286
未定职级 No-ranking	2340	2275	876

中等职业学校(机构)

Number of Educational Personnel in Secondary

	教职工数 Educational		
	合计 Total	校本部 Educational Personnel	
		小计 Subtotal	专任教师 Full-time Teachers
总　计	**375370**	**372249**	**301440**
其中:女 of Which: Female	179125	177555	152069
正高级 Senior	1526	1513	1009
副高级 Sub-senior	74326	74266	63049
中　级 Middle	136650	136152	120933
初　级 Junior	101103	100752	89214
未定职级 No-ranking	61765	59566	27235
总计中:聘任制 of the Total: Part-time	78924	78489	63416
其中:女 of Which: Female	37187	36978	31093
正高级 Senior	557	556	405
副高级 Sub-senior	13838	13831	12051
中　级 Middle	27148	27046	24122
初　级 Junior	21423	21360	18978
未定职级 No-ranking	15958	15696	7860

教职工数（成人中专学校）

Vocational Schools (Institutions) (Adult SSSs)

单位：人
unit: person

Personnel 教 职 工 in Main Campus 行政人员 Adm. Personnel	教辅人员 Supporting Staff	工勤人员 Workers	校办企业职工 Employees in School-run Factories & Farms	其他附设机构人员 Personnel in Others Subsidiary Units	聘请校外教师 Part-time Teachers
8102	**6161**	**5324**	**745**	**362**	**22590**
2591	2926	1647	379	138	7543
120	7				787
2349	690	26		44	6168
2610	2520	142		72	12182
1222	1809	157	5	26	2792
1801	1135	4999	740	220	661
1220	1180	814	43	22	
403	575	315	26	7	
18					
271	125	7			
362	444	12			
223	336	17			
346	275	778	43	22	

教职工数（职业高中学校）

Vocational Schools (Institutions) (Vocational High Schools)

单位：人
unit: person

Personnel 教 职 工 in Main Campus 行政人员 Adm. Personnel	教辅人员 Supporting Staff	工勤人员 Workers	校办企业职工 Employees in School-run Factories & Farms	其他附设机构人员 Personnel in Others Subsidiary Units	聘请校外教师 Part-time Teachers
25802	**21902**	**23105**	**1826**	**1295**	**29634**
8218	9706	7562	960	610	12411
451	42	11		13	723
8558	2418	241	6	54	4725
7287	7302	630	94	404	9419
3768	7073	697	117	234	5414
5738	5067	21526	1609	590	9353
5546	4458	5069	190	245	
1995	2030	1860	69	140	
136	15			1	
1364	387	29		7	
1489	1322	113	2	100	
835	1330	217	10	53	
1722	1404	4710	178	84	

中等职业学校(机构)

Number of Educational Personnel in Secondary

	教职工数 Educational		
	合计 Total	校本部 Educational Personnel	
		小计 Subtotal	专任教师 Full-time Teachers
总　计	**16559**	**16511**	**11708**
其中:女 of Which: Female	7543	7523	5860
正高级 Senior	127	127	90
副高级 Sub-senior	3842	3840	3037
中　级 Middle	6277	6272	5032
初　级 Junior	3618	3611	2727
未定职级 No-ranking	2695	2661	822
总计中:聘任制 of the Total: Part-time	3861	3848	2826
其中:女 of Which: Female	1963	1957	1496
正高级 Senior	37	37	30
副高级 Sub-senior	743	742	609
中　级 Middle	1422	1421	1218
初　级 Junior	1022	1015	751
未定职级 No-ranking	637	633	218

教职工数(其他机构)
Vocational Schools (Institutions) (Other Institutions)

单位：人
unit：person

Personnel 教　职　工 in Main Campus			校办企业职工 Employees in School-run Factories & Farms	其他附设机构人员 Personnel in Others Subsidiary Units	聘请校外教师 Part-time Teachers
行政人员 Adm. Personnel	教辅人员 Supporting Staff	工勤人员 Workers			
2093	**1484**	**1226**	**21**	**27**	**1970**
617	695	351	13	7	803
25	12				32
592	205	6		2	488
764	435	41	2	3	864
364	477	43	5	2	392
348	355	1136	14	20	194
347	416	259	5	8	
142	220	99		6	
4	3				
65	68			1	
98	99	6		1	
83	159	22	5	2	
97	87	231		4	

中等职业学校(机构)分科专任教师数(总计)

Number of Full-time Teachers by Field of Education in Secondary Vocational Schools (Institutions) (Total)

单位：人

unit: person

	合计 Total	其中:女 of Which: Female	正高级 Senior	副高级 Sub-Senior	中级 Middle	初级 Junior	未定职级 No-ranking
总　计 Total	**668754**	**339176**	**3383**	**155455**	**268628**	**182596**	**58692**
其中:女 of Which: Female	339176		1295	70033	137307	98828	31713
文化基础课 Common Required Subject	283547	153633	960	74120	118081	71737	18649
专业课 Specialized Subjects	362148	177749	2336	77931	141521	103772	36588
农林牧渔类 Agriculture, Forestry, Animal Husbandry & Fisheries	22813	9547	165	6252	9741	5380	1275
资源环境类 Resources & Environment09	1941	752	14	518	682	507	220
能源与新能源类 Energy Resources & New ER	3125	1255	29	898	1140	761	297
土木水利类 Civil Engineering & Water Conservancy	10838	4624	49	2545	4050	2866	1328
加工制造类 Manufacturing	50679	18367	322	11516	19459	14242	5140
石油化工类 Petroleum & Chemical Industries	2682	1196	14	754	1010	659	245
轻纺食品类 Light, Textile & Food Industries	3989	2177	10	832	1429	1177	541
交通运输类 Communication & Transport	16924	5013	182	2925	6080	5161	2576
信息技术类 Information Technology	64099	30585	242	11544	26986	19443	5884
医药卫生类 Medicine, Pharmacy & Health Care	25035	15437	498	6757	9485	6211	2084
休闲保健类 Recreation Services & Make-up Artists	1233	664	4	171	528	338	192
财经商贸类 Finance, Economics, Commerce & Trade	36194	22696	128	8517	14165	9981	3403
旅游服务类 Tourist Services	16402	10429	58	3038	6289	5081	1936
文化艺术类 Culture & Arts	32749	20041	319	5168	11896	11126	4240
体育与健身 Sports & Body-building	14271	3956	54	2857	5679	4465	1216
教育类 Educational Services	36876	20504	160	9144	14381	9970	3221
司法服务类 Legal Services	1686	747	11	296	587	496	296
公共管理与服务类 Public Administration & Services	5964	2993	33	1177	2291	1736	727
其他 Others	14648	6766	44	3022	5643	4172	1767
实习指导课 Practice Guidance Lessons	23059	7794	87	3404	9026	7087	3455

中等职业学校(机构)分科专任教师数(普通中专学校)

Number of Full-time Teachers by Field of Education in Secondary Vocational Schools (Institutions) (Regular SSSs)

单位：人

unit: person

	合计 Total	其中:女 of Which: Female	正高级 Senior	副高级 Sub-Senior	中级 Middle	初级 Junior	未定职级 No-ranking
总　计 Total	**303585**	**154955**	**1909**	**74596**	**119116**	**79912**	**28052**
其中:女 of Which: Female	154955		739	34699	60895	43329	15293
文化基础课 Common Required Subject	111285	60968	444	30690	45452	26843	7856
专业课 Specialized Subjects	179839	89822	1413	42051	68918	49133	18324
农林牧渔类 Agriculture, Forestry, Animal Husbandry & Fisheries	7909	3185	86	2586	3086	1680	471
资源环境类 Resources & Environment09	1079	450	4	323	388	234	130
能源与新能源类 Energy Resources & New ER	2055	856	23	653	735	428	216
土木水利类 Civil Engineering & Water Conservancy	6309	2868	35	1664	2316	1545	749
加工制造类 Manufacturing	25514	9539	203	6143	9770	6834	2564
石油化工类 Petroleum & Chemical Industries	1632	729	9	509	606	374	134
轻纺食品类 Light, Textile & Food Industries	1841	1065	3	425	671	476	266
交通运输类 Communication & Transport	8355	2470	90	1540	2856	2425	1444
信息技术类 Information Technology	28717	13544	137	5599	12376	8092	2513
医药卫生类 Medicine, Pharmacy & Health Care	19428	12383	370	5634	7084	4719	1621
休闲保健类 Recreation Services & Make-up Artists	413	222	2	37	179	99	96
财经商贸类 Finance, Economics, Commerce & Trade	20144	12682	70	5195	7753	5353	1773
旅游服务类 Tourist Services	6785	4226	23	1339	2606	1968	849
文化艺术类 Culture & Arts	16978	10320	226	2840	6182	5606	2124
体育与健身 Sports & Body-building	8276	2319	45	1912	3250	2465	604
教育类 Educational Services	14862	8330	56	3580	5515	4130	1581
司法服务类 Legal Services	836	395	3	172	299	220	142
公共管理与服务类 Public Administration & Services	2520	1315	13	503	950	771	283
其他 Others	6186	2924	15	1397	2296	1714	764
实习指导课 Practice Guidance Lessons	12461	4165	52	1855	4746	3936	1872

中等职业学校(机构)分科专任教师数(成人中专学校)

Number of Full-time Teachers by Field of Education in Secondary Vocational Schools (Institutions) (Adult SSSs)

单位：人

unit：person

	合计 Total	其中:女 of Which: Female	正高级 Senior	副高级 Sub-Senior	中级 Middle	初级 Junior	未定职级 No-ranking
总　计 Total	**52021**	**26292**	**375**	**14773**	**23547**	**10743**	**2583**
其中:女 of Which: Female	26292		146	6714	12478	5790	1164
文化基础课 Common Required Subject	28508	15201	129	9015	13007	5356	1001
专业课 Specialized Subjects	22145	10547	237	5536	9891	5079	1402
农林牧渔类 Agriculture, Forestry, Animal Husbandry & Fisheries	4430	1833	53	957	2131	1089	200
资源环境类 Resources & Environment09	216	70	1	70	75	56	14
能源与新能源类 Energy Resources & New ER	155	36		38	80	33	4
土木水利类 Civil Engineering & Water Conservancy	582	248	1	124	254	124	79
加工制造类 Manufacturing	1264	429	12	334	450	323	145
石油化工类 Petroleum & Chemical Industries	42	20		5	25	6	6
轻纺食品类 Light, Textile & Food Industries	130	30	2	30	58	32	8
交通运输类 Communication & Transport	738	262	17	121	297	190	113
信息技术类 Information Technology	1913	880	11	335	885	494	188
医药卫生类 Medicine, Pharmacy & Health Care	960	529	41	270	398	222	29
休闲保健类 Recreation Services & Make-up Artists	46	24		9	24	11	2
财经商贸类 Finance, Economics, Commerce & Trade	1210	737	12	294	533	289	82
旅游服务类 Tourist Services	318	186	1	50	117	93	57
文化艺术类 Culture & Arts	850	501	12	140	342	264	92
体育与健身 Sports & Body-building	363	71	1	31	188	82	61
教育类 Educational Services	7114	3906	61	2342	3231	1305	175
司法服务类 Legal Services	87	29	3	14	32	30	8
公共管理与服务类 Public Administration & Services	346	151	4	67	152	87	36
其他 Others	1381	605	5	305	619	349	103
实习指导课 Practice Guidance Lessons	1368	544	9	222	649	308	180

中等职业学校(机构)分科专任教师数(职业高中学校)

Number of Full-time Teachers by Field of Education in Secondary Vocational Schools (Institutions) (Vocational High Schools)

单位：人

unit：person

	合计 Total	其中:女 of Which: Female	正高级 Senior	副高级 Sub-Senior	中级 Middle	初级 Junior	未定职级 No-ranking
总 计 Total	**301440**	**152069**	**1009**	**63049**	**120933**	**89214**	**27235**
其中:女 of Which: Female	152069		363	27291	61469	48217	14729
文化基础课 Common Required Subject	138960	74863	353	33067	57608	38496	9436
专业课 Specialized Subjects	153645	74244	631	28730	59883	47974	16427
农林牧渔类 Agriculture, Forestry, Animal Husbandry & Fisheries	10227	4420	19	2628	4421	2566	593
资源环境类 Resources & Environment09	609	223	9	112	205	207	76
能源与新能源类 Energy Resources & New ER	906	356	6	203	324	296	77
土木水利类 Civil Engineering & Water Conservancy	3815	1458	12	732	1432	1162	477
加工制造类 Manufacturing	23209	8164	101	4888	8967	6846	2407
石油化工类 Petroleum & Chemical Industries	990	441	5	239	371	272	103
轻纺食品类 Light, Textile & Food Industries	1980	1061	4	368	681	660	267
交通运输类 Communication & Transport	7641	2190	73	1226	2858	2487	997
信息技术类 Information Technology	32628	15770	85	5486	13345	10599	3113
医药卫生类 Medicine, Pharmacy & Health Care	4078	2322	80	727	1651	1201	419
休闲保健类 Recreation Services & Make-up Artists	773	418	2	124	325	228	94
财经商贸类 Finance, Economics, Commerce & Trade	14323	8978	42	2945	5639	4198	1499
旅游服务类 Tourist Services	9153	5931	33	1627	3508	2970	1015
文化艺术类 Culture & Arts	14437	8929	80	2111	5167	5136	1943
体育与健身 Sports & Body-building	5316	1475	8	835	2121	1824	528
教育类 Educational Services	13015	7192	32	2566	4877	4147	1393
司法服务类 Legal Services	747	317	4	105	249	246	143
公共管理与服务类 Public Administration & Services	3014	1490	15	589	1142	868	400
其他 Others	6784	3109	21	1219	2600	2061	883
实习指导课 Practice Guidance Lessons	8835	2962	25	1252	3442	2744	1372

中等职业学校(机构)分科专任教师数(其他机构)

Number of Full-time Teachers by Field of Education in Secondary Vocational Schools (Institutions) (Other Institutions)

单位：人

unit：person

	合计 Total	其中:女 of Which: Female	正高级 Senior	副高级 Sub-Senior	中级 Middle	初级 Junior	未定职级 No-ranking
总　计 Total	**11708**	**5860**	**90**	**3037**	**5032**	**2727**	**822**
其中:女 of Which: Female	5860		47	1329	2465	1492	527
文化基础课 Common Required Subject	4794	2601	34	1348	2014	1042	356
专业课 Specialized Subjects	6519	3136	55	1614	2829	1586	435
农林牧渔类 Agriculture, Forestry, Animal Husbandry & Fisheries	247	109	7	81	103	45	11
资源环境类 Resources & Environment09	37	9		13	14	10	
能源与新能源类 Energy Resources & New ER	9	7		4	1	4	
土木水利类 Civil Engineering & Water Conservancy	132	50	1	25	48	35	23
加工制造类 Manufacturing	692	235	6	151	272	239	24
石油化工类 Petroleum & Chemical Industries	18	6		1	8	7	2
轻纺食品类 Light, Textile & Food Industries	38	21	1	9	19	9	
交通运输类 Communication & Transport	190	91	2	38	69	59	22
信息技术类 Information Technology	841	391	9	124	380	258	70
医药卫生类 Medicine, Pharmacy & Health Care	569	203	7	126	352	69	15
休闲保健类 Recreation Services & Make-up Artists	1			1			
财经商贸类 Finance, Economics, Commerce & Trade	517	299	4	83	240	141	49
旅游服务类 Tourist Services	146	86	1	22	58	50	15
文化艺术类 Culture & Arts	484	291	1	77	205	120	81
体育与健身 Sports & Body-building	316	91		79	120	94	23
教育类 Educational Services	1885	1076	11	656	758	388	72
司法服务类 Legal Services	16	6	1	5	7		3
公共管理与服务类 Public Administration & Services	84	37	1	18	47	10	8
其他 Others	297	128	3	101	128	48	17
实习指导课 Practice Guidance Lessons	395	123	1	75	189	99	31

中等职业学校（机构）专任教师、聘请校外教师学历情况（合计）
Number of Full-time and Part-time Teachers by Academic Qualifications in Secondary Vocational Schools（Institutions）（Total）

单位：人
unit：person

	合计 Total	博士研究生 Doctors	硕士研究生 Masters	本科 Normal Courses	专科 Short-cycle Courses	高中阶段及以下 Below High School Graduate
1. 专任教师 Full-time Teacher	**668754**	**915**	**37383**	**549795**	**76891**	**3770**
其中：女 of Which：Female	339176	383	21959	284866	30909	1059
实习指导课教师 Practice Course Teacher	23059	13	614	15676	6173	583
正高级 Senior	3383	140	604	2302	322	15
副高级 Sub-senior	155455	297	10640	135204	9079	235
中　级 Middle	268628	244	14942	223333	28818	1291
初　级 Junior	182596	89	6968	149464	24789	1286
未定职级 No-ranking	58692	145	4229	39492	13883	943
2. 聘请校外教师 Part-time Teacher	**96619**	**559**	**6778**	**68933**	**18693**	**1656**
其中：女 of Which：Female	39789	218	3115	29234	6816	406
实习指导课教师 Practice Course Teacher	9678	109	471	6465	2360	273
外籍教师 Foreign Teachers Among Part-time Teachers	297	4	38	236	15	4
正高级 Senior	3021	198	704	1903	160	56
副高级 Sub-senior	20639	208	2092	16189	1955	195
中　级 Middle	37918	120	2189	27807	7247	555
初　级 Junior	16248	12	826	11230	3970	210
未定职级 No-ranking	18793	21	967	11804	5361	640

中等职业学校(机构)专任教师、聘请校外教师学历情况(普通中专学校)

Number of Full-time and Part-time Teachers by Academic Qualifications in Secondary Vocational Schools (Institutions) (Regular SSSs)

单位：人

unit: person

	合计 Total	博士研究生 Doctors	硕士研究生 Masters	本科 Normal Courses	专科 Short-cycle Courses	高中阶段及以下 Below High School Graduate
1. 专任教师 Full-time Teacher	**303585**	**458**	**24945**	**247088**	**29055**	**2039**
其中:女 of Which: Female	154955	212	14888	127996	11303	556
实习指导课教师 Practice Course Teacher	12461	10	402	8173	3456	420
正高级 Senior	1909	71	328	1291	210	9
副高级 Sub-senior	74596	140	7299	63755	3241	161
中 级 Middle	119116	116	10143	97624	10529	704
初 级 Junior	79912	38	4566	65637	9035	636
未定职级 No-ranking	28052	93	2609	18781	6040	529
2. 聘请校外教师 Part-time Teacher	**42425**	**334**	**3953**	**31567**	**5942**	**629**
其中:女 of Which: Female	19032	141	1927	14412	2342	210
实习指导课教师 Practice Course Teacher	4026	100	274	2603	904	145
外籍教师 Foreign Teachers Among Part-time Teachers	136	2	17	108	8	1
正高级 Senior	1479	87	308	950	86	48
副高级 Sub-senior	9258	133	1096	7182	772	75
中 级 Middle	15453	93	1253	12041	1907	159
初 级 Junior	7650	10	572	5720	1287	61
未定职级 No-ranking	8585	11	724	5674	1890	286

中等职业学校(机构)专任教师、聘请校外教师学历情况(成人中专学校)

Number of Full-time and Part-time Teachers by Academic Qualifications in Secondary Vocational Schools (Institutions) (Adult SSSs)

单位：人

unit: person

	合计 Total	博士研究生 Doctors	硕士研究生 Masters	本科 Normal Courses	专科 Short-cycle Courses	高中阶段及以下 Below High School Graduate
1. 专任教师 Full-time Teacher	**52021**	**79**	**1810**	**39316**	**10328**	**488**
其中:女 of Which: Female	26292	29	975	20230	4898	160
实习指导课教师 Practice Course Teacher	1368	1	53	873	402	39
正高级 Senior	375	18	72	264	18	3
副高级 Sub-senior	14773	19	613	12586	1524	31
中 级 Middle	23547	11	731	17752	4811	242
初 级 Junior	10743	6	248	7329	3013	147
未定职级 No-ranking	2583	25	146	1385	962	65
2. 聘请校外教师 Part-time Teacher	**22590**	**115**	**1077**	**15275**	**5627**	**496**
其中:女 of Which: Female	7543	32	382	5134	1918	77
实习指导课教师 Practice Course Teacher	2101	2	40	1578	431	50
外籍教师 Foreign Teachers Among Part-time Teachers	38		9	28	1	
正高级 Senior	787	69	199	490	29	
副高级 Sub-senior	6168	38	506	4817	714	93
中 级 Middle	12182	8	261	8085	3513	315
初 级 Junior	2792		70	1524	1117	81
未定职级 No-ranking	661		41	359	254	7

中等职业学校(机构)专任教师、聘请校外教师学历情况(职业高中学校)

Number of Full-time and Part-time Teachers by Academic Qualifications in Secondary Vocational Schools (Institutions) (Vocational High Schools)

单位：人

unit：person

	合计 Total	博士研究生 Doctors	硕士研究生 Masters	本科 Normal Courses	专科 Short-cycle Courses	高中阶段及以下 Below High School Graduate
1. 专任教师 Full-time Teacher	**301440**	**346**	**9411**	**254268**	**36203**	**1212**
其中：女 of Which：Female	152069	132	5411	132047	14146	333
实习指导课教师 Practice Course Teacher	8835	2	139	6333	2238	123
正高级 Senior	1009	45	182	689	90	3
副高级 Sub-senior	63049	117	2364	56357	4174	37
中　级 Middle	120933	114	3545	104024	12916	334
初　级 Junior	89214	45	1960	74384	12332	493
未定职级 No-ranking	27235	25	1360	18814	6691	345
2. 聘请校外教师 Part-time Teacher	**29634**	**95**	**1434**	**20768**	**6830**	**507**
其中：女 of Which：Female	12411	42	667	9168	2428	106
实习指导课教师 Practice Course Teacher	3441	7	144	2211	1004	75
外籍教师 Foreign Teachers Among Part-time Teachers	121	2	10	100	6	3
正高级 Senior	723	40	189	445	42	7
副高级 Sub-senior	4725	29	407	3810	455	24
中　级 Middle	9419	14	521	7096	1719	69
初　级 Junior	5414	2	134	3749	1467	62
未定职级 No-ranking	9353	10	183	5668	3147	345

中等职业学校(机构)专任教师、聘请校外教师学历情况(其他机构)

Number of Full-time and Part-time Teachers by Academic Qualifications in Secondary Vocational Schools (Institutions) (Other Institutions)

单位：人
unit：person

	合计 Total	博士研究生 Doctors	硕士研究生 Masters	本科 Normal Courses	专科 Short-cycle Courses	高中阶段及以下 Below High School Graduate
1. 专任教师 Full-time Teacher	**11708**	**32**	**1217**	**9123**	**1305**	**31**
其中:女 of Which: Female	5860	10	685	4593	562	10
实习指导课教师 Practice Course Teacher	395		20	297	77	1
正高级 Senior	90	6	22	58	4	
副高级 Sub-senior	3037	21	364	2506	140	6
中　级 Middle	5032	3	523	3933	562	11
初　级 Junior	2727		194	2114	409	10
未定职级 No-ranking	822	2	114	512	190	4
2. 聘请校外教师 Part-time Teacher	**1970**	**15**	**314**	**1323**	**294**	**24**
其中:女 of Which: Female	803	3	139	520	128	13
实习指导课教师 Practice Course Teacher	110		13	73	21	3
外籍教师 Foreign Teachers Among Part-time Teachers	2		2			
正高级 Senior	32	2	8	18	3	1
副高级 Sub-senior	488	8	83	380	14	3
中　级 Middle	864	5	154	585	108	12
初　级 Junior	392		50	237	99	6
未定职级 No-ranking	194		19	103	70	2

中等职业学校(机构)

Number of Full-time Teachers by Age in

	合计 Total	29 岁及以下 29 and Under	30－34 岁 30 to 34	35－39 岁 35 to 39
总 计 Total	**668754**	**130743**	**132810**	**123434**
其中:女 of Which: Female	339176	77743	75847	65911
正高级 Senior	3383	12	21	271
副高级 Sub-senior	155455	60	2150	17570
中 级 Middle	268628	13292	60589	75639
初 级 Junior	182596	73933	61321	26846
未定职级 No-ranking	58692	43446	8729	3108
普通中专学校 Regular SSSs	303585	63863	61165	51870
其中:女 of Which: Female	154955	38352	34923	27286
正高级 Senior	1909	3	11	144
副高级 Sub-senior	74596	37	1072	8486
中 级 Middle	119116	7082	30587	31726
初 级 Junior	79912	35959	25349	10087
未定职级 No-ranking	28052	20782	4146	1427
成人中专学校 Adult SSSs	52021	5845	7628	9397
其中:女 of Which: Female	26292	3219	4213	5368
正高级 Senior	375		1	44
副高级 Sub-senior	14773	14	192	1148
中 级 Middle	23547	968	3545	5936
初 级 Junior	10743	3106	3459	2074
未定职级 No-ranking	2583	1757	431	195
职业高中学校 Vocational High Schools	301440	58893	61708	60182
其中:女 of Which: Female	152069	34849	35325	32195
正高级 Senior	1009	9	9	81
副高级 Sub-senior	63049	9	818	7620
中 级 Middle	120933	4920	25301	36641
初 级 Junior	89214	33644	31589	14382
未定职级 No-ranking	27235	20311	3991	1458
其他机构 Other Institutions	11708	2142	2309	1985
其中:女 of Which: Female	5860	1323	1386	1062
正高级 Senior	90			2
副高级 Sub-senior	3037		68	316
中 级 Middle	5032	322	1156	1336
初 级 Junior	2727	1224	924	303
未定职级 No-ranking	822	596	161	28

专任教师分年龄情况

Secondary Vocational Schools (Institutions)

单位：人

unit: person

40－44 岁 40 to 44	45－49 岁 45 to 49	50－54 岁 50 to 54	55－59 岁 55 to 59	60 岁及以上 60 and over
117057	**96235**	**46355**	**20877**	**1243**
58140	42382	17906	989	258
528	778	897	594	282
42883	51822	28025	12365	580
60129	35648	15911	7133	287
11759	6826	1268	612	31
1758	1161	254	173	63
50918	43591	21824	9697	657
25122	19727	8882	521	142
259	448	520	352	172
20323	24920	13583	5866	309
24714	14940	6927	3030	110
4801	2730	640	326	20
821	553	154	123	46
10363	10166	5905	2645	72
5832	5092	2479	77	12
69	70	119	55	17
3227	5127	3454	1584	27
5864	4094	2171	949	20
1099	801	148	53	3
104	74	13	4	5
53624	40648	17775	8102	508
26145	16848	6229	374	104
181	222	236	180	91
18419	20836	10458	4648	241
28512	15864	6536	3003	156
5695	3207	461	228	8
817	519	84	43	12
2152	1830	851	433	6
1041	715	316	17	
19	38	22	7	2
914	939	530	267	3
1039	750	277	151	1
164	88	19	5	
16	15	3	3	

中等职业学校(机构)专任教师、

Number of Full-time and Part-time Teachers

	本学年授课专任教师 Full-time Teacher by Teaching Content			
	合计 Total	文化基础课 Common Required Subject	专业课、实习指导课 Special Subject and Practice Course	
			小计 Subtotal	其中:双师型 of Which: Double-teacher Type
总　计 Total	**662385**	**280941**	**381444**	**175955**
其中:女 of Which: Female	336490	152580	183910	77605
正高级 Senior	3341	951	2390	1123
副高级 Sub-senior	153794	73352	80442	45253
中　级 Middle	266138	117057	149081	79262
初　级 Junior	180849	71062	109787	43401
未定职级 No-ranking	58263	18519	39744	6916
普通中专学校 Regular SSSs	300620	110075	190545	91989
其中:女 of Which: Female	153787	60504	93283	41640
正高级 Senior	1883	438	1445	738
副高级 Sub-senior	73828	30319	43509	26106
中　级 Middle	118039	45008	73031	41396
初　级 Junior	79093	26545	52548	20324
未定职级 No-ranking	27777	7765	20012	3425
成人中专学校 Adult SSSs	51128	28275	22853	5837
其中:女 of Which: Female	25847	15098	10749	2234
正高级 Senior	370	128	242	70
副高级 Sub-senior	14522	8944	5578	1483
中　级 Middle	23147	12894	10253	2925
初　级 Junior	10534	5318	5216	1146
未定职级 No-ranking	2555	991	1564	213
职业高中学校 Vocational High Schools	299024	137800	161224	75833
其中:女 of Which: Female	151031	74377	76654	32873
正高级 Senior	1003	351	652	287
副高级 Sub-senior	62433	32744	29689	17098
中　级 Middle	119958	57141	62817	33793
初　级 Junior	88504	38157	50347	21482
未定职级 No-ranking	27126	9407	17719	3173
其他机构 Other Institutions	11613	4791	6822	2296
其中:女 of Which: Female	5825	2601	3224	858
正高级 Senior	85	34	51	28
副高级 Sub-senior	3011	1345	1666	566
中　级 Middle	4994	2014	2980	1148
初　级 Junior	2718	1042	1676	449
未定职级 No-ranking	805	356	449	105

聘请校外教师岗位分类情况

by Teaching Course in Secondary Vocational Schools (Institutions)

单位：人

unit: person

本学年授课聘请校外教师 Part-time Teacher by Teaching Content				本学年授课专任教师 Full-time Teacher by Non - teaching			
合计 Total	文化基础课 Common Required Subject	专业课、实习指导课 Special Subject and Practice Course		合计 Total	进修 In-service	病休 Sick-Leave	其他 Others
		小计 Subtotal	其中：双师型 of Which: Double-teacher Type				
96619	**23015**	**73604**	**24748**	**6369**	**860**	**757**	**4752**
39789	11578	28211	8720	2686	440	351	1895
3021	526	2495	794	42		5	37
20639	4345	16294	7186	1661	170	162	1329
37918	8512	29406	11287	2490	362	305	1823
16248	4655	11593	3267	1747	230	256	1261
18793	4977	13816	2214	429	98	29	302
42425	10072	32353	11046	2965	406	317	2242
19032	5298	13734	4298	1168	212	160	796
1479	176	1303	410	26		4	22
9258	1772	7486	3413	768	55	79	634
15453	3632	11821	4619	1077	134	125	818
7650	2117	5533	1580	819	147	95	577
8585	2375	6210	1024	275	70	14	191
22590	5298	17292	5811	893	112	19	762
7543	2333	5210	1825	445	66	6	373
787	141	646	161	5			5
6168	1428	4740	1801	251	37	5	209
12182	2612	9570	3228	400	61	8	331
2792	877	1915	581	209	9	6	194
661	240	421	40	28	5		23
29634	6977	22657	7518	2416	324	405	1687
12411	3623	8788	2504	1038	155	179	704
723	195	528	214	6			6
4725	926	3799	1878	616	73	74	469
9419	2033	7386	3213	975	157	165	653
5414	1531	3883	1074	710	72	153	485
9353	2292	7061	1139	109	22	13	74
1970	668	1302	373	95	18	16	61
803	324	479	93	35	7	6	22
32	14	18	9	5		1	4
488	219	269	94	26	5	4	17
864	235	629	227	38	10	7	21
392	130	262	32	9	2	2	5
194	70	124	11	17	1	2	14

中等职业学校(机构)

Changes of Full – time Teachers in Secondary

	上学年初报表专任教师数 Number of Full-time Teachers at Beginning of Previous Academic Year	增加专任 Factors of				
		合计 Total	录用毕业生 New Recruits from Current Year Graduates			外单位 Teachers Recruited
			小计 Subtotal	研究生 Completing Doc, & Mas. Deg. Prog.	本科生 Completing 1st Degree Courses	小计 Subtotal
总　计 Total	**684067**	**58278**	**16985**	**2188**	**13114**	**24264**
其中:女 of Which: Female	341750	30131	10188	1567	7960	12269
普通中专学校 Regular SSSs	308168	24123	7925	1393	5812	8684
其中:女 of Which: Female	154891	12834	4870	990	3548	4457
成人中专学校 Adult SSSs	54669	4644	523	77	372	2688
其中:女 of Which: Female	27088	2356	283	53	200	1430
职业高中学校 Vocational High Schools	307717	28022	8343	657	6806	12146
其中:女 of Which: Female	153309	14121	4898	476	4128	6010
其他机构 Other Institutions	13513	1489	194	61	124	746
其中:女 of Which: Female	6462	820	137	48	84	372

专任教师变动情况

Vocational Schools (Institutions)

单位：人
unit: person

教师数 Increase					减少专任教师数 Factors of Decrease				本学年初报表专任教师数 Number of Full-time Teachers at Beginning of Current Academic Year
教师调入 from Other Units	非教师调入 Non-teaching Personnel Changed into Teachers								
其中：中职学校调入 of Which: from Other SVSs	小计 Subtotal	其中：本校调整 of Which: with Change of Status in Their Own Institutions	其他 Others	合计 Total	自然减员 Retired from Their Posts during Previcus Academic Year	调离教师岗位 Transferred from Teaching to Non-teaching Posts	其他 Others		
8801	**7658**	**5496**	**9371**	**73591**	**14264**	**19635**	**39692**	**668754**	
4391	3362	2288	4312	32705	6410	8152	18143	339176	
4317	2924	2012	4590	28706	6205	7316	15185	303585	
2134	1402	921	2105	12770	2758	2928	7084	154955	
453	535	371	898	7292	2274	1421	3597	52021	
256	226	144	417	3152	986	655	1511	26292	
3860	3996	2955	3537	34299	5524	10168	18607	301440	
1922	1630	1152	1583	15361	2558	4333	8470	152069	
171	203	158	346	3294	261	730	2303	11708	
79	104	71	207	1422	108	236	1078	5860	

中等职业学校

Condition of Fixed Assets and Teaching Resources in

	学校占地面积(平方米) Area of School sites (m^2)			图书(册) Books (volume)	
	合计 Total	其中:绿化用地面积 of Which: Green Areas	其中:运动场地面积 of Which: Sports Areas	合计 Total	当年新增 New Added in Current Year
总　计 Total					
学校产权 Owned by SVSs	498656332	116378052	77377424	350295948	18619046
非学校产权中独立使用 Not Owned by SVSs	42630074	7868279	6947480	11545367	950646
普通中专学校 Regular SSSs					
学校产权 Owned by SSSs	251185698	63039786	37431439	189341020	8530154
非学校产权中独立使用 Not Owned by SSSs	20827035	3980307	3233645	6009170	601512
成人中专学校 Adult SSSs					
学校产权 Owned by Adult SSSs	25636397	4982588	3490715	23149171	1224456
非学校产权中独立使用 Not Owned by Adult SSSs	2598026	412206	496670	1493118	64223
职业高中学校 Vocational High Schools					
学校产权 Owned by VHSs	210842926	45552188	34807846	130568470	8310044
非学校产权中独立使用 Not Owned by VHSs	18304246	3290735	3074867	3740410	276861
其他机构 Other Institutions					
学校产权 Owned by SVSs	10991311	2803490	1647424	7237287	554392
非学校产权中独立使用 Not Owned by SVSs	900767	185031	142298	302669	8050

(机构)资产情况
Secondary Vocational Schools (Institutions)

计算机数(台) No. of Computers			教室中:普通教室(间) of Which: General Classroom				
合计 Total	其中:教学用计算机 of Which: No. of Computers Used for Instruction — 小计 Subtotal	其中:教学用计算机 — 其中:平板电脑 of Which: Tablet PC	合计 Total	其中:网络多媒体教室 of Which: Network Multimedia Classroom	合计 Total	其中:教学、科研仪器设备资产值 of Which: Teaching Equipment & Instruments — 小计 Subtotal	当年新增 New Added in Current Year
2990717	2497229	110663	410934	145692	26573194. 20	5558781. 52	720711. 99
115298	93243	4312	44163	14034	1535418. 97	188690. 54	28118. 91
1564040	1309610	58607	200809	78598	14506467. 98	3077153. 97	371827. 72
49570	38649	2248	18619	5886	817744. 99	103231. 71	13228. 99
170004	132938	4486	26304	9897	1080686. 45	200169. 69	21523. 23
14848	12414	509	5451	2877	95461. 80	13309. 31	2321. 58
1202739	1010387	44667	177275	54235	10311025. 58	2193033. 70	320800. 18
47167	39479	1525	19340	4987	555829. 74	65956. 99	12466. 54
53934	44294	2903	6546	2962	675014. 19	88424. 16	6560. 86
3713	2701	30	753	284	66382. 44	6192. 53	101. 80

中等职业学校(机构)教职工其他情况
Supplementary Information on Educational Personnel in Secondary Vocational Schools (Institutions)

单位:人
unit: person

	共产党员 Member of C. P. A	共青团员 Member of C. Y. L	民主党派 Member of Non-Communist Part	华侨 Overseas Chinese	港澳台 From H. K, Macao and Taiwan	少数民族 Minorities
总计 Total						
教职工 Educational Personnel	303033	59081	11544	85	44	48329
其中:女 of Which: Female	121767	32067	5962	37	22	23120
专任教师 Full-time Teachers	219422	46482	9494	49	20	36064
其中:女 of Which: Female	95933	26250	5078	23	13	18089
普通中专学校 Regular SSSs						
教职工 Educational Personnel	155618	29479	6849	63	31	25523
其中:女 of Which: Female	65472	16089	3544	26	13	12021
专任教师 Full-time Teachers	107982	22642	5734	34	12	18487
其中:女 of Which: Female	49916	12847	3031	13	7	9168
成人中专学校 Adult SSSs						
教职工 Educational Personnel	27937	2889	610		4	3973
其中:女 of Which: Female	10478	1418	309		1	1891
专任教师 Full-time Teachers	19823	2101	461		1	3002
其中:女 of Which: Female	8156	1050	249			1500
职业高中学校 Vocational High Schools						
教职工 Educational Personnel	112626	25570	3771	20	9	18447
其中:女 of Which: Female	43227	13953	1935	10	8	9006
专任教师 Full-time Teachers	86802	20851	3053	14	7	14310
其中:女 of Which: Female	35848	11853	1649	9	6	7272
其他机构 Other Institutions						
教职工 Educational Personnel	6852	1143	314	2		386
其中:女 of Which: Female	2590	607	174	1		202
专任教师 Full-time Teachers	4815	888	246	1		265
其中:女 of Which: Female	2013	500	149	1		149

中等职业学校(机构)校舍情况
Condition of School Buildings in Secondary Vocational Schools (Institutions) (Total)

单位：平方米
unit: m^2

	学校产权建筑面积 Floor Area of School Building Owned by SVSs				正在施工校舍建筑面积 Floor Area Under Construction	独立使用非学校产权校舍建筑面积 Floor Area of School Building Not Owned by SVSs
	合计 Total	其中：危房 of Which: Dilapidated Buildings	其中：当年新增 of Which: New Added in Current Year	其中：被外单位借用 of Which: Floor Space Hired by Other Schools or Units		
总　计 Total	**214011336**	**2236475**	**8377962**	**564126**	**12097881**	**19670540**
一、教学及辅助用房 Buildings for Instruction and Ancillary Uses	102762636	913510	4470660	251274	6762059	9684456
教室 Classroom	50822858	575090	1721842	157189	2668398	5017747
图书馆 Library	7018349	43883	283424	5098	761150	691646
实验室、实习场所 Lab. and Practice Facilities	36032845	232416	2075857	79346	2756843	2852286
体育馆 Gymnasium	5824601	21913	275100	7989	475612	737239
会堂 Hall	3063983	40208	114437	1652	100056	385538
二、行政办公用房 Administrative	15008785	181563	457715	53940	765751	1241783
三、生活用房 Residential Buildings	79542191	958405	3066326	231042	3864599	8193560
学生宿舍(公寓) Students' Dormitories	52900207	624829	2150672	191010	2738914	5624381
学生食堂 Students' Dining Halls	12926542	100504	558770	20259	650737	1148338
教工宿舍(公寓) Apartments for Single	5136465	113542	196984	5355	335316	657456
教工食堂 Dining Halls for Teachers, Staff and Workers	1212423	6688	40776	258	12638	115017
生活福利及附属用房 Residential, Welfare and Anxiliary Buildings	7366554	112842	119124	14160	126994	648368
四、教工住宅 Residential Quarters for Teachers & Workers	12305761	146867	93606	12286	390797	
五、其他用房 Other	4391963	36130	289655	15584	314675	550591

中等职业学校(机构)校舍情况(普通中专学校)

Condition of School Buildings in Secondary Vocational Schools (Institutions)(Regular SSSs)

单位:平方米

unit: m^2

	学校产权建筑面积 Floor Area of School Building Owned by Regular SSSs				正在施工校舍建筑面积 Floor Area Under Construction	独立使用非学校产权校舍建筑面积 Floor Area of School Building Not Owned by Regular SSSs
	合计 Total	其中:危房 of Which: Dilapidated Buildings	其中:当年新增 of Which: New Added in Current Year	其中:被外单位借用 of Which: Floor Space Hired by Other Schools or Units		
总　计 Total	**114488231**	**1194515**	**3975913**	**291165**	**7790520**	**9783560**
一、教学及辅助用房 Buildings for Instruction and Ancillary Uses	54345589	474209	2090076	129815	4086429	4802050
教室 Classroom	25774703	269775	769679	68747	1754716	2308459
图书馆 Library	4038880	27625	165047	2459	504286	322364
实验室、实习场所 Lab. and Practice Facilities	19327578	136084	973043	55856	1536913	1519190
体育馆 Gymnasium	3679501	16925	129395	1880	222233	466970
会堂 Hall	1524927	23800	52912	873	68281	185067
二、行政办公用房 Administrative	7277096	94062	237913	8030	533803	531747
三、生活用房 Residential Buildings	42709207	520515	1488784	130059	2625708	4209783
学生宿舍(公寓) Students' Dormitories	29264844	360886	1113425	107876	1837046	2981950
学生食堂 Students' Dining Halls	6719085	57963	234462	13394	443518	546401
教工宿舍(公寓) Apartments for Single	2318839	45457	77641	1933	226484	331814
教工食堂 Dining Halls for Teachers, Staff and Workers	621980	2449	26196	119	10172	58592
生活福利及附属用房 Residential, Welfare and Anxiliary Buildings	3784459	53760	37060	6737	108488	291026
四、教工住宅 Residential Quarters for Teachers & Workers	8091611	81116	32469	8610	275200	
五、其他用房 Other	2064728	24613	126671	14651	269380	239980

中等职业学校(机构)校舍情况(成人中专学校)

Condition of School Buildings in Secondary Vocational Schools (Institutions) (Adult SSSs)

单位:平方米

unit: m^2

	学校产权建筑面积 Floor Area of School Building Owned by Adult SSSs				正在施工校舍建筑面积 Floor Area Under Construction	独立使用非学校产权校舍建筑面积 Floor Area of School Building Not Owned by Adult SSSs
	合计 Total	其中:危房 of Which: Dilapidated Buildings	其中:当年新增 of Which: New Added in Current Year	其中:被外单位借用 of Which: Floor Space Hired by Other Schools or Units		
总　计 Total	**10243625**	**167923**	**163317**	**62099**	**212791**	**1543844**
一、教学及辅助用房 Buildings for Instruction and Ancillary Uses	4546033	70102	95487	30089	130518	748551
教室 Classroom	2880459	59373	45675	27319	65451	419184
图书馆 Library	301779	1441	7345	1090	27288	80688
实验室、实习场所 Lab. and Practice Facilities	957502	6121	31558	1630	33341	166597
体育馆 Gymnasium	172601		4080	50	3473	43203
会堂 Hall	233692	3167	6829		965	38879
二、行政办公用房 Administrative	1309415	22853	8335	11433	15657	155891
三、生活用房 Residential Buildings	3582192	63797	41569	19649	57648	601494
学生宿舍(公寓) Students' Dormitories	2131049	30710	21505	16073	47774	424768
学生食堂 Students' Dining Halls	538006	5052	10042	2305	7080	97538
教工宿舍(公寓) Apartments for Single	257287	12939	2010	80	1661	34937
教工食堂 Dining Halls for Teachers, Staff and Workers	91825	1024	2333		1133	8944
生活福利及附属用房 Residential, Welfare and Anxiliary Buildings	564025	14072	5679	1191		35307
四、教工住宅 Residential Quarters for Teachers & Workers	600854	9596	6520	778	1000	
五、其他用房 Other	205131	1575	11406	150	7968	37908

中等职业学校(机构)校舍情况(职业高中学校)

Condition of School Buildings in Secondary Vocational Schools (Institutions) (Vocational High Schools)

单位：平方米
unit：m^2

	学校产权建筑面积 Floor Area of School Building Owned by VHSs				正在施工校舍建筑面积 Floor Area Under Construction	独立使用非学校产权校舍建筑面积 Floor Area of School Building Not Owned by VHSs
	合计 Total	其中：危房 of Which：Dilapidated Buildings	其中：当年新增 of Which：New Added in Current Year	其中：被外单位借用 of Which：Floor Space Hired by Other Schools or Units		
总　计 Total	**84535391**	**865157**	**4143449**	**208411**	**3766522**	**7851516**
一、教学及辅助用房 Buildings for Instruction and Ancillary Uses	41793656	366512	2222241	90264	2413731	3917699
教室 Classroom	21037853	243423	879203	60017	791960	2139380
图书馆 Library	2499284	14767	100964	1549	210472	271368
实验室、实习场所 Lab. and Practice Facilities	15239816	90093	1067420	21860	1153987	1135754
体育馆 Gymnasium	1784241	4988	120336	6059	228906	218456
会堂 Hall	1232462	13241	54318	779	28406	152741
二、行政办公用房 Administrative	6027746	63333	206887	34477	209001	470255
三、生活用房 Residential Buildings	31549966	369226	1512422	79989	1085661	3207557
学生宿舍(公寓) Students' Dormitories	20395435	229503	998178	67061	777987	2112488
学生食堂 Students' Dining Halls	5349214	37152	308909	4560	183327	472635
教工宿舍(公寓) Apartments for Single	2472218	54346	117109	2502	107171	276438
教工食堂 Dining Halls for Teachers, Staff and Workers	463150	3215	11941	139	1333	44758
生活福利及附属用房 Residential, Welfare and Anxiliary Buildings	2869949	45010	76285	5727	15843	301238
四、教工住宅 Residential Quarters for Teachers & Workers	3192196	56144	54613	2898	23327	
五、其他用房 Other	1971827	9942	147286	783	34802	256005

中等职业学校(机构)校舍情况(其他机构)

Condition of School Buildings in Secondary Vocational Schools (Institutions)(Other Institutions)

单位：平方米

unit：m²

	学校产权建筑面积 Floor Area of School Building Owned by SVSs				正在施工校舍建筑面积 Floor Area Under Construction	独立使用非学校产权校舍建筑面积 Floor Area of School Building Not Owned by SVSs
	合计 Total	其中：危房 of Which：Dilapidated Buildings	其中：当年新增 of Which：New Added in Current Year	其中：被外单位借用 of Which：Floor Space Hired by Other Schools or Units		
总　计 Total	**4744089**	**8880**	**95283**	**2451**	**328048**	**491620**
一、教学及辅助用房 Buildings for Instruction and Ancillary Uses	2077358	2687	62856	1106	131381	216156
教室 Classroom	1129843	2519	27285	1106	56271	150724
图书馆 Library	178406	50	10068		19104	17226
实验室、实习场所 Lab. and Practice Facilities	507949	118	3836		32602	30745
体育馆 Gymnasium	188258		21289		21000	8610
会堂 Hall	72902		378		2404	8851
二、行政办公用房 Administrative	394528	1315	4580		7290	83890
三、生活用房 Residential Buildings	1700826	4867	23551	1345	95582	174726
学生宿舍(公寓) Students' Dormitories	1108879	3730	17564		76107	105175
学生食堂 Students' Dining Halls	320237	337	5357		16812	31764
教工宿舍(公寓) Apartments for Single	88121	800	224	840		14267
教工食堂 Dining Halls for Teachers, Staff and Workers	35468		306			2723
生活福利及附属用房 Residential, Welfare and Anxiliary Buildings	148121		100	505	2663	20797
四、教工住宅 Residential Quarters for Teachers & Workers	421100	11	4		91270	
五、其他用房 Other	150277		4292		2525	16848

职业技术培训
Basic Statistics of Vocational-Technical

	学校数（所）Schools	教学班（点）（个）External Teaching Sites (class)	结业生数 合计 Total
总　计 Total	**112293**	**536037**	**47155968**
职工技术培训学校（机构）Vocational Technical Training Schools	2982	36513	2945587
教育部门办 Run by Ed. Dept.	1172	16716	1424911
其他部门办 Run by Non-Ed. Dept.	1145	14465	1246713
民办 Non-government	665	5332	273963
农村成人文化技术培训学校（机构）Technical Training Schools for Peasants	89014	265130	34160351
教育部门办 Run by Ed. Dept.	85245	246526	31890903
其中：县办 of Which：County-run	2349	23296	3094009
乡办 Township-run	14306	95125	15769477
村办 Village-run	68590	128105	13027417
其他部门办 Run by Non-Ed. Dept.	2721	8933	2001394
民办 Non-government	1048	9671	268054
其他培训机构（含社会培训机构）Others	20297	234394	10050030
教育部门办 Run by Ed. Dept.	776	9249	1116926
其他部门办 Run by Non-Ed. Dept.	1130	12846	1527813
民办 Non-government	18391	212299	7405291
总计中：少数民族 of the Total：Minority			3577441
培训形式：资格证书培训			6225492
Mode of Training：for Certificates of Vocational Qualifications			
岗位证书培训 for Certificates of Job-related Qualifications			10733536
按产业结构分：第一产业类培训 by Industry：Training for First Industry			19442773
第二产业类培训 Training for Second Industry			7317079
第三产业类培训 Training for Third Industry			20396116
按培训时间分：by Lengh of Training：			
一个月以内 1 Month			29686597
一个月至三个月以内 1 Month to 3 Months			7272658
三个月至半年以内 3 Months to 6 Months			4392090
半年至一年以内 6 Months to 1 Year			4847142
一年及以上 1 Year and Over			957481

机构基本情况
Training Institutions

单位：人次
unit：person

Graduates	注册学生数 Enrolment		教职工数 Educational Personnel		聘请校外教师 Part-time Teachers
其中:女 of Which: Female	合计 Total	其中:女 of Which: Female	合计 Total	其中:专任教师 of Which: Full-time Teacher	
22563938	**45159599**	**21759819**	**482211**	**274311**	**272832**
1244481	3055051	1315952	62083	45591	17848
712736	1449522	734007	39387	31017	9183
397693	1301886	416886	12464	7942	4968
134052	303643	165059	10232	6632	3697
16402966	30430375	14535051	167308	90112	159048
15259442	28693051	13632347	156599	84250	149314
1454312	3006223	1416835	20098	14885	15452
7354948	14119215	6523421	58825	34405	60977
6450182	11567613	5692091	77676	34960	72885
1008754	1453188	759392	6083	3142	8200
134770	284136	143312	4626	2720	1534
4916491	11674173	5908816	252820	138608	95936
577116	1185610	620562	12943	8731	5760
830841	1640738	862339	25198	9595	14137
3508534	8847825	4425915	214679	120282	76039
1620205	3577700	1645028	11295	4516	7356
2712592	6270678	2810590			
4869871	10487492	4734469			
9197418	18037123	8478907			
3247600	6685435	2905170			
10118920	20437041	10375742			
14127062	26258458	12366615			
3504302	7838021	4018771			
2188497	4757267	2278986			
2283374	4800622	2329667			
460703	1505231	765780			

职业技术培训机构资产情况

Condition of Fixed Assets and Teaching Resources in Vocational Technical Training Institutions

	合 计 Total	职工技术培训学校(机构) Vocational Technical Training Schools (Institutions)	农村成人文化技术培训学校(机构) Technical Training Schools for Peasants	其他培训机构(含社会培训机构) Others
占地面积(平方米) Area of School Sites (m^2)	116835277	27737561	57039966	32057750
教学行政用房建筑面积(平方米) Administrative (m^2)	44814552	9253820	17232948	18327784
图书(册) Books (volume)	154785708	20604194	43168190	91013324
计算机数(台) No. of Computers	1020419	171570	509589	339260
其中:教学用计算机 No. of Computers Used for Instruction	649513	139570	220399	289544
其中:平板电脑 of Which: Tablet PC	54152	5609	12857	35686
教室(间) Classroom (room)	511948	54586	195829	261533
其中:网络多媒体教室 of Which: Network Multimedia Classroom	283657	17005	78436	188216
固定资产总值(万元) Fixed Assets (in 10,000 yuan)	23873492.53	2789902.91	12615546.01	8468043.61
其中:教学、实习仪器设备资产值 of Which: Teaching Equipment &Instruments	7044833.46	815283.82	2742193.23	3487356.41

（二）初中阶段教育
Junior Secondary Education

初中阶段校数、班数

Number of Schools, Classes of Junior Secondary Education

	学校数(所) Schools				班数(个) Classes				
	合计 Total	初级中学 Regular Junior Secondary Schools	九年一贯制学校 9-year Schools	职业初中 Vocational Junior Secondary Schools	合计 Total	一年级 Grade 1	二年级 Grade 2	三年级 Grade 3	四年级 Grade 4
总　计 Total	**52804**	**38747**	**14017**	**40**	**909570**	**305192**	**300677**	**293544**	**10157**
教育部门 Run by Ed. Dept.	47693	37181	10473	39	811117	270727	268125	263079	9186
其他部门 Run by Non-ed. Dept.	552	187	364	1	6726	2186	2160	2151	229
地方企业办 Run by Local Enterprises	24	5	19		385	133	126	125	1
民办 Non-government	4535	1374	3161		91342	32146	30266	28189	741
城区 Urban Area	11124	7533	3587	4	293969	98836	96376	92716	6041
教育部门 Run by Ed. Dept.	8843	6860	1980	3	242853	80859	79483	77193	5318
其他部门 Run by Non-ed. Dept.	144	71	72	1	2098	687	689	685	37
地方企业办 Run by Local Enterprises	11	2	9		179	66	55	57	1
民办 Non-government	2126	600	1526		48839	17224	16149	14781	685
其中:城乡结合区 of Which: Urban-rural Transitional Area	2390	1466	923	1	47908	16519	15809	14913	667
教育部门 Run by Ed. Dept.	1760	1349	410	1	36439	12273	11980	11559	627
其他部门 Run by Non-ed. Dept.	24	14	10		241	74	80	78	9
地方企业办 Run by Local Enterprises	1		1		22	14	4	4	
民办 Non-government	605	103	502		11206	4158	3745	3272	31
镇区 Counties & Towns Area	23195	18437	4737	21	437638	146930	145089	142709	2910
教育部门 Run by Ed. Dept.	21150	17784	3345	21	398281	133274	132081	130240	2686
其他部门 Run by Non-ed. Dept.	342	96	246		4072	1315	1286	1279	192
地方企业办 Run by Local Enterprises	10	2	8		199	65	68	66	
民办 Non-government	1693	555	1138		35086	12276	11654	11124	32
其中:镇乡结合区 of Which: County-town Transitional Area	6047	4777	1264	6	110648	37677	36719	35565	687
教育部门 Run by Ed. Dept.	5387	4577	804	6	97664	33033	32402	31559	670
其他部门 Run by Non-ed. Dept.	16	8	8		160	70	45	43	2
地方企业办 Run by Local Enterprises					12	4	4	4	
民办 Non-government	644	192	452		12812	4570	4268	3959	15
乡村 Rural Area	18485	12777	5693	15	177963	59426	59212	58119	1206
教育部门 Run by Ed. Dept.	17700	12537	5148	15	169983	56594	56561	55646	1182
其他部门 Run by Non-ed. Dept.	66	20	46		556	184	185	187	
地方企业办 Run by Local Enterprises	3	1	2		7	2	3	2	
民办 Non-government	716	219	497		7417	2646	2463	2284	24
总计中:四年制 of the Total:4-year					41642	10556	10594	10341	10151
其他学校附设班 Classes Attached to Others Schools					5535	1839	1849	1802	45
独立设置少数民族学校 Inde. Sec. Schools for Minorities	1617	1075	538	4	28732	9961	9460	9266	45

初中班额情况

Size of Junior Secondary Schools Education Classes

单位:个

unit:class

	合计 Total	一年级 Grade 1	二年级 Grade 2	三年级 Grade 3	四年级 Grade 4
总 计 Total	**909570**	**305192**	**300677**	**293544**	**10157**
城区 Urban Area					
25 人及以下 Under 25 Persons	7856	2360	2195	2696	605
26 - 35 人 Between 26 - 35	31163	9620	9725	10444	1374
36 - 45 人 Between 36 - 45	74728	25544	23836	23739	1609
46 - 55 人 Between 46 - 55	110404	38537	36616	33824	1427
56 - 65 人 Between 56 - 65	46037	15029	15792	14494	722
66 人及以上 Over 66 Persons	23781	7746	8212	7519	304
其中:城乡结合区 of Which:Urban-rural Transitional Area					
25 人及以下 Under 25 Persons	1152	369	331	425	27
26 - 35 人 Between 26 - 35	4974	1586	1586	1690	112
36 - 45 人 Between 36 - 45	12415	4302	3922	3994	197
46 - 55 人 Between 46 - 55	19442	6993	6537	5682	230
56 - 65 人 Between 56 - 65	6466	2040	2276	2062	88
66 人及以上 Over 66 Persons	3459	1229	1157	1060	13
镇区 Counties & Towns Area					
25 人及以下 Under 25 Persons	7859	2606	2514	2565	174
26 - 35 人 Between 26 - 35	39487	13090	12524	13148	725
36 - 45 人 Between 36 - 45	107898	35870	35527	35529	972
46 - 55 人 Between 46 - 55	161580	53209	53811	53793	767
56 - 65 人 Between 56 - 65	71667	24491	23921	23048	207
66 人及以上 Over 66 Persons	49147	17664	16792	14626	65
其中:镇乡结合区 of Which: County-town Transitional Area					
25 人及以下 Under 25 Persons	1837	591	569	628	49
26 - 35 人 Between 26 - 35	9444	3127	2950	3240	127
36 - 45 人 Between 36 - 45	27192	9259	8947	8724	262
46 - 55 人 Between 46 - 55	41695	13741	13943	13785	226
56 - 65 人 Between 56 - 65	17960	6249	6099	5589	23
66 人及以上 Over 66 Persons	12520	4710	4211	3599	
乡村 Rural Area					
25 人及以下 Under 25 Persons	8116	2705	2535	2753	123
26 - 35 人 Between 26 - 35	26498	8658	8593	8944	303
36 - 45 人 Between 36 - 45	53293	17499	17571	17854	369
46 - 55 人 Between 46 - 55	56722	18469	19340	18593	320
56 - 65 人 Between 56 - 65	21155	7479	7014	6578	84
66 人及以上 Over 66 Persons	12179	4616	4159	3397	7

初　中

Number of Students in Junior

	毕业生数 Graduates	招生数 Entrants		
			合计 Total	其中:女 of Which: Female
总　计 Total	**15615452**	**14960867**	**44401248**	**20836306**
其中:女 of Which: Female	7427221	6958625	20836306	
少数民族学生 Minority Students	1542653	1662122	4710203	2224493
四年制 4-year	482988	449353	1752404	836837
九年一贯制学校 9-year Schools	1760777	1804465	5256281	2376171
十二年一贯制学校 12-year Schools	206450	231841	666538	273558
完全中学 Complete Secondary Schools	2081587	2057158	6127520	2869994
附设普通初中班 Junior Sec. Classes Attached	95566	84197	252633	113683
附设职业初中班 Vocational Junior Sec. Classes Attached	2789	157	417	152
独立设置少数民族学校 Inde. Sec. Schools for Minorities	452563	479937	1361743	657455
随迁子女 Migrant Children	920214	1526070	4267777	1814719
其中:外省迁入 of Which: from Other Province	320245	621567	1641187	693302
本省外县迁入 From Other County	599969	904503	2626590	1121417
进城务工人员随迁子女 Children of Migrant Workers	751856	1238665	3463140	1455939
其中:外省迁入 of Which: from Other Province	252791	493892	1296986	541032
本省外县迁入 From Other County	499065	744773	2166154	914907
农村留守儿童 Children Left Behind	1851794	2317864	6862774	3145814
教育部门 Run by Ed. Dept.	14119204	13244816	39491299	18782928
其他部门 Run by Non-ed. Dept.	105900	88755	269398	124336
地方企业办 Run by Local Enterprises	5431	6183	17069	8291
民办 Non-government	1384917	1621113	4623482	1920751
城区 Urban Area	4590441	4814726	14300203	6623498
教育部门 Run by Ed. Dept.	3870973	3939113	11804325	5548637
其他部门 Run by Non-ed. Dept.	33584	31554	96035	42267
地方企业办 Run by Local Enterprises	2526	3007	8163	3961
民办 Non-government	683358	841052	2391680	1028633
其中:城乡结合区 of Which:Urban-rural Transitional Area	733117	799024	2312158	1043894
教育部门 Run by Ed. Dept.	580822	592302	1753079	818985
其他部门 Run by Non-ed. Dept.	4047	2964	9729	4375
地方企业办 Run by Local Enterprises	177	495	875	405
民办 Non-government	148071	203263	548475	220129
镇区 Counties & Towns Area	7885935	7400752	21955710	10344810
教育部门 Run by Ed. Dept.	7233829	6695695	19926269	9517557
其他部门 Run by Non-ed. Dept.	63490	49946	151969	72004
地方企业办 Run by Local Enterprises	2714	3116	8690	4294
民办 Non-government	585902	651995	1868782	750955
其中:镇乡结合区 of Which: County-town Transitional Area	1953974	1914145	5586443	2609804
教育部门 Run by Ed. Dept.	1748154	1672343	4903283	2340430
其他部门 Run by Non-ed. Dept.	2330	3100	6817	3105
地方企业办 Run by Local Enterprises	184	203	580	275
民办 Non-government	203306	238499	675763	265994
乡村 Rural Area	3139076	2745389	8145335	3867998
教育部门 Run by Ed. Dept.	3014402	2610008	7760705	3716734
其他部门 Run by Non-ed. Dept.	8826	7255	21394	10065
地方企业办 Run by Local Enterprises	191	60	216	36
民办 Non-government	115657	128066	363020	141163

学　生　数
Secondary Schools

单位：人

unit：person

在校生数 Enrolment				预计毕业生数 Estimated Graduates for Next Year
一年级 Grade 1	二年级 Grade 2	三年级 Grade 3	四年级 Grade 4	
14972216	**14771466**	**14237562**	**420004**	**14225162**
6962278	6921858	6750100	202070	6737781
1663207	1560155	1479896	6945	1479477
449563	450433	432404	420004	420004
1806619	1745540	1630203	73919	1627373
232140	221455	208809	4134	208331
2058925	2043732	1989501	35362	1987336
84201	85835	80883	1714	81612
157	99	151	10	120
480566	450053	429496	1628	429586
1541621	1430536	1230917	64703	1186613
628831	549231	431775	31350	406763
912790	881305	799142	33353	779850
1251769	1161123	996920	53328	964244
499592	433898	339993	23503	320700
752177	727225	656927	29825	643544
2326912	2306247	2216512	13103	2190595
13254694	13135037	12719852	381716	12709494
88824	87482	85166	7926	85059
6183	5392	5473	21	5488
1622515	1543555	1427071	30341	1425121
4817167	4740435	4487427	255174	4470557
3940465	3907155	3731147	225558	3716518
31563	31565	31347	1560	31222
3007	2641	2494	21	2509
842132	799074	722439	28035	720308
799456	769442	712445	30815	711945
592400	581088	550224	29367	550003
2972	3124	3245	388	3086
495	180	200		200
203589	185050	158776	1060	158656
7408877	7311812	7115884	119137	7118296
6703460	6637037	6474427	111345	6476627
50006	48708	46889	6366	46907
3116	2681	2893		2893
652295	623386	591675	1426	591869
1915515	1863051	1779085	28792	1781005
1673628	1634581	1566994	28080	1568858
3100	2016	1621	80	1661
203	200	177		177
238584	226254	210293	632	210309
2746172	2719219	2634251	45693	2636309
2610769	2590845	2514278	44813	2516349
7255	7209	6930		6930
60	70	86		86
128088	121095	112957	880	112944

初中学龄人口及在校学生情况

Number of School-age Population and Enrolment of Junior Secondary Schools

单位：人
unit：person

	在校学龄人口数 School-age Population		在校生数 Enrolment					
	合计 Total	其中：女 of Which：Female	合计 Total	其中：女 of Which：Female	一年级 Grade 1	二年级 Grade 2	三年级 Grade 3	四年级 Grade 4
总　计 Total	**38876531**	**18314214**	**44401248**	**20836306**	**14972216**	**14771466**	**14237562**	**420004**
10 岁及以下 Under 10 Years			25428	12941	22596	2274	536	22
11 岁 11 Years	295418	142998	907425	449422	872163	32418	2834	10
12 岁 12 Years	8596908	4080234	9338985	4451746	8365622	932296	40912	155
13 岁 13 Years	13904272	6549780	13904272	6549780	4738142	8206645	950971	8514
14 岁 14 Years	13373048	6260890	13380541	6264331	790093	4597378	7728663	264407
15 岁 15 Years	2706885	1280312	5678586	2604495	144845	828469	4576491	128781
16 岁 16 Years			961514	415123	28120	137101	780119	16174
17 岁 17 Years			162809	69404	7130	26052	127958	1669
18 岁及以上 Over 18 Years			41688	19064	3505	8833	29078	272
城区 Urban Area	12548795	5843737	14300203	6623498	4817167	4740435	4487427	255174
10 岁及以下 Under 10 Years			9824	5032	9037	654	118	15
11 岁 11 Years	202863	97872	418121	209263	404016	13054	1045	6
12 岁 12 Years	3176883	1503645	3384615	1608654	2934084	430638	19793	100
13 岁 13 Years	4562836	2127904	4562836	2127904	1259005	2854287	444152	5392
14 岁 14 Years	4199998	1929024	4205260	1931397	179826	1223499	2625467	176468
15 岁 15 Years	406215	185292	1463313	638763	25390	187512	1185774	64637
16 岁 16 Years			219123	87943	4424	25390	181714	7595
17 岁 17 Years			30642	11926	899	4216	24708	819
18 岁及以上 Over 18 Years			6469	2616	486	1185	4656	142
其中：城乡结合区 of Which：Urban-rural Transitional Area	2016003	914367	2312158	1043894	799456	769442	712445	30815
10 岁及以下 Under 10 Years			1226	616	1095	74	47	10
11 岁 11 Years	22761	11094	55203	27239	53050	2021	132	
12 岁 12 Years	477208	220330	513655	238273	452944	57445	3260	6
13 岁 13 Years	725673	328869	725673	328869	245659	423052	56520	442
14 岁 14 Years	680668	304681	680958	304832	39263	239364	381143	21188
15 岁 15 Years	109693	49393	282011	122563	5824	40236	227410	8541
16 岁 16 Years			44514	17881	1261	5956	36750	547
17 岁 17 Years			7280	2930	261	1020	5938	61
18 岁及以上 Over 18 Years			1638	691	99	274	1245	20

初中学龄人口及在校学生情况(续)

Number of School-age Population and Enrolment of Junior Secondary Schools (Cont.)

单位:人

unit: person

	在校学龄人口数 School-age Population		在校学生数 Enrolment					
	合计 Total	其中:女 of Which: Female	合计 Total	其中:女 of Which: Female	一年级 Grade 1	二年级 Grade 2	三年级 Grade 3	四年级 Grade 4
镇区 Counties & Towns Area	19239285	9094146	21955710	10344810	7408877	7311812	7115884	119137
10 岁及以下 Under 10 Years			11260	5744	9729	1196	335	
11 岁 11 Years	68822	33557	359480	176386	343263	14860	1355	2
12 岁 12 Years	4089526	1939919	4472143	2131614	4085865	370311	15917	50
13 岁 13 Years	6844104	3234174	6844104	3234174	2457548	4009458	374419	2679
14 岁 14 Years	6697583	3155451	6699704	3156473	417106	2385200	3832396	65002
15 岁 15 Years	1539250	731045	2952934	1371322	76294	440264	2391250	45126
16 岁 16 Years			511328	223829	13979	73362	418359	5628
17 岁 17 Years			84719	36143	3553	12971	67628	567
18 岁及以上 Over 18 Years			20038	9125	1540	4190	14225	83
其中:镇乡结合区 of Which: County-town Transitional Area	4922850	2308905	5586443	2609804	1915515	1863051	1779085	28792
10 岁及以下 Under 10 Years			2045	1102	1835	180	30	
11 岁 11 Years	19065	9527	92323	44589	88979	3090	254	
12 岁 12 Years	1116026	523727	1195149	563262	1096835	93988	4324	2
13 岁 13 Years	1752373	822734	1752373	822734	604021	1055007	93178	167
14 岁 14 Years	1686495	788507	1686893	788690	101156	581380	986387	17970
15 岁 15 Years	348891	164410	711588	327098	18312	107382	576096	9798
16 岁 16 Years			122465	52349	3439	18051	100209	766
17 岁 17 Years			19783	8293	650	3155	15898	80
18 岁及以上 Over 18 Years			3824	1687	288	818	2709	9
乡村 Rural Area	7088451	3376331	8145335	3867998	2746172	2719219	2634251	45693
10 岁及以下 Under 10 Years			4344	2165	3830	424	83	7
11 岁 11 Years	23733	11569	129824	63773	124884	4504	434	2
12 岁 12 Years	1330499	636670	1482227	711478	1345673	131347	5202	5
13 岁 13 Years	2497332	1187702	2497332	1187702	1021589	1342900	132400	443
14 岁 14 Years	2475467	1176415	2475577	1176461	193161	988679	1270800	22937
15 岁 15 Years	761420	363975	1262339	594410	43161	200693	999467	19018
16 岁 16 Years			231063	103351	9717	38349	180046	2951
17 岁 17 Years			47448	21335	2678	8865	35622	283
18 岁及以上 Over 18 Years			15181	7323	1479	3458	10197	47

初中分课程专任

Number of Full-time Teachers in Junior Secondary

	合计 Total	其中:女 of Which: Female	思想品德(政治) Politics	语文 Language & Literature	数学 Mathematics	外语 Foreign Languages				科学 Science	物理 Physics
						小计 Subtotal	英语 English	日语 Japanese	俄语 Russian		
总 计 Total	**3480979**	**1799565**	**228736**	**626568**	**600285**	**544081**	**540991**	**360**	**247**	**31595**	**235706**
其中:女 of Which:Female	1799565		110769	375612	282802	413478	411437	291	193	13450	78649
少数民族 Minorities	311437	154936	22509	57719	51807	39878	39469	155	29	611	21741
研究生毕业 Graduate	45138	30994	3271	8306	6902	7901	7821	29	11	562	2698
本科毕业 Under-graduate	2561050	1427476	165340	491341	453184	430151	427802	269	196	25259	173434
专科毕业 Associate Bachelor	849842	335890	58602	124726	137597	104874	104228	61	38	5518	58763
高中阶段毕业 High School Graduate	24180	5111	1487	2158	2565	1134	1120	1	2	245	798
高中阶段以下毕业 Below High School Graduate	769	94	36	37	37	21	20			11	13
城区 Urban Area	1046324	659999	64346	184223	180140	174747	173421	262	135	12008	70915
其中:城乡结合区 of Which: Urban-rural Transitional Area	174350	99941	11036	31243	29945	28360	28209	26	2	2285	11311
镇区 Counties & Towns Area	1703507	825693	114484	307367	293693	263408	262117	76	70	14970	114672
其中:镇乡结合区 of Which: County-town Transitional Area	430033	214820	29199	78002	74099	66492	66174	13	7	4699	28205
乡村 Rural Area	731148	313873	49906	134978	126452	105926	105453	22	42	4617	50119

教师学历情况

Schools by Subject Taught & Educational Attainment

单位：人

unit：person

化学 Chem-istry	生物 Biology	历史与社会 History and Society	地理 Geogr-aphy	历史 History	体育与健康 Physical Training and Healthy	艺术 Art	音乐 Music	美术 Fine Arts	综合实践活动 Comprehensive Practice			其他 Others	当年不任课 No Teaching Load in Current Year
									小计 Subtotal	信息技术 Information Technique	劳动与技术 Skills Teaching		
150654	**140358**	**32157**	**133025**	**172030**	**181900**	**6362**	**87319**	**83759**	**127474**	**86193**	**36173**	**46065**	**52905**
66832	71842	14229	61046	82319	35382	2978	61455	42878	45006	32360	11041	20924	19914
13908	12622	1473	11578	15169	17264	312	8123	6937	10192	7512	2435	13041	6553
2260	2158	537	1599	2626	2134	37	767	856	1289	1109	139	718	517
112994	95304	22489	86564	119362	127252	3510	60734	57219	83436	62405	17761	25609	27868
34941	41595	8821	43421	48581	50110	2657	25024	24734	40287	22083	16517	17688	21903
450	1268	303	1406	1432	2314	152	765	917	2363	571	1687	1929	2494
9	33	7	35	29	90	6	29	33	99	25	69	121	123
45083	39546	9532	36480	49031	60692	1134	26977	25400	37300	26449	8902	11783	16987
7207	6863	1842	6318	8206	9537	256	4492	4291	6317	4197	1627	2228	2613
72845	70082	15767	67301	86179	86070	3423	42343	40676	62438	41015	19051	21803	25986
17804	18057	4234	17304	21861	21361	906	10516	10172	15535	10155	4793	5244	6343
32726	30730	6858	29244	36820	35138	1805	17999	17683	27736	18729	8220	12479	9932

初中专任教师专业技术
Number of Full-time Teachers in Junior Secondary

	合 计 Total	其中:女 of Which: Female	24岁及以下 24 Years and Under	25－29 25 to 29	30－34 30 to 34
总 计 Total	**3480979**	**1799565**	**134501**	**487371**	**688041**
其中:女 of Which:Female	1799565		94509	323577	406341
少数民族 Minorities	311437	154936	11593	49509	66724
中学高级 Senior	556896	243002	13	91	3464
中学一级 1st Grade	1502837	725514	779	27210	240385
中学二级 2nd Grade	1126940	644328	33788	326857	408093
中学三级 3rd Grade	57287	32131	10138	27394	12495
未定职级 No-ranking	237019	154590	89783	105819	23604
城区 Urban Area	1046324	659999	38234	132408	200393
其中:城乡结合区 of Which: Urban-rural Transitional Area	174350	99941	7996	23541	34083
镇区 Counties & Towns Area	1703507	825693	60823	230762	335111
其中:镇乡结合区 of Which: County-town Transitional Area	430033	214820	16132	57359	85325
乡村 Rural Area	731148	313873	35444	124201	152537

职称、年龄结构情况
Schools by Professional Rank and Age

单位：人
unit：person

35－39 35 to 39	40－44 40 to 44	45－49 45 to 49	50－54 50 to 54	55－59 55 to 59	60 岁及以上 60 Years and Over
735673	**621753**	**465307**	**224485**	**122111**	**1737**
391170	300762	202919	78094	1690	503
68357	54399	38116	15629	7035	75
50183	155554	191293	104406	50975	917
453940	378346	236210	104498	60880	589
219454	81596	34188	13878	9031	55
4093	1354	810	550	442	11
8003	4903	2806	1153	783	165
212725	203911	156413	72451	28782	1007
37312	31967	23852	10463	5008	128
370619	305715	227982	109086	62863	546
96811	77014	54983	26407	15841	161
152329	112127	80912	42948	30466	184

	上学年初报表专任教师数 Number of Full-time Teachers at Beginning of Previous Academic Year	增加教师 Factors of Increase					
		合计 Total	录用毕业生 New Recruits from Current Year Graduates		调入 Teachers Recruited from Other Units	校内调整 of Which: with Change of Status in Their Own Institutions	其他 Others
			小计 Subtotal	其中:师范生 of Which: Students Enrolled in Teacher Training Institutions			
总　计 Total	**3504433**	**327292**	**78139**	**58412**	**170757**	**57435**	**20961**
其中:女 of Which: Female	1784644	179785	54155	40782	89550	24779	11301
城区 Urban Area	1026587	106227	23079	18807	53906	19098	10144
其中:女 of Which: Female	643332	64705	16594	13560	32323	9623	6165
其中:城乡结合区 of Which: Urban-rural Transitional Area	170379	20281	4614	3731	10249	3314	2104
其中:女 of Which: Female	96853	11459	3106	2505	5717	1484	1152
镇区 Counties & Towns Area	1723481	153968	33472	24869	84737	28005	7754
其中:女 of Which: Female	823503	80795	23148	17380	42551	11348	3748
其中:镇乡结合区 of Which: County-town Transitional Area	432206	42480	8647	6444	24163	7313	2357
其中:女 of Which: Female	212582	22355	5973	4514	12318	2953	1111
乡村 Rural Area	754365	67097	21588	14736	32114	10332	3063
其中:女 of Which: Female	317809	34285	14413	9842	14676	3808	1388

教师变动情况
Junior Secondary Schools

单位：人
unit：person

减少教师 Factors of Decrease					本学年初报表专任教师数 Number of Full-time Teachers at Beginning of Current Academic Year
合计 Total	自然减员 Retired from Their Posts during Previous Academic Year	调出 Transferred from Teaching to Non-Teaching Posts	校内调整 of Which：with Change of Status in Their Own Institutions	其他 Others	
350746	**38837**	**213350**	**71568**	**26991**	**3480979**
164864	16562	104283	30858	13161	1799565
86490	13258	42751	20643	9838	1046324
48038	7481	24281	10571	5705	659999
16310	2089	9129	3119	1973	174350
8371	1060	4869	1437	1005	99941
173942	17714	108987	35107	12134	1703507
78605	6714	52079	14477	5335	825693
44653	4434	28231	8634	3354	430033
20117	1750	13485	3508	1374	214820
90314	7865	61612	15818	5019	731148
38221	2367	27923	5810	2121	313873

初中学生、专任教师政治面貌及其他

Supplementary Information on Students and Full-time Teachers of Junior Secondary Schools

单位：人

unit：person

	在校学生中 of Total Students				专任教师中 of Total Full-time Teachers			
	共产党员 Member of C. P. C.	共青团员 Member of C. Y. L.	华侨 Overseas Chinese	港澳台 From H. K, Macao and Taiwan	共产党员 Member of C. P. C.	共青团员 Member of C. Y. L.	民主党派 Member of Non-Communist Part	华侨 Overseas Chinese
总　计 Total		**13421941**	**2871**	**10276**	**997485**	**203003**	**22685**	**286**
其中：女 of Which：Female		6832991	1207	4617	371754	128507	13078	139
城区 Urban Area		3424418	1527	9366	332075	63590	17865	132
其中：女 of Which：Female		1788870	617	4217	178727	44160	10966	75
其中：城乡结合区 of Which：Urban-rural Transitional Area		595556	237	2055	49754	11353	1256	24
其中：女 of Which：Female		299809	73	875	22399	7497	658	14
镇区 Counties & Towns Area		7226067	1142	599	458239	93762	3823	144
其中：女 of Which：Female		3648905	509	271	140027	57161	1741	60
其中：镇乡结合区 of Which：County-town Transitional Area		1843664	290	190	112378	24336	628	20
其中：女 of Which：Female		920084	112	81	34421	15224	279	6
乡村 Rural Area		2771456	202	311	207171	45651	997	10
其中：女 of Which：Female		1395216	81	129	53000	27186	371	4

初中办学条件(一)

Condition of School Buildings in Junior Secondary Schools (1)

单位:平方米

unit:m^2

	合计 Total	城区 Urban Area	其中:城乡结合区 of Which: Urban-rural Transitional Area	镇区 Counties & Towns Area	其中:镇乡结合区 of Which: County-town Transitional Area	乡村 Rural Area
总　计 Total	**500794117**	**140951367**	**28357296**	**244555274**	**64405048**	**115287476**
其中:危房 of Which: Floor Space of Dilapidated Buildings	16751734	1659626	296241	8298010	1839125	6794098
当年新增校舍 New Floor Space Added in Current Year	20621688	5129216	1095283	10300592	3013059	5191880
一、教学及辅助用房 Teaching & Assistant Buildings	210620608	67111017	12840138	97294142	25657223	46215449
教室 Classroom	150532914	45091099	8877349	71026532	18682102	34415283
实验室 Laboratory	29816473	9748348	1800803	13812520	3662626	6255605
图书室 Library	10784947	3891290	664143	4727852	1276814	2165805
微机室 PC-room	9288544	2761007	517266	4288893	1101714	2238644
语音室 Linguistic	3119487	985288	196269	1510513	395480	623686
体育馆 Gymnasium	7078243	4633985	784308	1927832	538487	516426
二、行政办公用房 Administrative	46145315	16173309	2771400	20798580	5563536	9173426
其中:教师办公室 of Which: for Teachers	29534737	9730833	1648452	13517610	3579472	6286294
三、生活用房 Residential and Welfare	207285242	40599826	9864647	112743807	29323573	53941609
教工宿舍 Apartments for Single	52078883	7243161	2005833	29116951	7062003	15718771
其中:教师周转宿舍 of Which: Accommodation for Circulation of Teachers	8924370	901361	242712	5098019	1144243	2924990
学生宿舍 Students' Dormitories	92564615	15794300	4148207	52964392	13879823	23805923
食堂 Dining Halls	35898012	8451548	2006715	18887298	5208450	8559166
厕所 Toilet	14173001	4454249	858071	6444357	1783111	3274395
其他 Others	12570731	4656568	845821	5330809	1390186	2583354
四、其他用房 Rooms for Other Purposes	36742952	17067215	2881111	13718745	3860716	5956992

初中办学

Condition of School Buildings in

	占地面积(平方米) Areas Occupied(m^2)			图书(册) Books & Magazines in Libraries (volume)	计算机 No.
	合计 Total	其中 of Which			合计 Total
		绿化用地面积 Green Areas	运动场地面积 Sports Areas		
总 计 Total	**1516915508**	**294026542**	**404381041**	**1253642999**	**5444028**
城区 Urban Area	321018052	69729025	98425400	366287680	2002450
其中:城乡结合区 of Which: Urban-rural Transitional Area	75618767	17248138	21424111	69371395	348631
镇区 Counties & Towns Area	765260389	148704065	198506931	593967687	2365703
其中:镇乡结合区 of Which: County-town Transitional Area	197622498	38178189	50673898	156449794	615614
乡村 Rural Area	430637067	75593452	107448710	293387632	1075875

初中办学

Condition of School Buildings in

	体育运动场(馆)面积达标校数 Schools No: Sprots Areas Reached Standard	体育器械配备达标校数 Schools No: Sports Equip. Reached Standard
总 计 Total	**36796**	**38464**
城区 Urban Area	8652	9247
其中:城乡结合区 of Which: Urban-rural Transitional Area	1820	1910
镇区 Counties & Towns Area	16690	17338
其中:镇乡结合区 of Which: County-town Transitional Area	4315	4433
乡村 Rural Area	11454	11879

条件(二)
Junior Secondary Schools (2)

数(台) of Computers		教室(间) Classroom(room)		教室中:普通教室(间) of Which: General Classroom		固定资产总值(万元) Total Volue of Fixed Asset (10,000 yuan)		
其中:教学用计算机 No. of Computers Used for Instruction		合计 Total	其中:网络多媒体教室 of Which: Network Multimedia Classroom	合计 Total	其中:网络多媒体教室 of Which: Network Multimedia Classroom	合计 Total	其中:教学仪器设备资产值 of Which: Total Volue of Equip & Instru.	
小计 Subtotal	其中:平板电脑 of Which: Tablet PC						小计 Subtotal	其中:实验设备 for Profession
4403086	**179595**	**1494000**	**621389**	**1170499**	**531718**	**51235003. 07**	**5778797. 33**	**2127300. 15**
1597213	64884	427307	253588	329812	213341	18464113. 51	2459937. 56	731025. 40
281785	14319	85419	47073	66200	40241	3625060. 84	424538. 45	147417. 45
1925934	79277	699302	269062	539863	233344	23489628. 51	2336719. 33	963601. 37
504062	22766	200700	73167	142299	62888	6503892. 86	609499. 99	258683. 45
879939	35434	367391	98739	300824	85033	9281261. 05	982140. 43	432673. 38

条件(三)
Junior Secondary Schools (3)

单位:所
unit: school

音乐器械配备达标校数 Schools No: Musical Instru. Reached Standard	美术器械配备达标校数 Schools No: Fine Arts Instru. Reached Standard	理科实验仪器达标校数 Schools No: Equip. of Natural Sci. Reached Standard	建立校园网校数 Schools No: Campus Networks Set	接入互联网校数 Schools No: Internet Access
37140	**36986**	**40960**	**29502**	**48809**
9109	9065	9407	8377	10604
1864	1857	1926	1605	2267
16709	16658	18591	13430	21691
4252	4254	4768	3461	5570
11322	11263	12962	7695	16514

成人初中基本情况

Basic Statistics of Adult Junior Secondary Schools

单位：人(人次)
unit:person

	学校数(所) Schools	教学班(点)(个) External Teaching Sites	毕(结)业生数 Graduates		注册学生数 Enrolment		教职工数 Educational Personnel		专任教师 Full-time Teachers		聘请校外教师 Part-time Teachers
			合计 Total	其中:女 of Which: Female	合计 Total	其中:女 of Which: Female	合计 Total	其中:女 of Which: Female	合计 Total	其中:女 of Which: Female	
总计 Total	**1768**	**3783**	**433891**	**214341**	**482278**	**221798**	**7281**	**2518**	**5833**	**1932**	**5364**
职工初中 Junior Secondary Schools for Staff & workers	208	372	22344	11457	37923	17276	1388	522	1259	470	939
农民初中 Junior Secondary Schools for Peasants	1560	3411	411547	202884	444355	204522	5893	1996	4574	1462	4425

四、初等教育(小学)

Primary Education

(Primary Schools)

小学校数、教学点数及班数

Number of Schools, External Teaching Sites & Classes in Primary Schools

	学校数(所) Schools	教学点数(个) External Teaching Sites	班数(个) Classes
总　计 Total	**213529**	**82768**	**2499098**
教育部门 Run by Ed. Dept.	207614	82221	2340465
其他部门 Run by Non-ed. Dept.	468	135	11807
地方企业办 Run by Local Enterprises	40		676
民办 Non-government	5407	412	146150
城区 Urban Area	26049	1151	595913
教育部门 Run by Ed. Dept.	23930	1130	515718
其他部门 Run by Non-ed. Dept.	158	1	3184
地方企业办 Run by Local Enterprises	14		286
民办 Non-government	1947	20	76725
其中:城乡结合区 of Which: Urban-rural Transitional Area	8134	881	123431
教育部门 Run by Ed. Dept.	7540	874	98343
其他部门 Run by Non-ed. Dept.	36		464
地方企业办 Run by Local Enterprises	3		47
民办 Non-government	555	7	24577
镇区 Counties & Towns Area	47152	8062	764511
教育部门 Run by Ed. Dept.	45125	7969	710333
其他部门 Run by Non-ed. Dept.	193	25	6839
地方企业办 Run by Local Enterprises	13		297
民办 Non-government	1821	68	47042
其中:镇乡结合区 of Which: County-town Transitional Area	22102	6035	260611
教育部门 Run by Ed. Dept.	21308	5981	241411
其他部门 Run by Non-ed. Dept.	18	4	246
地方企业办 Run by Local Enterprises	5		46
民办 Non-government	771	50	18908
乡村 Rural Area	140328	73555	1138674
教育部门 Run by Ed. Dept.	138559	73122	1114414
其他部门 Run by Non-ed. Dept.	117	109	1784
地方企业办 Run by Local Enterprises	13		93
民办 Non-government	1639	324	22383
总计中:五年制 of the Total: 5-year			61587
九年一贯制学校 9-year Schools			187217
十二年一贯制学校 12-year Schools			17063
其他学校附设 Other Primary Schools Attached			7604
独立设置的少数民族学校 Inde. Sec. Schools for Minorities	8141		77887

小学班额情况

Size of Primary Classes

单位：个

unit：class

	合计 Total	一年级 Grade 1	二年级 Grade 2	三年级 Grade 3	四年级 Grade 4	五年级 Grade 5	六年级 Grade 6	复式班 Multiple-grade Classes
总　计 Total	**2499098**	**475667**	**452855**	**423580**	**398959**	**376069**	**359006**	**12962**
城区 Urban Area								
25 人及以下 Under 25 Persons	31644	5297	5526	5116	5475	5600	4587	43
26 – 35 人 Between 26 – 35	72163	12205	12868	11887	12031	12659	10511	2
36 – 45 人 Between 36 – 45	178626	37414	32742	29962	27522	26625	24359	2
46 – 55 人 Between 46 – 55	187126	36624	33357	32447	30431	27679	26587	1
56 – 65 人 Between 56 – 65	82287	14215	13552	14607	14078	12574	13254	7
66 人及以上 Over 66 Persons	44067	6749	7200	7967	7703	6672	7776	
其中：城乡结合区 of Which: Urban-rural Transitional Area								
25 人及以下 Under 25 Persons	14914	2694	2650	2494	2498	2463	2089	26
26 – 35 人 Between 26 – 35	19552	3553	3276	3162	3136	3328	3096	1
36 – 45 人 Between 36 – 45	37202	7643	6682	6135	5696	5538	5506	2
46 – 55 人 Between 46 – 55	34625	6787	6492	6144	5748	4940	4513	1
56 – 65 人 Between 56 – 65	12097	1915	2073	2266	2101	1897	1844	1
66 人及以上 Over 66 Persons	5041	874	884	873	836	758	816	
镇区 Counties & Towns Area								
25 人及以下 Under 25 Persons	86553	17865	16522	14605	13497	12483	10853	728
26 – 35 人 Between 26 – 35	115456	21232	20111	19210	18700	18462	17684	57
36 – 45 人 Between 36 – 45	219392	40588	38560	36225	34940	34468	34602	9
46 – 55 人 Between 46 – 55	186052	32435	31003	30758	30704	30188	30963	1
56 – 65 人 Between 56 – 65	90440	14744	15030	15240	15062	14873	15488	3
66 人及以上 Over 66 Persons	66618	10656	11022	11653	11535	10402	11350	
其中：镇乡结合区 of Which: County-town Transitional Area								
25 人及以下 Under 25 Persons	52783	10998	10273	9080	8252	7454	6248	478
26 – 35 人 Between 26 – 35	51162	9531	9118	8582	8228	7941	7735	27
36 – 45 人 Between 36 – 45	70345	13084	12526	11859	11229	10937	10708	2
46 – 55 人 Between 46 – 55	51517	8848	8681	8571	8542	8223	8652	
56 – 65 人 Between 56 – 65	21499	3553	3521	3578	3578	3486	3781	2
66 人及以上 Over 66 Persons	13305	2162	2186	2307	2312	2043	2295	
乡村 Rural Area								
25 人及以下 Under 25 Persons	507681	112979	104955	86054	74740	64388	53429	11136
26 – 35 人 Between 26 – 35	267422	48932	48647	46363	43493	40950	38368	669
36 – 45 人 Between 36 – 45	211657	38033	36785	36232	34301	33207	32854	245
46 – 55 人 Between 46 – 55	104143	17503	17464	17339	17130	16941	17726	40
56 – 65 人 Between 56 – 65	34672	5920	5508	5799	5525	5782	6125	13
66 人及以上 Over 66 Persons	13099	2276	2003	2116	2092	2116	2490	6

小 学
Number of Students

	毕业生数 Graduates	招生数 Entrants			
		合计 Total	其中:受过学前教育 of Which: Those Received the Pre-school Education	合计 Total	其中:女 of Which: Female
总 计 Total	**15810583**	**16953556**	**16417268**	**93605487**	**43312688**
其中:女 of Which: Female	7330087	7876592	7628092	43312688	
少数民族 Minorities	1671908	1857971	1599065	10409488	4834232
五年制 5-year	475675	505017	502063	2371040	1112465
九年一贯制学校 9-year Schools	1372707	1381950	1345457	7920436	3553566
十二年一贯制学校 12-year Schools	122193	120177	117707	686227	281835
附设小学班 Primary School Classes	173283	27094	25898	347899	153361
复式班 Morning & Afternoon Shift Classes	3393	53320	44071	165163	79024
小学教学点 External Teaching Sites	373556	1066657	993782	3803710	1802716
独立设置少数民族学校 Inde. Sec. Schools for Minorities	493329	494482	394129	2857242	1364767
随迁子女 Migrant Children	1375052	2261306	2230385	11868126	5072272
其中:外省迁入 of Which: from Other Province	656091	1130014	1114550	5794822	2451392
本省外县迁入 From Other County	718961	1131292	1115835	6073304	2620880
进城务工人员随迁子女 Children of Migrant Workers	1087292	1771957	1751593	9308533	3963615
其中:外省迁入 of Which: from Other Province	495128	844605	835793	4334820	1828928
本省外县迁入 From Other County	592164	927352	915800	4973713	2134687
农村留守儿童 Children Left Behind	1669302	2558053	2460515	14404725	6469154
教育部门 Run by Ed. Dept.	14711594	15760639	15251074	86861496	40528034
其他部门 Run by Non-ed. Dept.	86551	75677	73960	433095	203150
地方企业办 Run by Local Enterprises	4147	4394	4387	24881	11561
民办 Non-government	1008291	1112846	1087847	6286015	2569943
城区 Urban Area	4439115	5184555	5124551	27729719	12658832
教育部门 Run by Ed. Dept.	3908306	4517956	4475098	24249130	11191223
其他部门 Run by Non-ed. Dept.	26053	24521	24338	136108	62832
地方企业办 Run by Local Enterprises	1684	1989	1983	10692	4942
民办 Non-government	503072	640089	623132	3333789	1399835
其中:城乡结合区 of Which: Urban-rural Transitional Area	801391	984018	967014	5198647	2329474
教育部门 Run by Ed. Dept.	638983	763102	753882	4056776	1862269
其他部门 Run by Non-ed. Dept.	2752	2865	2861	14979	6983
地方企业办 Run by Local Enterprises	202	458	458	1852	844
民办 Non-government	159454	217593	209813	1125040	459378
镇区 Counties & Towns Area	5768325	5850940	5740292	33705362	15474206
教育部门 Run by Ed. Dept.	5351738	5496043	5391597	31404520	14555937
其他部门 Run by Non-ed. Dept.	50341	41151	40164	242794	114754
地方企业办 Run by Local Enterprises	2019	1994	1993	11900	5513
民办 Non-government	364227	311752	306538	2046148	798002
其中:镇乡结合区 of Which: County-town Transitional Area	1726225	1791826	1761412	10119773	4648285
教育部门 Run by Ed. Dept.	1585005	1666681	1638099	9296095	4325868
其他部门 Run by Non-ed. Dept.	1501	1564	1563	8855	4110
地方企业办 Run by Local Enterprises	351	237	236	1539	695
民办 Non-government	139368	123344	121514	813284	317612
乡村 Rural Area	5603143	5918061	5552425	32170406	15179650
教育部门 Run by Ed. Dept.	5451550	5746640	5384379	31207846	14780874
其他部门 Run by Non-ed. Dept.	10157	10005	9458	54193	25564
地方企业办 Run by Local Enterprises	444	411	411	2289	1106
民办 Non-government	140992	161005	158177	906078	372106

学　生　数
in Primary Schools

单位：人

unit：person

在校生数 Enrolment						预计毕业生数 Estimated Graduates for Next Year
一年级 Grade 1	二年级 Grade 2	三年级 Grade 3	四年级 Grade 4	五年级 Grade 5	六年级 Grade 6	
17014194	**16452428**	**15968628**	**15277067**	**14523683**	**14369487**	**14798022**
7901631	7640390	7382127	7077514	6677216	6633810	6830425
1868081	1813235	1742169	1681549	1649811	1654643	1660532
505179	484762	500991	451573	428535		428535
1382927	1335638	1316331	1297862	1279316	1308362	1370668
120231	110225	111475	113125	112075	119096	122506
27097	24905	27524	33758	49656	184959	187436
54894	58433	25541	14661	7292	4342	4333
1074024	980718	686684	474578	335570	252136	259207
499235	486832	470167	462899	471060	467049	469470
2286546	2192882	2076655	1933040	1773391	1605612	1689157
1143571	1100969	1025413	946650	853044	725175	787114
1142975	1091913	1051242	986390	920347	880437	902043
1787878	1720569	1628621	1517971	1394310	1259184	1328231
852779	823343	766981	708650	640126	542941	590782
935099	897226	861640	809321	754184	716243	737449
2581692	2530354	2427844	2345846	2267875	2251114	2253083
15821511	15309580	14851656	14166702	13435312	13276735	13669882
75696	73410	72550	71961	70162	69316	75170
4394	3826	4215	4273	3930	4243	4285
1112593	1065612	1040207	1034131	1014279	1019193	1048685
5187427	4866502	4791725	4548640	4220127	4115298	4368939
4521326	4246362	4204503	3986097	3688816	3602026	3832084
24519	22355	22291	22104	21321	23518	23882
1989	1610	1847	1867	1606	1773	1803
639593	596175	563084	538572	508384	487981	511170
982350	933953	898972	847193	786197	749982	785292
764247	724882	703444	660553	612953	590697	617443
2862	2384	2524	2469	2298	2442	2447
458	200	284	340	288	282	282
214783	206487	192720	183831	170658	156561	165120
5873081	5754084	5651059	5551434	5386020	5489684	5597511
5518453	5395201	5281123	5161147	4983917	5064679	5163690
41167	41195	41084	41186	40548	37614	43091
1994	1878	1966	2035	1930	2097	2097
311467	315810	326886	347066	359625	385294	388633
1799079	1760821	1707320	1658341	1587451	1606761	1632031
1674321	1633639	1574713	1517298	1443498	1452626	1476506
1564	1411	1404	1411	1545	1520	1532
237	253	269	256	242	282	282
122957	125518	130934	139376	142166	152333	153711
5953686	5831842	5525844	5176993	4917536	4764505	4831572
5781732	5668017	5366030	5019458	4762579	4610030	4674108
10010	9860	9175	8671	8293	8184	8197
411	338	402	371	394	373	385
161533	153627	150237	148493	146270	145918	148882

小学学龄人口入学

Number of Schools-age Population

	在校学龄人口数 School-age Population		招生数 Entrants		
	合计 Total	其中:女 of Which: Female	合计 Total	其中:受过学前教育 of Which: Those Received the Pre-school Education	合计 Total
总　计 Total	**89357005**	**41418251**	**16953556**	**16417268**	**93605487**
5 岁及以下 Under 5 Years			265791		272557
6 岁 6 Years	11887431	5555195	12572274		12973127
7 岁 7 Years	16088130	7487846	3840765		16088130
8 岁 8 Years	15736245	7307030	215910		15736245
9 岁 9 Years	15241719	7064716	41412		15241719
10 岁 10 Years	14246698	6584861	9705		14246698
11 岁 11 Years	13687164	6278359	4153		13752514
12 岁 12 Years	2469618	1140244	2405		4509273
13 岁 13 Years			697		609576
14 岁 14 Years			240		131157
15 岁及以上 Over 15 Years			204		44491
城区 Urban Area	26626664	12181527	5184555	5124551	27729719
5 岁及以下 Under 5 Years			65927		66966
6 岁 6 Years	4093371	1905537	4234878		4345272
7 岁 7 Years	4829011	2213277	837343		4829011
8 岁 8 Years	4743900	2170352	36109		4743900
9 岁 9 Years	4573220	2092003	7395		4573220
10 岁 10 Years	4148548	1887811	1649		4148548
11 岁 11 Years	3942512	1781488	792		3980509
12 岁 12 Years	296102	131059	299		909721
13 岁 13 Years			108		107388
14 岁 14 Years			46		19949
15 岁及以上 Over 15 Years			9		5235
其中:城乡结合区 of Which: Urban-rural Transitional Area	4960868	2229202	984018	967014	5198647
5 岁及以下 Under 5 Years			12233		12711
6 岁 6 Years	741146	339808	772887		795936
7 岁 7 Years	920630	415594	184404		920630
8 岁 8 Years	889641	400312	10727		889641
9 岁 9 Years	846590	379625	2039		846590
10 岁 10 Years	774000	345244	826		774000
11 岁 11 Years	713506	315346	572		718884
12 岁 12 Years	75355	33273	208		203549
13 岁 13 Years			75		29487
14 岁 14 Years			41		5549
15 岁及以上 Over 15 Years			6		1670

及在校生情况

of Primary Schools

单位：人

unit：person

在校学生数 Enrolment						
其中：女 of Which： Female	一年级 Grade 1	二年级 Grade 2	三年级 Grade 3	四年级 Grade 4	五年级 Grade 5	六年级 Grade 6
43312688	**17014194**	**16452428**	**15968628**	**15277067**	**14523683**	**14369487**
138522	267067	5317	173			
6085675	12604766	359748	8365	248		
7487846	3865625	11816497	395265	10413	330	
7307030	220319	3889663	11162798	450448	12663	354
7064716	41039	301636	3928032	10517827	436196	16989
6584861	8940	56169	369802	3755968	9569186	486633
6306767	3375	14745	75342	418072	3885460	9355520
2009005	2084	5426	19810	93486	488010	3900457
253485	579	1948	5671	21529	99865	479984
54748	204	680	1944	5779	22823	99727
20033	196	599	1426	3297	9150	29823
12658832	5187427	4866502	4791725	4548640	4220127	4115298
36217	66053	872	41			
2028126	4238851	104779	1579	63		
2213277	839512	3866804	120176	2438	81	
2170352	35136	835142	3724269	146328	2934	91
2092003	6570	48703	867771	3510219	135816	4141
1887811	950	8022	64080	800010	3113123	162363
1797680	213	1517	10880	72744	862678	3032477
382610	85	396	2051	13348	85614	808227
41037	36	159	573	2622	15871	88127
7642	15	56	192	578	3043	16065
2077	6	52	113	290	967	3807
2329474	982350	933953	898972	847193	786197	749982
6419	12421	278	12			
365761	773929	21599	384	24		
415594	184335	711111	24623	547	14	
400312	9992	185291	664978	28647	703	30
379625	1325	13362	187681	615756	27574	892
345244	213	1739	17773	177439	546500	30336
317591	74	367	2660	20304	182339	513140
84984	35	126	571	3407	23621	175789
11055	12	52	192	783	4178	24270
2169	11	21	62	193	933	4329
720	3	7	36	93	335	1196

小学学龄人口入学

Number of Schools-age Population

	在校学龄人口数 School-age Population		招生数 Entrants		
	合计 Total	其中:女 of Which: Female	合计 Total	其中:受过学前教育 of Which: Those Received the Pre-school Education	合计 Total
镇区 Counties & Towns Area	32121372	14773756	5850940	5740292	33705362
5 岁及以下 Under 5 Years			96344		98534
6 岁 6 Years	4086697	1896544	4346227		4497074
7 岁 7 Years	5641040	2608424	1318510		5641040
8 岁 8 Years	5569737	2567398	73856		5569737
9 岁 9 Years	5501390	2529344	11883		5501390
10 岁 10 Years	5267536	2417508	2159		5267536
11 岁 11 Years	5172246	2351857	1045		5190171
12 岁 12 Years	882726	402681	681		1674129
13 岁 13 Years			157		214698
14 岁 14 Years			38		40652
15 岁及以上 Over 15 Years			40		10401
其中:镇乡结合区 of Which: County-town Transitional Area	9667456	4451559	1791826	1761412	10119773
5 岁及以下 Under 5 Years			28614		29411
6 岁 6 Years	1276771	593110	1328854		1374712
7 岁 7 years	1728841	799232	407813		1728841
8 岁 8 Years	1686385	779378	21506		1686385
9 岁 9 Years	1646101	758411	3578		1646101
10 岁 10 Years	1556645	714327	812		1556645
11 岁 11 Years	1517851	690652	350		1523152
12 岁 12 Years	254862	116449	179		494786
13 岁 13 Years			91		64323
14 岁 14 Years			10		12169
15 岁及以上 Over 15 Years			19		3248
乡村 Rural Area	30608969	14462968	5918061	5552425	32170406
5 岁及以下 Under 5 Years			103520		107057
6 岁 6 Years	3707363	1753114	3991169		4130781
7 岁 7 Years	5618079	2666145	1684912		5618079
8 岁 8 Years	5422608	2569280	105945		5422608
9 岁 9 Years	5167109	2443369	22134		5167109
10 岁 10 Years	4830614	2279542	5897		4830614
11 岁 11 Years	4572406	2145014	2316		4581834
12 岁 12 Years	1290790	606504	1425		1925423
13 岁 13 Years			432		287490
14 岁 14 Years			156		70556
15 岁及以上 Over 15 Years			155		28855

及在校生情况(续)

of Primary Schools (Cont.)

单位：人

unit：person

在校学生数 Enrolment						
其中:女 of Which: Female	一年级 Grade 1	二年级 Grade 2	三年级 Grade 3	四年级 Grade 4	五年级 Grade 5	六年级 Grade 6
15474206	5873081	5754084	5651059	5551434	5386020	5489684
49830	96784	1688	62			
2096843	4360454	133705	2821	94		
2608424	1325588	4161785	149923	3636	108	
2567398	75070	1333422	3981454	175062	4598	131
2529344	11740	101838	1361521	3848585	171581	6125
2417508	1922	16276	126674	1342014	3586665	193985
2359856	803	3349	21926	145883	1407097	3611113
737602	560	1389	4930	28992	175867	1462391
86950	99	377	1156	5265	32099	175702
16018	31	136	319	1282	5997	32887
4433	30	119	273	621	2008	7350
4648285	1799079	1760821	1707320	1658341	1587451	1606761
14699	28770	623	18			
640514	1334893	38792	1000	27		
799232	409507	1275320	42777	1213	24	
779378	21566	409837	1204855	48863	1241	23
758411	3395	30170	411203	1152433	47026	1874
714327	640	4465	38558	400323	1061230	51429
693059	189	1035	6757	44076	413906	1057189
217375	69	409	1609	8976	51683	432040
25317	36	103	365	1811	9720	52288
4613	5	37	95	415	2011	9606
1360	9	30	83	204	610	2312
15179650	5953686	5831842	5525844	5176993	4917536	4764505
52475	104230	2757	70			
1960706	4005461	121264	3965	91		
2666145	1700525	3787908	125166	4339	141	
2569280	110113	1721099	3457075	129058	5131	132
2443369	22729	151095	1698740	3159023	128799	6723
2279542	6068	31871	179048	1613944	2869398	130285
2149231	2359	9879	42536	199445	1615685	2711930
888793	1439	3641	12829	51146	226529	1629839
125498	444	1412	3942	13642	51895	216155
31088	158	488	1433	3919	13783	50775
13523	160	428	1040	2386	6175	18666

小学教

Number of Educational

	教　职 Educational			
	合计 Total	专任教师 Full-time Teachers	行政人员 Adm. Personnel	教辅人员 Supporting Staff
总　计 Total	**5494877**	**5096634**	**176119**	**96889**
其中:女 of Which:Female	3209818	3066446	49568	41525
少数民族 Minorities	588411	543760	17562	9666
教育部门 Run by Ed. Dept.	5267442	4925710	163661	88813
其他部门 Run by Non-ed. Dept.	21370	18074	1031	637
地方企业办 Run by Local Enterprises	1204	1050	56	33
民办 Non-government	204861	151800	11371	7406
城区 Urban Area	1413266	1293251	55850	27252
教育部门 Run by Ed. Dept.	1302990	1209499	49474	23104
其他部门 Run by Non-ed. Dept.	6895	5966	358	217
地方企业办 Run by Local Enterprises	686	582	29	23
民办 Non-government	102695	77204	5989	3908
其中:城乡结合区 of Which: Urban-rural Transitional Area	263432	241211	10176	4160
教育部门 Run by Ed. Dept.	235390	219868	8443	3310
其他部门 Run by Non-ed. Dept.	1488	1257	90	36
地方企业办 Run by Local Enterprises	81	77	1	
民办 Non-government	26473	20009	1642	814
镇区 Counties & Towns Area	1892651	1742138	59059	41773
教育部门 Run by Ed. Dept.	1812057	1683420	54862	38819
其他部门 Run by Non-ed. Dept.	11538	9436	582	381
地方企业办 Run by Local Enterprises	272	252	7	4
民办 Non-government	68784	49030	3608	2569
其中:镇乡结合区 of Which: County-town Transitional Area	594567	555470	16824	9449
教育部门 Run by Ed. Dept.	568026	536166	15374	8695
其他部门 Run by Non-ed. Dept.	501	435	28	12
地方企业办 Run by Local Enterprises	85	75	5	3
民办 Non-government	25955	18794	1417	739
乡村 Rural Area	2188960	2061245	61210	27864
教育部门 Run by Ed. Dept.	2152395	2032791	59325	26890
其他部门 Run by Non-ed. Dept.	2937	2672	91	39
地方企业办 Run by Local Enterprises	246	216	20	6
民办 Non-government	33382	25566	1774	929

职工数

Personnel in Primary Schools

单位：人
unit：person

职工数 Personnel		代课教师 Substitute Teachers	兼任教师 Part-time Teachers
工勤人员 Workers	校办企业职工 Employees in School-run Factories & Farms		
124430	**805**	**167253**	**25854**
51903	376	122013	15201
17382	41	15700	6833
88765	493	153989	23441
1614	14	455	59
65		9	60
33986	298	12800	2294
36667	246	32788	4923
20765	148	30297	3991
354		239	29
52		4	4
15496	98	2248	899
7858	27	5213	921
3751	18	4887	552
105		13	
3		3	
3999	9	310	369
49259	422	44573	4828
34690	266	37890	4115
1125	14	121	21
9		5	42
13435	142	6557	650
12723	101	16962	1657
7732	59	14267	1149
26			
2			
4963	42	2695	508
38504	137	89892	16103
33310	79	85802	15335
135		95	9
4			14
5055	58	3995	745

小学分课程专任教师
Number of Full-time Teachers in Primary School

	合 计 Total	其中:女 of Which: Female	品德与生活(社会) Virtue Education	语 文 Language & Literature	数 学 Mathematics	外语 Foreign		
						小计 Subtotal	英语 English	日语 Japanese
总 计 Total	**5584644**	**3388375**	**217012**	**2091617**	**1687700**	**381025**	**379253**	**135**
其中:女 Female	3388375		98333	1459260	954464	316258	315225	112
少数民族 Minorities	589984	324806	22725	224914	179575	24350	24077	78
研究生毕业 Graduate	20228	15477	640	6935	3920	2987	2973	4
本科毕业 Under-graduate	2059660	1504951	56385	809035	563936	216438	215619	71
专科毕业 Associate Bachelor	2797184	1657671	114766	1045223	889797	152560	151791	57
高中阶段毕业 High School Graduate	697973	208295	44545	227365	227002	8971	8802	3
高中阶段以下毕业 Below High School Graduate	9599	1981	676	3059	3045	69	68	

小学专任教师专业
Number of Full-time Teachers in Primary

	合 计 Total	其中:女 of Which Female	24岁及以下 24 Years and Under	25－29 25 to 29	30－34 30 to 34
总 计 Total	**5584644**	**3388375**	**276220**	**736869**	**1049492**
女 Female	3388375		226635	562631	751259
少数民族 Minorities	589984	324806	24564	87229	114131
中学高级 Senior Secondary	114805	58860		102	1519
小学高级 Senior Primary	2919927	1618333	950	34895	339841
小学一级 1st Grade Primary	1880106	1213032	47322	432702	619288
小学二级 2nd Grade Primary	177237	118172	28526	76261	38383
小学三级 3rd Grade Primary	12469	8414	3295	4328	1971
未定职级 No-ranking	480100	371564	196127	188581	48490

学历情况

by Subject Taught and Educational Attainment

单位：人
unit: person

Languages 俄语 Russian	体　育 Physical	科　学 Science	艺　术 Art	音　乐 Music	美　术 Fine Arts	综合实践活动 Practical Activities 小　计 Subtotal	信息技术 Information Technique	劳动与技术 Skills Teaching	其他 Others	当年不任课 No Teaching Load in Current Year
37	**263827**	**179163**	**23342**	**183922**	**170420**	**176472**	**115220**	**54562**	**128400**	**81744**
27	58319	72151	13578	139202	100244	66245	40877	22224	74838	35483
11	25264	17055	1884	17576	14844	15450	9818	4988	33645	12702
1	1654	708	54	847	965	811	681	103	431	276
18	97885	50462	6010	80465	68082	60521	46838	11664	32225	18216
14	124506	95881	13661	84597	79163	90189	57901	28873	69191	37650
4	39239	31808	3569	17838	21943	24635	9709	13724	25955	25103
	543	304	48	175	267	316	91	198	598	499

技术职称、年龄结构情况

Schools by Professional Rank and Age

单位：人
unit: person

35－39 35 to 39	40－44 40 to 44	45－49 45 to 49	50－54 50 to 54	55－59 55 to 59	60 岁及以上 60 Years and Over
961730	**801147**	**693089**	**617108**	**446391**	**2598**
649309	514103	395180	285061	3597	600
106133	89391	77308	54458	36664	106
11641	28506	32343	26342	14203	149
563360	581792	531234	498559	367462	1834
349240	170385	117086	84540	59281	262
16123	6797	4641	3606	2859	41
969	511	462	437	486	10
20397	13156	7323	3624	2100	302

小学专任教

Changes of Full-time

	上学年初报表专任教师数 Number of Full-time Teachers at Beginning of Previous Academic Year	增加教师 Factors of Increase				
		合计 Total	录用毕业生 New Recruits from Current Year Graduates		调入 Teachers Recruited from Other Units	校内调整 of Which: with Change of Status in Their Own Institutions
			小计 Subtotal	其中:师范生 of Which: Students Enrolled in Teacher Training Institutions		
总计 Total	**5585475**	**728872**	**151220**	**106853**	**410419**	**127313**
其中:女 of Which: Female	3328014	441615	119492	85005	238206	57939
城区 Urban Area	1423469	170283	39202	30797	94003	21585
其中:女 of Which: Female	1100517	123836	32124	25357	67805	12528
城乡结合区 Urban-rural Transitional Area	277759	40958	9443	7258	21802	5591
其中:女 of Which: Female	195809	27994	7533	5815	14588	2949
镇区 Counties & Towns Area	1899563	243360	43607	30133	145055	42469
其中:女 of Which: Female	1220838	153283	35377	24580	89648	20388
镇乡结合区 County-town Transitional Area	597288	80679	13555	9448	49453	13705
其中:女 of Which: Female	372388	50963	11082	7810	30399	6747
乡村 Rural Area	2262443	315229	68411	45923	171361	63259
其中:女 of Which: Female	1006659	164496	51991	35068	80753	25023

小学学生、教职工

Supplementary Information on Students and

	在校学生中 of Total Students			教职 of Total Educational	
	共青团员 Member of C. Y. L.	华侨 Overseas Chinese	港澳台 From H. K, Macao and Taiwan	共产党员 Member of C. P. C.	共青团员 Member of C. Y. L.
总计 Total	**110107**	**13689**	**45345**	**1410773**	**257865**
其中:女 of Which: Female	51736	6353	20663	628725	201761
城区 Urban Area	26901	7222	39105	427773	101771
其中:女 of Which: Female	13417	3338	17821	289530	84613
城乡结合区 Urban-rural Transitional Area	4243	1176	6556	69802	17274
其中:女 of Which: Female	2090	518	3081	38322	14130
镇区 Counties & Towns Area	48210	4148	3939	469640	78236
其中:女 of Which: Female	22027	1899	1745	200849	62206
镇乡结合区 County-town Transitional Area	20502	745	1256	134515	22616
其中:女 of Which: Female	9091	317	547	54129	18058
乡村 Rural Area	34996	2319	2301	513360	77858
其中:女 of Which: Female	16292	1116	1097	138346	54942

师变动情况
Teachers in Primary Schools

单位：人
unit：person

其他 Others	减少教师 Factors of Decrease 合计 Total	自然减员 Retired from Their Posts during Previous Academic Year	调出 Transferred from Teaching to Non-teaching Posts	校内调整 of Which：with Change of Status in Their Own Institutions	其他 Others	本学年初报表专任教师数 Number of Full-time Teachers at Beginning of Current Academic Year
39920	**729703**	**132965**	**413194**	**137610**	**45934**	**5584644**
25978	381254	62719	228882	64269	25384	3388375
15493	127106	25764	67082	19697	14563	1466646
11379	86462	18086	46647	12105	9624	1137891
4122	33468	6283	17603	5662	3920	285249
2924	20895	3895	11346	3244	2410	202908
12229	223706	42238	126913	40308	14247	1919217
7870	127843	22405	76804	20247	8387	1246278
3966	78501	14316	46465	13193	4527	599466
2735	43451	7159	27156	6558	2578	379900
12198	378891	64963	219199	77605	17124	2198781
6729	166949	22228	105431	31917	7373	1004206

政治面貌及其他
Educational Personnel of Primary Schools

单位：人
unit：person

工　中 Personnel 民主党派 Member of Dem. Parties	华　侨 Overseas Chinese	专任教师中 of Total Full-time Teachers 共产党员 Member of C. P. C.	共青团员 Member of C. Y. L.	民主党派 Member of Dem. Parties	华　侨 Overseas Chinese
13001	**609**	**1384504**	**301082**	**13001**	**575**
9015	339	646142	237076	9129	329
8710	236	422703	123808	8600	216
6536	166	293992	103067	6502	157
543	39	69796	24466	540	46
354	27	40614	20065	359	33
2550	149	459281	91287	2697	143
1719	92	208251	72868	1871	91
515	18	129815	26651	526	17
316	14	55496	21387	345	15
1741	224	502520	85987	1704	216
760	81	143899	61141	756	81

小学办学
Condition of School Buildings

	合计 Total	城区 Urban Area
总　计 Total	**620648517**	**158066383**
其中:危房 of Which:Floor Space of Dilapidated Buildings	29504829	2407818
当年新增 New Floor Space Added in Current Year	29095493	6896918
一、教学及辅助用房 Teaching & Assistant Buildings	349119945	88145120
教室 Classroom	294287815	70883164
实验室 Laboratory	17652404	4647815
图书室 Library	15125683	3866696
微机室 PC-room	12127654	3378494
语音室 Linguistic	3462403	1131049
体育馆 Gymnasium	6463986	4237902
二、行政办公用房 Administrative	60730192	17763554
其中:教师办公室 of Which: for Teachers	42720733	11086720
三、生活用房 Residential and Welfare	152410495	27332642
教工宿舍 Apartments for Single	50586522	5947865
其中:教师周转宿舍 Accommodation for Circulation of Teachers	7860712	653544
学生宿舍 Students' Dormitories	33645001	3988895
食堂 Dining Halls	26165162	5704024
厕所 Toilet	25437191	6123364
其他 Others	16576619	5568494
四、其他用房 Rooms for Other Purposes	58387885	24825067

条件(一)
in Primary Schools (1)

单位：平方米
unit: m^2

其中:城乡结合区 of Which: Urban-rural Transitional Area	镇区 Counties & Towns Area	其中:镇乡结合区 of Which: County-town Transitional Area	乡村 Rural Area
32615007	**198103692**	**66227971**	**264478442**
569345	7188366	2720233	19908645
1565893	10565762	3217069	11632813
18136929	108699448	37857532	152275377
14724798	92016373	32028048	131388278
995151	5466119	1941028	7538470
819655	4429209	1646863	6829778
690999	3924688	1349410	4824472
222259	1313888	403921	1017466
684067	1549171	488262	676913
3300421	19541085	6556798	23425553
2106552	13512583	4676437	18121430
6528773	53812282	16242151	71265571
1872661	17861886	5317952	26776771
181794	2953232	698048	4253936
1043753	14179572	3593902	15476534
1254825	9486869	2892117	10974269
1323831	7269017	2722162	12044810
1033703	5014938	1716018	5993187
4648884	16050877	5571490	17511941

小学办学

Condition of School Buildings

	占地面积(平方米) Areas Occupied			图书(册) Books & Magazines in Libraries (volume)	计算机数(台)	
	合计 Total	其中 of Which			合计 Total	其中:教学用 No. of Computers
		绿化用地面积 Green Areas	运动场地面积 Sports Areas			小计 Subtotal
总　计 Total	**2274275122**	**375972161**	**676434475**	**1770876638**	**7317496**	**5930713**
城区 Urban Area	352991477	68220128	124592219	549450846	2917061	2376205
其中:城乡结合区 of Which: Urban-rural Transitional Area	101483728	20871626	33855146	98772353	504470	414255
镇区 Counties & Towns Area	652119160	109951629	196560102	600533487	2353456	1926288
其中:镇乡结合区 of Which: County-town Transitional Area	242374743	40528406	73311155	190930876	726296	599846
乡村 Rural Area	1269164485	197800404	355282154	620892305	2046979	1628220

小学办学条件(三)

Condition of School Buildings in Primary Schools (3)

单位：所
unit：school

	体育运动场(馆)面积达标校数 Schools No: Sprots Areas Reached Standard	体育器械配备达标校数 Schools No: Sports Equip. Reached Standard	音乐器械配备达标校数 Schools No: Musical Instru. Reached Standard	美术器械配备达标校数 Schools No: Fine Arts Instru. Reached Standard	教学自然实验仪器达标校数 Schools No: Equip. of Natural Sci. Reached Standard	建立校园网校数 Schools No: Campus Networks Set	接入互联网校数 Schools No: Internet Access
总　计 Total	**109844**	**111314**	**107047**	**106955**	**115710**	**54489**	**145338**
城区 Urban Area	18207	20442	20216	20153	20343	16260	23908
其中:城乡结合区 of Which: Urban-rural Transitional Area	5322	5660	5517	5494	5681	3664	7020
镇区 Counties & Towns Area	27487	28929	28082	27894	29715	16475	38128
其中:镇乡结合区 of Which: County-town Transitional Area	11538	11748	11292	11241	12098	5744	16371
乡村 Rural Area	64150	61943	58749	58908	65652	21754	83302

条件(二)
in Primary Schools (2)

No. of Computers 计算机 Used for Instruction 其中:平板电脑 of Which: Tablet PC	教室(间)Classroom(room) 合计 Total	其中:网络多媒体教室 of Which: Network Multimedia Classroom	教室中:普通教室(间) of Which: General Classroom 合计 Total	其中:网络多媒体教室 of Which: Network Multimedia Classroom	固定资产总值(万元) Total Volue of Fixed Asset (10,000 yuan) 合计 Total	其中:教学仪器设备资产值 of Which: Total Volue of Equip & Instru. 小计 Subtotal	其中:实验设备 of Which: for Profession
227025	**3471445**	**939436**	**2879225**	**809045**	**60201121.29**	**7171039.00**	**1886206.23**
92236	726896	420053	572990	353673	21037378.31	3386930.99	681385.76
15682	158371	70278	121514	58616	3973362.44	522996.48	132898.61
77225	998650	309230	839245	276524	19562091.76	2049322.30	610374.31
24296	371666	91071	313319	80698	6015437.92	598978.09	192130.13
57564	1745899	210153	1466990	178848	19601651.22	1734785.71	594446.16

成人小学基本情况
Basic Statistics of Adult Primary Schools by Province

单位:人(人次)
unit: person

	学校数(所) Schools	教学班(点)(个) External Teaching Sites	毕(结)业生数 Graduates 合计 Total	其中:女 of Which: Female	注册学生数 Enrolment 合计 Total	其中:女 of Which: Female	教职工数 Educational Personnel 合计 Total	其中:女 of Which: Female	专任教师 Full-time Teachers 合计 Total	其中:女 of Which: Female	聘请校外教师 Part-time Teachers
总 计 Total	**21840**	**39259**	**1177918**	**599231**	**1242563**	**666796**	**43603**	**18374**	**22639**	**10882**	**26187**
其中:少数民族 of Which: Minority	1125	3818	111293	52608	132102	65003	3544	1331	1175	502	4068
职工小学 General Primary Schools for Staff & Workers	525	608	27504	12762	21106	9504	600	355	363	246	467
农民小学 General Primary Shools for Peasants	21315	38651	1150414	586469	1221457	657292	43003	18019	22276	10636	25720
小学班 Primary Classes	6211	10687	644537	316077	602229	324680	10345	4117	6877	3098	6242
扫盲班 Literacy Classes	15104	27964	505877	270392	619228	332612	32658	13902	15399	7538	19478

五、工读学校
Correctional Work-study Schools

工读学校基本情况
Basic Statistics of Correctional Work-study Schools

单位：人
unit: person

	学校数（所）Schools	班 数（个）Classes	离校人数 Sclools Leavers	入校人数 No. of Persons Enrolled	在校生数 Enrolment	教职工数 Educational Personnel	
						合计 Total	其中:专任教师 of Which: Full-time Teachers
总　计 Total	**78**	**373**	**3596**	**3891**	**9307**	**2687**	**1851**
其中:女 of Which: Female			480	436	1265	971	711

六、特殊教育
Special Education

特殊教育
Basic Statistics of

	学校数（所）Schools	班 数（个）Classes	毕业生数 Graduates	招生数 Entrants	合计 Total	其中:女 of Which: Female	小学 一年级 Grade 1	二年级 Grade 2
总 计 Total	**1933**	**18909**	**50739**	**65977**	**368103**	**132523**	**45138**	**45848**
女 Female			17409	24163	132523		16539	16444
少数民族学生 Minority Students			3097	5940	28536	11449	4477	3944
寄宿生 Of the TotalBoarders			11313	21101	125797	48712	15769	15181
特殊教育学校中:寄宿生 of the Special Education Schools: Boarders			7362	15299	101322	39257	14989	14146
职业技术班 Vocational and Technical Classes			1081	895	4114	1271	15	27
视力残疾 Visual Impairment	32	1098	7024	8681	40094	14962	2957	3372
听力残疾 Hearing Impairment	446	7721	14332	13419	89173	36864	10096	10303
智力残疾 Intellectual Disability	428	9640	22376	32551	185047	62976	26217	25965
其他残疾 Other Disability	1027	456	7007	11326	53789	17721	5868	6208
特殊教育学校 Schools for Special Edu.		18337	21557	30894	177195	68106	27947	24577
视力残疾 Visual Impairment		1076	1491	1668	8860	3161	1014	910
听力残疾 Hearing Impariment		7668	11591	10255	71614	31122	8342	8094
智力残疾 Intellecutual Disability		9193	8057	18037	92870	32481	17712	14957
其他残疾 Other Disability		400	418	934	3851	1342	879	616
小学附设特教班 Classes Attached to Primary Schools		532	469	468	3150	1226	611	505
视力残疾 Visual Impairment		21	3	28	76	33	29	19
听力残疾 Hearing Impariment		46	26	88	333	157	90	59
智力残疾 Intellecutual Disability		409	408	315	2490	934	460	345
其他残疾 Other Disability		56	32	37	251	102	32	82
小学随班就读 Followers In Primary Schools			14238	16093	129508	42750	16563	20750
视力残疾 Visual Impairment			1708	1866	15837	5502	1914	2443
听力残疾 Hearing Impariment			1260	1608	12334	3927	1655	2145
智力残疾 Intellecutual Disability			8389	7764	68846	22794	8037	10652
其他残疾 Other Disability			2881	4855	32491	10527	4957	5510
初中附设特教班 Special Classes Attached to Junior High Schools		40	23	6	147	47	6	11
视力残疾 Visual Impairment		1			5	1		
听力残疾 Hearing Impariment		6	4	4	32	10	4	5
智力残疾 Intellecutual Disability		33	19	2	110	36	2	6
其他残疾 Other Disability								
初中随班就读 Followers in Junior High Schools			14422	18482	58026	20361		
视力残疾 Visual Impairment			3822	5119	15316	6265		
听力残疾 Hearing Impariment			1451	1460	4855	1645		
智力残疾 Intellecutual Disability			5473	6403	20659	6701		
其他残疾 Other Disability			3676	5500	17196	5750		
其他学校附设特教班 Special Classes Attached to Other Schools		695	30	34	77	33	11	5
视力残疾 Visual Impairment		34						
听力残疾 Hearing Impariment		74		4	5	3	5	
智力残疾 Intellecutual Disability		525	30	30	72	30	6	5
其他残疾 Other Disability		62						
城区 Urban Area	942	11257	22003	26340	155918	57984	18552	17325
其中:城乡结合区 of Which: Urban-rural Transitional Area	135	1685	3254	4705	25213	9346	3154	2992
镇区 County and Town Area	872	6677	20164	26694	139421	50618	17468	18179
其中:镇乡结合区 of Which: County-town Transitional Area	293	2141	4723	7431	38335	13667	5357	5749
乡村 Rural Area	119	975	8572	12943	72764	23921	9118	10344

基本情况
Special Education

单位：人
unit: person

在校生数 Enrolment										
阶段 Primary Education				初中阶段 Junior Secondary Education				高中阶段 Senior Secondary Education		
三年级 Grade 3	四年级 Grade 4	五年级 Grade 5	六年级 Grade 6	一年级 Grade 1	二年级 Grade 2	三年级 Grade 3	四年级 Grade 4	一年级 Grade 1	二年级 Grade 2	三年级及以上 Over 3 Grade
43204	**42693**	**42086**	**40098**	**32948**	**32625**	**31574**	**1894**	**3803**	**3232**	**2960**
15402	15072	14707	13888	12242	11908	11480	698	1525	1371	1247
3555	3407	3090	3033	2129	2171	2203	29	183	153	162
13458	12586	12444	11588	13334	12728	12131	393	2363	2013	1809
12174	10997	10430	9292	8293	7485	6939	392	2363	2013	1809
47	61	61	62	178	156	209	20	1110	1076	1092
3416	3889	3876	3945	5898	5625	5784	50	465	409	408
9595	9566	9414	9118	8133	8155	7959	383	2303	2134	2014
24317	23476	22900	20895	13039	12762	11886	1356	1031	680	523
5876	5762	5896	6140	5878	6083	5945	105	4	9	15
21114	19232	17774	15722	14265	13000	12264	1362	3788	3190	2960
976	931	851	855	747	626	635	33	465	409	408
7413	7313	7141	7098	6651	6437	6327	347	2303	2134	2014
12225	10621	9413	7491	6535	5727	5084	928	1016	638	523
500	367	369	278	332	210	218	54	4	9	15
427	445	542	508	63	12	37				
3	10	6	9							
52	53	42	24	13						
336	361	457	433	50	12	36				
36	21	37	42			1				
21634	22996	23722	23843							
2432	2948	3019	3081							
2125	2192	2224	1993							
11737	12482	12989	12949							
5340	5374	5490	5820							
29	16	48	25	11		1				
5										
5	8	7	3							
19	8	41	22	11		1				
				18609	19613	19272	532			
				5151	4999	5149	17			
				1469	1718	1632	36			
				6443	7023	6765	428			
				5546	5873	5726	51			
	4							15	42	
	4							15	42	
17164	16672	16884	15593	14623	14331	14158	1563	3446	2876	2731
2743	2726	2574	2486	2625	2604	2380	75	377	281	196
16141	16117	15181	14848	13738	13782	12930	260	309	266	202
4881	4697	4226	4025	3153	3008	2879	75	109	84	92
9899	9904	10021	9657	4587	4512	4486	71	48	90	27

特殊教育学

Number of Educational Personnel

	教　职 Educational		
	合计 Total	专任教师 Full-time Teachers	行政人员 Adm. Personnel
总　计 Total	**55096**	**45653**	**3561**
其中:女 of Which:Female	37685	33079	1676
少数民族 Minorities	4070	3356	272

特殊教育学校专任

Number of Full-time Teachers in Special Education

	合计 Total	按学历分 By Educational Attainment				
		研究生毕业 Graduate	本科毕业 Under-graduate	专科毕业 Associate Bachelor	高中阶段毕业 High School Graduate	高中阶段以下毕业 Below High School Graduate
总　计 Total	**45653**	**703**	**25068**	**17569**	**2257**	**56**
其中:女 of Which:Female	33079	536	18544	12651	1310	38
受过特教专业培训 Trained in Special Education	27854	492	16002	10239	1095	26

特殊教育专任

Changes of Full-time Teachers in

	上学年初报表专任教师数 Number of Full-time Teachers at Beginning of Previous Academic Year	增　加　教　师 Factors of Increase					
		合计 Total	录用毕业生 New Recruits from Current Year Graduates		调入 Teachers Recruited from Other Units	校内调整 of Which: with Change of Status in Their Own Institutions	其　他 Others
			小计 Subtotal	其中:师范生 of Which: Students Enrolled in Teacher Training Institutions			
总　计 Total	**43697**	**4608**	**1381**	**1046**	**2324**	**613**	**290**
其中:女 of Which: Female	31624	3182	1132	871	1517	334	199

校教职工数
in Special Education Schools

单位：人
unit：person

工　数 Personnel		代课教师 Substitute Teachers	兼任教师 Part-time Teachers
教辅人员 Supporting Staff	工勤人员 Workers		
2325	**3557**	**1171**	**201**
1490	1440	872	90
191	251	84	6

教师学历、职称情况
Schools by Educational Attainment and Professional Rank

单位：人
unit：person

按职称分 By Professional Rank					
中学高级 Senior Secondary	小学高级 Senior Primary	小学一级 1st Grade Primary	小学二级 2nd Grade Primary	小学三级 3rd Grade Primary	未定职级 No-ranking
4013	**22891**	**13415**	**1447**	**118**	**3769**
2331	16499	9984	1094	104	3067
2161	13499	8666	941	92	2495

教师变动情况
Special Education Schools

单位：人
unit：person

减　少　教　师 Factors of Decrease					本学年初报表专任教师数 Number of Full-time Teachers at Beginning of Current Academic Year
合计 Total	自然减员 Retired from Their Posts during Previous Academic Year	调出 Transferred from Teaching to Non-Teaching Posts	校内调整 of Which：with Change of Status in Their Own Institutions	其　他 Others	
2652	**763**	**982**	**606**	**301**	**45653**
1727	547	630	351	199	33079

特殊教育学校办学条件(一)
Condition of School Buildings in Special Education Schools (1)

单位:平方米
unit: m^2

	合计 Total
总　计 Total	**7418850**
其中:危房 of Which:Floor Space of Dilapidated Buildings	96641
当年新增校舍 New Added in Current Year	709026
一、教学及辅助用房 Teaching & Assistant Buildings	3381342
教室 Classroom Only	1979042
专用教室 Classroom	999427
实验室 Laboratory	137448
微机室 PC-room	128719
图书室 Library	136706
二、行政办公用房 Administrative	784388
其中:教师办公室 of Which: for Teachers	457414
三、生活用房 Residential and Welfare	2168672
四、其他用房 Rooms for Other Purposes	1084448

特殊教育学校办学条件(二)
Condition of School Buildings in Special Education Schools (2)

	占地面积(平方米) Areas Occupied (m^2)			图书(册) Books & Magazines in Libraries (volume)	数字资源(GB) Digital Resources
	合计 Total	其中 of Which			
		绿化用地面积 Green Areas	运动场地面积 Sports Areas		
总　计 Total	**16677524**	**3451599**	**3850577**	**7368327**	**372981**

七、幼儿教育
Pre-primary Education

幼儿园园数、班数

Number of Kindergartens, Classes in Pre-Primary Education

	园数(所) Kindergartens		班数(个) Classes
	合计 Total	其中:少数民族幼儿园 of Which: Minorities	
总　计 Total	**198553**	**4339**	**1343042**
教育部门 Run by Ed. Dept.	45037	3644	499800
其他部门办 Run by Non-ed. Dept.	1854	29	20589
地方企业 Run by Local Enterprises	1413		11216
事业单位 Run by Public Institutions	3364	34	19060
部队 Run by Army	491	1	4088
集体办 Run by Communities	12943	49	64743
民办 Non-government	133451	582	723546
城区 Urban Area	61239	339	471208
教育部门 Run by Ed. Dept.	7455	133	90766
其他部门办 Run by Non-ed. Dept.	1155	3	15094
地方企业 Run by Local Enterprises	1142		9408
事业单位 Run by Public Institutions	999	17	7835
部队 Run by Army	465	1	3957
集体办 Run by Communities	3861	17	26947
民办 Non-government	46162	168	317201
其中:城乡结合区 of Which: Urban-rural Transitional Area	12067	63	80927
教育部门 Run by Ed. Dept.	1293	45	14333
其他部门办 Run by Non-ed. Dept.	53		498
地方企业 Run by Local Enterprises	78		578
事业单位 Run by Public Institutions	128	1	655
部队 Run by Army	11		70
集体办 Run by Communities	1682	3	9569
民办 Non-government	8822	14	55224

幼儿园园数、班数(续)

Number of Kindergartens, Classes in Pre-Primary Education(Cont.)

	园数(所) Kindergartens		班数(个) Classes
	合计 Total	其中:少数民族幼儿园 of Which:Minorities	
镇区 Counties & Towns Area	67436	836	463356
教育部门 Run by Ed. Dept.	15879	570	178812
其他部门办 Run by Non-ed. Dept.	569	11	4797
地方企业 Run by Local Enterprises	222		1561
事业单位 Run by Public Institutions	952	10	5857
部队 Run by Army	12		67
集体办 Run by Communities	2824	10	17859
民办 Non-government	46978	235	254403
其中:镇乡结合区 of Which: County-town Transitional Area	21248	194	136362
教育部门 Run by Ed. Dept.	4637	138	51379
其他部门办 Run by Non-ed. Dept.	54	1	464
地方企业 Run by Local Enterprises	47		298
事业单位 Run by Public Institutions	247	1	1481
部队 Run by Army	1		6
集体办 Run by Communities	1450	6	7495
民办 Non-government	14812	48	75239
乡村 Rural Area	69878	3164	408478
教育部门 Run by Ed. Dept.	21703	2941	230222
其他部门办 Run by Non-ed. Dept.	130	15	698
地方企业 Run by Local Enterprises	49		247
事业单位 Run by Public Institutions	1413	7	5368
部队 Run by Army	14		64
集体办 Run by Communities	6258	22	19937
民办 Non-government	40311	179	151942
总计中:独立设置幼儿园 of the Total:Inde. Kinder.			1103844
附设幼儿班 Kinder. Classes Attached to School			239198

学前(幼儿)教育分年龄学生数

Number of Students in Pre-school Education by Age

单位：人

unit：person

	入园(班)人数 Entrants	在园(班)人数 Enrolment	离园(班)人数 Leavers
总　计 Total	**19700271**	**38946903**	**14917314**
其中:女 of Which:Female	9139790	17982284	7092734
少数民族 Minorities	1882904	3155937	1498934
残疾人 Disability	11794	32527	12961
教育部门 Run by Ed. Dept.	9235621	15484717	7299649
2 岁以下 2 Years and Under	169020	178852	
3 岁 3 Years	2437221	2689122	
4 岁 4 Years	1874342	4212137	
5 岁 5 Years	3547400	6664087	1606241
6 岁及以上 6 Years and Over	1207638	1740519	5693408
其他部门 Run by Non-ed. Dept.	251118	625535	210712
2 岁以下 2 Years and Under	26320	28061	
3 岁 3 Years	124716	158347	
4 岁 4 years	44896	192194	
5 岁 5 Years	44592	217913	42802
6 岁及以上 6 Years and Over	10594	29020	167910
地方企业 Run by Local Enterprises	120196	338144	110332
2 岁以下 2 Years and Under	16149	17831	
3 岁 3 Years	63477	88775	
4 岁 4 Years	20815	106569	
5 岁 5 Years	17679	115518	22068
6 岁及以上 6 Years and Over	2076	9451	88264
事业单位 Run by Public Institutions	277086	568988	246705
2 岁以下 2 Years and Under	15359	16793	
3 岁 3 Years	87010	112051	
4 岁 4 Years	57876	160920	
5 岁 5 Years	93632	235984	44177
6 岁及以上 6 Years and Over	23209	43240	202528
部队 Run by Army	45259	134487	38865
2 岁以下 2 Years and Under	8092	8578	
3 岁 3 Years	28184	39425	
4 岁 4 Years	4897	42744	
5 岁 5 Years	3844	41562	6074
6 岁及以上 6 Years and Over	242	2178	32791
集体 Run by Communities	691416	1892496	664004
2 岁以下 2 Years and Under	40057	45109	
3 岁 3 Years	390181	474010	
4 岁 4 Years	131564	607118	
5 岁 5 Years	111626	700547	77227
6 岁及以上 6 Years and Over	17988	65712	586777
民办 Non-government	9079575	19902536	6347047
2 岁以下 2 Years and Under	820937	958304	
3 岁 3 Years	3320355	4608967	
4 岁 4 Years	2365137	6362596	
5 岁 5 Years	2217807	7040600	1534201
6 岁及以上 6 Years and Over	355339	932069	4812846

学前(幼儿)教育分年龄学生数(续)(城区)

Number of Students in Pre-school Education by Age (Urban Area)

单位:人

unit: person

	入园(班)人数 Entrants	在园(班)人数 Enrolment	离园(班)人数 Leavers
总 计 Total	**5284877**	**13175629**	**4308058**
其中:女 of Which:Female	2441126	6050646	2019730
少数民族 Minorities	222104	507831	199144
残疾人 Disability	3793	12498	6532
教育部门 Run by Ed. Dept.	1441221	3117629	1203089
2 岁以下 2 Years and Under	61475	64664	
3 岁 3 Years	679655	768101	
4 岁 4 Years	214514	925142	
5 岁 5 Years	387538	1205825	241555
6 岁及以上 6 Years and Over	98039	153897	961534
其他部门 Run by Non-ed. Dept.	161759	444586	138686
2 岁以下 2 Years and Under	22254	23671	
3 岁 3 Years	95043	122168	
4 岁 4 Years	22512	138399	
5 岁 5 Years	19740	149823	28577
6 岁及以上 6 Years and Over	2210	10525	110109
地方企业 Run by Local Enterprises	95842	281422	90390
2 岁以下 2 Years and Under	14192	15723	
3 岁 3 Years	51688	74142	
4 岁 4 Years	15725	88299	
5 岁 5 Years	12588	95211	16935
6 岁及以上 6 Years and Over	1649	8047	73455
事业单位 Run by Public Institutions	105949	256819	96643
2 岁以下 2 Years and Under	11808	12760	
3 岁 3 Years	43729	61497	
4 岁 4 Years	15829	74296	
5 岁 5 Years	28395	95999	21686
6 岁及以上 6 and Over	6188	12267	74957
部队 Run by Army	44077	130571	37838
2 岁以下 2 Years and Under	7865	8346	
3 岁 3 Years	27386	38339	
4 岁 4 Years	4802	41439	
5 岁 5 Years	3796	40417	6001
6 岁及以上 6 Years and Over	228	2030	31837
集体 Run by Communities	295729	843041	282088
2 岁以下 2 Years and Under	24260	27207	
3 岁 3 Years	171897	220327	
4 岁 4 Years	49515	268561	
5 岁 5 Years	43897	305913	38899
6 岁及以上 6 Years and Over	6160	21033	243189
民办 Non-government	3140300	8101561	2459324
2 岁以下 2 Years and Under	417232	495478	
3 岁 3 Years	1235074	1919283	
4 岁 4 Years	712198	2509595	
5 岁 5 Years	678389	2854073	504778
6 岁及以上 6 Years and Over	97407	323132	1954546

幼儿教育分年龄学生数(城乡结合区)

Number of Students in Pre-school Education by Age (Urban-rural Transitional Area)

单位：人

unit：person

	入园(班)人数 Entrants	在园(班)人数 Enrolment	离园(班)人数 Leavers
总　计 Total	**955612**	**2289332**	**756518**
其中:女 of Which:Female	438871	1041219	347350
少数民族 Minorities	34684	72152	31413
残疾人 Disability	1154	2656	1579
教育部门 Run by Ed. Dept.	240560	432802	182614
2 岁以下 2 Years and Under	7593	8092	
3 岁 3 Years	75486	86559	
4 岁 4 Years	46318	120025	
5 岁 5 Years	85379	180937	38107
6 岁及以上 6 Years and Over	25784	37189	144507
其他部门 Run by Non-ed. Dept.	7403	17416	5297
2 岁以下 2 Years and Under	453	476	
3 岁 3 Years	4223	4746	
4 岁 4 Years	1200	5579	
5 岁 5 Years	1397	6088	1864
6 岁及以上 6 Years and Over	130	527	3433
地方企业 Run by Local Enterprises	6437	17381	5559
2 岁以下 2 Years and Under	939	960	
3 岁 3 Years	3132	4513	
4 岁 4 Years	1293	5459	
5 岁 5 Years	833	5758	1231
6 岁及以上 6 Years and Over	240	691	4328
事业单位 Run by Public Institutions	12215	23290	10331
2 岁以下 2 Years and Under	281	329	
3 岁 3 Years	3878	4583	
4 岁 4 Years	2937	6747	
5 岁 5 Years	4240	10232	2803
6 岁及以上 6 Years and Over	879	1399	7528
部队 Run by Army	1134	2129	606
2 岁以下 2 Years and Under	203	203	
3 岁 3 Years	446	615	
4 岁 4 Years	231	662	
5 岁 5 Years	247	572	95
6 岁及以上 6 Years and Over	7	77	511
集体 Run by Communities	97339	280690	91713
2 岁以下 2 Years and Under	6417	7624	
3 岁 3 Years	54863	72284	
4 岁 4 Years	18391	89289	
5 岁 5 Years	15606	103389	13710
6 岁及以上 6 Years and Over	2062	8104	78003
民办 Non-government	590524	1515624	460398
2 岁以下 2 Years and Under	64539	77449	
3 岁 3 Years	235452	354401	
4 岁 4 Years	142585	481549	
5 岁 5 Years	128767	544799	94014
6 岁及以上 6 Years and Over	19181	57426	366384

幼儿教育分年龄学生数(镇区)

Number of Students in Pre-school Education by Age (Counties & Towns Area)

单位:人

unit: person

	入园(班)人数 Entrants	在园(班)人数 Enrolment	离园(班)人数 Leavers
总　计 Total	**7791227**	**14978832**	**5728075**
其中:女 of Which:Female	3598240	6897167	2720514
少数民族 Minorities	703378	1251833	546629
残疾人 Disability	4745	12024	3529
教育部门 Run by Ed. Dept.	3622373	6369261	2856761
2 岁以下 2 Years and Under	77171	81723	
3 岁 3 Years	1076845	1191476	
4 岁 4 Years	784233	1825937	
5 岁 5 Years	1296212	2678749	663393
6 岁及以上 6 Years and Over	387912	591376	2193368
其他部门 Run by Non-ed. Dept.	77539	160155	63391
2 岁以下 2 Years and Under	3835	4154	
3 岁 3 Years	26766	32703	
4 岁 4 Years	19327	47608	
5 岁 5 Years	20654	59695	12032
6 岁及以上 6 Years and Over	6957	15995	51359
地方企业 Run by Local Enterprises	21661	49494	17290
2 岁以下 2 Years and Under	1631	1762	
3 岁 3 Years	10702	12987	
4 岁 4 Years	4467	16178	
5 岁 5 Years	4456	17525	4473
6 岁及以上 6 Years and Over	405	1042	12817
事业单位 Run by Public Institutions	93216	177798	86123
2 岁以下 2 Years and Under	2279	2557	
3 岁 3 Years	24422	29270	
4 岁 4 Years	20978	48133	
5 岁 5 Years	34605	79048	13136
6 岁及以上 6 Years and Over	10932	18790	72987
部队 Run by Army	697	2130	568
2 岁以下 2 Years and Under	119	121	
3 岁 3 Years	453	612	
4 岁 4 Years	85	740	
5 岁 5 Years	39	611	32
6 岁及以上 6 Years and Over	1	46	536
集体 Run by Communities	218546	582069	205072
2 岁以下 2 Years and Under	10153	11205	
3 岁 3 Years	123819	143615	
4 岁 4 Years	41561	186455	
5 岁 5 Years	36083	215308	22519
6 岁及以上 6 Years and Over	6930	25486	182553
民办 Non-government	3757195	7637925	2498870
2 岁以下 2 Years and Under	285817	329111	
3 岁 3 Years	1313827	1732481	
4 岁 4 Years	1026717	2461833	
5 岁 5 Years	964084	2713599	649384
6 岁及以上 6 Years and Over	166750	400901	1849486

幼儿教育分年龄学生数(镇乡结合区)

Number of Students in Pre-school Education by Age (County-town Transitional Area)

单位:人
unit: person

	入园(班)人数 Entrants	在园(班)人数 Enrolment	离园(班)人数 Leavers
总　计 Total	**2209254**	**4163989**	**1609659**
其中:女 of Which: Female	1021857	1918793	762160
少数民族 Minorities	139264	231656	112438
残疾人 Disability	1278	3903	1468
教育部门 Run by Ed. Dept.	1022192	1669571	796840
2 岁以下 2 Years and Under	15654	16682	
3 岁 3 Years	262380	286693	
4 岁 4 Years	214859	463877	
5 岁 5 Years	402725	731700	184715
6 岁及以上 6 Years and Over	126574	170619	612125
其他部门 Run by Non-ed. Dept.	8101	17256	5704
2 岁以下 2 Years and Under	405	415	
3 岁 3 Years	3293	3843	
4 岁 4 Years	2031	5504	
5 岁 5 Years	2283	6597	1406
6 岁及以上 6 Years and Over	89	897	4298
地方企业 Run by Local Enterprises	3560	10101	3205
2 岁以下 2 Years and Under	225	242	
3 岁 3 Years	2337	2768	
4 岁 4 Years	643	3594	
5 岁 5 Years	345	3378	786
6 岁及以上 6 Years and Over	10	119	2419
事业单位 Run by Public Institutions	17054	37871	16358
2 岁以下 2 Years and Under	297	364	
3 岁 3 Years	5896	6754	
4 岁 4 Years	4049	11530	
5 岁 5 Years	5751	17016	2316
6 岁及以上 6 Years and Over	1061	2207	14042
部队 Run by Army	65	198	63
2 岁以下 2 Years and Under	4	4	
3 岁 3 Years	35	52	
4 岁 4 Years	17	33	
5 岁 5 Years	9	79	
6 岁及以上 6 Years and Over		30	63
集体 Run by Communities	83010	227156	79496
2 岁以下 2 Years and Under	3714	4094	
3 岁 3 Years	47098	55592	
4 岁 4 Years	16063	72734	
5 岁 5 Years	13648	84593	7491
6 岁及以上 6 Years and Over	2487	10143	72005
民办 Non-government	1075272	2201836	707993
2 岁以下 2 Years and Under	78493	89721	
3 岁 3 Years	388654	510496	
4 岁 4 Years	294126	718149	
5 岁 5 Years	270875	779961	182230
6 岁及以上 6 Years and Over	43124	103509	525763

幼儿教育分年龄学生数(乡村)

Number of Students in Pre-school Education by Age (Rural Area)

单位：人

unit：person

	入园(班)人数 Entrants	在园(班)人数 Enrolment	离园(班)人数 Leavers
总　计 Total	**6624167**	**10792442**	**4881181**
其中:女 of Which:Female	3100424	5034471	2352490
少数民族 Minorities	957422	1396273	753161
残疾人 Disability	3256	8005	2900
教育部门 Run by Ed. Dept.	4172027	5997827	3239799
2 岁以下 2 Years and Under	30374	32465	
3 岁 3 Years	680721	729545	
4 岁 4 Years	875595	1461058	
5 岁 5 Years	1863650	2779513	701293
6 岁及以上 6 Years and Over	721687	995246	2538506
其他部门 Run by Non-ed. Dept.	11820	20794	8635
2 岁以下 2 Years and Under	231	236	
3 岁 3 Years	2907	3476	
4 岁 4 Years	3057	6187	
5 岁 5 Years	4198	8395	2193
6 岁及以上 6 Years and Over	1427	2500	6442
地方企业 Run by Local Enterprises	2693	7228	2652
2 岁以下 2 Years and Under	326	346	
3 岁 3 Years	1087	1646	
4 岁 4 Years	623	2092	
5 岁 5 Years	635	2782	660
6 岁及以上 6 Years and Over	22	362	1992
事业单位 Run by Public Institutions	77921	134371	63939
2 岁以下 2 Years and Under	1272	1476	
3 岁 3 Years	18859	21284	
4 岁 4 Years	21069	38491	
5 岁 5 Years	30632	60937	9355
6 岁及以上 6 Years and Over	6089	12183	54584
部队 Run by Army	485	1786	459
2 岁以下 2 Years and Under	108	111	
3 岁 3 Years	345	474	
4 岁 4 Years	10	565	
5 岁 5 Years	9	534	41
6 岁及以上 6 Years and Over	13	102	418
集体 Run by Communities	177141	467386	176844
2 岁以下 2 Years and Under	5644	6697	
3 岁 3 Years	94465	110068	
4 岁 4 Years	40488	152102	
5 岁 5 Years	31646	179326	15809
6 岁及以上 6 Years and Over	4898	19193	161035
民办 Non-government	2182080	4163050	1388853
2 岁以下 2 Years and Under	117888	133715	
3 岁 3 Years	771454	957203	
4 岁 4 Years	626222	1391168	
5 岁 5 Years	575334	1472928	380039
6 岁及以上 6 Years and Over	91182	208036	1008814

幼儿园教

Number of Educational Personnel

	教职 Educational	
	合计 Total	园长 Kindergarten Heads
总计 Total	**2826753**	**221606**
其中:女 of Which: Female	2591701	200861
少数民族 Minorities	158839	14946
学前教育专业 Pre-primary Education Programmes	1255416	118071
教育部门 Run by Ed. Dept.	638390	43789
其他部门办 Run by Non-ed. Dept.	71828	3481
地方企业 Run by Local Enterprises	43696	2337
事业单位 Run by Public Institutions	42266	3173
部队 Run by Army	18645	863
集体办 Run by Communities	163174	12138
民办 Non-government	1848754	155825
城区 Urban Area	1423614	86600
教育部门 Run by Ed. Dept.	246437	11693
其他部门办 Run by Non-ed. Dept.	55753	2581
地方企业 Run by Local Enterprises	36750	1958
事业单位 Run by Public Institutions	27654	1540
部队 Run by Army	18192	828
集体办 Run by Communities	87610	4973
民办 Non-government	951218	63027
其中:城乡结合区 of Which: Urban-rural Transitional Area	218244	15155
教育部门 Run by Ed. Dept.	22682	1450
其他部门办 Run by Non-ed. Dept.	2005	98
地方企业 Run by Local Enterprises	2456	132
事业单位 Run by Public Institutions	1407	131
部队 Run by Army	309	17
集体办 Run by Communities	28185	1920
民办 Non-government	161200	11407
镇区 Counties & Towns Area	958790	76070
教育部门 Run by Ed. Dept.	279147	17476
其他部门办 Run by Non-ed. Dept.	14834	791
地方企业 Run by Local Enterprises	6005	312
事业单位 Run by Public Institutions	9201	792
部队 Run by Army	202	18
集体办 Run by Communities	43836	2875
民办 Non-government	605565	53806
其中:镇乡结合区 of Which: County-town Transitional Area	255254	22612
教育部门 Run by Ed. Dept.	57343	4545
其他部门办 Run by Non-ed. Dept.	1481	74
地方企业 Run by Local Enterprises	1242	71
事业单位 Run by Public Institutions	1974	212
部队 Run by Army	15	1
集体办 Run by Communities	16829	1320
民办 Non-government	176370	16389
乡村 Rural Area	444349	58936
教育部门 Run by Ed. Dept.	112806	14620
其他部门办 Run by Non-ed. Dept.	1241	109
地方企业 Run by Local Enterprises	941	67
事业单位 Run by Public Institutions	5411	841
部队 Run by Army	251	17
集体办 Run by Communities	31728	4290
民办 Non-government	291971	38992

职工数

in Kindergarten

单位：人
unit：person

工　数 Personnel				代课教师 Substitute Teachers	兼任教师 Part-time Teachers
专任教师 Full-time Teachers	保健医 Health Physician	保育员 Caretaker	其他 Other		
1663487	**72633**	**484534**	**384493**	**163689**	**24025**
1630288	64002	472132	224418	153340	19952
102672	2432	21713	17076	9080	3234
1062990	8035	46584	19736	56191	6075
444015	11043	77640	61903	100351	9204
39516	2006	13444	13381	2691	270
24057	1165	8003	8134	1426	333
25761	931	6575	5826	4286	2110
9358	619	3786	4019	208	135
100565	3331	25130	22010	7294	1123
1020215	53538	349956	269220	47433	10850
802174	41299	266927	226614	41473	8639
163209	6155	33769	31611	22695	2024
30385	1628	10476	10683	1561	139
20255	1032	6616	6889	1157	150
15367	785	5118	4844	1495	802
9093	603	3714	3954	205	135
50623	2216	15767	14031	1604	241
513242	28880	191467	154602	12756	5148
122268	6018	40650	34153	6992	1234
15204	428	3079	2521	3076	292
1146	55	327	379	56	5
1352	65	396	511	41	6
855	28	224	169	536	71
142	11	63	76	14	
16466	651	4831	4317	557	56
87103	4780	31730	26180	2712	804
592986	21414	157142	111178	81513	9501
200440	3805	33991	23435	53821	4264
8439	348	2753	2503	968	110
3321	107	1176	1089	252	181
6606	106	1036	661	1359	822
123	6	30	25		
28748	718	6454	5041	2612	624
345309	16324	111702	78424	22501	3500
154313	5993	42152	30184	23098	2128
40163	732	7433	4470	13732	877
930	34	256	187	103	2
732	18	226	195	29	1
1384	25	210	143	457	150
14					
11130	305	2159	1915	1413	145
99960	4879	31868	23274	7364	953
268327	9920	60465	46701	40703	5885
80366	1083	9880	6857	23835	2916
692	30	215	195	162	21
481	26	211	156	17	2
3788	40	421	321	1432	486
142	10	42	40	3	
21194	397	2909	2938	3078	258
161664	8334	46787	36194	12176	2202

幼儿园园长、专任教师
Number of Kindergarten Heads, Full-time Teachers

	合计 Total	按学历分 By Educational Attainment				
		研究生毕业 Graduate	本科毕业 Under-graduate	专科毕业 Associate Bachelor	高中阶段毕业 High School Graduate	高中阶段以下毕业 Below High School Graduate
总　计 Total	**1885093**	**4291**	**313650**	**989945**	**526263**	**50944**
园长 Kindergarten Heads	221606	2047	53819	118404	43517	3819
专任教师 Full-time Teachers	1663487	2244	259831	871541	482746	47125
城区 Urban Area	888774	3589	188166	491664	193836	11519
园长 Kindergarten Heads	86600	1704	28907	44660	10645	684
专任教师 Full-time Teachers	802174	1885	159259	447004	183191	10835
其中:城乡结合区 of Which: Urban-rural Transitional Area	137423	220	17040	72985	43831	3347
园长 Kindergarten Heads	15155	129	3589	8396	2829	212
专任教师 Full-time Teachers	122268	91	13451	64589	41002	3135
镇区 Counties & Towns Area	669056	558	97888	349284	201116	20210
园长 Kindergarten Heads	76070	277	17008	42498	15147	1140
专任教师 Full-time Teachers	592986	281	80880	306786	185969	19070
其中:镇乡结合区 of Which: County-town Transitional Area	176925	157	20805	88274	60752	6937
园长 Kindergarten Heads	22612	65	4335	12578	5200	434
专任教师 Full-time Teachers	154313	92	16470	75696	55552	6503
乡村 Rural Area	327263	144	27596	148997	131311	19215
园长 Kindergarten Heads	58936	66	7904	31246	17725	1995
专任教师 Full-time Teachers	268327	78	19692	117751	113586	17220

学历、职称情况

by Educational Attainment and Professional Rank

单位：人

unit：person

按职称分 By Professional Rank					
中学高级 Senior Secondary	小学高级 Senior Primary	小学一级 1st Grade Primary	小学二级 2nd Grade Primary	小学三级 3rd Grade Primary	未定职级 No-ranking
13574	**210850**	**242836**	**75699**	**14742**	**1327392**
7519	42615	24957	6687	1496	138332
6055	168235	217879	69012	13246	1189060
7736	103443	119074	38968	8179	611374
4632	18879	10613	2958	722	48796
3104	84564	108461	36010	7457	562578
465	7542	11892	4434	1018	112072
295	2032	1804	609	125	10290
170	5510	10088	3825	893	101782
4557	79555	89201	25712	4600	465431
2224	14752	7499	1893	486	49216
2333	64803	81702	23819	4114	416215
915	15681	19743	5959	1123	133504
444	3645	2277	548	122	15576
471	12036	17466	5411	1001	117928
1281	27852	34561	11019	1963	250587
663	8984	6845	1836	288	40320
618	18868	27716	9183	1675	210267

	教职工中 of Total Educational Personnel		
	共产党员 Member of C. P. C.	共青团员 Member of C. Y. L.	民主党派 Member of Dem. Parties
总　计 Total	**197582**	**568237**	**4549**
其中:女 of Which: Female	172775	556872	4184
城区 Urban Area	106742	345339	2842
其中:女 of Which: Female	97731	339399	2628
城乡结合区 Urban-rural Transitional Area	9644	55821	218
其中:女 of Which: Female	8337	54759	195
镇区 Counties & Towns Area	65758	160534	1439
其中:女 of Which: Female	57086	157463	1330
镇乡结合区 County-town Transitional Area	13689	44203	244
其中:女 of Which: Female	11392	43371	214
乡村 Rural Area	25082	62364	268
其中:女 of Which: Female	17958	60010	226

政治面貌及其他
and Educational Personnel of Kindergarten

单位：人
unit: person

	专任教师中 of Total Full-time Teachers			
华侨 Overseas Chinese	共产党员 Member of C. P. C.	共青团员 Member of C. Y. L.	民主党派 Member of Dem. Parties	华侨 Overseas Chinese
436	**130488**	**490665**	**2275**	**199**
404	123590	485998	2246	197
291	69370	300028	1398	119
274	67644	297502	1379	119
88	5872	47080	112	31
85	5621	46720	108	31
114	46268	138083	746	60
102	43360	137017	738	58
21	8947	37659	110	12
17	8270	37419	109	11
31	14850	52554	131	20
28	12586	51479	129	20

幼儿园办学条件(一)

Condition of Kindergarten Buildings (1)

单位: 平方米
unit: m^2

	合计 Total	城区 Urban Area	其中:城乡结合区 of Which: Urban-rural Transitional Area	镇区 Counties & Towns Area	其中:镇乡结合区 of Which: County-town Transitional Area	乡村 Rural Area
总　计 Total	**201842763**	**91763492**	**14994349**	**72995278**	**19661350**	**37083993**
其中:of Which :						
危房 Floor Space of Dilapidated Buildings	1383596	423900	39291	567253	108630	392443
当年新增 New Added in Current Year	10329816	3198013	587818	4717606	1119336	2414197
一、教学及辅助用房 Teaching & Assistant Buildings	139832114	62968201	10145482	51078886	13717949	25785027
活动室 Recreational	82156769	36439121	5934345	30151166	8131944	15566482
洗手间 Toilet	12213689	5676849	922078	4396768	1194830	2140072
睡眠室 Bedroom	35699014	17259753	2629322	12747820	3300615	5691441
保健室 Health Care Room	4377890	1521202	281359	1720985	493656	1135703
图书室 Reading Room	5384752	2071276	378378	2062147	596904	1251329
二、行政办公用房 Administrative	14598530	5992106	958342	5492840	1506546	3113584
其中:教师办公室 of Which: for Teachers	8818278	3078830	529388	3506142	982727	2233306
三、生活用房 Residential and Welfare	21480593	9745877	1767836	7556583	2046580	4178133
其中:厨房 of Which:Kitchen	10020688	4560133	751846	3487739	948758	1972816
四、其他用房 Rooms for Other Purposes	25931526	13057308	2122689	8866969	2390275	4007249

幼儿园办学条件(二)

Condition of Kindergarten Buildings (2)

	占地面积(平方米)Areas Occupied(m^2)			图书(册)Books & Magazines in Libraries (volume)	数字资源(GB) Digital Resources
	合计 Total	其中 of Which			
		绿化用地面积 Green Areas	运动场地面积 Sports Areas		
总　计 Total	**392967185**	**65117166**	**131194736**	**218970675**	**38352308.24**
城区 Urban Area	140052343	24816576	47692703	100194643	23472420.88
其中:城乡结合区 of Which: Urban-rural Transitional Area	25051029	4599247	8539896	15252436	6891437.73
镇区 Counties & Towns Area	144485657	23435359	47703678	80781764	10316227.46
其中:镇乡结合区 of Which: County-town Transitional Area	42071204	6781857	13878453	21899073	3326228.06
乡村 Rural Area	108429185	16865231	35798355	37994268	4563659.90

八、各级各类学校分布情况

Geographical Distribution of Schools by Type and Level

高等教育学校(机构)数
Number of Higher Education Institutions

单位:所
unit: institution

地 区 Region	普通高校 Regular HEIs				成人高等学校 Adult HEIs		民办的其他高等教育机构 Other Non-government HEIs
	合计 Total	其中:中央部门 of Which: HEIs under Central Ministries & Agencies	本科院校 HEIs Offering Degree Programs	高职(专科)院校 Higher Vocational Colleges	合计 Total	其中:中央部门 of Which: HEIs under Central Ministries & Agencies	
总 计 Total	**2491**	**113**	**1170**	**1321**	**297**	**13**	**802**
北 京 Beijing	89	35	63	26	24	8	69
天 津 Tianjin	55	3	29	26	14		
河 北 Hebei	118	4	57	61	7	1	36
山 西 Shanxi	78		29	49	12		49
内蒙古 Inner Mongolia	49		15	34	2		
辽 宁 Liaoning	115	5	63	52	20	2	70
吉 林 Jilin	58	2	37	21	14		14
黑龙江 Heilongjiang	80	3	37	43	22		36
上 海 Shanghai	68	10	36	32	15		219
江 苏 Jiangsu	156	10	74	82	9	1	
浙 江 Zhejiang	102	2	56	46	9		22
安 徽 Anhui	117	2	44	73	6		7
福 建 Fujian	87	2	32	55	3		
江 西 Jiangxi	92		40	52	8		23
山 东 Shandong	139	2	63	76	11		91
河 南 Henan	127	1	50	77	13		50
湖 北 Hubei	123	8	67	56	14		19

高等教育学校(机构)数(续)

Number of Higher Education Institutions (Cont.)

单位:所

unit: institution

地 区 Region	普通高校 Regular HEIs 合计 Total	其中:中央部门 of Which: HEIs under Central Ministries & Agencies	本科院校 HEIs Offering Degree Programs	高职(专科)院校 Higher Vocational Colleges	成人高等学校 Adult HEIs 合计 Total	其中:中央部门 of Which: HEIs under Central Ministries & Agencies	民办的其他高等教育机构 Other Non-government HEIs
湖 南 Hunan	122	3	47	75	12		13
广 东 Guangdong	138	4	58	80	15		31
广 西 Guangxi	70		32	38	6		
海 南 Hainan	17		6	11	1		
重 庆 Chongqing	63	2	24	39	4		7
四 川 Sichuan	103	6	48	55	18	1	16
贵 州 Guizhou	52		26	26	4		
云 南 Yunnan	67		29	38	2		
西 藏 Tibet	6		3	3			
陕 西 Shaanxi	92	6	54	38	16		
甘 肃 Gansu	42	2	21	21	6		30
青 海 Qinghai	9		4	5	2		
宁 夏 Ningxia	16	1	8	8	1		
新 疆 Xinjiang	41		18	23	7		

高等学校(机

Number of Postgraduate Students in

地区 Region	毕(结)业生数 Graduates				授予学位数 Degrees Awarded	招生数	
	合计 Total	其中:女 of Which: Female	博士 Doctor's Degree	硕士 Master's Degree		合计 Total	其中:女 of Which: Female
总计 Total	**513626**	**257314**	**53139**	**460487**	**509520**	**611381**	**305184**
北京 Beijing	74165	36486	13809	60356	73526	92256	44839
天津 Tianjin	14959	8222	1708	13251	14590	17117	9157
河北 Hebei	11231	6422	412	10819	11209	12933	7368
山西 Shanxi	7754	4244	320	7434	7764	9384	5370
内蒙古 Inner Mongolia	5125	2965	175	4950	5081	5886	3535
辽宁 Liaoning	28780	15449	2243	26537	28421	32824	17363
吉林 Jilin	17489	9779	2161	15328	17504	18942	10763
黑龙江 Heilongjiang	18439	9109	1893	16546	18420	20824	10505
上海 Shanghai	35669	17224	5238	30431	35388	46223	22061
江苏 Jiangsu	40287	19363	3989	36298	39847	47985	22101
浙江 Zhejiang	15592	7500	1661	13931	15589	19535	9524
安徽 Anhui	13205	5708	1229	11976	12465	16312	7028
福建 Fujian	10179	5633	979	9200	10086	12620	6602
江西 Jiangxi	7853	3837	140	7713	7825	9407	4700
山东 Shandong	22623	12782	1557	21066	22679	26404	14726
河南 Henan	10660	5852	250	10410	10532	12185	6968
湖北 Hubei	34585	16779	3948	30637	34505	39027	18631
湖南 Hunan	17236	8619	1491	15745	17337	20538	10368
广东 Guangdong	24353	11977	2907	21446	23943	29255	14368
广西 Guangxi	7518	2975	140	7378	7735	8787	3676
海南 Hainan	1029	575	23	1006	1026	1309	788
重庆 Chongqing	14189	7319	895	13294	14131	16324	8285
四川 Sichuan	24384	11237	2243	22141	23778	28123	12674
贵州 Guizhou	4093	2085	52	4041	4028	4937	2648
云南 Yunnan	8933	4597	426	8507	8916	10411	5591
西藏 Tibet	274	144	3	271	274	517	301
陕西 Shaanxi	27566	12396	2269	25297	27916	32326	15136
甘肃 Gansu	8629	4098	762	7867	8343	10116	4992
青海 Qinghai	820	429	22	798	739	1136	615
宁夏 Ningxia	1232	729	22	1210	1232	1516	892
新疆 Xinjiang	4775	2780	172	4603	4691	6222	3609

构)研究生数

Higher Education Institutions

单位：人

unit：person

Entrants		在校生数 Enrolment				预计毕业生数 Estimated Graduates for Next Year			
博 士 Doctor's Degree	硕 士 Master's Degree	合计 Total	其中:女 of Which: Female	博 士 Doctor's Degree	硕 士 Master' Degree	合计 Total	其中:女 of Which: Female	博 士 Doctor's Degree	硕 士 Master's Degree
70462	**540919**	**1793953**	**878484**	**298283**	**1495670**	**665984**	**312590**	**146941**	**519043**
17962	74294	268107	126277	72204	195903	99353	45923	31385	67968
2036	15081	50622	26997	8014	42608	19095	10027	3967	15128
552	12381	37823	21133	2337	35486	13990	7564	1242	12748
479	8905	27473	15235	2315	25158	10035	5008	1368	8667
246	5640	16897	10014	1102	15795	6548	3503	415	6133
2959	29865	93189	49369	13848	79341	34364	17684	5435	28929
2469	16473	56992	31892	10345	46647	19740	10759	5159	14581
2467	18357	62249	30350	10570	51679	25951	11363	5772	20179
7014	39209	134799	62870	28840	105959	50563	22306	14684	35879
5670	42315	145947	67511	25091	120856	56068	25414	13183	42885
2346	17189	57801	27192	10038	47763	20738	9344	5402	15336
1585	14727	46506	19943	5394	41112	15452	6719	2283	13169
1256	11364	38190	19648	5205	32985	14052	6778	2649	11403
224	9183	26330	13103	920	25410	8745	4117	493	8252
2033	24371	72962	39951	8495	64467	25476	14075	3332	22144
415	11770	33317	18843	1380	31937	10773	6155	568	10205
5070	33957	112707	52395	22367	90340	43603	19449	12199	31404
2065	18473	65276	31301	10822	54454	25811	11380	6734	19077
3566	25689	85180	40639	14351	70829	33034	15259	6972	26062
216	8571	24905	12116	831	24074	9417	3403	409	9008
37	1272	3959	2259	174	3785	1492	744	99	1393
1240	15084	48210	23913	5435	42775	17093	8586	1836	15257
2953	25170	88237	38711	13405	74832	34437	14120	7511	26926
97	4840	14057	7390	340	13717	4723	2413	156	4567
576	9835	30595	16088	2562	28033	10433	5252	1438	8995
4	513	1244	693	15	1229	317	180	6	311
3562	28764	97014	44661	16785	80229	35631	15104	9784	25847
973	9143	29412	14234	3746	25666	10742	5264	1834	8908
45	1091	3074	1662	135	2939	958	510	50	908
34	1482	4012	2403	88	3924	1372	822	25	1347
311	5911	16867	9691	1129	15738	5978	3365	551	5427

普通高校

Number of Postgraduate Students in

地 区 Region	毕(结)业生数 Graduates				授予学位数 Degrees Awarded	招生数	
	合计 Total	其中:女 of Which: Female	博 士 Doctor's Degree	硕 士 Master's Degree		合计 Total	其中:女 of Which: Female
总 计 Total	**502426**	**253132**	**49405**	**453021**	**498339**	**596368**	**299371**
北 京 Beijing	69773	34668	12539	57234	69141	86616	42500
天 津 Tianjin	14959	8222	1708	13251	14590	17117	9157
河 北 Hebei	11201	6413	412	10789	11179	12895	7360
山 西 Shanxi	7708	4216	320	7388	7718	9324	5341
内蒙古 Inner Mongolia	5120	2965	175	4945	5076	5883	3535
辽 宁 Liaoning	28243	15274	1975	26268	27885	32034	17082
吉 林 Jilin	17088	9631	1893	15195	17088	18269	10532
黑龙江 Heilongjiang	18263	9044	1874	16389	18244	20566	10408
上 海 Shanghai	34148	16704	4561	29587	33847	43659	21065
江 苏 Jiangsu	39936	19249	3891	36045	39493	47588	21953
浙 江 Zhejiang	15519	7472	1660	13859	15519	19460	9504
安 徽 Anhui	12956	5646	1098	11858	12216	15957	6923
福 建 Fujian	10065	5595	932	9133	9972	12433	6531
江 西 Jiangxi	7853	3837	140	7713	7825	9407	4700
山 东 Shandong	22427	12684	1488	20939	22456	26189	14615
河 南 Henan	10588	5846	242	10346	10460	12120	6957
湖 北 Hubei	33935	16557	3788	30147	33881	38248	18351
湖 南 Hunan	17173	8602	1481	15692	17273	20466	10345
广 东 Guangdong	23902	11788	2732	21170	23506	28710	14137
广 西 Guangxi	7518	2975	140	7378	7735	8787	3676
海 南 Hainan	1029	575	23	1006	1026	1309	788
重 庆 Chongqing	14168	7315	895	13273	14110	16300	8278
四 川 Sichuan	23782	11021	2092	21690	23202	27445	12438
贵 州 Guizhou	4064	2076	52	4012	3999	4881	2636
云 南 Yunnan	8710	4487	338	8372	8675	10092	5450
西 藏 Tibet	274	144	3	271	274	517	301
陕 西 Shaanxi	27120	12278	2196	24924	27462	31817	14972
甘 肃 Gansu	8297	3995	617	7680	8044	9689	4833
青 海 Qinghai	760	401	4	756	679	1052	581
宁 夏 Ningxia	1232	729	22	1210	1232	1516	892
新 疆 Xinjiang	4615	2723	114	4501	4532	6022	3530

研究生数

Regular Higher Education Institutions

单位：人

unit：person

Entrants		在校生数 Enrolment				预计毕业生数 Estimated Graduates for Next Year			
博　士 Doctor's Degree	硕　士 Master's Degree	合计 Total	其中:女 of Which: Female	博　士 Doctor's Degree	硕　士 Master's Degree	合计 Total	其中:女 of Which: Female	博　士 Doctor's Degree	硕　士 Master's Degree
65785	**530583**	**1749864**	**861561**	**281959**	**1467905**	**650683**	**306740**	**139957**	**510726**
16355	70261	251676	119525	66625	185051	93299	43425	29010	64289
2036	15081	50622	26997	8014	42608	19095	10027	3967	15128
552	12343	37716	21111	2337	35379	13957	7559	1242	12715
479	8845	27300	15148	2315	24985	9980	4976	1368	8612
246	5637	16886	10013	1102	15784	6544	3503	415	6129
2625	29409	90683	48425	12517	78166	33482	17364	4832	28650
2177	16092	55040	31167	9366	45674	19109	10506	4767	14342
2443	18123	61437	30038	10449	50988	25660	11260	5706	19954
6181	37478	127803	60275	26046	101757	48397	21533	13477	34920
5543	42045	144699	67069	24627	120072	55636	25267	12989	42647
2345	17115	57571	27121	10032	47539	20664	9329	5401	15263
1443	14514	45434	19622	4902	40532	15090	6617	2074	13016
1206	11227	37735	19461	5059	32676	13916	6729	2600	11316
224	9183	26330	13103	920	25410	8745	4117	493	8252
1954	24235	72333	39650	8274	64059	25236	13968	3233	22003
413	11707	33116	18807	1374	31742	10706	6143	567	10139
4841	33407	110345	51523	21548	88797	42808	19174	11841	30967
2046	18420	65061	31228	10753	54308	25737	11355	6702	19035
3368	25342	83522	39947	13659	69863	32451	15018	6672	25779
216	8571	24905	12116	831	24074	9417	3403	409	9008
37	1272	3959	2259	174	3785	1492	744	99	1393
1240	15060	48141	23890	5435	42706	17074	8578	1836	15238
2775	24670	86178	38006	12765	73413	33760	13874	7253	26507
97	4784	13914	7350	340	13574	4692	2403	156	4536
448	9644	29588	15653	2104	27484	10051	5097	1232	8819
4	513	1244	693	15	1229	317	180	6	311
3434	28383	95396	44188	16265	79131	35063	14924	9560	25503
776	8913	28141	13772	3111	25030	10304	5103	1577	8727
15	1037	2820	1552	43	2777	876	471	16	860
34	1482	4012	2403	88	3924	1372	822	25	1347
232	5790	16257	9449	869	15388	5753	3271	432	5321

地 区 Region	毕(结)业生数 Graduates				授予学位数 Degrees Awarded	招生数	
	合计 Total	其中:女 of Which: Female	博 士 Doctor's Degree	硕 士 Master's Degree		合计 Total	其中:女 of Which: Female
总 计 Total	**11200**	**4182**	**3734**	**7466**	**11181**	**15013**	**5813**
北 京 Beijing	4392	1818	1270	3122	4385	5640	2339
天 津 Tianjin							
河 北 Hebei	30	9		30	30	38	8
山 西 Shanxi	46	28		46	46	60	29
内蒙古 Inner Mongolia	5			5	5	3	
辽 宁 Liaoning	537	175	268	269	536	790	281
吉 林 Jilin	401	148	268	133	416	673	231
黑龙江 Heilongjiang	176	65	19	157	176	258	97
上 海 Shanghai	1521	520	677	844	1541	2564	996
江 苏 Jiangsu	351	114	98	253	354	397	148
浙 江 Zhejiang	73	28	1	72	70	75	20
安 徽 Anhui	249	62	131	118	249	355	105
福 建 Fujian	114	38	47	67	114	187	71
江 西 Jiangxi							
山 东 Shandong	196	98	69	127	223	215	111
河 南 Henan	72	6	8	64	72	65	11
湖 北 Hubei	650	222	160	490	624	779	280
湖 南 Hunan	63	17	10	53	64	72	23
广 东 Guangdong	451	189	175	276	437	545	231
广 西 Guangxi							
海 南 Hainan							
重 庆 Chongqing	21	4		21	21	24	7
四 川 Sichuan	602	216	151	451	576	678	236
贵 州 Guizhou	29	9		29	29	56	12
云 南 Yunnan	223	110	88	135	241	319	141
西 藏 Tibet							
陕 西 Shaanxi	446	118	73	373	454	509	164
甘 肃 Gansu	332	103	145	187	299	427	159
青 海 Qinghai	60	28	18	42	60	84	34
宁 夏 Ningxia							
新 疆 Xinjiang	160	57	58	102	159	200	79

研究生数

Research Institutes

单位：人

unit：person

Entrants		在校生数 Enrolment				预计毕业生数 Estimated Graduates for Next Year			
博士 Doctor's Degree	硕士 Master's Degree	合计 Total	其中:女 of Which: Female	博士 Doctor's Degree	硕士 Master's Degree	合计 Total	其中:女 of Which: Female	博士 Doctor's Degree	硕士 Master's Degree
4677	**10336**	**44089**	**16923**	**16324**	**27765**	**15301**	**5850**	**6984**	**8317**
1607	4033	16431	6752	5579	10852	6054	2498	2375	3679
	38	107	22		107	33	5		33
	60	173	87		173	55	32		55
	3	11	1		11	4			4
334	456	2506	944	1331	1175	882	320	603	279
292	381	1952	725	979	973	631	253	392	239
24	234	812	312	121	691	291	103	66	225
833	1731	6996	2595	2794	4202	2166	773	1207	959
127	270	1248	442	464	784	432	147	194	238
1	74	230	71	6	224	74	15	1	73
142	213	1072	321	492	580	362	102	209	153
50	137	455	187	146	309	136	49	49	87
79	136	629	301	221	408	240	107	99	141
2	63	201	36	6	195	67	12	1	66
229	550	2362	872	819	1543	795	275	358	437
19	53	215	73	69	146	74	25	32	42
198	347	1658	692	692	966	583	241	300	283
	24	69	23		69	19	8		19
178	500	2059	705	640	1419	677	246	258	419
	56	143	40		143	31	10		31
128	191	1007	435	458	549	382	155	206	176
128	381	1618	473	520	1098	568	180	224	344
197	230	1271	462	635	636	438	161	257	181
30	54	254	110	92	162	82	39	34	48
79	121	610	242	260	350	225	94	119	106

Number of Students Enrolled in Normal and

地 区 Region	毕(结)业生数 Graduates				授予学位数 Degrees Awarded	招生数	
	合计 Total	其中:女 of Which: Female	本 科 Normal Courses	专 科 Short-cycle Courses		合计 Total	其中:女 of Which: Female
总 计 Total	**8384939**	**4354290**	**4010875**	**4374064**	**3256472**	**9563264**	**5277144**
北 京 Beijing	247345	131943	167578	79767	127270	263518	140454
天 津 Tianjin	146630	75809	79507	67123	65441	171347	90473
河 北 Hebei	416380	231077	184656	231724	150476	444271	255547
山 西 Shanxi	226641	117355	100771	125870	76946	269904	147492
内蒙古 Inner Mongolia	141764	73786	62645	79119	49541	166855	92313
辽 宁 Liaoning	320131	161749	175318	144813	149992	361429	189018
吉 林 Jilin	214982	109820	132660	82322	101714	253462	136976
黑龙江 Heilongjiang	249368	130529	146065	103303	119437	286744	150083
上 海 Shanghai	187788	102867	122207	65581	90646	191607	104108
江 苏 Jiangsu	624310	322884	304972	319338	254426	607869	344676
浙 江 Zhejiang	345942	193760	162800	183142	131509	393064	227696
安 徽 Anhui	347717	174969	148293	199424	121945	404668	223532
福 建 Fujian	221760	121072	109621	112139	96790	270546	150538
江 西 Jiangxi	277436	127889	118578	158858	101452	316918	167115
山 东 Shandong	604155	313745	271385	332770	214934	657079	377745
河 南 Henan	556065	296933	226901	329164	186957	620801	355280
湖 北 Hubei	466210	229095	215247	250963	180632	513480	253427
湖 南 Hunan	395535	201452	177242	218293	141743	419571	222613
广 东 Guangdong	568592	303117	255464	313128	204039	732637	413651
广 西 Guangxi	236741	123373	91825	144916	72598	298205	167409
海 南 Hainan	51211	27648	23586	27625	19299	57307	31264
重 庆 Chongqing	188785	95173	92277	96508	79960	246581	136975
四 川 Sichuan	443317	228244	198243	245074	163914	523000	297409
贵 州 Guizhou	110717	60618	55171	55546	40741	158102	93910
云 南 Yunnan	180442	95621	89471	90971	64864	231854	136095
西 藏 Tibet	12326	6229	6516	5810	5539	14727	7986
陕 西 Shaanxi	323290	156698	156617	166673	135411	354859	187921
甘 肃 Gansu	138170	65345	71752	66418	58939	155735	75035
青 海 Qinghai	17567	8747	9518	8049	7293	20556	11486
宁 夏 Ningxia	34549	16982	15704	18845	12106	44124	23672
新 疆 Xinjiang	89073	49761	38285	50788	29918	112444	65245

本、专科学生数

Short-cycle Courses in Higher Education

单位：人

unit：person

Entrants		在校生数 Enrolment				预计毕业生数 Estimated Graduates for Next Year			
本　科 Normal Courses	专　科 Short-cycle Courses	合计 Total	其中:女 of Which: Female	本　科 Normal Courses	专　科 Short-cycle Courses	合计 Total	其中:女 of Which: Female	本　科 Normal Courses	专　科 Short-cycle Courses
4852489	**4710775**	**30944871**	**16231957**	**17598949**	**13345922**	**9099668**	**4507799**	**4437487**	**4662181**
183685	79833	863348	453737	650052	213296	264471	133472	179659	84812
98247	73100	563491	288629	358924	204567	159354	80715	90124	69230
222389	221882	1498192	827451	815610	682582	450457	241769	205080	245377
134497	135407	865711	458627	468253	397458	241296	117095	112990	128306
83690	83165	515181	276843	281643	233538	164092	84701	73507	90585
206449	154980	1181075	599393	757453	423622	343231	166083	190423	152808
150731	102731	776974	408666	536086	240888	227554	117152	138424	89130
168917	117827	907193	470574	602557	304636	272312	138277	159884	112428
128432	63175	679355	360301	488145	191210	198996	100128	131078	67918
328078	279791	2082376	1038036	1208820	873556	660654	311182	331996	328658
184178	208886	1236207	685648	672699	563508	382653	202028	178906	203747
195251	209417	1272765	644453	675028	597737	394382	199719	170240	224142
142194	128352	874433	463318	511145	363288	237696	117418	122153	115543
149702	167216	1045891	505186	562147	483744	296071	133355	137708	158363
322900	334179	2158348	1150201	1175714	982634	620439	298447	284717	335722
299050	321751	1954715	1035687	1049439	905276	583163	293958	259314	323849
257325	256155	1704260	832359	962386	741874	527308	247182	243084	284224
206526	213045	1332998	682096	743231	589767	415305	196782	195485	219820
313120	419517	2244257	1226311	1113681	1130576	615681	317115	270480	345201
126033	172172	883143	487797	417703	465440	267698	138567	105819	161879
29654	27653	195844	109507	115335	80509	53471	27925	28329	25142
117653	128928	804074	422730	452717	351357	219941	109801	108077	111864
222522	300478	1640036	877248	834033	806003	503800	239544	219369	284431
82766	75336	520738	280037	304235	216503	130909	66028	66539	64370
127274	104580	743874	414642	444258	299616	204486	109781	101927	102559
9208	5519	45803	24204	29555	16248	12256	6100	7019	5237
196372	158487	1258594	641704	756498	502096	348852	166240	176907	171945
84785	70950	536019	254719	319671	216348	151478	63892	78285	73193
11756	8800	63500	34214	40377	23123	18630	9639	10291	8339
21613	22511	138001	72411	76195	61806	40995	21366	18491	22504
47492	64952	358475	205228	175359	183116	92037	52338	41182	50855

Number of Regular Students Enrolled in Normal and

地　区 Region	毕(结)业生数 Graduates				授予学位数 Degrees Awarded	招生数	
	合计 Total	其中:女 of Which: Female	本　科 Normal Courses	专　科 Short-cycle Courses		合计 Total	其中:女 of Which: Female
总　计 Total	**6387210**	**3274056**	**3199716**	**3187494**	**3130415**	**6998330**	**3843225**
北　京 Beijing	150929	77748	114149	36780	112233	159813	85119
天　津 Tianjin	120996	61616	67160	53836	64913	138556	73495
河　北 Hebei	334278	187059	146201	188077	144468	325886	192479
山　西 Shanxi	173259	90857	76375	96884	74220	206939	119324
内蒙古 Inner Mongolia	108272	56804	50275	57997	49308	112409	62179
辽　宁 Liaoning	241049	125085	146687	94362	145225	271346	143377
吉　林 Jilin	146379	73830	103426	42953	99708	166248	88968
黑龙江 Heilongjiang	184085	95221	116544	67541	115093	197331	103742
上　海 Shanghai	133794	70864	84636	49158	82405	137160	74813
江　苏 Jiangsu	473843	240496	236363	237480	227949	439506	255557
浙　江 Zhejiang	244860	132163	128186	116674	125495	268946	156377
安　徽 Anhui	280106	137805	121965	158141	119565	296557	159360
福　建 Fujian	187230	100742	94450	92780	93714	213564	116537
江　西 Jiangxi	240601	107649	101020	139581	98642	247389	124146
山　东 Shandong	475858	244250	211661	264197	209249	491557	285034
河　南 Henan	450194	238468	184178	266016	180755	466695	266888
湖　北 Hubei	361572	176630	180278	181294	176401	398854	194445
湖　南 Hunan	294355	148836	142030	152325	139466	313650	164852
广　东 Guangdong	412315	209077	200491	211824	198225	516866	276722
广　西 Guangxi	169543	80935	65083	104460	63664	198528	105815
海　南 Hainan	43804	23088	19986	23818	19024	49296	25539
重　庆 Chongqing	148684	77619	82490	66194	79396	184909	104040
四　川 Sichuan	318407	161176	164906	153501	162809	357802	200982
贵　州 Guizhou	88060	48245	43091	44969	40420	119734	71912
云　南 Yunnan	127932	69263	64950	62982	62725	162911	95251
西　藏 Tibet	9139	4688	4818	4321	4713	9286	4989
陕　西 Shaanxi	253823	127886	136062	117761	133635	297854	162897
甘　肃 Gansu	109192	50618	60848	48344	58859	122285	59533
青　海 Qinghai	12447	6285	6813	5634	6576	14805	7934
宁　夏 Ningxia	22221	11013	12574	9647	12106	30664	16395
新　疆 Xinjiang	69983	38040	32020	37963	29454	80984	44524

普通本、专科学生数
Short-cycle Courses in Higher Education

单位：人
unit：person

Entrants		在校生数 Enrolment				预计毕业生数 Estimated Graduates for Next Year			
本 科 Normal Courses	专 科 Short-cycle Courses	合计 Total	其中：女 of Which：Female	本 科 Normal Courses	专 科 Short-cycle Courses	合计 Total	其中：女 of Which：Female	本 科 Normal Courses	专 科 Short-cycle Courses
3814331	**3183999**	**24680726**	**12769199**	**14944353**	**9736373**	**6737474**	**3288432**	**3497450**	**3240024**
125282	34531	598904	306796	491776	107128	155595	78485	120070	35525
81851	56705	489919	250140	323170	166749	128204	64246	76521	51683
160751	165135	1174374	653506	645385	528989	349014	188793	155624	193390
110032	96907	676817	372421	390654	286163	174811	86592	85217	89594
58417	53992	399201	212035	230040	169161	114662	58175	54932	59730
175111	96235	968034	489628	675819	292215	254431	126421	157724	96707
115705	50543	599526	313872	454357	145169	150948	77226	103733	47215
125341	71990	717856	370890	509894	207962	188077	96577	121406	66671
90189	46971	504771	264512	362742	142029	140353	71629	91174	49179
244501	195005	1684455	831573	1000820	683635	492672	226388	252051	240621
147532	121414	959629	527934	587410	372219	262539	139015	139796	122743
149012	147545	1052123	513552	583089	469034	303343	147075	135437	167906
121637	91927	730510	375309	457241	273269	196815	94555	106147	90668
122658	124731	861849	395704	481211	380638	244520	107535	113694	130826
237463	254094	1698545	893683	935480	763065	472405	226455	218940	253465
235931	230764	1618320	847088	910156	708164	447026	217786	209613	237413
215220	183634	1421434	691157	857489	563945	396887	189106	200997	195890
163936	149714	1100770	559194	651789	448981	302592	137630	155381	147211
251684	265182	1709881	888119	949585	760296	454682	215973	217874	236808
88389	110139	656127	347777	330734	325393	178225	86944	71938	106287
25655	23641	172143	93140	102993	69150	46071	23345	24391	21680
105163	79746	659400	352213	420129	239271	170415	84582	95437	74978
182840	174962	1270818	664566	735441	535377	349184	164136	181117	168067
66804	52930	419040	223391	257209	161831	100910	50222	53041	47869
99176	63735	548577	306203	358914	189663	143960	77655	75603	68357
5702	3584	33562	17387	21388	12174	9087	4298	4903	4184
171768	126086	1077627	561918	687369	390258	281368	138497	153663	127705
71619	50666	442963	211161	280071	162892	120036	51068	65275	54761
8848	5957	50675	26618	33308	17367	13220	6485	7403	5817
18188	12476	104451	54197	67369	37082	25537	12952	14180	11357
37926	43058	278425	153515	151321	127104	69885	38586	34168	35717

Number of Adult Students Enrolled in Normal and

地 区 Region	毕(结)业生数 Graduates				授予学位数 Degrees Awarded	招生数	
	合计 Total	其中:女 of Which: Female	本 科 Normal Courses	专 科 Short - cycle Courses		合计 Total	其中:女 of Which: Female
总 计 Total	**1997729**	**1080234**	**811159**	**1186570**	**126057**	**2564934**	**1433919**
北 京 Beijing	96416	54195	53429	42987	15037	103705	55335
天 津 Tianjin	25634	14193	12347	13287	528	32791	16978
河 北 Hebei	82102	44018	38455	43647	6008	118385	63068
山 西 Shanxi	53382	26498	24396	28986	2726	62965	28168
内蒙古 Inner Mongolia	33492	16982	12370	21122	233	54446	30134
辽 宁 Liaoning	79082	36664	28631	50451	4767	90083	45641
吉 林 Jilin	68603	35990	29234	39369	2006	87214	48008
黑龙江 Heilongjiang	65283	35308	29521	35762	4344	89413	46341
上 海 Shanghai	53994	32003	37571	16423	8241	54447	29295
江 苏 Jiangsu	150467	82388	68609	81858	26477	168363	89119
浙 江 Zhejiang	101082	61597	34614	66468	6014	124118	71319
安 徽 Anhui	67611	37164	26328	41283	2380	108111	64172
福 建 Fujian	34530	20330	15171	19359	3076	56982	34001
江 西 Jiangxi	36835	20240	17558	19277	2810	69529	42969
山 东 Shandong	128297	69495	59724	68573	5685	165522	92711
河 南 Henan	105871	58465	42723	63148	6202	154106	88392
湖 北 Hubei	104638	52465	34969	69669	4231	114626	58982
湖 南 Hunan	101180	52616	35212	65968	2277	105921	57761
广 东 Guangdong	156277	94040	54973	101304	5814	215771	136929
广 西 Guangxi	67198	42438	26742	40456	8934	99677	61594
海 南 Hainan	7407	4560	3600	3807	275	8011	5725
重 庆 Chongqing	40101	17554	9787	30314	564	61672	32935
四 川 Sichuan	124910	67068	33337	91573	1105	165198	96427
贵 州 Guizhou	22657	12373	12080	10577	321	38368	21998
云 南 Yunnan	52510	26358	24521	27989	2139	68943	40844
西 藏 Tibet	3187	1541	1698	1489	826	5441	2997
陕 西 Shaanxi	69467	28812	20555	48912	1776	57005	25024
甘 肃 Gansu	28978	14727	10904	18074	80	33450	15502
青 海 Qinghai	5120	2462	2705	2415	717	5751	3552
宁 夏 Ningxia	12328	5969	3130	9198		13460	7277
新 疆 Xinjiang	19090	11721	6265	12825	464	31460	20721

成人本、专科学生数
Short-cycle Courses in Higher Education

单位：人
unit：person

Entrants		在校生数 Enrolment				预计毕业生数 Estimated Graduates for Next Year			
本 科 Normal Courses	专 科 Short-cycle Courses	合计 Total	其中：女 of Which：Female	本 科 Normal Courses	专 科 Short-cycle Courses	合计 Total	其中：女 of Which：Female	本 科 Normal Courses	专 科 Short-cycle Courses
1038158	**1526776**	**6264145**	**3462758**	**2654596**	**3609549**	**2362194**	**1219367**	**940037**	**1422157**
58403	45302	264444	146941	158276	106168	108876	54987	59589	49287
16396	16395	73572	38489	35754	37818	31150	16469	13603	17547
61638	56747	323818	173945	170225	153593	101443	52976	49456	51987
24465	38500	188894	86206	77599	111295	66485	30503	27773	38712
25273	29173	115980	64808	51603	64377	49430	26526	18575	30855
31338	58745	213041	109765	81634	131407	88800	39662	32699	56101
35026	52188	177448	94794	81729	95719	76606	39926	34691	41915
43576	45837	189337	99684	92663	96674	84235	41700	38478	45757
38243	16204	174584	95789	125403	49181	58643	28499	39904	18739
83577	84786	397921	206463	208000	189921	167982	84794	79945	88037
36646	87472	276578	157714	85289	191289	120114	63013	39110	81004
46239	61872	220642	130901	91939	128703	91039	52644	34803	56236
20557	36425	143923	88009	53904	90019	40881	22863	16006	24875
27044	42485	184042	109482	80936	103106	51551	25820	24014	27537
85437	80085	459803	256518	240234	219569	148034	71992	65777	82257
63119	90987	336395	188599	139283	197112	136137	76172	49701	86436
42105	72521	282826	141202	104897	177929	130421	58076	42087	88334
42590	63331	232228	122902	91442	140786	112713	59152	40104	72609
61436	154335	534376	338192	164096	370280	160999	101142	52606	108393
37644	62033	227016	140020	86969	140047	89473	51623	33881	55592
3999	4012	23701	16367	12342	11359	7400	4580	3938	3462
12490	49182	144674	70517	32588	112086	49526	25219	12640	36886
39682	125516	369218	212682	98592	270626	154616	75408	38252	116364
15962	22406	101698	56646	47026	54672	29999	15806	13498	16501
28098	40845	195297	108439	85344	109953	60526	32126	26324	34202
3506	1935	12241	6817	8167	4074	3169	1802	2116	1053
24604	32401	180967	79786	69129	111838	67484	27743	23244	44240
13166	20284	93056	43558	39600	53456	31442	12824	13010	18432
2908	2843	12825	7596	7069	5756	5410	3154	2888	2522
3425	10035	33550	18214	8826	24724	15458	8414	4311	11147
9566	21894	80050	51713	24038	56012	22152	13752	7014	15138

高等教育网络本科、专科

Number of Web-based Students Enrolled in Normal and

地 区 Region	毕(结)业生数 Graduates				授予学位数 Degrees Awarded	招生
	合计 Total	其中:女 of Which: Female	本 科 Normal Courses	专 科 Short-cycle Courses		合计 Total
总 计 Total	**1560762**	**799193**	**536702**	**1024060**	**40267**	**2200729**
北 京 Beijing	955161	503330	287497	667664	19112	1326622
天 津 Tianjin	20243	9899	7849	12394	400	26697
河 北 Hebei						
山 西 Shanxi						
内蒙古 Inner Mongolia						
辽 宁 Liaoning	66645	29324	31085	35560	3306	108705
吉 林 Jilin	36458	20615	14525	21933	357	59800
黑龙江 Heilongjiang	22861	8883	5456	17405	599	26856
上 海 Shanghai	53096	30691	15808	37288	1329	50338
江 苏 Jiangsu	16991	9019	8662	8329	3593	26863
浙 江 Zhejiang	15965	10005	12821	3144	1041	18743
安 徽 Anhui	209	72	199	10	26	427
福 建 Fujian	24598	14933	13308	11290	666	29634
江 西 Jiangxi						
山 东 Shandong	37808	15030	15640	22168	1741	56271
河 南 Henan	19463	9442	8116	11347	818	50488
湖 北 Hubei	55404	21303	18883	36521	2322	73796
湖 南 Hunan	24050	13273	9131	14919	591	30040
广 东 Guangdong	24698	15296	11204	13494	390	37773
广 西 Guangxi						
海 南 Hainan						
重 庆 Chongqing	51105	22484	21939	29166	191	73978
四 川 Sichuan	79325	35811	29296	50029	2397	109826
贵 州 Guizhou						
云 南 Yunnan						
西 藏 Tibet						
陕 西 Shaanxi	45415	23595	20217	25198	1388	72527
甘 肃 Gansu	11267	6188	5066	6201		21345
青 海 Qinghai						
宁 夏 Ningxia						
新 疆 Xinjiang						

生学生数

Short-cycle Courses in Higher Education

单位：人
unit：person

数 Entrants			在校生数 Enrolment			
其中:女 of Which： Female	本 科 Normal Courses	专 科 Short-cycle Courses	合计 Total	其中:女 of Which： Female	本 科 Normal Courses	专 科 Short-cycle Courses
1081450	**804378**	**1396351**	**6146406**	**3015989**	**2175100**	**3971306**
666017	422739	903883	4253105	2130367	1333806	2919299
13302	12274	14423	71705	34788	32891	38814
44265	55729	52976	258143	105656	132811	125332
34300	27780	32020	115387	64025	53677	61710
10096	9404	17452	51659	18844	18012	33647
27751	14450	35888	132038	70611	32516	99522
14139	14839	12024	53721	27851	31093	22628
11097	13516	5227	49549	29362	37789	11760
126	427		2118	701	1185	933
17082	15767	13867	61206	35587	34030	27176
23093	26321	29950	124139	51985	57381	66758
26812	18042	32446	84574	46424	37430	47144
30415	28343	45453	183149	71653	68623	114526
15433	11998	18042	63985	32959	25193	38792
23023	15902	21871	94952	54242	41302	53650
28866	33147	40831	137060	58372	62573	74487
47592	43164	66662	234086	96287	96267	137819
35867	30889	41638	129312	60344	55115	74197
12174	9647	11698	46518	25931	23406	23112

综合大学本科、专科生
Number of Students of

地 区 Region	毕(结)业生数 Graduates			招生数 Entrants		
	合计 Total	本 科 Normal Courses	专 科 Short-cycle Courses	合计 Total	本 科 Normal Courses	专 科 Short-cycle Courses
总 计 Total	**1724029**	**899984**	**824045**	**1870525**	**1045126**	**825399**
北 京 Beijing	19118	14778	4340	18602	15538	3064
天 津 Tianjin	34195	10467	23728	36313	13163	23150
河 北 Hebei	58176	23053	35123	58171	25510	32661
山 西 Shanxi	48746	21158	27588	53688	31303	22385
内蒙古 Inner Mongolia	45420	24859	20561	49858	31415	18443
辽 宁 Liaoning	43996	21125	22871	41409	22907	18502
吉 林 Jilin	26380	24218	2162	28691	26512	2179
黑龙江 Heilongjiang	50859	29970	20889	54257	32558	21699
上 海 Shanghai	13468	12224	1244	12723	12485	238
江 苏 Jiangsu	81758	64842	16916	73976	66721	7255
浙 江 Zhejiang	90987	36750	54237	100870	41551	59319
安 徽 Anhui	29219	19493	9726	31877	24277	7600
福 建 Fujian	63564	37378	26186	71761	46471	25290
江 西 Jiangxi	93913	33112	60801	93780	41351	52429
山 东 Shandong	235937	97185	138752	235862	105943	129919
河 南 Henan	64544	44317	20227	64204	49621	14583
湖 北 Hubei	41403	36711	4692	43549	40586	2963
湖 南 Hunan	136338	76122	60216	138123	83233	54890
广 东 Guangdong	195722	83491	112231	252534	107891	144643
广 西 Guangxi	45792	23845	21947	49350	27915	21435
海 南 Hainan	6461	6461		8655	8655	
重 庆 Chongqing	42809	25696	17113	48216	30285	17931
四 川 Sichuan	97584	44120	53464	117276	47120	70156
贵 州 Guizhou	30493	14163	16330	41031	16700	24331
云 南 Yunnan	25721	14916	10805	31606	22134	9472
西 藏 Tibet	3731	1834	1897	3626	2168	1458
陕 西 Shaanxi	49290	25768	23522	56331	33058	23273
甘 肃 Gansu	20574	12673	7901	22677	14637	8040
青 海 Qinghai	3453	2964	489	4395	4395	
宁 夏 Ningxia	6802	4785	2017	7616	5697	1919
新 疆 Xinjiang	17576	11506	6070	19498	13326	6172

学生数
Comprehensive Universities

单位：人
unit：person

在校生数 Enrolment			预计毕业生数 Estimated Graduates for Next Year		
合计 Total	本科 Normal Courses	专科 Short-cycle Courses	合计 Total	本科 Normal Courses	专科 Short-cycle Courses
6661910	**4132844**	**2529066**	**1808603**	**977727**	**830876**
74041	63371	10670	19823	15933	3890
123662	51197	72465	34868	11748	23120
213295	103502	109793	63970	24968	39002
187150	110490	76660	49802	23991	25811
178688	119800	58888	48837	27763	21074
153866	91265	62601	45302	22567	22735
112840	106354	6486	27273	25028	2245
192054	128974	63080	51379	31052	20327
55325	52487	2838	15390	13992	1398
313900	274983	38917	85919	69417	16502
346507	166855	179652	98343	40291	58052
118980	93143	25837	31537	21691	9846
252705	179501	73204	67792	42753	25039
319852	164576	155276	91490	38324	53166
806827	413176	393651	230760	99116	131644
241596	193174	48422	63233	46259	16974
181239	169981	11258	44546	40270	4276
503089	334361	168728	134543	79668	54875
814445	401101	413344	215429	89960	125469
174857	111403	63454	47372	24966	22406
33748	33748		8011	8011	
177256	122209	55047	47010	28756	18254
406874	196730	210144	113308	49055	64253
141447	72374	69073	33862	16644	17218
111854	83058	28796	28528	17723	10805
13482	8054	5428	3682	1859	1823
214232	138636	75596	55916	31226	24690
82188	56864	25324	22657	13756	8901
17354	16942	412	3882	3470	412
28751	21974	6777	7534	5133	2401
69806	52561	17245	16605	12337	4268

高等理工院校本科、

Number of Students of Institutions

地 区 Region	毕(结)业生数 Graduates			招生数	
	合计 Total	本 科 Normal Courses	专 科 Short-cycle Courses	合计 Total	本 科 Normal Courses
总 计 Total	**2338763**	**1010016**	**1328747**	**2547398**	**1194961**
北 京 Beijing	63529	48016	15513	67340	53294
天 津 Tianjin	45604	25775	19829	54157	32182
河 北 Hebei	129717	56021	73696	127693	61449
山 西 Shanxi	52868	24066	28802	63260	31984
内蒙古 Inner Mongolia	31258	5282	25976	30178	5375
辽 宁 Liaoning	108894	73490	35404	127038	86231
吉 林 Jilin	52125	29550	22575	62002	32487
黑龙江 Heilongjiang	52652	34970	17682	55782	37581
上 海 Shanghai	57532	35880	21652	56656	36875
江 苏 Jiangsu	267025	103009	164016	245362	105662
浙 江 Zhejiang	64193	37938	26255	68345	42047
安 徽 Anhui	122118	37096	85022	128622	47253
福 建 Fujian	53791	24717	29074	62676	33312
江 西 Jiangxi	75012	34275	40737	80684	43533
山 东 Shandong	114580	48509	66071	119783	54969
河 南 Henan	208439	61564	146875	212008	80808
湖 北 Hubei	224369	86072	138297	250713	105592
湖 南 Hunan	82561	34699	47862	90051	37852
广 东 Guangdong	94202	31571	62631	124928	43818
广 西 Guangxi	54796	16136	38660	65691	23983
海 南 Hainan	8956		8956	9144	
重 庆 Chongqing	50355	19515	30840	66829	24610
四 川 Sichuan	106768	53239	53529	120247	61570
贵 州 Guizhou	9957		9957	15473	2909
云 南 Yunnan	26095	8004	18091	30818	10131
西 藏 Tibet					
陕 西 Shaanxi	115339	62479	52860	132879	75904
甘 肃 Gansu	37748	15713	22035	41779	17329
青 海 Qinghai	2661		2661	3355	
宁 夏 Ningxia	5442	2333	3109	8746	5023
新 疆 Xinjiang	20177	97	20080	25159	1198

专科生学生数
of Science & Technology

单位：人
unit: person

Entrants	在校生数 Enrolment			预计毕业生数 Estimated Graduates for Next Year		
专科 Short-cycle Courses	合计 Total	本科 Normal Courses	专科 Short-cycle Courses	合计 Total	本科 Normal Courses	专科 Short-cycle Courses
1352437	**8760295**	**4654955**	**4105340**	**2475999**	**1107807**	**1368192**
14046	254640	208535	46105	66116	50719	15397
21975	186478	124660	61818	49178	30526	18652
66244	449488	245343	204145	132338	59614	72724
31276	203992	115507	88485	55111	27018	28093
24803	98597	21911	76686	32271	5408	26863
40807	451323	333309	118014	115534	78757	36777
29515	209664	127148	82516	54267	27693	26574
18201	203368	149986	53382	53290	35973	17317
19781	211039	151250	59789	58640	38041	20599
139700	913225	434217	479008	276144	111098	165046
26298	248673	167969	80704	68944	41512	27432
81369	431735	179274	252461	132092	41980	90112
29364	210057	124803	85254	56699	29553	27146
37151	278946	167112	111834	77938	39324	38614
64814	404807	214103	190704	112994	49709	63285
131200	709088	311404	397684	206498	72973	133525
145121	851991	415303	436688	247732	97868	149864
52199	304566	151671	152895	89073	38454	50619
81110	389239	157282	231957	110105	34836	75269
41708	207313	82941	124372	58004	17644	40360
9144	26767		26767	8262		8262
42219	224911	100849	124062	59453	23091	36362
58677	423126	242298	180828	118314	59581	58733
12564	42326	2909	39417	12134		12134
20687	98829	37674	61155	29827	9003	20824
56975	472051	302203	169848	123330	68601	54729
24450	145260	66598	78662	41719	15687	26032
3355	9180		9180	2857		2857
3723	28622	16520	12102	6891	2928	3963
23961	70994	2176	68818	20244	216	20028

高等农业院校本科、
Number of Students of

地　区 Region	毕(结)业生数 Graduates			招生数	
	合计 Total	本　科 Normal Courses	专　科 Short-cycle Courses	合计 Total	本　科 Normal Courses
总　计 Total	**257382**	**151718**	**105664**	**281988**	**177141**
北　京 Beijing	6411	4730	1681	5933	4338
天　津 Tianjin	3055	2297	758	3109	2541
河　北 Hebei	11560	7906	3654	11262	8411
山　西 Shanxi	5905	5198	707	10305	9686
内蒙古 Inner Mongolia	7629	6630	999	7946	6880
辽　宁 Liaoning	9828	4623	5205	12814	6308
吉　林 Jilin	10588	7973	2615	11947	9117
黑龙江 Heilongjiang	18887	9568	9319	22618	11341
上　海 Shanghai	4557	3004	1553	4001	2938
江　苏 Jiangsu	18848	4019	14829	16565	4512
浙　江 Zhejiang	4462	3410	1052	5886	3783
安　徽 Anhui	4596	4496	100	4333	4333
福　建 Fujian	11588	6042	5546	11735	5966
江　西 Jiangxi	7427	4601	2826	6243	4789
山　东 Shandong	18427	11947	6480	21513	16072
河　南 Henan	25639	8909	16730	28200	12541
湖　北 Hubei	4335	4335		4774	4774
湖　南 Hunan	9449	6410	3039	9409	6386
广　东 Guangdong	18536	17583	953	21329	20913
广　西 Guangxi	6279		6279	7560	
海　南 Hainan					
重　庆 Chongqing					
四　川 Sichuan	11599	7896	3703	11641	8384
贵　州 Guizhou					
云　南 Yunnan	7347	3181	4166	8446	4324
西　藏 Tibet	1201	805	396	1462	1164
陕　西 Shaanxi	9921	5442	4479	11549	5523
甘　肃 Gansu	7852	3793	4059	8161	4182
青　海 Qinghai	778		778	1039	
宁　夏 Ningxia					
新　疆 Xinjiang	10678	6920	3758	12208	7935

专科生学生数
Institutions of Agriculture

单位：人
unit：person

Entrants	在校生数 Enrolment			预计毕业生数 Estimated Graduates for Next Year		
专　科 Short-cycle Courses	合计 Total	本　科 Normal Courses	专　科 Short-cycle Courses	合计 Total	本　科 Normal Courses	专　科 Short-cycle Courses
104847	**1002655**	**682505**	**320150**	**268104**	**161638**	**106466**
1595	23386	18123	5263	6517	4718	1799
568	12443	10608	1835	3187	2571	616
2851	43045	33647	9398	11872	8438	3434
619	35693	33926	1767	7135	6656	479
1066	31293	28095	3198	8145	7069	1076
6506	40941	22924	18017	10523	5147	5376
2830	43407	34633	8774	11195	8109	3086
11277	76821	45659	31162	19445	10039	9406
1063	15804	12050	3754	4347	2876	1471
12053	58266	17422	40844	19449	4157	15292
2103	19763	14128	5635	4809	3310	1499
	18626	18626		4622	4622	
5769	40039	23040	16999	11275	5858	5417
1454	23967	18091	5876	6984	4448	2536
5441	70526	56678	13848	17379	12512	4867
15659	96866	45408	51458	28256	10399	17857
	18625	18625		4529	4529	
3023	34593	26049	8544	9301	6651	2650
416	82541	80657	1884	20554	19816	738
7560	20754		20754	6522		6522
3257	42893	32023	10870	12181	8361	3820
4122	27884	16075	11809	7401	3423	3978
298	5553	4659	894	1583	1237	346
6026	40125	21895	18230	11214	5333	5881
3979	29816	16615	13201	8064	4011	4053
1039	2911		2911	811		811
4273	46074	32849	13225	10804	7348	3456

高等林业院校本科、
Number of Students of

地 区 Region	毕(结)业生数 Graduates			招生数	
	合计 Total	本 科 Normal Courses	专 科 Short-cycle Courses	合计 Total	本 科 Normal Courses
总 计 Total	**47391**	**26631**	**20760**	**54824**	**30064**
北 京 Beijing	3195	3195		3441	3441
天 津 Tianjin					
河 北 Hebei					
山 西 Shanxi	1705		1705	1761	
内蒙古 Inner Mongolia					
辽 宁 Liaoning	1464		1464	1915	
吉 林 Jilin					
黑龙江 Heilongjiang	8324	4722	3602	8867	4676
上 海 Shanghai					
江 苏 Jiangsu	5891	5891		6618	6618
浙 江 Zhejiang	4966	4966		5067	5067
安 徽 Anhui	1049		1049	1051	
福 建 Fujian	1601		1601	2351	
江 西 Jiangxi	2009		2009	1820	
山 东 Shandong					
河 南 Henan				262	
湖 北 Hubei	2045		2045	3629	
湖 南 Hunan	5732	4999	733	6472	5890
广 东 Guangdong					
广 西 Guangxi	1922		1922	2132	
海 南 Hainan					
重 庆 Chongqing					
四 川 Sichuan					
贵 州 Guizhou					
云 南 Yunnan	4817	2858	1959	6496	4372
西 藏 Tibet					
陕 西 Shaanxi					
甘 肃 Gansu	2671		2671	2739	
青 海 Qinghai					
宁 夏 Ningxia				203	
新 疆 Xinjiang					

专科生学生数
Institutions of Forestry

单位：人
unit：person

Entrants	在校生数 Enrolment			预计毕业生数 Estimated Graduates for Next Year		
专科 Short-cycle Courses	合计 Total	本科 Normal Courses	专科 Short-cycle Courses	合计 Total	本科 Normal Courses	专科 Short-cycle Courses
24760	**187360**	**117504**	**69856**	**50781**	**28461**	**22320**
	13282	13282		3294	3294	
1761	5430		5430	1652		1652
1915	5661		5661	1599		1599
4191	30372	18846	11526	8293	4502	3791
	26507	26507		6531	6531	
	20121	20121		4923	4923	
1051	3090		3090	1069		1069
2351	6286		6286	1761		1761
1820	6007		6007	2072		2072
262	262		262			
3629	8740		8740	2420		2420
582	25034	22968	2066	6312	5537	775
2132	5526		5526	1972		1972
2124	21937	15780	6157	5840	3674	2166
2739	8483		8483	2833		2833
203	622		622	210		210

高等医药院校本科、
Number of Students of Institutions

地 区 Region	毕(结)业生数 Graduates			招生数	
	合计 Total	本 科 Normal Courses	专 科 Short-cycle Courses	合计 Total	本 科 Normal Courses
总 计 Total	**361848**	**174004**	**187844**	**408283**	**214059**
北 京 Beijing	3021	2077	944	3688	2402
天 津 Tianjin	7071	3527	3544	8701	4456
河 北 Hebei	29653	9842	19811	28759	10055
山 西 Shanxi	9593	5960	3633	12409	8517
内蒙古 Inner Mongolia	4016	2169	1847	3695	2303
辽 宁 Liaoning	16402	11402	5000	21203	16525
吉 林 Jilin	8051	3324	4727	8638	3415
黑龙江 Heilongjiang	12909	7717	5192	14227	8857
上 海 Shanghai	2937	824	2113	3980	824
江 苏 Jiangsu	15416	9338	6078	18965	11891
浙 江 Zhejiang	12323	6195	6128	12658	6247
安 徽 Anhui	20878	9522	11356	21277	11558
福 建 Fujian	11383	4631	6752	14838	5291
江 西 Jiangxi	11116	5176	5940	11507	6057
山 东 Shandong	38835	17216	21619	41480	18178
河 南 Henan	28378	7479	20899	27754	8676
湖 北 Hubei	9682	5410	4272	10759	6896
湖 南 Hunan	16526	6878	9648	19093	7925
广 东 Guangdong	21139	16589	4550	22953	16456
广 西 Guangxi	11803	5429	6374	15227	8859
海 南 Hainan	2136	1213	923	2539	1529
重 庆 Chongqing	10145	3291	6854	11753	4387
四 川 Sichuan	17025	10442	6583	17602	11772
贵 州 Guizhou	12468	6080	6388	19245	12091
云 南 Yunnan	8649	3946	4703	13776	7135
西 藏 Tibet	216	107	109	257	222
陕 西 Shaanxi	7462	3827	3635	8753	6073
甘 肃 Gansu	5296	1201	4095	5682	1896
青 海 Qinghai	1133		1133	747	
宁 夏 Ningxia	1282	911	371	1449	1025
新 疆 Xinjiang	4904	2281	2623	4669	2541

专科生学生数

of Medicine & Pharmacy

单位：人

unit：person

Entrants	在校生数 Enrolment			预计毕业生数 Estimated Graduates for Next Year		
专 科 Short-cycle Courses	合计 Total	本 科 Normal Courses	专 科 Short-cycle Courses	合计 Total	本 科 Normal Courses	专 科 Short-cycle Courses
194224	**1529433**	**929868**	**599565**	**384103**	**189011**	**195092**
1286	13244	9854	3390	2758	1917	841
4245	31053	18962	12091	7577	3936	3641
18704	106280	48636	57644	30774	10128	20646
3892	43455	32712	10743	9905	6789	3116
1392	15963	10535	5428	4187	2197	1990
4678	80863	65968	14895	16982	12025	4957
5223	31431	16308	15123	8217	3673	4544
5370	56792	41531	15261	13014	8413	4601
3156	12576	3749	8827	3482	922	2560
7074	70055	49014	21041	17850	11014	6836
6411	47268	27932	19336	12170	6042	6128
9719	83521	51565	31956	21564	9943	11621
9547	48458	22780	25678	12320	4870	7450
5450	46357	27527	18830	12436	5805	6631
23302	160962	88726	72236	41341	18312	23029
19078	104458	41673	62785	29484	8946	20538
3863	41375	28997	12378	10284	5970	4314
11168	68271	35834	32437	18092	7788	10304
6497	91693	74636	17057	22377	17323	5054
6368	56040	35805	20235	12510	6204	6306
1010	9862	6842	3020	2450	1469	981
7366	42319	20210	22109	10905	3771	7134
5830	70634	50426	20208	16616	10449	6167
7154	64683	43349	21334	14137	7414	6723
6641	43942	26533	17409	9884	4614	5270
35	1066	847	219	270	123	147
2680	37313	24197	13116	9822	4505	5317
3786	20725	8136	12589	5839	1540	4299
747	2378		2378	945		945
424	6282	5053	1229	1306	910	396
2128	20114	11531	8583	4605	1999	2606

高等师范院校本科、

Number of Students of

地 区 Region	毕(结)业生数 Graduates			招生数	
	合计 Total	本 科 Normal Courses	专 科 Short-cycle Courses	合计 Total	本 科 Normal Courses
总 计 Total	**655598**	**457456**	**198142**	**698142**	**536202**
北 京 Beijing	4530	4530		5400	5232
天 津 Tianjin	10010	9195	815	10268	9609
河 北 Hebei	51405	28154	23251	46946	30781
山 西 Shanxi	22239	11987	10252	25801	14794
内蒙古 Inner Mongolia	10493	7236	3257	11160	8064
辽 宁 Liaoning	19868	11487	8381	20415	12942
吉 林 Jilin	23206	20153	3053	24427	21200
黑龙江 Heilongjiang	19701	16373	3328	18224	14191
上 海 Shanghai	8721	8204	517	9226	8636
江 苏 Jiangsu	44548	30945	13603	34537	28482
浙 江 Zhejiang	23177	20352	2825	23613	22433
安 徽 Anhui	52502	42731	9771	55190	48964
福 建 Fujian	21332	15444	5888	23008	19208
江 西 Jiangxi	22612	15701	6911	21865	16874
山 东 Shandong	18409	13356	5053	21901	17481
河 南 Henan	55556	42304	13252	65096	51805
湖 北 Hubei	22605	13157	9448	24262	14611
湖 南 Hunan	12593	8302	4291	13196	11010
广 东 Guangdong	23963	18242	5721	27918	22698
广 西 Guangxi	18820	10664	8156	22144	14716
海 南 Hainan	9252	5690	3562	10546	7015
重 庆 Chongqing	12086	9144	2942	15958	13854
四 川 Sichuan	44337	27502	16835	42901	29270
贵 州 Guizhou	22128	14802	7326	27446	22669
云 南 Yunnan	22623	12183	10440	26872	18092
西 藏 Tibet	927		927	933	
陕 西 Shaanxi	28262	18753	9509	32453	24751
甘 肃 Gansu	15643	11193	4450	19269	15496
青 海 Qinghai	2060	1967	93	2561	2120
宁 夏 Ningxia	1367	885	482	1979	1548
新 疆 Xinjiang	10623	6820	3803	12627	7656

专科生学生数

Institutions of Teachers

单位：人

unit：person

Entrants	在校生数 Enrolment			预计毕业生数 Estimated Graduates for Next Year		
专 科 Short-cycle Courses	合计 Total	本 科 Normal Courses	专 科 Short-cycle Courses	合计 Total	本 科 Normal Courses	专 科 Short-cycle Courses
161940	**2635628**	**2086949**	**548679**	**695863**	**498837**	**197026**
168	19930	19659	271	4839	4736	103
659	41816	39637	2179	10206	9374	832
16165	181601	123771	57830	55408	31282	24126
11007	83078	52891	30187	21148	12411	8737
3096	41254	31796	9458	11358	8036	3322
7473	75375	50395	24980	21385	12228	9157
3227	92868	83208	9660	23089	19894	3195
4033	72032	61171	10861	19378	15891	3487
590	36855	35236	1619	9684	9159	525
6055	156597	119762	36835	46257	30827	15430
1180	95387	89656	5731	23454	20985	2469
6226	222674	193566	29108	58298	46862	11436
3800	86988	71832	15156	22232	16567	5665
4991	85575	64848	20727	24171	16540	7631
4420	81232	66621	14611	20599	15331	5268
13291	236786	201462	35324	58349	47502	10847
9651	89303	59599	29704	24776	14458	10318
2186	47487	39699	7788	11958	9059	2899
5220	101706	85678	16028	25785	20050	5735
7428	78159	55584	22575	20668	13186	7482
3531	39209	27879	11330	10611	6836	3775
2104	58236	49026	9210	14531	11253	3278
13631	158596	114679	43917	43708	29233	14475
4777	106403	90265	16138	25323	19277	6046
8780	90906	62850	28056	24772	13999	10773
933	2628		2628	833		833
7702	120733	93254	27479	30995	20815	10180
3773	69544	57225	12319	16308	11974	4334
441	9588	8127	1461	2455	1995	460
431	6690	5527	1163	1424	1109	315
4971	46392	32046	14346	11861	7968	3893

高等语文院校本科、

Number of Students of Institutions

地 区 Region	毕(结)业生数 Graduates			招生数	
	合计 Total	本 科 Normal Courses	专 科 Short-cycle Courses	合计 Total	本 科 Normal Courses
总 计 Total	**97632**	**46420**	**51212**	**116439**	**65523**
北 京 Beijing	11242	8284	2958	11802	8669
天 津 Tianjin	4414	3138	1276	4933	3596
河 北 Hebei	6538		6538	8101	1533
山 西 Shanxi	5304		5304	6786	1008
内蒙古 Inner Mongolia	43		43	82	
辽 宁 Liaoning	3787	3114	673	3630	3380
吉 林 Jilin	4248	4248		5335	5335
黑龙江 Heilongjiang	1924	1924		2326	2326
上 海 Shanghai	5097	1482	3615	5644	1522
江 苏 Jiangsu					
浙 江 Zhejiang	5850	4095	1755	9498	8828
安 徽 Anhui	3864		3864	4693	1364
福 建 Fujian	2302		2302	2534	
江 西 Jiangxi					
山 东 Shandong	1745		1745	3229	
河 南 Henan					
湖 北 Hubei					
湖 南 Hunan	8719		8719	10964	2538
广 东 Guangdong	7232	7232		7209	7209
广 西 Guangxi	2438		2438	3855	1723
海 南 Hainan	2338		2338	1125	
重 庆 Chongqing	5553	4734	819	6657	6657
四 川 Sichuan	3531	2761	770	4198	2583
贵 州 Guizhou					
云 南 Yunnan				433	
西 藏 Tibet					
陕 西 Shaanxi	9274	5408	3866	10535	7252
甘 肃 Gansu	2189		2189	2870	
青 海 Qinghai					
宁 夏 Ningxia					
新 疆 Xinjiang					

专科生学生数
of Languages & Literatures

单位：人
unit: person

Entrants	在校生数 Enrolment			预计毕业生数 Estimated Graduates for Next Year		
专科 Short-cycle Courses	合计 Total	本科 Normal Courses	专科 Short-cycle Courses	合计 Total	本科 Normal Courses	专科 Short-cycle Courses
50916	**387639**	**236941**	**150698**	**102514**	**50640**	**51874**
3133	42629	33917	8712	11167	8137	3030
1337	17310	14261	3049	4369	3500	869
6568	22626	2291	20335	7331		7331
5778	18945	1008	17937	5531		5531
82	212		212	64		64
250	14544	13624	920	3656	3268	388
	19846	19846		4470	4470	
	8840	8840		1923	1923	
4122	17512	5986	11526	5347	1513	3834
670	33293	30571	2722	7503	6107	1396
3329	13026	2773	10253	4259		4259
2534	7306		7306	2417		2417
3229	7427		7427	2015		2015
8426	32589	7644	24945	9681	1243	8438
	28668	28668		6944	6944	
2132	11016	3489	7527	3052		3052
1125	3943		3943	1376		1376
	25959	25393	566	5804	5238	566
1615	13829	10811	3018	3232	2683	549
433	555		555			
3283	38396	27819	10577	9185	5614	3571
2870	9168		9168	3188		3188

高等财经院校本科、
Number of Students of Institutions

地 区 Region	毕(结)业生数 Graduates			招生数	
	合计 Total	本 科 Normal Courses	专 科 Short-cycle Courses	合计 Total	本 科 Normal Courses
总 计 Total	**614251**	**283487**	**330764**	**689307**	**360720**
北 京 Beijing	22128	13937	8191	23037	15071
天 津 Tianjin	11937	9952	1985	14460	12000
河 北 Hebei	25705	14668	11037	23636	15137
山 西 Shanxi	19976	8006	11970	25244	12740
内蒙古 Inner Mongolia	8864	4099	4765	8769	4380
辽 宁 Liaoning	17533	8229	9304	20443	10863
吉 林 Jilin	12201	8570	3631	13152	10136
黑龙江 Heilongjiang	14356	9933	4423	15626	12349
上 海 Shanghai	30776	15626	15150	33428	18742
江 苏 Jiangsu	28734	11320	17414	29969	11075
浙 江 Zhejiang	31875	12357	19518	34630	14502
安 徽 Anhui	39223	8627	30596	42952	11263
福 建 Fujian	17944	5355	12589	21687	10341
江 西 Jiangxi	22455	8155	14300	22534	8037
山 东 Shandong	35322	16155	19167	31434	15125
河 南 Henan	50359	19605	30754	58262	30702
湖 北 Hubei	33885	17891	15994	35372	22621
湖 南 Hunan	14656	4620	10036	16381	7437
广 东 Guangdong	42431	20982	21449	49124	27653
广 西 Guangxi	14633	3422	11211	17386	3985
海 南 Hainan	13360	6622	6738	15789	8456
重 庆 Chongqing	21814	14334	7480	27544	18466
四 川 Sichuan	15817	5053	10764	16784	5219
贵 州 Guizhou	6719	3263	3456	9684	6818
云 南 Yunnan	22966	12557	10409	32025	22837
西 藏 Tibet	436		436	274	76
陕 西 Shaanxi	23194	7552	15642	32769	11385
甘 肃 Gansu	8983	8983		9316	9316
青 海 Qinghai					
宁 夏 Ningxia	2355		2355	3608	
新 疆 Xinjiang	3614	3614		3988	3988

专科生学生数
of Finance & Economies

单位：人
unit：person

Entrants	在校生数 Enrolment			预计毕业生数 Estimated Graduates for Next Year		
专 科 Short-cycle Courses	合计 Total	本 科 Normal Courses	专 科 Short-cycle Courses	合计 Total	本 科 Normal Courses	专 科 Short-cycle Courses
328587	**2375104**	**1386859**	**988245**	**643789**	**317477**	**326312**
7966	83633	60312	23321	22178	14802	7376
2460	55354	48257	7097	13625	11545	2080
8499	87943	59272	28671	25856	15002	10854
12504	79612	44120	35492	19062	8352	10710
4389	31652	17903	13749	9223	4459	4764
9580	68508	40048	28460	18667	9116	9551
3016	48093	38564	9529	12026	8741	3285
3277	61292	49218	12074	16805	12259	4546
14686	113756	69980	43776	31804	16842	14962
18894	98487	44435	54052	28089	11194	16895
20128	121267	58457	62810	34343	13724	20619
31689	139903	44142	95761	42882	10339	32543
11346	70055	33045	37010	19027	5903	13124
14497	76134	33064	43070	23287	8589	14698
16309	113488	61672	51816	33689	16408	17281
27560	189875	112402	77473	47452	22828	24624
12751	130324	85841	44483	36297	19790	16507
8944	55153	28881	26272	15001	6378	8623
21471	163066	100274	62792	43268	24097	19171
13401	54373	15115	39258	15684	3800	11884
7333	54590	34524	20066	14160	8075	6085
9078	101097	76023	25074	25236	17182	8054
11565	57164	21742	35422	16149	5384	10765
2866	37876	27420	10456	7956	4532	3424
9188	106760	78284	28476	26269	14328	11941
198	924	204	720	251		251
21384	109003	47518	61485	29007	9998	19009
	40204	40204		10275	10275	
3608	9580		9580	2686		2686
	15938	15938		3535	3535	

高等政法院校本科、
Number of Students of Institutions of

地 区 Region	毕(结)业生数 Graduates			招生数	
	合计 Total	本 科 Normal Courses	专 科 Short-cycle Courses	合计 Total	本 科 Normal Courses
总 计 Total	**84052**	**34005**	**50047**	**101261**	**49506**
北 京 Beijing	9118	6299	2819	11069	8184
天 津 Tianjin	726		726	793	
河 北 Hebei	8340	2376	5964	8050	2469
山 西 Shanxi	2458		2458	3018	
内蒙古 Inner Mongolia	282		282	308	
辽 宁 Liaoning	2341	1456	885	5186	2821
吉 林 Jilin	1915		1915	3031	975
黑龙江 Heilongjiang	859		859	1068	
上 海 Shanghai	6143	4930	1213	6378	5246
江 苏 Jiangsu	2215	1554	661	2976	2976
浙 江 Zhejiang	1927	516	1411	2690	1378
安 徽 Anhui	2722		2722	2844	
福 建 Fujian	1185	883	302	1310	1048
江 西 Jiangxi	3176		3176	3268	1040
山 东 Shandong	4523	2345	2178	6672	3354
河 南 Henan	6266		6266	5353	1778
湖 北 Hubei	2995	531	2464	4105	931
湖 南 Hunan	2081		2081	3754	1665
广 东 Guangdong	2239	1075	1164	2626	1032
广 西 Guangxi	674		674	1620	
海 南 Hainan	1301		1301	1498	
重 庆 Chongqing	4350	4296	54	5131	5119
四 川 Sichuan	2673	1436	1237	2861	1556
贵 州 Guizhou	1351		1351	1104	
云 南 Yunnan	1896	1114	782	2454	1486
西 藏 Tibet	203		203	322	
陕 西 Shaanxi	4340	2656	1684	5489	3407
甘 肃 Gansu	3188	2538	650	3310	2633
青 海 Qinghai	219		219	264	
宁 夏 Ningxia	717		717	922	
新 疆 Xinjiang	1629		1629	1787	408

专科生学生数

Political Science & Law

单位：人
unit:person

Entrants	在校生数 Enrolment			预计毕业生数 Estimated Graduates for Next Year		
专 科 Short-cycle Courses	合计 Total	本 科 Normal Courses	专 科 Short-cycle Courses	合计 Total	本 科 Normal Courses	专 科 Short-cycle Courses
51755	**335717**	**179996**	**155721**	**95705**	**41855**	**53850**
2885	37513	29268	8245	9902	7333	2569
793	2025		2025	540		540
5581	25260	9156	16104	7473	1918	5555
3018	7806		7806	1983		1983
308	610		610	302		302
2365	14525	8788	5737	3934	2665	1269
2056	9446	3616	5830	2291	455	1836
1068	2830		2830	989		989
1132	23856	20599	3257	6722	5108	1614
	9858	9208	650	2558	2045	513
1312	8521	4849	3672	2572	1183	1389
2844	8572		8572	2836		2836
262	2752	2240	512	815	643	172
2228	10748	3554	7194	3050	664	2386
3318	21034	11633	9401	5562	2680	2882
3575	18548	4633	13915	6269	706	5563
3174	12284	2676	9608	4006	356	3650
2089	10411	4682	5729	2653	603	2050
1594	11082	5853	5229	3121	1256	1865
1620	3884		3884	1427		1427
1498	4024		4024	1201		1201
12	20852	19854	998	5599	4613	986
1305	12527	7461	5066	4158	2335	1823
1104	5067		5067	2203		2203
968	8839	6000	2839	2297	1442	855
322	959		959	368		368
2082	20560	14431	6129	5143	3316	1827
677	12674	10721	1953	3340	2534	806
264	731		731	246		246
922	2579		2579	707		707
1379	5340	774	4566	1438		1438

高等体育院校本科、
Number of Students of Institutions

地 区 Region	毕(结)业生数 Graduates			招生数	
	合计 Total	本 科 Normal Courses	专 科 Short-cycle Courses	合计 Total	本 科 Normal Courses
总 计 Total	**28531**	**21933**	**6598**	**30907**	**25960**
北 京 Beijing	2555	2482	73	3043	3021
天 津 Tianjin	1415	1290	125	2692	2460
河 北 Hebei	1401	1228	173	1274	1219
山 西 Shanxi	567		567	522	
内蒙古 Inner Mongolia	114		114	170	
辽 宁 Liaoning	1980	1849	131	2034	1973
吉 林 Jilin	1727	1727		1541	1541
黑龙江 Heilongjiang	1367	1367		1462	1462
上 海 Shanghai	1081	976	105	1139	1038
江 苏 Jiangsu	507	448	59	1511	1455
浙 江 Zhejiang	262		262	128	
安 徽 Anhui	650		650	336	
福 建 Fujian	368		368	276	
江 西 Jiangxi					
山 东 Shandong	1660	1558	102	1861	1861
河 南 Henan	462		462	355	
湖 北 Hubei	3787	3458	329	4150	3906
湖 南 Hunan	852		852	507	
广 东 Guangdong	2656	1564	1092	2731	1682
广 西 Guangxi	616		616	388	
海 南 Hainan					
重 庆 Chongqing					
四 川 Sichuan	2059	2059		2225	2225
贵 州 Guizhou					
云 南 Yunnan	491		491	312	
西 藏 Tibet					
陕 西 Shaanxi	1954	1927	27	2117	2117
甘 肃 Gansu					
青 海 Qinghai					
宁 夏 Ningxia					
新 疆 Xinjiang				133	

专科生学生数

of Physical Culture

单位：人

unit：person

Entrants	在校生数 Enrolment			预计毕业生数 Estimated Graduates for Next Year		
专　科 Short-cycle Courses	合计 Total	本　科 Normal Courses	专　科 Short-cycle Courses	合计 Total	本　科 Normal Courses	专　科 Short-cycle Courses
4947	117749	98929	18820	29757	22867	6890
22	11343	11147	196	2665	2558	107
232	8867	8365	502	1834	1661	173
55	5095	4882	213	1367	1241	126
522	1183		1183	570		570
170	433		433	145		145
61	7968	7782	186	1982	1857	125
	6192	6192		1533	1533	
	5669	5669		1354	1354	
101	4497	4052	445	1220	1033	187
56	4809	4593	216	701	614	87
128	708		708	298		298
336	1466		1466	609		609
276	1351		1351	581		581
	6875	6875		1556	1556	
355	2644		2644	614		614
244	16692	15814	878	4171	3884	287
507	1677		1677	589		589
1049	10449	6430	4019	2812	1418	1394
388	1223		1223	434		434
	8927	8927		2143	2143	
312	1293		1293	564		564
	8201	8201		2015	2015	
133	187		187			

高等艺术院校本科、
Number of Students of

地 区 Region	毕(结)业生数 Graduates			招生数	
	合计 Total	本 科 Normal Courses	专 科 Short-cycle Courses	合计 Total	本 科 Normal Courses
总 计 Total	**86190**	**48623**	**37567**	**104287**	**59399**
北 京 Beijing	3359	3098	261	3609	3243
天 津 Tianjin	2569	1519	1050	3069	1844
河 北 Hebei	5569	2953	2616	7060	4187
山 西 Shanxi	1015		1015	761	
内蒙古 Inner Mongolia	153		153	243	
辽 宁 Liaoning	9934	6213	3721	11226	7128
吉 林 Jilin	3717	3663	54	5041	4987
黑龙江 Heilongjiang	387		387	567	
上 海 Shanghai	3482	1486	1996	3985	1883
江 苏 Jiangsu	7885	4997	2888	8750	5109
浙 江 Zhejiang	3871	1607	2264	4617	1696
安 徽 Anhui	723		723	822	
福 建 Fujian	1175		1175	1258	
江 西 Jiangxi	2359		2359	3418	977
山 东 Shandong	3810	3390	420	5220	4480
河 南 Henan	1505		1505	1487	
湖 北 Hubei	7208	4023	3185	6522	4918
湖 南 Hunan	2465		2465	2901	
广 东 Guangdong	4195	2162	2033	5514	2332
广 西 Guangxi	3672	2244	1428	4828	3355
海 南 Hainan					
重 庆 Chongqing	1572	1480	92	2821	1785
四 川 Sichuan	9195	4516	4679	12705	4861
贵 州 Guizhou					
云 南 Yunnan	3139	2240	899	4414	3442
西 藏 Tibet					
陕 西 Shaanxi	2449	2250	199	2534	2298
甘 肃 Gansu					
青 海 Qinghai					
宁 夏 Ningxia					
新 疆 Xinjiang	782	782		915	874

专科生学生数
Institutions of Art

单位：人
unit: person

Entrants	在校生数 Enrolment			预计毕业生数 Estimated Graduates for Next Year		
专 科 Short-cycle Courses	合计 Total	本 科 Normal Courses	专 科 Short-cycle Courses	合计 Total	本 科 Normal Courses	专 科 Short-cycle Courses
44888	**354619**	**225575**	**129044**	**92596**	**52113**	**40483**
366	13951	12996	955	3541	3128	413
1225	10779	7223	3556	2785	1660	1125
2873	24056	14885	9171	6532	3033	3499
761	2072		2072	600		600
243	499		499	130		130
4098	38350	26857	11493	10171	6649	3522
54	18594	18488	106	4189	4137	52
567	1454		1454	368		368
2102	13551	7353	6198	3717	1688	2029
3641	30882	20679	10203	8089	5154	2935
2921	15114	6872	8242	4177	1719	2458
822	2680		2680	957		957
1258	3361		3361	966		966
2441	9529	2439	7090	2519		2519
740	17500	15996	1504	3824	3316	508
1487	5358		5358	1906		1906
1604	27532	19679	7853	7850	4638	3212
2901	7761		7761	2325		2325
3182	16992	9006	7986	4287	2174	2113
1473	15250	11632	3618	3434	2482	952
1036	8770	6565	2205	1877	1533	344
7844	41864	19521	22343	11333	5020	6313
972	15278	12723	2555	3607	2777	830
236	9862	9215	647	2619	2240	379
41	3580	3446	134	793	765	28

高等民族院校本科、

Number of Students of

地 区 Region	毕(结)业生数 Graduates			招生数	
	合计 Total	本 科 Normal Courses	专 科 Short-cycle Courses	合计 Total	本 科 Normal Courses
总 计 Total	**51160**	**45439**	**5721**	**61982**	**55670**
北 京 Beijing	2723	2723		2849	2849
天 津 Tianjin					
河 北 Hebei					
山 西 Shanxi					
内蒙古 Inner Mongolia					
辽 宁 Liaoning	3699	3699		4033	4033
吉 林 Jilin					
黑龙江 Heilongjiang	338		338	1022	
上 海 Shanghai					
江 苏 Jiangsu					
浙 江 Zhejiang					
安 徽 Anhui					
福 建 Fujian					
江 西 Jiangxi					
山 东 Shandong					
河 南 Henan					
湖 北 Hubei	8690	8690		10385	10385
湖 南 Hunan	1689		1689	2220	
广 东 Guangdong					
广 西 Guangxi	3769	3343	426	4082	3853
海 南 Hainan					
重 庆 Chongqing					
四 川 Sichuan	7542	5882	1660	9254	8280
贵 州 Guizhou	4944	4783	161	5751	5617
云 南 Yunnan	4188	3951	237	5259	5223
西 藏 Tibet	2425	2072	353	2412	2072
陕 西 Shaanxi					
甘 肃 Gansu	4754	4754		6130	6130
青 海 Qinghai	2143	1882	261	2444	2333
宁 夏 Ningxia	4256	3660	596	6141	4895
新 疆 Xinjiang					

专科生学生数

Nationalities Institutions

单位：人

unit：person

Entrants	在校生数 Enrolment			预计毕业生数 Estimated Graduates for Next Year		
专　科 Short-cycle Courses	合计 Total	本　科 Normal Courses	专　科 Short-cycle Courses	合计 Total	本　科 Normal Courses	专　科 Short-cycle Courses
6312	**232102**	**211428**	**20674**	**55331**	**49017**	**6314**
	11312	11312		2795	2795	
	14859	14859		3445	3445	
1022	2373		2373	630		630
	40989	40974	15	9244	9234	10
2220	8686		8686	2588		2588
229	15766	14765	1001	4106	3656	450
974	33863	30823	3040	7856	6873	983
134	21238	20892	346	5295	5174	121
36	20500	19937	563	4971	4620	351
340	8950	7624	1326	2100	1684	416
	23708	23708		5498	5498	
111	8533	8239	294	2024	1938	86
1246	21325	18295	3030	4779	4100	679

高等职业学校本科、

Number of Students of Higher

地区 Region	毕(结)业生数 Graduates			招生数	
	合计 Total	本 科 Normal Courses	专 科 Short-cycle Courses	合计 Total	本 科 Normal Courses
总 计 Total	**2169276**	**97**	**2169179**	**2351367**	
北 京 Beijing	24264		24264	23039	
天 津 Tianjin	47321		47321	49870	
河 北 Hebei	102264		102264	100885	
山 西 Shanxi	56899		56899	67770	
内蒙古 Inner Mongolia	43690		43690	42553	
辽 宁 Liaoning	55362		55362	68514	
吉 林 Jilin	21023		21023	26694	
黑龙江 Heilongjiang	47100		47100	54287	
上 海 Shanghai	31683		31683	33298	
江 苏 Jiangsu	219200		219200	187293	
浙 江 Zhejiang	97431		97431	107436	
安 徽 Anhui	120154		120154	119493	
福 建 Fujian	64670		64670	74282	
江 西 Jiangxi	82594		82594	75787	
山 东 Shandong	172026		172026	167033	
河 南 Henan	147343		147343	135133	
湖 北 Hubei	118430		118430	138274	
湖 南 Hunan	127134		127134	130735	
广 东 Guangdong	171137		171137	232705	
广 西 Guangxi	62120		62120	67741	
海 南 Hainan	16366		16366	16349	
重 庆 Chongqing	47274		47274	66105	
四 川 Sichuan	92558		92558	115649	
贵 州 Guizhou	27262		27262	39263	
云 南 Yunnan	36821		36821	39285	
西 藏 Tibet	1591		1591	1315	
陕 西 Shaanxi	65652		65652	87759	
甘 肃 Gansu	31877		31877	37443	
青 海 Qinghai	4791		4791	5405	
宁 夏 Ningxia	6673		6673	9655	
新 疆 Xinjiang	26566	97	26469	30317	

专科生学生数
Vocational Colleges

单位：人
unit：person

Entrants	在校生数 Enrolment			预计毕业生数 Estimated Graduates for Next Year		
专科 Short-cycle Courses	合计 Total	本 科 Normal Courses	专 科 Short-cycle Courses	合计 Total	本 科 Normal Courses	专 科 Short-cycle Courses
2351367	**6982063**	**168**	**6981895**	**2253012**	**114**	**2252898**
23039	71707		71707	23226		23226
49870	147212		147212	45457		45457
100885	306905		306905	105809		105809
67770	188919		188919	57439		57439
42553	128398		128398	44295		44295
68514	192873		192873	57599		57599
26694	76599		76599	24599		24599
54287	152316		152316	47704		47704
33298	93571		93571	31006		31006
187293	637236		637236	221038		221038
107436	324070		324070	104786		104786
119493	366260		366260	128610		128610
74282	205817		205817	63968		63968
75787	220885		220885	74989		74989
167033	496614		496614	162508		162508
135133	408325		408325	135243		135243
138274	403177		403177	134503		134503
130735	386804		386804	124174		124174
232705	658730		658730	198414		198414
67741	195450		195450	63318		63318
16349	47487		47487	14922		14922
66105	190077		190077	56594		56594
115649	348391		348391	108363		108363
39263	114979		114979	32101		32101
39285	113925		113925	40490		40490
1315	5018		5018	1664		1664
87759	252268		252268	75247		75247
37443	116777		116777	37997		37997
5405	15200		15200	4859		4859
9655	27030		27030	7922		7922
30317	89043	168	88875	24168	114	24054

广播电视大学本、

Number of Students in Radio/TV

地 区 Region	毕业生数 Graduates			招生数	
	合 计 Total	本 科 Normal Courses	专 科 Short-cycle Courses	合 计 Total	本 科 Normal Courses
总 计 Total	**54894**	**1144**	**53750**	**68296**	**1521**
北 京 Beijing	754		754	500	
天 津 Tianjin	136		136	81	
河 北 Hebei	757		757	2387	
山 西 Shanxi	970		970	1429	
内蒙古 Inner Mongolia	804		804	906	
辽 宁 Liaoning	2399		2399	3500	
吉 林 Jilin	1963		1963	1601	
黑龙江 Heilongjiang	1248		1248	972	
上 海 Shanghai					
江 苏 Jiangsu	3370		3370	2755	
浙 江 Zhejiang	4536		4536	6376	
安 徽 Anhui	434	16	418	586	164
福 建 Fujian	2218		2218	4092	
江 西 Jiangxi	300		300	683	
山 东 Shandong	393		393	1494	
河 南 Henan	1055	4	1051	272	22
湖 北 Hubei	2007	244	1763	1769	400
湖 南 Hunan	1785		1785	1017	
广 东 Guangdong	4359		4359	3387	
广 西 Guangxi	379	205	174	388	235
海 南 Hainan	412		412	105	
重 庆 Chongqing	4413		4413	9003	
四 川 Sichuan	9291	656	8635	10553	601
贵 州 Guizhou	1404		1404	3873	
云 南 Yunnan	1629	19	1610	2613	33
西 藏 Tibet					
陕 西 Shaanxi	2608		2608	1686	66
甘 肃 Gansu	2457		2457	1928	
青 海 Qinghai	196		196	396	
宁 夏 Ningxia	1439		1439	1918	
新 疆 Xinjiang	1178		1178	2026	

专科学生数
Universities

单位：人
unit：person

Entrants	在校生数 Enrolment			预计毕业生数 Estimated Graduates for Next Year		
专　科 Short-cycle Courses	合　计 Total	本　科 Normal Courses	专　科 Short-cycle Courses	合　计 Total	本　科 Normal Courses	专　科 Short-cycle Courses
66775	**163761**	**3775**	**159986**	**69122**	**1715**	**67407**
500	1762		1762	914		914
81	351		351	270		270
2387	4791		4791	1815		1815
1429	2964		2964	1228		1228
906	1835		1835	929		929
3500	7214		7214	3714		3714
1601	3246		3246	1645		1645
972	2815		2815	1251		1251
2755	6271		6271	2647		2647
6376	15176		15176	4958		4958
422	1820	443	1377	836	157	679
4092	9601		9601	1489		1489
683	1269		1269	586		586
1494	2970		2970	1446		1446
250	948	36	912	676	14	662
1369	4319	923	3396	2326	349	1977
1017	3935		3935	2886		2886
3387	9196		9196	3493		3493
153	982	478	504			
105	413		413	308		308
9003	20730		20730	4699		4699
9952	27683	1777	25906	16855	1176	15679
3873	8648		8648	4460		4460
2580	5042	52	4990	1934	19	1915
1620	5985	66	5919	2440		2440
1928	4800		4800	1809		1809
396	622		622	206		206
1918	4564		4564	2035		2035
2026	3809		3809	1267		1267

职工高等学校本、

Number of Students in

地　区 Region	毕业生数 Graduates			招生数	
	合　计 Total	本　科 Normal Courses	专　科 Short-cycle Courses	合　计 Total	本科 Normal Courses
总　计 Total	**60623**	**3402**	**57221**	**67458**	**2021**
北　京 Beijing	3952	243	3709	5195	219
天　津 Tianjin	3980		3980	4882	
河　北 Hebei	136		136	747	
山　西 Shanxi	4860	1225	3635	7628	1071
内蒙古 Inner Mongolia					
辽　宁 Liaoning	7155		7155	9189	
吉　林 Jilin	4292	1867	2425	3408	612
黑龙江 Heilongjiang	3376		3376	2492	
上　海 Shanghai	3213		3213	2933	
江　苏 Jiangsu	802		802	921	
浙　江 Zhejiang	2183		2183	1881	
安　徽 Anhui	673		673	727	
福　建 Fujian					
江　西 Jiangxi	736		736	885	
山　东 Shandong	499		499	1458	
河　南 Henan	5850		5850	6367	
湖　北 Hubei	9		9	12	
湖　南 Hunan	4004		4004	2703	
广　东 Guangdong	2330		2330	2178	
广　西 Guangxi	222		222	346	
海　南 Hainan					
重　庆 Chongqing	422		422	178	
四　川 Sichuan	4817	32	4785	6981	76
贵　州 Guizhou	813		813	1417	
云　南 Yunnan					
西　藏 Tibet					
陕　西 Shaanxi	5286	35	5251	3391	43
甘　肃 Gansu	196		196	356	
青　海 Qinghai	804		804	1042	
宁　夏 Ningxia					
新　疆 Xinjiang	13		13	141	

专科学生数
Workers' Colleges

单位：人
unit: person

Entrants	在校生数 Enrolment			预计毕业生数 Estimated Graduates for Next Year		
专 科 Short-cycle Courses	合 计 Total	本 科 Normal Courses	专 科 Short-cycle Courses	合 计 Total	本 科 Normal Courses	专 科 Short-cycle Courses
65437	**156032**	**6941**	**149091**	**67896**	**4161**	**63735**
4976	12022	876	11146	4898	270	4628
4882	10540		10540	5658		5658
747	1148		1148	231		231
6557	17126	2354	14772	6234	915	5319
9189	18512		18512	6888		6888
2796	8927	3502	5425	5519	2890	2629
2492	8085		8085	3699		3699
2933	8150		8150	4708		4708
921	1400		1400	521		521
1881	4396		4396	2430		2430
727	1403		1403	676		676
885	2089		2089	997		997
1458	3394		3394	1220		1220
6367	13306		13306	6340		6340
12	38		38	26		26
2703	5325		5325	2541		2541
2178	5498		5498	2673		2673
346	546		546	249		249
178	758		758	387		387
6905	15249	133	15116	5433	57	5376
1417	2809		2809	1222		1222
3348	11981	76	11905	3754	29	3725
356	1173		1173	681		681
1042	1780		1780	713		713
141	377		377	198		198

教育学院本、

Number of Students in

地　区 Region	毕业生数 Graduates			招生数	
	合　计 Total	本　科 Normal Courses	专　科 Short-cycle Courses	合　计 Total	本　科 Normal Courses
总　计 Total	**20149**	**6580**	**13569**	**35166**	**7011**
北　京 Beijing	1787	640	1147	1003	366
天　津 Tianjin					
河　北 Hebei					
山　西 Shanxi	155		155	207	
内蒙古 Inner Mongolia					
辽　宁 Liaoning	1411	401	1010	2149	433
吉　林 Jilin	791	438	353	2691	960
黑龙江 Heilongjiang	2725	1005	1720	5222	1758
上　海 Shanghai					
江　苏 Jiangsu	1331		1331	1489	
浙　江 Zhejiang	2132	771	1361	2948	860
安　徽 Anhui					
福　建 Fujian	2878	1533	1345	8774	1147
江　西 Jiangxi	289		289	749	
山　东 Shandong	10		10	10	
河　南 Henan	2901	999	1902	4476	387
湖　北 Hubei	1235		1235	1302	
湖　南 Hunan	775		775	565	
广　东 Guangdong	178		178	667	
广　西 Guangxi	918	793	125	2084	1100
海　南 Hainan					
重　庆 Chongqing					
四　川 Sichuan					
贵　州 Guizhou					
云　南 Yunnan					
西　藏 Tibet					
陕　西 Shaanxi	148		148	255	
甘　肃 Gansu					
青　海 Qinghai					
宁　夏 Ningxia					
新　疆 Xinjiang	485		485	575	

专科学生数
Educational Colleges

单位：人
unit：person

Entrants	在校生数 Enrolment			预计毕业生数 Estimated Graduates for Next Year		
专 科 Short-cycle Courses	合 计 Total	本 科 Normal Courses	专 科 Short-cycle Courses	合 计 Total	本 科 Normal Courses	专 科 Short-cycle Courses
28155	**80504**	**18534**	**61970**	**30058**	**7594**	**22464**
637	4212	1321	2891	1720	570	1150
207	680		680	473		473
1716	3872	981	2891	1723	548	1175
1731	4644	2101	2543	1703	891	812
3464	9509	3246	6263	3818	1309	2509
1489	3197		3197	1708		1708
2088	8076	3327	4749	2986	917	2069
7627	24431	4400	20031	6259	1749	4510
749	1204		1204	247		247
10	15		15	5		5
4089	9617	1157	8460	4689	709	3980
1302	2435		2435	1078		1078
565	1400		1400	835		835
667	2109		2109	901		901
984	3109	2001	1108	1025	901	124
255	357		357	101		101
575	1637		1637	787		787

管理干部学院本、

Number of Students in Institutes

地　区 Region	毕业生数 Graduates			招生数	
	合　计 Total	本　科 Normal Courses	专　科 Short-cycle Courses	合　计 Total	本　科 Normal Courses
总　计 Total	**17757**	**2771**	**14986**	**20775**	**3770**
北　京 Beijing	2730	383	2347	2454	188
天　津 Tianjin	187		187	59	
河　北 Hebei	92		92	59	
山　西 Shanxi	2427		2427	4110	
内蒙古 Inner Mongolia					
辽　宁 Liaoning	209	171	38	144	132
吉　林 Jilin	580	176	404	776	179
黑龙江 Heilongjiang	2498	255	2243	2884	550
上　海 Shanghai	507		507	350	
江　苏 Jiangsu	3241		3241	2626	
浙　江 Zhejiang					
安　徽 Anhui	252		252	395	
福　建 Fujian					
江　西 Jiangxi	1227	548	679	2288	987
山　东 Shandong	2598	846	1752	2932	1401
河　南 Henan					
湖　北 Hubei	227	72	155	83	
湖　南 Hunan					
广　东 Guangdong					
广　西 Guangxi	724	320	404	695	333
海　南 Hainan					
重　庆 Chongqing					
四　川 Sichuan					
贵　州 Guizhou					
云　南 Yunnan					
西　藏 Tibet					
陕　西 Shaanxi	258		258	920	
甘　肃 Gansu					
青　海 Qinghai					
宁　夏 Ningxia					
新　疆 Xinjiang					

专科学生数
for Administration

单位：人
unit：person

Entrants	在校生数 Enrolment			预计毕业生数 Estimated Graduates for Next Year		
专 科 Short-cycle Courses	合 计 Total	本 科 Normal Courses	专 科 Short-cycle Courses	合 计 Total	本 科 Normal Courses	专 科 Short-cycle Courses
17005	**46044**	**8033**	**38011**	**18695**	**2637**	**16058**
2266	5602	815	4787	2751	230	2521
59	177		177	75		75
59	150		150	87		87
4110	10178		10178	3271		3271
12	438	403	35	213	190	23
597	1362	348	1014	586	169	417
2334	5917	845	5072	2898	151	2747
350	999		999	318		318
2626	4886		4886	2260		2260
395	857		857	462		462
1301	3929	1747	2182	1420	567	853
1531	7844	2732	5112	2681	821	1860
83	382	93	289	299	93	206
362	2086	1050	1036	1057	416	641
920	1237		1237	317		317

其他机构本、

Number of Students in

地　区 Region	毕业生数 Graduates			招生数	
	合　计 Total	本　科 Normal Courses	专　科 Short-cycle Courses	合　计 Total	本　科 Normal Courses
总　计 Total	**173**		**173**	**6**	
北　京 Beijing					
天　津 Tianjin					
河　北 Hebei					
山　西 Shanxi					
内蒙古 Inner Mongolia					
辽　宁 Liaoning					
吉　林 Jilin					
黑龙江 Heilongjiang					
上　海 Shanghai					
江　苏 Jiangsu					
浙　江 Zhejiang	32		32	6	
安　徽 Anhui					
福　建 Fujian					
江　西 Jiangxi					
山　东 Shandong					
河　南 Henan	108		108		
湖　北 Hubei					
湖　南 Hunan	33		33		
广　东 Guangdong					
广　西 Guangxi					
海　南 Hainan					
重　庆 Chongqing					
四　川 Sichuan					
贵　州 Guizhou					
云　南 Yunnan					
西　藏 Tibet					
陕　西 Shaanxi					
甘　肃 Gansu					
青　海 Qinghai					
宁　夏 Ningxia					
新　疆 Xinjiang					

专科学生数

Other Insitutes

单位：人
unit: person

Entrants	在校生数 Enrolment			预计毕业生数 Estimated Graduates for Next Year		
专 科 Short-cycle Courses	合 计 Total	本 科 Normal Courses	专 科 Short-cycle Courses	合 计 Total	本 科 Normal Courses	专 科 Short-cycle Courses
6	**203**		**203**	**191**		**191**
6	33		33	21		21
	150		150	150		150
	20		20	20		20

普通高等学校举办函授、业余、

Number of Students in Correspondence Courses for Adults run

地区 Region	函授、业余 Divisions of Correspondence, Sparetime Schools							
	毕业生数 Graduates			招生数 Entrants			在校生数 Enrolment	
	合计 Total	本科 Normal Courses	专科 Short-cycle Courses	合计 Total	本科 Normal Courses	专科 Short-cycle Courses	合计 Total	本科 Normal Courses
总计 Total	**1836655**	**795213**	**1041442**	**2360659**	**1019738**	**1340921**	**5791903**	**2608320**
北京 Beijing	87185	52159	35026	94553	57630	36923	240818	155260
天津 Tianjin	20546	12347	8199	27769	16396	11373	62504	35754
河北 Hebei	80182	38037	42145	114563	61110	53453	314716	168508
山西 Shanxi	44947	23171	21776	49578	23394	26184	157910	75245
内蒙古 Inner Mongolia	32688	12370	20318	53540	25273	28267	114145	51603
辽宁 Liaoning	67859	28010	39849	75101	30773	44328	183004	80249
吉林 Jilin	60382	26753	33629	78081	33275	44806	158095	75778
黑龙江 Heilongjiang	55310	28135	27175	77843	41268	36575	163008	88572
上海 Shanghai	50272	37569	12703	51164	38243	12921	165431	125403
江苏 Jiangsu	141618	68602	73016	160522	83577	76945	382090	208000
浙江 Zhejiang	92011	33843	58168	112800	35679	77121	247735	81428
安徽 Anhui	66250	26310	39940	106403	46075	60328	216562	91496
福建 Fujian	29433	13638	15795	44116	19410	24706	109891	49504
江西 Jiangxi	31510	16069	15441	55099	22752	32347	158930	73266
山东 Shandong	124459	58836	65623	159628	84036	75592	445517	237475
河南 Henan	95912	41720	54192	142515	62710	79805	311868	138090
湖北 Hubei	101012	34518	66494	111460	41705	69755	275179	103602
湖南 Hunan	94370	35206	59164	101636	42590	59046	221475	91442
广东 Guangdong	149250	54973	94277	209539	61436	148103	517573	164096
广西 Guangxi	64936	25417	39519	96164	35976	60188	220255	83418
海南 Hainan	6995	3600	3395	7906	3999	3907	23288	12342
重庆 Chongqing	35243	9767	25476	52491	12490	40001	123186	32588
四川 Sichuan	110647	32571	78076	147664	39005	108659	325526	96545
贵州 Guizhou	20439	12080	8359	33078	15962	17116	90120	46968
云南 Yunnan	50881	24502	26379	66330	28065	38265	190255	85292
西藏 Tibet	3120	1698	1422	5413	3506	1907	12087	8167
陕西 Shaanxi	61108	20465	40643	50739	24495	26244	161335	68987
甘肃 Gansu	26249	10904	15345	31166	13166	18000	87083	39600
青海 Qinghai	4120	2705	1415	4313	2908	1405	10423	7069
宁夏 Ningxia	10889	3130	7759	11542	3425	8117	28986	8826
新疆 Xinjiang	16832	6108	10724	27943	9409	18534	72908	23747

脱产分本专科学生数

divisions, Sparetime Schools & Short-cycle by Regular HEIs

单位：人
unit：person

	脱产 Short-cycle Courses for Adults								
	毕业生数 Graduates			招生数 Entrants			在校生数 Enrolment		
专科 Short-cycle Courses	合计 Total	本科 Normal Courses	专科 Short-cycle Courses	合计 Total	本科 Normal Courses	专科 Short-cycle Courses	合计 Total	本科 Normal Courses	专科 Short-cycle Courses
3183583	**6938**	**2049**	**4889**	**11917**	**4097**	**7820**	**24530**	**8993**	**15537**
85558	8	4	4				28	4	24
26750	785		785						
146208	935	418	517	629	528	101	3013	1717	1296
82665	23		23	13		13	36		36
62542									
102755	49	49					1	1	
82317	55		55				6		6
74436	126	126					3		3
40028	2	2					4		4
174090	105	7	98	50		50	77		77
166307	188		188	107	107		1162	534	628
125066	2	2							
60387	1		1						
85664	2773	941	1832	9825	3305	6520	16621	5923	10698
208042	338	42	296				63	27	36
173778	45		45	476		476	506		506
171577	148	135	13				473	279	194
130033	213	6	207				73		73
353477	160		160						
136837	19	7	12				38	22	16
10946									
90598	23	20	3						
228981	155	78	77				760	137	623
43152	1		1				121	58	63
104963									
3920	67		67	28		28	154		154
92348	59	55	4	14		14	72		72
47483	76		76						
3354									
20160									
49161	582	157	425	775	157	618	1319	291	1028

在职人员攻读硕士

Number of On-the-job

地　区 Region	授予学位数 Degrees Awarded
总　计 Total	**103468**
北　京 Beijing	14699
天　津 Tianjin	2827
河　北 Hebei	2071
山　西 Shanxi	990
内蒙古 Inner Mongolia	1617
辽　宁 Liaoning	4337
吉　林 Jilin	3434
黑龙江 Heilongjiang	3043
上　海 Shanghai	8181
江　苏 Jiangsu	9082
浙　江 Zhejiang	3596
安　徽 Anhui	1842
福　建 Fujian	2663
江　西 Jiangxi	1863
山　东 Shandong	6150
河　南 Henan	1683
湖　北 Hubei	7754
湖　南 Hunan	2836
广　东 Guangdong	3856
广　西 Guangxi	627
海　南 Hainan	214
重　庆 Chongqing	2993
四　川 Sichuan	7493
贵　州 Guizhou	607
云　南 Yunnan	3070
西　藏 Tibet	9
陕　西 Shaanxi	4065
甘　肃 Gansu	899
青　海 Qinghai	209
宁　夏 Ningxia	238
新　疆 Xinjiang	520

学位学生数

Students Studying for Master's Degree

单位:人
unit: person

招生数(人) Entrants	在校生数(人) Enrolment
167576	**558730**
23550	83358
5671	15512
3083	9217
2526	6287
2107	6127
6828	21507
5987	16294
4543	15881
9843	37230
12617	44759
3715	15686
3523	9812
4089	14099
2692	10041
9605	30187
3646	10351
15328	48521
5735	20226
6272	19162
1170	4026
595	1868
8179	19581
7475	27856
840	2772
5147	15040
6	28
9284	42183
1531	5033
432	978
446	1266
1111	3842

高等教育非学历

Number of Students in Non-formal Education

地 区 Region	毕(结)业生数 Graduates												
	自考助学班 Classes Run by Non-government HEIs for Students Preparing for Self-directed State-administered Examinations	普通预科生 College-preparatory Classes	研究生课程进修班 Postgraduate Courses	进修及培训 In-service Training									
				合计 Total	其中:资格证书培训 of Which: For Certificates of Vocational Qualifications	岗位证书培训 For Certificates of Job-related Qualifications	其中:第一产业类培训 of Which: Training for First Industry	第二产业类培训 Training for Second Industry	第三产业类培训 Training for Third Industry	一个月以内 1 Month Under	一个月至三个月以内 1 Month to 3 Months Under	三个月至半年以内 3 Months to 6 Months Under	半年至一年以内 6 Months to 1 Year Under
总 计 Total	**194882**		**48329**	**9094537**	**2351305**	**2504684**	**419587**	**1188577**	**7486373**	**5807915**	**1912224**	**646283**	**441010**
北 京 Beijing	16793		12980	774950	71757	179116	31565	49925	693460	536907	108508	60524	42324
天 津 Tianjin	2454		1199	179411	55265	65139	22801	29163	127447	136519	20522	10688	10747
河 北 Hebei	4543		1226	110370	33838	10673	14285	22663	73422	98953	6389	2895	1383
山 西 Shanxi	3619			58866	33430	14565	909	16851	41106	31069	1072	1785	9702
内蒙古 Inner Mongolia			70	64131	29044	34871	3184	25527	35420	57763	4626	334	1283
辽 宁 Liaoning	11739		1637	188749	52672	114144	7623	73941	107185	145939	20340	7529	14724
吉 林 Jilin	41329		4806	81640	23278	20999	3016	38543	40081	71831	4702	4061	124
黑龙江 Heilongjiang	1822			99435	21159	50532	25926	44241	29268	76799	3543	2396	16625
上 海 Shanghai	4477		2988	765379	101021	151827	5876	71800	687703	323521	84099	266980	51309
江 苏 Jiangsu	11487		2354	516770	230991	118402	70654	126844	319272	336196	103181	53003	16819
浙 江 Zhejiang	9012		1894	775044	192817	202763	40783	53169	681092	669067	46397	35718	21639
安 徽 Anhui	469		925	297684	68162	40437	7347	42370	247967	114239	14891	16128	147955
福 建 Fujian	3889		676	359541	67600	143554	8959	13706	336876	59936	145785	6939	15673
江 西 Jiangxi	7233		151	59827	28103	19765	10455	7952	41420	41956	9922	2593	3212
山 东 Shandong	5802		3444	331484	132280	139259	8925	74104	248455	248795	51050	19045	5527
河 南 Henan	3764		2774	370385	259540	88355	5734	17550	347101	312679	45523	3212	7226
湖 北 Hubei	24623		2356	279936	103468	66024	12542	87011	180383	199977	41775	18576	17632
湖 南 Hunan	9456		358	239434	162609	50275	23839	41319	174276	184543	35035	15818	2721
广 东 Guangdong	6660		4170	825883	98697	593142	5861	56277	763745	290287	493371	25245	12067
广 西 Guangxi	4916		1141	204628	81183	68720	8351	58556	137721	173746	25137	4617	922
海 南 Hainan	4352			10726	2782			604	10122	8887	202	317	1086
重 庆 Chongqing	5930		383	546223	57726	17108	3268	12815	530140	79679	445959	10007	8506
四 川 Sichuan	5776		1262	1259045	106394	108019	20131	44757	1194157	1170190	44295	28836	11820
贵 州 Guizhou	2153		97	79188	24965	19605	8740	12568	57880	39276	7969	7839	86
云 南 Yunnan	444		393	168791	60075	47837	33484	83149	52158	88475	73668	2974	3674
西 藏 Tibet				6577	1613	3494	352		6225	3464	2850		21
陕 西 Shaanxi	62		438	148378	53955	60294	13423	47785	87170	83648	30982	28663	1924
甘 肃 Gansu	1129		258	185446	151365	33007	8024	5596	171826	143652	28990	3205	8831
青 海 Qinghai	383			13747	3570	2346		4584	9163	12447	695		163
宁 夏 Ningxia			78	23822	10008	11749	3353	10199	10270	14399	3526	4265	1262
新 疆 Xinjiang	566		271	69047	31938	28663	10177	15008	43862	53076	7220	2091	4023

注:包含民办的其他高等教育机构数据。

Note: Data of Non-government HEIs are included.

教育学生情况(总计)

of HEIs (Total)

单位:人,人次

unit: person

一年及以上 1 Year and Over	注册学生数 Enrolment													
	自考助学班 Classes Run by Non-government HEIs for Students Preparing for Self-directed State-administered Examinations	普通预科生 College-preparatory Classes	研究生课程进修班 Postgraduate Courses	进修及培训 In-service Training										
				合计 Total	其中:资格证书培训 of Which: For Certificates of Vocational Qualifications	岗位证书培训 For Certificates of Job-related Qualifications	其中:第一产业类培训 of Which: Training for First Industry	第二产业类培训 Training for Second Industry	第三产业类培训 Training for Third Industry	一个月以内 1 Month Under	一个月至三个月以内 1 Month to 3 Months Under	三个月至半年以内 3 Months to 6 Months Under	半年至一年以内 6 Months to 1 Year Under	一年及以上 1 Year and Over
287105	**405329**	**42514**	**69321**	**6268398**	**1979966**	**1713103**	**281679**	**1028161**	**4958558**	**3759314**	**1106380**	**598034**	**446463**	**358207**
26687	34586	2333	14982	760371	79913	159070	25164	47312	687895	472539	105874	54880	81770	45308
935	6130	158	1635	152017	55779	60021	24575	28463	98979	120848	16963	8444	5461	301
750	8740	842	876	89954	35108	10264	14306	23156	52492	74910	7941	3871	1558	1674
15238	6634		134	62463	37923	13893	2842	18698	40923	27206	3407	3146	10211	18493
125		1191	339	66113	30389	35573	3238	25051	37824	58700	4875	961	1517	60
217	21590	1664	1634	99504	22188	59289	7664	61560	30280	86256	7435	1522	3238	1053
922	39677	1648	4868	77198	20864	21174	1179	38661	37358	67860	4966	3174	204	994
72	2513	343	206	37886	12854	24329	8742	17925	11219	28882	3358	3000	2355	291
39470	8811	30	5858	771293	103378	125792	4903	85463	680927	304664	77223	289094	48336	51976
7571	26233	78	3097	306761	163295	76929	59062	74181	173518	182945	68124	28437	18690	8565
2223	31012	88	4052	473778	147333	81850	8341	37923	427514	400274	17249	24402	26233	5620
4471	1191	215	1988	291926	73644	34688	7424	35777	248725	103839	13978	16148	148026	9935
131208	6301	745	1546	336944	49251	129205	8133	6979	321832	21197	141899	6572	14973	152303
2144	9335	4475	445	54992	26509	19574	2260	6518	46214	33072	12415	5759	1137	2609
7067	11933	412	4319	279575	81812	78812	19153	89637	170785	216246	39318	12239	4729	7043
1745	14829	2963	2773	383851	255851	85868	4463	22798	356590	316220	52310	9000	1478	4843
1976	83825	4039	3334	208939	86577	52867	10515	74665	123759	125801	44529	17464	18934	2211
1317	29386	2210	2	206948	138492	48451	21797	33030	152121	168106	24715	9393	3100	1634
4913	14448	742	9199	478825	73854	279755	1073	34902	442850	248896	191955	21705	11140	5129
206	10647	1549	3954	137075	66656	30098	1641	50125	85309	109069	22932	2576	2149	349
234	7783	118		14311	5133	1378		1798	12513	10059	366	2010	1642	234
2072	5222	1175	555	131544	56975	26322	1549	28774	101221	79939	40564	6577	4464	
3904	10283	2750	910	286781	92325	78702	9872	46694	230215	191145	56335	18968	14510	5823
24018	5287	2914	120	56328	16195	16115	2286	10638	43404	19594	4636	7994	86	24018
	860	2458	1047	115262	28416	31185	7466	74005	33791	38325	70204	2819	3914	
242				4257	258	2563	352		3905	2006	2022	8	21	200
3161	588	509	400	113236	41156	56945	4942	23280	85014	46423	31355	29575	2740	3143
768	5053	2202	333	188788	151496	34423	8827	6106	173855	143372	29022	3173	11519	1702
442	1271	1098		6519	144				6519	6375				144
370		3565	114	25132	10802	12128	3410	10417	11305	14732	4142	4458	1430	370
2637	1161		601	49827	15396	25840	6500	13625	29702	39814	6268	665	898	2182

地 区 Region	毕(结)业生数 Graduates												
	自考助学班 Classes Run by Non-government HEIs for Students Preparing for Self-directed State-administered Examinations	普通预科生 College-preparatory Classes	研究生课程进修班 Postgraduate Courses	进修及培训 In-service Training									
				合计 Total	其中:资格证书培训 of Which: For Certificates of Vocational Qualifications	岗位证书培训 For Certificates of Job-related Qualific-ations	其中:第一产业类培训 of Which: Training for First Industry	第二产业类培训 Training for Second Industry	第三产业类培训 Training for Third Industry	一个月以内 1 Month Under	一个月至三个月以内 1 Month to 3 Months Under	三个月至半年以内 3 Months to 6 Months Under	半年至一年以内 6 Months to 1 Year Under
总 计 Total	**122961**		**48040**	**4839106**	**1595881**	**1596498**	**320812**	**973662**	**3544632**	**3569099**	**745043**	**278021**	**205726**
北 京 Beijing	1770		12691	421945	43576	103634	13544	32726	375675	284815	65813	25029	32225
天 津 Tianjin	1595		1199	117837	36142	34347	1074	21328	95435	89610	14813	6948	6323
河 北 Hebei	1487		1226	82637	29911	10282	11964	22605	48068	74541	5812	1653	578
山 西 Shanxi				29563	15969	7906	581	16091	12891	25746	80		3737
内蒙古 Inner Mongolia			70	64131	29044	34871	3184	25527	35420	57763	4626	334	1283
辽 宁 Liaoning	1774		1637	115037	26904	68361	7623	71462	35952	92646	5178	2320	14724
吉 林 Jilin	37850		4806	60335	17679	5765	2981	22291	35063	51358	4051	4043	3
黑龙江 Heilongjiang	1397			88708	18808	42156	17791	43625	27292	67099	3543	1369	16625
上 海 Shanghai	1957		2988	173068	36649	44345	3404	11743	157921	111940	22202	21389	16196
江 苏 Jiangsu	11487		2354	438138	213186	99654	63054	114243	260841	281090	94661	43002	14564
浙 江 Zhejiang	3073		1894	692503	187388	194040	33069	48817	610617	612494	41471	31006	6636
安 徽 Anhui			925	123514	49279	36640	6021	40681	76812	94092	12037	15135	1839
福 建 Fujian	3889		676	93317	46841	32664	5000	13669	74648	56266	12994	6674	15005
江 西 Jiangxi	5175		151	55300	26883	19321	10234	7465	37601	41596	9173	1826	2595
山 东 Shandong	1059		3444	258891	109983	101513	7533	63484	187874	208164	40373	6309	1107
河 南 Henan	2173		2774	105939	30518	57366	4502	17120	84317	88211	8006	2827	6776
湖 北 Hubei	19796		2356	279323	103112	65767	12542	86929	179852	199977	41395	18576	17632
湖 南 Hunan	5926		358	186667	120013	42104	21299	41155	124213	134119	34819	14275	2137
广 东 Guangdong	3789		4170	489940	83094	287241	2507	50743	436690	268585	187683	22705	9306
广 西 Guangxi	4872		1141	174345	80967	67682	7313	58556	108476	144065	24845	4307	922
海 南 Hainan	346			2860	2716			604	2256	1087	136	317	1086
重 庆 Chongqing	3483		383	111410	43114	12632	1729	11237	98444	73648	22796	8160	4734
四 川 Sichuan	5426		1262	320041	85790	93270	19178	40584	260279	258196	32615	14799	11302
贵 州 Guizhou	2153		97	52890	24404	17886	8740	12568	31582	39276	5689	7839	86
云 南 Yunnan	444		393	119788	60075	47837	33484	34146	52158	88475	24665	2974	3674
西 藏 Tibet				6577	1613	3494	352		6225	3464	2850		21
陕 西 Shaanxi	62		438	69491	30906	20748	4723	30176	34592	51094	9899	7222	1181
甘 肃 Gansu	1029		258	17215	11402	5533	7503	5396	4316	4563	2616	2055	7981
青 海 Qinghai	383			13747	3570	2346		4584	9163	12447	695		163
宁 夏 Ningxia			78	22722	10008	10649	3353	9099	10270	13299	3526	4265	1262
新 疆 Xinjiang	566		271	51227	16337	26444	6530	15008	29689	39373	5981	663	4023

教育学生情况(普通高校)
Education of Regular HEIs

单位: 人,人次
unit: person

	注册学生数 Enrolment													
				进修及培训 In-service Training										
一年及以上 1 Year and Over	自考助学班 Classes Run by Non-government HEIs for Students Preparing for Self-directed State-administered Examinations	普通预科生 College-preparatory Classes	研究生课程进修班 Postgraduate Courses	合计 Total	其中:资格证书培训 of Which: For Certificates of Vocational Qualifications	岗位证书培训 ForCertificates of Job-related Qualifications	其中:第一产业类培训 of Which: Training for First Industry	第二产业类培训 Training for Second Industry	第三产业类培训 Training for Third Industry	一个月以内 1 Month Under	一个月至三个月以内 1 Month to 3 Months Under	三个月至半年以内 3 Months to 6 Months Under	半年至一年以内 6 Months to 1 Year Under	一年及以上 1 Year and Over
41217	**244670**	**42514**	**69007**	**3843074**	**1341684**	**1218271**	**206286**	**847005**	**2789783**	**2673979**	**690671**	**244997**	**181392**	**52035**
14063	2771	2333	14668	384426	53801	85018	7593	39421	337412	248265	65975	18021	32999	19166
143	6068	158	1635	104680	41535	33070	1418	22734	80528	79478	15192	7173	2696	141
53	2843	842	876	86871	34222	9816	13096	23073	50702	74378	7288	2990	942	1273
			134	30747	19573	9926	2652	17123	10972	24940	2070		3737	
125		1191	339	66113	30389	35573	3238	25051	37824	58700	4875	961	1517	60
169	2148	1664	1634	98089	21495	59289	7664	60867	29558	86256	6742	1522	3238	331
880	37710	1648	4868	57838	17560	5940	1134	22397	34307	49682	4286	3144	2	724
72	1055	343	206	29521	10621	18197	1404	17925	10192	21544	3358	1973	2355	291
1341	447	30	5858	135946	36592	32140	2480	13999	119467	78370	19947	19574	15895	2160
4821	26233	78	3097	292555	155706	70655	58309	68792	165454	179112	65102	28000	14526	5815
896	9926	88	4052	411659	143202	75282	5865	34991	370803	358688	12677	20834	14578	4882
411		215	1988	112179	48934	31145	6021	33759	72399	83685	11118	15129	1969	278
2378	6301	745	1546	47853	28089	13610	3829	6919	37105	17527	9108	6307	14305	606
110	5445	4475	445	48654	25484	19546	2100	6343	40211	32584	9952	5271	789	58
2938	4796	412	4319	246730	74004	64982	18782	86886	141062	194989	38116	7105	3218	3302
119	9458	2963	2773	116074	26802	54879	3231	21813	91030	91744	14681	8564	985	100
1743	66911	4039	3334	206801	85699	52607	10515	74601	121685	125801	43124	17464	18934	1478
1317	16501	2210	2	168264	106526	42133	19257	32710	116297	132418	23955	7850	2516	1525
1661	10550	742	9199	465428	69428	275605	1073	34902	429453	248308	186258	19322	9527	2013
206	10647	1549	3954	107154	66492	29060	603	50125	56426	79440	22640	2576	2149	349
234	540	118		6439	5061	1378		1798	4641	2259	294	2010	1642	234
2072	2688	1175	555	117481	45260	24209	645	27766	89070	79939	30409	4728	2405	
3129	7928	2750	910	250233	83902	62262	7065	42521	200647	172741	41853	18348	13015	4276
	5287	2914	120	32310	16195	16115	2286	10638	19386	19594	4636	7994	86	
	860	2458	1047	66259	28416	31185	7466	25002	33791	38325	21201	2819	3914	
242				4257	258	2563	352		3905	2006	2022	8	21	200
95	588	509	400	49908	28452	18635	15	16031	33862	29102	10734	8055	1940	77
	4537	2202	333	18227	11644	6583	8283	5876	4068	4283	2648	2132	9164	
442	1271	1098		6519	144				6519	6375				144
370		3565	114	24032	10802	11028	3410	9317	11305	13632	4142	4458	1430	370
1187	1161		601	49827	15396	25840	6500	13625	29702	39814	6268	665	898	2182

高等教育非学历
Number of Students in Non-formal

地区 Region	毕(结)业生数 Graduates												
	自考助学班 Classes Run by Non-government HEIs for Students Preparing for Self-directed State-administered Examinations	普通预科生 College-preparatory Classes	研究生课程进修班 Postgraduate Courses	进修及培训 In-service Training									
				合计 Total	其中:资格证书培训 of Which: For Certificates of Vocational Qualifications	岗位证书培训 For Certificates of Job-related Qualific-ations	其中:第一产业类培训 of Which: Training for First Industry	第二产业类培训 Training for Second Industry	第三产业类培训 Training for Third Industry	一个月以内 1 Month Under	一个月至三个月以内 1 Month to 3 Months Under	三个月至半年以内 3 Months to 6 Months Under	半年至一年以内 6 Months to 1 Year Under
总　计 Total	**7878**			**3511603**	**620188**	**791068**	**66962**	**134536**	**3310105**	**1983682**	**1087498**	**102643**	**172899**
北　京 Beijing				289421	19150	72253		12567	276854	205560	39402	33569	7786
天　津 Tianjin	859			61574	19123	30792	21727	7835	32012	46909	5709	3740	4424
河　北 Hebei				23600	2532		374		23226	23600			
山　西 Shanxi				3107		3107			3107	3107			
内蒙古 Inner Mongolia													
辽　宁 Liaoning				73712	25768	45783		2479	71233	53293	15162	5209	
吉　林 Jilin	2969			17444	2210	15234		16234	1210	17084	360		
黑龙江 Heilongjiang				10509	2233	8276	8049	562	1898	9482		1027	
上　海 Shanghai				87544	17228	42997		5872	81672	55808	10512	19610	1573
江　苏 Jiangsu				78632	17805	18748	7600	12601	58431	55106	8520	10001	2255
浙　江 Zhejiang				65377	2376	3340	7444	2021	55912	53151	2165	568	9015
安　徽 Anhui				166132	12994	1648	80	301	165751	19904	1385	474	144298
福　建 Fujian				266224	20759	110890	3959	37	262228	3670	132791	265	668
江　西 Jiangxi				487	132				487	360	92	35	
山　东 Shandong				20907	3403	12655			20907	17584	866	2457	
河　南 Henan				261004	228663	30789	1152		259852	224241	36763		
湖　北 Hubei				490	233	257		82	408		257		
湖　南 Hunan				50767	42596	8171	2540	164	48063	48424	216	1543	584
广　东 Guangdong				307129	5593	299975		1700	305429	6151	300435	458	85
广　西 Guangxi	44			30283	216	1038	1038		29245	29681	292	310	
海　南 Hainan	4006			7866	66				7866	7800	66		
重　庆 Chongqing				430652	12988	2285	652	196	429804	6031	423163	210	1248
四　川 Sichuan				920171	5820	11872		4173	915998	910290	9363	298	220
贵　州 Guizhou				26298	561	1719			26298		2280		
云　南 Yunnan				49003				49003			49003		
西　藏 Tibet													
陕　西 Shaanxi				78887	23049	39546	8700	17609	52578	32554	21083	21441	743
甘　肃 Gansu				165463	139089	26374			165463	139089	26374		
青　海 Qinghai													
宁　夏 Ningxia				1100		1100		1100		1100			
新　疆 Xinjiang				17820	15601	2219	3647		14173	13703	1239	1428	

教育学生情况（成人高校）
Education of Adults HEIs

单位：人，人次
unit：person

一年及以上 1 Year and Over	注册学生数 Enrolment 自考助学班 Classes Run by Non-government HEIs for Students Preparing for Self-directed State-administered Examinations	普通预科生 College-preparatory Classes	研究生课程进修班 Postgraduate Courses	进修及培训 In-service Training 合计 Total	其中：资格证书培训 of Which：For Certificates of Vocational Qualifications	岗位证书培训 For Certificates of Job-related Qualifications	其中：第一产业类培训 of Which：Training for First Industry	第二产业类培训 Training for Second Industry	第三产业类培训 Training for Third Industry	一个月以内 1 Month Under	一个月至三个月以内 1 Month to 3 Months Under	三个月至半年以内 3 Months to 6 Months Under	半年至一年以内 6 Months to 1 Year Under	一年及以上 1 Year and Over
164881	**8494**			**1697567**	**534868**	**423361**	**47483**	**99390**	**1550694**	**855352**	**353170**	**89790**	**212190**	**187065**
3104				303129	17088	73150		2310	300819	178234	38266	35373	47559	3697
792	62			47337	14244	26951	23157	5729	18451	41370	1771	1271	2765	160
48				1415	693			693	722		693			722
				17444	2210	15234		16234	1210	17084	360			
				8365	2233	6132	7338		1027	7338		1027		
41				93166	18433	43034		5872	87294	56441	11033	24078	1573	41
2750				14206	7589	6274	753	5389	8064	3833	3022	437	4164	2750
478				50825	1766	2648	2194	893	47738	38237	1985	651	9474	478
71				166132	12994	1648	80	301	165751	19904	1385	474	144298	71
128830				289091	21162	115595	4304	60	284727	3670	132791	265	668	151697
	1100													
				20907	3403	12655			20907	17584	866	2457		
				261004	228663	30789	1152		259852	224241	36763			
233				516	256	260		64	452		260			256
	89			38684	31966	6318	2540	320	35824	35688	760	1543	584	109
				4681	3827	854			4681	200	4256	140	85	
				29921	164	1038	1038		28883	29629	292			
	7243			7872	72				7872	7800	72			
				10365	10365				10365		10155	210		
				29595	5947	14997		4173	25422	16589	12442	344	220	
24018				24018					24018					24018
				49003				49003			49003			
3066				63328	12704	38310	4927	7249	51152	17321	20621	21520	800	3066
				165463	139089	26374			165463	139089	26374			
				1100		1100		1100		1100				
1450														

高等教育非学历

Number of Students in Non-formal

地 区 Region	毕(结)业生数 Graduates												
	自考助学班 Classes Run by Non-government HEIs for Students Preparing for Self-directed State-administered Examinations	普通预科生 College-preparatory Classes	研究生课程进修班 Postgraduate Courses	进修及培训 In-service Training 合计 Total	其中:资格证书培训 of Which: For Certificates of Vocational Qualifications	岗位证书培训 For Certificates of Job-related Qualific-ations	其中:第一产业类培训 of Which: Training for First Industry	第二产业类培训 Training for Second Industry	第三产业类培训 Training for Third Industry	一个月以内 1 Month Under	一个月至三个月以内 1 Month to 3 Months Under	三个月至半年以内 3 Months to 6 Months Under	半年至一年以内 6 Months to 1 Year Under
总 计 Total			**289**										
北 京 Beijing			289										
天 津 Tianjin													
河 北 Hebei													
山 西 Shanxi													
内蒙古 Inner Mongolia													
辽 宁 Liaoning													
吉 林 Jilin													
黑龙江 Heilongjiang													
上 海 Shanghai													
江 苏 Jiangsu													
浙 江 Zhejiang													
安 徽 Anhui													
福 建 Fujian													
江 西 Jiangxi													
山 东 Shandong													
河 南 Henan													
湖 北 Hubei													
湖 南 Hunan													
广 东 Guangdong													
广 西 Guangxi													
海 南 Hainan													
重 庆 Chongqing													
四 川 Sichuan													
贵 州 Guizhou													
云 南 Yunnan													
西 藏 Tibet													
陕 西 Shaanxi													
甘 肃 Gansu													
青 海 Qinghai													
宁 夏 Ningxia													
新 疆 Xinjiang													

教育学生情况(科研机构)

Education of Research Institutes

单位：人,人次

unit: person

	注册学生数 Enrolment														
				进修及培训 In-service Training											
一年及以上 1 Year and Over	自考助学班 Classes Run by Non-government HEIs for Students Preparing for Self-directed State-administered Examinations	普通预科生 College-preparatory Classes	研究生课程进修班 Postgraduate Courses	合计 Total	其中:资格证书培训 of Which: For Certificates of Vocational Qualifications	岗位证书培训 ForCertificates of Job-related Qualifications	其中:第一产业类培训 of Which: Training for First Industry	第二产业类培训 Training for Second Industry	第三产业类培训 Training for Third Industry	一个月以内 1 Month Under	一个月至三个月以内 1 Month to 3 Months Under	三个月至半年以内 3 Months to 6 Months Under	半年至一年以内 6 Months to 1 Year Under	一年及以上 1 Year and Over
			314											
			314											

高等教育非学历

Number of Students in Non-formal Education

地区 Region	毕(结)业生数 Graduates												
	自考助学班 Classes Run by Non-government HEIs for Students Preparing for Self-directed State-administered Examinations	普通预科生 College-preparatory Classes	研究生课程进修班 Postgraduate Courses	进修及培训 In-service Training									
				合计 Total	其中:资格证书培训 of Which: For Certificates of Vocational Qualifications	岗位证书培训 For Certificates of Job-related Qualifications	其中:第一产业类培训 of Which: Training for First Industry	第二产业类培训 Training for Second Industry	第三产业类培训 Training for Third Industry	一个月以内 1 Month Under	一个月至三个月以内 1 Month to 3 Months Under	三个月至半年以内 3 Months to 6 Months Under	半年至一年以内 6 Months to 1 Year Under
总　计 Total	**64043**			**743828**	**135236**	**117118**	**31813**	**80379**	**631636**	**255134**	**79683**	**265619**	**62385**
北　京 Beijing	15023			63584	9031	3229	18021	4632	40931	46532	3293	1926	2313
天　津 Tianjin													
河　北 Hebei	3056			4133	1395	391	1947	58	2128	812	577	1242	805
山　西 Shanxi	3619			26196	17461	3552	328	760	25108	2216	992	1785	5965
内蒙古 Inner Mongolia													
辽　宁 Liaoning	9965												
吉　林 Jilin	510			3861	3389		35	18	3808	3389	291	18	121
黑龙江 Heilongjiang	425			218	118	100	86	54	78	218			
上　海 Shanghai	2520			504767	47144	64485	2472	54185	448110	155773	51385	225981	33540
江　苏 Jiangsu													
浙　江 Zhejiang	5939			17164	3053	5383	270	2331	14563	3422	2761	4144	5988
安　徽 Anhui	469			8038	5889	2149	1246	1388	5404	243	1469	519	1818
福　建 Fujian													
江　西 Jiangxi	2058			4040	1088	444	221	487	3332		657	732	617
山　东 Shandong	4743			51686	18894	25091	1392	10620	39674	23047	9811	10279	4420
河　南 Henan	1591			3442	359	200	80	430	2932	227	754	385	450
湖　北 Hubei	4827			123	123				123		123		
湖　南 Hunan	3530			2000					2000	2000			
广　东 Guangdong	2871			28814	10010	5926	3354	3834	21626	15551	5253	2082	2676
广　西 Guangxi													
海　南 Hainan													
重　庆 Chongqing	2447			4161	1624	2191	887	1382	1892			1637	2524
四　川 Sichuan	350			18833	14784	2877	953		17880	1704	2317	13739	298
贵　州 Guizhou													
云　南 Yunnan													
西　藏 Tibet													
陕　西 Shaanxi													
甘　肃 Gansu	100			2768	874	1100	521	200	2047			1150	850
青　海 Qinghai													
宁　夏 Ningxia													
新　疆 Xinjiang													

教育学生情况（民办的其他高等教育机构）
of Other Non-government HEIs

单位：人，人次

unit：person

	注册学生数 Enrolment													
				进修及培训 In-service Training										
一年及以上 1 Year and Over	自考助学班 Classes run by Non-government HEIs for Students Preparing for Self-directed State-administered Examinations	普通预科生 College-preparatory Classes	研究生课程进修班 Postgraduate Courses	合计 Total	其中：资格证书培训 of Which：For Certificates of Vocational Qualifications	岗位证书培训 ForCertificates of Job-related Qualifications	其中：第一产业类培训 of Which：Training for First Industry	第二产业类培训 Training for Second Industry	第三产业类培训 Training for Third Industry	一个月以内 1 Month Under	一个月至三个月以内 1 Month to 3 Months Under	三个月至半年以内 3 Months to 6 Months Under	半年至一年以内 6 Months to 1 Year Under	一年及以上 1 Year and Over
81007	**152165**			**727757**	**103414**	**71471**	**27910**	**81766**	**618081**	**229983**	**62539**	**263247**	**52881**	**119107**
9520	31815			72816	9024	902	17571	5581	49664	46040	1633	1486	1212	22445
697	5897			3083	886	448	1210	83	1790	532	653	881	616	401
15238	6634			31716	18350	3967	190	1575	29951	2266	1337	3146	6474	18493
	19442													
42	1967			1916	1094		45	30	1841	1094	320	30	202	270
	1458													
38088	8364			542181	48353	50618	2423	65592	474166	169853	46243	245442	30868	49775
849	21086			11294	2365	3920	282	2039	8973	3349	2587	2917	2181	260
3989	1191			13615	11716	1895	1323	1717	10575	250	1475	545	1759	9586
2034	2790			6338	1025	28	160	175	6003	488	2463	488	348	2551
4129	7137			11938	4405	1175	371	2751	8816	3673	336	2677	1511	3741
1626	5371			6773	386	200	80	985	5708	235	866	436	493	4743
	16914			1622	622				1622		1145			477
	12796													
3252	3898			8716	599	3296			8716	388	1441	2243	1528	3116
	2534			3698	1350	2113	904	1008	1786			1639	2059	
775	2355			6953	2476	1443	2807		4146	1815	2040	276	1275	1547
768	516			5098	763	1466	544	230	4324			1041	2355	1702

外国留

Information on

地　区 Region	毕(结)业生数 Graduates	授予学位数 Degrees Awarded	招生数 Entrants	
			合计 Total	其中:春季招生 of Which:Spring Term
总　计 Total	**91251**	**19025**	**106448**	**31008**
北　京 Beijing	26373	4720	29821	6793
天　津 Tianjin	4559	599	3897	1616
河　北 Hebei	575	253	853	342
山　西 Shanxi	79	3	86	35
内蒙古 Inner Mongolia	311	173	645	7
辽　宁 Liaoning	3663	1055	5147	1400
吉　林 Jilin	2320	664	2435	800
黑龙江 Heilongjiang	2574	546	3316	1125
上　海 Shanghai	9534	2187	10641	3879
江　苏 Jiangsu	6457	1401	7722	2296
浙　江 Zhejiang	6153	613	7080	2759
安　徽 Anhui	346	56	644	238
福　建 Fujian	3764	515	3735	894
江　西 Jiangxi	777	442	539	112
山　东 Shandong	4538	535	5143	2107
河　南 Henan	677	254	254	14
湖　北 Hubei	2886	1147	3822	779
湖　南 Hunan	1277	259	1479	344
广　东 Guangdong	2957	802	3936	831
广　西 Guangxi	2160	789	2575	806
海　南 Hainan	279	32	558	210
重　庆 Chongqing	1671	308	1993	626
四　川 Sichuan	1490	328	1963	605
贵　州 Guizhou	309	22	561	58
云　南 Yunnan	1576	538	2288	771
西　藏 Tibet	12		17	
陕　西 Shaanxi	1893	488	2644	927
甘　肃 Gansu	486	134	515	157
青　海 Qinghai	113	2	105	24
宁　夏 Ningxia	134	6	394	171
新　疆 Xinjiang	1308	154	1640	282

学生情况
Foreign Students

单位:人
unit: person

在校生数 Enrolment					
合计 Total	第一年 1st Year	第二年 2nd Year	第三年 3rd Year	第四年 4th year	第五年及以上 5th year
174806	**92412**	**34990**	**22473**	**15217**	**9714**
43183	25776	7484	4858	3429	1636
6566	3217	1324	837	586	602
2204	795	409	394	383	223
119	85	18	4	7	5
1758	640	414	357	192	155
9873	4458	2304	1591	1078	442
4688	2008	1187	594	554	345
4540	2393	1005	618	347	177
18970	9597	3967	2617	2077	712
13115	7176	2298	1656	980	1005
10588	6299	1844	1204	667	574
1138	720	223	104	82	9
2719	1681	514	222	159	143
2163	549	602	446	163	403
6428	4269	896	549	372	342
1354	482	371	224	143	134
8177	3525	1926	1195	726	805
2386	1339	465	359	145	78
7545	3285	1669	1292	742	557
4645	2194	986	782	565	118
787	516	189	18	55	9
3225	1645	849	378	183	170
4072	1978	918	529	399	248
718	561	99	28	30	
4554	2310	1139	471	382	252
29	17	12			
4422	2444	794	542	391	251
991	483	175	129	110	94
257	105	61	48	20	23
517	225	161	105	25	1
3075	1640	687	322	225	201

高等教育学校(机构)
Number of Educational Personnel

地 区 Region	合计 Total	教职 Educational — 校本部 Educational Personnel				
		小计 Subtotal	专任教师 Full-time Teachers			
			小计 Subtotal	正高级 Senior	副高级 Sub-senior	中级 Middle
总 计 Total	**2352679**	**2235200**	**1530512**	**182982**	**442685**	**611226**
北 京 Beijing	142708	125143	68394	16718	23734	23126
天 津 Tianjin	49079	47811	31983	4520	10324	12576
河 北 Hebei	102535	99124	67624	9156	19731	26513
山 西 Shanxi	63684	60712	42267	3036	10965	15689
内蒙古 Inner Mongolia	37858	36849	24828	2468	7630	9347
辽 宁 Liaoning	101554	98719	65127	8776	20270	26201
吉 林 Jilin	65525	61922	39600	5844	12482	15055
黑龙江 Heilongjiang	80470	77111	48226	7261	15403	19627
上 海 Shanghai	74971	68793	41151	7116	13129	16612
江 苏 Jiangsu	167571	157320	109046	12822	34417	47036
浙 江 Zhejiang	87054	82650	57072	7623	17565	25090
安 徽 Anhui	77486	74847	55644	4448	14846	21272
福 建 Fujian	65634	62737	43368	4783	11989	16710
江 西 Jiangxi	75957	72462	53328	5366	14407	21473
山 东 Shandong	145083	139765	100667	10229	28018	43230
河 南 Henan	128522	123374	93107	7831	24713	37180
湖 北 Hubei	129849	122735	82890	10247	25336	31596
湖 南 Hunan	98407	93541	64845	7089	18647	27117
广 东 Guangdong	138404	132773	93841	10899	24146	38724
广 西 Guangxi	56752	51739	37437	3880	10047	14559
海 南 Hainan	13671	13446	8543	925	2040	3226
重 庆 Chongqing	54989	53041	37728	4105	10387	15388
四 川 Sichuan	116021	110301	78222	8015	20171	31190
贵 州 Guizhou	35682	35243	25719	2515	8103	9000
云 南 Yunnan	47805	46651	34494	3607	9170	12950
西 藏 Tibet	3623	3561	2472	183	781	1018
陕 西 Shaanxi	104835	99986	65910	7807	17873	27311
甘 肃 Gansu	36201	34014	24820	2660	7212	9772
青 海 Qinghai	7115	6198	3951	795	1362	1123
宁 夏 Ningxia	10603	10168	7181	1032	1967	2266
新 疆 Xinjiang	33031	32464	21027	1226	5820	9249

注:不含民办的其他高等教育机构数据。

Note: Data of Non-government HEIs are not included.

教职工情况(总计)
in HEIs (Total)

单位：人
unit：person

工　数 Personnel								
教职工 in Main Campus					科研机构人员 Personnel in Affiliated Research Org.	校办企业职工 Employees in School-run Factories & Farms	其他附设机构人员 Personnel in Others Subsidiary Units
		行政人员 Adm. Personnel	教辅人员 Supporting Staff	工勤人员 Workers			
初级 Junior	未定职级 No-Ranking						
209963	**83656**	**323388**	**211969**	**169331**	**29918**	**31076**	**56485**
2916	1900	23788	18163	14798	7402	1712	8451
3495	1068	7637	4714	3477	476	481	311
8896	3328	14236	8870	8394	307	1158	1946
8914	3663	8258	5491	4696	598	506	1868
3953	1430	5586	3809	2626	97	249	663
6978	2902	15936	8607	9049	679	924	1232
5699	520	8585	6640	7097	955	973	1675
4477	1458	11701	8226	8958	1255	682	1422
2893	1401	12698	9111	5833	1776	2338	2064
11341	3430	22793	15336	10145	2796	2215	5240
3659	3135	14005	8068	3505	1495	968	1941
11909	3169	8335	6141	4727	710	461	1468
7462	2424	9928	6087	3354	811	1380	706
9389	2693	9073	5843	4218	512	1657	1326
15454	3736	18001	12145	8952	1170	2635	1513
18598	4785	12800	8694	8773	468	961	3719
11477	4234	18810	11998	9037	1676	2440	2998
7900	4092	13548	9010	6138	686	1618	2562
10975	9097	19982	12578	6372	1369	1258	3004
4952	3999	6767	4229	3306	140	757	4116
1644	708	2259	1248	1396	44	25	156
5153	2695	7757	4043	3513	271	494	1183
14128	4718	14162	8941	8976	900	2184	2636
3663	2438	5171	2686	1667	227	61	151
5839	2928	5340	3439	3378	348	431	375
378	112	479	309	301	27		35
9771	3148	14532	10258	9286	1580	1425	1844
3704	1472	4074	2719	2401	592	340	1255
455	216	845	779	623	342	561	14
981	935	1504	843	640	135		300
2910	1822	4798	2944	3695	74	182	311

高等教育学校(机构)

Number of Female Educational Personnel

地 区 Region	合计 Total	小计 Subtotal	专任教师 Full-time Teachers 小计 Subtotal	正高级 Senior	副高级 Sub-senior	中级 Middle
	教职 Educational					
		校本部 Educational				
总 计 Total	**1097490**	**1047550**	**732219**	**53118**	**195330**	**320996**
北 京 Beijing	69599	60196	31005	4078	11250	12977
天 津 Tianjin	23679	23271	16079	1455	5010	7026
河 北 Hebei	52935	51563	37579	3928	10526	15486
山 西 Shanxi	32391	30945	23039	1189	5534	8787
内蒙古 Inner Mongolia	19370	18998	13783	1060	4083	5434
辽 宁 Liaoning	50146	49094	35025	3326	10680	15316
吉 林 Jilin	30834	29647	20747	2304	6390	8453
黑龙江 Heilongjiang	38609	37146	25449	3013	7813	11134
上 海 Shanghai	34087	32199	19262	1395	5859	9574
江 苏 Jiangsu	76006	71532	49446	2784	13926	24676
浙 江 Zhejiang	39787	38341	25681	1787	7048	13161
安 徽 Anhui	31814	30980	23193	878	5004	9659
福 建 Fujian	30877	29722	20663	1181	4959	8805
江 西 Jiangxi	32123	30867	22729	1636	5490	9643
山 东 Shandong	67153	65267	49483	3079	12266	22979
河 南 Henan	58834	56145	43899	2508	10491	18287
湖 北 Hubei	57365	54348	36433	2338	9979	15667
湖 南 Hunan	45567	43857	30363	1646	7870	14056
广 东 Guangdong	65471	62653	43632	2776	10107	19946
广 西 Guangxi	27745	24586	17696	1244	4296	7360
海 南 Hainan	6834	6706	4292	296	868	1808
重 庆 Chongqing	24724	24062	17227	961	4152	7869
四 川 Sichuan	52553	50521	36107	2053	8217	15777
贵 州 Guizhou	17469	17293	12787	937	4020	4625
云 南 Yunnan	24073	23554	17980	1225	4396	7154
西 藏 Tibet	1668	1639	1197	56	338	534
陕 西 Shaanxi	46078	44270	29712	2021	7323	13302
甘 肃 Gansu	15301	14456	10874	718	2782	4586
青 海 Qinghai	3191	2864	2007	352	720	575
宁 夏 Ningxia	5319	5188	3803	420	996	1242
新 疆 Xinjiang	15888	15640	11047	474	2937	5098

注:不含民办的其他高等教育机构数据。

Note:Data of Non-government HEIs are not included.

女教职工情况(总计)

in HEIs (Total)

单位:人

unit:person

工数(人)

Personnel

教职工 Personnel in Main Campus					科研机构人员 Personnel in Affiliated Research Org.	校办企业职工 Employees in School-run Factories & Farms	其他附设机构人员 Personnel in Others Subsidiary Units
初　级 Junior	未定职级 No-Ranking	行政人员 Adm. Personnel	教辅人员 Supporting Staff	工勤人员 Workers			
118270	**44505**	**149109**	**115630**	**50592**	**11166**	**9163**	**29611**
1702	998	13121	11114	4956	3118	435	5850
2015	573	3763	2419	1010	146	93	169
5497	2142	6284	5072	2628	142	318	912
5209	2320	3480	3179	1247	205	217	1024
2418	788	2323	2214	678	45	56	271
4069	1634	7332	4829	1908	251	235	566
3322	278	3510	3669	1721	405	291	491
2679	810	4951	4348	2398	609	165	689
1734	700	6959	4652	1326	638	555	695
6356	1704	10682	8240	3164	915	581	2978
2044	1641	7237	4451	972	426	268	752
6212	1440	3342	3096	1349	190	149	495
4447	1271	4784	3200	1075	258	515	382
4780	1180	3872	2850	1416	159	630	467
9105	2054	6506	6740	2538	521	619	746
10237	2376	5329	4565	2352	171	281	2237
6297	2152	8663	6488	2764	555	1013	1449
4573	2218	6326	5288	1880	258	404	1048
5892	4911	9889	6748	2384	541	359	1918
2551	2245	3303	2279	1308	58	294	2807
890	430	1062	634	718	19	3	106
2976	1269	3782	2106	947	85	107	470
7746	2314	6679	4500	3235	330	725	977
2016	1189	2419	1602	485	86	29	61
3502	1703	2402	1894	1278	135	116	268
199	70	205	178	59	7		22
5399	1667	6249	5432	2877	527	392	889
2068	720	1578	1302	702	159	68	618
246	114	272	435	150	125	192	10
542	603	687	516	182	45		86
1547	991	2118	1590	885	37	53	158

高等教育学校(机构)

Number of Educational Personnel

地区 Region	合计 Total	教职 Educational					
		校本部 Educational Personnel					
		小计 Subtotal	专任教师 Full-time Teachers				
			小计 Subtotal	正高级 Senior	副高级 Sub-senior	中级 Middle
总　计 Total	**2296262**	**2179314**	**1496865**	**181501**	**432356**	**596954**
北　京 Beijing	139305	121783	66871	16611	23257	22362
天　津 Tianjin	47123	45855	30900	4469	9854	12143
河　北 Hebei	101072	97669	66825	9100	19514	26186
山　西 Shanxi	61009	58074	40764	2990	10430	15138
内蒙古 Inner Mongolia	37296	36287	24554	2459	7512	9237
辽　宁 Liaoning	97536	94705	62706	8653	19315	25296
吉　林 Jilin	63002	59457	38003	5720	11930	14439
黑龙江 Heilongjiang	77234	73890	46215	7111	14510	18914
上　海 Shanghai	73361	67209	40297	7089	12941	16118
江　苏 Jiangsu	166223	155976	108272	12719	34178	46712
浙　江 Zhejiang	85381	81020	56000	7579	17233	24547
安　徽 Anhui	76178	73573	54903	4430	14650	20916
福　建 Fujian	64744	61847	42905	4766	11816	16553
江　西 Jiangxi	74396	70920	52434	5275	14146	21228
山　东 Shandong	142240	136930	98685	10130	27418	42432
河　南 Henan	125170	120038	90949	7752	24120	36213
湖　北 Hubei	128185	121086	81784	10217	24959	31147
湖　南 Hunan	96915	92065	63869	7064	18334	26642
广　东 Guangdong	133719	128161	91099	10843	23603	37501
广　西 Guangxi	55283	50274	36425	3799	9745	14094
海　南 Hainan	13513	13288	8458	921	2028	3196
重　庆 Chongqing	53790	51868	37130	4078	10225	15105
四　川 Sichuan	113553	107835	76795	8002	19794	30564
贵　州 Guizhou	35102	34663	25351	2499	8008	8867
云　南 Yunnan	47592	46438	34421	3602	9148	12917
西　藏 Tibet	3623	3561	2472	183	781	1018
陕　西 Shaanxi	102017	97194	64171	7770	17442	26471
甘　肃 Gansu	35582	33403	24384	2650	7076	9568
青　海 Qinghai	6851	5934	3785	787	1323	1039
宁　夏 Ningxia	10486	10051	7111	1024	1936	2240
新　疆 Xinjiang	28781	28260	18327	1209	5130	8151

教职工情况(普通高校)
in Regular HEIs

单位：人
unit:person

工数(人) Personnel							
教职工 in Main Campus					科研机构人员 Personnel in Affiliated Research Org.	校办企业职工 Employees in School-run Factories & Farms	其他附设机构人员 Personnel in Others Subsidiary Units
初 级 Junior	未定职级 No-Ranking	行政人员 Adm. Personnel	教辅人员 Supporting Staff	工勤人员 Workers			
203713	**82341**	**312606**	**205280**	**164563**	**29789**	**30864**	**56295**
2786	1855	22617	17721	14574	7388	1708	8426
3374	1060	7294	4373	3288	476	481	311
8723	3302	13889	8698	8257	299	1158	1946
8633	3573	7722	5146	4442	594	488	1853
3920	1426	5476	3694	2563	97	249	663
6623	2819	15209	8115	8675	679	924	1228
5413	501	8231	6321	6902	937	973	1635
4266	1414	11136	7913	8626	1255	667	1422
2772	1377	12397	8822	5693	1768	2322	2062
11241	3422	22568	15056	10080	2792	2215	5240
3559	3082	13712	7878	3430	1487	968	1906
11771	3136	8105	5947	4618	710	461	1434
7373	2397	9719	5909	3314	811	1380	706
9131	2654	8739	5693	4054	497	1653	1326
14992	3713	17617	11989	8639	1162	2635	1513
18085	4779	12213	8306	8570	468	945	3719
11242	4219	18500	11842	8960	1661	2440	2998
7776	4053	13286	8908	6002	681	1609	2560
10383	8769	19079	12021	5962	1359	1195	3004
4829	3958	6564	4096	3189	136	757	4116
1626	687	2210	1237	1383	44	25	156
5039	2683	7470	3828	3440	271	476	1175
13788	4647	13600	8756	8684	900	2184	2634
3549	2428	5054	2609	1649	227	61	151
5827	2927	5263	3394	3360	348	431	375
378	112	479	309	301	27		35
9387	3101	14037	10007	8979	1580	1410	1833
3623	1467	3966	2680	2373	592	334	1253
434	202	806	740	603	342	561	14
979	932	1474	835	631	135		300
2191	1646	4174	2437	3322	66	154	301

高等教育学校(机构)

Number of Female Educational

地区 Region	合计 Total	教职 Educational				
		校本部 Educational Personnel				
		小计 Subtotal	专任教师 Full-time Teachers			
			小计 Subtotal	正高级 Senior	副高级 Sub-senior	中级 Middle
总计 Total	**1070126**	**1020402**	**714450**	**52494**	**190283**	**313104**
北京 Beijing	67656	58280	30022	4032	10949	12453
天津 Tianjin	22681	22273	15422	1433	4749	6740
河北 Hebei	52175	50808	37097	3899	10404	15276
山西 Shanxi	31041	29603	22189	1171	5262	8434
内蒙古 Inner Mongolia	19081	18709	13619	1057	4010	5362
辽宁 Liaoning	48014	46964	33568	3257	10097	14764
吉林 Jilin	29481	28337	19819	2221	6102	8075
黑龙江 Heilongjiang	37095	35632	24392	2940	7373	10756
上海 Shanghai	33278	31394	18768	1387	5764	9274
江苏 Jiangsu	75366	70896	49076	2758	13813	24501
浙江 Zhejiang	39006	37567	25138	1775	6902	12876
安徽 Anhui	31258	30437	22870	874	4927	9510
福建 Fujian	30447	29292	20441	1176	4896	8709
江西 Jiangxi	31495	30245	22356	1604	5387	9543
山东 Shandong	65983	64100	48575	3043	12041	22570
河南 Henan	57149	54467	42705	2469	10194	17726
湖北 Hubei	56572	53562	35884	2331	9813	15425
湖南 Hunan	44931	43225	29907	1633	7734	13835
广东 Guangdong	63117	60347	42199	2753	9846	19305
广西 Guangxi	27051	23893	17195	1218	4159	7105
海南 Hainan	6759	6631	4244	294	858	1792
重庆 Chongqing	24210	23552	16953	954	4098	7710
四川 Sichuan	51512	49480	35473	2051	8053	15497
贵州 Guizhou	17172	16996	12591	929	3980	4573
云南 Yunnan	23970	23451	17939	1223	4382	7137
西藏 Tibet	1668	1639	1197	56	338	534
陕西 Shaanxi	44770	42971	28867	2009	7137	12899
甘肃 Gansu	15041	14198	10675	715	2730	4486
青海 Qinghai	3088	2761	1931	348	699	537
宁夏 Ningxia	5266	5135	3772	415	984	1231
新疆 Xinjiang	13793	13557	9566	469	2602	4469

女教职工情况(普通高校)
Personnel in Regular HEIs

单位：人
unit:person

工 数 Personnel							
教职工 in Main Campus					科研机构人员 Personnel in Affiliated Research Org.	校办企业职工 Employees in School-run Factories & Farms	其他附设机构人员 Personnel in Others Subsidiary Units
初级 Junior	未定职级 No-ranking	行政人员 Adm. Personnel	教辅人员 Supporting Staff	工勤人员 Workers			
114819	**43750**	**144446**	**112138**	**49368**	**11096**	**9091**	**29537**
1621	967	12497	10843	4918	3107	433	5836
1933	567	3621	2250	980	146	93	169
5392	2126	6149	4962	2600	137	318	912
5055	2267	3269	2982	1163	201	215	1022
2402	788	2286	2143	661	45	56	271
3854	1596	7006	4562	1828	251	235	564
3158	263	3362	3469	1687	392	291	461
2548	775	4708	4200	2332	609	165	689
1656	687	6801	4517	1308	635	555	694
6302	1702	10578	8098	3144	911	581	2978
1988	1597	7120	4365	944	421	268	750
6136	1423	3251	2993	1323	190	149	482
4410	1250	4690	3106	1055	258	515	382
4659	1163	3737	2776	1376	155	628	467
8883	2038	6386	6680	2459	518	619	746
9945	2371	5094	4376	2292	171	274	2237
6170	2145	8534	6402	2742	548	1013	1449
4510	2195	6229	5240	1849	256	402	1048
5538	4757	9492	6440	2216	536	316	1918
2492	2221	3207	2220	1271	57	294	2807
882	418	1039	633	715	19	3	106
2927	1264	3633	2030	936	85	105	468
7595	2277	6428	4411	3168	330	725	977
1927	1182	2377	1545	483	86	29	61
3494	1703	2370	1865	1277	135	116	268
199	70	205	178	59	7		22
5190	1632	6031	5294	2779	527	386	886
2027	717	1546	1285	692	159	67	617
236	111	267	419	144	125	192	10
540	602	670	512	181	45		86
1150	876	1863	1342	786	34	48	154

高等教育学校(机构)

Number of Educational Personnel

地　区 Region	合计 Total	教　职 Educational 校本部 Educational Personnel 小计 Subtotal	专任教师 Full-time Teachers 小计 Subtotal	正高级 Senior	副高级 Sub-senior	中级 Middle
总　计 Total	**56417**	**55886**	**33647**	**1481**	**10329**	**14272**
北　京 Beijing	3403	3360	1523	107	477	764
天　津 Tianjin	1956	1956	1083	51	470	433
河　北 Hebei	1463	1455	799	56	217	327
山　西 Shanxi	2675	2638	1503	46	535	551
内蒙古 Inner Mongolia	562	562	274	9	118	110
辽　宁 Liaoning	4018	4014	2421	123	955	905
吉　林 Jilin	2523	2465	1597	124	552	616
黑龙江 Heilongjiang	3236	3221	2011	150	893	713
上　海 Shanghai	1610	1584	854	27	188	494
江　苏 Jiangsu	1348	1344	774	103	239	324
浙　江 Zhejiang	1673	1630	1072	44	332	543
安　徽 Anhui	1308	1274	741	18	196	356
福　建 Fujian	890	890	463	17	173	157
江　西 Jiangxi	1561	1542	894	91	261	245
山　东 Shandong	2843	2835	1982	99	600	798
河　南 Henan	3352	3336	2158	79	593	967
湖　北 Hubei	1664	1649	1106	30	377	449
湖　南 Hunan	1492	1476	976	25	313	475
广　东 Guangdong	4685	4612	2742	56	543	1223
广　西 Guangxi	1469	1465	1012	81	302	465
海　南 Hainan	158	158	85	4	12	30
重　庆 Chongqing	1199	1173	598	27	162	283
四　川 Sichuan	2468	2466	1427	13	377	626
贵　州 Guizhou	580	580	368	16	95	133
云　南 Yunnan	213	213	73	5	22	33
西　藏 Tibet						
陕　西 Shaanxi	2818	2792	1739	37	431	840
甘　肃 Gansu	619	611	436	10	136	204
青　海 Qinghai	264	264	166	8	39	84
宁　夏 Ningxia	117	117	70	8	31	26
新　疆 Xinjiang	4250	4204	2700	17	690	1098

教职工情况（成人高校）

in Adult HEIs

单位：人
unit：person

工 数 Personnel							
教职工 in Main Campus					科研机构人员 Personnel in Affiliated Research Org.	校办企业职工 Employees in School-run Factories & Farms	其他附设机构人员 Personnel in Others Subsidiary Units
		行政人员 Adm. Personnel	教辅人员 Supporting Staff	工勤人员 Workers			
初 级 Junior	未定职级 No-ranking						
6250	**1315**	**10782**	**6689**	**4768**	**129**	**212**	**190**
130	45	1171	442	224	14	4	25
121	8	343	341	189			
173	26	347	172	137	8		
281	90	536	345	254	4	18	15
33	4	110	115	63			
355	83	727	492	374			4
286	19	354	319	195	18		40
211	44	565	313	332		15	
121	24	301	289	140	8	16	2
100	8	225	280	65	4		
100	53	293	190	75	8		35
138	33	230	194	109			34
89	27	209	178	40			
258	39	334	150	164	15	4	
462	23	384	156	313	8		
513	6	587	388	203		16	
235	15	310	156	77	15		
124	39	262	102	136	5	9	2
592	328	903	557	410	10	63	
123	41	203	133	117	4		
18	21	49	11	13			
114	12	287	215	73		18	8
340	71	562	185	292			2
114	10	117	77	18			
12	1	77	45	18			
384	47	495	251	307		15	11
81	5	108	39	28		6	2
21	14	39	39	20			
2	3	30	8	9			
719	176	624	507	373	8	28	10

高等教育学校(机构)

Number of Female Educational

地区 Region	合计 Total	教职 Educational 校本部 Educational Personnel 小计 Subtotal	专任教师 Full-time Teachers 小计 Subtotal	正高级 Senior	副高级 Sub-senior	中级 Middle
总计 Total	**27364**	**27148**	**17769**	**624**	**5047**	**7892**
北京 Beijing	1943	1916	983	46	301	524
天津 Tianjin	998	998	657	22	261	286
河北 Hebei	760	755	482	29	122	210
山西 Shanxi	1350	1342	850	18	272	353
内蒙古 Inner Mongolia	289	289	164	3	73	72
辽宁 Liaoning	2132	2130	1457	69	583	552
吉林 Jilin	1353	1310	928	83	288	378
黑龙江 Heilongjiang	1514	1514	1057	73	440	378
上海 Shanghai	809	805	494	8	95	300
江苏 Jiangsu	640	636	370	26	113	175
浙江 Zhejiang	781	774	543	12	146	285
安徽 Anhui	556	543	323	4	77	149
福建 Fujian	430	430	222	5	63	96
江西 Jiangxi	628	622	373	32	103	100
山东 Shandong	1170	1167	908	36	225	409
河南 Henan	1685	1678	1194	39	297	561
湖北 Hubei	793	786	549	7	166	242
湖南 Hunan	636	632	456	13	136	221
广东 Guangdong	2354	2306	1433	23	261	641
广西 Guangxi	694	693	501	26	137	255
海南 Hainan	75	75	48	2	10	16
重庆 Chongqing	514	510	274	7	54	159
四川 Sichuan	1041	1041	634	2	164	280
贵州 Guizhou	297	297	196	8	40	52
云南 Yunnan	103	103	41	2	14	17
西藏 Tibet						
陕西 Shaanxi	1308	1299	845	12	186	403
甘肃 Gansu	260	258	199	3	52	100
青海 Qinghai	103	103	76	4	21	38
宁夏 Ningxia	53	53	31	5	12	11
新疆 Xinjiang	2095	2083	1481	5	335	629

女教职工情况(成人高校)

Personnel in Adult HEIs

单位：人
unit：person

工　数 Personnel							
教职工 in Main Campus					科研机构人员 Personnel in Affiliated Research Org.	校办企业职工 Employees in School-run Factories & Farms	其他附设机构人员 Personnel in Others Subsidiary Units
		行政人员 Adm. Personnel	教辅人员 Supporting Staff	工勤人员 Workers			
初　级 Junior	未定职级 No-ranking						
3451	**755**	**4663**	**3492**	**1224**	**70**	**72**	**74**
81	31	624	271	38	11	2	14
82	6	142	169	30			
105	16	135	110	28	5		
154	53	211	197	84	4	2	2
16		37	71	17			
215	38	326	267	80			2
164	15	148	200	34	13		30
131	35	243	148	66			
78	13	158	135	18	3		1
54	2	104	142	20	4		
56	44	117	86	28	5		2
76	17	91	103	26			13
37	21	94	94	20			
121	17	135	74	40	4	2	
222	16	120	60	79	3		
292	5	235	189	60		7	
127	7	129	86	22	7		
63	23	97	48	31	2	2	
354	154	397	308	168	5	43	
59	24	96	59	37	1		
8	12	23	1	3			
49	5	149	76	11		2	2
151	37	251	89	67			
89	7	42	57	2			
8		32	29	1			
209	35	218	138	98		6	3
41	3	32	17	10		1	1
10	3	5	16	6			
2	1	17	4	1			
397	115	255	248	99	3	5	4

高等教育学校(机构)教职工

Number of Educational Personnel

地区 Region	合计 Total	教职 Educational 校本部 Educational Personnel 小计 Subtotal	专任教师 Full-time Teachers 小计 Subtotal	正高级 Senior	副高级 Sub-senior	中级 Middle
总 计 Total	**28394**	**28001**	**13350**	**1203**	**2524**	**4244**
北 京 Beijing	5036	5018	2076	294	444	612
天 津 Tianjin						
河 北 Hebei	893	887	502	83	119	176
山 西 Shanxi	1859	1673	1039	127	172	320
内蒙古 Inner Mongolia						
辽 宁 Liaoning	1514	1514	945	53	232	545
吉 林 Jilin	374	374	205	24	59	73
黑龙江 Heilongjiang	130	130	49	2	16	9
上 海 Shanghai	6393	6381	2102	184	308	410
江 苏 Jiangsu						
浙 江 Zhejiang	1946	1944	794	23	89	307
安 徽 Anhui	1007	984	688	13	44	80
福 建 Fujian						
江 西 Jiangxi	712	679	352	41	60	149
山 东 Shandong	4370	4274	2646	224	562	917
河 南 Henan	335	335	131	10	25	48
湖 北 Hubei	726	726	220	25	82	69
湖 南 Hunan	256	256	105	11	20	38
广 东 Guangdong	1142	1140	609	29	103	234
广 西 Guangxi						
海 南 Hainan						
重 庆 Chongqing	647	636	317	13	93	141
四 川 Sichuan	611	611	361	20	32	72
贵 州 Guizhou						
云 南 Yunnan						
西 藏 Tibet						
陕 西 Shaanxi						
甘 肃 Gansu	443	439	209	27	64	44
青 海 Qinghai						
宁 夏 Ningxia						
新 疆 Xinjiang						

情况（民办的其他高等教育机构）
in Other Non-government HEIs

单位：人
unit：person

工　数 Personnel							
教职工 in Main Campus					科研机构人员 Personnel in Affiliated Research Org.	校办企业职工 Employees in School-run Factories & Farms	其他附设机构人员 Personnel in Others Subsidiary Units
初　级 Junior	未定职级 No-ranking	行政人员 Adm. Personnel	教辅人员 Supporting Staff	工勤人员 Workers			
1961	**3418**	**7995**	**4029**	**2627**	**32**	**238**	**123**
276	450	1540	802	600		4	14
96	28	171	128	86			6
179	241	333	156	145	3	170	13
110	5	333	154	82			
18	31	93	39	37			
15	7	31	23	27			
96	1104	2509	1382	388	11	1	
222	153	580	279	291	2		
39	512	149	91	56	7	16	
81	21	156	78	93		20	13
514	429	946	334	348	7	24	65
23	25	110	54	40			
30	14	249	151	106			
18	18	80	46	25			
90	153	309	112	110	2		
41	29	170	77	72		3	8
71	166	120	42	88			
42	32	116	81	33			4

高等教育学校(机构)

Number of Female Educational Personnel

地区 Region	合计 Total	小计 Subtotal	小计 Subtotal	正高级 Senior	副高级 Sub-senior	中级 Middle
		教职 Educational				
		校本部 Educational Personnel				
			专任教师 Full-time Teachers			
总计 Total	**14936**	**14706**	**6777**	**396**	**1133**	**2107**
北京 Beijing	2612	2606	1011	86	202	305
天津 Tianjin						
河北 Hebei	481	475	267	26	50	105
山西 Shanxi	932	808	511	58	88	154
内蒙古 Inner Mongolia						
辽宁 Liaoning	843	843	512	37	134	289
吉林 Jilin	210	210	120	8	33	46
黑龙江 Heilongjiang	98	98	36	1	12	6
上海 Shanghai	3865	3858	1168	43	113	211
江苏 Jiangsu						
浙江 Zhejiang	1171	1170	485	11	52	186
安徽 Anhui	424	414	307	2	6	28
福建 Fujian						
江西 Jiangxi	293	273	147	9	19	71
山东 Shandong	2054	2003	1297	76	257	424
河南 Henan	160	160	61	2	8	22
湖北 Hubei	379	379	96	11	34	25
湖南 Hunan	131	131	62	7	9	25
广东 Guangdong	502	501	253	6	33	85
广西 Guangxi						
海南 Hainan						
重庆 Chongqing	300	296	145	4	32	68
四川 Sichuan	291	291	189	3	11	37
贵州 Guizhou						
云南 Yunnan						
西藏 Tibet						
陕西 Shaanxi						
甘肃 Gansu	190	190	110	6	40	20
青海 Qinghai						
宁夏 Ningxia						
新疆 Xinjiang						

女教职工情况(民办的其他高等教育机构)

in Other Non-government HEIs

单位：人

unit：person

工　数 Personnel							
教职工 in Main Campus					科研机构人员 Personnel in Affiliated Research Org.	校办企业职工 Employees in School-run Factories & Farms	其他附设机构人员 Personnel in Others Subsidiary Units
初　级 Junior	未定职级 No-ranking	行政人员 Adm. Personnel	教辅人员 Supporting Staff	工勤人员 Workers			
1139	**2002**	**4381**	**2395**	**1153**	**12**	**143**	**75**
176	242	845	465	285		2	4
73	13	86	77	45			6
108	103	152	94	51	1	114	9
49	3	186	95	50			
11	22	56	24	10			
12	5	22	23	17			
57	744	1541	971	178	6	1	
132	104	351	174	160	1		
19	252	65	23	19	1	9	
38	10	58	32	36		13	7
291	249	455	141	110	2	4	45
13	16	58	27	14			
16	10	146	84	53			
14	7	35	25	9			
42	87	156	57	35	1		
24	17	72	40	39			4
37	101	51	20	31			
27	17	46	23	11			

专任教师学历、职称情况(总计)

Number of Full-time Teacher by Academic Qualification and Professional Rank(Total)

单位：人

unit：person

地　区 Region	合计 Total	按学历分 By Academic Qualification				按职称分 By Professional Rank				
		博　士 Doctor's Degrees	硕　士 Master's Degrees	本　科 Normal Courses	专科及以下 Short-cycle Courses and Under	正高级 Senior	副高级 Sub-Senior	中　级 Middle	初　级 Junior	未定职级 No-ranking
总　计 Total	**1530512**	**286148**	**542792**	**678793**	**22779**	**182982**	**442685**	**611226**	**209963**	**83656**
北　京 Beijing	68394	35958	18648	13144	644	16718	23734	23126	2916	1900
天　津 Tianjin	31983	8789	11332	11585	277	4520	10324	12576	3495	1068
河　北 Hebei	67624	8057	23417	35353	797	9156	19731	26513	8896	3328
山　西 Shanxi	42267	3863	15241	22295	868	3036	10965	15689	8914	3663
内蒙古 Inner Mongolia	24828	2352	8797	13119	560	2468	7630	9347	3953	1430
辽　宁 Liaoning	65127	12254	24000	27864	1009	8776	20270	26201	6978	2902
吉　林 Jilin	39600	7603	15266	16236	495	5844	12482	15055	5699	520
黑龙江 Heilongjiang	48226	9263	16161	22432	370	7261	15403	19627	4477	1458
上　海 Shanghai	41151	17723	13332	9495	601	7116	13129	16612	2893	1401
江　苏 Jiangsu	109046	25898	36516	45748	884	12822	34417	47036	11341	3430
浙　江 Zhejiang	57072	14060	19376	23060	576	7623	17565	25090	3659	3135
安　徽 Anhui	55644	6823	23221	25105	495	4448	14846	21272	11909	3169
福　建 Fujian	43368	7790	15442	19666	470	4783	11989	16710	7462	2424
江　西 Jiangxi	53328	5277	16471	30775	805	5366	14407	21473	9389	2693
山　东 Shandong	100667	15692	35655	47808	1512	10229	28018	43230	15454	3736
河　南 Henan	93107	10950	34584	46328	1245	7831	24713	37180	18598	4785
湖　北 Hubei	82890	17106	30128	34323	1333	10247	25336	31596	11477	4234
湖　南 Hunan	64845	9639	20402	33709	1095	7089	18647	27117	7900	4092
广　东 Guangdong	93841	18519	34572	38993	1757	10899	24146	38724	10975	9097
广　西 Guangxi	37437	3905	15962	17071	499	3880	10047	14559	4952	3999
海　南 Hainan	8543	1074	3016	4315	138	925	2040	3226	1644	708
重　庆 Chongqing	37728	6457	14719	15834	718	4105	10387	15388	5153	2695
四　川 Sichuan	78222	11607	28784	35695	2136	8015	20171	31190	14128	4718
贵　州 Guizhou	25719	2109	8833	14282	495	2515	8103	9000	3663	2438
云　南 Yunnan	34494	4288	12429	16787	990	3607	9170	12950	5839	2928
西　藏 Tibet	2472	190	1082	1122	78	183	781	1018	378	112
陕　西 Shaanxi	65910	13233	25143	26740	794	7807	17873	27311	9771	3148
甘　肃 Gansu	24820	2916	9643	11923	338	2660	7212	9772	3704	1472
青　海 Qinghai	3951	260	1027	2522	142	795	1362	1123	455	216
宁　夏 Ningxia	7181	720	2404	3909	148	1032	1967	2266	981	935
新　疆 Xinjiang	21027	1773	7189	11555	510	1226	5820	9249	2910	1822

注：不含民办的其他高等教育机构数据。

Note：Data of Non-government HEIs are not included.

专任教师学历、职称情况（普通高校）

Number of Full-time Teacher by Academic Qualification and Professional Rank (Regular HEIs)

单位：人

unit：person

地区 Region	合计 Total	按学历分 By Academic Qualification				按职称分 By Professional Rank				
		博士 Doctor's Degrees	硕士 Master's Degrees	本科 Normal Courses	专科及以下 Short-cycle Courses and Under	正高级 Senior	副高级 Sub-Senior	中级 Middle	初级 Junior	未定职级 No-ranking
总计 Total	**1496865**	**285353**	**535784**	**654660**	**21068**	**181501**	**432356**	**596954**	**203713**	**82341**
北京 Beijing	66871	35734	18078	12437	622	16611	23257	22362	2786	1855
天津 Tianjin	30900	8748	11178	10736	238	4469	9854	12143	3374	1060
河北 Hebei	66825	8034	23122	34878	791	9100	19514	26186	8723	3302
山西 Shanxi	40764	3856	14992	21139	777	2990	10430	15138	8633	3573
内蒙古 Inner Mongolia	24554	2350	8754	12893	557	2459	7512	9237	3920	1426
辽宁 Liaoning	62706	12231	23573	26013	889	8653	19315	25296	6623	2819
吉林 Jilin	38003	7543	14776	15287	397	5720	11930	14439	5413	501
黑龙江 Heilongjiang	46215	9247	15976	20705	287	7111	14510	18914	4266	1414
上海 Shanghai	40297	17683	13044	8980	590	7089	12941	16118	2772	1377
江苏 Jiangsu	108272	25846	36265	45299	862	12719	34178	46712	11241	3422
浙江 Zhejiang	56000	14003	19128	22316	553	7579	17233	24547	3559	3082
安徽 Anhui	54903	6814	23070	24546	473	4430	14650	20916	11771	3136
福建 Fujian	42905	7772	15287	19376	470	4766	11816	16553	7373	2397
江西 Jiangxi	52434	5247	16296	30091	800	5275	14146	21228	9131	2654
山东 Shandong	98685	15680	35211	46401	1393	10130	27418	42432	14992	3713
河南 Henan	90949	10920	34218	44620	1191	7752	24120	36213	18085	4779
湖北 Hubei	81784	17099	29826	33540	1319	10217	24959	31147	11242	4219
湖南 Hunan	63869	9626	20295	32938	1010	7064	18334	26642	7776	4053
广东 Guangdong	91099	18475	34000	37025	1599	10843	23603	37501	10383	8769
广西 Guangxi	36425	3860	15590	16482	493	3799	9745	14094	4829	3958
海南 Hainan	8458	1074	3002	4245	137	921	2028	3196	1626	687
重庆 Chongqing	37130	6448	14518	15503	661	4078	10225	15105	5039	2683
四川 Sichuan	76795	11595	28575	34839	1786	8002	19794	30564	13788	4647
贵州 Guizhou	25351	2106	8775	13991	479	2499	8008	8867	3549	2428
云南 Yunnan	34421	4286	12426	16727	982	3602	9148	12917	5827	2927
西藏 Tibet	2472	190	1082	1122	78	183	781	1018	378	112
陕西 Shaanxi	64171	13229	24778	25463	701	7770	17442	26471	9387	3101
甘肃 Gansu	24384	2915	9577	11592	300	2650	7076	9568	3623	1467
青海 Qinghai	3785	260	1005	2419	101	787	1323	1039	434	202
宁夏 Ningxia	7111	720	2402	3844	145	1024	1936	2240	979	932
新疆 Xinjiang	18327	1762	6965	9213	387	1209	5130	8151	2191	1646

专任教师学历、职称情况(成人高校)

Number of Full-time Teacher by Academic Qualification and Professional Rank (Adult HEIs)

单位：人

unit：person

地区 Region	合计 Total	按学历分 By Academic Qualification				按职称分 By Professional Rank				
		博士 Doctor's Degrees	硕士 Master's Degrees	本科 Normal Courses	专科及以下 Short-cycle Courses and Under	正高级 Senior	副高级 Sub-Senior	中级 Middle	初级 Junior	未定职级 No-ranking
总计 Total	**33647**	**795**	**7008**	**24133**	**1711**	**1481**	**10329**	**14272**	**6250**	**1315**
北京 Beijing	1523	224	570	707	22	107	477	764	130	45
天津 Tianjin	1083	41	154	849	39	51	470	433	121	8
河北 Hebei	799	23	295	475	6	56	217	327	173	26
山西 Shanxi	1503	7	249	1156	91	46	535	551	281	90
内蒙古 Inner Mongolia	274	2	43	226	3	9	118	110	33	4
辽宁 Liaoning	2421	23	427	1851	120	123	955	905	355	83
吉林 Jilin	1597	60	490	949	98	124	552	616	286	19
黑龙江 Heilongjiang	2011	16	185	1727	83	150	893	713	211	44
上海 Shanghai	854	40	288	515	11	27	188	494	121	24
江苏 Jiangsu	774	52	251	449	22	103	239	324	100	8
浙江 Zhejiang	1072	57	248	744	23	44	332	543	100	53
安徽 Anhui	741	9	151	559	22	18	196	356	138	33
福建 Fujian	463	18	155	290		17	173	157	89	27
江西 Jiangxi	894	30	175	684	5	91	261	245	258	39
山东 Shandong	1982	12	444	1407	119	99	600	798	462	23
河南 Henan	2158	30	366	1708	54	79	593	967	513	6
湖北 Hubei	1106	7	302	783	14	30	377	449	235	15
湖南 Hunan	976	13	107	771	85	25	313	475	124	39
广东 Guangdong	2742	44	572	1968	158	56	543	1223	592	328
广西 Guangxi	1012	45	372	589	6	81	302	465	123	41
海南 Hainan	85		14	70	1	4	12	30	18	21
重庆 Chongqing	598	9	201	331	57	27	162	283	114	12
四川 Sichuan	1427	12	209	856	350	13	377	626	340	71
贵州 Guizhou	368	3	58	291	16	16	95	133	114	10
云南 Yunnan	73	2	3	60	8	5	22	33	12	1
西藏 Tibet										
陕西 Shaanxi	1739	4	365	1277	93	37	431	840	384	47
甘肃 Gansu	436	1	66	331	38	10	136	204	81	5
青海 Qinghai	166		22	103	41	8	39	84	21	14
宁夏 Ningxia	70		2	65	3	8	31	26	2	3
新疆 Xinjiang	2700	11	224	2342	123	17	690	1098	719	176

专任教师学历、职称情况(民办的其他高等教育机构)
Number of Full-time Teacher by Academic Qualification and Professional Rank (Other Non-government HEIs)

单位：人
unit：person

地区 Region	合计 Total	按学历分 By Academic Qualification				按职称分 By Professional Rank				
		博士 Doctor's Degrees	硕士 Master's Degrees	本科 Normal Courses	专科及以下 Short-cycle Courses and Under	正高级 Senior	副高级 Sub-Senior	中级 Middle	初级 Junior	未定职级 No-ranking
总计 Total	**13350**	**427**	**2606**	**9341**	**976**	**1203**	**2524**	**4244**	**1961**	**3418**
北京 Beijing	2076	137	556	1287	96	294	444	612	276	450
天津 Tianjin										
河北 Hebei	502	7	66	360	69	83	119	176	96	28
山西 Shanxi	1039	31	216	696	96	127	172	320	179	241
内蒙古 Inner Mongolia										
辽宁 Liaoning	945		187	740	18	53	232	545	110	5
吉林 Jilin	205	32	67	94	12	24	59	73	18	31
黑龙江 Heilongjiang	49		1	45	3	2	16	9	15	7
上海 Shanghai	2102	95	464	1420	123	184	308	410	96	1104
江苏 Jiangsu										
浙江 Zhejiang	794	3	125	634	32	23	89	307	222	153
安徽 Anhui	688	7	67	580	34	13	44	80	39	512
福建 Fujian										
江西 Jiangxi	352	10	76	233	33	41	60	149	81	21
山东 Shandong	2646	50	403	1860	333	224	562	917	514	429
河南 Henan	131	3	27	91	10	10	25	48	23	25
湖北 Hubei	220	19	55	138	8	25	82	69	30	14
湖南 Hunan	105	8	31	64	2	11	20	38	18	18
广东 Guangdong	609	18	175	366	50	29	103	234	90	153
广西 Guangxi										
海南 Hainan										
重庆 Chongqing	317		24	276	17	13	93	141	41	29
四川 Sichuan	361	5	39	284	33	20	32	72	71	166
贵州 Guizhou										
云南 Yunnan										
西藏 Tibet										
陕西 Shaanxi										
甘肃 Gansu	209	2	27	173	7	27	64	44	42	32
青海 Qinghai										
宁夏 Ningxia										
新疆 Xinjiang										

聘请校外教师学历情况(总计)

Number of Part-time Teacher by Academic Qualification (Total)

单位：人
unit: person

地　区 Region	合计 Total	博　士 Doctor's Degrees	硕　士 Master's Degrees	本　科 Normal Courses	专科及以下 Short-cycle Courses and Under
总　计 Total	**442176**	**62778**	**143739**	**212387**	**23272**
北　京 Beijing	16980	5810	5272	5375	523
天　津 Tianjin	9279	985	2946	4841	507
河　北 Hebei	17094	2333	5394	8473	894
山　西 Shanxi	6581	673	2282	3331	295
内蒙古 Inner Mongolia	6977	733	2265	3681	298
辽　宁 Liaoning	14192	1994	4804	6702	692
吉　林 Jilin	8181	1409	2190	4064	518
黑龙江 Heilongjiang	16368	3248	5651	7003	466
上　海 Shanghai	13052	3947	4124	4584	397
江　苏 Jiangsu	39481	6054	12226	18793	2408
浙　江 Zhejiang	23725	2341	6052	13218	2114
安　徽 Anhui	17110	2706	7114	6982	308
福　建 Fujian	10081	1821	2735	4690	835
江　西 Jiangxi	11632	1199	3988	6037	408
山　东 Shandong	34700	4058	10372	18409	1861
河　南 Henan	21309	2071	8937	9927	374
湖　北 Hubei	26630	3954	10064	11109	1503
湖　南 Hunan	18372	2317	5860	9742	453
广　东 Guangdong	30194	2305	7761	16763	3365
广　西 Guangxi	10035	929	3561	4871	674
海　南 Hainan	2960	335	925	1508	192
重　庆 Chongqing	14116	2161	4961	6476	518
四　川 Sichuan	21558	2933	6411	11205	1009
贵　州 Guizhou	5856	348	1982	3259	267
云　南 Yunnan	9418	972	2904	4498	1044
西　藏 Tibet	189	37	60	92	
陕　西 Shaanxi	19859	2637	7762	9000	460
甘　肃 Gansu	7066	1690	2203	2976	197
青　海 Qinghai	677	22	57	440	158
宁　夏 Ningxia	1439	40	508	798	93
新　疆 Xinjiang	7065	716	2368	3540	441

注:不含民办的其他高等教育机构数据。

Note: Data of Non-government HEIs are not included.

聘请校外教师学历情况（普通高校）

Number of Part-time Teacher by Academic Qualification（Regular HEIs）

单位：人

unit：person

地　区 Region	合计 Total	博　士 Doctor's Degrees	硕　士 Master's Degrees	本　科 Normal Courses	专科及以下 Short-cycle Courses and Under
总　计 Total	**403330**	**62086**	**136231**	**183065**	**21948**
北　京 Beijing	16483	5773	5110	5090	510
天　津 Tianjin	7430	978	2650	3307	495
河　北 Hebei	15702	2310	5129	7456	807
山　西 Shanxi	5855	661	2081	2843	270
内蒙古 Inner Mongolia	6851	733	2242	3590	286
辽　宁 Liaoning	12371	1989	4349	5407	626
吉　林 Jilin	6993	1408	2140	2979	466
黑龙江 Heilongjiang	15024	3220	5453	5922	429
上　海 Shanghai	12551	3900	3924	4331	396
江　苏 Jiangsu	35747	6032	11797	15583	2335
浙　江 Zhejiang	19709	2290	5280	10120	2019
安　徽 Anhui	16856	2703	7020	6825	308
福　建 Fujian	10037	1821	2721	4661	834
江　西 Jiangxi	11460	1199	3901	5952	408
山　东 Shandong	34071	4046	10268	17904	1853
河　南 Henan	19151	2043	8587	8190	331
湖　北 Hubei	26373	3938	9890	11047	1498
湖　南 Hunan	18193	2312	5823	9622	436
广　东 Guangdong	25605	2273	7004	13221	3107
广　西 Guangxi	9809	920	3507	4710	672
海　南 Hainan	2886	334	906	1459	187
重　庆 Chongqing	13639	2157	4626	6347	509
四　川 Sichuan	16163	2736	5569	7121	737
贵　州 Guizhou	5595	348	1934	3046	267
云　南 Yunnan	9418	972	2904	4498	1044
西　藏 Tibet	189	37	60	92	
陕　西 Shaanxi	15742	2561	6579	6290	312
甘　肃 Gansu	5854	1660	2066	1954	174
青　海 Qinghai	637	22	57	418	140
宁　夏 Ningxia	1336	40	504	699	93
新　疆 Xinjiang	5600	670	2150	2381	399

聘请校外教师学历情况(成人高校)
Number of Part-time Teacher by Academic Qualification (Adult HEIs)

单位：人
unit：person

地　区 Region	合计 Total	博　士 Doctor's Degrees	硕　士 Master's Degrees	本　科 Normal Courses	专科及以下 Short-cycle Courses and Under
总　计 Total	**38846**	**692**	**7508**	**29322**	**1324**
北　京 Beijing	497	37	162	285	13
天　津 Tianjin	1849	7	296	1534	12
河　北 Hebei	1392	23	265	1017	87
山　西 Shanxi	726	12	201	488	25
内蒙古 Inner Mongolia	126		23	91	12
辽　宁 Liaoning	1821	5	455	1295	66
吉　林 Jilin	1188	1	50	1085	52
黑龙江 Heilongjiang	1344	28	198	1081	37
上　海 Shanghai	501	47	200	253	1
江　苏 Jiangsu	3734	22	429	3210	73
浙　江 Zhejiang	4016	51	772	3098	95
安　徽 Anhui	254	3	94	157	
福　建 Fujian	44		14	29	1
江　西 Jiangxi	172		87	85	
山　东 Shandong	629	12	104	505	8
河　南 Henan	2158	28	350	1737	43
湖　北 Hubei	257	16	174	62	5
湖　南 Hunan	179	5	37	120	17
广　东 Guangdong	4589	32	757	3542	258
广　西 Guangxi	226	9	54	161	2
海　南 Hainan	74	1	19	49	5
重　庆 Chongqing	477	4	335	129	9
四　川 Sichuan	5395	197	842	4084	272
贵　州 Guizhou	261		48	213	
云　南 Yunnan					
西　藏 Tibet					
陕　西 Shaanxi	4117	76	1183	2710	148
甘　肃 Gansu	1212	30	137	1022	23
青　海 Qinghai	40			22	18
宁　夏 Ningxia	103		4	99	
新　疆 Xinjiang	1465	46	218	1159	42

聘请校外教师学历情况(民办的其他高等教育机构)

Number of Part-time Teacher by Academic Qualification (Other Non-government HEIs)

单位：人
unit：person

地 区 Region	合计 Total	博 士 Doctor's Degrees	硕 士 Master's Degrees	本 科 Normal Courses	专科及以下 Short-cycle Courses and Under
总 计 Total	**13327**	**1360**	**4114**	**7231**	**622**
北 京 Beijing	1838	183	600	972	83
天 津 Tianjin					
河 北 Hebei	323	32	113	176	2
山 西 Shanxi	503	31	128	303	41
内蒙古 Inner Mongolia					
辽 宁 Liaoning	412	35	123	254	
吉 林 Jilin	149	32	47	53	17
黑龙江 Heilongjiang	92		15	54	23
上 海 Shanghai	5205	671	1279	3010	245
江 苏 Jiangsu					
浙 江 Zhejiang	779	30	187	532	30
安 徽 Anhui	365	36	105	220	4
福 建 Fujian					
江 西 Jiangxi	128		51	75	2
山 东 Shandong	1295	113	420	610	152
河 南 Henan	441	45	217	168	11
湖 北 Hubei	666	55	302	306	3
湖 南 Hunan	5		5		
广 东 Guangdong	389	56	161	167	5
广 西 Guangxi					
海 南 Hainan					
重 庆 Chongqing	288	8	191	89	
四 川 Sichuan	163	13	65	81	4
贵 州 Guizhou					
云 南 Yunnan					
西 藏 Tibet					
陕 西 Shaanxi					
甘 肃 Gansu	286	20	105	161	
青 海 Qinghai					
宁 夏 Ningxia					
新 疆 Xinjiang					

资产情况(学校

Condition of Fixed Assets and Teaching

地　区 Region	占地面积(平方米) Area of School Sites (m^2)			图书(万册) Books & Magazines in Libraries (10,000 volume)		
	合计 Total	其中:绿化用地面积 of Which: Green Areas	其中:运动场地面积 of Which: Sports Areas	合计 Total	当年新增 New Added in Current Year	合计 Total
总　计 Total	**1699129270**	**521398682**	**127870363**	**225394.17**	**12100.87**	**9720437**
北　京 Beijing	43625473	13722393	3493887	10999.52	487.43	670054
天　津 Tianjin	35860698	9047852	2745681	4876.70	234.02	201052
河　北 Hebei	68704326	18203586	7415224	9308.90	488.41	362527
山　西 Shanxi	34746965	7740918	3450717	5446.73	308.83	172934
内蒙古 Inner Mongolia	34356823	8112884	2473988	3326.29	160.76	133547
辽　宁 Liaoning	66726213	18409792	5440014	8596.11	419.38	417575
吉　林 Jilin	41841393	11555167	3192459	5797.71	320.81	240179
黑龙江 Heilongjiang	58139244	14503880	4401009	7185.52	290.52	294968
上　海 Shanghai	34318828	11908429	2787898	6944.99	244.91	415543
江　苏 Jiangsu	130893121	44521809	8809724	16003.84	765.08	872193
浙　江 Zhejiang	57128555	17642747	4877410	9420.31	530.79	505670
安　徽 Anhui	66281511	21046802	5558035	8066.49	426.84	301938
福　建 Fujian	49622996	15568447	3822912	6657.18	443.48	281690
江　西 Jiangxi	67883270	26548774	5099183	7973.30	404.64	300356
山　东 Shandong	129154613	41141305	8780419	15929.02	773.84	579214
河　南 Henan	108323744	30107499	7536022	13693.01	733.34	490851
湖　北 Hubei	89133244	29938382	6597594	12548	610.60	529066
湖　南 Hunan	74317015	22679230	5684356	9774.45	475.35	377097
广　东 Guangdong	96312964	31111775	7091122	13549.62	718.36	614288
广　西 Guangxi	42564997	12749135	2909344	5322.97	282.36	213825
海　南 Hainan	12769892	4618713	811043	1400.35	110.03	53686
重　庆 Chongqing	50140505	18265413	3556418	5549	480.23	246224
四　川 Sichuan	88168132	27007549	5934877	10854.86	682.78	434607
贵　州 Guizhou	36169468	11334153	2378424	3633.67	335.33	125733
云　南 Yunnan	38564467	12902016	2927499	4994.04	429.41	182019
西　藏 Tibet	3244265	842032	244209	338.23	16.49	11633
陕　西 Shaanxi	63464315	15552534	4675302	9804.01	525.80	394053
甘　肃 Gansu	26242046	7205402	1922935	3204.28	241.27	127072
青　海 Qinghai	3954320	1251618	344892	484.58	17.30	16993
宁　夏 Ningxia	10856121	3747520	739134	828.98	51.30	44232
新　疆 Xinjiang	35619746	12410926	2168632	2881.51	91.17	109618

注:不含民办的其他高等教育机构数据。

Note: Data of Non-government HEIs are not included.

产权)(总计)

Resources (Owned by HEIs) (Total)

计算机数(台) No. of Computers		教室(间) Classroom(room)		固定资产值(万元) Fixed Assets (10,000 yuan)				
其中:教学用计算机 of Which: No. of Computers Used for Instruction		合计 Total	其中:网络多媒体教室 of Which: Network Multimedia Classroom	合计 Total	其中:教学、科研仪器设备资产 of Which: Teaching Equipment & Instruments		其中:信息化设备资产值 of Which: Assets of Information Facilities	
小计 Subtotal	其中:平板电脑 of Which: Tablet PC				小计 Subtotal	当年新增 New Added in Current Year	小计 Subtotal	其中:软件 of Which: Software
7400120	**45816**	**592115**	**268851**	**151608742.67**	**32830625.18**	**3935309.70**	**9196778.12**	**1305119.28**
404547	4553	19149	12789	12040523.19	4134529.40	468492.69	1064847.56	212050.92
146052	646	9826	4223	2977309.53	835668.05	91147.17	183997.24	25238
293831	1168	22651	10217	5197689.91	1009780.58	96993.02	251119.33	26748.95
145716	230	18829	6325	2542397.86	543763.11	57110.76	147388.39	15002.31
113088	954	11940	4490	2410922.97	448653.24	69700.26	107212.71	13215.49
330522	858	29877	9180	6165949.52	1180799.03	158145.20	381833.79	51304.43
167791	2843	12873	4183	3698306.28	791084.54	93222.01	231937.91	21813.58
240174	340	19585	6360	5259147.28	1118251.29	121026.24	242231.39	31987.85
286103	1311	14464	8431	6783249.58	1917669.81	264890.76	513338.27	88759.23
684872	7372	39493	23200	14076022.13	2874232.69	357975.96	817850.10	97439.12
377833	1544	22198	13579	7508667.25	1662792.45	204644.97	502189.60	75274.64
239424	1399	25186	9049	4420239.38	992146.16	131174.06	207611.97	23027.07
215372	547	16711	7929	4398492.93	848298.89	96705.89	251450.71	36714.73
244434	3710	21665	7251	4369434.60	716198.16	80255.09	215958.34	25188.76
456094	1761	42556	17258	9884224.34	1802176.38	178614.03	532942.43	56040.58
399898	2903	37532	15486	6479943.63	1248823.27	140713.75	384306.83	33520.91
396442	1211	25575	12909	7863683.58	1655064	186488.63	423354.38	54965.21
299586	2027	26499	14175	5366813.45	1075062.45	131018.77	313272.98	38571.34
477411	2208	24937	16341	8785197.20	1922533.44	207784.44	622499.16	104707.55
180184	2421	13408	5900	2409085.49	602455.84	82608.68	141055.41	16660.91
43174	31	7950	1900	988829.65	161929.92	28531.29	45112.47	5339.20
186205	1001	14392	7934	4715934.27	657008.23	91582.77	241169.35	28873.27
323766	1263	28213	13445	6932742.36	1501449.84	189826.20	448292.80	113630.19
102506	79	14402	4805	1738173.55	356840.65	61999.86	121158.35	12410.28
142668	79	13148	5750	3698811.55	446217.71	61299.51	175969.87	18150.21
9815	49	778	396	230038.01	40260.17	4516.69	17073.19	2422.56
269105	901	24901	8887	6608634.28	1382202.80	172204.89	355433.89	48167.49
92287	1176	7853	2734	1846393.99	393484.97	36968.32	95320.27	7537.96
13707	22	1236	316	181555.68	56335.22	13706.98	19899.84	2249.18
34407	738	9348	5938	619173.50	131372.10	20554.49	43914.78	6160.47
83106	471	14940	7471	1411155.73	323540.79	35406.32	97034.81	11946.89

资产情况(学校

Condition of Fixed Assets and Teaching

地　区 Region	占地面积(平方米) Area of School Sites (m²)			图书(万册) Books & Magazines in Libraries (10,000 volume)		
	合计 Total	其中:绿化用地面积 of Which: Green Areas	其中:运动场地面积 of Which: Sports Areas	合计 Total	当年新增 New Added in Current Year	合计 Total
总　计 Total	**1670982872**	**514972205**	**124993256**	**221300.86**	**12000.96**	**9515032**
北　京 Beijing	42340698	13428845	3415635	10779.56	483.34	654799
天　津 Tianjin	35290735	8928593	2589823	4694.54	232.17	194143
河　北 Hebei	67731310	18086541	7298669	9195.80	474.39	355977
山　西 Shanxi	33841706	7529712	3318778	5284.49	307.96	166258
内蒙古 Inner Mongolia	34072636	8079224	2442688	3287.25	160.76	131013
辽　宁 Liaoning	65570790	18245822	5215179	8337.56	416.56	401907
吉　林 Jilin	40500069	11194720	3044611	5646.33	318.09	233447
黑龙江 Heilongjiang	57173845	14322807	4278267	6962.25	287.09	288474
上　海 Shanghai	33568492	11823319	2746456	6783.53	243.74	402753
江　苏 Jiangsu	130224417	44390915	8744167	15899.22	762.73	864418
浙　江 Zhejiang	56581928	17492421	4809396	9290.64	527.41	497365
安　徽 Anhui	65572456	20930644	5502245	7973.95	424.94	296582
福　建 Fujian	49427186	15536312	3808290	6593.31	443.19	279720
江　西 Jiangxi	66543092	26072987	5018160	7798.54	399.38	294292
山　东 Shandong	126469606	40562802	8613889	15751.24	761.37	569808
河　南 Henan	106124493	29671997	7275273	13343.50	727.98	479122
湖　北 Hubei	88282335	29741302	6523472	12386.60	608.19	525207
湖　南 Hunan	73572018	22486469	5614909	9635.76	466.27	369717
广　东 Guangdong	95416262	30871293	7025941	13444.26	715.31	603966
广　西 Guangxi	41986998	12626962	2864965	5158.27	280.14	207351
海　南 Hainan	12694902	4586148	808523	1391.71	109.68	53019
重　庆 Chongqing	49088183	17874370	3466778	5461.72	476.83	239999
四　川 Sichuan	86565023	26652203	5702078	10718.34	681.84	428128
贵　州 Guizhou	35669425	11169587	2332784	3580.26	333.83	121995
云　南 Yunnan	38415383	12850437	2918649	4906.02	429.41	178091
西　藏 Tibet	3244265	842032	244209	338.23	16.49	11633
陕　西 Shaanxi	61924987	15204932	4502391	9587.94	523.17	385885
甘　肃 Gansu	26037655	7187562	1915334	3160.37	240.14	124546
青　海 Qinghai	3871352	1235324	324783	472.84	17.30	16006
宁　夏 Ningxia	10833644	3740720	735514	825.68	51.30	43330
新　疆 Xinjiang	32346981	11605203	1891400	2611.15	79.96	96081

产权)(普通高校)
Resources (Owned by HEIs)(Regular HEIs)

计算机数(台) No. of Computers		教室(间) Classroom(room)		固定资产值(万元) Fixed Assets (10,000 yuan)				
其中:教学用计算机 of Which: No. of Computers Used for Instruction		合计 Total	其中:网络多媒体教室 of Which: Network Multimedia Classroom	合计 Total	其中:教学、科研仪器设备资产 of Which: Teaching Equipment & Instruments		其中:信息化设备资产值 of Which: Assets of Information Facilities	
小计 Subtotal	其中:平板电脑 of Which: Tablet PC				小计 Subtotal	当年新增 New Added in Current Year	小计 Subtotal	其中:软件 of Which: Software
7247088	**44777**	**561191**	**256364**	**149637264.76**	**32411012.86**	**3904708.65**	**9029793.45**	**1290660.78**
394442	4509	18167	12097	11755653.35	4104667.34	465119.92	1042155.01	211013.40
140762	646	9165	4025	2937964.65	822020.44	90744.77	179255.94	25051.16
289196	1168	22139	9943	5153600.89	996147.64	93469.03	246326.52	26528.61
140300	230	17638	5967	2491302.74	530797.75	56019.30	143258.50	14643.16
111405	954	9712	4154	2399921.47	445465.74	69700.26	105514.91	13146.80
319402	858	28009	8597	6052858.34	1160299.45	157129.71	374724.34	50838.49
163004	2733	12160	3989	3628651.74	772303	91927.43	226280.88	20942.38
235249	330	18615	6137	5201843.11	1105794.90	119824.72	236084.44	31402.49
276330	1239	12703	7837	6661931.98	1888249.44	263411.36	496151.77	88235.86
679504	7372	39082	22972	13972774.43	2865418.83	357660.27	812013.40	96833.43
371534	1542	21709	13218	7454095.61	1650610.63	203914.79	492108.35	74246.33
235382	1385	24786	8894	4381481.04	984827.10	130793.10	202665.07	22756.40
214083	547	16576	7857	4368538.63	842170.99	96274.56	249563.14	36426.58
239484	3530	21233	7097	4285408.81	703779.08	79418.84	211944.42	24480.88
449143	1749	40587	16828	9771328.84	1781476.34	177187.82	527239.89	55549.73
390427	2843	36280	15203	6393432.27	1223079.49	139653.57	377451.68	32608.77
393056	1181	25010	12659	7819881.60	1643319.86	186239.33	420861.47	54895.58
293143	1945	25545	13548	5313415.43	1059717.38	129980.30	310165.96	38230.04
469355	2146	24373	16009	8719298.58	1896849.82	206614.65	613480.12	104493.39
175045	2417	13087	5720	2375946.41	593250.66	81679.35	138164.47	16303.33
42667	31	7915	1879	985262.26	160527.96	28527.93	43757.28	5322.20
181698	993	14081	7797	4637907.76	645240.71	90742.88	235206.91	28419.44
318917	1227	27258	13245	6833490.39	1480037.19	188134.16	443255.16	112433.99
99489	79	13995	4720	1660933.74	348615.98	61830.86	114258.99	11788.78
141067	79	13096	5729	3670834.21	438212.67	61299.51	173545.47	18030.21
9815	49	778	396	230038.01	40260.17	4516.69	17073.19	2422.56
263152	835	23451	8628	6522164.78	1356629.99	170564.93	350774.64	47337.06
90506	1168	7619	2697	1832706.38	389943.34	36630.60	92985.50	7388.46
13140	18	1201	289	176608.68	55062.22	13662.98	19074.84	2234.18
33522	518	8512	5793	616722.19	130664.70	20554.49	43455.78	6022.99
72869	456	6709	2440	1331266.44	295572.05	31480.54	90995.41	10634.10

资产情况(学校

Condition of Fixed Assets and Teaching

地　区 Region	占地面积(平方米) Area of School Sites (m^2)			图书(万册) Books & Magazines in Libraries (10,000 volume)		
	合计 Total	其中:绿化用地面积 of Which: Green Areas	其中:运动场地面积 of Which: Sports Areas	合计 Total	当年新增 New Added in Current Year	合计 Total
总　计 Total	**28146398**	**6426477**	**2877107**	**4093.31**	**99.91**	**205405**
北　京 Beijing	1284775	293548	78252	219.96	4.09	15255
天　津 Tianjin	569963	119259	155858	182.16	1.85	6909
河　北 Hebei	973016	117045	116555	113.10	14.02	6550
山　西 Shanxi	905259	211206	131939	162.24	0.87	6676
内蒙古 Inner Mongolia	284187	33660	31300	39.04		2534
辽　宁 Liaoning	1155423	163970	224835	258.55	2.83	15668
吉　林 Jilin	1341324	360447	147848	151.38	2.72	6732
黑龙江 Heilongjiang	965399	181073	122742	223.27	3.43	6494
上　海 Shanghai	750336	85110	41442	161.46	1.17	12790
江　苏 Jiangsu	668704	130894	65557	104.62	2.35	7775
浙　江 Zhejiang	546627	150326	68014	129.67	3.39	8305
安　徽 Anhui	709055	116158	55790	92.54	1.90	5356
福　建 Fujian	195810	32135	14622	63.87	0.29	1970
江　西 Jiangxi	1340178	475787	81023	174.76	5.26	6064
山　东 Shandong	2685007	578503	166530	177.78	12.47	9406
河　南 Henan	2199251	435502	260749	349.51	5.36	11729
湖　北 Hubei	850909	197080	74122	161.40	2.41	3859
湖　南 Hunan	744997	192761	69447	138.69	9.08	7380
广　东 Guangdong	896702	240482	65181	105.36	3.05	10322
广　西 Guangxi	577999	122173	44379	164.70	2.22	6474
海　南 Hainan	74990	32565	2520	8.64	0.35	667
重　庆 Chongqing	1052322	391043	89640	87.28	3.40	6225
四　川 Sichuan	1603109	355346	232799	136.52	0.94	6479
贵　州 Guizhou	500043	164566	45640	53.41	1.50	3738
云　南 Yunnan	149084	51579	8850	88.02		3928
西　藏 Tibet						
陕　西 Shaanxi	1539328	347602	172911	216.07	2.63	8168
甘　肃 Gansu	204391	17840	7601	43.91	1.13	2526
青　海 Qinghai	82968	16294	20109	11.74		987
宁　夏 Ningxia	22477	6800	3620	3.30		902
新　疆 Xinjiang	3272765	805723	277232	270.36	11.21	13537

产权)(成人高校)
Resources (Owned by HEIs) (Adult HEIs)

计算机数(台) No. of Computers		教室(间) Classroom(room)		固定资产值(万元) Fixed Assets (10,000 yuan)				
其中:教学用计算机 of Which: No. of Computers Used for Instruction		合计 Total	其中:网络多媒体教室 of Which: Network Multimedia Classroom	合计 Total	其中:教学、科研仪器设备资产 of Which: Teaching Equipment & Instruments		其中:信息化设备资产值 of Which: Assets of Information Facilities	
小计 Subtotal	其中:平板电脑 of Which: Tablet PC				小计 Subtotal	当年新增 New Added in Current Year	小计 Subtotal	其中:软件 of Which: Software
153032	**1039**	**30924**	**12487**	**1971477.91**	**419612.32**	**30601.05**	**166984.67**	**14458.50**
10105	44	982	692	284869.84	29862.06	3372.77	22692.55	1037.52
5290		661	198	39344.88	13647.61	402.40	4741.30	186.84
4635		512	274	44089.02	13632.94	3523.99	4792.81	220.34
5416		1191	358	51095.12	12965.36	1091.46	4129.89	359.15
1683		2228	336	11001.50	3187.50		1697.80	68.69
11120		1868	583	113091.18	20499.58	1015.49	7109.45	465.94
4787	110	713	194	69654.54	18781.54	1294.58	5657.03	871.20
4925	10	970	223	57304.17	12456.39	1201.52	6146.95	585.36
9773	72	1761	594	121317.60	29420.37	1479.40	17186.50	523.37
5368		411	228	103247.70	8813.86	315.69	5836.70	605.69
6299	2	489	361	54571.64	12181.82	730.18	10081.25	1028.31
4042	14	400	155	38758.34	7319.06	380.96	4946.90	270.67
1289		135	72	29954.30	6127.90	431.33	1887.57	288.15
4950	180	432	154	84025.79	12419.08	836.25	4013.92	707.88
6951	12	1969	430	112895.50	20700.04	1426.21	5702.54	490.85
9471	60	1252	283	86511.36	25743.78	1060.18	6855.15	912.14
3386	30	565	250	43801.98	11744.14	249.30	2492.91	69.63
6443	82	954	627	53398.02	15345.07	1038.47	3107.02	341.30
8056	62	564	332	65898.62	25683.62	1169.79	9019.04	214.16
5139	4	321	180	33139.08	9205.18	929.33	2890.94	357.58
507		35	21	3567.39	1401.96	3.36	1355.19	17
4507	8	311	137	78026.51	11767.52	839.89	5962.44	453.83
4849	36	955	200	99251.97	21412.65	1692.04	5037.64	1196.20
3017		407	85	77239.81	8224.67	169	6899.36	621.50
1601		52	21	27977.34	8005.04		2424.40	120
5953	66	1450	259	86469.50	25572.81	1639.96	4659.25	830.43
1781	8	234	37	13687.61	3541.63	337.72	2334.77	149.50
567	4	35	27	4947	1273	44	825	15
885	220	836	145	2451.31	707.40		459	137.48
10237	15	8231	5031	79889.29	27968.74	3925.78	6039.40	1312.79

资产情况(学校

Condition of Fixed Assets and Teaching

地 区 Region	占地面积(平方米) Area of School Sites (m^2)			图书(万册) Books & Magazines in Libraries (10,000 volume)		
	合计 Total	其中:绿化用地面积 of Which: Green Areas	其中:运动场地面积 of Which: Sports Areas	合计 Total	当年新增 New Added in Current Year	合计 Total
总 计 Total	**6288591**	**1386442**	**616512**	**1269.56**	**70.46**	**79993**
北 京 Beijing	772724	133047	43672	263.95	10.12	19085
天 津 Tianjin						
河 北 Hebei	275383	74095	34800	41.82	0.42	2064
山 西 Shanxi	454829	48822	40974	132.91	20.76	3601
内蒙古 Inner Mongolia						
辽 宁 Liaoning	128850	24402	14800	157.60		432
吉 林 Jilin	29086	3000	10000	16.80	0.90	715
黑龙江 Heilongjiang	21942	2000	5000	5		324
上 海 Shanghai	176812	43419	21701	48	2.79	9323
江 苏 Jiangsu						
浙 江 Zhejiang	147060	87648	19385	48.14	1.95	5842
安 徽 Anhui	374997	86970	23844	72.25	1	7321
福 建 Fujian						
江 西 Jiangxi	805794	169747	123827	59.19	4.93	3849
山 东 Shandong	2191011	425319	178735	227.87	4.80	13973
河 南 Henan	4567	680	280	21.65	2.45	683
湖 北 Hubei	164035	37774	17056	26.98	1.58	2631
湖 南 Hunan				18.65		1129
广 东 Guangdong	225113	43409	20000	51.77	2.52	3539
广 西 Guangxi						
海 南 Hainan						
重 庆 Chongqing	63186	12179	10755	38.17	3.74	2789
四 川 Sichuan	450536	193531	51017	28.60	10.85	2375
贵 州 Guizhou						
云 南 Yunnan						
西 藏 Tibet						
陕 西 Shaanxi						
甘 肃 Gansu	2666	400	666	10.21	1.65	318
青 海 Qinghai						
宁 夏 Ningxia						
新 疆 Xinjiang						

产权)(民办的其他高等教育机构)
Resources (Owned by HEIs) (Other Non-government HEIs)

计算机数(台) No. of Computers: 其中:教学用计算机 of Which: No. of Computers Used for Instruction — 小计 Subtotal	计算机数(台) No. of Computers: 其中:教学用计算机 — 其中:平板电脑 of Which: Tablet PC	教室(间) Classroom(room): 合计 Total	教室(间) Classroom(room): 其中:网络多媒体教室 of Which: Network Multimedia Classroom	固定资产值(万元) Fixed Assets (10,000 yuan): 合计 Total	固定资产值: 其中:教学、科研仪器设备资产 of Which: Teaching Equipment & Instruments — 小计 Subtotal	固定资产值: 其中:教学、科研仪器设备资产 — 当年新增 New Added in Current Year	固定资产值: 其中:信息化设备资产值 of Which: Assets of Information Facilities — 小计 Subtotal	固定资产值: 其中:信息化设备资产值 — 其中:软件 of Which: Software
65957	**971**	**6910**	**1582**	**478510.78**	**93881.92**	**7481.76**	**29814.87**	**4901.01**
15178	78	1377	174	126478.90	22289.47	649.59	8129.95	590.15
1670		69	32	14577.05	2653.54	319.20	975.04	301.65
2981	38	344	67	13891.23	3908.89	416.48	1376.06	286.19
339		641		15689.40	5093	5	234	1.20
619		310	120	1052.10	548.20	1.50	93	10
290		48	4	1228	271	2	68.71	10.19
7688	73	784	236	17672.14	6762.68	1078.95	2083.77	260.41
4691		633	155	36834.09	9234.77	654.63	2617.53	393.25
6737		365	234	14969.20	7740.60	1476	3497.80	163.80
3361	50	528	59	32846.57	3253.69	186	1263	336.69
10850	431	853	139	112590.34	18678.10	1590.61	6294.06	1946.22
497	5	18	4	2701.29	706.40	39.38	942.91	140.76
2191	75	223	76	35553.82	3650.79	108.80	739.57	44
987		116	80	1436	811	100	170	15
3238	21	280	144	22202.57	3645.49	266.23	302.57	3.70
2251	200	81	8	18508.08	3014.70	255.79	741.10	344.60
2160		237	50	9135	1180	319	243	46.50
229		3		1145	439.60	12.60	42.80	6.70

地　区 Region	占地面积(平方米) Area of School Sites (m^2)			图书(万册) Books & Magazines in Libraries (10,000 volume)		
	合计 Total	其中:绿化用地面积 of Which: Green Areas	其中:运动场地面积 of Which: Sports Areas	合计 Total	当年新增 New Added in Current Year	合计 Total
总　计 Total	**214403118**	**47280419**	**14578461**	**5660.61**	**165.21**	**351634**
北　京 Beijing	13039703	1610381	596269	27.20		444
天　津 Tianjin	2812768	123100	144734	187.11	8.29	10464
河　北 Hebei	5499443	804452	458384	266.84	10.65	15659
山　西 Shanxi	4476282	912284	547982	129.18	0.39	8163
内蒙古 Inner Mongolia	1424758	106800	188366	5.96	0.38	138
辽　宁 Liaoning	6137065	990467	436999	213.75	3.18	10707
吉　林 Jilin	6096596	1565909	283975	56	0.30	3947
黑龙江 Heilongjiang	6083386	947413	663241	172.37		8178
上　海 Shanghai	5550858	1569175	296149	121.40	1.34	5119
江　苏 Jiangsu	19131867	5646951	1682011	649.30	27.76	40953
浙　江 Zhejiang	9085538	2214633	742559	333.69	17.60	30274
安　徽 Anhui	3936094	656917	251717	163.28	4.50	11930
福　建 Fujian	9188571	2256187	697801	70.50	5.89	9761
江　西 Jiangxi	7051780	1007021	447445	120.26	4	2690
山　东 Shandong	12623488	2971967	967811	144.66		3325
河　南 Henan	7438667	1463339	334571	450.14	4.60	15884
湖　北 Hubei	10639006	2097655	610744	366.97	5.60	13094
湖　南 Hunan	7499639	1416029	325205	333.22	4.49	3721
广　东 Guangdong	28220379	7379555	1760678	636.18	6.46	54840
广　西 Guangxi	6540500	1581388	313644	177.25	15.50	45930
海　南 Hainan	1159340	298923	41185			63
重　庆 Chongqing	2767576	572825	87886	16.28	0.30	663
四　川 Sichuan	13868884	3088107	1018040	227.48	2.01	21937
贵　州 Guizhou	1167403	434937	62749	43.20		
云　南 Yunnan	5972764	823711	179831	50.76		1380
西　藏 Tibet				0.67		
陕　西 Shaanxi	13436178	3997812	1032680	495.43	30.35	16698
甘　肃 Gansu	3139132	696523	393685	161.28	11.58	14728
青　海 Qinghai	33333				369	
宁　夏 Ningxia	66670			32		
新　疆 Xinjiang	315450	45958	12120	8.25	0.05	575

注:不含民办的其他高等教育机构数据。

Note: Data of Non-government HEIs are not included.

(非学校产权独立使用)
Resources (Not Owned by HEIs)

计算机数(台) No. of Computers		教室(间) Classroom(room)		固定资产值(万元) Fixed Assets (10,000 yuan)				
其中:教学用计算机 of Which: No. of Computers Used for Instruction		合计 Total	其中:网络多媒体教室 of Which: Network Multimedia Classroom	合计 Total	其中:教学、科研仪器设备资产 of Which: Teaching Equipment & Instruments		其中:信息化设备资产值 of Which: Assets of Information Facilities	
小计 Subtotal	其中:平板电脑 of Which: Tablet PC				小计 Subtotal	当年新增 New Added in Current Year	小计 Subtotal	其中:软件 of Which: Software
234498	**4394**	**51272**	**24489**	**8679861.83**	**1035565.76**	**73235.13**		
305		666	350	291742.27	221762	15202		
9377	35	2246	1319	136142.22	21129.83	1020.06		
13851		2134	1159	245074.29	42191.50	2007.47		
7117	126	1129	593	157979.34	11887.93	2472		
113		163	30	29270.31	65.74	65.74		
7850	1063	2314	835	651103.80	29231.89	1635.91		
2898	11	803	198	81389.79	4099	391		
6622		1925	1043	63025.57	13599.72	3240		
2915	1	1162	530	283491.72	26084.45	992.88		
30645	244	10561	4821	954769.83	101549.23	9947.47		
23561		4224	2741	318469.90	48511.04	2376.82		
10164		2797	1043	226939.67	20633.40	2488.36		
7933		749	430	396657.29	37391.71	1923.77		
1680	180	3293	720	422281.31	13797.50	285		
2291		1206	381	417863.15	8491.18	212		
2935		325	161	246061.50	31184.02	1910.35		
10358		1810	793	409399.21	30836.62	82.28		
3475		383	201	289777.55	29502.44	3820.10		
42904	2618	8270	5140	1620783.35	91845.52	4429.17		
4781		379	170	173003.50	12881.01	946.70		
		261	157	3135.58				
570		51	16	104215.18	15141.53	708		
16303	12	1109	523	625369.60	109570.38	9281.72		
				14749.80	7266.60	1276		
1240		1060	581	208318.99	60737.89	824.33		
13074		1582	436	175457.49	23120.23	2565.35		
10737	104	526	80	116494.37	21493.24	3091.65		
300				3772	993	2		
				7556				
499		144	38	5567.25	567.16	37		

地　区 Region	占地面积(平方米) Area of School Sites (m^2)			图书(万册) Books & Magazines in Libraries (10,000 volume)		
	合计 Total	其中:绿化用地面积 of Which: Green Areas	其中:运动场地面积 of Which: Sports Areas	合计 Total	当年新增 New Added in Current Year	合计 Total
总　计 Total	**188357322**	**41031564**	**11210157**	**2291.65**	**94.31**	**79693**
北　京 Beijing	12957600	1550381	589669	25		393
天　津 Tianjin	2162304	81700	22000	17.63	0.16	950
河　北 Hebei	4806528	624680	406330	148.37	7.46	6058
山　西 Shanxi	4322833	897794	523612	93.20	0.05	4488
内蒙古 Inner Mongolia	1424758	106800	188366	5.96	0.38	138
辽　宁 Liaoning	4463019	619583	231674	8.90		405
吉　林 Jilin	5695340	1460635	187886			
黑龙江 Heilongjiang	5124598	848825	434691	8.90		128
上　海 Shanghai	5550730	1569175	296149	121.40	1.34	5119
江　苏 Jiangsu	14845061	4331448	1041108	115.90	4	10837
浙　江 Zhejiang	6090927	1388728	370853	11.49	4.50	317
安　徽 Anhui	2185710	424173	149913	68	4.50	3310
福　建 Fujian	9188571	2256187	697801	70.50	5.89	9761
江　西 Jiangxi	6948220	977021	407445	120.26	4	2490
山　东 Shandong	12623488	2971967	967811	144.66		3325
河　南 Henan	5678545	968472	208249	126.20	4.60	6428
湖　北 Hubei	8555863	1730331	413371	64.54	3.36	961
湖　南 Hunan	7454639	1391029	325205	325.02	4.49	3453
广　东 Guangdong	24604805	6306318	1184497	112.65	3.26	3362
广　西 Guangxi	6385490	1558407	287816	110	15.50	1327
海　南 Hainan	1159340	298923	41185			63
重　庆 Chongqing	2767576	572825	87886	16.28	0.30	663
四　川 Sichuan	12787324	2930181	895354	105.07	2.01	8671
贵　州 Guizhou	1167403	434937	62749	43.20		
云　南 Yunnan	5914407	818867	176525	47.91		975
西　藏 Tibet				0.67		
陕　西 Shaanxi	11933297	3625618	919760	346.63	28.52	5867
甘　肃 Gansu	1272278	252347	92252	1.31		180
青　海 Qinghai	33333					
宁　夏 Ningxia	66670			32		
新　疆 Xinjiang	186665	34212			24	

(非学校产权独立使用)(普通高校)
Resources (Not Owned by HEIs)(Regular HEIs)

计算机数(台) No. of Computers		教室(间) Classroom(room)		固定资产值(万元) Fixed Assets (10,000 yuan)				
其中:教学用计算机 of Which: No. of Computers Used for Instruction		合计 Total	其中:网络多媒体教室 of Which: Network Multimedia Classroom	合计 Total	其中:教学、科研仪器设备资产 of Which: Teaching Equipment & Instruments		其中:信息化设备资产值 of Which: Assets of Information Facilities	
小计 Subtotal	其中:平板电脑 of Which: Tablet PC				小计 Subtotal	当年新增 New Added in Current Year	小计 Subtotal	其中:软件 of Which: Software
62536	**143**	**31829**	**14615**	**7257796.21**	**684801.25**	**53851.30**		
301		666	350	291701.27	221756	15202		
842		286	126	112903.21	10340.97	265.06		
5662		968	341	187778.79	29956.01	1038.85		
4359	126	902	516	143732.09	8929.70	2447		
113		163	30	29270.31	65.74	65.74		
256		1567	481	523939.52	2988.02	387		
		295	60	63477.75				
115		575	101	21709.37	3846.77	3240		
2915	1	1162	530	283491.72	26084.45	992.88		
9080	4	5991	3476	684663.17	40283.44	3815.88		
235		2609	1610	134149.34	1210.35			
3005		1232	408	154968.28	7250.36	2488.36		
7933		749	430	396657.29	37391.71	1923.77		
1500		3247	717	415531.31	13461.90	260		
2291		1206	381	417863.15	8491.18	212		
2935		287	155	171138.22	10868.17	1910.35		
835		1561	635	339205.46	12390.09	62.28		
3207		323	166	286976.55	28367.39	3730.10		
2836		4571	2740	1358791.24	20435.78	266.97		
1294		368	159	142998.49	8002.43	643		
		261	157	3135.58				
570		51	16	104215.18	15141.53	708		
6195	12	745	225	570352.99	96915.47	9220.72		
				14749.80	7266.60	1276		
945		1060	581	204014.49	60248.89	824.33		
4977		880	210	137206.33	11280.94	2340.13		
120		3	1	49506.06	1794.20	511.88		
				1106	6	2		
				7556				
15		101	13	5007.25	27.16	17		

地 区 Region	占地面积(平方米) Area of School Sites (m^2)			图书(万册) Books & Magazines in Libraries (10,000 volume)		
	合计 Total	其中:绿化用地面积 of Which: Green Areas	其中:运动场地面积 of Which: Sports Areas	合计 Total	当年新增 New Added in Current Year	合计 Total
总 计 Total	**26045796**	**6248855**	**3368304**	**3368.96**	**70.90**	**271941**
北 京 Beijing	82103	60000	6600	2.20		51
天 津 Tianjin	650464	41400	122734	169.48	8.13	9514
河 北 Hebei	692915	179772	52054	118.47	3.19	9601
山 西 Shanxi	153449	14490	24370	35.98	0.34	3675
内蒙古 Inner Mongolia						
辽 宁 Liaoning	1674046	370884	205325	204.85	3.18	10302
吉 林 Jilin	401256	105274	96089	56	0.30	3947
黑龙江 Heilongjiang	958788	98588	228550	163.47		8050
上 海 Shanghai	128					
江 苏 Jiangsu	4286806	1315503	640903	533.40	23.76	30116
浙 江 Zhejiang	2994611	825905	371706	322.20	13.10	29957
安 徽 Anhui	1750384	232744	101804	95.28		8620
福 建 Fujian						
江 西 Jiangxi	103560	30000	40000			200
山 东 Shandong						
河 南 Henan	1760122	494867	126322	323.94		9456
湖 北 Hubei	2083143	367324	197373	302.43	2.24	12133
湖 南 Hunan	45000	25000		8.20		268
广 东 Guangdong	3615574	1073237	576181	523.53	3.20	51478
广 西 Guangxi	155010	22981	25828	67.25		44603
海 南 Hainan						
重 庆 Chongqing						
四 川 Sichuan	1081560	157926	122686	122.41		13266
贵 州 Guizhou						
云 南 Yunnan	58357	4844	3306	2.85		405
西 藏 Tibet						
陕 西 Shaanxi	1502881	372194	112920	148.80	1.83	10831
甘 肃 Gansu	1866854	444176	301433	159.97	11.58	14548
青 海 Qinghai					369	
宁 夏 Ningxia						
新 疆 Xinjiang	128785	11746	12120	8.25	0.05	551

(非学校产权独立使用)(成人高校)
Resources (Not Owned by HEIs)(Adult HEIs)

计算机数(台) No. of Computers		教室(间) Classroom(room)		固定资产值(万元) Fixed Assets (10,000 yuan)				
其中:教学用计算机 of Which: No. of Computers Used for Instruction		合计 Total	其中:网络多媒体教室 of Which: Network Multimedia Classroom	合计 Total	其中:教学、科研仪器设备资产 of Which: Teaching Equipment & Instruments		其中:信息化设备资产值 of Which: Assets of Information Facilities	
小计 Subtotal	其中:平板电脑 of Which: Tablet PC				小计 Subtotal	当年新增 New Added in Current Year	小计 Subtotal	其中:软件 of Which: Software
171962	**4251**	**19443**	**9874**	**1422065.62**	**350764.51**	**19383.83**		
4				41	6			
8535	35	1960	1193	23239.01	10788.86	755		
8189		1166	818	57295.50	12235.49	968.62		
2758		227	77	14247.25	2958.23	25		
7594	1063	747	354	127164.28	26243.87	1248.91		
2898	11	508	138	17912.04	4099	391		
6507		1350	942	41316.20	9752.95			
21565	240	4570	1345	270106.66	61265.79	6131.59		
23326		1615	1131	184320.56	47300.69	2376.82		
7159		1565	635	71971.39	13383.04			
180	180	46	3	6750	335.60	25		
		38	6	74923.28	20315.85			
9523		249	158	70193.75	18446.53	20		
268		60	35	2801	1135.05	90		
40068	2618	3699	2400	261992.11	71409.74	4162.20		
3487		11	11	30005.01	4878.58	303.70		
10108		364	298	55016.61	12654.91	61		
295				4304.50	489			
8097		702	226	38251.16	11839.29	225.22		
10617	104	523	79	66988.31	19699.04	2579.77		
300				2666	987			
484		43	25	560	540	20		

地 区 Region	占地面积(平方米) Area of School Sites (m^2)			图书(万册) Books & Magazines in Libraries (10,000 volume)		
	合计 Total	其中:绿化用地面积 of Which: Green Areas	其中:运动场地面积 of Which: Sports Areas	合计 Total	当年新增 New Added in Current Year	合计 Total
总 计 Total	**7540177**	**1794857**	**1034781**	**62237.64**	**507.69**	**16985**
北 京 Beijing	2271093	784452	419248	6.13	0.01	1565
天 津 Tianjin						
河 北 Hebei	414158	60730	32919	36.75	0.20	1454
山 西 Shanxi	615676	146597	62310	60023.36	1.01	1225
内蒙古 Inner Mongolia						
辽 宁 Liaoning	71186	5240	8450	3.53		2216
吉 林 Jilin	1031914	7370	10750	11.60	0.10	125
黑龙江 Heilongjiang	11000	370	1500			100
上 海 Shanghai	338543	93513	110357	41.35	2.63	1994
江 苏 Jiangsu						
浙 江 Zhejiang	337356	96385	54964	2.05	0.05	766
安 徽 Anhui	148310	20000	10000	6.70		5
福 建 Fujian						
江 西 Jiangxi	362046	208221	16432	6		115
山 东 Shandong	992404	193040	165673	71.43	0.29	1442
河 南 Henan	164185	23385	26818	2001.43	500.10	848
湖 北 Hubei	103103	20168	19974	1.50		300
湖 南 Hunan	22754	600	300	0.50		10
广 东 Guangdong	301033	42658	43826	8.31	1.10	2234
广 西 Guangxi						
海 南 Hainan						
重 庆 Chongqing	230491	64055	28740	11	0.70	2060
四 川 Sichuan	104341	25275	18054	4	1	163
贵 州 Guizhou						
云 南 Yunnan						
西 藏 Tibet						
陕 西 Shaanxi						
甘 肃 Gansu	20584	2798	4466	2	0.50	363
青 海 Qinghai						
宁 夏 Ningxia						
新 疆 Xinjiang						

(非学校产权独立使用)(民办的其他高等教育机构)
(Not Owned by HEIs)(Other Non-government HEIs)

计算机数(台) No. of Computers		教室(间) Classroom(room)		固定资产值(万元) Fixed Assets (10,000 yuan)				
其中:教学用计算机 of Which: No. of Computers Used for Instruction		合计 Total	其中:网络多媒体教室 of Which: Network Multimedia Classroom	合计 Total	其中:教学、科研仪器设备资产 of Which: Teaching Equipment & Instruments		其中:信息化设备资产值 of Which: Assets of Information Facilities	
小计 Subtotal	其中:平板电脑 of Which: Tablet PC				小计 Subtotal	当年新增 New Added in Current Year	小计 Subtotal	其中:软件 of Which: Software
12404	**97**	**5391**	**1101**	**205045.16**	**28802.12**	**5435.63**		
1112		1254	137	25412.22	1867.35	293.30		
1037	13	112	36	7659.13	1101.92	91.40		
1037		389	33	8588.08	2292.12	175.50		
1515	65	497	2	8404.72	4840.50	3		
114		171	10	840	39	0.50		
78		146	3					
1628	8	701	371	4535.16	2458.13	1089.72		
684		565	25	9706.26	1759.09	369.51		
3		82	33	3883	1.20	1.20		
34		129	4	6342	246			
991		350	79	29519.40	2322.19	83.30		
729		122	41	6892.40	3174.68	23.20		
200		54	15	2391.65	800			
		137	114	840	840			
1191		347	113	1163	781	180		
1588		208	72	10009	1586	105		
103	11	28	13	78161.84	4401.84	3010		
360		99		697.30	291.10	10		

校舍情况(总计)
Condition of School Buidings (Total)

单位:平方米
unit: m^2

地区 Region	学校产权建筑面积 Floor Area of School Building Owned by HEIs				正在施工面积 Floor Area Under Construction	独立使用非学校产权建筑面积 Floor Area of School Building Not Owned by HEIs
	合计 Total	其中:危房 of Which: Dilapidated Buildings	其中:当年新增 of Which: New Added in Current Year	其中:被外单位借用 of Which: Floor Space Hired by Other Schools or Units		
总　计 Total	**768812285**	**1242170**	**29077842**	**527849**	**55544866**	**100332587**
北　京 Beijing	34850708	94293	681725	59879	3070896	2462682
天　津 Tianjin	15360085	203	338362		623100	1215852
河　北 Hebei	33669233	4583	638219		1715959	2441350
山　西 Shanxi	19292586	11086	1889465	13590	2452082	1889198
内蒙古 Inner Mongolia	12843095	17957	603005	6000	684457	668751
辽　宁 Liaoning	27879711	24278	1126006	2048	2708616	3957797
吉　林 Jilin	18937142	1497	442038	1024	1123505	1819567
黑龙江 Heilongjiang	25547588	35036	349267	16405	1850699	1226084
上　海 Shanghai	18993541		400854	42378	1237826	3858885
江　苏 Jiangsu	53334784	85192	1114549	122899	2901619	9731796
浙　江 Zhejiang	27648925	185	1688335	112489	2541240	7062628
安　徽 Anhui	30660357	126819	1624964	2727	1524826	1919887
福　建 Fujian	19470867	12786	1554216		1446278	4932737
江　西 Jiangxi	29328521	1573	1083422	8881	912069	3326088
山　东 Shandong	54510415	61059	930118	25186	2074287	5430074
河　南 Henan	55162199	13130	2567452	6908	3492126	2754013
湖　北 Hubei	46072153	38655	912596	24959	2354136	6110541
湖　南 Hunan	33770496	104435	988978		1226515	3763495
广　东 Guangdong	38121631	14719	773243	10732	1775803	13417962
广　西 Guangxi	18003644	61135	852231	19449	2328245	3368869
海　南 Hainan	3947400	15600	104156		205208	1458076
重　庆 Chongqing	21698031	54672	952459		1515152	1390211
四　川 Sichuan	36498386	70578	2296228	2000	2985213	5073885
贵　州 Guizhou	14008137	8794	1710409	8431	3409871	473116
云　南 Yunnan	14786264	138355	890862		1776935	3286773
西　藏 Tibet	1102509	6602	46127	6265	57421	
陕　西 Shaanxi	35158670	57906	1385799		4254531	5667889
甘　肃 Gansu	12171944	67884	555280		1658193	1442271
青　海 Qinghai	1640042	2309	58896		295589	19461
宁　夏 Ningxia	3130321	43	125273	32349	129650	12491
新　疆 Xinjiang	11212900	110806	393308	3250	1212819	150158

注:不含民办的其他高等教育机构数据。

Note: Data of Non-government HEIs are not included.

校舍情况(普通高校)
Condition of School Buidings (Regular HEIs)

单位:平方米
unit: m^2

地 区 Region	学校产权建筑面积 Floor Area of School Building Owned by HEIs 合计 Total	其中:危房 of Which: Dilapidated Buildings	其中:当年新增 of Which: New Added in Current Year	其中:被外单位借用 of Which: Floor Space Hired by Other Schools or Units	正在施工面积 Floor Area Under Construction	独立使用非学校产权建筑面积 Floor Area of School Building Not Owned by HEIs
总 计 Total	**753806412**	**1184374**	**28819559**	**498713**	**54600804**	**87743134**
北 京 Beijing	33981714	94293	678674	59879	3030896	2453654
天 津 Tianjin	15004703	203	338362		622830	715991
河 北 Hebei	33231656	2149	638219		1561925	2016563
山 西 Shanxi	18539320	11086	1772055	13590	2452082	1876983
内蒙古 Inner Mongolia	12748457	17957	603005	6000	684457	668751
辽 宁 Liaoning	27181687	24278	1121006	2048	2688616	3215990
吉 林 Jilin	18324471		416039	1024	841582	1615124
黑龙江 Heilongjiang	24856971	35036	349267	1690	1850699	741074
上 海 Shanghai	18394730		400854	35407	1234163	3833215
江 苏 Jiangsu	52927054	85192	1114549	122899	2901619	7912667
浙 江 Zhejiang	27293806		1688335	112489	2424720	5468202
安 徽 Anhui	30272656	126819	1624964	2727	1485453	1470280
福 建 Fujian	19348505	12786	1554216		1426654	4932737
江 西 Jiangxi	28774934	1573	1083422	8881	878963	3268653
山 东 Shandong	53602229	61059	930118	25186	1992975	5430074
河 南 Henan	53957525	13130	2541832	6908	3492126	1455213
湖 北 Hubei	45609843	38655	912596	20759	2354136	5296367
湖 南 Hunan	33257821	104435	983203		1146648	3746120
广 东 Guangdong	37683742	14719	773243	10732	1775803	11487208
广 西 Guangxi	17541958	33363	849172	19449	2325186	3235518
海 南 Hainan	3913260	15600	104156		185208	1458076
重 庆 Chongqing	21217170	54672	929715		1493693	1390211
四 川 Sichuan	35578222	70119	2263769	2000	2964813	4543191
贵 州 Guizhou	13712544	8794	1710409	8431	3409871	351836
云 南 Yunnan	14665874	136404	890862		1776935	3118841
西 藏 Tibet	1102509	6602	46127	6265	57421	
陕 西 Shaanxi	34107176	57906	1385799		4254531	5142660
甘 肃 Gansu	12047177	67884	555280		1658193	732369
青 海 Qinghai	1607587	2309	58896		295589	19461
宁 夏 Ningxia	3101450	43	125273	32349	129650	12491
新 疆 Xinjiang	10219661	87308	376142		1203367	133614

校舍情况(成人高校)

Condition of School Buidings (Adult HEIs)

单位:平方米

unit: m^2

地 区 Region	学校产权建筑面积 Floor Area of School Building Owned by HEIs				正在施工面积 Floor Area Under Construction	独立使用非学校产权建筑面积 Floor Area of School Building Not Owned by HEIs
	合计 Total	其中:危房 of Which: Dilapidated Buildings	其中:当年新增 of Which: New Added in Current Year	其中:被外单位借用 of Which: Floor Space Hired by Other Schools or Units		
总 计 Total	**15005873**	**57796**	**258283**	**29136**	**944062**	**12589453**
北 京 Beijing	868994		3051		40000	9028
天 津 Tianjin	355382				270	499861
河 北 Hebei	437577	2434			154034	424787
山 西 Shanxi	753266		117410			12215
内蒙古 Inner Mongolia	94638					
辽 宁 Liaoning	698024		5000		20000	741807
吉 林 Jilin	612671	1497	25999		281923	204443
黑龙江 Heilongjiang	690617			14715		485010
上 海 Shanghai	598811			6971	3663	25670
江 苏 Jiangsu	407730					1819129
浙 江 Zhejiang	355119	185			116520	1594426
安 徽 Anhui	387701				39373	449607
福 建 Fujian	122362				19624	
江 西 Jiangxi	553587				33106	57435
山 东 Shandong	908186				81312	
河 南 Henan	1204674		25620			1298800
湖 北 Hubei	462310			4200		814174
湖 南 Hunan	512675		5775		79867	17375
广 东 Guangdong	437889					1930754
广 西 Guangxi	461686	27772	3059		3059	133351
海 南 Hainan	34140				20000	
重 庆 Chongqing	480861		22744		21459	
四 川 Sichuan	920164	459	32459		20400	530694
贵 州 Guizhou	295593					121280
云 南 Yunnan	120390	1951				167932
西 藏 Tibet						
陕 西 Shaanxi	1051494					525229
甘 肃 Gansu	124767					709902
青 海 Qinghai	32455					
宁 夏 Ningxia	28871					
新 疆 Xinjiang	993239	23498	17166	3250	9452	16544

校舍情况(民办的其他高等教育机构)

Condition of School Buidings (Other Non-government HEIs)

单位:平方米

unit: m^2

地区 Region	学校产权建筑面积 Floor Area of School Building Owned by HEIs				正在施工面积 Floor Area Under Construction	独立使用非学校产权建筑面积 Floor Area of School Building Not Owned by HEIs
	合计 Total	其中:危房 of Which: Dilapidated Buildings	其中:当年新增 of Which: New Added in Current Year	其中:被外单位借用 of Which: Floor Space Hired by Other Schools or Units		
总　计 Total	**2940264**		**173729**	**1000**	**263097**	**4509597**
北　京 Beijing	428047					1433512
天　津 Tianjin						
河　北 Hebei	224182				120416	203652
山　西 Shanxi	279546				6520	166532
内蒙古 Inner Mongolia						
辽　宁 Liaoning	178363					107694
吉　林 Jilin	43524					305327
黑龙江 Heilongjiang	10651					11460
上　海 Shanghai	59391			1000	1000	435154
江　苏 Jiangsu						
浙　江 Zhejiang	166252		750			384522
安　徽 Anhui	214000					44852
福　建 Fujian						
江　西 Jiangxi	311064		31000		38596	190128
山　东 Shandong	502407				61000	498586
河　南 Henan	4154					96906
湖　北 Hubei	147120					113622
湖　南 Hunan	3100					58376
广　东 Guangdong	87379					223437
广　西 Guangxi						
海　南 Hainan						
重　庆 Chongqing	75091					169524
四　川 Sichuan	203129		141979		35565	39612
贵　州 Guizhou						
云　南 Yunnan						
西　藏 Tibet						
陕　西 Shaanxi						
甘　肃 Gansu	2864					26701
青　海 Qinghai						
宁　夏 Ningxia						
新　疆 Xinjiang						

普通高中校数、班数(总计)
Number of Schools and Classes in Regular Senior Secondary Schools (Total)

地 区 Region	学校数(所) Schools				班数(个) Classes			
	合计 Total	完全中学 Combined Secondary Schools	高级中学 Regular High Schools	十二年一贯制学校 12 - year Schools	合计 Total	一年级 Grade 1	二年级 Grade 2	三年级 Grade 3
总 计 Total	**13352**	**5861**	**6591**	**900**	**443170**	**148513**	**146820**	**147837**
北 京 Beijing	291	200	41	50	5897	1904	2000	1993
天 津 Tianjin	193	105	82	6	4078	1277	1364	1437
河 北 Hebei	563	186	352	25	19213	6411	6233	6569
山 西 Shanxi	504	223	245	36	15645	5351	5221	5073
内蒙古 Inner Mongolia	277	114	146	17	9252	3138	3104	3010
辽 宁 Liaoning	416	73	333	10	13428	4477	4482	4469
吉 林 Jilin	243	70	167	6	8406	2798	2759	2849
黑龙江 Heilongjiang	379	104	258	17	10973	3627	3628	3718
上 海 Shanghai	243	92	134	17	4565	1517	1512	1536
江 苏 Jiangsu	578	157	383	38	23586	7439	7838	8309
浙 江 Zhejiang	569	84	448	37	18215	5977	6050	6188
安 徽 Anhui	698	377	262	59	23002	7272	7913	7817
福 建 Fujian	544	418	103	23	13546	4331	4473	4742
江 西 Jiangxi	436	248	138	50	15223	5209	5031	4983
山 东 Shandong	547	98	421	28	30071	10342	10039	9690
河 南 Henan	776	154	563	59	28440	9837	9308	9295
湖 北 Hubei	563	89	438	36	17387	5503	5623	6261
湖 南 Hunan	577	224	310	43	17764	6068	5929	5767
广 东 Guangdong	1015	597	330	88	40925	13618	13675	13632
广 西 Guangxi	453	186	254	13	13401	4706	4351	4344
海 南 Hainan	102	75	11	16	3235	1122	1101	1012
重 庆 Chongqing	261	240	21		11307	3776	3739	3792
四 川 Sichuan	735	546	145	44	25787	8541	8504	8742
贵 州 Guizhou	448	232	189	27	14293	5392	4747	4154
云 南 Yunnan	440	287	135	18	13062	4548	4355	4159
西 藏 Tibet	29	4	23	2	975	345	327	303
陕 西 Shaanxi	511	212	261	38	15726	5138	5123	5465
甘 肃 Gansu	428	217	199	12	11653	3922	3813	3918
青 海 Qinghai	105	46	37	22	2089	715	713	661
宁 夏 Ningxia	62	21	41		2811	941	916	954
新 疆 Xinjiang	366	182	121	63	9215	3271	2949	2995

普通高中校数、班数(城区)

Number of Schools and Classes in Regular Senior Secondary Schools (Urban Area)

地 区 Region	学校数(所) Schools				班数(个) Classes			
	合计 Total	完全中学 Combined Secondary Schools	高级中学 Regular High Schools	十二年一贯制学校 12 - year Schools	合计 Total	一年级 Grade 1	二年级 Grade 2	三年级 Grade 3
总 计 Total	**6348**	**2774**	**3026**	**548**	**211249**	**70749**	**70176**	**70324**
北 京 Beijing	255	178	32	45	5168	1675	1753	1740
天 津 Tianjin	137	93	40	4	2826	890	953	983
河 北 Hebei	239	109	117	13	8087	2710	2626	2751
山 西 Shanxi	246	148	81	17	6832	2340	2294	2198
内蒙古 Inner Mongolia	150	61	77	12	4954	1683	1673	1598
辽 宁 Liaoning	315	65	246	4	9572	3187	3213	3172
吉 林 Jilin	156	43	108	5	5983	2000	1961	2022
黑龙江 Heilongjiang	211	54	145	12	6483	2155	2143	2185
上 海 Shanghai	212	84	111	17	3941	1305	1306	1330
江 苏 Jiangsu	318	89	208	21	12350	3941	4116	4293
浙 江 Zhejiang	290	47	216	27	9684	3200	3233	3251
安 徽 Anhui	224	112	89	23	7597	2478	2571	2548
福 建 Fujian	201	143	45	13	5726	1863	1897	1966
江 西 Jiangxi	143	96	32	15	5053	1721	1689	1643
山 东 Shandong	295	56	221	18	16082	5509	5373	5200
河 南 Henan	334	82	222	30	11347	3967	3730	3650
湖 北 Hubei	318	57	235	26	10061	3222	3263	3576
湖 南 Hunan	210	102	87	21	6640	2250	2205	2185
广 东 Guangdong	594	309	214	71	25054	8408	8334	8312
广 西 Guangxi	163	68	89	6	4981	1699	1644	1638
海 南 Hainan	57	41	4	12	1933	672	646	615
重 庆 Chongqing	121	114	7		5280	1753	1778	1749
四 川 Sichuan	253	175	49	29	10063	3357	3335	3371
贵 州 Guizhou	148	67	68	13	4675	1708	1551	1416
云 南 Yunnan	148	93	44	11	4259	1461	1437	1361
西 藏 Tibet	10	2	6	2	313	103	104	106
陕 西 Shaanxi	231	133	69	29	5616	1854	1861	1901
甘 肃 Gansu	135	60	71	4	3739	1310	1206	1223
青 海 Qinghai	37	13	15	9	600	201	207	192
宁 夏 Ningxia	34	11	23		1610	541	530	539
新 疆 Xinjiang	163	69	55	39	4740	1586	1544	1610

普通高中校数、班数(城乡结合区)
Number of Schools and Classes in Regular Senior Secondary Schools (Urban-rural Transitional Area)

地区 Region	学校数(所) Schools				班数(个) Classes			
	合计 Total	完全中学 Combined Secondary Schools	高级中学 Regular High Schools	十二年一贯制学校 12 - year Schools	合计 Total	一年级 Grade 1	二年级 Grade 2	三年级 Grade 3
总　计 Total	**917**	**333**	**457**	**127**	**32056**	**10924**	**10584**	**10548**
北　京 Beijing	19	8	4	7	318	107	104	107
天　津 Tianjin	9	5	4		190	61	64	65
河　北 Hebei	42	8	29	5	1705	581	532	592
山　西 Shanxi	33	14	18	1	847	307	275	265
内蒙古 Inner Mongolia	7	2	5		233	86	81	66
辽　宁 Liaoning	34	6	28		1295	443	440	412
吉　林 Jilin	13	7	5	1	246	87	81	78
黑龙江 Heilongjiang	21	8	12	1	547	183	185	179
上　海 Shanghai	11	3	5	3	194	66	65	63
江　苏 Jiangsu	36	11	21	4	1587	511	523	553
浙　江 Zhejiang	69	7	53	9	2237	752	738	747
安　徽 Anhui	36	22	11	3	1065	339	350	376
福　建 Fujian	30	20	6	4	819	268	266	285
江　西 Jiangxi	13	7	3	3	461	165	155	141
山　东 Shandong	73	6	60	7	4278	1455	1435	1388
河　南 Henan	55	8	38	9	1890	670	612	608
湖　北 Hubei	40	8	26	6	1315	402	414	499
湖　南 Hunan	38	19	14	5	1211	408	412	391
广　东 Guangdong	156	77	53	26	6102	2073	2033	1996
广　西 Guangxi	26	12	11	3	951	322	311	318
海　南 Hainan	6	4	1	1	143	64	50	29
重　庆 Chongqing	6	5	1		346	114	117	115
四　川 Sichuan	35	18	7	10	1337	457	441	439
贵　州 Guizhou	28	16	8	4	778	314	256	208
云　南 Yunnan	29	18	8	3	891	319	291	281
西　藏 Tibet								
陕　西 Shaanxi	22	4	13	5	516	183	172	161
甘　肃 Gansu	8	4	4		124	39	41	44
青　海 Qinghai	5	2	3		61	23	20	18
宁　夏 Ningxia	3	1	2		132	42	44	46
新　疆 Xinjiang	14	3	4	7	237	83	76	78

普通高中校数、班数(镇区)
Number of Schools and Classes in Regular Senior Secondary Schools (Counties & Towns Area)

地 区 Region	学校数(所) Schools				班数(个) Classes			
	合计 Total	完全中学 Combined Secondary Schools	高级中学 Regular High Schools	十二年一贯制学校 12 - year Schools	合计 Total	一年级 Grade 1	二年级 Grade 2	三年级 Grade 3
总 计 Total	**6296**	**2722**	**3294**	**280**	**216618**	**72567**	**71542**	**72509**
北 京 Beijing	26	16	6	4	555	178	189	188
天 津 Tianjin	49	11	37	1	1131	349	372	410
河 北 Hebei	295	68	219	8	10429	3467	3382	3580
山 西 Shanxi	218	54	148	16	7821	2662	2607	2552
内蒙古 Inner Mongolia	120	48	69	3	4231	1429	1407	1395
辽 宁 Liaoning	93	7	82	4	3653	1226	1200	1227
吉 林 Jilin	81	24	56	1	2364	781	781	802
黑龙江 Heilongjiang	159	45	110	4	4301	1409	1423	1469
上 海 Shanghai	26	6	20		564	188	188	188
江 苏 Jiangsu	255	68	172	15	11110	3457	3680	3973
浙 江 Zhejiang	247	28	212	7	7740	2516	2547	2677
安 徽 Anhui	435	245	159	31	14243	4450	4921	4872
福 建 Fujian	283	222	53	8	6914	2191	2278	2445
江 西 Jiangxi	272	141	103	28	9855	3373	3241	3241
山 东 Shandong	243	39	195	9	13625	4704	4540	4381
河 南 Henan	411	68	316	27	16618	5710	5416	5492
湖 北 Hubei	212	30	174	8	6496	2041	2084	2371
湖 南 Hunan	326	110	197	19	10301	3526	3443	3332
广 东 Guangdong	356	252	96	8	13750	4508	4625	4617
广 西 Guangxi	259	101	152	6	7510	2662	2419	2429
海 南 Hainan	40	32	6	2	1216	419	427	370
重 庆 Chongqing	131	117	14		5672	1892	1849	1931
四 川 Sichuan	454	350	92	12	15180	5007	4989	5184
贵 州 Guizhou	275	146	115	14	9228	3500	3074	2654
云 南 Yunnan	260	174	82	4	8223	2878	2720	2625
西 藏 Tibet	11	1	10		440	157	144	139
陕 西 Shaanxi	255	70	177	8	9378	3051	3016	3311
甘 肃 Gansu	251	125	121	5	7428	2436	2447	2545
青 海 Qinghai	64	30	21	13	1418	489	483	446
宁 夏 Ningxia	26	10	16		1117	370	357	390
新 疆 Xinjiang	163	84	64	15	4107	1541	1293	1273

普通高中校数、班数(镇乡结合区)
Number of Schools and Classes in Regular Senior Secondary Schools (County-town Transitional Area)

地 区 Region	学校数(所) Schools				班数(个) Classes			
	合计 Total	完全中学 Combined Secondary Schools	高级中学 Regular High Schools	十二年一贯制学校 12 - year Schools	合计 Total	一年级 Grade 1	二年级 Grade 2	三年级 Grade 3
总 计 Total	**1592**	**592**	**903**	**97**	**55663**	**18791**	**18376**	**18496**
北 京 Beijing	9	6	1	2	170	54	58	58
天 津 Tianjin	20	2	17	1	482	148	155	179
河 北 Hebei	123	31	86	6	4060	1334	1319	1407
山 西 Shanxi	77	15	53	9	2494	864	822	808
内蒙古 Inner Mongolia	10	3	6	1	384	130	128	126
辽 宁 Liaoning	17	3	14		649	226	211	212
吉 林 Jilin	3	2	1		56	18	19	19
黑龙江 Heilongjiang	14	2	11	1	388	118	133	137
上 海 Shanghai	4	2	2		81	26	28	27
江 苏 Jiangsu	58	13	37	8	2475	798	813	864
浙 江 Zhejiang	85	11	72	2	2613	857	864	892
安 徽 Anhui	105	53	40	12	3119	998	1073	1048
福 建 Fujian	64	52	7	5	1453	454	481	518
江 西 Jiangxi	42	18	17	7	1463	504	477	482
山 东 Shandong	110	16	90	4	6378	2182	2118	2078
河 南 Henan	134	16	112	6	5190	1775	1715	1700
湖 北 Hubei	53	7	43	3	1465	486	469	510
湖 南 Hunan	103	28	65	10	3042	1029	1012	1001
广 东 Guangdong	133	85	45	3	5462	1810	1829	1823
广 西 Guangxi	27	11	15	1	642	240	213	189
海 南 Hainan	12	10	2		318	120	114	84
重 庆 Chongqing	24	21	3		1276	435	407	434
四 川 Sichuan	64	42	19	3	2356	775	764	817
贵 州 Guizhou	69	36	27	6	1839	752	603	484
云 南 Yunnan	84	52	31	1	2929	1012	968	949
西 藏 Tibet	2		2		91	30	35	26
陕 西 Shaanxi	59	17	39	3	2167	725	693	749
甘 肃 Gansu	54	24	30		1733	561	574	598
青 海 Qinghai	11	6	3	2	295	99	101	95
宁 夏 Ningxia	2	1	1		126	42	40	44
新 疆 Xinjiang	20	7	12	1	467	189	140	138

普通高中校数、班数(乡村)
Number of Schools and Classes in Regular Senior Secondary Schools (Rural Area)

地区 Region	学校数(所) Schools				班数(个) Classes			
	合计 Total	完全中学 Combined Secondary Schools	高级中学 Regular High Schools	十二年一贯制学校 12 - year Schools	合计 Total	一年级 Grade 1	二年级 Grade 2	三年级 Grade 3
总　计 Total	**708**	**365**	**271**	**72**	**15303**	**5197**	**5102**	**5004**
北　京 Beijing	10	6	3	1	174	51	58	65
天　津 Tianjin	7	1	5	1	121	38	39	44
河　北 Hebei	29	9	16	4	697	234	225	238
山　西 Shanxi	40	21	16	3	992	349	320	323
内蒙古 Inner Mongolia	7	5		2	67	26	24	17
辽　宁 Liaoning	8	1	5	2	203	64	69	70
吉　林 Jilin	6	3	3		59	17	17	25
黑龙江 Heilongjiang	9	5	3	1	189	63	62	64
上　海 Shanghai	5	2	3		60	24	18	18
江　苏 Jiangsu	5		3	2	126	41	42	43
浙　江 Zhejiang	32	9	20	3	791	261	270	260
安　徽 Anhui	39	20	14	5	1162	344	421	397
福　建 Fujian	60	53	5	2	906	277	298	331
江　西 Jiangxi	21	11	3	7	315	115	101	99
山　东 Shandong	9	3	5	1	364	129	126	109
河　南 Henan	31	4	25	2	475	160	162	153
湖　北 Hubei	33	2	29	2	830	240	276	314
湖　南 Hunan	41	12	26	3	823	292	281	250
广　东 Guangdong	65	36	20	9	2121	702	716	703
广　西 Guangxi	31	17	13	1	910	345	288	277
海　南 Hainan	5	2	1	2	86	31	28	27
重　庆 Chongqing	9	9			355	131	112	112
四　川 Sichuan	28	21	4	3	544	177	180	187
贵　州 Guizhou	25	19	6		390	184	122	84
云　南 Yunnan	32	20	9	3	580	209	198	173
西　藏 Tibet	8	1	7		222	85	79	58
陕　西 Shaanxi	25	9	15	1	732	233	246	253
甘　肃 Gansu	42	32	7	3	486	176	160	150
青　海 Qinghai	4	3	1		71	25	23	23
宁　夏 Ningxia	2		2		84	30	29	25
新　疆 Xinjiang	40	29	2	9	368	144	112	112

普通高中学生数(总计)

Number of Students in Regular Senior Secondary Schools (Total)

单位:人
unit: person

地　区 Region	毕业生数 Graduates	招生数 Entrants	在校生数 Enrolment 合　计 Total	其中:女 of Which: Female	一年级 Grade 1	二年级 Grade 2	三年级 Grade 3	预计毕业生数 Estimated Graduates for Next Year
总　计 Total	**7989789**	**8226961**	**24358817**	**12118900**	**8233790**	**8084933**	**8040094**	**8040094**
北　京 Beijing	58072	59983	187586	96621	60357	63665	63564	63564
天　津 Tianjin	61167	55116	175144	90621	55125	58789	61230	61230
河　北 Hebei	404522	375572	1092815	574005	375625	354327	362863	362863
山　西 Shanxi	286103	288826	848464	435434	288839	285853	273772	273772
内蒙古 Inner Mongolia	161587	164232	494243	255412	164232	167991	162020	162020
辽　宁 Liaoning	231626	222938	681460	352310	222966	226234	232260	232260
吉　林 Jilin	157117	151131	453171	234830	151173	147528	154470	154470
黑龙江 Heilongjiang	206088	193979	589379	307281	193980	195220	200179	200179
上　海 Shanghai	52675	53092	156817	82099	53380	52306	51131	51131
江　苏 Jiangsu	425924	341417	1109899	530825	341589	369904	398406	398406
浙　江 Zhejiang	296105	265198	839755	425533	265337	276586	297832	297832
安　徽 Anhui	416723	380526	1255132	584105	381717	441119	432296	432296
福　建 Fujian	231800	209370	656488	322774	209493	215467	231528	231528
江　西 Jiangxi	240907	310514	876722	372187	310829	289401	276492	276492
山　东 Shandong	509383	588897	1705043	856406	588900	572835	543308	543308
河　南 Henan	631289	661063	1892306	935079	661065	624122	607119	607119
湖　北 Hubei	391211	316471	988159	449170	316553	319321	352285	352285
湖　南 Hunan	316720	373754	1041044	509338	373804	346907	320333	320333
广　东 Guangdong	723659	730784	2204473	1084546	731806	739229	733438	733438
广　西 Guangxi	241922	297665	818878	432602	298440	265359	255079	255079
海　南 Hainan	53651	60171	179047	84980	60188	60738	58121	58121
重　庆 Chongqing	214128	221024	661384	339700	221306	217580	222498	222498
四　川 Sichuan	485487	511492	1516027	772875	511746	497023	507258	507258
贵　州 Guizhou	210409	330212	857077	425058	330244	287005	239828	239828
云　南 Yunnan	209987	267407	737426	392372	267613	246906	222907	222907
西　藏 Tibet	14734	19648	53092	28448	19678	17097	16317	16317
陕　西 Shaanxi	317569	299383	899424	437403	299437	295267	304720	304720
甘　肃 Gansu	216530	218143	666556	318414	218151	221128	227277	227277
青　海 Qinghai	33081	39592	109026	55978	40091	35547	33388	33388
宁　夏 Ningxia	49770	55779	165240	87167	55793	53805	55642	55642
新　疆 Xinjiang	139843	163582	447540	245327	164333	140674	142533	142533

普通高中学生数(城区)

Number of Students in Regular Senior Secondary Schools (Urban Area)

单位:人
unit: person

地　区 Region	毕业生数 Graduates	招生数 Entrants	在校生数 Enrolment					预计毕业生数 Estimated Graduates for Next Year
			合　计 Total	其中:女 of Which: Female	一年级 Grade 1	二年级 Grade 2	三年级 Grade 3	
总　计 Total	**3661366**	**3735274**	**11144953**	**5599740**	**3739333**	**3707881**	**3697739**	**3697739**
北　京 Beijing	50683	52342	162784	83813	52678	55051	55055	55055
天　津 Tianjin	39896	36310	114521	59417	36319	38734	39468	39468
河　北 Hebei	162367	156091	452910	238704	156098	146482	150330	150330
山　西 Shanxi	122540	125528	369360	191094	125538	125053	118769	118769
内蒙古 Inner Mongolia	88419	90270	270828	140862	90270	92023	88535	88535
辽　宁 Liaoning	158243	152483	467340	241655	152502	156384	158454	158454
吉　林 Jilin	109274	107864	323499	167814	107872	105142	110485	110485
黑龙江 Heilongjiang	120013	112633	342831	178686	112633	113147	117051	117051
上　海 Shanghai	44520	45459	134093	69909	45676	44767	43650	43650
江　苏 Jiangsu	207082	173652	559943	274421	173739	187879	198325	198325
浙　江 Zhejiang	152074	141463	442048	224484	141523	146228	154297	154297
安　徽 Anhui	134543	129804	411323	195967	129808	141559	139956	139956
福　建 Fujian	93713	91088	278511	139991	91120	91973	95418	95418
江　西 Jiangxi	78037	100771	288088	123660	100813	95947	91328	91328
山　东 Shandong	267599	306871	897312	455535	306874	301740	288698	288698
河　南 Henan	225026	246984	704960	354009	246986	232796	225178	225178
湖　北 Hubei	216067	179553	555182	254177	179607	179908	195667	195667
湖　南 Hunan	118513	132814	378545	185701	132835	126622	119088	119088
广　东 Guangdong	431550	445892	1333875	655323	446880	445529	441466	441466
广　西 Guangxi	87897	102618	294315	154031	103332	97109	93874	93874
海　南 Hainan	31680	35945	106149	49087	35961	35660	34528	34528
重　庆 Chongqing	95090	97149	293453	154021	97279	98220	97954	97954
四　川 Sichuan	187894	194276	578746	298152	194375	191387	192984	192984
贵　州 Guizhou	70213	98595	265360	135014	98599	88540	78221	78221
云　南 Yunnan	70683	80433	230275	124633	80463	77903	71909	71909
西　藏 Tibet	5199	5696	16670	8903	5715	5220	5735	5735
陕　西 Shaanxi	110478	103264	310113	153687	103276	102104	104733	104733
甘　肃 Gansu	66314	66646	200665	95681	66646	67097	66922	66922
青　海 Qinghai	8963	10429	29840	15301	10818	9941	9081	9081
宁　夏 Ningxia	28787	31858	94210	49491	31870	30993	31347	31347
新　疆 Xinjiang	78009	80493	237204	126517	81228	76743	79233	79233

普通高中学生数(城乡结合区)
Number of Students in Regular Senior Secondary Schools (Urban-rural Transitional Area)

单位:人
unit: person

地　区 Region	毕业生数 Graduates	招生数 Entrants	在校生数 Enrolment					预计毕业生数 Estimated Graduates for Next Year
			合计 Total	其中:女 of Which: Female	一年级 Grade 1	二年级 Grade 2	三年级 Grade 3	
总　计 Total	**559728**	**593986**	**1738362**	**857742**	**594093**	**577471**	**566798**	**566798**
北　京 Beijing	3208	3542	10065	5141	3550	3257	3258	3258
天　津 Tianjin	2994	2538	8374	4621	2538	2849	2987	2987
河　北 Hebei	37255	34428	99647	51890	34428	31330	33889	33889
山　西 Shanxi	14597	16534	46646	23946	16534	15510	14602	14602
内蒙古 Inner Mongolia	4303	4383	11525	6008	4383	4192	2950	2950
辽　宁 Liaoning	20009	20896	64544	32958	20899	22027	21618	21618
吉　林 Jilin	4123	4443	12734	6691	4444	4082	4208	4208
黑龙江 Heilongjiang	9990	9062	27723	14504	9062	9278	9383	9383
上　海 Shanghai	2093	2292	6588	3598	2302	2180	2106	2106
江　苏 Jiangsu	27420	21907	71672	34120	21907	24368	25397	25397
浙　江 Zhejiang	34695	33812	101810	50511	33821	33098	34891	34891
安　徽 Anhui	18343	17370	57912	27167	17372	20010	20530	20530
福　建 Fujian	14266	13139	40374	18990	13143	13181	14050	14050
江　西 Jiangxi	7886	10633	29090	11734	10633	9608	8849	8849
山　东 Shandong	68809	81094	238479	118230	81094	80222	77163	77163
河　南 Henan	38089	42502	120774	60279	42502	39150	39122	39122
湖　北 Hubei	33255	22756	73795	33007	22756	23651	27388	27388
湖　南 Hunan	22928	25067	70356	33825	25067	24018	21271	21271
广　东 Guangdong	102587	111701	328561	157795	111745	110180	106636	106636
广　西 Guangxi	18073	20274	57983	30029	20274	18885	18824	18824
海　南 Hainan	1025	4010	8696	3535	4010	3031	1655	1655
重　庆 Chongqing	6733	6817	19997	10090	6820	6674	6503	6503
四　川 Sichuan	20493	25519	72954	37635	25519	24045	23390	23390
贵　州 Guizhou	9853	19688	46755	24220	19688	15345	11722	11722
云　南 Yunnan	16805	19613	53836	28375	19628	18073	16135	16135
西　藏 Tibet								
陕　西 Shaanxi	9984	10029	28843	14280	10037	9589	9217	9217
甘　肃 Gansu	2147	2112	6457	3122	2112	2099	2246	2246
青　海 Qinghai	751	1194	2975	1568	1194	1000	781	781
宁　夏 Ningxia	2476	2444	7336	3910	2444	2496	2396	2396
新　疆 Xinjiang	4538	4187	11861	5963	4187	4043	3631	3631

普通高中学生数(镇区)

Number of Students in Regular Senior Secondary Schools (Counties & Towns Area)

单位:人
unit: person

地 区 Region	毕业生数 Graduates	招生数 Entrants	在校生数 Enrolment					预计毕业生数 Estimated Graduates for Next Year
			合 计 Total	其中:女 of Which: Female	一年级 Grade 1	二年级 Grade 2	三年级 Grade 3	
总 计 Total	**4068002**	**4210455**	**12398955**	**6120642**	**4213158**	**4105850**	**4079947**	**4079947**
北 京 Beijing	5767	6084	19595	10270	6102	6876	6617	6617
天 津 Tianjin	19224	17109	54842	28197	17109	18148	19585	19585
河 北 Hebei	227899	205658	598612	313653	205704	194206	198702	198702
山 西 Shanxi	145831	143750	426165	218689	143753	144344	138068	138068
内蒙古 Inner Mongolia	72350	72822	220457	113188	72822	74920	72715	72715
辽 宁 Liaoning	69824	67310	203887	105651	67319	66320	70248	70248
吉 林 Jilin	47137	42493	127339	65907	42527	41796	43016	43016
黑龙江 Heilongjiang	82196	77732	236283	123523	77733	78771	79779	79779
上 海 Shanghai	7437	6850	20644	11099	6919	6906	6819	6819
江 苏 Jiangsu	216515	165835	543488	253282	165915	179807	197766	197766
浙 江 Zhejiang	131314	112182	361367	183001	112257	117921	131189	131189
安 徽 Anhui	262366	232932	782224	358663	234117	277151	270956	270956
福 建 Fujian	121610	105578	336222	164262	105667	109976	120579	120579
江 西 Jiangxi	158888	203151	571900	242803	203424	188298	180178	180178
山 东 Shandong	236621	275243	788461	391543	275243	264473	248745	248745
河 南 Henan	396705	403622	1158375	567055	403622	381645	373108	373108
湖 北 Hubei	157143	123402	386923	175250	123430	124195	139298	139298
湖 南 Hunan	185120	223101	615418	301261	223130	204518	187770	187770
广 东 Guangdong	255858	247931	758265	372983	247965	255429	254871	254871
广 西 Guangxi	139652	176559	472228	251881	176620	151049	144559	144559
海 南 Hainan	20476	22619	68253	33681	22620	23617	22016	22016
重 庆 Chongqing	112249	116309	347185	175348	116455	112869	117861	117861
四 川 Sichuan	288130	307581	908463	459651	307730	296000	304733	304733
贵 州 Guizhou	136456	220770	569898	279299	220798	191687	157413	157413
云 南 Yunnan	130954	174984	475323	250233	175140	158091	142092	142092
西 藏 Tibet	6675	8778	23780	12754	8789	7835	7156	7156
陕 西 Shaanxi	192132	182393	548457	264797	182435	179148	186874	186874
甘 肃 Gansu	141154	141470	438355	209389	141478	144678	152199	152199
青 海 Qinghai	23001	27690	75446	38695	27800	24406	23240	23240
宁 夏 Ningxia	19738	22115	66059	35046	22117	21093	22849	22849
新 疆 Xinjiang	57580	76402	195041	109588	76418	59677	58946	58946

普通高中学生数(镇乡结合区)
Number of Students in Regular Senior Secondary Schools (County-town Transitional Area)

单位:人
unit: person

地 区 Region	毕业生数 Graduates	招生数 Entrants	在校生数 Enrolment					预计毕业生数 Estimated Graduates for Next Year
			合 计 Total	其中:女 of Which: Female	一年级 Grade 1	二年级 Grade 2	三年级 Grade 3	
总 计 Total	**1033340**	**1076048**	**3154717**	**1557127**	**1077586**	**1044035**	**1033096**	**1033096**
北 京 Beijing	1538	1613	5322	2715	1620	1827	1875	1875
天 津 Tianjin	8150	7493	23704	12326	7493	7726	8485	8485
河 北 Hebei	91976	78440	230562	121438	78469	73514	78579	78579
山 西 Shanxi	42809	44375	130153	67010	44378	43338	42437	42437
内蒙古 Inner Mongolia	6316	6719	20609	10136	6719	7373	6517	6517
辽 宁 Liaoning	12230	12796	36994	19557	12796	11961	12237	12237
吉 林 Jilin	1256	777	2534	1313	777	848	909	909
黑龙江 Heilongjiang	8220	6666	21189	11305	6667	7000	7522	7522
上 海 Shanghai	1000	996	2978	1498	998	1013	967	967
江 苏 Jiangsu	47472	38257	122282	55399	38282	40594	43406	43406
浙 江 Zhejiang	44017	38069	121828	61561	38104	40542	43182	43182
安 徽 Anhui	54619	48458	163325	74646	49508	58050	55767	55767
福 建 Fujian	26987	22052	71280	33694	22063	23379	25838	25838
江 西 Jiangxi	21224	29783	82835	34254	29812	26932	26091	26091
山 东 Shandong	110808	126229	365203	182174	126229	122150	116824	116824
河 南 Henan	120725	120143	344912	169545	120143	114626	110143	110143
湖 北 Hubei	33705	30589	88532	41221	30596	27976	29960	29960
湖 南 Hunan	55478	65813	183854	89789	65831	60819	57204	57204
广 东 Guangdong	99998	99950	301256	146496	99954	101445	99857	99857
广 西 Guangxi	10287	13900	36836	19718	13902	12236	10698	10698
海 南 Hainan	4649	6101	17926	8619	6101	6456	5369	5369
重 庆 Chongqing	25619	28215	81832	42015	28336	25997	27499	27499
四 川 Sichuan	45082	46521	139430	72397	46554	44210	48666	48666
贵 州 Guizhou	24521	46291	110649	53987	46295	36350	28004	28004
云 南 Yunnan	46137	59943	166232	86519	60027	54960	51245	51245
西 藏 Tibet	1234	1823	5486	2816	1823	2051	1612	1612
陕 西 Shaanxi	42846	42747	126865	60144	42786	41983	42096	42096
甘 肃 Gansu	30549	33353	103439	48894	33355	33773	36311	36311
青 海 Qinghai	4153	5412	15249	7916	5444	5332	4473	4473
宁 夏 Ningxia	2609	2777	7937	4401	2777	2632	2528	2528
新 疆 Xinjiang	7126	9747	23484	13624	9747	6942	6795	6795

普通高中学生数(乡村)
Number of Students in Regular Senior Secondary Schools (Rural Area)

单位:人
unit: person

地区 Region	毕业生数 Graduates	招生数 Entrants	在校生数 Enrolment 合计 Total	其中:女 of Which: Female	一年级 Grade 1	二年级 Grade 2	三年级 Grade 3	预计毕业生数 Estimated Graduates for Next Year
总　计 Total	**260421**	**281232**	**814909**	**398518**	**281299**	**271202**	**262408**	**262408**
北　京 Beijing	1622	1557	5207	2538	1577	1738	1892	1892
天　津 Tianjin	2047	1697	5781	3007	1697	1907	2177	2177
河　北 Hebei	14256	13823	41293	21648	13823	13639	13831	13831
山　西 Shanxi	17732	19548	52939	25651	19548	16456	16935	16935
内蒙古 Inner Mongolia	818	1140	2958	1362	1140	1048	770	770
辽　宁 Liaoning	3559	3145	10233	5004	3145	3530	3558	3558
吉　林 Jilin	706	774	2333	1109	774	590	969	969
黑龙江 Heilongjiang	3879	3614	10265	5072	3614	3302	3349	3349
上　海 Shanghai	718	783	2080	1091	785	633	662	662
江　苏 Jiangsu	2327	1930	6468	3122	1935	2218	2315	2315
浙　江 Zhejiang	12717	11553	36340	18048	11557	12437	12346	12346
安　徽 Anhui	19814	17790	61585	29475	17792	22409	21384	21384
福　建 Fujian	16477	12704	41755	18521	12706	13518	15531	15531
江　西 Jiangxi	3982	6592	16734	5724	6592	5156	4986	4986
山　东 Shandong	5163	6783	19270	9328	6783	6622	5865	5865
河　南 Henan	9558	10457	28971	14015	10457	9681	8833	8833
湖　北 Hubei	18001	13516	46054	19743	13516	15218	17320	17320
湖　南 Hunan	13087	17839	47081	22376	17839	15767	13475	13475
广　东 Guangdong	36251	36961	112333	56240	36961	38271	37101	37101
广　西 Guangxi	14373	18488	52335	26690	18488	17201	16646	16646
海　南 Hainan	1495	1607	4645	2212	1607	1461	1577	1577
重　庆 Chongqing	6789	7566	20746	10331	7572	6491	6683	6683
四　川 Sichuan	9463	9635	28818	15072	9641	9636	9541	9541
贵　州 Guizhou	3740	10847	21819	10745	10847	6778	4194	4194
云　南 Yunnan	8350	11990	31828	17506	12010	10912	8906	8906
西　藏 Tibet	2860	5174	12642	6791	5174	4042	3426	3426
陕　西 Shaanxi	14959	13726	40854	18919	13726	14015	13113	13113
甘　肃 Gansu	9062	10027	27536	13344	10027	9353	8156	8156
青　海 Qinghai	1117	1473	3740	1982	1473	1200	1067	1067
宁　夏 Ningxia	1245	1806	4971	2630	1806	1719	1446	1446
新　疆 Xinjiang	4254	6687	15295	9222	6687	4254	4354	4354

普通高中女学生数

Number of Female Students in Regular Senior Secondary Schools

单位：人
unit: person

地 区 Region	毕业生数 Graduates	招生数 Entrants	在校生数 Enrolment 合计 Total	一年级 Grade 1	二年级 Grade 2	三年级 Grade 3	预计毕业生数 Estimated Graduates for Next Year
总 计 Total	**3946201**	**4086357**	**12118900**	**4089303**	**4028315**	**4001282**	**4001282**
北 京 Beijing	31277	30904	96621	31078	32542	33001	33001
天 津 Tianjin	32194	28268	90621	28269	30303	32049	32049
河 北 Hebei	213609	196765	574005	196788	186601	190616	190616
山 西 Shanxi	146103	148399	435434	148404	146682	140348	140348
内蒙古 Inner Mongolia	83293	84704	255412	84704	86372	84336	84336
辽 宁 Liaoning	120374	115334	352310	115342	116418	120550	120550
吉 林 Jilin	81223	77584	234830	77601	77111	80118	80118
黑龙江 Heilongjiang	107164	101043	307281	101043	102595	103643	103643
上 海 Shanghai	27449	27705	82099	27797	27311	26991	26991
江 苏 Jiangsu	201132	163562	530825	163641	177480	189704	189704
浙 江 Zhejiang	150522	134499	425533	134543	140002	150988	150988
安 徽 Anhui	187379	177235	584105	177747	206325	200033	200033
福 建 Fujian	114123	103504	322774	103535	105939	113300	113300
江 西 Jiangxi	100448	131311	372187	131366	123114	117707	117707
山 东 Shandong	250936	296681	856406	296681	288203	271522	271522
河 南 Henan	305769	327434	935079	327434	309416	298229	298229
湖 北 Hubei	176835	144821	449170	144856	145798	158516	158516
湖 南 Hunan	158048	178952	509338	178960	170163	160215	160215
广 东 Guangdong	354676	356237	1084546	356856	364861	362829	362829
广 西 Guangxi	128210	157329	432602	157632	139968	135002	135002
海 南 Hainan	24647	28899	84980	28904	28571	27505	27505
重 庆 Chongqing	109820	113105	339700	113221	111872	114607	114607
四 川 Sichuan	245984	258877	772875	258967	254538	259370	259370
贵 州 Guizhou	102103	163607	425058	163622	142704	118732	118732
云 南 Yunnan	110259	140638	392372	140701	131670	120001	120001
西 藏 Tibet	8085	10554	28448	10561	9254	8633	8633
陕 西 Shaanxi	154861	145458	437403	145480	142748	149175	149175
甘 肃 Gansu	100091	104670	318414	104670	105747	107997	107997
青 海 Qinghai	16817	20001	55978	20216	18564	17198	17198
宁 夏 Ningxia	25588	29435	87167	29441	28475	29251	29251
新 疆 Xinjiang	77182	88842	245327	89243	76968	79116	79116

普通中学教职工数(总计)
Number of Educational Personnel in General Secondary Schools (Total)

单位:人
unit: person

地 区 Region	教职工数 Educational Personnel						代课教师 Substitute Teachers	兼任教师 Part-time Teachers
	合计 Total	专任教师 Full-time Teachers	行政人员 Adm. Personnel	教辅人员 Supporting Staff	工勤人员 Workers	校办企业职工 Employees in School-run Factories & Farms		
总 计 Total	**6402356**	**5597997**	**231675**	**270626**	**298012**	**4046**	**81802**	**20900**
北 京 Beijing	80511	58963	8730	8652	4056	110		1062
天 津 Tianjin	53120	43163	4323	3893	1707	34	289	724
河 北 Hebei	306697	262271	12315	18520	13304	287	7949	500
山 西 Shanxi	222483	191005	6729	9688	14220	841	13061	1387
内蒙古 Inner Mongolia	131991	104838	7540	10975	8578	60	3175	211
辽 宁 Liaoning	205009	172255	22258	5056	5408	32	330	22
吉 林 Jilin	133273	106471	9724	12461	4509	108	1209	246
黑龙江 Heilongjiang	184400	155482	10112	9287	9474	45	1316	449
上 海 Shanghai	76598	61055	5358	5877	4234	74	631	492
江 苏 Jiangsu	344331	297685	8899	19302	18157	288	1247	271
浙 江 Zhejiang	229656	201078	6262	10113	12075	128		1382
安 徽 Anhui	284131	250093	8551	7835	17582	70	4522	877
福 建 Fujian	175034	154832	5858	7103	7093	148	1263	205
江 西 Jiangxi	203903	187006	3388	4104	9253	152	2065	452
山 东 Shandong	466088	408407	12886	28078	16566	151	2480	478
河 南 Henan	459767	408312	14913	14541	21916	85	13610	832
湖 北 Hubei	254716	218569	7834	13900	14027	386	5221	285
湖 南 Hunan	301044	266555	9799	11820	12786	84	2713	980
广 东 Guangdong	539181	478919	19319	16095	24362	486	3234	354
广 西 Guangxi	196577	169750	5770	9355	11687	15	1170	1224
海 南 Hainan	50220	42754	1286	1365	4689	126	472	769
重 庆 Chongqing	133838	120052	4414	3861	5436	75	577	692
四 川 Sichuan	386393	351145	8593	8508	18124	23	4715	270
贵 州 Guizhou	189727	173664	5141	3141	7725	56	202	5085
云 南 Yunnan	193206	176051	2898	4252	9961	44	152	764
西 藏 Tibet	13625	13086	136	43	360		112	1
陕 西 Shaanxi	206168	178554	10556	9443	7568	47	4159	160
甘 肃 Gansu	148159	136856	3266	4186	3826	25	1305	491
青 海 Qinghai	30396	28556	374	571	865	30	1460	58
宁 夏 Ningxia	33686	30990	513	1132	1049	2	595	86
新 疆 Xinjiang	168428	149580	3930	7469	7415	34	2568	91

普通中学教职工数(城区)
Number of Educational Personnel in General Secondary Schools (Urban Area)

单位:人
unit: person

地区 Region	教职工数 Educational Personnel						代课教师 Substitute Teachers	兼任教师 Part-time Teachers
	合计 Total	专任教师 Full-time Teachers	行政人员 Adm. Personnel	教辅人员 Supporting Staff	工勤人员 Workers	校办企业职工 Employees in School-run Factories & Farms		
总 计 Total	**2327960**	**1993435**	**105457**	**112720**	**114451**	**1897**	**33203**	**8384**
北 京 Beijing	63303	46914	6931	6315	3033	110		1034
天 津 Tianjin	33528	26629	2928	2714	1230	27	155	470
河 北 Hebei	97510	83022	4035	5707	4560	186	2274	137
山 西 Shanxi	75395	63252	3346	3538	5134	125	4611	820
内蒙古 Inner Mongolia	53557	43095	4415	3710	2322	15	1962	183
辽 宁 Liaoning	107417	90501	11622	2459	2816	19	116	15
吉 林 Jilin	59315	47943	4022	5135	2152	63	751	135
黑龙江 Heilongjiang	79490	67597	4577	4086	3222	8	703	289
上 海 Shanghai	61844	49154	4235	5062	3325	68	542	422
江 苏 Jiangsu	157827	137666	4500	8371	7202	88	884	67
浙 江 Zhejiang	109228	94270	3123	4864	6876	95		813
安 徽 Anhui	69502	60639	2246	2214	4388	15	2099	440
福 建 Fujian	60160	52447	2193	2395	3075	50	911	50
江 西 Jiangxi	48553	44507	1029	961	2010	46	529	148
山 东 Shandong	184951	160730	5818	11898	6462	43	971	293
河 南 Henan	130036	112909	6160	5084	5838	45	4213	318
湖 北 Hubei	105801	90230	3926	5771	5607	267	2441	185
湖 南 Hunan	73827	63379	2659	3872	3900	17	1127	284
广 东 Guangdong	292694	253695	10531	11544	16566	358	3046	206
广 西 Guangxi	46918	40432	1516	2252	2715	3	631	393
海 南 Hainan	20672	16919	765	680	2235	73	340	247
重 庆 Chongqing	47626	42343	1619	1502	2126	36	250	606
四 川 Sichuan	101356	88505	2963	3512	6371	5	1267	125
贵 州 Guizhou	41188	36616	1513	810	2197	52	163	387
云 南 Yunnan	38939	34467	1076	1235	2125	36	6	44
西 藏 Tibet	2727	2541	70	12	104		102	
陕 西 Shaanxi	58806	48894	4530	2742	2616	24	1274	110
甘 肃 Gansu	32641	28853	1295	1183	1296	14	72	99
青 海 Qinghai	6587	6155	100	110	222		232	2
宁 夏 Ningxia	13991	12898	229	428	435	1	279	9
新 疆 Xinjiang	52571	46233	1485	2554	2291	8	1252	53

普通中学教职工数(城乡结合区)
Number of Educational Personnel in General Secondary Schools (Urban – rural Transitional Area)

单位:人
unit: person

地 区 Region	教职工数 Educational Personnel						代课教师 Substitute Teachers	兼任教师 Part-time Teachers
	合计 Total	专任教师 Full-time Teachers	行政人员 Adm. Personnel	教辅人员 Supporting Staff	工勤人员 Workers	校办企业职工 Employees in School-run Factories & Farms		
总 计 Total	**394094**	**336734**	**15366**	**17157**	**24547**	**290**	**4524**	**1387**
北 京 Beijing	5509	3674	603	753	479			21
天 津 Tianjin	2382	1955	173	190	63	1		
河 北 Hebei	22243	18927	752	1262	1293	9	336	19
山 西 Shanxi	8242	7090	289	411	442	10	954	59
内蒙古 Inner Mongolia	1998	1650	130	122	96		24	
辽 宁 Liaoning	11804	9990	1310	163	336	5	8	5
吉 林 Jilin	3498	2765	319	255	159		40	
黑龙江 Heilongjiang	8264	6865	499	425	475		16	
上 海 Shanghai	3921	3298	208	239	174	2	42	
江 苏 Jiangsu	20334	17633	546	1145	979	31	52	1
浙 江 Zhejiang	25200	20887	771	1016	2475	51		344
安 徽 Anhui	10222	8629	373	300	916	4	321	103
福 建 Fujian	10530	8513	428	461	1107	21	121	1
江 西 Jiangxi	6131	5540	141	177	273		14	15
山 东 Shandong	46980	40943	1367	3010	1658	2	293	114
河 南 Henan	23449	20717	860	607	1237	28	571	41
湖 北 Hubei	14394	12133	425	829	1001	6	195	1
湖 南 Hunan	16029	13588	575	795	1071		151	35
广 东 Guangdong	89850	77237	3398	3006	6100	109	794	31
广 西 Guangxi	8559	7511	254	360	434		83	17
海 南 Hainan	1657	1355	18	50	234		3	64
重 庆 Chongqing	3349	2860	140	60	289		8	347
四 川 Sichuan	15970	13255	518	676	1519	2	171	20
贵 州 Guizhou	7519	6771	233	79	430	6	66	80
云 南 Yunnan	7508	6676	237	136	458	1	4	17
西 藏 Tibet								
陕 西 Shaanxi	7712	6450	567	390	303	2	89	22
甘 肃 Gansu	2703	2474	61	81	87		36	
青 海 Qinghai	865	809	13	7	36		32	
宁 夏 Ningxia	1791	1725	18	11	37			
新 疆 Xinjiang	5481	4814	140	141	386		100	30

普通中学教职工数(镇区)

Number of Educational Personnel in General Secondary Schools (Counties & Towns Area)

单位:人

unit: person

地 区 Region	教职工数 Educational Personnel						代课教师 Substitute Teachers	兼任教师 Part-time Teachers
	合计 Total	专任教师 Full-time Teachers	行政人员 Adm. Personnel	教辅人员 Supporting Staff	工勤人员 Workers	校办企业职工 Employees in School-run Factories & Farms		
总 计 Total	**3052946**	**2680712**	**93677**	**131273**	**145500**	**1784**	**34789**	**8120**
北 京 Beijing	11998	8410	1126	1771	691			9
天 津 Tianjin	14536	12277	966	923	366	4	10	252
河 北 Hebei	161543	137142	6092	10992	7232	85	3682	246
山 西 Shanxi	106368	92404	2298	4716	6289	661	5503	432
内蒙古 Inner Mongolia	68260	53616	2692	6433	5486	33	1091	19
辽 宁 Liaoning	74818	62417	8011	2174	2204	12	186	1
吉 林 Jilin	47568	37299	3487	4966	1789	27	314	37
黑龙江 Heilongjiang	75967	62764	4008	4000	5179	16	414	119
上 海 Shanghai	12675	10212	973	705	779	6	80	63
江 苏 Jiangsu	171790	147438	3982	10165	10006	199	335	203
浙 江 Zhejiang	101229	89722	2609	4490	4379	29		349
安 徽 Anhui	152439	132513	4634	4524	10713	55	1820	345
福 建 Fujian	81151	72104	2447	3574	2930	96	208	80
江 西 Jiangxi	113957	103660	1808	2800	5590	99	1045	204
山 东 Shandong	233094	205036	5950	13458	8542	108	1332	170
河 南 Henan	238207	210264	6605	8122	13216		7959	413
湖 北 Hubei	110983	95392	2784	6142	6591	74	1965	61
湖 南 Hunan	151996	133952	4610	6645	6729	60	893	652
广 东 Guangdong	196020	180069	6527	3856	5521	47	143	99
广 西 Guangxi	117280	101114	3130	5905	7121	10	450	549
海 南 Hainan	26469	23123	463	643	2187	53	72	506
重 庆 Chongqing	73411	66115	2336	2146	2776	38	244	21
四 川 Sichuan	203974	186532	3939	4496	8989	18	1789	121
贵 州 Guizhou	100711	92251	2430	1988	4038	4	25	2288
云 南 Yunnan	100646	91449	1214	2534	5446	3	74	446
西 藏 Tibet	8262	8012	49	17	184		10	1
陕 西 Shaanxi	127314	111844	5089	6060	4298	23	2429	36
甘 肃 Gansu	69954	64181	1397	2488	1879	9	600	281
青 海 Qinghai	17266	16086	246	407	526	1	903	56
宁 夏 Ningxia	14446	13032	249	652	512	1	224	44
新 疆 Xinjiang	68614	60282	1526	3481	3312	13	989	17

普通中学教职工数(镇乡结合区)

Number of Educational Personnel in General Secondary Schools (County-town Transitional Area)

单位:人

unit: person

地区 Region	教职工数 Educational Personnel						代课教师 Substitute Teachers	兼任教师 Part-time Teachers
	合计 Total	专任教师 Full-time Teachers	行政人员 Adm. Personnel	教辅人员 Supporting Staff	工勤人员 Workers	校办企业职工 Employees in School-run Factories & Farms		
总计 Total	**779219**	**682838**	**23882**	**32837**	**38739**	**923**	**9751**	**2100**
北京 Beijing	3503	2411	477	441	174			9
天津 Tianjin	5433	4602	385	318	128		4	3
河北 Hebei	68218	57913	2726	4208	3369	2	1532	28
山西 Shanxi	31059	26024	718	1517	2298	502	2041	166
内蒙古 Inner Mongolia	6096	4738	229	625	504		246	3
辽宁 Liaoning	10999	9240	1116	336	303	4	163	
吉林 Jilin	4092	3329	287	325	151		3	1
黑龙江 Heilongjiang	6497	5651	290	353	203		52	5
上海 Shanghai	3020	2467	168	161	220	4	19	4
江苏 Jiangsu	39800	34260	969	2326	2199	46	126	66
浙江 Zhejiang	33354	29846	827	1370	1293	18		161
安徽 Anhui	36575	30657	1325	1129	3427	37	483	106
福建 Fujian	18678	16479	669	732	741	57	75	34
江西 Jiangxi	21422	18845	377	558	1565	77	169	84
山东 Shandong	94698	83148	2326	5625	3521	78	343	120
河南 Henan	79612	69704	2273	3005	4630		2316	94
湖北 Hubei	25326	21518	685	1319	1762	42	606	13
湖南 Hunan	49781	44402	1448	1687	2234	10	334	336
广东 Guangdong	63449	58020	2326	1274	1813	16	68	27
广西 Guangxi	18090	15890	496	747	957		48	57
海南 Hainan	4233	3538	85	97	513		20	174
重庆 Chongqing	14241	12947	388	430	475	1	61	2
四川 Sichuan	34609	30967	946	913	1772	11	407	53
贵州 Guizhou	21701	19770	501	300	1130		8	336
云南 Yunnan	28170	25391	313	843	1623		7	197
西藏 Tibet	1036	1003	9	4	20			
陕西 Shaanxi	26402	23221	1084	1152	931	14	369	1
甘肃 Gansu	14895	13720	245	529	397	4	68	12
青海 Qinghai	3607	3522	20	42	23		142	5
宁夏 Ningxia	2373	2191	32	91	59		4	
新疆 Xinjiang	8250	7424	142	380	304		37	3

普通中学教职工数(乡村)

Number of Educational Personnel in General Secondary Schools (Rural Area)

单位：人
unit: person

地区 Region	教职工数 Educational Personnel						代课教师 Substitute Teachers	兼任教师 Part-time Teachers
	合计 Total	专任教师 Full-time Teachers	行政人员 Adm. Personnel	教辅人员 Supporting Staff	工勤人员 Workers	校办企业职工 Employees in School-run Factories & Farms		
总　计 Total	**1021450**	**923850**	**32541**	**26633**	**38061**	**365**	**13810**	**4396**
北　京 Beijing	5210	3639	673	566	332			19
天　津 Tianjin	5056	4257	429	256	111	3	124	2
河　北 Hebei	47644	42107	2188	1821	1512	16	1993	117
山　西 Shanxi	40720	35349	1085	1434	2797	55	2947	135
内蒙古 Inner Mongolia	10174	8127	433	832	770	12	122	9
辽　宁 Liaoning	22774	19337	2625	423	388	1	28	6
吉　林 Jilin	26390	21229	2215	2360	568	18	144	74
黑龙江 Heilongjiang	28943	25121	1527	1201	1073	21	199	41
上　海 Shanghai	2079	1689	150	110	130		9	7
江　苏 Jiangsu	14714	12581	417	766	949	1	28	1
浙　江 Zhejiang	19199	17086	530	759	820	4		220
安　徽 Anhui	62190	56941	1671	1097	2481		603	92
福　建 Fujian	33723	30281	1218	1134	1088	2	144	75
江　西 Jiangxi	41393	38839	551	343	1653	7	491	100
山　东 Shandong	48043	42641	1118	2722	1562		177	15
河　南 Henan	91524	85139	2148	1335	2862	40	1438	101
湖　北 Hubei	37932	32947	1124	1987	1829	45	815	39
湖　南 Hunan	75221	69224	2530	1303	2157	7	693	44
广　东 Guangdong	50467	45155	2261	695	2275	81	45	49
广　西 Guangxi	32379	28204	1124	1198	1851	2	89	282
海　南 Hainan	3079	2712	58	42	267		60	16
重　庆 Chongqing	12801	11594	459	213	534	1	83	65
四　川 Sichuan	81063	76108	1691	500	2764		1659	24
贵　州 Guizhou	47828	44797	1198	343	1490		14	2410
云　南 Yunnan	53621	50135	608	483	2390	5	72	274
西　藏 Tibet	2636	2533	17	14	72			
陕　西 Shaanxi	20048	17816	937	641	654		456	14
甘　肃 Gansu	45564	43822	574	515	651	2	633	111
青　海 Qinghai	6543	6315	28	54	117	29	325	
宁　夏 Ningxia	5249	5060	35	52	102		92	33
新　疆 Xinjiang	47243	43065	919	1434	1812	13	327	21

普通中学女教职工数

Number of Female Educational Personnel in General Secondary Schools

单位：人

unit: person

地区 Region	教职工数 Educational Personnel						代课教师 Substitute Teachers	兼任教师 Part-time Teachers
	合计 Total	专任教师 Full-time Teachers	行政人员 Adm. Personnel	教辅人员 Supporting Staff	工勤人员 Workers	校办企业职工 Employees in School-run Factories & Farms		
总　计 Total	**3229805**	**2933435**	**56442**	**127010**	**111368**	**1550**	**50189**	**10606**
北　京 Beijing	54396	43677	4375	5100	1205	39		761
天　津 Tianjin	33223	29232	1553	2059	370	9	204	484
河　北 Hebei	188549	171849	2548	9336	4703	113	5730	229
山　西 Shanxi	134243	121108	1800	4866	6150	319	8536	793
内蒙古 Inner Mongolia	74312	64675	2232	5137	2240	28	2075	92
辽　宁 Liaoning	125617	114135	7486	2981	1011	4	246	16
吉　林 Jilin	78542	68793	2587	5814	1327	21	808	149
黑龙江 Heilongjiang	109602	98402	3285	4391	3513	11	897	224
上　海 Shanghai	51186	43338	2720	3860	1235	33	343	241
江　苏 Jiangsu	163378	148422	1508	7281	6069	98	749	118
浙　江 Zhejiang	124816	112135	1457	5044	6132	48		787
安　徽 Anhui	108224	95943	1338	3390	7520	33	2194	267
福　建 Fujian	78500	71026	1219	3348	2856	51	832	56
江　西 Jiangxi	82199	75472	616	1907	4149	55	1281	178
山　东 Shandong	225226	208506	2293	10406	3983	38	1239	192
河　南 Henan	242111	223852	3355	6749	8113	42	8251	333
湖　北 Hubei	100944	89371	1433	5104	4845	191	2539	108
湖　南 Hunan	131902	121230	1084	5194	4351	43	1707	412
广　东 Guangdong	291825	266976	3698	9647	11289	215	1657	127
广　西 Guangxi	95732	85231	1045	4332	5117	7	848	631
海　南 Hainan	24743	21175	399	763	2349	57	342	440
重　庆 Chongqing	60363	56669	863	1552	1267	12	323	346
四　川 Sichuan	172690	161131	1685	4163	5705	6	3200	145
贵　州 Guizhou	77374	71132	922	1448	3853	19	116	2739
云　南 Yunnan	91927	84521	686	2080	4625	15	75	377
西　藏 Tibet	6518	6290	50	28	150		50	1
陕　西 Shaanxi	106089	96591	2456	4331	2703	8	2478	72
甘　肃 Gansu	58947	55761	373	1678	1126	9	617	176
青　海 Qinghai	15439	14725	80	239	382	13	784	20
宁　夏 Ningxia	16719	15794	67	477	380	1	260	53
新　疆 Xinjiang	104469	96273	1229	4305	2650	12	1808	39

普通中学教职工总数中

Number of General Secondary Schools Educational

地 区 Region	教职工数 Educational Personnel		
	合计 Total	专任教师 Full-time Teachers	行政人员 Adm. Personnel
总 计 Total	**665808**	**499088**	**34890**
北 京 Beijing	8246	5188	1182
天 津 Tianjin	2658	1745	281
河 北 Hebei	29038	22113	1456
山 西 Shanxi	40212	28686	1782
内蒙古 Inner Mongolia	4730	3473	435
辽 宁 Liaoning	8958	7646	885
吉 林 Jilin	7826	6192	428
黑龙江 Heilongjiang	6042	4500	413
上 海 Shanghai	9235	6808	646
江 苏 Jiangsu	40504	32054	1474
浙 江 Zhejiang	42197	31276	1574
安 徽 Anhui	51109	36445	2645
福 建 Fujian	20817	15680	1233
江 西 Jiangxi	24344	16822	1207
山 东 Shandong	34544	27009	1792
河 南 Henan	65369	49740	3396
湖 北 Hubei	21189	15274	1047
湖 南 Hunan	23391	18376	918
广 东 Guangdong	108646	85315	4979
广 西 Guangxi	14437	10021	831
海 南 Hainan	8236	5423	427
重 庆 Chongqing	7731	5740	435
四 川 Sichuan	33327	24305	1669
贵 州 Guizhou	18330	13575	1078
云 南 Yunnan	8166	6251	626
西 藏 Tibet	46	39	3
陕 西 Shaanxi	19012	13802	1601
甘 肃 Gansu	3331	2553	228
青 海 Qinghai	371	287	26
宁 夏 Ningxia	741	584	40
新 疆 Xinjiang	3025	2166	153

民办教职工数
Personnel Maintained by the Communties

单位:人
unit:person

教辅人员 Supporting Staff	工勤人员 Workers	校办企业职工 Employees in School-run Factories & Farms	代课教师 Substitute Teachers	兼任教师 Part-time Teachers
30804	**99289**	**1737**	**22774**	**7374**
845	1001	30		45
389	243		231	558
1497	3953	19	664	180
1879	7611	254	5190	1020
192	603	27	387	41
272	151	4	9	12
382	818	6	111	4
277	844	8	122	131
877	865	39	240	376
1960	4987	29	333	91
2315	6972	60		1259
2153	9810	56	1819	422
1008	2794	102	200	76
936	5253	126	130	190
1926	3772	45	931	96
2574	9600	59	9310	429
929	3759	180	1038	99
1065	2991	41	55	657
3884	14007	461	115	117
735	2848	2	50	295
240	2054	92	1	40
301	1236	19	165	559
2040	5307	6		76
486	3166	25	34	143
218	1036	35	26	339
1	3		2	1
1075	2524	10	1053	92
156	392	2	381	20
3	55		6	2
34	83		135	4
155	551		36	

普通高中专任教师

Number of Full-time Teachers in Regular Senior Secondary Schools

地 区 Region	合 计 Total	其中:女 of Which: Female	按学历分 By Academic Qualification			
			研究生毕业 Graduate	本科毕业 Under-graduate	专科毕业 Associate Bachelor	高中阶段毕业 High School Graduate
总 计 Total	**1629008**	**811941**	**93703**	**1483256**	**50736**	**1269**
北 京 Beijing	20840	14710	4003	16720	115	2
天 津 Tianjin	15589	10646	1838	13543	200	8
河 北 Hebei	82273	50929	3972	75587	2641	73
山 西 Shanxi	59910	35888	3836	53622	2393	59
内蒙古 Inner Mongolia	33080	19200	2405	29588	1066	21
辽 宁 Liaoning	48320	32138	3515	44021	730	52
吉 林 Jilin	27518	17394	2055	24944	497	21
黑龙江 Heilongjiang	41997	26427	2099	38911	968	18
上 海 Shanghai	16600	10715	2111	14423	62	4
江 苏 Jiangsu	97293	46120	8914	87339	1011	29
浙 江 Zhejiang	64983	32784	4392	60002	569	20
安 徽 Anhui	73844	27400	3357	68516	1943	28
福 建 Fujian	51602	23757	1940	47947	1688	27
江 西 Jiangxi	49762	18657	2664	43263	3768	66
山 东 Shandong	119011	58943	6812	109935	2169	95
河 南 Henan	108063	52726	6840	97399	3775	49
湖 北 Hubei	69726	26325	4028	62933	2618	127
湖 南 Hunan	67420	26962	2185	63449	1681	101
广 东 Guangdong	144756	75744	9784	129462	5405	99
广 西 Guangxi	46752	23602	2479	42682	1572	19
海 南 Hainan	11444	5792	382	10560	502	
重 庆 Chongqing	37698	17448	1805	34960	892	40
四 川 Sichuan	89964	38945	2934	83627	3346	57
贵 州 Guizhou	46964	19864	1093	43977	1828	64
云 南 Yunnan	47285	22596	1369	44600	1282	33
西 藏 Tibet	3871	1831	186	3598	83	4
陕 西 Shaanxi	56952	29051	3746	51202	1951	50
甘 肃 Gansu	42469	16111	1593	38146	2690	39
青 海 Qinghai	7996	3875	227	7032	724	13
宁 夏 Ningxia	10006	4921	443	9244	306	13
新 疆 Xinjiang	35020	20440	696	32024	2261	38

学历、职称情况（总计）

by Academic Qualification and Professional Rank (Total)

单位：人

unit: person

	按职称分 By Professional Rank				
高中阶段毕业以下 Below High School Graduate	中学高级 Senior Secondary	中学一级 1st Grade	中学二级 2nd Grade	中学三级 3rd Grade	未定职级 No-ranking
44	**430223**	**588678**	**483894**	**11925**	**114288**
	7364	6762	4980	40	1694
	5825	6857	2345	25	537
	19217	32394	25546	833	4283
	11313	17251	22559	847	7940
	11107	10579	8477	186	2731
2	18109	16523	9870	322	3496
1	7273	11590	6942	136	1577
1	13904	15336	10598	238	1921
	5367	7786	2873	7	567
	31808	38926	23058	32	3469
	20097	24960	15596	180	4150
	20930	24661	20472	1228	6553
	15087	18738	16066	257	1454
1	17649	17162	11060	665	3226
	25382	42860	44035	398	6336
	24156	35425	41190	1989	5303
20	21629	27191	17462	910	2534
4	19418	28557	16099	412	2934
6	31065	58559	39342	702	15088
	9616	19833	13370	404	3529
	2988	3790	3438	29	1199
1	7835	12536	14288	80	2959
	24980	32897	26673	90	5324
2	9662	14001	15171	425	7705
1	13221	14692	15835	175	3362
	387	1470	1532	47	435
3	12739	18516	21079	467	4151
1	7397	13810	17768	281	3213
	2615	2716	1768	195	702
	2795	2810	3244	189	968
1	9288	9490	11158	136	4948

普通高中专任教师

Number of Full-time Teachers in Regular Senior Secondary Schools

地　区 Region	合　计 Total	其中:女 of Which: Female	按学历分 By Academic Qualifications			
			研究生毕业 Graduate	本科毕业 Under-graduate	专科毕业 Associate Bachelor	高中阶段毕业 High School Graduate
总　计 Total	**773716**	**420577**	**63425**	**693948**	**15917**	**415**
北　京 Beijing	18057	12891	3576	14375	104	2
天　津 Tianjin	10919	7744	1610	9203	102	4
河　北 Hebei	34195	22104	2067	31122	951	55
山　西 Shanxi	25478	16125	2168	22682	613	15
内蒙古 Inner Mongolia	17519	10557	1650	15451	413	5
辽　宁 Liaoning	34632	23618	2862	31340	405	24
吉　林 Jilin	18638	11998	1728	16628	272	9
黑龙江 Heilongjiang	24870	16128	1707	22607	548	8
上　海 Shanghai	14272	9325	1923	12306	39	4
江　苏 Jiangsu	51050	25804	5921	44643	462	24
浙　江 Zhejiang	34684	17878	2757	31695	223	9
安　徽 Anhui	24112	10518	1536	22058	508	10
福　建 Fujian	21212	11466	1306	19493	403	10
江　西 Jiangxi	17282	7553	1374	14963	931	14
山　东 Shandong	63322	33668	4677	57801	821	23
河　南 Henan	41600	21724	3816	37086	689	9
湖　北 Hubei	40383	16628	3202	36096	1062	23
湖　南 Hunan	24947	11069	1228	23192	504	21
广　东 Guangdong	89315	48233	8321	78976	1978	36
广　西 Guangxi	17161	9394	1526	15319	310	6
海　南 Hainan	6941	3681	242	6468	231	
重　庆 Chongqing	18276	8972	1328	16632	298	18
四　川 Sichuan	35023	16103	1780	32321	896	26
贵　州 Guizhou	15264	7723	637	14221	396	9
云　南 Yunnan	15132	7913	767	14088	271	6
西　藏 Tibet	1279	594	85	1170	23	1
陕　西 Shaanxi	19308	10622	1896	16629	764	19
甘　肃 Gansu	13016	5715	778	11664	569	4
青　海 Qinghai	2184	1178	78	1903	197	6
宁　夏 Ningxia	5912	3072	346	5435	130	1
新　疆 Xinjiang	17733	10579	533	16381	804	14

学历、职称情况(城区)

by Academic Qualification and Professional Rank (Urban Area)

单位:人

unit: person

	按职称分 By Professional Rank				
高中阶段毕业以下 Below High School Graduate	中学高级 Senior Secondary	中学一级 1st Grade	中学二级 2nd Grade	中学三级 3rd Grade	未定职级 No-ranking
11	**236476**	**283857**	**199019**	**4384**	**49980**
	6656	6014	4113	31	1243
	4235	4722	1553	19	390
	9162	13766	9110	341	1816
	5574	7605	8283	304	3712
	6183	5591	4255	140	1350
1	13338	12184	6460	236	2414
1	5206	7648	4573	63	1148
	8845	9230	5553	131	1111
	4714	6728	2324	6	500
	19177	20479	9684	18	1692
	11915	13071	7331	127	2240
	7359	8098	6132	375	2148
	7047	7262	6165	91	647
	6784	5966	3490	91	951
	14187	23020	22385	166	3564
	11234	14351	13489	613	1913
	14485	14621	9341	473	1463
2	8520	10490	4745	159	1033
4	23203	35606	22724	205	7577
	4512	6730	4393	101	1425
	1968	2346	1912	16	699
	4535	6149	6247	8	1337
	10887	13251	9090	18	1777
1	4072	4428	4415	98	2251
	5190	4805	4187	43	907
	201	528	404	24	122
	5530	6735	5625	131	1287
1	3435	4777	4025	49	730
	875	710	400	98	101
	1898	1705	1637	138	534
1	5549	5241	4974	71	1898

普通高中专任教师

Number of Full-time Teachers in Regular Senior Secondary Schools

地 区 Region	合 计 Total	其中：女 of Which: Female	按学历分 By Academic Qualifications			
			研究生毕业 Graduate	本科毕业 Under-graduate	专科毕业 Associate Bachelor	高中阶段毕业 High School Graduate
总 计 Total	**118346**	**60903**	**8778**	**106848**	**2664**	**56**
北 京 Beijing	1030	635	169	852	9	
天 津 Tianjin	795	550	76	710	6	3
河 北 Hebei	7551	4853	383	6829	335	4
山 西 Shanxi	3050	1852	276	2691	80	3
内蒙古 Inner Mongolia	858	476	90	744	24	
辽 宁 Liaoning	4422	2894	338	4042	38	4
吉 林 Jilin	963	568	125	819	19	
黑龙江 Heilongjiang	2134	1402	186	1893	55	
上 海 Shanghai	762	497	97	660	5	
江 苏 Jiangsu	6789	3187	556	6182	51	
浙 江 Zhejiang	7797	3986	570	7168	55	4
安 徽 Anhui	3434	1299	113	3212	108	1
福 建 Fujian	3103	1556	132	2916	55	
江 西 Jiangxi	1626	635	54	1533	39	
山 东 Shandong	16332	8205	1308	14718	299	7
河 南 Henan	7156	3648	809	6246	100	1
湖 北 Hubei	5483	2104	405	4971	106	1
湖 南 Hunan	4571	1739	189	4318	55	9
广 东 Guangdong	21549	11267	1821	19056	660	12
广 西 Guangxi	3301	1823	204	3025	72	
海 南 Hainan	524	263	28	480	16	
重 庆 Chongqing	876	410	63	783	29	1
四 川 Sichuan	4645	2178	393	4163	87	2
贵 州 Guizhou	2233	1142	68	2094	71	
云 南 Yunnan	3274	1653	93	3102	77	2
西 藏 Tibet						
陕 西 Shaanxi	1986	1062	172	1767	47	
甘 肃 Gansu	493	214	21	427	45	
青 海 Qinghai	203	95	10	172	19	2
宁 夏 Ningxia	576	254	14	543	19	
新 疆 Xinjiang	830	456	15	732	83	

学历、职称情况(城乡结合区)

by Academic Qualification and Professional Rank (Urban-rural Transitional Area)

单位:人

unit: person

	按职称分 By Professional Rank				
高中阶段毕业以下 Below High School Graduate	中学高级 Senior Secondary	中学一级 1st Grade	中学二级 2nd Grade	中学三级 3rd Grade	未定职级 No-ranking
	30950	**42112**	**34287**	**773**	**10224**
	341	309	251	10	119
	302	358	104		31
	1917	2996	2164	61	413
	526	816	1080	41	587
	363	296	146	6	47
	1657	1511	886	43	325
	310	418	209		26
	826	641	537	23	107
	289	317	122	1	33
	2265	2673	1461		390
	2307	2853	1992	91	554
	863	1054	902	82	533
	1032	1095	883	1	92
	542	538	353		193
	3039	5157	6882	40	1214
	1739	2403	2543	176	295
	1987	2013	1240	44	199
	1497	1884	912	9	269
	4731	8847	5327	64	2580
	651	1169	1178	19	284
	75	88	187		174
	162	272	346	1	95
	1147	1655	1471	2	370
	425	495	700	13	600
	945	999	1064	4	262
	455	570	680	13	268
	112	162	205	6	8
	72	77	43	3	8
	224	221	77		54
	149	225	342	20	94

普通高中专任教师

Number of Full-time Teachers in Regular Senior Secondary Schools

地 区 Region	合 计 Total	其中:女 of Which: Female	按学历分 By Academic Qualification			
			研究生毕业 Graduate	本科毕业 Under-graduate	专科毕业 Associate Bachelor	高中阶段毕业 High School Graduate
总 计 Total	**800126**	**365912**	**27791**	**739059**	**32461**	**782**
北 京 Beijing	2072	1370	321	1742	9	
天 津 Tianjin	4225	2651	209	3917	95	4
河 北 Hebei	45008	27031	1726	41663	1602	17
山 西 Shanxi	30856	17880	1462	27839	1533	22
内蒙古 Inner Mongolia	15339	8545	729	13944	650	16
辽 宁 Liaoning	13089	8170	609	12131	320	28
吉 林 Jilin	8511	5204	317	7973	209	12
黑龙江 Heilongjiang	16328	9806	380	15553	384	10
上 海 Shanghai	2093	1245	163	1909	21	
江 苏 Jiangsu	45719	20070	2943	42235	536	5
浙 江 Zhejiang	27682	13657	1468	25890	313	11
安 徽 Anhui	46413	15770	1679	43372	1344	18
福 建 Fujian	26729	10878	583	24981	1149	16
江 西 Jiangxi	31672	10862	1255	27666	2710	40
山 东 Shandong	54187	24457	2084	50765	1266	72
河 南 Henan	64279	30048	2851	58358	3030	40
湖 北 Hubei	26097	8545	646	23918	1429	84
湖 南 Hunan	39438	14761	877	37365	1115	79
广 东 Guangdong	48262	24128	1007	44148	3050	55
广 西 Guangxi	26668	12733	874	24661	1120	13
海 南 Hainan	4207	1966	126	3814	267	
重 庆 Chongqing	18397	7980	474	17355	546	21
四 川 Sichuan	52860	21887	1058	49465	2306	31
贵 州 Guizhou	30320	11575	447	28436	1381	55
云 南 Yunnan	30153	13764	564	28617	945	26
西 藏 Tibet	1637	761	75	1533	27	2
陕 西 Shaanxi	34999	17017	1681	32168	1116	31
甘 肃 Gansu	27685	9780	789	24862	1999	35
青 海 Qinghai	5555	2600	146	4902	501	6
宁 夏 Ningxia	3762	1684	97	3492	161	12
新 疆 Xinjiang	15884	9087	151	14385	1327	21

学历、职称情况（镇区）

by Academic Qualification and Professional Rank（Counties & Towns Area）

单位：人

unit：person

	按职称分 By Professional Rank				
高中阶段毕业以下 Below High School Graduate	中学高级 Senior Secondary	中学一级 1st Grade	中学二级 2nd Grade	中学三级 3rd Grade	未定职级 No-ranking
33	**183689**	**285135**	**266429**	**6917**	**57956**
	527	515	626	8	396
	1443	1893	741	6	142
	9419	17555	15411	449	2174
	5238	8691	13056	425	3446
	4863	4923	4177	46	1330
1	4627	4162	3252	83	965
	2000	3743	2274	69	425
1	4803	5879	4766	107	773
	574	953	504	1	61
	12492	18259	13194	14	1760
	7585	10824	7522	52	1699
	12957	15619	13109	817	3911
	7331	10029	8563	145	661
1	10715	10966	7329	522	2140
	10939	19390	21009	227	2622
	12540	20459	26758	1352	3170
20	6506	11179	7060	390	962
2	10261	16729	10484	216	1748
2	6880	19807	14783	445	6347
	4737	11909	8064	225	1733
	890	1366	1460	13	478
1	3184	6081	7616	64	1452
	13541	18782	17004	71	3462
1	5366	9197	10312	322	5123
1	7563	9240	10958	125	2267
	132	654	683	2	166
3	6724	10926	14488	314	2547
	3776	8501	12875	203	2330
	1681	1886	1305	91	592
	881	1078	1408	51	344
	3514	3940	5638	62	2730

普通高中专任教师
Number of Full-time Teachers in Regular Senior Secondary Schools

地 区 Region	合 计 Total	其中:女 of Which: Female	按学历分 By Academic Qualifications			
			研究生毕业 Graduate	本科毕业 Under-graduate	专科毕业 Associate Bachelor	高中阶段毕业 High School Graduate
总 计 Total	**208809**	**97302**	**6972**	**192717**	**8919**	**196**
北 京 Beijing	623	371	130	492	1	
天 津 Tianjin	1779	1093	86	1633	58	2
河 北 Hebei	17723	10689	703	16274	735	11
山 西 Shanxi	9878	5825	378	8839	654	7
内蒙古 Inner Mongolia	1453	801	80	1233	134	6
辽 宁 Liaoning	2236	1402	93	2088	51	4
吉 林 Jilin	257	153	4	244	9	
黑龙江 Heilongjiang	1325	807	42	1264	19	
上 海 Shanghai	260	155	15	245		
江 苏 Jiangsu	10049	4536	685	9290	73	1
浙 江 Zhejiang	9236	4567	422	8627	180	7
安 徽 Anhui	10211	3415	427	9505	274	5
福 建 Fujian	5326	2117	103	4946	273	4
江 西 Jiangxi	4694	1615	152	4009	523	10
山 东 Shandong	25817	11706	895	24401	496	25
河 南 Henan	20510	9821	820	18338	1336	16
湖 北 Hubei	5941	1859	134	5558	242	7
湖 南 Hunan	11488	4304	271	10882	318	17
广 东 Guangdong	18834	9531	354	17222	1245	13
广 西 Guangxi	2290	1161	53	2141	92	4
海 南 Hainan	1118	566	32	1035	51	
重 庆 Chongqing	4219	1844	83	3974	150	11
四 川 Sichuan	8470	3652	203	8014	247	6
贵 州 Guizhou	6174	2251	72	5762	336	4
云 南 Yunnan	10684	5017	181	10245	249	8
西 藏 Tibet	366	182	11	348	6	1
陕 西 Shaanxi	7894	3683	339	7183	357	12
甘 肃 Gansu	6465	2292	167	5791	499	8
青 海 Qinghai	1189	565	17	1054	115	3
宁 夏 Ningxia	408	228	8	392	8	
新 疆 Xinjiang	1892	1094	12	1688	188	4

学历、职称情况（镇乡结合区）

by Academic Qualification and Professional Rank (County-town Transitional Area)

单位：人

unit: person

	按职称分 By Professional Rank				
高中阶段毕业以下 Below High School Graduate	中学高级 Senior Secondary	中学一级 1st Grade	中学二级 2nd Grade	中学三级 3rd Grade	未定职级 No-ranking
5	**43799**	**73421**	**72685**	**2021**	**16883**
	116	140	170		197
	584	779	337	5	74
	3649	6624	6290	184	976
	1619	2678	4076	163	1342
	472	449	388	2	142
	752	650	666	18	150
	53	115	69		20
	416	447	427	4	31
	74	131	42	1	12
	2670	3710	3071	10	588
	2226	3578	2776	41	615
	2558	3335	2867	343	1108
	1355	1985	1770	26	190
	1344	1506	1206	118	520
	4935	9555	10114	53	1160
	3895	6654	8606	361	994
	1478	2536	1617	91	219
	2846	4808	3245	50	539
	2652	7758	5721	165	2538
	308	1033	678	69	202
	222	272	427	6	191
1	635	1254	1907	3	420
	2175	2865	2836	6	588
	1005	1911	1983	47	1228
1	2716	3480	3738	30	720
	31	124	135		76
3	1519	2359	3186	76	754
	773	1735	3077	101	779
	304	402	283	35	165
	92	120	171	2	23
	325	428	806	11	322

普通高中专任教师

Number of Full-time Teachers in Regular Senior Secondary Schools

地 区 Region	合 计 Total	其中：女 of Which: Female	按学历分 By Academic Qualifications			
			研究生毕业 Graduate	本科毕业 Under-graduate	专科毕业 Associate Bachelor	高中阶段毕业 High School Graduate
总 计 Total	**55166**	**25452**	**2487**	**50249**	**2358**	**72**
北 京 Beijing	711	449	106	603	2	
天 津 Tianjin	445	251	19	423	3	
河 北 Hebei	3070	1794	179	2802	88	1
山 西 Shanxi	3576	1883	206	3101	247	22
内蒙古 Inner Mongolia	222	98	26	193	3	
辽 宁 Liaoning	599	350	44	550	5	
吉 林 Jilin	369	192	10	343	16	
黑龙江 Heilongjiang	799	493	12	751	36	
上 海 Shanghai	235	145	25	208	2	
江 苏 Jiangsu	524	246	50	461	13	
浙 江 Zhejiang	2617	1249	167	2417	33	
安 徽 Anhui	3319	1112	142	3086	91	
福 建 Fujian	3661	1413	51	3473	136	1
江 西 Jiangxi	808	242	35	634	127	12
山 东 Shandong	1502	818	51	1369	82	
河 南 Henan	2184	954	173	1955	56	
湖 北 Hubei	3246	1152	180	2919	127	20
湖 南 Hunan	3035	1132	80	2892	62	1
广 东 Guangdong	7179	3383	456	6338	377	8
广 西 Guangxi	2923	1475	79	2702	142	
海 南 Hainan	296	145	14	278	4	
重 庆 Chongqing	1025	496	3	973	48	1
四 川 Sichuan	2081	955	96	1841	144	
贵 州 Guizhou	1380	566	9	1320	51	
云 南 Yunnan	2000	919	38	1895	66	1
西 藏 Tibet	955	476	26	895	33	1
陕 西 Shaanxi	2645	1412	169	2405	71	
甘 肃 Gansu	1768	616	26	1620	122	
青 海 Qinghai	257	97	3	227	26	1
宁 夏 Ningxia	332	165		317	15	
新 疆 Xinjiang	1403	774	12	1258	130	3

学历、职称情况(乡村)

by Academic Qualification and Professional Rank (Rural Area)

单位:人

unit: person

高中阶段毕业以下 Below High School Graduate	按职称分 By Professional Rank				
	中学高级 Senior Secondary	中学一级 1st Grade	中学二级 2nd Grade	中学三级 3rd Grade	未定职级 No-ranking
	10058	**19686**	**18446**	**624**	**6352**
	181	233	241	1	55
	147	242	51		5
	636	1073	1025	43	293
	501	955	1220	118	782
	61	65	45		51
	144	177	158	3	117
	67	199	95	4	4
	256	227	279		37
	79	105	45		6
	139	188	180		17
	597	1065	743	1	211
	614	944	1231	36	494
	709	1447	1338	21	146
	150	230	241	52	135
	256	450	641	5	150
	382	615	943	24	220
	638	1391	1061	47	109
	637	1338	870	37	153
	982	3146	1835	52	1164
	367	1194	913	78	371
	130	78	66		22
	116	306	425	8	170
	552	864	579	1	85
	224	376	444	5	331
	468	647	690	7	188
	54	288	445	21	147
	485	855	966	22	317
	186	532	868	29	153
	59	120	63	6	9
	16	27	199		90
	225	309	546	3	320

普通高中办学
Condition of School Buildings in Regular Senior

地 区 Region	校舍建筑面积 Floor Space	教学及辅助用房 Teaching & Assistant Buildings							行政办公用房 Administrative	
		合计 Total	其中 of Which：						合计 Total	其中：教师办公室 of Which: for Teachers
			教室 Classroom	实验室 Laboratory	图书室 Library	微机室 PC-room	语音室 Linguistic	体育馆 Gymnasium		
总 计 Total	**435601377**	**170626465**	**107534129**	**27009096**	**13564788**	**6509647**	**2622970**	**13385835**	**36174459**	**21965305**
北 京 Beijing	8485057	2949922	1651970	498963	236399	129099	27148	406343	856709	447799
天 津 Tianjin	4196173	1624473	898563	260839	135825	68022	24957	236267	527514	345638
河 北 Hebei	19510624	7740149	4751554	1465829	670615	294321	135013	422817	1631236	1200505
山 西 Shanxi	15311976	5702849	3589803	973613	503351	213782	94373	327927	1310227	857295
内蒙古 Inner Mongolia	8345055	3448097	2144525	459084	254538	135900	73335	380715	846792	592212
辽 宁 Liaoning	10063703	3817778	2190249	530010	362572	158288	74857	501802	1088445	581157
吉 林 Jilin	5431394	2156215	1400043	240847	129610	83691	39193	262831	631466	349264
黑龙江 Heilongjiang	7656696	3522090	2177646	499506	214526	130669	65578	434165	877429	578618
上 海 Shanghai	6121921	2561964	1282371	450402	256114	98335	41562	433180	641883	285448
江 苏 Jiangsu	27548829	11785530	6414037	2033863	1225954	579066	189336	1343274	2604534	1592110
浙 江 Zhejiang	21934105	8549837	4364035	1541232	943782	280911	116346	1303531	1747381	1041360
安 徽 Anhui	21530127	8397367	5607734	1270943	598891	336063	122496	461240	1644384	897533
福 建 Fujian	16721823	7330880	4010152	1642559	806358	251328	84656	535827	1252571	649657
江 西 Jiangxi	15137455	6436478	4358455	827090	499493	232026	120001	399413	1119706	706984
山 东 Shandong	25927629	9030250	5489484	1697279	730436	388338	144886	579827	2565895	1394652
河 南 Henan	26443398	9432767	6482881	1357526	726185	348844	131875	385456	2324555	1656348
湖 北 Hubei	18099661	6159185	4033954	941193	455708	198868	109064	420398	1431367	851069
湖 南 Hunan	21447707	8275885	5329399	1114834	674420	285318	128472	743442	1291403	738057
广 东 Guangdong	43831583	18188439	11930054	2617009	1255117	589456	251645	1545158	3132236	1761468
广 西 Guangxi	13238172	4426750	2970806	617957	378042	168075	55612	236258	754536	526188
海 南 Hainan	3761159	1395508	903731	213866	118836	50308	17718	91049	203764	116716
重 庆 Chongqing	12333920	4715868	3248885	657900	283181	161562	57531	306809	792692	462643
四 川 Sichuan	24902252	9543099	6617005	1303397	580340	380927	157552	503878	1676507	1041781
贵 州 Guizhou	10489107	4016015	2803106	608373	259083	137713	55928	151812	809165	484663
云 南 Yunnan	12142192	4908685	3251769	824274	367183	203337	74854	187268	766766	459218
西 藏 Tibet	1049963	358647	251531	37563	20830	5914	4160	38649	69068	31105
陕 西 Shaanxi	12785830	5059775	3296510	919111	319899	200165	96217	227873	1331566	858063
甘 肃 Gansu	8241448	3546153	2527383	522119	191970	144834	47893	111954	846731	603842
青 海 Qinghai	1720478	733737	522365	102498	38846	28940	10221	30867	169865	119535
宁 夏 Ningxia	2492993	1152093	638675	232847	93118	62422	28884	96147	306018	236877
新 疆 Xinjiang	8698947	3659980	2395454	546570	233566	163125	41607	279658	922048	497500

条件(一)(总计)

Secondary Schools (1) (Total)

单位:平方米

unit: m^2

生活用房 Residential and Welfare							其他用房 Rooms for Other Purposes	校舍面积中 of the Floor Space	
合计 Total	教工宿舍 Apartments for Single		学生宿舍 Students' Dormitories	食堂 Dining Halls	厕所 Toilet	其他 Others		危房面积 Floor Space of Dilapidated Buildings	当年新增校舍 New Floor Space Added in Current Year
	小计 Subtotal	其中:教师周转宿舍 of Which: Accommodation for Circulation of Teachers							
200756503	**39237741**	**6417595**	**108763702**	**33768838**	**9645644**	**9340578**	**28043950**	**8972702**	**14904471**
2549094	366488	62575	1058180	511519	270467	342440	2129332	200	368751
1443278	106435	11152	622859	282131	142589	289264	600908		255419
9132523	1105483	154852	5446015	1716713	399180	465132	1006716	5416	268783
7142828	1191872	110583	3829091	1328601	385318	407946	1156072	193238	669039
3472153	159396	42418	2168713	707035	191861	245148	578013	41679	535459
4198888	218938	29701	2427298	937125	292973	322554	958592	19472	173339
2152017	60464	1419	1212741	483283	188665	206864	491696	53539	79500
2655073	99838	29280	1656616	568345	170213	160061	602104	104633	121445
2063704	110087	12680	953632	431153	242693	326139	854370		68905
11485884	1660024	280227	6359094	2415084	525153	526529	1672881		914737
10082171	1322148	209032	5789415	2008202	566910	395496	1554716		614074
10633804	2600934	220688	5642482	1646508	389767	354113	854572	201207	413228
6921427	1881313	343239	3414684	1065386	274376	285668	1216945	58725	672861
6950652	1428408	208501	3900631	1175951	244124	201538	630619	637671	418756
12750135	1871698	425896	6986465	2601946	718425	571601	1581349	163066	789302
13598669	2439690	285157	7906761	2305872	528015	418331	1087407	238012	292531
9686847	3094946	417808	4501505	1404651	334199	351546	822262	333629	451567
10732413	3329172	605611	4974074	1656321	390814	382032	1148006	460936	219411
18750014	4717494	505343	9705433	2460284	990406	876397	3760894	145249	924196
7569847	2261060	330571	3966131	872914	216956	252786	487039	787092	578341
1955227	694995	152222	887778	230492	66647	75315	206660	190760	138820
6365351	1694200	232129	3412274	892320	187847	178710	460009	358817	376550
12812220	2447710	661292	7359314	2022010	611707	371479	870426	464356	1163672
5081653	907620	211520	3052985	723586	217112	180350	582274	11927	1416106
5876217	1111238	307866	3397917	868790	233703	264569	590524	2141503	613017
555363	211590	165049	234319	95550	8596	5308	66885		32848
5635685	1269020	152593	2987362	883875	266026	229402	758804	158356	334418
3399085	435861	61665	1952475	509750	255127	245872	449479	2089874	510932
705918	105213	41822	380325	94364	51984	74032	110958	9519	192617
930542	20291	7831	602166	207409	56600	44076	104340	77850	54589
3467821	314115	136873	1974967	661668	227191	289880	649098	25976	1241258

普通高中办学

Condition of School Buildings in Regular Senior

地 区 Region	校舍建筑面积 Floor Space	教学及辅助用房 Teaching & Assistant Buildings							行政办公用房 Administrative	
		合计 Total	其中 of Which:						合计 Total	其中:教师办公室 of Which: for Teachers
			教室 Classroom	实验室 Laboratory	图书室 Library	微机室 PC-room	语音室 Linguistic	体育馆 Gymnasium		
总 计 Total	**217767962**	**88954031**	**53258200**	**14252434**	**7551241**	**3446803**	**1298359**	**9146994**	**19967044**	**11758148**
北 京 Beijing	7445368	2572906	1440289	410737	209516	111734	23398	377232	766592	392810
天 津 Tianjin	3252918	1270207	673680	197060	108906	53285	17198	220078	430045	287085
河 北 Hebei	8556144	3579504	2145540	651154	336580	143902	62126	240202	771812	589321
山 西 Shanxi	6736427	2611295	1621595	449292	241944	92415	37419	168630	695272	430452
内蒙古 Inner Mongolia	4711571	1965850	1192439	253114	159575	74948	39354	246420	504614	351717
辽 宁 Liaoning	7283538	2807778	1536452	398695	274845	119350	55208	423228	792892	416675
吉 林 Jilin	3897006	1574944	992739	170879	96624	59054	26514	229134	460834	245454
黑龙江 Heilongjiang	4547692	2148246	1271777	311280	137485	75601	36183	315920	538595	336506
上 海 Shanghai	5216021	2253949	1133345	393052	225964	83871	37602	380115	531458	248230
江 苏 Jiangsu	15175180	6778103	3631856	1152557	731634	323458	99908	838690	1510856	940280
浙 江 Zhejiang	12759460	4975269	2500047	850294	556200	168187	67483	833058	1037673	585485
安 徽 Anhui	6606560	2946025	1808723	513456	242609	130152	37472	213613	619945	333344
福 建 Fujian	6802671	3195693	1638985	720648	364280	102249	30981	338550	609484	322883
江 西 Jiangxi	5303805	2451907	1509766	356000	199116	93315	53549	240161	434505	293632
山 东 Shandong	14284018	5119101	2977728	1010708	457266	239966	82286	351147	1454367	825595
河 南 Henan	11173206	4339141	2757535	683730	369060	151254	49709	327853	1040541	676894
湖 北 Hubei	10198045	3715273	2335707	585625	288709	120026	63323	321883	897690	536324
湖 南 Hunan	8707743	3740146	2300243	538693	297853	130195	47190	425972	570953	300669
广 东 Guangdong	28313160	11771977	7392964	1733724	865622	399750	154783	1225134	2206628	1222863
广 西 Guangxi	5131707	1862456	1169333	265295	172949	80317	21684	152878	331298	217385
海 南 Hainan	2323563	880749	544013	142379	81184	31835	13038	68300	146459	86916
重 庆 Chongqing	6100858	2518268	1733314	323490	164309	93550	29207	174398	455108	253206
四 川 Sichuan	10401510	4253236	2840282	579834	281313	165129	69068	317610	769527	457164
贵 州 Guizhou	3418497	1315469	881018	188481	99196	49580	17759	79435	310354	181278
云 南 Yunnan	4843267	1968318	1187756	338869	179773	92838	36777	132305	374441	206089
西 藏 Tibet	351341	142095	102194	10834	5741	1933	1144	20249	24294	4582
陕 西 Shaanxi	5190861	2168352	1357272	417348	127068	83402	38293	144969	579921	335464
甘 肃 Gansu	2741652	1252612	856474	185377	82432	48688	18984	60657	328082	227991
青 海 Qinghai	510598	245001	160164	36751	15256	10611	3358	18861	63854	38044
宁 夏 Ningxia	1493479	704196	393867	132424	65137	37486	13317	61965	205643	156376
新 疆 Xinjiang	4290096	1825965	1171103	250654	113095	78722	14044	198347	503307	257434

条件(一)(城区)

Secondary Schools (1) (Urban Area)

单位:平方米

unit: m^2

生活用房 Residential and Welfare							其他用房 Rooms for Other Purposes	校舍面积中 of the Floor Space	
合计 Total	教工宿舍 Apartments for Single		学生宿舍 Students' Dormitories	食堂 Dining Halls	厕所 Toilet	其他 Others		危房面积 Floor Space of Dilapidated Buildings	当年新增校舍 New Floor Space Added in Current Year
	小计 Subtotal	其中:教师周转宿舍 of Which: Accommodation for Circulation of Teachers							
90875407	**14648870**	**2371715**	**49318094**	**16167201**	**5317551**	**5423691**	**17971480**	**3011354**	**6434854**
2122217	311775	62012	821251	438600	242856	307735	1983653	200	261830
992440	67783	5875	364341	204570	110631	245115	560226		217728
3631924	389295	45525	2126895	668628	182916	264190	572904	3197	121241
2861608	480200	42606	1468547	546042	172708	194111	568252	71367	434797
1862450	91059	40268	1164167	377995	114425	114804	378657	1680	358195
2896155	171087	19574	1585995	658790	226700	253583	786713	16398	139111
1467669	50331	1097	774631	320217	142351	180139	393559	18422	79485
1477661	56487	6989	878580	333499	110165	98930	383190	71017	60090
1709831	87638	10470	759919	349635	208670	303969	720783		59742
5921191	506488	98486	3440157	1317683	335498	321365	965030		500193
5738919	684686	114617	3296687	1142462	324342	290742	1007599		155513
2636992	430669	28179	1509206	455237	128025	113855	403598	47376	173596
2417520	499497	125810	1281517	382192	126564	127750	579974	13479	322604
2178057	496009	137629	1135051	379004	92238	75755	239336	189613	80851
6649447	670022	184417	3701375	1498686	424245	355119	1061103	42904	538809
5197664	796426	120057	3047580	942472	227823	183363	595860	96862	160104
5103627	1462809	139511	2432164	771270	215683	221701	481455	113863	169928
3806842	1041322	216251	1845829	600693	164208	154790	589802	80930	98510
11497987	2487611	305900	6128647	1615078	702898	563753	2836568	69169	727588
2771663	753688	93222	1468752	325110	92164	131949	166290	104733	139104
1185734	363761	85971	581786	151362	43895	44930	110621	160739	76608
2880531	587923	60410	1709196	390232	101043	92137	246951	210885	184094
4978776	792570	196945	2876734	859994	282386	167092	399971	78458	489115
1476156	230828	20858	887948	209749	72924	74707	316518	6246	159712
2139469	370037	74531	1204375	326340	100219	138498	361039	822778	216017
161713	68135	45357	69493	19036	3634	1415	23239		14443
1934976	433937	31334	1008805	285012	122273	84949	507612	60556	63862
951028	97704	12314	536506	148358	82780	85680	209930	693310	78709
149328	10388	1570	57444	18186	20608	42702	52415		27905
507329	15944	7651	305510	123011	37676	25188	76311	30140	19948
1568503	142761	36279	849006	308058	105003	163675	392321	7032	305422

普通高中办学

Condition of School Buildings in Regular Senior

地　区 Region	校舍建筑面　积 Floor Space	教学及辅助用房 Teaching & Assistant Buildings							行政办公用房 Administrative	
		合计 Total	其中 of Which:						合计 Total	其中:教师办公室 of Which: for Teachers
			教室 Classroom	实验室 Laboratory	图书室 Library	微机室 PC-room	语音室 Linguistic	体育馆 Gymnasium		
总　计 Total	**38830159**	**14773180**	**9056985**	**2324065**	**1218385**	**534429**	**237697**	**1401619**	**3078417**	**1833145**
北　京 Beijing	613518	212215	107384	19025	10730	6099	3075	65902	45607	24636
天　津 Tianjin	193447	62560	32303	7394	5614	2804	784	13661	14651	6422
河　北 Hebei	2149573	844676	473293	179403	76545	29143	15925	70367	157642	127728
山　西 Shanxi	685725	237366	159576	37299	26606	7695	2096	4094	66809	48515
内蒙古 Inner Mongolia	398904	124620	66652	15303	8846	2512	12374	18933	29239	22995
辽　宁 Liaoning	1150573	379671	208280	50858	35882	18689	5616	60346	94956	48356
吉　林 Jilin	408605	114744	69354	10994	4538	3389	1835	24634	29647	22899
黑龙江 Heilongjiang	454991	229360	139867	34103	13697	7566	6032	28095	54951	34542
上　海 Shanghai	511733	216626	128189	21391	23582	6673	4646	32145	53211	17950
江　苏 Jiangsu	2170591	940200	515509	185929	97061	45332	16478	79891	205621	125280
浙　江 Zhejiang	3254585	1236983	653681	186519	137036	29790	12945	217012	223595	136389
安　徽 Anhui	993169	412076	300039	56639	26764	10282	4577	13775	65967	37673
福　建 Fujian	1216790	510402	284007	104213	61973	13338	5039	41832	73232	41098
江　西 Jiangxi	560996	212767	136593	28746	15655	13435	6447	11891	26334	20474
山　东 Shandong	4184911	1478347	837130	323457	119797	78899	30777	88287	374572	228851
河　南 Henan	2030236	665039	458584	94790	58619	28302	8361	16383	175388	123123
湖　北 Hubei	1459167	521754	334612	55518	39792	17566	18043	56223	119423	61466
湖　南 Hunan	2103594	945028	591923	129014	86679	23299	7914	106199	110849	57061
广　东 Guangdong	7875828	3096446	2003516	427514	211025	101203	44497	308691	632689	343073
广　西 Guangxi	976856	290826	205481	37559	20590	10256	3985	12955	54638	37701
海　南 Hainan	190130	62937	38120	8541	6919	1297	1150	6910	12088	5084
重　庆 Chongqing	456101	212047	169389	19933	8254	6559	1740	6172	20902	8625
四　川 Sichuan	1892965	670292	451481	96350	38286	28955	5806	49414	138125	64443
贵　州 Guizhou	664292	262301	166177	51626	22764	6645	1823	13266	54392	30774
云　南 Yunnan	1047824	371223	215858	80784	30089	17142	8416	18934	96747	47244
西　藏 Tibet										
陕　西 Shaanxi	527505	192322	131670	25540	11668	7234	3495	12715	59275	43253
甘　肃 Gansu	138220	62363	46406	7176	1425	2490	2191	2675	14148	9643
青　海 Qinghai	37340	16250	7705	6000	1612	753	120	60	2455	1618
宁　夏 Ningxia	128379	41368	23911	8644	3198	1771	1005	2839	40567	39267
新　疆 Xinjiang	353611	150371	100295	13803	13139	5311	505	17318	30697	16962

条件(一)(城乡结合区)
Secondary Schools (1) (Urban-rural Transitional Area)

单位:平方米
unit: m²

生活用房 Residential and Welfare								其他用房 Rooms for Other Purposes	校舍面积中 of the Floor Space	
合计 Total	教工宿舍 Apartments for Single: 小计 Subtotal	教工宿舍 Apartments for Single: 其中:教师周转宿舍 of Which: Accommodation for Circulation of Teachers	学生宿舍 Students' Dormitories	食堂 Dining Halls	厕所 Toilet	其他 Others			危房面积 Floor Space of Dilapidated Buildings	当年新增校舍 New Floor Space Added in Current Year
18292511	**3116315**	**560937**	**10077469**	**3344355**	**895915**	**858457**		**2686051**	**261086**	**919820**
311422	66529	3447	164634	51385	14428	14446		44274		21528
66443	6862	2234	37463	15288	4012	2818		49793		
971948	103891	11148	565584	175797	47475	79201		175307	699	13789
335040	48349	2563	169930	85726	16106	14929		46510	800	18858
185318	10272	561	93628	28314	5908	47196		59727		
508701	34776	3722	307200	104991	29459	32275		167245	3259	12328
187228	4707	24	85466	36013	17212	43830		76986		13590
155488	8525	50	94636	34117	5630	12580		15192	4021	3220
222132	16109		134709	32358	16814	22142		19764		
945134	72318	22901	569184	220385	41175	42072		79636		14437
1544343	226440	50296	902248	282730	80311	52614		249664		41572
453425	69609	12085	256707	94895	17142	15072		61701	9472	28596
529846	125419	23013	283432	87585	22427	10983		103310		40116
302059	79675	25908	139291	62710	7191	13192		19836	13092	5330
2069915	172139	76028	1150906	492927	127523	126420		262077	465	225700
1102649	170378	26505	659632	208992	38422	25225		87160	780	8558
788167	204468	8661	369635	142383	33265	38416		29823	19133	23480
912523	190209	31380	494320	181637	34795	11562		135194	20562	42505
3412105	839892	96383	1748663	502427	201727	119396		734588	1527	164672
596493	148344	26626	322036	77268	19875	28970		34899	16623	34466
111365	24528	4092	66202	13709	5175	1751		3740		18195
217416	34885	449	144105	25443	8502	4481		5736	15046	
1041252	221668	90737	588733	174070	39878	16903		43296	2404	84581
297749	59037	5097	166891	43036	14043	14742		49850		16451
499024	104197	31923	281083	81366	16003	16375		80830	110476	58357
253754	53090	210	140873	38081	9288	12422		22154	1265	7741
59882	7172		37077	9508	3530	2595		1827	41462	
15233	880	320	6558	1320	2940	3535		3402		9100
40905	200		17403	8487	5418	9397		5539		
155552	11747	4574	79240	31407	10241	22917		16991		12650

普通高中办学

Condition of School Buildings in Regular Senio

地 区 Region	校舍建筑面积 Floor Space	教学及辅助用房 Teaching & Assistant Buildings 合计 Total	其中 of Which: 教室 Classroom	实验室 Laboratory	图书室 Library	微机室 PC-room	语音室 Linguistic	体育馆 Gymnasium	行政办公用房 Administrative 合计 Total	其中:教师办公室 of Which: for Teacher
总 计 Total	**198648220**	**74850311**	**49618454**	**11831405**	**5547604**	**2826094**	**1224565**	**3802189**	**14941864**	**9432025**
北 京 Beijing	807231	307081	172420	70820	21341	14479	3120	24901	61305	40372
天 津 Tianjin	825878	313487	198325	59134	25952	13576	6517	9983	84786	52444
河 北 Hebei	9989187	3820105	2384290	773560	311293	139138	62325	149499	794518	560102
山 西 Shanxi	7229617	2713340	1715589	476943	226714	103669	45246	145179	528210	361655
内蒙古 Inner Mongolia	3431030	1403960	900894	198772	92648	59429	33101	119116	327077	233936
辽 宁 Liaoning	2439938	910436	582271	121895	81591	34225	17795	72659	275438	153652
吉 林 Jilin	1477583	558296	388673	67461	32395	23912	12158	33697	164494	100978
黑龙江 Heilongjiang	2944270	1302756	853076	180996	73771	52452	27998	114463	323890	231222
上 海 Shanghai	767240	264607	129980	52436	24866	12445	3246	41634	101867	33668
江 苏 Jiangsu	12012872	4874213	2706714	850208	484840	252824	88877	490750	1072654	641050
浙 江 Zhejiang	8187893	3212795	1679476	623935	352410	100223	45579	411172	640204	405003
安 徽 Anhui	13660569	5062347	3503475	714053	329114	192012	80565	243128	930152	515876
福 建 Fujian	8193854	3467887	1953797	794078	373285	126220	46948	173559	549738	275949
江 西 Jiangxi	9141243	3684134	2583687	457527	294898	133704	63003	151315	648527	396210
山 东 Shandong	11233525	3765923	2443101	661295	251646	140877	61334	207670	1074711	548583
河 南 Henan	14724875	4925502	3597516	653746	348176	189452	79069	57543	1226130	938466
湖 北 Hubei	6917933	2111714	1454994	312461	146071	70658	41673	85857	476460	282996
湖 南 Hunan	11675870	4171295	2775537	531054	351852	147589	73909	291354	662331	411882
广 东 Guangdong	12926268	5383329	3817376	751840	330581	163495	84667	235370	771816	445459
广 西 Guangxi	7399789	2337113	1645840	334324	190340	79283	29136	58190	389197	285052
海 南 Hainan	1267786	476241	338983	67764	33429	16284	4168	15613	49343	25741
重 庆 Chongqing	5890205	2098533	1446921	319184	109349	63820	26848	132411	324526	199580
四 川 Sichuan	13753890	5027503	3584084	682158	285765	207740	86478	181278	866196	561453
贵 州 Guizhou	6620038	2555486	1805768	404052	154998	82609	35802	72257	469619	283315
云 南 Yunnan	6709527	2711963	1899104	453469	174314	97884	36229	50963	363796	237863
西 藏 Tibet	415853	137786	94733	17805	9103	2665	2332	11148	30168	19474
陕 西 Shaanxi	6977067	2635851	1786695	464668	175782	106361	52198	50147	709847	496246
甘 肃 Gansu	5072688	2141669	1553471	317748	103035	88162	27956	51297	468995	335996
青 海 Qinghai	1163049	469236	346657	63457	23239	17301	6576	12006	102649	78833
宁 夏 Ningxia	925837	419264	222592	95329	27461	24413	15507	33962	89367	71288
新 疆 Xinjiang	3865615	1586459	1052415	259233	107345	69193	24205	74068	363853	207681

条件(一)(镇区)

Secondary Schools (1) (Counties & Towns Area)

单位:平方米
unit: m^2

生活用房 Residential and Welfare							其他用房 Rooms for Other Purposes	校舍面积中 of the Floor Space	
合计 Total	教工宿舍 Apartments for Single: 小计 Subtotal	教工宿舍 Apartments for Single: 其中:教师周转宿舍 of Which: Accommodation for Circulation of Teachers	学生宿舍 Students' Dormitories	食堂 Dining Halls	厕所 Toilet	其他 Others		危房面积 Floor Space of Dilapidated Buildings	当年新增校舍 New Floor Space Added in Current Year
100078821	**22050915**	**3536647**	**54367490**	**16150803**	**3918925**	**3590688**	**8777224**	**5488150**	**7550898**
316633	37331	513	184286	57365	20317	17334	122212		101723
394899	33592	5121	225266	68895	26710	40436	32706		13768
5034343	617457	91589	3071725	972011	196180	176970	340221	2219	134647
3567844	593043	38837	1952140	669757	170762	182142	420223	116654	185771
1539002	52201	1800	965427	317934	74356	129084	160991	39999	176032
1133895	35583	6575	730470	244388	56487	66967	120169	3074	34228
661238	10033	322	423256	157049	44813	26087	93555	35117	15
1106884	39327	22235	731721	219940	55995	59901	210740	20996	61355
285855	22089	2010	163994	55890	22395	21487	114911		9163
5376310	1113178	153941	2815651	1075962	177883	193636	689695		256544
3866658	535332	86233	2250573	773326	215111	92316	468236		376647
7266477	1966634	176216	3731661	1099931	240445	227806	401593	136231	225212
3674660	1113306	177094	1748108	545851	127604	139791	501569	45246	299211
4464687	873524	61569	2584865	750008	139227	117063	343895	431047	277403
5886780	1169241	229561	3154544	1066885	282696	213414	506111	120162	250493
8113386	1579577	161920	4706259	1314405	291585	221560	459857	116879	128999
4018211	1450889	256818	1792337	563240	103345	108400	311548	218334	277263
6337434	2075292	337149	2872555	973082	202594	213911	504810	335894	117452
6021657	1858791	119203	2985803	687486	223783	265794	749466	65349	180216
4381099	1372400	205565	2279767	501222	114813	112897	292380	646357	411265
687247	297924	65061	271448	69243	19772	28860	54955	30021	38213
3259370	1041372	167375	1578374	470758	83119	85747	207776	123372	163381
7404675	1543350	436935	4246624	1101089	317721	195891	455516	368810	598262
3371640	614955	167335	2045884	478029	134092	98680	223293	2539	1174670
3432060	654986	216179	2030782	504204	124289	117799	201708	1162125	363318
222942	79100	70050	90766	49277	2276	1523	24957		9466
3397539	758635	111864	1820795	561545	134409	122155	233830	97800	209614
2240892	292042	45703	1302553	330525	161975	153797	221132	1298246	409859
536399	91395	40252	310311	73737	30515	30441	54765	9519	162892
389177	4347	180	268674	79424	18084	18648	28029	47710	34521
1688928	123989	81442	1030871	318345	105572	110151	226375	14450	869295

普通高中办学

Condition of School Buildings in Regular Senior

地 区 Region	校舍建筑面积 Floor Space	教学及辅助用房 Teaching & Assistant Buildings							行政办公用房 Administrative	
		合计 Total	其中 of Which:						合计 Total	其中:教师办公室 of Which: for Teachers
			教室 Classroom	实验室 Laboratory	图书室 Library	微机室 PC-room	语音室 Linguistic	体育馆 Gymnasium		
总 计 Total	**53452872**	**19752780**	**13022807**	**3200277**	**1447388**	**718508**	**312742**	**1051058**	**3941707**	**2523202**
北 京 Beijing	285528	93082	46138	29371	8347	4794	1253	3179	17464	9262
天 津 Tianjin	286270	103631	73745	19842	3950	4111	1871	112	31015	17059
河 北 Hebei	3944641	1445757	930587	300207	98269	53328	26152	37214	326447	220771
山 西 Shanxi	2513675	978037	569894	163497	68147	33879	14628	127992	194395	134410
内蒙古 Inner Mongolia	420920	169830	96576	31155	14429	4336	1042	22292	26102	19761
辽 宁 Liaoning	423442	138600	89874	18513	11706	8052	1841	8614	42034	28845
吉 林 Jilin	59730	20964	16698	2369	806	813	278		7234	4411
黑龙江 Heilongjiang	321838	144546	92577	24732	5452	8703	1609	11473	38074	25325
上 海 Shanghai	112851	32136	18421	8140	2207	1136	175	2057	10964	4634
江 苏 Jiangsu	2699302	1073194	641476	191256	100653	46656	15256	77897	212727	130354
浙 江 Zhejiang	2696131	1071936	596314	188194	108651	32943	18357	127477	204008	116690
安 徽 Anhui	3560378	1229028	866779	164883	85870	42908	23529	45059	259124	127011
福 建 Fujian	1870808	714129	400466	172821	74400	22595	7064	36783	118429	64243
江 西 Jiangxi	1430835	506447	360032	64036	42936	22095	8050	9298	72865	48270
山 东 Shandong	5525027	1858748	1195463	329823	126809	70788	27007	108858	461785	276045
河 南 Henan	4618814	1532990	1126210	201109	119738	52867	19186	13880	406337	326696
湖 北 Hubei	1796156	543551	380583	77661	35699	15484	11344	22780	112325	62774
湖 南 Hunan	3706676	1297565	860576	177051	102878	51746	28998	76316	225206	152861
广 东 Guangdong	4670660	2057143	1427776	263410	139349	63293	32195	131120	323140	191849
广 西 Guangxi	651862	237333	167928	33242	23979	6729	2296	3159	32642	20548
海 南 Hainan	337049	125316	87605	13358	11783	5495	687	6388	10830	4740
重 庆 Chongqing	1411027	475231	343956	62161	18259	16292	7259	27304	85800	43935
四 川 Sichuan	2366794	840722	548017	121726	54904	36505	9839	69731	142482	97054
贵 州 Guizhou	1561987	637122	449341	98523	28261	17598	9736	33663	93517	58717
云 南 Yunnan	2397894	942459	647720	167807	65339	36067	11553	13973	148122	95975
西 藏 Tibet	85274	31161	17124	4880	3559	663	753	4182	4260	4260
陕 西 Shaanxi	1719877	623484	403331	119888	43676	31041	19443	6105	176800	123195
甘 肃 Gansu	1195669	492301	353740	84659	28083	16548	6626	2645	101074	77908
青 海 Qinghai	206497	77611	59475	10926	2665	2584	1565	396	12363	9790
宁 夏 Ningxia	109773	46857	30191	9973	2466	2545	1482	200	12889	12252
新 疆 Xinjiang	465487	211869	124194	45064	14118	5914	1668	20911	31253	13557

条件(一)(镇乡结合区)

Secondary Schools (1) (County-town Transitional Area)

单位:平方米
unit: m²

生活用房 Residential and Welfare							其他用房 Rooms for Other Purposes	校舍面积中 of the Floor Space	
合计 Total	教工宿舍 Apartments for Single		学生宿舍 Students' Dormitories	食堂 Dining Halls	厕所 Toilet	其他 Others		危房面积 Floor Space of Dilapidated Buildings	当年新增校舍 New Floor Space Added in Current Year
	小计 Subtotal	其中:教师周转宿舍 of Which: Accommodation for Circulation of Teachers							
27343488	**5626271**	**954478**	**15076447**	**4598377**	**1071213**	**971180**	**2414897**	**1222133**	**2141907**
137143	21243		77291	25354	5575	7680	37839		68
143474	16798	3141	85343	23417	8409	9507	8150		71
2058711	252505	41996	1271448	380663	79755	74340	113726		83641
1191726	198205	15379	680771	204691	47258	60801	149517	60097	63585
198187	10770	810	119221	44063	5603	18530	26801		4571
199373	8669	4978	125490	39275	9073	16866	43435	3074	
28692			15894	7965	2251	2582	2840		
130305	12914	8388	85431	24378	3989	3593	8913		300
43011	1765		21521	7830	3123	8772	26740		
1279099	281599	41067	646327	251665	41781	57727	134282		85388
1266033	172061	30964	738771	254900	74616	25685	154154		175739
1940634	420545	44031	1073805	305354	60615	80315	131592	29561	62482
926351	271883	34211	466407	138150	35633	14278	111899		58808
829648	152223	8034	511854	138827	18262	8482	21875	44881	61903
2929070	538174	102975	1615740	565506	109269	100381	275424	95959	93956
2577875	490485	66340	1505347	419382	89877	72784	101612	51015	16778
1015538	303724	99089	502051	148102	31877	29784	124742	34088	193536
2000871	602381	50252	916954	335824	79731	65981	183034	113966	66898
2021333	546330	48793	1016441	271395	103323	83844	269044	1160	84946
361612	115567	9654	187926	47375	6614	4130	20275	25665	24360
200230	79685	37386	75722	17836	6931	20056	673	3751	17427
781565	241006	56966	370939	118295	22138	29187	68431	20326	64621
1274268	246591	85944	739515	195317	61546	31299	109322	14740	119458
778769	117987	41072	468401	132044	34855	25482	52579		329675
1204781	241092	71203	693540	185975	42941	41233	102532	437434	151123
49087	16349	16349	23143	9283	312		766		4182
877505	169792	14251	496113	150306	31193	30101	42088	28374	100186
553016	66875	8243	328220	88603	37322	31996	49278	257962	88092
103024	18619	7564	59267	12321	6932	5885	13499		4758
47827			34995	10957	286	1589	2200		
194730	10434	5398	122559	43324	10123	8290	27635	80	185355

普通高中办学
Condition of School Buildings in Regular Senior

地区 Region	校舍建筑面积 Floor Space	教学及辅助用房 Teaching & Assistant Buildings							行政办公用房 Administrative	
		合计 Total	其中 of Which:						合计 Total	其中：教师办公室 of Which: for Teachers
			教室 Classroom	实验室 Laboratory	图书室 Library	微机室 PC-room	语音室 Linguistic	体育馆 Gymnasium		
总　计 Total	**19185195**	**6822123**	**4657475**	**925257**	**465943**	**236750**	**100046**	**436652**	**1265551**	**775132**
北　京 Beijing	232458	69935	39261	17406	5542	2886	630	4210	28812	14617
天　津 Tianjin	117377	40779	26558	4645	967	1161	1242	6206	12683	6109
河　北 Hebei	965293	340540	221724	41115	22742	11281	10562	33116	64906	51082
山　西 Shanxi	1345932	378214	252619	47378	34693	17698	11708	14118	86745	65188
内蒙古 Inner Mongolia	202454	78287	51192	7198	2315	1523	880	15179	15101	6559
辽　宁 Liaoning	340227	99564	71526	9420	6136	4713	1854	5915	20115	10830
吉　林 Jilin	56805	22975	18631	2507	591	725	521		6138	2832
黑龙江 Heilongjiang	164734	71088	52793	7230	3270	2616	1397	3782	14944	10890
上　海 Shanghai	138660	43408	19046	4914	5284	2019	714	11431	8558	3550
江　苏 Jiangsu	360777	133214	75467	31098	9480	2784	551	13834	21024	10780
浙　江 Zhejiang	986752	361773	184512	67003	35172	12501	3284	59301	69504	50872
安　徽 Anhui	1262998	388995	295536	43434	27168	13899	4459	4499	94287	48313
福　建 Fujian	1725298	667300	417370	127833	68793	22859	6727	23718	93349	50825
江　西 Jiangxi	692407	300437	265002	13563	5479	5007	3449	7937	36674	17142
山　东 Shandong	410086	145226	68655	25276	21524	7495	1266	21010	36817	20474
河　南 Henan	545317	168124	127830	20050	8949	8138	3097	60	57884	40988
湖　北 Hubei	983683	332198	243253	43107	20928	8184	4068	12658	57217	31749
湖　南 Hunan	1064094	364444	253619	45087	24715	7534	7373	26116	58119	25506
广　东 Guangdong	2592155	1033133	719714	131445	58914	26211	12195	84654	153792	93146
广　西 Guangxi	706676	227181	155633	18338	14753	8475	4792	25190	34041	23751
海　南 Hainan	169810	38518	20735	3723	4223	2189	512	7136	7962	4059
重　庆 Chongqing	342857	99067	68650	15226	9523	4192	1476		13058	9857
四　川 Sichuan	746852	262360	192639	41405	13262	8058	2006	4990	40784	23164
贵　州 Guizhou	450572	145060	116320	15840	4889	5524	2367	120	29192	20070
云　南 Yunnan	589398	228404	164909	31936	13096	12615	1848	4000	28529	15266
西　藏 Tibet	282769	78766	54604	8924	5986	1316	684	7252	14606	7049
陕　西 Shaanxi	617902	255572	152543	37095	17049	10402	5726	32757	41798	26353
甘　肃 Gansu	427108	151872	117438	18994	6503	7984	953		49654	39855
青　海 Qinghai	46831	19500	15544	2290	351	1028	287		3362	2658
宁　夏 Ningxia	73677	28633	22216	5094	520	523	60	220	11008	9213
新　疆 Xinjiang	543236	247556	171936	36683	13126	15210	3358	7243	54888	32385

条件(一)(乡村)
Secondary Schools (1) (Rural Area)

单位:平方米
unit: m^2

生活用房 Residential and Welfare							其他用房 Rooms for Other Purposes	校舍面积中 of the Floor Space	
	教工宿舍 Apartments for Single								
合计 Total	小计 Subtotal	其中:教师周转宿舍 of Which: Accommodation for Circulation of Teachers	学生宿舍 Students' Dormitories	食堂 Dining Halls	厕所 Toilet	其他 Others		危房面积 Floor Space of Dilapidated Buildings	当年新增校舍 New Floor Space Added in Current Year
9802275	**2537956**	**509233**	**5078118**	**1450834**	**409168**	**326199**	**1295246**	**473198**	**918719**
110244	17382	50	52643	15554	7294	17371	23467		5198
55939	5060	156	33252	8666	5248	3713	7976		23923
466256	98731	17738	247395	76074	20084	23972	93591		12895
713376	118629	29140	408404	112802	41848	31693	167597	5217	48471
70701	16136	350	39119	11106	3080	1260	38365		1232
168838	12268	3552	110833	33947	9786	2004	51710		
23110	100		14854	6017	1501	638	4582		
70528	4024	56	46315	14906	4053	1230	8174	12620	
68018	360	200	29719	25628	11628	683	18676		
188383	40358	27800	103286	21439	11772	11528	18156		158000
476594	102130	8182	242155	92414	27457	12438	78881		81914
730335	203631	16293	401615	91340	21297	12452	49381	17600	14420
829247	268510	40335	385059	137343	20208	18127	135402		51046
307908	58875	9303	180715	46939	12659	8720	47388	17011	60502
213908	32435	11918	130546	36375	11484	3068	14135		
287619	63687	3180	152922	48995	8607	13408	31690	24271	3428
565009	181248	21479	277004	70141	15171	21445	29259	1432	4376
588137	212558	52211	255690	82546	24012	13331	53394	44112	3449
1230370	371092	80240	590983	157720	63725	46850	174860	10731	16392
417085	134972	31784	217612	46582	9979	7940	28369	36002	27972
82246	33310	1190	34544	9887	2980	1525	41084		23999
225450	64905	4344	124704	31330	3685	826	5282	24560	29075
428769	111790	27412	235956	60927	11600	8496	14939	17088	76295
233857	61837	23327	119153	35808	10096	6963	42463	3142	81724
304688	86215	17156	162760	38246	9195	8272	27777	156600	33682
170708	64355	49642	74060	27237	2686	2370	18689		8939
303170	76448	9395	157762	37318	9344	22298	17362		60942
207165	46115	3648	113416	30867	10372	6395	18417	98318	22364
20191	3430		12570	2441	861	889	3778		1820
34036			27982	4974	840	240			120
210390	47365	19152	95090	35265	16616	16054	30402	4494	66541

普通高中办

Condition of School Buildings in Regular Senior

地　区 Region	占地面积(平方米) Areas of School Sites (m^2)			图书(册) Books & Magazines in Libraries (volume)	
	合计 Total	其中 of Which			合计 Total
		绿化用地面积 Green Areas	运动场地面积 Sports Areas		
总　计 Total	**940695586**	**238491391**	**209433965**	**738857314**	**4123799**
北　京 Beijing	12798987	2619642	4044828	17951125	162849
天　津 Tianjin	8363375	1299241	2266733	9583494	54441
河　北 Hebei	42877253	7987254	9611638	31310572	172027
山　西 Shanxi	31527492	5292063	6520568	19509227	118747
内蒙古 Inner Mongolia	21414324	3400656	5342363	11226404	65425
辽　宁 Liaoning	22187198	3811851	6117863	15343058	110092
吉　林 Jilin	12383531	2414427	3682738	8520038	55215
黑龙江 Heilongjiang	20769920	3116102	5463605	7492524	75414
上　海 Shanghai	9587095	3146510	2284139	13146520	105917
江　苏 Jiangsu	54245584	18013315	12088488	51207902	297491
浙　江 Zhejiang	44359516	14347909	9857654	37234172	230653
安　徽 Anhui	51429221	11557927	10083149	30574336	161024
福　建 Fujian	34950664	9588431	9698194	42718517	168658
江　西 Jiangxi	35722516	10529947	7007498	23440967	124287
山　东 Shandong	58937513	16842806	13808548	50069950	268034
河　南 Henan	56668579	11195233	11089741	32743083	153506
湖　北 Hubei	38541221	11041384	7525031	20149275	115188
湖　南 Hunan	44717422	13170290	8274585	27599496	145849
广　东 Guangdong	87453349	28034166	18942922	98646318	574633
广　西 Guangxi	30153850	7657004	6104643	21600175	92189
海　南 Hainan	9051280	2513022	1877823	5429278	30191
重　庆 Chongqing	21799098	6223892	4860489	14963729	98966
四　川 Sichuan	47510607	11640434	11598989	43818232	200872
贵　州 Guizhou	26359759	5839344	5561460	22314741	78350
云　南 Yunnan	33018210	9341495	5772787	18659788	105279
西　藏 Tibet	2907427	439560	328369	1630684	6003
陕　西 Shaanxi	24301330	4734888	6442247	26359456	134825
甘　肃 Gansu	18484227	3088973	4814411	15671311	83213
青　海 Qinghai	5065670	703345	1198454	4124449	22844
宁　夏 Ningxia	7441071	2271215	1280481	4616183	29457
新　疆 Xinjiang	25668297	6629065	5883527	11202310	82160

学条件(二)(总计)

Secondary Schools (2) (Total)

计算机数(台) No. of Computers(set)		教室(间) Classroom(room)		教室中:普通教室(间) of Which: General Classroom (room)		固定资产总值(万元) Total Volue of Fixed Asset (10,000 yuan)		
其中:教学用计算机 No. of Computers Used for Instruction		合计 Total	其中:网络多媒体教室 of Which: Network Multimedia Classroom	合计 Total	其中:网络多媒体教室 of Which: Network Multimedia Classroom	合计 Total	其中:教学仪器设备资产值 of Which: Total Volue of Equip & Instru.	
小计 Subtotal	其中:平板电脑 of Which: Tablet PC						小计 Subtotal	其中:实验设备 of Which: for Profession
3146203	**158288**	**847051**	**445296**	**686706**	**389986**	**55903115.75**	**5841188.02**	**2186292.82**
138323	2512	20395	16697	13404	12246	1752713.85	391300.61	49343.97
40919	1395	8773	5217	6767	4765	585116.06	81417.87	18786.00
137050	7865	41485	20904	31387	18284	2144701.23	187697.32	86228.35
95706	1818	28617	14925	22879	13919	1740206.61	169211.99	83434.09
50982		15145	8990	13013	8373	1265206.74	99726.69	42498.39
78687	6951	22711	10774	18588	9723	1388315.51	149621.22	57183.42
40441	1896	11791	4940	9863	4470	653095.66	68108.87	32818.70
57482	2507	18584	7382	14333	6664	950733.86	108757.48	52995.13
87100	2188	12643	10203	8503	7556	1489306.54	227111.93	65796.21
230707	9853	46481	31684	33122	26733	4950547.49	447682.85	157353.91
190862	6184	32350	25994	23689	21940	3368702.66	309084.67	92527.05
125884	12636	48094	15053	40512	13686	2423767.44	220223.74	101690.65
130647	593	33102	20988	25699	17876	1959234.08	235417.64	92131.24
99536	9562	26296	11725	24074	11765	1501749.98	137328.40	56723.71
208923	8888	48185	33104	38621	29664	3522644.25	344698.82	102053.08
127411	7624	56123	20768	47312	18556	2383778.44	171624.77	86834.83
88882	6184	26930	12426	22408	11153	2231860.44	203254.60	90673.95
117097	10198	26754	15916	21666	14532	2417102.92	248325.46	111704.51
338678	26435	85689	52429	64833	42292	5398955.00	676261.00	260153.00
70853	796	20362	9363	18144	9359	1051331.76	109457.77	48082.63
22826	4673	6578	3506	5708	3131	515257.65	54101.60	20252.46
77833	6171	18924	12819	16332	11951	1421239.21	134492.85	42522.06
161805	2498	59858	21115	49168	18846	3179785.66	341827.89	129766.86
64759	4200	25897	9467	21914	9182	1405145.85	124582.93	54569.16
85855	3120	25588	11273	21109	10504	1622010.38	122285.27	42188.05
4311	220	1158	343	1021	258	147600.80	7673.17	3744.61
106655	6535	30173	13293	24373	11752	1707506.02	213499.62	105555.75
63733	3284	18637	9735	24889	8085	983276.09	89497.72	38625.82
17695	1060	5170	1838	3610	1581	242540.64	26836.18	8864.86
21433	230	4091	3132	3268	2718	345095.46	36451.01	11514.31
63128	212	20467	9293	16497	8422	1154587.47	103626.08	39676.06

普通高中办

Condition of School Buildings in Regular Senior

地 区 Region	占地面积(平方米) Areas of School Sites (m^2)			图书(册) Books & Magazines in Libraries (volume)	
	合计 Total	其中 of Which			合计 Total
		绿化用地面积 Green Areas	运动场地面积 Sports Areas		
总 计 Total	**419516153**	**113552344**	**98693985**	**379950833**	**2447141**
北 京 Beijing	10271576	1910570	3323175	16304924	148326
天 津 Tianjin	5682930	928344	1583073	7469216	44593
河 北 Hebei	16554699	3355194	3882396	14308747	86556
山 西 Shanxi	12931930	2253107	2954473	10310865	62819
内蒙古 Inner Mongolia	10451899	1821033	2635797	6490109	39201
辽 宁 Liaoning	15437896	2724104	4391589	11944683	86306
吉 林 Jilin	7834758	1578226	2263428	6048593	39456
黑龙江 Heilongjiang	10769973	1687068	2860987	4492343	45724
上 海 Shanghai	7764165	2552688	1884251	11622011	93260
江 苏 Jiangsu	29260837	10117564	6285691	26966588	173635
浙 江 Zhejiang	24269782	7967003	5327798	20218857	134297
安 徽 Anhui	13880051	3645314	2837022	9351978	56591
福 建 Fujian	11999396	3503402	3321019	18212132	83945
江 西 Jiangxi	10917968	3423386	2362809	8280955	55433
山 东 Shandong	31387823	9201118	7499259	29120141	158303
河 南 Henan	21894957	4952626	4705852	14940315	78454
湖 北 Hubei	21214765	6388345	4426897	12042391	71085
湖 南 Hunan	15452763	4877390	3096788	10282039	62773
广 东 Guangdong	48869907	16257174	11092823	60912582	457874
广 西 Guangxi	10275978	2689334	2480466	8647306	43135
海 南 Hainan	4937797	1332305	1143718	3264390	20142
重 庆 Chongqing	9943179	3115088	2408815	8018857	58141
四 川 Sichuan	18608477	4934064	4708994	17537125	95299
贵 州 Guizhou	7536753	1696857	1598904	6302937	31065
云 南 Yunnan	10233375	3205603	2038854	7620390	47366
西 藏 Tibet	899221	140558	117670	484529	2437
陕 西 Shaanxi	8682776	1791800	2501544	12490142	65060
甘 肃 Gansu	5244206	1042648	1373590	6252832	30686
青 海 Qinghai	1518222	246597	337698	1338601	9321
宁 夏 Ningxia	4116038	1306929	740589	2851320	18839
新 疆 Xinjiang	10672056	2906905	2508016	5822935	47019

学条件(二)(城区)

Secondary Schools (2) (Urban Area)

计算机数(台) No. of Computers(set) 其中:教学用计算机 No. of Computers Used for Instruction 小计 Subtotal	其中:平板电脑 of Which: Tablet PC	教室(间) Classroom(room) 合计 Total	其中:网络多媒体教室 of Which: Network Multimedia Classroom	教室中:普通教室(间) of Which: General Classroom (room) 合计 Total	其中:网络多媒体教室 of Which: Network Multimedia Classroom	固定资产总值(万元) Total Volue of Fixed Asset (10,000 yuan) 合计 Total	其中:教学仪器设备资产值 of Which: Total Value of Equip & Instru. 小计 Subtotal	其中:实验设备 of Which: for Profession
1802746	**87882**	**410631**	**255846**	**325901**	**221342**	**30698477.98**	**3655603.95**	**1212676.19**
125454	2499	18224	15005	11869	10918	1620208.19	363223.11	45550.32
33924	1203	6621	4139	5065	3760	468353.25	69303.09	14387.94
68950	2715	18447	10560	13681	9106	996773.27	102476.45	43430.85
48850	918	13718	8179	10755	7380	869989.05	97866.02	45169.82
30420		8330	5481	7234	5005	742748.83	60670.94	21847.12
62506	5456	16215	8493	13292	7672	1088349.31	117227.52	44056.52
28884	1501	8113	3710	6876	3400	489542.47	52302.22	24608.10
33525	1476	10530	4689	8094	4206	602032.55	67075.48	31985.47
76944	2185	11094	9069	7497	6736	1230933.97	206500.01	60702.02
134880	6122	24813	17778	17696	14795	3110716.00	289821.13	90409.93
109408	3419	18443	15182	13386	12550	1937179.76	187461.93	49533.23
43740	5098	15333	5591	12990	5025	747887.28	80426.47	38226.25
63887	142	13486	9982	10519	8545	895174.48	118523.06	42470.07
44068	5149	8731	5044	7979	5197	548322.45	62533.76	21738.99
120618	3709	26451	20089	20877	17978	2044321.00	212596.94	55976.77
65321	5530	21778	9977	18224	8931	995413.03	91232.84	43473.79
55811	2855	16133	7998	13283	7186	1363112.96	125491.55	55895.07
49357	3944	11318	7182	9381	6569	1090269.21	119781.88	46812.76
241463	15613	49085	35609	39177	29915	3683462.00	514926.00	185859.00
33250	572	7796	4005	6886	4132	448371.42	58160.34	20741.45
14533	3527	3996	2316	3450	1971	319243.96	37992.83	12603.01
46270	3580	9681	7116	8458	6852	820817.27	76224.16	20009.05
77415	2190	24321	11174	19615	9866	1470307.43	176399.83	59919.78
25143	2333	7742	3805	6615	3737	489407.66	54863.76	18846.53
38104	2149	8362	4928	7424	4588	683675.16	64465.31	18344.53
1554	30	426	115	442	96	34868.67	3286.55	2019.66
49234	2916	12405	6729	10034	5861	693815.91	113718.91	51094.56
23416	842	5474	4243	4240	2443	370367.95	43271.58	15400.07
6717	70	1456	690	1094	588	59065.57	8972.50	2919.47
13448		2468	1990	1942	1760	196393.09	22807.98	7123.49
35652	139	9641	4978	7826	4574	587354.83	55999.80	21520.57

普通高中办

Condition of School Buildings in Regular Senior

地　区 Region	占地面积(平方米) Areas of School Sites (m²)			图书(册) Books & Magazines in Libraries (volume)	
	合计 Total	其中 of Which			合计 Total
		绿化用地面积 Green Areas	运动场地面积 Sports Areas		
总　计 Total	**80743435**	**23586112**	**17417115**	**57634787**	**468886**
北　京 Beijing	1400930	233223	366505	583760	5705
天　津 Tianjin	425375	53054	119037	465037	2425
河　北 Hebei	4096658	1084119	887303	2636742	16375
山　西 Shanxi	1516838	219585	366396	1244714	6943
内蒙古 Inner Mongolia	863478	218877	125638	419327	2742
辽　宁 Liaoning	2384605	480780	541825	1256386	9573
吉　林 Jilin	914375	202553	199123	494942	2210
黑龙江 Heilongjiang	1259747	302170	324377	559560	4324
上　海 Shanghai	952687	346515	150426	595642	4968
江　苏 Jiangsu	4466194	1348670	854973	3544644	20730
浙　江 Zhejiang	6312355	1951932	1396987	4305676	29151
安　徽 Anhui	2556194	704804	434073	1308202	5667
福　建 Fujian	2364427	730933	664495	2820452	10978
江　西 Jiangxi	1403818	392685	258186	910579	4947
山　东 Shandong	9942945	3243548	2174978	7624333	37940
河　南 Henan	5014364	1049018	1024613	1987210	12491
湖　北 Hubei	3134149	1092936	663243	1649224	9616
湖　南 Hunan	4157665	1306416	672207	2016750	12424
广　东 Guangdong	14301590	5017258	3141394	15043739	221071
广　西 Guangxi	1774762	487201	561396	1214452	6409
海　南 Hainan	527429	166505	102100	187397	1348
重　庆 Chongqing	745842	290504	176760	365260	3154
四　川 Sichuan	3542953	917827	804849	2193034	14125
贵　州 Guizhou	1702549	373802	281984	827945	3926
云　南 Yunnan	2358480	744977	427981	1365430	8420
西　藏 Tibet					
陕　西 Shaanxi	1046335	261794	309154	1074253	4646
甘　肃 Gansu	276579	27198	98587	272780	1199
青　海 Qinghai	155952	34124	26260	118017	878
宁　夏 Ningxia	358521	66472	70900	231479	768
新　疆 Xinjiang	785639	236632	191365	317821	3733

学条件(二)(城乡结合区)
Secondary Schools (2) (Urban-rural Transitional Area)

计算机数(台) No. of Computers(set)		教室(间) Classroom(room)		教室中:普通教室(间) of Which: General Classroom (room)		固定资产总值(万元) Total Value of Fixed Asset (10,000 yuan)		
其中:教学用计算机 No. of Computers Used for Instruction		合计 Total	其中:网络多媒体教室 of Which: Network Multimedia Classroom	合计 Total	其中:网络多媒体教室 of Which: Network Multimedia Classroom	合计 Total	其中:教学仪器设备资产值 of Which: Total Volue of Equip & Instru.	
小计 Subtotal	其中:平板电脑 of Which: Tablet PC						小计 Subtotal	其中:实验设备 of Which: for Profession
250115	**11068**	**65663**	**37299**	**51837**	**33147**	**5439062.94**	**484097.67**	**186291.01**
4301	176	1040	739	808	595	110858.61	9084.85	1354.95
1553	90	360	214	273	147	37532.20	3624.30	492.81
13508	420	4599	2235	3037	2263	233774.49	17200.99	9376.17
5820	196	1319	723	1074	629	72414.23	6472.29	4867.66
2383		471	441	418	418	95633.30	1958.00	594.05
7405	800	2257	1064	1785	912	191997.56	14923.99	6448.89
1730	33	451	132	365	123	32870.00	2852.50	952.30
3051	61	844	362	661	340	68910.25	9556.52	4381.17
3883	430	736	588	546	470	68395.06	11865.68	2117.92
16132	608	3203	1977	2278	1736	503138.00	38169.28	14996.74
24692	756	4220	3359	3021	2802	486799.12	38421.72	13338.48
4772	110	2698	650	2298	618	115690.74	9557.97	4172.37
7761		2049	1265	1561	1055	155141.34	10825.62	5546.42
3770	290	842	339	822	487	49696.59	5068.02	1266.26
29603	388	7613	5397	6059	4788	562524.68	47266.81	16872.13
9633	871	4123	1632	3126	1425	193537.20	13146.32	6392.89
6873	167	2316	1091	1943	1048	167044.10	17178.72	5918.47
9969	1096	2388	1510	2042	1430	271606.65	23852.70	7333.50
55272	3741	12672	8433	10147	7165	1127097.00	128071.00	48929.00
4844	20	1431	781	1295	754	77523.99	5528.19	2919.31
970	1	384	84	326	60	47801.00	4611.00	1331.00
2471		690	560	606	540	74021.20	3654.60	800.90
11370	56	3689	1404	2881	1179	319182.28	26098.69	9597.91
3245	383	1301	477	1090	416	73409.79	6906.56	2106.81
6786	343	1725	831	1519	803	154883.58	10085.63	4896.23
3838	32	1034	468	891	436	52248.15	11130.26	6316.29
912		290	115	219	118	7898.84	2019.24	655.35
665		129	64	75	60	12401.00	528.00	302.00
722		176	132	153	117	20860.02	1846.14	508.91
2181		613	232	518	213	54171.97	2592.08	1504.12

普通高中办

Condition of School Buildings in Regular Senior

地　区 Region	占地面积(平方米) Areas of School Sites (m²)			图书(册) Books & Magazines in Libraries (volume)	
	合计 Total	其中 of Which			合计 Total
		绿化用地面积 Green Areas	运动场地面积 Sports Areas		
总　计 Total	**470936164**	**112156286**	**100526974**	**331517837**	**1542931**
北　京 Beijing	1847263	472326	530022	1247119	10327
天　津 Tianjin	2353316	294392	597311	1874078	8943
河　北 Hebei	23703720	4135191	5273519	16031562	77970
山　西 Shanxi	15778716	2614152	3000232	8107479	50146
内蒙古 Inner Mongolia	10282323	1401573	2572058	4652790	25615
辽　宁 Liaoning	6067451	959421	1646567	3095198	22085
吉　林 Jilin	4182532	737336	1337867	2349313	15161
黑龙江 Heilongjiang	9554811	1343884	2442155	2808396	28274
上　海 Shanghai	1539212	532693	363853	1346123	10654
江　苏 Jiangsu	24514267	7717397	5704696	23863236	121460
浙　江 Zhejiang	17825505	5707954	4120173	15446457	87451
安　徽 Anhui	34122262	7146299	6681756	19668071	97646
福　建 Fujian	18560223	5015197	5247299	20526933	73305
江　西 Jiangxi	23181294	6680532	4179907	14502199	65952
山　东 Shandong	26259076	7108318	5991353	20340736	106726
河　南 Henan	33125898	6012785	6190543	17217243	72409
湖　北 Hubei	15333860	4187024	2719000	7169480	39629
湖　南 Hunan	27134446	7791828	4793206	16061489	77074
广　东 Guangdong	31223493	9276497	6445995	33035768	98108
广　西 Guangxi	17873691	4456516	3264690	11924016	43370
海　南 Hainan	3647773	1020892	676542	2046612	8895
重　庆 Chongqing	11077415	2907424	2291151	6699280	38654
四　川 Sichuan	27316558	6231530	6453059	25116691	99036
贵　州 Guizhou	17228369	3828130	3735071	15148858	45357
云　南 Yunnan	20481723	5621511	3369273	9975441	51355
西　藏 Tibet	1256709	121368	115745	864364	2322
陕　西 Shaanxi	14316940	2695078	3602761	12908648	64712
甘　肃 Gansu	12032151	1838136	3123405	8721305	48410
青　海 Qinghai	3376048	411106	824286	2732874	12891
宁　夏 Ningxia	2883838	831978	472657	1693822	10073
新　疆 Xinjiang	12855281	3057818	2760822	4342256	28921

学条件(二)(镇区)
Secondary Schools (2) (Counties & Towns Area)

计算机数(台) No. of Computers(set)		教室(间) Classroom(room)		教室中:普通教室(间) of Which: General Classroom (room)		固定资产总值(万元) Total Volue of Fixed Asset (10,000 yuan)		
其中:教学用计算机 No. of Computers Used for Instruction		合计 Total	其中:网络多媒体教室 of Which: Network Multimedia Classroom	合计 Total	其中:网络多媒体教室 of Which: Network Multimedia Classroom	合计 Total	其中:教学仪器设备资产值 of Which: Total Volue of Equip & Instru.	
小计 Subtotal	其中:平板电脑 of Which: Tablet PC						小计 Subtotal	其中:实验设备 of Which: for Profession
1236058	**64908**	**402572**	**174939**	**333792**	**156130**	**22899232.76**	**1995072.31**	**897609.79**
8865	13	1613	1259	1166	1031	91620.52	18698.23	2808.80
6501	147	1937	968	1531	912	94986.49	10372.25	4188.86
62245	5098	21343	9587	16772	8706	1027858.78	79147.29	40592.34
42162	735	12835	5966	10656	5736	708195.11	60844.78	32689.33
20046		6368	3458	5371	3321	495320.11	37917.75	19973.83
15053	1303	5844	2086	4722	1863	271124.20	27536.20	12168.90
11066	395	3576	1226	2910	1069	157216.19	15360.75	8071.40
22641	789	7602	2503	5910	2295	330612.01	39822.60	20124.26
8713	3	1326	1003	825	720	215089.69	16474.92	4204.54
93882	3731	21031	13721	14911	11783	1763521.11	150193.07	63588.20
74160	2338	12418	9722	9233	8526	1258705.19	111647.43	39856.61
76599	7051	30122	9000	25269	8256	1550993.66	131726.57	59437.30
57455	409	16483	9602	12857	8201	857959.96	96033.83	42101.06
53381	4283	16498	6238	15097	6143	892503.83	71785.58	33524.04
85763	5179	21207	12754	17315	11474	1404681.25	128481.47	45069.04
60425	2049	33111	10447	28022	9308	1356121.83	78297.43	42119.02
29461	3239	9482	3956	8021	3601	751048.36	69189.47	31088.22
63607	5794	14251	8168	11276	7356	1240147.50	121610.61	61142.53
81685	8563	32279	14156	22123	10035	1396980.00	134244.00	64288.00
33414	223	11414	4900	10228	4820	547333.04	46745.49	25602.03
7339	1001	2360	1125	2064	1063	177143.24	13411.84	6026.48
30134	2591	8715	5379	7566	4912	568913.58	54927.86	21135.01
79049	144	34048	9266	28409	8391	1632953.15	154383.24	66239.55
37960	1803	17172	5519	14414	5316	862535.55	66652.85	33782.83
42168	921	15886	5883	12545	5498	864796.35	50394.53	21480.60
1698	190	482	160	348	94	64578.50	2647.82	998.15
53286	3558	16710	6135	13421	5494	936623.82	91793.33	49534.61
36718	2085	12283	5213	19923	5400	559795.80	42537.27	20806.58
10396	990	3543	1107	2385	956	178202.39	17496.28	5694.79
7555	210	1519	1048	1240	872	129279.57	13106.83	4048.22
22631	73	9114	3384	7262	2978	512391.98	41590.74	15224.66

普通高中办

Condition of School Buildings in Regular Senior

地 区 Region	占地面积(平方米) Areas of School Sites (m²)			图书(册) Books & Magazines in Libraries (volume)	
	合计 Total	其中 of Which			合计 Total
		绿化用地面积 Green Areas	运动场地面积 Sports Areas		
总 计 Total	**128281205**	**31790510**	**26394927**	**84304699**	**402253**
北 京 Beijing	626237	166823	184220	414458	3538
天 津 Tianjin	926596	101245	255140	727582	3649
河 北 Hebei	9602712	1560922	2083957	6373550	29599
山 西 Shanxi	5813428	928871	1018191	2637318	17710
内蒙古 Inner Mongolia	1044677	72200	219959	418626	1952
辽 宁 Liaoning	1163432	147473	269954	369895	3330
吉 林 Jilin	187995	40853	48672	69770	442
黑龙江 Heilongjiang	983559	88060	224828	206659	2444
上 海 Shanghai	235534	78151	43539	166811	1251
江 苏 Jiangsu	5831148	1875726	1366822	5363480	28251
浙 江 Zhejiang	6182814	1804254	1331592	4969871	26972
安 徽 Anhui	8583674	2065646	1664753	4190239	20538
福 建 Fujian	4271786	1234023	1155295	4241211	16139
江 西 Jiangxi	3677858	1173846	514238	1804674	7594
山 东 Shandong	12549914	3411884	3001485	9697878	50230
河 南 Henan	11192534	1983939	1948868	5579456	22158
湖 北 Hubei	4208802	1324348	745878	1495731	9993
湖 南 Hunan	9269066	2982417	1561975	4605190	23104
广 东 Guangdong	11296872	3198529	2377260	11853340	38989
广 西 Guangxi	1709012	446611	309997	1108621	4458
海 南 Hainan	902079	232901	123960	419394	2179
重 庆 Chongqing	2927437	1034204	454663	1343486	7333
四 川 Sichuan	4333434	1046817	1189626	3988984	19009
贵 州 Guizhou	4343601	871259	996902	3414022	10488
云 南 Yunnan	7005613	2058124	1067627	3202665	16578
西 藏 Tibet	207336	58990	22841	110535	328
陕 西 Shaanxi	3836505	857827	848568	2674875	15043
甘 肃 Gansu	2997930	437607	783478	2023320	12899
青 海 Qinghai	593590	106689	156960	359790	2344
宁 夏 Ningxia	312077	36970	53316	184000	645
新 疆 Xinjiang	1463953	363301	370363	289268	3066

学条件(二)(镇乡结合区)
Secondary Schools (2)(County-Town Transitional Area)

计算机数(台) No. of Computers(set) 其中:教学用计算机 No. of Computers Used for Instruction 小计 Subtotal	其中:平板电脑 of Which: Tablet PC	教室(间) Classroom(room) 合计 Total	其中:网络多媒体教室 of Which: Network Multimedia Classroom	教室中:普通教室(间) of Which: General Classroom (room) 合计 Total	其中:网络多媒体教室 of Which: Network Multimedia Classroom	固定资产总值(万元) Total Volue of Fixed Asset (10,000 yuan) 合计 Total	其中:教学仪器设备资产值 of Which: Total Volue of Equip & Instru. 小计 Subtotal	其中:实验设备 of Which: for Profession
325078	**19367**	**106910**	**48552**	**82778**	**41113**	**6486324.65**	**525816.32**	**239967.13**
3068	13	548	372	413	296	19533.89	6270.79	1468.26
2680	8	784	400	702	372	24813.76	3042.83	1252.51
23489	2462	8897	3844	6704	3103	386617.88	29379.58	16575.70
13949	146	4690	2149	3723	2170	199470.53	20955.34	10755.67
1544		679	362	496	340	61013.20	4418.00	2561.60
2668	73	907	383	829	365	67043.20	5721.00	3078.00
347		213	7	106	2	4212.10	262.50	77.80
2057	140	752	141	549	103	47732.90	3623.62	2342.63
1077		240	164	105	76	39783.75	2823.49	627.58
21346	948	4725	3576	3394	2962	385852.63	36042.09	15804.67
23233	829	4138	3315	3061	2931	444413.97	35641.70	12673.83
16838	1212	7084	1577	5736	1447	432536.15	25016.93	11987.32
13003	7	4194	2545	3433	2183	217905.81	19450.09	10117.40
6444	616	1952	621	1894	600	143186.13	12118.04	6695.46
41685	2119	9717	6555	8308	6115	673520.50	63158.39	23324.66
18089	520	10242	2974	8486	2555	412997.98	22539.13	12535.24
7935	1031	2245	835	1866	747	234080.11	13680.22	6269.33
18079	2571	4230	2394	3262	1907	394539.56	34801.72	16577.15
33796	4048	15809	6593	8894	3867	615392.00	56080.00	25938.00
3148	31	1056	360	963	407	46547.27	2994.00	1839.58
1561	177	602	261	526	242	49024.00	3308.10	1194.00
5552	842	1655	1301	1501	1161	156056.89	14585.03	7182.78
14912	2	4934	1935	3996	1733	326124.65	36610.75	12606.21
9261	354	4078	1256	3180	1130	227800.16	14970.22	6787.57
13669	303	4845	2088	4327	1976	359116.83	18241.99	10250.28
314		84	3	38	2	12484.00	369.00	357.00
11926	383	4060	960	3213	853	248912.62	22364.02	13260.06
7972	232	1948	861	1734	811	139168.16	10052.84	3734.12
2118	300	478	308	415	291	32805.95	1299.25	604.56
580		196	66	174	66	18268.92	1518.14	325.17
2738		928	346	750	300	65369.15	4477.52	1162.99

普通高中办

Condition of School Buildings in Regular Senior

地 区 Region	占地面积(平方米) Areas of School Sites (m²)			图书(册) Books & Magazines in Libraries (volume)	
	合计 Total	其中 of Which			合计 Total
		绿化用地面积 Green Areas	运动场地面积 Sports Areas		
总 计 Total	**50243269**	**12782761**	**10213006**	**27388644**	**133727**
北 京 Beijing	680148	236746	191631	399082	4196
天 津 Tianjin	327129	76505	86349	240200	905
河 北 Hebei	2618834	496869	455723	970263	7501
山 西 Shanxi	2816846	424804	565863	1090883	5782
内蒙古 Inner Mongolia	680102	178050	134508	83505	609
辽 宁 Liaoning	681851	128326	79707	303177	1701
吉 林 Jilin	366241	98865	81443	122132	598
黑龙江 Heilongjiang	445136	85150	160463	191785	1416
上 海 Shanghai	283718	61129	36035	178386	2003
江 苏 Jiangsu	470480	178354	98101	378078	2396
浙 江 Zhejiang	2264229	672952	409683	1568858	8905
安 徽 Anhui	3426908	766314	564371	1554287	6787
福 建 Fujian	4391045	1069832	1129876	3979452	11408
江 西 Jiangxi	1623254	426029	464782	657813	2902
山 东 Shandong	1290614	533370	317936	609073	3005
河 南 Henan	1647724	229822	193346	585525	2643
湖 北 Hubei	1992596	466015	379134	937404	4474
湖 南 Hunan	2130213	501072	384591	1255968	6002
广 东 Guangdong	7359949	2500495	1404104	4697968	18651
广 西 Guangxi	2004181	511154	359487	1028853	5684
海 南 Hainan	465710	159825	57563	118276	1154
重 庆 Chongqing	778504	201380	160523	245592	2171
四 川 Sichuan	1585572	474840	436936	1164416	6537
贵 州 Guizhou	1594637	314357	227485	862946	1928
云 南 Yunnan	2303112	514381	364660	1063957	6558
西 藏 Tibet	751497	177634	94954	281791	1244
陕 西 Shaanxi	1301614	248010	337942	960666	5053
甘 肃 Gansu	1207870	208189	317416	697174	4117
青 海 Qinghai	171400	45642	36470	52974	632
宁 夏 Ningxia	441195	132308	67235	71041	545
新 疆 Xinjiang	2140960	664342	614689	1037119	6220

学条件(二)(乡村)
Secondary Schools (2) (Rural Area)

计算机数(台) No. of Computers(set)		教室(间) Classroom(room)		教室中:普通教室(间) of Which: General Classroom (room)		固定资产总值(万元) Total Volue of Fixed Asset (10,000 yuan)		
其中:教学用计算机 No. of Computers Used for Instruction		合计 Total	其中:网络多媒体教室 of Which: Network Multimedia Classroom	合计 Total	其中:网络多媒体教室 of Which: Network Multimedia Classroom	合计 Total	其中:教学仪器设备资产值 of Which: Total Volue of Equip & Instru.	
小计 Subtotal	其中:平板电脑 of Which: Tablet PC						小计 Subtotal	其中:实验设备 of Which: for Profession
107399	**5498**	**33848**	**14511**	**27013**	**12514**	**2305405.01**	**190511.76**	**76006.84**
4004		558	433	369	297	40885.14	9379.27	984.85
494	45	215	110	171	93	21776.32	1742.53	209.20
5855	52	1695	757	934	472	120069.18	6073.58	2205.16
4694	165	2064	780	1468	803	162022.45	10501.19	5574.94
516		447	51	408	47	27137.80	1138.00	677.44
1128	192	652	195	574	188	28842.00	4857.50	958.00
491		102	4	77	1	6337.00	445.90	139.20
1316	242	452	190	329	163	18089.30	1859.40	885.40
1443		223	131	181	100	43282.88	4137.00	889.65
1945		637	185	515	155	76310.38	7668.65	3355.78
7294	427	1489	1090	1070	864	172817.71	9975.31	3137.21
5545	487	2639	462	2253	405	124886.50	8070.70	4027.10
9305	42	3133	1404	2323	1130	206099.64	20860.75	7560.11
2087	130	1067	443	998	425	60923.70	3009.06	1460.68
2542		527	261	429	212	73642.00	3620.41	1007.27
1665	45	1234	344	1066	317	32243.58	2094.50	1242.02
3610	90	1315	472	1104	366	117699.12	8573.58	3690.66
4133	460	1185	566	1009	607	86686.21	6932.97	3749.22
15530	2259	4325	2664	3533	2342	318513.00	27091.00	10006.00
4189	1	1152	458	1030	407	55627.30	4551.94	1739.15
954	145	222	65	194	97	18870.45	2696.93	1622.97
1429		528	324	308	187	31508.36	3340.83	1378.00
5341	164	1489	675	1144	589	76525.08	11044.82	3607.53
1656	64	983	143	885	129	53202.64	3066.32	1939.80
5583	50	1340	462	1140	418	73538.87	7425.43	2362.92
1059		250	68	231	68	48153.63	1738.80	726.80
4135	61	1058	429	918	397	77066.29	7987.38	4926.58
3599	357	880	279	726	242	53112.34	3688.87	2419.17
582		171	41	131	37	5272.68	367.40	250.60
430	20	104	94	86	86	19422.80	536.20	342.60
4845		1712	931	1409	870	54840.66	6035.54	2930.83

中等职业学

Number of Secondary

地 区 Region	合计 Total	其中：中央部门 of Which: under Central Ministries & Agencies	其中：地方部门 of Which: under Local Auth.	其中：民办 of Which: Non-government	中等职业学校 普通中等专业学校 Reg. Specialized Sec. Schools 小计 Subtotal	其中：中央部门 of Which: under Central Ministries & Agencies	其中：地方部门 of Which: under Local Auth.
总 计 Total	**9380**	**23**	**6875**	**2482**	**3577**	**18**	**2667**
北 京 Beijing	97	7	67	23	31	6	25
天 津 Tianjin	83		76	7	39		39
河 北 Hebei	636	1	443	192	265	1	103
山 西 Shanxi	445		350	95	92		79
内蒙古 Inner Mongolia	264		193	71	81		41
辽 宁 Liaoning	311		223	88	120		109
吉 林 Jilin	302		225	77	54		49
黑龙江 Heilongjiang	373		311	62	73		40
上 海 Shanghai	111	2	102	7	62	2	57
江 苏 Jiangsu	269		246	23	170		154
浙 江 Zhejiang	337		249	88	48		43
安 徽 Anhui	463		336	127	115		97
福 建 Fujian	230		187	43	230		187
江 西 Jiangxi	429	1	272	156	78	1	58
山 东 Shandong	525		385	140	247		197
河 南 Henan	716	2	496	218	145	1	134
湖 北 Hubei	308	2	236	70	226	2	173
湖 南 Hunan	496		286	210	46		41
广 东 Guangdong	502		378	124	384		280
广 西 Guangxi	309		217	92	309		217
海 南 Hainan	87		54	33	29		25
重 庆 Chongqing	141		118	23	23		21
四 川 Sichuan	503	1	272	230	249	1	77
贵 州 Guizhou	218		154	64	58		56
云 南 Yunnan	390	2	336	52	83	1	69
西 藏 Tibet	6		6		6		6
陕 西 Shaanxi	316	1	199	116	45	1	42
甘 肃 Gansu	260	1	227	32	125		119
青 海 Qinghai	38		33	5	32		29
宁 夏 Ningxia	35		29	6	19		13
新 疆 Xinjiang	180	3	169	8	93	2	87

注：未含技工学校数据（下同）

Note: Data on Skilled Workers are not included (Same as the Followings)

校(机构)数
Vocational Schools (Institutions)

单位:所
unit: institution

Secondary Vocational Schools

其中:民办 of Which: Non-government	成人中等专业学校 Adults Specialized Sec. Schools				职业高中学校 Vocational High Schools			
	小计 Subtotal	其中:中央部门 of Which: under Central Ministries & Agencies	其中:地方部门 of Which: under Local Auth.	其中:民办 of Which: Non-government	小计 Subtotal	其中:中央部门 of Which: under Central Ministries & Agencies	其中:地方部门 of Which: under Local Auth.	其中:民办 of Which: Non-government
892	**1536**	**3**	**1384**	**149**	**4267**	**2**	**2824**	**1441**
	11	1	9	1	55		33	22
	19		19		25		18	7
161	165		153	12	206		187	19
13	119		119		234		152	82
40	61		61		122		91	31
11	1		1		190		113	77
5	82		82		166		94	72
33	156		153	3	144		118	26
3	21		20	1	28		25	3
16	34		33	1	65		59	6
5	37		36	1	252		170	82
18	61		55	6	287		184	103
43								
19	91		91		260		123	137
50	89		69	20	189		119	70
10	190		123	67	381	1	239	141
51	13		10	3	69		53	16
5	90		72	18	360		173	187
104	13		13		105		85	20
92								
4	5		5		53		24	29
2	47		44	3	71		53	18
171	23		13	10	231		182	49
2	14		13	1	146		85	61
13	130	1	129		177		138	39
2	8		8		263		149	114
6	33	1	30	2	102		78	24
3	2		2		4		2	2
6	3		3		13		13	
4	18		18		69	1	64	4

中等职业学校

Number of students in Secondary

地 区 Region	毕业生数 Graduates		招生数 Entrants			
	合计 Total	其中:获得职业资格证书 of Which: Recipients of Vocational Qualifications	合计 Total	其中:应届毕业 of Which: Graduates of Current Year		其中:五年制高职中职段 of Which: 5 - year Secondary Vocational Education
				小计 Subtotal	其中:初中毕业生 of Which: Junior Secondary School Graduates	
总 计 Total	**5575587**	**4336937**	**5412624**	**4631934**	**4446788**	**371335**
北 京 Beijing	75618	60640	55427	25807	25428	4236
天 津 Tianjin	39270	31939	33786	32294	30607	4032
河 北 Hebei	337100	233535	220896	184199	177530	7446
山 西 Shanxi	159749	129099	142943	127629	121787	14048
内蒙古 Inner Mongolia	95508	71732	83852	72874	71019	11817
辽 宁 Liaoning	127767	83504	117987	97290	93168	7131
吉 林 Jilin	83932	50643	61055	48762	43362	3494
黑龙江 Heilongjiang	91783	72294	83261	64930	62785	3251
上 海 Shanghai	48508	40627	44377	42294	40712	3075
江 苏 Jiangsu	306146	261097	259053	233324	231148	53694
浙 江 Zhejiang	207272	197082	191505	182651	181650	19689
安 徽 Anhui	324927	285670	369049	318227	310440	22042
福 建 Fujian	150811	139327	155040	108404	104153	7561
江 西 Jiangxi	159155	126287	167380	150410	146449	24131
山 东 Shandong	378626	292790	363547	329236	317857	50853
河 南 Henan	511694	391210	422209	373102	351845	19650
湖 北 Hubei	199722	166889	130826	126107	122930	2283
湖 南 Hunan	237097	205913	228627	214142	208189	25491
广 东 Guangdong	488286	285803	474927	429938	400958	9662
广 西 Guangxi	267471	167349	303601	190426	171543	17401
海 南 Hainan	40386	18879	51756	40834	39209	1523
重 庆 Chongqing	102518	84080	122154	117702	116717	5408
四 川 Sichuan	414213	383817	489969	397318	377589	7931
贵 州 Guizhou	100281	87800	247135	191503	190409	4872
云 南 Yunnan	210191	145918	179685	166614	162940	19863
西 藏 Tibet	6412	5063	6471	4320	4020	
陕 西 Shaanxi	177319	147287	163984	148364	139751	13516
甘 肃 Gansu	105043	82698	98604	90552	85806	2050
青 海 Qinghai	22386	15788	29277	20886	20015	520
宁 夏 Ningxia	31536	21289	30348	27132	26293	1204
新 疆 Xinjiang	74860	50888	83893	74663	70479	3461

(机构)学生数
Vocational Schools (Institutions)

单位:人
unit: person

在校学生数 Enrolment					预计毕业生数 Estimated Graduates for Next Year	
合计 Total	一年级 Grade 1	二年级 Grade 2	三年级 Grade 3	四年级及以上 Grade 4 and Over	合计 Total	其中:五年制高职中职段 of Which: 5 - year Secondary Vocational Education
15363842	**5418413**	**5028833**	**4817693**	**98903**	**5392971**	**254986**
164892	55463	56310	38025	15094	78492	3166
97443	33651	33538	30123	131	34365	2622
752285	221572	258754	269429	2530	304227	9159
436393	142928	138289	153239	1937	155480	3776
245414	83852	84249	76089	1224	83589	7725
349912	118204	112374	109449	9885	120537	7257
192672	61017	62677	68727	251	76607	2419
274020	83277	97642	91703	1398	102468	766
153298	44497	50986	42883	14932	55018	986
793716	259163	258568	269979	6006	276705	53348
578523	191544	188754	195677	2548	203961	13123
967746	369484	327137	264660	6465	348601	18398
525051	156470	190707	177086	788	194383	4886
484628	167343	162080	154272	933	159974	13874
1031585	363746	336642	322502	8695	360144	28171
1193105	422209	402634	367349	913	425708	19286
410795	130889	134535	143831	1540	148633	722
650569	228673	220418	196437	5041	204274	17392
1408894	474485	453785	475436	5188	484031	9449
822241	303996	276528	240345	1372	257768	2068
140225	51756	44546	43378	545	44262	971
362827	122911	118778	119952	1186	118159	2033
1195085	489843	352702	351748	792	475213	8108
475512	247135	123552	104807	18	118953	1884
494103	179710	160791	152735	867	155852	6086
17491	6559	6550	4382		6448	
454858	163944	144392	145734	788	167457	13280
289531	99230	98483	88517	3301	96700	983
77784	29277	26649	20224	1634	21535	713
93950	30358	28793	34740	59	38080	645
229294	85227	76990	64235	2842	75347	1690

中等职业学校

Number of Female students in Secondary

地 区 Region	毕业生数 Graduates		招生数 Entrants			
	合计 Total	其中:获得职业资格证书 of Which: Reciptents of Vocational Qualifications	合计 Total	其中:应届毕业 of Which: Graduates of Current Year		其中:五年制高职中职段 of Which:5 - year Secondary Vocational Education
				小计 Subtotal	其中:初中毕业生 of Which: Junior Secondary School Graduates	
总 计 Total	**2756207**	**2105777**	**2634661**	**2278446**	**2195851**	**204078**
北 京 Beijing	41692	33514	34685	11431	11197	1764
天 津 Tianjin	17106	13687	14229	13762	13146	1650
河 北 Hebei	165678	112711	111489	90843	87698	5047
山 西 Shanxi	82583	66559	73947	68055	65374	7446
内蒙古 Inner Mongolia	45522	34155	37666	33088	32492	5507
辽 宁 Liaoning	62159	38562	52800	44816	43124	4196
吉 林 Jilin	38473	22822	29534	24386	21803	1902
黑龙江 Heilongjiang	43765	34752	38379	31840	31221	2025
上 海 Shanghai	21957	17369	18388	17818	16927	1145
江 苏 Jiangsu	149522	123425	122336	110663	109795	29635
浙 江 Zhejiang	99810	94134	86540	83368	82735	10313
安 徽 Anhui	153187	132510	173579	152750	149546	13735
福 建 Fujian	71486	65947	68142	49697	47675	3955
江 西 Jiangxi	83763	67313	92547	84616	83174	15971
山 东 Shandong	180886	132776	171623	156581	151816	24953
河 南 Henan	261518	202130	223252	197127	187066	10572
湖 北 Hubei	99896	81627	61355	59449	58151	2084
湖 南 Hunan	119507	100848	112327	104900	101866	14043
广 东 Guangdong	250866	146183	235915	211634	198313	5471
广 西 Guangxi	119030	69054	128993	86965	80037	6530
海 南 Hainan	21451	10009	23619	18660	18234	628
重 庆 Chongqing	52492	44195	59938	57406	57153	3184
四 川 Sichuan	200834	181992	242081	198525	188039	5160
贵 州 Guizhou	51083	44432	127993	101471	101286	3891
云 南 Yunnan	107740	73874	91400	85142	83541	12035
西 藏 Tibet	2576	2093	1797	1767	1618	
陕 西 Shaanxi	91195	72678	80184	73108	69414	8028
甘 肃 Gansu	57609	44467	53707	50388	47838	1066
青 海 Qinghai	10146	6572	11999	8971	8688	217
宁 夏 Ningxia	16634	11332	16910	15390	15055	741
新 疆 Xinjiang	36041	24055	37307	33829	31829	1184

(机构)女学生数
Vocational Schools (Institutions)

单位:人
unit: person

在校学生数 Enrolment					预计毕业生数 Estimated Graduates for Next Year	
合计 Total	一年级 Grade 1	二年级 Grade 2	三年级 Grade 3	四年级及以上 Grade 4 and Over	合计 Total	其中:五年制高职中职段 of Which: 5 - year Secondary Vocational Education
7646365	**2636321**	**2514584**	**2437947**	**57513**	**2601593**	**148528**
93760	34715	32635	18378	8032	53464	1033
41705	14092	14082	13434	97	14433	1268
390001	111712	138366	138965	958	148391	5324
227537	73927	73406	79428	776	71571	3231
110994	37666	37072	35317	939	37683	4387
170041	52972	54358	54273	8438	57466	5006
92990	29528	29914	33345	203	35320	1783
130985	38379	46584	45384	638	45892	525
66061	18426	21216	18845	7574	23375	449
379507	122114	124191	128748	4454	127647	28869
266256	86548	87123	91809	776	93892	6710
468940	173745	159224	133039	2932	163203	12414
245026	69421	89759	85190	656	87669	3290
267521	92535	89664	84701	621	84461	9329
500297	171532	165156	158593	5016	168779	16694
633334	223252	209238	200464	380	219344	11266
198409	61368	65017	71109	915	68333	689
323605	112268	108812	99828	2697	99599	9419
717211	235305	234544	244650	2712	241591	5024
360169	129031	122206	108452	480	108817	934
68847	23648	22297	22647	255	19888	690
180225	60261	58872	60138	954	58908	1245
612327	241949	186154	183541	683	235361	5130
252847	127993	66819	58017	18	62847	1326
254838	91322	83158	79725	633	76774	3449
6902	1824	3040	2038		2083	
232504	79719	74106	78163	516	81340	7679
158871	53909	54259	48717	1986	50651	556
34274	11979	11527	10043	725	9265	157
51726	16916	15638	19120	52	17878	113
108655	38265	36147	31846	2397	35668	539

地区 Region	毕业生数 Graduates		招生数 Entrants			
	合计 Total	其中:获得职业资格证书 of Which: Reciptents of Vocational Qualifications	合计 Total	其中:应届毕业 of Which: Graduates of Current Year		其中:五年制高职中职段 of Which:5 - year Secondary Vocational Education
				小计 Subtotal	其中:初中毕业生 of Which: Junior Secondary School Graduates	
总 计 Total	**2652082**	**1982561**	**2714716**	**2501162**	**2397610**	**342770**
北 京 Beijing	17002	12165	14029	13535	13276	3874
天 津 Tianjin	26063	20947	23460	22629	21711	3554
河 北 Hebei	161125	108422	101168	89285	85187	6737
山 西 Shanxi	69722	58297	64007	57267	53242	12238
内蒙古 Inner Mongolia	45571	30718	36926	33643	32407	10761
辽 宁 Liaoning	68035	47435	60734	50877	47950	7131
吉 林 Jilin	31273	15736	22747	19948	17010	3275
黑龙江 Heilongjiang	37314	23631	40612	33416	32279	3251
上 海 Shanghai	30615	26849	27591	27263	27188	2615
江 苏 Jiangsu	210476	177421	184013	182384	180896	53042
浙 江 Zhejiang	36987	35899	32204	32022	31849	6433
安 徽 Anhui	89586	76858	87825	84822	82098	22042
福 建 Fujian	102250	96633	101328	96373	94255	7466
江 西 Jiangxi	72198	55899	94538	85834	84119	23998
山 东 Shandong	201035	152481	228620	217226	210237	47410
河 南 Henan	231438	155365	233108	207172	191724	19650
湖 北 Hubei	152374	127635	96585	92843	90100	2283
湖 南 Hunan	63037	45483	82674	78693	75475	24687
广 东 Guangdong	300289	196359	381335	348122	329714	9161
广 西 Guangxi	126528	91899	162382	150503	142727	17399
海 南 Hainan	25821	9820	30657	23919	23286	1444
重 庆 Chongqing	27590	20791	30509	28876	28421	3439
四 川 Sichuan	163943	142120	177021	164463	156021	7613
贵 州 Guizhou	50400	43551	91983	79839	79445	4872
云 南 Yunnan	107167	66411	109455	100817	97658	18377
西 藏 Tibet	6276	5063	6471	4320	4020	
陕 西 Shaanxi	44145	26095	30374	25222	23324	12910
甘 肃 Gansu	64896	47624	63627	60669	58388	2050
青 海 Qinghai	19679	14053	20807	17601	16979	520
宁 夏 Ningxia	19219	13726	20479	18598	17759	1077
新 疆 Xinjiang	50028	37175	57447	52981	48865	3461

专业学生数
Specialized Sec. Schools

单位:人
unit: person

在校学生数 Enrolment					预计毕业生数 Estimated Graduates for Next Year	
合计 Total	一年级 Grade 1	二年级 Grade 2	三年级 Grade 3	四年级及以上 Grade 4 and Over	合计 Total	其中:五年制高职中职段 of Which: 5 - year Secondary Vocational Education
7721842	**2716550**	**2524646**	**2400163**	**80483**	**2537549**	**237489**
56275	14022	14723	14969	12561	16878	3143
69818	23324	23241	23122	131	23636	1924
338928	101681	111870	122917	2460	133560	8839
182644	63992	62185	54530	1937	64942	3776
120783	36926	44603	38030	1224	41237	6612
183128	60951	56572	56403	9202	65096	7257
76937	22766	24035	30044	92	31776	2351
119341	40613	41969	35361	1398	37508	766
100403	27679	29696	28706	14322	37486	906
565935	184120	187918	187979	5918	190215	52144
100002	32209	31667	34995	1131	35036	5982
256912	87825	80713	83401	4973	86097	18398
297044	101275	94191	100790	788	104608	4000
260665	94596	88730	76406	933	79008	13723
622644	228620	204814	182473	6737	198379	26858
637875	233108	211093	192773	901	215075	19286
303138	96648	98001	106987	1502	111067	722
219464	82685	73013	61511	2255	65360	16304
1018550	380836	341219	294587	1908	298686	7647
405466	162672	126735	115326	733	121610	2068
84080	30657	27066	26122	235	26891	971
99335	30255	33966	33933	1181	32135	1793
507182	176898	166862	162658	764	166879	7743
204053	91983	57086	54966	18	55877	1884
301317	109480	100715	90260	862	91541	5686
17377	6559	6506	4312		6334	
107875	30383	33248	43656	588	46034	13235
191223	63737	64927	60658	1901	63482	431
56815	20807	18403	16481	1124	17782	713
56265	20489	17608	18109	59	19151	637
160368	58754	51271	47698	2645	54183	1690

普通中等专业

Number of Female students in Reg.

地　区 Region	毕业生数 Graduates		招生数 Entrants			
	合计 Total	其中:获得职业资格证书 of Which: Reciptents of Vocational Qualifications	合计 Total	其中:应届毕业 of Which: Graduates of Current Year		其中:五年制高职中职段 of Which:5 – year Secondary Vocational Education
				小计 Subtotal	其中:初中毕业生 of Which: Junior Secondary School Graduates	
总　计 Total	**1403900**	**1022619**	**1417207**	**1314924**	**1266410**	**190268**
北　京 Beijing	8352	6372	6171	5923	5777	1592
天　津 Tianjin	11016	8898	9340	9139	8734	1366
河　北 Hebei	78458	52658	50861	44801	43144	4741
山　西 Shanxi	39026	31136	36124	33664	31698	6657
内蒙古 Inner Mongolia	22089	14909	17175	15641	15173	4894
辽　宁 Liaoning	34729	22568	28181	24717	23469	4196
吉　林 Jilin	16032	7926	12538	11732	10360	1851
黑龙江 Heilongjiang	19303	12710	20914	18510	18247	2025
上　海 Shanghai	13673	11394	11618	11459	11410	1051
江　苏 Jiangsu	105031	84554	90738	89935	89435	29363
浙　江 Zhejiang	20828	20155	17517	17493	17366	3996
安　徽 Anhui	49631	41485	48179	47243	46131	13735
福　建 Fujian	51987	48827	45157	44210	43187	3955
江　西 Jiangxi	43148	33414	57908	53616	52684	15898
山　东 Shandong	107038	76592	114202	109096	106254	23182
河　南 Henan	127038	89268	132626	118297	110863	10572
湖　北 Hubei	76477	62298	46594	45070	43980	2084
湖　南 Hunan	39115	27143	50061	47325	45515	13356
广　东 Guangdong	161762	102978	195536	177046	168438	5335
广　西 Guangxi	61248	39165	76673	71639	68108	6530
海　南 Hainan	13592	5260	15384	12446	12291	628
重　庆 Chongqing	16263	12786	16966	15812	15621	2721
四　川 Sichuan	89299	75140	99981	92254	87111	4941
贵　州 Guizhou	26496	22653	51395	44862	44849	3891
云　南 Yunnan	59452	37424	63753	58725	57302	10750
西　藏 Tibet	2540	2093	1797	1767	1618	
陕　西 Shaanxi	26165	13872	16844	14194	13186	7844
甘　肃 Gansu	37851	26921	35649	34443	33101	1066
青　海 Qinghai	9209	6090	9242	7987	7802	217
宁　夏 Ningxia	10046	7538	11292	10838	10503	647
新　疆 Xinjiang	27006	18392	26791	25040	23053	1184

学校女学生数
Specialized Sec. Schools

单位：人
unit: person

在校学生数 Enrolment					预计毕业生数 Estimated Graduates for Next Year	
合计 Total	一年级 Grade 1	二年级 Grade 2	三年级 Grade 3	四年级及以上 Grade 4 and Over	合计 Total	其中：五年制高职中职段 of Which: 5 - year Secondary Vocational Education
4136989	**1416994**	**1359554**	**1311406**	**49035**	**1302569**	**139978**
26421	6189	6832	7118	6282	7678	1026
28788	9203	9672	9816	97	9709	862
173107	51048	58632	62492	935	61463	5169
106349	36124	36433	33016	776	33469	3231
55957	17175	19985	17858	939	18705	3779
94045	28353	28125	29704	7863	32166	5006
43456	12579	13516	17296	65	17811	1764
63216	20914	22243	19421	638	18088	525
44753	11652	12891	12877	7333	15975	422
280981	90586	92993	93035	4367	90483	28584
55018	17517	17834	19138	529	18898	3567
145922	48179	45712	49181	2850	48197	12414
140964	45081	44434	50793	656	48455	2489
162979	58075	56158	48125	621	48153	9258
319820	114230	104711	96650	4229	99155	15988
367700	132626	119872	114826	376	118156	11266
150532	46607	48550	54488	887	51471	689
135665	50060	45277	39397	931	38623	8908
538431	194926	183418	158785	1302	155805	4145
199451	76656	64155	58211	429	56664	934
44576	15387	14431	14585	173	12333	690
55502	16691	19548	18314	949	16783	1170
295960	99858	99677	95768	657	96548	4873
115569	51395	32090	32066	18	32286	1326
175121	63699	58630	52160	632	51729	3212
6858	1824	3024	2010		2039	
61205	16589	18527	25686	403	23862	7658
108654	35502	37122	34708	1322	33686	214
26625	9222	8313	8632	458	8130	157
30792	11298	9734	9708	52	8338	113
82572	27749	27015	25542	2266	27711	539

成人中等
Number of Students in Adult

地 区 Region	毕业生数 Graduates		招生数 Entrants			
	合计 Total	其中:获得职业资格证书 of Which: Reciptents of Vocational Qualifications	合计 Total	其中:应届毕业 of Which: Graduates of Current Year		其中:五年制高职中职段 of Which:5 - year Secondary Vocational Education
				小计 Subtotal	其中:初中毕业生 of Which: Junior Secondary School Graduates	
总 计 Total	**878323**	**596059**	**862591**	**397783**	**352537**	**2254**
北 京 Beijing	40786	33327	34392	5544	5502	
天 津 Tianjin	4376	3936	3191	2974	2928	
河 北 Hebei	38150	20811	31470	13904	13218	
山 西 Shanxi	7713		5353	100	90	
内蒙古 Inner Mongolia	10795	7963	7994	4394	4203	
辽 宁 Liaoning	7699	2225	10245	2447	2204	
吉 林 Jilin	12597	5434	10991	4905	4881	
黑龙江 Heilongjiang	15125	11107	16213	8119	7312	
上 海 Shanghai	7755	4404	6162	4407	2900	
江 苏 Jiangsu	26951	17001	25731	12588	12123	
浙 江 Zhejiang	13931	9606	13112	5142	4395	79
安 徽 Anhui	85645	75856	121282	78032	74460	
福 建 Fujian	48561	42694	53712	12031	9898	95
江 西 Jiangxi	3645	1850	3909	2422	1648	
山 东 Shandong	54475	39351	39775	25432	24178	1686
河 南 Henan	48549	34713	47975	29673	27502	
湖 北 Hubei	4205	2461	3304	2725	2612	
湖 南 Hunan	45316	41403	18999	12788	11870	
广 东 Guangdong	107415	41256	19463	15278	9284	
广 西 Guangxi	140943	75450	141219	39923	28816	2
海 南 Hainan	777		2891	102	91	
重 庆 Chongqing	9390	6048	8278	8026	8007	308
四 川 Sichuan	105205	100669	163481	85708	75010	84
贵 州 Guizhou	5000	2711	43930	9209	8588	
云 南 Yunnan	1217	711	2012	146	146	
西 藏 Tibet	136					
陕 西 Shaanxi	3983	1469	1587	444	444	
甘 肃 Gansu	13240	10522	12049	7877	7033	
青 海 Qinghai	2558	1586	8196	3041	2793	
宁 夏 Ningxia	4610	1113	1172	24	24	
新 疆 Xinjiang	7575	382	4503	378	377	

专业学生数
Specialized Sec. Schools

单位:人
unit: person

在校学生数 Enrolment					预计毕业生数 Estimated Graduates for Next Year	
合计 Total	一年级 Grade 1	二年级 Grade 2	三年级 Grade 3	四年级及以上 Grade 4 and Over	合计 Total	其中:五年制高职中职段 of Which: 5 – year Secondary Vocational Education
2299806	**865279**	**757926**	**667977**	**8624**	**1031010**	**2449**
59871	34392	21243	3545	691	41943	
7440	3191	3953	296		3498	
99874	31469	38523	29812	70	50782	94
26409	5353	11149	9907		12240	
19933	7994	5103	6836		10320	
28291	10245	10468	7578		9144	
30768	11001	11712	8055		10834	
61396	16213	23393	21790		27313	
20617	6164	10330	4007	116	6942	
77182	25731	24464	26899	88	31389	
30877	13112	13609	4156		13003	127
254199	121717	89376	42006	1100	110014	
228007	55195	96516	76296		89775	886
16894	3954	4711	8229		10504	
108346	39818	38704	29824		39681	933
93922	47975	29084	16863		40964	
12016	3304	4581	4093	38	4622	
82483	19035	29865	32184	1399	31567	
176924	19463	36968	117213	3280	115016	
416775	141324	149793	125019	639	136158	
8578	2891	2260	3427		3361	
23965	8278	6598	9089		9089	
273209	163481	56985	52743		171099	32
50574	43930	4909	1735		13627	
5781	2012	2412	1357		2871	
114		44	70		114	
7398	1587	2264	3547		3997	24
32805	12579	10623	8910	693	12171	353
20243	8196	7922	3615	510	3625	
9960	1172	2174	6614		8643	
14955	4503	8190	2262		6704	

成人中等

Number of Female Students

地 区 Region	毕业生数 Graduates 合计 Total	毕业生数 Graduates 其中：获得职业资格证书 of Which: Reciptents of Vocational Qualifications	招生数 Entrants 合计 Total	招生数 Entrants 其中：应届毕业 of Which: Graduates of Current Year 小计 Subtotal	招生数 Entrants 其中：应届毕业 of Which: Graduates of Current Year 其中：初中毕业生 of Which: Junior Secondary School Graduates	其中：五年制高职中职段 of Which:5 - year Secondary Vocational Education
总 计 Total	**394311**	**264098**	**390020**	**179731**	**160347**	**1195**
北 京 Beijing	24622	19691	25304	2537	2521	
天 津 Tianjin	1495	1235	1310	1235	1225	
河 北 Hebei	20027	10255	18900	7958	7439	
山 西 Shanxi	2432		2130	40	30	
内蒙古 Inner Mongolia	4951	3714	3290	1888	1851	
辽 宁 Liaoning	3200	942	4164	1093	1048	
吉 林 Jilin	4981	1275	4418	1691	1687	
黑龙江 Heilongjiang	6395	4633	6188	3424	3079	
上 海 Shanghai	3309	1412	2395	1984	1142	
江 苏 Jiangsu	12493	7955	10729	4976	4739	
浙 江 Zhejiang	7160	4961	5833	2874	2415	79
安 徽 Anhui	35881	30863	51529	33822	32302	
福 建 Fujian	19499	17120	22985	5487	4488	
江 西 Jiangxi	1343	901	2019	1009	845	
山 东 Shandong	25378	16994	18733	11407	10759	1028
河 南 Henan	24378	17435	23784	14261	12861	
湖 北 Hubei	2582	1809	2267	1957	1849	
湖 南 Hunan	18640	16581	8948	5687	5318	
广 东 Guangdong	50080	20144	8026	6384	3881	
广 西 Guangxi	57782	29889	52320	15326	11929	
海 南 Hainan	522		1504	67	67	
重 庆 Chongqing	5526	4249	5196	5126	5108	36
四 川 Sichuan	47137	44696	75245	40188	35089	52
贵 州 Guizhou	2441	1461	20345	3924	3762	
云 南 Yunnan	296	179	507	24	24	
西 藏 Tibet	36					
陕 西 Shaanxi	1113	181	604	125	125	
甘 肃 Gansu	5624	4537	6010	4134	3759	
青 海 Qinghai	856	401	2625	882	784	
宁 夏 Ningxia	2416	432	931	4	4	
新 疆 Xinjiang	1716	153	1781	217	217	

专业女学生数

in Adult Specialized Sec. Schools

单位:人
unit: person

在校学生数 Enrolment					预计毕业生数 Estimated Graduates for Next Year	
合计 Total	一年级 Grade 1	二年级 Grade 2	三年级 Grade 3	四年级及以上 Grade 4 and Over	合计 Total	其中:五年制高职中职段 of Which: 5 - year Secondary Vocational Education
1036081	**391867**	**341418**	**299243**	**3553**	**466448**	**1753**
42610	25304	15441	1510	355	36040	
2925	1310	1417	198		1181	
57809	18900	22182	16704	23	27144	48
10163	2130	4950	3083		3351	
7869	3290	1690	2889		4131	
11523	4164	4358	3001		3633	
11048	4423	4059	2566		3075	
25681	6188	9952	9541		11114	
7236	2395	3453	1343	45	2602	
32834	10729	10363	11655	87	12792	
14852	5833	6556	2463		6144	125
111472	51695	40394	19383		46768	
104062	24340	45325	34397		39214	801
7470	2025	1831	3614		4212	
52086	18771	20027	13288		19057	536
42866	23784	11479	7603		20394	
6927	2267	2852	1780	28	2170	
36907	8961	12385	14474	1087	13969	
82454	8026	16887	56131	1410	54806	
160718	52375	58051	50241	51	52153	
4192	1504	1104	1584		1059	
13896	5196	3468	5232		5221	
127416	75245	27452	24719		76122	10
23810	20345	2390	1075		5893	
1581	507	824	250		596	
44		16	28		44	
2252	454	593	1205		1067	10
14882	6369	4898	3415	200	5244	223
7298	2625	3036	1370	267	1094	
5380	931	838	3611		3529	
5818	1781	3147	890		2629	

职业高中

Number of Students in

地 区 Region	毕业生数 Graduates		招生数 Entrants			
	合计 Total	其中:获得职业资格证书 of Which: Recipitents of Vocational Qualifications	合计 Total	其中:应届毕业 of Which: Graduates of Current Year		其中:五年制高职中职段 of Which:5 - year Secondary Vocational Education
				小计 Subtotal	其中:初中毕业生 of Which: Junior Secondary School Graduates	
总 计 Total	**2045182**	**1758317**	**1835317**	**1732989**	**1696641**	**26311**
北 京 Beijing	17830	15148	7006	6728	6650	362
天 津 Tianjin	8831	7056	7135	6691	5968	478
河 北 Hebei	137825	104302	88258	81010	79125	709
山 西 Shanxi	82314	70802	73583	70262	68455	1810
内蒙古 Inner Mongolia	39142	33051	38932	34837	34409	1056
辽 宁 Liaoning	52033	33844	47008	43966	43014	
吉 林 Jilin	40062	29473	27317	23909	21471	219
黑龙江 Heilongjiang	39344	37556	26436	23395	23194	
上 海 Shanghai	10138	9374	10624	10624	10624	460
江 苏 Jiangsu	68719	66675	49309	38352	38129	652
浙 江 Zhejiang	156354	151577	146189	145487	145406	13177
安 徽 Anhui	149696	132956	159942	155373	153882	
福 建 Fujian						
江 西 Jiangxi	83312	68538	68933	62154	60682	133
山 东 Shandong	123116	100958	95152	86578	83442	1757
河 南 Henan	231707	201132	141126	136257	132619	
湖 北 Hubei	43143	36793	30937	30539	30218	
湖 南 Hunan	128744	119027	126954	122661	120844	804
广 东 Guangdong	80582	48188	74129	66538	61960	501
广 西 Guangxi						
海 南 Hainan	13788	9059	18208	16813	15832	79
重 庆 Chongqing	65538	57241	83367	80800	80289	1661
四 川 Sichuan	145065	141028	149467	147147	146558	234
贵 州 Guizhou	44881	41538	111222	102455	102376	
云 南 Yunnan	101807	78796	68218	65651	65136	1486
西 藏 Tibet						
陕 西 Shaanxi	129191	119723	132023	122698	115983	606
甘 肃 Gansu	26907	24552	22928	22006	20385	
青 海 Qinghai	149	149	274	244	243	
宁 夏 Ningxia	7707	6450	8697	8510	8510	127
新 疆 Xinjiang	17257	13331	21943	21304	21237	

学生数
Vocational High Schools

单位：人

unit：person

在校学生数 Enrolment					预计毕业生数 Estimated Graduates for Next Year	
合计 Total	一年级 Grade 1	二年级 Grade 2	三年级 Grade 3	四年级及以上 Grade 4 and Over	合计 Total	其中：五年制高职中职段 of Which：5 - year Secondary Vocational Education
5342194	**1836584**	**1746261**	**1749553**	**9796**	**1824412**	**15048**
48746	7049	20344	19511	1842	19671	23
20185	7136	6344	6705		7231	698
313483	88422	108361	116700		119885	226
227340	73583	64955	88802		78298	
104698	38932	34543	31223		32032	1113
138493	47008	45334	45468	683	46297	
84967	27250	26930	30628	159	33997	68
93283	26451	32280	34552		37647	
32278	10654	10960	10170	494	10590	80
150599	49312	46186	55101		55101	1204
447644	146223	143478	156526	1417	155922	7014
456635	159942	157048	139253	392	152490	
207069	68793	68639	69637		70462	151
300595	95308	93124	110205	1958	122084	380
461308	141126	162457	157713	12	169669	
95641	30937	31953	32751		32944	
348622	126953	117540	102742	1387	107347	1088
213420	74186	75598	63636		70329	1802
47567	18208	15220	13829	310	14010	
239527	84378	78214	76930	5	76935	240
414694	149464	128855	136347	28	137235	333
220885	111222	61557	48106		49449	
187005	68218	57664	61118	5	61440	400
339585	131974	108880	98531	200	117426	21
65503	22914	22933	18949	707	21047	199
726	274	324	128		128	
27725	8697	9011	10017		10286	8
53971	21970	17529	14275	197	14460	

职业高中

Number of Female Students

地　区 Region	毕业生数 Graduates		招生数 Entrants			
	合计 Total	其中：获得职业资格证书 of Which: Recipients of Vocational Qualifications	合计 Total	其中：应届毕业 of Which: Graduates of Current Year		其中：五年制高职中职段 of Which: 5 – year Secondary Vocational Education
				小计 Subtotal	其中：初中毕业生 of Which: Junior Secondary School Graduates	
总　计 Total	**957996**	**819060**	**827434**	**783791**	**769094**	**12615**
北　京 Beijing	8718	7451	3210	2971	2899	172
天　津 Tianjin	4595	3554	3579	3388	3187	284
河　北 Hebei	67193	49798	41728	38084	37115	306
山　西 Shanxi	41125	35423	35693	34351	33646	789
内蒙古 Inner Mongolia	18482	15532	17201	15559	15468	613
辽　宁 Liaoning	24230	15052	20455	19006	18607	
吉　林 Jilin	17460	13621	12578	10963	9756	51
黑龙江 Heilongjiang	18067	17409	11277	9906	9895	
上　海 Shanghai	4975	4563	4375	4375	4375	94
江　苏 Jiangsu	31998	30916	20869	15752	15621	272
浙　江 Zhejiang	71822	69018	63190	63001	62954	6238
安　徽 Anhui	67675	60162	73871	71685	71113	
福　建 Fujian						
江　西 Jiangxi	39272	32998	32620	29991	29645	73
山　东 Shandong	48470	39190	38688	36078	34803	743
河　南 Henan	110102	95427	66842	64569	63342	
湖　北 Hubei	20837	17520	12494	12422	12322	
湖　南 Hunan	61752	57124	53318	51888	51033	687
广　东 Guangdong	39024	23061	32353	28204	25994	136
广　西 Guangxi						
海　南 Hainan	7337	4749	6731	6147	5876	
重　庆 Chongqing	30703	27160	37776	36468	36424	427
四　川 Sichuan	64398	62156	66855	66083	65839	167
贵　州 Guizhou	22146	20318	56253	52685	52675	
云　南 Yunnan	47992	36271	27140	26393	26215	1285
西　藏 Tibet						
陕　西 Shaanxi	63917	58625	62736	58789	56103	184
甘　肃 Gansu	14134	13009	12048	11811	10978	
青　海 Qinghai	81	81	132	102	102	
宁　夏 Ningxia	4172	3362	4687	4548	4548	94
新　疆 Xinjiang	7319	5510	8735	8572	8559	

女学生数
in Vocational High Schools

单位：人
unit: person

在校学生数 Enrolment					预计毕业生数 Estimated Graduates for Next Year	
合计 Total	一年级 Grade 1	二年级 Grade 2	三年级 Grade 3	四年级及以上 Grade 4 and Over	合计 Total	其中：五年制高职中职段 of Which: 5 - year Secondary Vocational Education
2473295	**827460**	**813612**	**827298**	**4925**	**832576**	**6797**
24729	3222	10362	9750	1395	9746	7
9992	3579	2993	3420		3543	406
159085	41764	57552	59769		59784	107
111025	35673	32023	43329		34751	
47168	17201	15397	14570		14847	608
64473	20455	21875	21568	575	21667	
38486	12526	12339	13483	138	14434	19
42088	11277	14389	16422		16690	
14072	4379	4872	4625	196	4798	27
65692	20799	20835	24058		24372	285
196386	63198	62733	70208	247	68850	3018
211546	73871	73118	64475	82	68238	
97072	32435	31675	32962		32096	71
128391	38531	40418	48655	787	50567	170
222768	66842	77887	78035	4	80794	
40950	12494	13615	14841		14692	
151033	53247	51150	45957	679	47007	511
96326	32353	34239	29734		30980	879
20079	6757	6762	6478	82	6496	
110827	38374	35856	36592	5	36904	75
188951	66846	59025	63054	26	62691	247
113468	56253	32339	24876		24668	
78136	27116	23704	27315	1	24449	237
169047	62676	54986	51272	113	56411	11
35335	12038	12239	10594	464	11721	119
351	132	178	41		41	
15554	4687	5066	5801		6011	
20265	8735	5985	5414	131	5328	

中等职业学校(机

Number of Students by Age in Secondary

地　区 Region	合计 Total	14 岁及以下 14 Years and Under	15 岁 15 Years	16 岁 16 Years	17 岁 17 Years
总　计 Total	**15363842**	**195634**	**1967604**	**3580388**	**3656138**
北　京 Beijing	164892	3945	15874	28595	32897
天　津 Tianjin	97443	714	8489	22075	26143
河　北 Hebei	752285	7209	68777	145860	164500
山　西 Shanxi	436393	5088	62972	107278	110311
内蒙古 Inner Mongolia	245414	1587	20320	46559	50786
辽　宁 Liaoning	349912	8741	38970	79618	85186
吉　林 Jilin	192672	2949	12888	26942	42040
黑龙江 Heilongjiang	274020	3216	21834	48701	54924
上　海 Shanghai	153298	1299	21974	36763	40642
江　苏 Jiangsu	793716	4637	116925	202942	215197
浙　江 Zhejiang	578523	5448	95727	166491	173331
安　徽 Anhui	967746	8792	148200	236840	227093
福　建 Fujian	525051	2650	38418	74169	85352
江　西 Jiangxi	484628	9714	86871	134035	125649
山　东 Shandong	1031585	13068	149424	245134	237455
河　南 Henan	1193105	14524	187874	305813	290229
湖　北 Hubei	410795	7235	66635	112336	115486
湖　南 Hunan	650569	24531	122909	168322	143189
广　东 Guangdong	1408894	12374	137374	314396	365930
广　西 Guangxi	822241	7409	49436	113998	122261
海　南 Hainan	140225	2042	10779	24275	28485
重　庆 Chongqing	362827	5433	47129	103146	105987
四　川 Sichuan	1195085	12140	203784	335948	294494
贵　州 Guizhou	475512	6625	58278	113551	105178
云　南 Yunnan	494103	7948	59491	128775	129537
西　藏 Tibet	17491	888	1610	3336	3827
陕　西 Shaanxi	454858	5324	54712	115952	126146
甘　肃 Gansu	289531	3090	22681	55743	70346
青　海 Qinghai	77784	902	5347	12174	14378
宁　夏 Ningxia	93950	807	8615	21323	21500
新　疆 Xinjiang	229294	5305	23287	49298	47659

构）分年龄学生数

Vocational Schools（Institutions）

单位：人

unit：person

18 岁 18 Years	19 岁 19 Years	20 岁 20 Years	21 岁 21 Years	22 岁及以上 22 Years and Over
2499463	**1096035**	**525189**	**336162**	**1507229**
36141	16660	13229	5227	12324
22442	8354	3055	2690	3481
110394	49428	20767	17312	168038
61052	20802	9229	6780	52881
41184	23854	11372	7236	42516
60193	30730	12842	7414	26218
37444	16451	11987	9904	32067
45549	25440	15637	12478	46241
30404	10857	2178	781	8400
130625	47531	20099	8359	47401
96308	23100	4217	1718	12183
142922	72560	36388	23213	71738
77070	38948	22030	17643	168771
68155	28462	9055	5512	17175
161458	65259	37013	25265	97509
184265	81407	37156	22116	69721
70448	20668	6186	2973	8828
80975	31415	17777	11903	49548
274202	126553	60697	32912	84456
107687	66480	41769	33064	280137
24372	14809	7399	4080	23984
64407	21093	7053	2777	5802
186104	79093	34944	18930	29648
77177	38355	18881	12287	45180
91706	34777	12591	6303	22975
3653	2719	692	358	408
86693	31284	12987	7255	14505
58262	29179	15754	8439	26037
12410	8710	4757	3312	15794
16464	9233	5240	3278	7490
39297	21824	12208	14643	15773

中等职业学校(机构)

Number of Female Students by Age in

	合计 Total	14 岁及以下 14 Years and Under	15 岁 15 Years	16 岁 16 Years
总　计 Total	**7646365**	**105447**	**996560**	**1814447**
北　京 Beijing	93760	2559	7772	13900
天　津 Tianjin	41705	387	3898	9358
河　北 Hebei	390001	3781	36162	72001
山　西 Shanxi	227537	2602	31002	58340
内蒙古 Inner Mongolia	110994	808	9538	22050
辽　宁 Liaoning	170041	5652	19159	40567
吉　林 Jilin	92990	1578	6300	13941
黑龙江 Heilongjiang	130985	1701	11573	26200
上　海 Shanghai	66061	760	9499	15637
江　苏 Jiangsu	379507	2744	56462	98523
浙　江 Zhejiang	266256	2820	45686	76877
安　徽 Anhui	468940	4426	72310	116809
福　建 Fujian	245026	1372	18304	35853
江　西 Jiangxi	267521	4890	50727	76176
山　东 Shandong	500297	6536	73864	118811
河　南 Henan	633334	7649	100298	163594
湖　北 Hubei	198409	3620	33832	57089
湖　南 Hunan	323605	14390	62046	85831
广　东 Guangdong	717211	7309	69140	159835
广　西 Guangxi	360169	3534	23358	55605
海　南 Hainan	68847	961	5478	12119
重　庆 Chongqing	180225	2902	23914	49226
四　川 Sichuan	612327	6496	105331	172398
贵　州 Guizhou	252847	3764	31557	62067
云　南 Yunnan	254838	4291	30908	67794
西　藏 Tibet	6902	369	697	1521
陕　西 Shaanxi	232504	2625	27481	59576
甘　肃 Gansu	158871	1697	12200	31288
青　海 Qinghai	34274	430	2467	5933
宁　夏 Ningxia	51726	485	5115	11724
新　疆 Xinjiang	108655	2309	10482	23804

分年龄女学生数

Secondary Vocational Schools (Institutions)

单位:人

unit: person

17 岁 17 Years	18 岁 18 Years	19 岁 19 Years	20 岁 20 Years	21 岁 21 Years	22 岁及以上 22 Years and Over
1854051	**1252549**	**536903**	**254212**	**156592**	**675604**
15831	23143	10649	11731	2699	5476
11147	9551	3815	1140	1042	1367
81695	57782	24489	10166	8639	95286
61962	33347	10965	4338	3361	21620
23876	19305	11133	5299	3352	15633
42414	29855	14694	5247	2844	9609
21370	18593	8184	4455	4360	14209
27648	22635	11191	6389	4565	19083
17729	13538	4669	921	295	3013
103409	62439	22848	9064	3560	20458
80088	43474	10645	1774	810	4082
115139	69949	34236	16808	10366	28897
41850	37326	18957	9980	7579	73805
70160	35542	14351	4853	2955	7867
113629	78338	32019	17952	12123	47025
151710	95180	41402	20203	11558	41740
56451	32057	8454	2425	1038	3443
72207	37247	13909	7432	5417	25126
190402	143331	63224	29442	14857	39671
59437	50434	30904	18983	15055	102859
14339	12135	7036	3358	1820	11601
51602	32029	11449	4118	1811	3174
154191	94480	38797	17242	9402	13990
58761	41073	20461	9218	5485	20461
68464	47400	17111	5938	2916	10016
1998	1129	611	216	167	194
64890	45141	15919	6763	3774	6335
40316	32852	15822	8502	4572	11622
6590	5333	3915	1960	1402	6244
11855	8498	4800	2820	1701	4728
22891	19413	10244	5475	7067	6970

中等职业学校(机

Number of Graduates in Secondary

地　区 Region	结业生数 合计 Total	其中:女 of Which: Female	其中:少数民族 of Which: Minority	其中:资格证书培训 of Which: Vocational Qualifications Training	其中:岗位证书培训 of Which: Job Certificate Training	其中:第一产业类培训 of Which: Training for First Industry
总　计 Total	**6247386**	**2818212**	**519980**	**2467512**	**2048427**	**1442486**
北　京 Beijing	63889	35772	1897	26419	10118	14974
天　津 Tianjin	44572	19023	917	36876	5237	8095
河　北 Hebei	294647	149560	21397	76978	74172	86799
山　西 Shanxi	166559	55400	267	38672	41623	21209
内蒙古 Inner Mongolia	90806	47220	16523	30301	34617	21710
辽　宁 Liaoning	317491	82246	77809	88538	146387	115710
吉　林 Jilin	30686	10129	976	8738	6222	4797
黑龙江 Heilongjiang	236604	99842	3234	122536	39386	108252
上　海 Shanghai	107467	41883	107	32530	52031	2286
江　苏 Jiangsu	539167	267109	373	215768	207786	53384
浙　江 Zhejiang	376348	162660	2784	174899	125327	55759
安　徽 Anhui	423592	197912	8961	187881	144367	97396
福　建 Fujian	193224	82982	1855	108235	46156	52021
江　西 Jiangxi	169860	81508	447	54362	68433	39446
山　东 Shandong	399572	143993	5507	102951	148119	43198
河　南 Henan	392585	186805	7595	144810	147575	80114
湖　北 Hubei	291357	168661	33489	51083	30601	203231
湖　南 Hunan	224134	97363	17623	103730	81770	59186
广　东 Guangdong	269164	141131	1064	117076	135523	30159
广　西 Guangxi	161480	65773	55721	78094	55668	31696
海　南 Hainan	41133	17992	5465	19582	12370	9902
重　庆 Chongqing	123790	58760	11219	59855	39257	18070
四　川 Sichuan	285379	129932	12481	157806	104093	47276
贵　州 Guizhou	171783	79675	49765	64331	59245	32462
云　南 Yunnan	409352	199098	115628	178561	119665	109500
西　藏 Tibet	4188	1074	3647	868	530	
陕　西 Shaanxi	185057	79750	791	59793	50531	39365
甘　肃 Gansu	86404	46969	8886	49507	20134	15566
青　海 Qinghai	38650	12345	13981	10314	19959	16531
宁　夏 Ningxia	35074	19023	5406	20322	5015	4810
新　疆 Xinjiang	73372	36622	34165	46096	16510	19582

构)培训结业学生情况

Vocational Schools (Institutions)

单位:人
unit: person

Graduates

其中:第二产业类培训 of Which: Training for Second Industry	其中:第三产业类培训 of Which: Training for Third Industry	一个月以内 1 Month Under	一个月至三个月以内 1 Month to 3 Months	三个月至半年以内 3 Months to 6 Months	半年至一年以内 6 Months to 1 Year	一年及以上 1 Year and Over
1373805	**3431095**	**3668855**	**1176721**	**540019**	**539712**	**322079**
8166	40749	23099	10605	2830	20786	6569
16730	19747	9788	18242	14474	1614	454
53611	154237	164457	40323	35022	39180	15665
18153	127197	64034	22433	10698	64648	4746
12965	56131	59894	15893	10287	2912	1820
60408	141373	237988	43022	19743	11885	4853
11131	14758	25349	4149	386	766	36
35487	92865	201231	19674	6688	3183	5828
31470	73711	56827	27285	17858	2743	2754
137864	347919	303106	115296	48283	49060	23422
102666	217923	190478	83288	30008	47615	24959
94862	231334	241751	100042	35699	29497	16603
31926	109277	110606	16198	15895	13339	37186
33011	97403	72692	25134	23561	35307	13166
105838	250536	267045	59983	22040	36187	14317
67032	245439	196504	73423	50002	46493	26163
27507	60619	237049	22208	11511	8356	12233
48098	116850	120868	50066	30107	12148	10945
67899	171106	133587	74273	22647	20001	18656
31805	97979	105951	43763	7424	737	3605
6574	24657	28094	9699	2456	884	
32149	73571	83275	22148	3723	5872	8772
102186	135917	132173	54350	36395	26781	35680
85828	53493	116035	40230	9033	5207	1278
48910	250942	249667	70135	38559	35222	15769
	4188	2152	1128	908		
48069	97623	83805	63500	20078	11366	6308
17208	53630	53659	15379	8571	5005	3790
6746	15373	27949	8166	1260	1047	228
7146	23118	23975	7143	1110	354	2492
22360	31430	45767	19543	2763	1517	3782

中等职业学校(机

Number of Enrolment in Secondary

注册学生数

地　区 Region	合计 Total	其中:女 of Which: Female	其中:少数民族 of Which: Minority	其中:资格证书培训 of Which: Vocational Qualifications Training	其中:岗位证书培训 of Which: Job Certificate Training	其中:第一产业类培训 of Which: Training for First Industry
总　计 Total	**3986943**	**1889212**	**333145**	**1757692**	**1182845**	**971664**
北　京 Beijing	34366	18999	626	21128	5037	2112
天　津 Tianjin	27179	10100	298	22156	4369	460
河　北 Hebei	133312	68785	1043	34234	33347	42701
山　西 Shanxi	58810	31724	270	26838	22652	15449
内蒙古 Inner Mongolia	51591	27264	8495	20918	18447	3657
辽　宁 Liaoning	121586	32010	47047	75969	20653	53169
吉　林 Jilin	18124	4743	1080	8792	1244	7140
黑龙江 Heilongjiang	148449	63727	1178	97579	14612	76432
上　海 Shanghai	74159	28637	139	29271	34827	2427
江　苏 Jiangsu	365668	173639	334	127092	155896	27596
浙　江 Zhejiang	262537	113723	2749	127381	91369	40221
安　徽 Anhui	430369	202958	9034	192680	144724	100335
福　建 Fujian	157505	67591	1693	89476	33281	37336
江　西 Jiangxi	97755	51449	357	36833	33401	22123
山　东 Shandong	173495	74722	685	68321	48490	25609
河　南 Henan	237806	113754	3056	88239	83373	51044
湖　北 Hubei	237669	144503	26986	25891	16140	197997
湖　南 Hunan	106270	49868	9991	58435	30951	30921
广　东 Guangdong	230969	124171	3459	103662	96729	25712
广　西 Guangxi	117019	50998	44082	66018	31997	22987
海　南 Hainan	17458	7516	5135	11037	3101	2875
重　庆 Chongqing	69434	34610	8631	41404	18190	8886
四　川 Sichuan	225743	107637	6903	125773	83198	39402
贵　州 Guizhou	165588	78230	48652	59330	53085	32042
云　南 Yunnan	199089	98758	62616	77293	53537	63196
西　藏 Tibet	3889	368	3824	1656	530	
陕　西 Shaanxi	101234	47984	1335	47760	29947	18287
甘　肃 Gansu	41166	19729	2429	26838	4433	7684
青　海 Qinghai	5374	1895	1287	3678	381	175
宁　夏 Ningxia	31070	18158	4457	16878	4290	4724
新　疆 Xinjiang	42260	20962	25274	25132	10614	8965

构）培训注册学生情况

Vocational Schools（Institutions）

单位：人

unit：person

Enrolment

其中：第二产业类培训 of Which：Training for Second Industry	其中：第三产业类培训 of Which：Training for Third Industry	一个月以内 1 Month Under	一个月至三个月以内 1 Month to 3 Months	三个月至半年以内 3 Months to 6 Months	半年至一年以内 6 Months to 1 Year	一年及以上 1 Year and Over
933231	**2082048**	**2034619**	**810081**	**391693**	**324267**	**426283**
7611	24643	19182	7004	1162	5245	1773
14471	12248	5321	13367	6370	1824	297
17309	73302	32210	16277	16787	25089	42949
11943	31418	28465	11871	871	10776	6827
6202	41732	25805	11066	2859	2361	9500
37517	30900	82965	16460	10957	2192	9012
5726	5258	11101	3881	2096	556	490
27097	44920	133230	3610	6430	727	4452
28475	43257	36208	21038	12020	3347	1546
95687	242385	193353	70103	41200	41669	19343
68921	153395	117091	62958	26767	30647	25074
97021	233013	242540	103508	35854	29833	18634
35060	85109	86384	11489	14701	7236	37695
17890	57742	35272	13849	15859	20942	11833
41219	106667	59608	33645	15853	38698	25691
41433	145329	97385	57798	28829	27311	26483
8138	31534	205455	9611	4860	4575	13168
23383	51966	42446	18087	17263	6829	21645
48950	156307	90879	73960	23925	12336	29869
25504	68528	61499	34952	15150	1321	4097
4134	10449	3992	7414	2588	2437	1027
12171	48377	36295	11340	5141	3835	12823
71329	115012	81074	40845	25124	18838	59862
87431	46115	104892	38915	11009	6239	4533
27160	108733	102504	51445	22860	9809	12471
	3889	866	200	2823		
33209	49738	33295	36871	16615	6277	8176
12076	21406	19935	8342	2853	1911	8125
3171	2028	1989	904	700	200	1581
6459	19887	22715	6735	910	510	200
16534	16761	20663	12536	1257	697	7107

中等职业学校(机构)

Changes of Enrolment in Secondary

地 区 Region	上学年初报表在校学生数 Enrolment at Beginning of Previous Academic Year	增加学生数 Factors of Increase			
		合计 Total	招 生 No. of Students Admitted	复 学 Students Resuming Studies	转 入 Transfers from Other Inst.
总 计 Total	**16898275**	**6101899**	**5412624**	**11185**	**481354**
北 京 Beijing	189195	58866	55427	173	2671
天 津 Tianjin	105735	36227	33786	10	1046
河 北 Hebei	934042	255549	220896	138	25063
山 西 Shanxi	483237	150334	142943	338	2684
内蒙古 Inner Mongolia	275527	102262	83852	137	17366
辽 宁 Liaoning	380601	122229	117987	239	1347
吉 林 Jilin	228866	73600	61055	36	2798
黑龙江 Heilongjiang	292987	88560	83261	39	3172
上 海 Shanghai	156490	56260	44377	169	6969
江 苏 Jiangsu	884549	310018	259053	163	48651
浙 江 Zhejiang	618597	200352	191505	285	4468
安 徽 Anhui	1002374	417674	369049	1131	41222
福 建 Fujian	582998	163103	155040	334	3495
江 西 Jiangxi	549084	179896	167380	1000	5375
山 东 Shandong	1147012	455562	363547	265	66597
河 南 Henan	1456626	496867	422209	657	53291
湖 北 Hubei	500540	140316	130826	446	4361
湖 南 Hunan	734242	271508	228627	1697	30394
广 东 Guangdong	1495738	552226	474927	516	46023
广 西 Guangxi	862445	306624	303601	389	570
海 南 Hainan	141876	65887	51756	13	4044
重 庆 Chongqing	372049	129177	122154	124	3876
四 川 Sichuan	1262600	546293	489969	1874	48688
贵 州 Guizhou	383367	258470	247135	220	5113
云 南 Yunnan	567843	194417	179685	268	11995
西 藏 Tibet	18291	6577	6471		88
陕 西 Shaanxi	526654	172118	163984	62	4730
甘 肃 Gansu	327834	121854	98604	42	22565
青 海 Qinghai	76842	29858	29277	5	204
宁 夏 Ningxia	104757	39888	30348	17	507
新 疆 Xinjiang	235277	99327	83893	398	11981

学生数变动情况

Vocational Schools (Institutions)

单位:人

unit: person

	减少学生数 Factors of Decrease									本学年初报表在校学生数 Enrolment at Beginning of Current Academic Year
其他 Others	合计 Total	毕业 Graduates	结业 Completers of Courses without Formal Awards	休学 Suspended	退学 Quitting	开除 Expelled	死亡 Dead	转出 Transfers to Other Inst.	其他 Others	
196736	**7636332**	**5575587**	**195185**	**36595**	**529651**	**10722**	**359**	**817400**	**470833**	**15363842**
595	83169	75618	89	321	3886	73	16	1881	1285	164892
1385	44519	39270	42	40	3335	29	4	1197	602	97443
9452	437306	337100	5480	353	30385	206	6	34980	28796	752285
4369	197178	159749	3560	598	10759	115	9	8667	13721	436393
907	132375	95508	4119	233	7569	237	4	21226	3479	245414
2656	152918	127767	1025	820	9585	453	9	3429	9830	349912
9711	109794	83932	563	153	11653	108	1	4897	8487	192672
2088	107527	91783	562	250	3645	77	4	7584	3622	274020
4745	59452	48508	238	392	3226		6	2868	4214	153298
2151	400851	306146	4210	1239	12092	188	17	73750	3209	793716
4094	240426	207272	935	694	12781	123	10	13101	5510	578523
6272	452302	324927	22087	903	20322	199	12	66959	16893	967746
4234	221050	150811	14132	3823	26809	283	8	4655	20529	525051
6141	244352	159155	8283	837	20594	297	7	22158	33021	484628
25153	570989	378626	11280	471	26230	490	18	59714	94160	1031585
20710	760388	511694	17775	1209	37850	1131	3	133248	57478	1193105
4683	230061	199722	929	1139	9872	280	21	10556	7542	410795
10790	355181	237097	7270	2105	23839	329	25	65133	19383	650569
30760	639070	488286	12646	2756	47632	632	23	61343	25752	1408894
2064	346828	267471	10227	5476	30752	523	12	5531	26836	822241
10074	67538	40386	1015	532	11429	510	2	10406	3258	140225
3023	138399	102518	689	1327	15606	349	21	10255	7634	362827
5762	613808	414213	45129	4691	40239	918	35	83156	25427	1195085
6002	166325	100281	8750	2080	25745	1609	19	15995	11846	475512
2469	268157	210191	1668	987	29438	399	29	18273	7172	494103
18	7377	6412		76	130	8		301	450	17491
3342	243914	177319	6909	1052	18041	330	4	27691	12568	454858
643	160157	105043	1435	242	13982	104	3	34900	4448	289531
372	28916	22386	459	270	3075	49	4	1052	1621	77784
9016	50695	31536	3331	414	4539	85	3	2079	8708	93950
3055	105310	74860	348	1112	14611	588	24	10415	3352	229294

中等职业学校(机构)

Changes of Female Enrolment in Secondary

地 区 Region	上学年初报表在校学生数 Total Enrolment at Beginning of Previous Academic Year	增加学生数 Factors of Increase			
		合计 Total	招 生 No. of Students Admitted	复 学 Students Resuming Studies	转 入 Transfers from Other Inst.
总 计 Total	**8411755**	**2949007**	**2634661**	**4172**	**221272**
北 京 Beijing	102665	36520	34685	80	1573
天 津 Tianjin	45901	15161	14229	3	461
河 北 Hebei	471130	129961	111489	65	12998
山 西 Shanxi	249795	76515	73947	110	979
内蒙古 Inner Mongolia	129074	46252	37666	26	8347
辽 宁 Liaoning	188900	54747	52800	29	557
吉 林 Jilin	105614	34314	29534	9	1096
黑龙江 Heilongjiang	141335	40645	38379	12	1155
上 海 Shanghai	71577	20837	18388	69	1315
江 苏 Jiangsu	426925	146643	122336	68	23427
浙 江 Zhejiang	290847	89357	86540	67	1517
安 徽 Anhui	487196	194109	173579	96	17176
福 建 Fujian	273027	72369	68142	125	1147
江 西 Jiangxi	292553	97223	92547	442	2056
山 东 Shandong	554056	218257	171623	119	33975
河 南 Henan	755574	254258	223252	255	22629
湖 北 Hubei	245836	65714	61355	260	1813
湖 南 Hunan	372745	130854	112327	732	13920
广 东 Guangdong	767880	269896	235915	152	21552
广 西 Guangxi	381912	130053	128993	22	80
海 南 Hainan	71614	31208	23619	8	1699
重 庆 Chongqing	187737	63096	59938	50	1541
四 川 Sichuan	645977	268335	242081	893	22130
贵 州 Guizhou	199383	134642	127993	131	2917
云 南 Yunnan	289961	97740	91400	91	5100
西 藏 Tibet	8100	1838	1797		34
陕 西 Shaanxi	270872	84418	80184	21	2464
甘 肃 Gansu	177966	65640	53707	24	11600
青 海 Qinghai	35122	12294	11999	3	105
宁 夏 Ningxia	56205	21705	16910	2	122
新 疆 Xinjiang	114276	44406	37307	208	5787

女学生数变动情况

Vocational Schools（Institutions）

单位：人
unit：person

其 他 Others	减少学生数 Factors of Decrease									本学年初报表在校学生数 Total Enrolment at Beginning of Current Academic Year
	合计 Total	毕业 Graduates	结业 Completers of Courses without Formal Awards	休学 Suspended	退学 Quitting	开除 Expelled	死亡 Dead	转出 Transfers to Other Inst.	其他 Others	
88902	**3714397**	**2756207**	**89480**	**17369**	**241480**	**3274**	**108**	**387711**	**218768**	**7646365**
182	45425	41692	34	111	1976	16	5	898	693	93760
468	19357	17106	29	16	1314	17	1	598	276	41705
5409	211090	165678	2397	168	12621	104	1	16078	14043	390001
1479	98773	82583	1779	335	5191	60	4	4338	4483	227537
213	64332	45522	1977	102	3727	62		11190	1752	110994
1361	73606	62159	348	419	4074	185	1	1432	4988	170041
3675	46938	38473	206	31	4974	33		1686	1535	92990
1099	50995	43765	313	106	1446	35		3905	1425	130985
1065	26353	21957	50	123	1145			1301	1777	66061
812	194061	149522	2102	545	5162	60	4	35410	1256	379507
1233	113948	99810	276	289	5093	45	6	5604	2825	266256
3258	212365	153187	10996	567	9887	91	8	30032	7597	468940
2955	100370	71486	3630	1430	11956	119	2	1750	9997	245026
2178	122255	83763	3925	330	9335	42	3	9492	15365	267521
12540	272016	180886	5218	219	12659	167	5	26922	45940	500297
8122	376498	261518	8293	420	20112	330	1	58480	27344	633334
2286	113141	99896	686	379	3967	58	7	4188	3960	198409
3875	179994	119507	3394	1086	10944	73	6	36327	8657	323605
12277	320565	250866	6536	1215	21516	141	10	28299	11982	717211
958	151796	119030	3960	2806	12927	137	5	2381	10550	360169
5882	33975	21451	747	285	4991	69		5464	968	68847
1567	70608	52492	253	564	7761	107	3	6296	3132	180225
3231	301985	200834	21421	2764	19249	390	11	42734	14582	612327
3601	81178	51083	3609	1005	11459	494	5	8291	5232	252847
1149	132863	107740	879	541	13244	128	7	7669	2655	254838
7	3036	2576		37	62	3		270	88	6902
1749	122786	91195	3716	525	9050	110	2	12376	5812	232504
309	84735	57609	713	106	6767	22	1	17351	2166	158871
187	13142	10146	139	68	1440	8		715	626	34274
4671	26184	16634	1595	213	1717	15		807	5203	51726
1104	50027	36041	259	564	5714	153	10	5427	1859	108655

中等职业学校(机

Number of Foreign Students in Secondary

地 区 Region	合计 Total	其中:女 of Which: Female	结业生数 分时间 一个月以内 1 Month Under	一个月至三个月以内 1 Month to 3 Months	三个月至半年以内 3 Months to 6 Months
总 计 Total	**1423**	**820**	**998**	**56**	**16**
北 京 Beijing	576	283	550		4
天 津 Tianjin					
河 北 Hebei					
山 西 Shanxi					
内蒙古 Inner Mongolia	10	3			
辽 宁 Liaoning	11	9			
吉 林 Jilin					
黑龙江 Heilongjiang					
上 海 Shanghai	28	18	8	14	
江 苏 Jiangsu					
浙 江 Zhejiang	4				
安 徽 Anhui					
福 建 Fujian	4	4			
江 西 Jiangxi					
山 东 Shandong	58	15		34	
河 南 Henan					
湖 北 Hubei					
湖 南 Hunan					
广 东 Guangdong	110	77			
广 西 Guangxi	573	389	440	8	12
海 南 Hainan					
重 庆 Chongqing					
四 川 Sichuan					
贵 州 Guizhou					
云 南 Yunnan	39	17			
西 藏 Tibet					
陕 西 Shaanxi					
甘 肃 Gansu					
青 海 Qinghai					
宁 夏 Ningxia					
新 疆 Xinjiang	10	5			

构）外国留学生情况
Vocational Schools（Institutions）

单位：人
unit：person

Graduates							
by Time		分地区 by Continent					
半年至一年以内 6 Months to 1 Year	一年及以上 1 Year and Over	亚洲 Asia	非洲 Africa	欧洲 Europe	北美洲 North America	南美洲 South America	大洋洲 Australia
131	**222**	**1152**	**10**	**219**	**23**	**13**	**6**
13	9	358		183	22	10	3
	10	10					
2	9	8	1			1	1
	6	3		24			1
	4		4				
4		4					
12	12	58					
30	80	89	5	12	1	2	1
56	57	573					
4	35	39					
10		10					

中等职业学校

Number of Educational Personnel in Secondary

地区 Region	教职工数 Educational		
	合计 Total	校本部教职工 Educational	
		小计 Subtotal	专任教师 Full-time Teachers
总　计 Total	**883959**	**874171**	**668754**
北　京 Beijing	11926	11722	7180
天　津 Tianjin	9798	9694	6939
河　北 Hebei	57812	57576	44211
山　西 Shanxi	33496	33200	25401
内蒙古 Inner Mongolia	20109	19929	14755
辽　宁 Liaoning	29499	29310	20750
吉　林 Jilin	25215	25127	18094
黑龙江 Heilongjiang	23790	23687	17173
上　海 Shanghai	13706	13586	8358
江　苏 Jiangsu	54527	54216	44164
浙　江 Zhejiang	38920	38665	32778
安　徽 Anhui	41317	40844	33973
福　建 Fujian	21614	21505	17187
江　西 Jiangxi	22454	21656	16315
山　东 Shandong	66810	65929	50243
河　南 Henan	69437	67772	52559
湖　北 Hubei	30619	30206	22384
湖　南 Hunan	33342	33201	24827
广　东 Guangdong	58927	58322	45443
广　西 Guangxi	28219	27427	20459
海　南 Hainan	7162	6882	4709
重　庆 Chongqing	18594	18430	14850
四　川 Sichuan	52690	52166	40292
贵　州 Guizhou	18188	17810	14326
云　南 Yunnan	27023	26959	21147
西　藏 Tibet	763	763	652
陕　西 Shaanxi	26374	26181	18368
甘　肃 Gansu	20825	20735	16008
青　海 Qinghai	3234	3167	2567
宁　夏 Ningxia	3474	3462	2611
新　疆 Xinjiang	14095	14042	10031

(机构)教职工数
Vocational Schools (Institutions)

单位:人
unit: person

Personnel					
Personnel in Main Campus			校办企业职工 Employees in School-run Factories & Farms	其他附设机构人员 Personnel in Others Subsidiary Units	聘请校外教师 Part-time Teachers
行政人员 Adm. Personnel	教辅人员 Supporting Staff	工勤人员 Workers			
82651	**57700**	**65066**	**5378**	**4410**	**96619**
2308	1036	1198	16	188	1431
1578	553	624	51	53	1012
5472	4075	3818	153	83	3384
3169	2164	2466	146	150	4563
1995	1739	1440	94	86	1288
3898	1993	2669	136	53	3405
3082	2482	1469	22	66	1012
2699	1717	2098	64	39	1602
2048	1528	1652	56	64	1156
2998	3269	3785	190	121	6238
1880	2131	1876	138	117	4786
2737	1795	2339	113	360	5246
1778	1303	1237	6	103	3684
2635	1155	1551	659	139	2931
6025	5483	4178	719	162	3276
5837	4446	4930	1055	610	8154
3262	2210	2350	293	120	3613
3576	2396	2402	62	79	2970
5302	3454	4123	69	536	5026
2626	1796	2546	172	620	4012
836	530	807	184	96	518
1492	939	1149	152	12	2986
4525	2649	4700	292	232	4576
1720	669	1095	256	122	5133
1706	1521	2585	22	42	4994
43	19	49			37
3608	2121	2084	149	44	2901
1794	1304	1629	56	34	1322
237	102	261	46	21	1131
299	238	314	6	6	741
1486	883	1642	1	52	3491

中等职业学校(机

Number of Female Educational Personnel in Secondary

地 区 Region	教职工数 Educational		
	合计 Total	校本部教职工 Educational	
		小计 Subtotal	专任教师 Full-time Teachers
总 计 Total	**420514**	**415993**	**339176**
北 京 Beijing	7126	7055	4972
天 津 Tianjin	5485	5437	4360
河 北 Hebei	32012	31877	27026
山 西 Shanxi	18005	17890	14992
内蒙古 Inner Mongolia	10125	10042	8179
辽 宁 Liaoning	16448	16329	12893
吉 林 Jilin	13797	13776	10827
黑龙江 Heilongjiang	12617	12578	10118
上 海 Shanghai	7094	7047	5059
江 苏 Jiangsu	26407	26276	22860
浙 江 Zhejiang	20267	20193	17785
安 徽 Anhui	14863	14684	12455
福 建 Fujian	10117	10084	8407
江 西 Jiangxi	8962	8570	6683
山 东 Shandong	29088	28805	23832
河 南 Henan	32718	31792	26441
湖 北 Hubei	12447	12287	9364
湖 南 Hunan	14327	14267	11375
广 东 Guangdong	28903	28620	23047
广 西 Guangxi	12758	12248	9404
海 南 Hainan	3242	3127	2229
重 庆 Chongqing	8818	8729	7438
四 川 Sichuan	23406	23187	18765
贵 州 Guizhou	7826	7622	6360
云 南 Yunnan	12763	12737	10261
西 藏 Tibet	316	316	266
陕 西 Shaanxi	12145	12054	9100
甘 肃 Gansu	8467	8441	6748
青 海 Qinghai	1346	1321	1110
宁 夏 Ningxia	1542	1539	1243
新 疆 Xinjiang	7077	7063	5577

构）女教职工数
Vocational Schools (Institutions)

单位：人
unit: person

Personnel					
Personnel in Main Campus			校办企业职工 Employees in School-run Factories & Farms	其他附设机构人员 Personnel in Others Subsidiary Units	聘请校外教师 Part-time Teachers
行政人员 Adm. Personnel	教辅人员 Supporting Staff	工勤人员 Workers			
28775	**27485**	**20557**	**2321**	**2200**	**39789**
1239	514	330	3	68	750
650	293	134	6	42	546
1782	1888	1181	98	37	1673
992	1098	808	51	64	1876
693	813	357	36	47	700
1591	1069	776	90	29	1617
1268	1329	352	5	16	476
1108	840	512	14	25	839
940	728	320	13	34	468
923	1528	965	65	66	2605
642	1045	721	23	51	1877
789	730	710	24	155	1840
626	627	424		33	1312
877	455	555	341	51	1144
1719	2230	1024	227	56	1347
1804	2081	1466	574	352	3469
1167	953	803	123	37	1273
971	1135	786	36	24	1137
1893	1984	1696	17	266	2118
921	897	1026	38	472	1420
333	235	330	66	49	250
528	443	320	82	7	1471
1602	1201	1619	116	103	2154
613	255	394	154	50	1600
646	770	1060	6	20	1763
13	15	22			15
1235	986	733	82	9	1232
489	691	513	12	14	628
67	46	98	16	9	430
93	95	108	3		395
561	511	414		14	1364

普通中等专业学

Number of Educational Personnel in Regular Specialized

地 区 Region	教职工数 Educational		
	合计 Total	校本部教职工 Educational	
		小计 Subtotal	专任教师 Full-time Teachers
总 计 Total	**419315**	**413803**	**303585**
北 京 Beijing	3701	3534	1995
天 津 Tianjin	6357	6261	4317
河 北 Hebei	19256	19085	13028
山 西 Shanxi	12239	12013	7943
内蒙古 Inner Mongolia	6750	6708	4494
辽 宁 Liaoning	14847	14793	10397
吉 林 Jilin	6277	6228	4508
黑龙江 Heilongjiang	7263	7199	4279
上 海 Shanghai	9211	9173	5293
江 苏 Jiangsu	36637	36474	30017
浙 江 Zhejiang	6993	6948	5796
安 徽 Anhui	13613	13297	10444
福 建 Fujian	21614	21505	17187
江 西 Jiangxi	8035	7933	5462
山 东 Shandong	36832	36044	27555
河 南 Henan	22583	21933	16152
湖 北 Hubei	22633	22254	16160
湖 南 Hunan	5886	5852	4197
广 东 Guangdong	45327	44979	34201
广 西 Guangxi	28162	27370	20448
海 南 Hainan	3514	3249	1998
重 庆 Chongqing	3960	3958	2871
四 川 Sichuan	25888	25603	17564
贵 州 Guizhou	6506	6393	4816
云 南 Yunnan	10636	10613	7560
西 藏 Tibet	763	763	652
陕 西 Shaanxi	5649	5626	3464
甘 肃 Gansu	13705	13633	10440
青 海 Qinghai	2772	2705	2227
宁 夏 Ningxia	1937	1925	1342
新 疆 Xinjiang	9769	9752	6778

校(机构)教职工数

Secondary Vocational Schools (Institutions)

单位:人
unit: person

Personnel					
Personnel in Main Campus			校办企业职工 Employees in School-run Factories & Farms	其他附设机构人员 Personnel in Others Subsidiary Units	聘请校外教师 Part-time Teachers
行政人员 Adm. Personnel	教辅人员 Supporting Staff	工勤人员 Workers			
46654	**28153**	**35411**	**2786**	**2726**	**42425**
876	279	384		167	557
1138	400	406	48	48	322
2869	1379	1809	122	49	1339
1919	964	1187	106	120	1301
1025	559	630	26	16	704
2004	954	1438	45	9	1309
875	397	448	12	37	45
1179	694	1047	58	6	907
1664	959	1257	36	2	820
2078	2067	2312	121	42	3651
385	430	337	13	32	855
1202	661	990	49	267	2067
1778	1303	1237	6	103	3684
1336	620	515	64	38	1558
3431	2814	2244	650	138	2061
2322	1445	2014	431	219	1275
2642	1596	1856	264	115	2073
793	389	473		34	482
4593	2766	3419	69	279	4207
2598	1782	2542	172	620	4012
558	339	354	184	81	330
518	324	245	2		621
3234	1694	3111	104	181	2344
837	259	481	85	28	1040
996	921	1136	8	15	1533
43	19	49			37
1006	537	619	15	8	635
1244	742	1207	44	28	623
182	91	205	46	21	514
217	133	233	6	6	439
1112	636	1226		17	1080

普通中等专业学

Number of Female Educational Personnel in Regular

地 区 Region	教职工数 Educational		
	合计 Total	校本部教职工 Educational	
		小计 Subtotal	专任教师 Full-time Teachers
总 计 Total	**199873**	**197459**	**154955**
北 京 Beijing	1978	1928	1270
天 津 Tianjin	3380	3337	2577
河 北 Hebei	10029	9927	7511
山 西 Shanxi	6175	6087	4629
内蒙古 Inner Mongolia	3551	3529	2580
辽 宁 Liaoning	8458	8424	6585
吉 林 Jilin	3513	3497	2814
黑龙江 Heilongjiang	3718	3699	2558
上 海 Shanghai	4489	4481	3075
江 苏 Jiangsu	18445	18384	16048
浙 江 Zhejiang	3769	3749	3187
安 徽 Anhui	5591	5444	4492
福 建 Fujian	10117	10084	8407
江 西 Jiangxi	3568	3522	2542
山 东 Shandong	15939	15714	13075
河 南 Henan	10829	10463	8383
湖 北 Hubei	9205	9056	6744
湖 南 Hunan	2630	2620	2051
广 东 Guangdong	22195	22036	17377
广 西 Guangxi	12737	12227	9400
海 南 Hainan	1585	1474	1015
重 庆 Chongqing	1906	1905	1460
四 川 Sichuan	11899	11782	8504
贵 州 Guizhou	2983	2979	2381
云 南 Yunnan	5448	5438	4092
西 藏 Tibet	316	316	266
陕 西 Shaanxi	2597	2589	1746
甘 肃 Gansu	5779	5756	4675
青 海 Qinghai	1177	1152	977
宁 夏 Ningxia	909	906	694
新 疆 Xinjiang	4958	4954	3840

校(机构)女教职工数

Specialized Secondary Schools (Institutions)

单位:人
unit: person

Personnel					
Personnel in Main Campus			校办企业职工 Employees in School-run Factories & Farms	其他附设机构人员 Personnel in Others Subsidiary Units	聘请校外教师 Part-time Teachers
行政人员 Adm. Personnel	教辅人员 Supporting Staff	工勤人员 Workers			
17349	**14158**	**10997**	**969**	**1445**	**19032**
440	140	78		50	308
456	216	88	6	37	157
1127	706	583	76	26	679
636	518	304	28	60	750
451	337	161	15	7	391
879	557	403	32	2	684
356	244	83		16	20
499	365	277	14	5	518
754	421	231	7	1	353
722	987	627	32	29	1506
171	251	140	6	14	406
385	300	267	9	138	851
626	627	424		33	1312
516	291	173	28	18	664
946	1187	506	189	36	899
809	751	520	218	148	625
948	734	630	114	35	941
254	187	128		10	231
1684	1578	1397	17	142	1760
911	890	1026	38	472	1420
214	135	110	66	45	163
222	162	61	1		354
1283	789	1206	37	80	1204
331	122	145		4	393
416	522	408	3	7	761
13	15	22			15
392	256	195	2	6	301
359	375	347	12	11	302
57	44	74	16	9	262
77	58	77	3		242
415	393	306		4	560

成人中等专业学校教

Number of Educational Personnel in

地 区 Region	教职工数 Educational		
	合计 Total	校本部教职工 Educational	
		小计 Subtotal	专任教师 Full-time Teachers
总 计 Total	**72715**	**71608**	**52021**
北 京 Beijing	572	570	313
天 津 Tianjin	679	674	454
河 北 Hebei	7349	7321	5557
山 西 Shanxi	4202	4202	3470
内蒙古 Inner Mongolia	2331	2270	1774
辽 宁 Liaoning	533	533	399
吉 林 Jilin	5874	5864	4424
黑龙江 Heilongjiang	6198	6191	4875
上 海 Shanghai	474	474	217
江 苏 Jiangsu	2633	2616	1464
浙 江 Zhejiang	1670	1670	1049
安 徽 Anhui	2153	2114	1609
福 建 Fujian			
江 西 Jiangxi	2428	1891	1615
山 东 Shandong	3743	3708	2627
河 南 Henan	11597	11296	8129
湖 北 Hubei	1384	1384	738
湖 南 Hunan	4286	4286	2990
广 东 Guangdong	639	639	498
广 西 Guangxi			
海 南 Hainan	177	166	126
重 庆 Chongqing	2582	2581	1850
四 川 Sichuan	1539	1508	1020
贵 州 Guizhou	1712	1697	1265
云 南 Yunnan	3307	3304	2713
西 藏 Tibet			
陕 西 Shaanxi	1308	1308	740
甘 肃 Gansu	1691	1687	923
青 海 Qinghai	396	396	295
宁 夏 Ningxia	185	185	112
新 疆 Xinjiang	1073	1073	775

职工数

Adult Specialized Sec. Schools

单位:人
unit: person

Personnel					
Personnel in Main Campus			校办企业职工 Employees in School-run Factories & Farms	其他附设机构人员 Personnel in Others Subsidiary Units	聘请校外教师 Part-time Teachers
行政人员 Adm. Personnel	教辅人员 Supporting Staff	工勤人员 Workers			
8102	**6161**	**5324**	**745**	**362**	**22590**
136	60	61		2	384
107	45	68		5	612
853	510	401		28	420
280	220	232			2229
203	181	112	61		11
92	26	16			1137
651	547	242		10	52
631	373	312		7	322
96	93	68			92
347	319	486	5	12	1512
260	190	171			1450
239	144	122	15	24	485
135	68	73	536	1	55
409	272	400	35		407
1113	1196	858	75	226	3767
242	276	128			1238
509	418	369			571
49	24	68			133
23	2	15		11	
306	226	199	1		189
219	139	130	17	14	153
245	84	103		15	1554
194	115	282		3	2210
255	202	111			738
275	344	145		4	313
54	9	38			591
40	14	19			118
139	64	95			1847

成人中等专业学校女

Number of Female Educational Personnel in

地　区 Region	教职工数 Educational		
	合计 Total	校本部教职工 Educational	
		小计 Subtotal	专任教师 Full-time Teachers
总　计 Total	**33973**	**33456**	**26292**
北　京 Beijing	330	330	191
天　津 Tianjin	317	312	239
河　北 Hebei	4089	4078	3464
山　西 Shanxi	2338	2338	2025
内蒙古 Inner Mongolia	1166	1150	970
辽　宁 Liaoning	271	271	220
吉　林 Jilin	3095	3095	2567
黑龙江 Heilongjiang	3310	3310	2837
上　海 Shanghai	222	222	109
江　苏 Jiangsu	942	941	638
浙　江 Zhejiang	634	634	401
安　徽 Anhui	827	823	631
福　建 Fujian			
江　西 Jiangxi	1016	724	655
山　东 Shandong	1628	1602	1229
河　南 Henan	5395	5249	4116
湖　北 Hubei	517	517	288
湖　南 Hunan	1619	1619	1151
广　东 Guangdong	236	236	179
广　西 Guangxi			
海　南 Hainan	58	55	46
重　庆 Chongqing	1118	1118	839
四　川 Sichuan	670	659	459
贵　州 Guizhou	626	626	533
云　南 Yunnan	1436	1436	1190
西　藏 Tibet			
陕　西 Shaanxi	578	578	359
甘　肃 Gansu	812	810	420
青　海 Qinghai	150	150	119
宁　夏 Ningxia	78	78	55
新　疆 Xinjiang	495	495	362

教职工数
Adult Specialized Sec. Schools

单位:人
unit: person

Personnel					
Personnel in Main Campus			校办企业职工 Employees in School-run Factories & Farms	其他附设机构人员 Personnel in Others Subsidiary Units	聘请校外教师 Part-time Teachers
行政人员 Adm. Personnel	教辅人员 Supporting Staff	工勤人员 Workers			
2591	**2926**	**1647**	**379**	**138**	**7543**
79	33	27			199
46	17	10		5	349
224	260	130		11	250
85	121	107			571
60	93	27	16		3
35	12	4			451
220	272	36			17
244	169	60			147
41	50	22			34
82	133	88		1	689
98	73	62			372
78	67	47	4		153
36	19	14	292		27
129	119	125	26		137
325	550	258	38	108	1405
83	97	49			208
125	206	137			80
11	13	33			37
6	1	2		3	
95	124	60			80
75	75	50	3	8	82
77	9	7			361
58	48	140			638
96	81	42			220
81	245	64		2	177
10	2	19			156
9	8	6			41
83	29	21			659

职业高中学

Number of Educational Personnel

地 区 Region	教职工数 Educational		
	合计 Total	校本部教职工 Educational	
		小计 Subtotal	专任教师 Full-time Teachers
总 计 Total	**375370**	**372249**	**301440**
北 京 Beijing	7653	7618	4872
天 津 Tianjin	2762	2759	2168
河 北 Hebei	30007	29970	24730
山 西 Shanxi	16809	16739	13806
内蒙古 Inner Mongolia	11028	10951	8487
辽 宁 Liaoning	14119	13984	9954
吉 林 Jilin	11302	11284	8069
黑龙江 Heilongjiang	10286	10254	7985
上 海 Shanghai	4021	3939	2848
江 苏 Jiangsu	12752	12626	10825
浙 江 Zhejiang	29228	29020	25155
安 徽 Anhui	23579	23461	20464
福 建 Fujian			
江 西 Jiangxi	11806	11647	9081
山 东 Shandong	24088	24038	18564
河 南 Henan	34157	33446	27560
湖 北 Hubei	6152	6127	5168
湖 南 Hunan	22126	22019	16977
广 东 Guangdong	11813	11556	9910
广 西 Guangxi			
海 南 Hainan	3436	3432	2554
重 庆 Chongqing	11603	11452	9790
四 川 Sichuan	24809	24601	21360
贵 州 Guizhou	9912	9662	8209
云 南 Yunnan	12676	12638	10614
西 藏 Tibet			
陕 西 Shaanxi	19380	19210	14128
甘 肃 Gansu	5332	5318	4570
青 海 Qinghai	66	66	45
宁 夏 Ningxia	1215	1215	1069
新 疆 Xinjiang	3253	3217	2478

校教职工数
in Vocational High Schools

单位：人
unit: person

Personnel					聘请校外教师 Part-time Teachers
Personnel in Main Campus			校办企业职工 Employees in School-run Factories & Farms	其他附设机构人员 Personnel in Others Subsidiary Units	
行政人员 Adm. Personnel	教辅人员 Supporting Staff	工勤人员 Workers			
25802	**21902**	**23105**	**1826**	**1295**	**29634**
1296	697	753	16	19	490
333	108	150	3		78
1626	2119	1495	31	6	1497
949	960	1024	40	30	1033
767	999	698	7	70	573
1802	1013	1215	91	44	959
1299	1282	634	10	8	861
884	646	739	6	26	371
288	476	327	20	62	244
363	653	785	62	64	577
1132	1447	1286	125	83	2296
1055	835	1107	49	69	2357
1156	459	951	59	100	1286
1938	2145	1391	28	22	714
2140	1727	2019	546	165	3037
337	301	321	22	3	253
2062	1483	1497	62	45	1752
532	567	547		257	599
253	189	436		4	188
617	370	675	146	5	2033
1033	782	1426	171	37	2072
616	326	511	171	79	2539
447	466	1111	14	24	1218
2346	1382	1354	134	36	1528
263	215	270	12	2	354
1	2	18			26
32	70	44			135
235	183	321	1	35	564

职业高中学校女

Number of Female Educational Personnel

地　区 Region	教职工数 Educational		
	合计 Total	校本部教职工 Educational	
		小计 Subtotal	专任教师 Full-time Teachers
总　计 Total	**179125**	**177555**	**152069**
北　京 Beijing	4818	4797	3511
天　津 Tianjin	1788	1788	1544
河　北 Hebei	17287	17265	15520
山　西 Shanxi	9391	9364	8259
内蒙古 Inner Mongolia	5408	5363	4629
辽　宁 Liaoning	7719	7634	6088
吉　林 Jilin	6185	6180	4734
黑龙江 Heilongjiang	5566	5546	4706
上　海 Shanghai	2383	2344	1875
江　苏 Jiangsu	5910	5843	5289
浙　江 Zhejiang	15327	15273	13754
安　徽 Anhui	7777	7749	6829
福　建 Fujian			
江　西 Jiangxi	4309	4255	3424
山　东 Shandong	10627	10597	8814
河　南 Henan	15980	15567	13535
湖　北 Hubei	2539	2536	2208
湖　南 Hunan	9627	9577	7852
广　东 Guangdong	5911	5787	5042
广　西 Guangxi			
海　南 Hainan	1590	1589	1160
重　庆 Chongqing	5557	5476	4961
四　川 Sichuan	10640	10549	9641
贵　州 Guizhou	4185	3985	3424
云　南 Yunnan	5689	5673	4842
西　藏 Tibet			
陕　西 Shaanxi	8949	8866	6974
甘　肃 Gansu	1839	1838	1624
青　海 Qinghai	19	19	14
宁　夏 Ningxia	481	481	441
新　疆 Xinjiang	1624	1614	1375

教职工数

in Vocational High Schools

单位：人
unit：person

Personnel					
Personnel in Main Campus			校办企业职工 Employees in School-run Factories & Farms	其他附设机构人员 Personnel in Others Subsidiary Units	聘请校外教师 Part-time Teachers
行政人员 Adm. Personnel	教辅人员 Supporting Staff	工勤人员 Workers			
8218	**9706**	**7562**	**960**	**610**	**12411**
720	341	225	3	18	243
148	60	36			40
407	897	441	22		681
263	450	392	23	4	555
182	383	169	5	40	306
677	500	369	58	27	482
584	666	196	5		426
362	303	175		20	174
145	257	67	6	33	81
61	294	199	31	36	212
353	683	483	17	37	987
249	306	365	11	17	759
324	141	366	21	33	440
602	816	365	11	19	268
616	742	674	317	96	1410
118	103	107	3		112
522	704	499	36	14	756
157	352	236		124	271
112	99	218		1	87
188	144	183	78	3	974
226	323	359	76	15	867
195	124	242	154	46	846
152	193	486	3	13	352
747	649	496	80	3	711
41	71	102		1	131
		5			12
4	16	20			83
63	89	87		10	145

其他机构

Number of Educational Personnel

地　区 Region	教职工数 Educational		
		校本部教职工 Educational	
	合计 Total	小计 Subtotal	专任教师 Full-time Teachers
总　计 Total	**16559**	**16511**	**11708**
北　京 Beijing			
天　津 Tianjin			
河　北 Hebei	1200	1200	896
山　西 Shanxi	246	246	182
内蒙古 Inner Mongolia			
辽　宁 Liaoning			
吉　林 Jilin	1762	1751	1093
黑龙江 Heilongjiang	43	43	34
上　海 Shanghai			
江　苏 Jiangsu	2505	2500	1858
浙　江 Zhejiang	1029	1027	778
安　徽 Anhui	1972	1972	1456
福　建 Fujian			
江　西 Jiangxi	185	185	157
山　东 Shandong	2147	2139	1497
河　南 Henan	1100	1097	718
湖　北 Hubei	450	441	318
湖　南 Hunan	1044	1044	663
广　东 Guangdong	1148	1148	834
广　西 Guangxi	57	57	11
海　南 Hainan	35	35	31
重　庆 Chongqing	449	439	339
四　川 Sichuan	454	454	348
贵　州 Guizhou	58	58	36
云　南 Yunnan	404	404	260
西　藏 Tibet			
陕　西 Shaanxi	37	37	36
甘　肃 Gansu	97	97	75
青　海 Qinghai			
宁　夏 Ningxia	137	137	88
新　疆 Xinjiang			

教职工数

in Other Institutions

单位：人
unit: person

Personnel					
Personnel in Main Campus			校办企业职工 Employees in School-run Factories & Farms	其他附设机构人员 Personnel in Others Subsidiary Units	聘请校外教师 Part-time Teachers
行政人员 Adm. Personnel	教辅人员 Supporting Staff	工勤人员 Workers			
2093	**1484**	**1226**	**21**	**27**	**1970**
124	67	113			128
21	20	23			
257	256	145		11	54
5	4				2
210	230	202	2	3	498
103	64	82		2	185
241	155	120			337
8	8	12			32
247	252	143	6	2	94
262	78	39	3		75
41	37	45	7	2	49
212	106	63			165
128	97	89			87
28	14	4			
2		2			
51	19	30	3	7	143
39	34	33			7
22					
69	19	56			33
1					
12	3	7			32
10	21	18			49

其他机构女

Number of Female Educational

地 区 Region	教职工数 Educational		
	合计 Total	校本部教职工 Educational	
		小计 Subtotal	专任教师 Full-time Teachers
总 计 Total	**7543**	**7523**	**5860**
北 京 Beijing			
天 津 Tianjin			
河 北 Hebei	607	607	531
山 西 Shanxi	101	101	79
内蒙古 Inner Mongolia			
辽 宁 Liaoning			
吉 林 Jilin	1004	1004	712
黑龙江 Heilongjiang	23	23	17
上 海 Shanghai			
江 苏 Jiangsu	1110	1108	885
浙 江 Zhejiang	537	537	443
安 徽 Anhui	668	668	503
福 建 Fujian			
江 西 Jiangxi	69	69	62
山 东 Shandong	894	892	714
河 南 Henan	514	513	407
湖 北 Hubei	186	178	124
湖 南 Hunan	451	451	321
广 东 Guangdong	561	561	449
广 西 Guangxi	21	21	4
海 南 Hainan	9	9	8
重 庆 Chongqing	237	230	178
四 川 Sichuan	197	197	161
贵 州 Guizhou	32	32	22
云 南 Yunnan	190	190	137
西 藏 Tibet			
陕 西 Shaanxi	21	21	21
甘 肃 Gansu	37	37	29
青 海 Qinghai			
宁 夏 Ningxia	74	74	53
新 疆 Xinjiang			

教职工数
Personnel in Other Institutions

单位:人
unit: person

Personnel					
Personnel in Main Campus			校办企业职工 Employees in School-run Factories & Farms	其他附设机构人员 Personnel in Others Subsidiary Units	聘请校外教师 Part-time Teachers
行政人员 Adm. Personnel	教辅人员 Supporting Staff	工勤人员 Workers			
617	**695**	**351**	**13**	**7**	**803**
24	25	27			63
8	9	5			
108	147	37			13
3	3				
58	114	51	2		198
20	38	36			112
77	57	31			77
1	4	2			13
42	108	28	1	1	43
54	38	14	1		29
18	19	17	6	2	12
70	38	22			70
41	41	30			50
10	7				
1					
23	13	16	3	4	63
18	14	4			1
10					
20	7	26			12
8					18
3	13	5			29

中等职业学校(机构)专

Number of Full-time Teachers By Professional Rank and Academic

地 区 Region	合计 Total	按职称分 By Professional Rank		
		正高级 Senior	副高级 Sub-Senior	中级 Middle
总 计 Total	**668754**	**3383**	**155455**	**268628**
北 京 Beijing	7180	37	1860	2925
天 津 Tianjin	6939	26	2694	2689
河 北 Hebei	44211	222	10811	19167
山 西 Shanxi	25401	106	3792	9617
内蒙古 Inner Mongolia	14755		4569	5321
辽 宁 Liaoning	20750	389	6779	8036
吉 林 Jilin	18094	196	5422	8042
黑龙江 Heilongjiang	17173	117	5904	6849
上 海 Shanghai	8358	31	1699	4307
江 苏 Jiangsu	44164	153	12192	18885
浙 江 Zhejiang	32778	39	7660	12541
安 徽 Anhui	33973	38	7994	13273
福 建 Fujian	17187	13	3910	6706
江 西 Jiangxi	16315	182	4369	5784
山 东 Shandong	50243	134	12796	19897
河 南 Henan	52559	214	10757	22213
湖 北 Hubei	22384	160	5275	10121
湖 南 Hunan	24827	148	5296	11168
广 东 Guangdong	45443	111	7338	19982
广 西 Guangxi	20459	220	3228	8792
海 南 Hainan	4709	32	795	1276
重 庆 Chongqing	14850	90	2918	5187
四 川 Sichuan	40292	422	8752	14317
贵 州 Guizhou	14326	22	2405	4775
云 南 Yunnan	21147	49	6065	7628
西 藏 Tibet	652		45	285
陕 西 Shaanxi	18368	155	3426	7357
甘 肃 Gansu	16008	45	2983	6034
青 海 Qinghai	2567	2	806	984
宁 夏 Ningxia	2611	19	627	803
新 疆 Xinjiang	10031	11	2288	3667

任教师职称、学历情况

Qualifications in Secondary Vocational Schools (Institutions)

单位:人
unit: person

		按学历分 By Academic Qualifications				
初级 Junior	未定职级 No-ranking	博士研究生 Doctor's Degree	硕士研究生 Master's Degree	本科 Normal Courses	专科 Short-cycle Courses	高中阶段及以下 Below High School Graduate
182596	**58692**	**915**	**37383**	**549795**	**76891**	**3770**
1657	701	32	800	5961	348	39
1327	203	3	600	5797	490	49
11166	2845	21	1556	37109	5318	207
9619	2267	54	997	20389	3776	185
3526	1339	40	687	11818	2166	44
4054	1492	18	1196	17587	1826	123
3747	687	31	1010	14993	1955	105
3439	864	24	426	14632	2037	54
1978	343	40	1114	6810	342	52
10328	2606	26	5396	36808	1833	101
9204	3334	3	1808	29259	1635	73
9196	3472	7	1224	29016	3620	106
5076	1482	6	768	14790	1513	110
4210	1770	40	925	12316	2898	136
14207	3209	71	3029	42927	3911	305
16177	3198	68	3439	42709	6157	186
5719	1109	7	964	18050	3130	233
5913	2302	15	930	20219	3529	134
12365	5647	38	3253	37181	4604	367
5947	2272	69	1434	15678	3095	183
1727	879	1	126	3954	565	63
4681	1974	110	657	12267	1753	63
11617	5184	112	1172	31529	7309	170
4099	3025	4	430	11238	2563	91
5500	1905	15	998	17145	2763	226
289	33		47	549	51	5
5935	1495	47	1038	14047	3130	106
5635	1311	7	628	13148	2128	97
597	178	1	60	1830	606	70
746	416	2	170	2149	279	11
2915	1150	3	501	7890	1561	76

普通中等专业学校专任

Number of Full-time Teachers By Professional Rank and Academic

地 区 Region	合计 Total	按职称分 By Professional Rank 正高级 Senior	副高级 Sub-Senior	中级 Middle
总 计 Total	**303585**	**1909**	**74596**	**119116**
北 京 Beijing	1995	20	507	839
天 津 Tianjin	4317	5	1612	1612
河 北 Hebei	13028	171	3450	4833
山 西 Shanxi	7943	28	1930	2976
内蒙古 Inner Mongolia	4494		1574	1458
辽 宁 Liaoning	10397	265	3444	4095
吉 林 Jilin	4508	60	1791	1733
黑龙江 Heilongjiang	4279	50	1424	1318
上 海 Shanghai	5293	28	1191	2561
江 苏 Jiangsu	30017	139	8156	13026
浙 江 Zhejiang	5796	22	1412	2218
安 徽 Anhui	10444	8	2922	3659
福 建 Fujian	17187	13	3910	6706
江 西 Jiangxi	5462	42	1425	1912
山 东 Shandong	27555	80	7485	10944
河 南 Henan	16152	57	4322	6492
湖 北 Hubei	16160	140	3951	7126
湖 南 Hunan	4197	44	1206	1582
广 东 Guangdong	34201	109	5220	14639
广 西 Guangxi	20448	220	3226	8784
海 南 Hainan	1998	1	434	524
重 庆 Chongqing	2871	35	709	1034
四 川 Sichuan	17564	303	3684	5800
贵 州 Guizhou	4816	1	1128	1585
云 南 Yunnan	7560	10	2362	2332
西 藏 Tibet	652		45	285
陕 西 Shaanxi	3464	20	1094	1327
甘 肃 Gansu	10440	16	2258	4047
青 海 Qinghai	2227		761	831
宁 夏 Ningxia	1342	15	332	318
新 疆 Xinjiang	6778	7	1631	2520

教师职称、学历情况
Qualifications in Reg. Specialized Sec. Schools

单位：人
unit：person

初级 Junior	未定职级 No-ranking	按学历分 By Academic Qualifications 博士研究生 Doctor's Degree	硕士研究生 Master's Degree	本科 Normal Courses	专科 Short-cycle Courses	高中阶段及以下 Below High School Graduate
79912	**28052**	**458**	**24945**	**247088**	**29055**	**2039**
483	146	26	478	1357	109	25
948	140	2	445	3505	333	32
3106	1468	18	766	10099	2019	126
2429	580	6	736	6445	664	92
1001	461	16	402	3438	617	21
2085	508	16	854	8808	646	73
835	89	10	397	3754	323	24
1049	438	22	264	3577	400	16
1271	242	25	916	4009	294	49
6867	1829	26	4412	24419	1103	57
1661	483	3	477	5052	256	8
2763	1092	7	699	8885	818	35
5076	1482	6	768	14790	1513	110
1611	472	6	592	4246	550	68
7259	1787	42	2048	23442	1859	164
4504	777	14	1712	13402	927	97
4071	872	7	739	12970	2292	152
916	449	3	330	3519	318	27
9649	4584	32	2654	27762	3461	292
5946	2272	69	1433	15668	3095	183
722	317	1	71	1813	97	16
643	450	6	236	2321	291	17
4594	3183	63	859	13226	3306	110
1274	828	1	286	3960	543	26
1895	961	6	710	6240	563	41
289	33		47	549	51	5
859	164	21	491	2594	333	25
3453	666	3	539	8924	927	47
483	152		60	1583	514	70
345	332		94	1118	122	8
1825	795	1	430	5613	711	23

成人中等专业学校专任

Number of Full-time Teachers By Professional Rank and Academic

地 区 Region	合计 Total	按职称分 By Professional Rank 正高级 Senior	副高级 Sub-Senior	中级 Middle
总 计 Total	**52021**	**375**	**14773**	**23547**
北 京 Beijing	313	2	81	138
天 津 Tianjin	454	9	157	185
河 北 Hebei	5557	29	1759	2691
山 西 Shanxi	3470	12	419	1761
内蒙古 Inner Mongolia	1774		851	636
辽 宁 Liaoning	399	28	107	193
吉 林 Jilin	4424	10	1426	2307
黑龙江 Heilongjiang	4875	50	2144	2082
上 海 Shanghai	217	1	28	146
江 苏 Jiangsu	1464	1	423	615
浙 江 Zhejiang	1049	8	432	445
安 徽 Anhui	1609	1	332	678
福 建 Fujian				
江 西 Jiangxi	1615		821	620
山 东 Shandong	2627	33	812	991
河 南 Henan	8129	91	1595	3658
湖 北 Hubei	738	9	118	412
湖 南 Hunan	2990	25	864	1550
广 东 Guangdong	498		43	207
广 西 Guangxi				
海 南 Hainan	126		60	43
重 庆 Chongqing	1850	32	579	675
四 川 Sichuan	1020	14	106	250
贵 州 Guizhou	1265	10	164	629
云 南 Yunnan	2713	4	906	1304
西 藏 Tibet				
陕 西 Shaanxi	740		73	340
甘 肃 Gansu	923	2	200	452
青 海 Qinghai	295	1	41	148
宁 夏 Ningxia	112		25	55
新 疆 Xinjiang	775	3	207	336

教师职称、学历情况

Qualifications in Adult Specialized Sec. Schools

单位：人
unit：person

		按学历分 By Academic Qualifications				
初级 Junior	未定职级 No-ranking	博士研究生 Doctor's Degree	硕士研究生 Master's Degree	本科 Normal Courses	专科 Short-cycle Courses	高中阶段及以下 Below High School Graduate
10743	**2583**	**79**	**1810**	**39316**	**10328**	**488**
71	21	2	11	272	28	
80	23		10	376	65	3
943	135	1	172	4158	1186	40
1174	104		21	2556	860	33
249	38		47	1410	305	12
55	16		10	294	92	3
614	67		97	3460	830	37
542	57	1	64	3884	901	25
38	4	15	7	171	24	
332	93		105	1215	136	8
120	44		69	871	108	1
414	184		48	1195	334	32
156	18		19	1252	329	15
621	170	2	103	2188	306	28
2062	723	46	543	5893	1621	26
193	6		15	421	249	53
444	107	1	59	2284	624	22
185	63		4	371	93	30
22	1		6	110	10	
428	136	2	179	1474	187	8
323	327	4	33	711	270	2
384	78		24	925	316	
473	26	3	79	1976	575	80
292	35		12	368	360	
245	24		24	653	239	7
95	10			208	87	
22	10	1	13	76	22	
166	63	1	36	544	171	23

职业高中学校专任教

Number of Full-time Teachers By Professional Rank and Academic

地　区 Region	合计 Total	按职称分 By Professional Rank 正高级 Senior	副高级 Sub-Senior	中级 Middle
总　计 Total	**301440**	**1009**	**63049**	**120933**
北　京 Beijing	4872	15	1272	1948
天　津 Tianjin	2168	12	925	892
河　北 Hebei	24730	14	5307	11253
山　西 Shanxi	13806	66	1406	4803
内蒙古 Inner Mongolia	8487		2144	3227
辽　宁 Liaoning	9954	96	3228	3748
吉　林 Jilin	8069	95	1828	3563
黑龙江 Heilongjiang	7985	14	2320	3434
上　海 Shanghai	2848	2	480	1600
江　苏 Jiangsu	10825	6	2986	4426
浙　江 Zhejiang	25155	9	5667	9551
安　徽 Anhui	20464	29	4424	8182
福　建 Fujian				
江　西 Jiangxi	9081	135	2085	3182
山　东 Shandong	18564	10	3999	7427
河　南 Henan	27560	62	4764	11807
湖　北 Hubei	5168	5	1124	2452
湖　南 Hunan	16977	74	3041	7723
广　东 Guangdong	9910	1	1910	4665
广　西 Guangxi				
海　南 Hainan	2554	31	293	696
重　庆 Chongqing	9790	21	1600	3360
四　川 Sichuan	21360	102	4918	8126
贵　州 Guizhou	8209	11	1112	2541
云　南 Yunnan	10614	35	2769	3939
西　藏 Tibet				
陕　西 Shaanxi	14128	135	2250	5674
甘　肃 Gansu	4570	27	507	1498
青　海 Qinghai	45	1	4	5
宁　夏 Ningxia	1069		236	400
新　疆 Xinjiang	2478	1	450	811

师职称、学历情况

Qualifications in Vocational High Schools

单位：人

unit: person

		按学历分 By Academic Qualifications				
初级 Junior	未定职级 No-ranking	博士研究生 Doctor's Degree	硕士研究生 Master's Degree	本科 Normal Courses	专科 Short-cycle Courses	高中阶段及以下 Below High School Graduate
89214	**27235**	**346**	**9411**	**254268**	**36203**	**1212**
1103	534	4	311	4332	211	14
299	40	1	145	1916	92	14
6983	1173	1	496	22141	2054	38
5949	1582	48	240	11261	2199	58
2276	840	24	238	6970	1244	11
1914	968	2	332	8485	1088	47
2065	518	21	380	6878	748	42
1848	369	1	96	7145	730	13
669	97		191	2630	24	3
2786	621		634	9709	454	28
7235	2693		1230	22662	1199	64
5658	2171		279	17872	2276	37
2411	1268	34	287	6690	2017	53
5931	1197	1	675	16202	1578	108
9381	1546	8	1137	22828	3527	60
1388	199		193	4479	473	23
4416	1723	8	498	13813	2573	85
2415	919	4	520	8383	959	44
973	561		49	2020	438	47
3471	1338	102	239	8226	1185	38
6562	1652	45	273	17346	3638	58
2430	2115	3	120	6327	1694	65
3038	833	6	187	8720	1596	105
4773	1296	26	532	11055	2434	81
1928	610	4	62	3506	955	43
19	16	1		39	5	
369	64	1	32	900	133	3
924	292	1	35	1733	679	30

其他机构专任教师

Number of Full-time Teachers By Professional Rank and Academic

地 区 Region	合计 Total	按职称分 By Professional Rank		
		正高级 Senior	副高级 Sub-Senior	中级 Middle
总 计 Total	**11708**	**90**	**3037**	**5032**
北 京 Beijing				
天 津 Tianjin				
河 北 Hebei	896	8	295	390
山 西 Shanxi	182		37	77
内蒙古 Inner Mongolia				
辽 宁 Liaoning				
吉 林 Jilin	1093	31	377	439
黑龙江 Heilongjiang	34	3	16	15
上 海 Shanghai				
江 苏 Jiangsu	1858	7	627	818
浙 江 Zhejiang	778		149	327
安 徽 Anhui	1456		316	754
福 建 Fujian				
江 西 Jiangxi	157	5	38	70
山 东 Shandong	1497	11	500	535
河 南 Henan	718	4	76	256
湖 北 Hubei	318	6	82	131
湖 南 Hunan	663	5	185	313
广 东 Guangdong	834	1	165	471
广 西 Guangxi	11		2	8
海 南 Hainan	31		8	13
重 庆 Chongqing	339	2	30	118
四 川 Sichuan	348	3	44	141
贵 州 Guizhou	36		1	20
云 南 Yunnan	260		28	53
西 藏 Tibet				
陕 西 Shaanxi	36		9	16
甘 肃 Gansu	75		18	37
青 海 Qinghai				
宁 夏 Ningxia	88	4	34	30
新 疆 Xinjiang				

职称、学历情况
Qualifications in Other Institutions

单位：人
unit: person

初级 Junior	未定职级 No-ranking	按学历分 By Academic Qualifications 博士研究生 Doctor's Degree	硕士研究生 Master's Degree	本科 Normal Courses	专科 Short-cycle Courses	高中阶段及以下 Below High School Graduate
2727	**822**	**32**	**1217**	**9123**	**1305**	**31**
134	69	1	122	711	59	3
67	1			127	53	2
233	13		136	901	54	2
			2	26	6	
343	63		245	1465	140	8
188	114		32	674	72	
361	25		198	1064	192	2
32	12		27	128	2	
396	55	26	203	1095	168	5
230	152		47	586	82	3
67	32		17	180	116	5
137	23	3	43	603	14	
116	81	2	75	665	91	1
1			1	10		
10				11	20	
139	50		3	246	90	
138	22		7	246	95	
11	4			26	10	
94	85		22	209	29	
11			3	30	3	
9	11		3	65	7	
10	10		31	55	2	

中等职业学校(机构)

Condition of Fixed Assets and Teaching Resources in Secondary

地区 Region	学校占地面积(平方米) Area of School Sites (m²)			图书(册) Books (volume)		
	合计 Total	其中:绿化用地面积 of Which: Green Areas	其中:运动场地面积 of Which: Sports Areas	合计 Total	当年新增 New Added in Current Year	合计 Total
总计 Total	**498656332**	**116378052**	**77377424**	**350295948**	**18619046**	**2990717**
北京 Beijing	4482579	949507	933341	4984050	405428	56056
天津 Tianjin	3817212	704119	566887	3587475	122095	29279
河北 Hebei	23804673	3917630	4696993	19412360	752138	154532
山西 Shanxi	14526041	2501983	2013244	9573709	312668	75925
内蒙古 Inner Mongolia	10595568	1918216	2084051	5800408	458651	46463
辽宁 Liaoning	11344723	1727385	2609895	8952655	110290	93782
吉林 Jilin	7170986	1399918	1563365	6296322	253165	44542
黑龙江 Heilongjiang	10456409	1979231	1902568	4770117	122999	51994
上海 Shanghai	3782079	1233286	786599	6568372	248016	81573
江苏 Jiangsu	35292551	10458250	5088137	26237354	1134104	226588
浙江 Zhejiang	19845976	5967512	3749443	15235586	795679	172979
安徽 Anhui	36664550	7674773	4703394	29263803	2894409	137043
福建 Fujian	13143703	3711914	2309127	10675003	627551	96249
江西 Jiangxi	23261634	5815752	2757569	11093432	402071	83684
山东 Shandong	38972690	9496184	6064747	24108442	1792219	196143
河南 Henan	35264097	6035989	4952653	27593806	1025429	192305
湖北 Hubei	19490904	5884621	2678120	12873860	285000	111537
湖南 Hunan	20600913	5582538	3116436	13603288	458316	139230
广东 Guangdong	30897182	9328236	5473882	28222751	1409896	283262
广西 Guangxi	24009320	5520909	2558163	14090801	520355	109013
海南 Hainan	3184772	834217	620667	1967120	110622	21177
重庆 Chongqing	11153151	2884378	1616729	7708337	441735	73191
四川 Sichuan	24634292	5452269	4650857	18678878	2197098	166531
贵州 Guizhou	11654331	3026369	1827123	5704705	533873	62104
云南 Yunnan	16218603	3140649	1867858	9164584	218434	86896
西藏 Tibet	873883	113511	81925	241628	38383	1990
陕西 Shaanxi	14124343	2427392	2151669	10306808	503733	78808
甘肃 Gansu	9878592	1947149	1632271	6260332	99044	55505
青海 Qinghai	2370975	571024	363085	1156408	27564	11567
宁夏 Ningxia	4898383	1146985	399925	1467963	129271	14364
新疆 Xinjiang	12241217	3026156	1556701	4695591	188810	36405

资产情况(学校产权)

Vocational Schools (Institutions) (Owned by SVSs)

计算机数(台) No. of Computers(set)		教室(间) Classroom(room)		固定资产值(万元) Fixed Assets (10,000 yuan)		
其中:教学用计算机 of Which:No. of Computers Used for Instruction		合计 Total	其中:网络多媒体教室 of Which: Network Multimedia Classroom	合计 Total	其中:教学、科研仪器设备资产值 of Which: Teaching Equipment & Instruments	
小计 Subtotal	其中:平板电脑 of Which: Tablet PC				小计 Subtotal	当年新增 New Added in Current Year
2497229	**110663**	**410934**	**145692**	**26573194.20**	**5558781.52**	**720711.99**
46275	548	4480	2551	522476.81	171861.42	27691.07
24535	1339	3145	1043	205699.03	65311.14	5213.62
125609	9576	25054	5681	1031172.73	243501.22	26615.21
64428	1104	11884	2931	659697.94	118847.95	17737.74
38396		6200	2327	522901.05	94734.58	13771.25
75546	3727	8723	3356	728566.60	167045.38	18029.55
32848	1291	6858	1513	370363.62	68901.98	8833.90
41978	1519	6911	1880	348819.11	78194.76	7427.90
66364	873	6431	3767	803466.89	222541.23	30708.97
191184	6451	23706	13134	2708845.62	479722.35	50622.98
145494	2075	17947	10792	1470801.22	336793.66	35254.59
114497	5938	29209	4700	1732648.30	329173.94	40028.02
81245	3125	9189	4070	658482.13	175823.30	24801.63
71407	4173	11107	3482	870614.92	150535.71	19429.15
157288	7973	32963	9735	2129394.43	376047.53	37981.34
163153	6018	38832	12151	1437896.83	292618.90	34502.35
96009	5298	12363	2815	903533.82	165878.95	18593.60
117025	5682	12954	3507	1028015.40	205252.35	22259.52
247896	14199	41345	26093	2083679.00	533214.00	65404.00
91394	6737	10763	3186	816715.68	227212.81	26830.46
16630	1706	2737	1154	185604.27	44409.61	10427.63
61471	3543	8986	4744	692999.39	138879.22	24830.07
137213	3593	30487	6040	1412713.39	278476.08	64885.26
53793	2863	8020	2315	512920.00	102353.90	22668.17
72017	119	9729	2319	777346.92	102064.27	16634.19
1385		215	71	32204.59	7458.16	3281.08
65615	5376	14535	5519	748247.82	143220.98	16095.38
47265	2625	6939	2738	447409.06	91403.55	10031.14
8565	676	1771	338	193512.69	25315.83	2785.58
11799	718	1738	423	145598.02	32801.77	4462.76
28905	1798	5713	1317	390846.92	89184.99	12873.88

中等职业学校(机构)

Condition of Fixed Assets and Teaching Resources in Secondary

地 区 Region	学校占地面积(平方米) Area of School Sites (m^2)			图书(册) Books (volume)		
	合计 Total	其中:绿化用地面积 of Which: Green Areas	其中:运动场地面积 of Which: Sports Areas	合计 Total	当年新增 New Added in Current Year	合计 Total
总 计 Total	**42630074**	**7868279**	**6947480**	**11545367**	**950646**	**115298**
北 京 Beijing	338407	47278	77483	48099	2600	382
天 津 Tianjin	331116	16582	68975	356671	2021	2462
河 北 Hebei	3153915	425643	378370	862999	29449	8021
山 西 Shanxi	1656029	141435	220905	657428	1700	2587
内蒙古 Inner Mongolia	809102	127751	292093	114084	650	1751
辽 宁 Liaoning	1202989	190098	279103	204800	3944	1430
吉 林 Jilin	735507	108805	151511	199092	3900	3691
黑龙江 Heilongjiang	793722	85938	198566	247892	11300	2339
上 海 Shanghai	238767	38884	23271	10000		180
江 苏 Jiangsu	1237227	258751	125054	805272	33070	6748
浙 江 Zhejiang	861128	143146	182121	210977	15460	2486
安 徽 Anhui	1676331	270426	190596	339000	11100	1715
福 建 Fujian	1172221	316679	202571	239817	1656	3304
江 西 Jiangxi	1558752	393198	266773	244337	21311	4711
山 东 Shandong	2672526	659472	493659	457310	18950	4601
河 南 Henan	2731872	408713	418436	667702	35561	13947
湖 北 Hubei	1038979	147801	180163	342350	7390	2143
湖 南 Hunan	2547276	748666	369985	551390	27326	12099
广 东 Guangdong	3025052	664985	655319	523166	45982	10341
广 西 Guangxi	2902647	486097	267868	2181163	173737	4216
海 南 Hainan	407274	69270	44848	25932	2400	801
重 庆 Chongqing	805013	165163	118421	49979	3478	1119
四 川 Sichuan	4302093	852055	817926	721067	385075	11194
贵 州 Guizhou	1214991	242479	232211	255745	21430	3184
云 南 Yunnan	2122859	298232	186788	146888	16226	1726
西 藏 Tibet						
陕 西 Shaanxi	1758848	263781	309624	899373	70330	6600
甘 肃 Gansu	706648	107901	169182	156768	4600	1276
青 海 Qinghai	126520	860	5000	3126		142
宁 夏 Ningxia	36179	8515	10458			
新 疆 Xinjiang	466084	179675	10200	22940		102

资产情况(非学校产权中独立使用)
Vocational Schools (Institutions)(Not Owned by SVSs)

计算机数(台) No. of Computers(set)		教室(间) Classroom(room)		固定资产值(万元) Fixed Assets (10,000 yuan)		
其中:教学用计算机 of Which:No. of Computers Used for Instruction		合计 Total	其中:网络多媒体教室 of Which: Network Multimedia Classroom	合计 Total	其中:教学、科研仪器设备资产值 of Which: Teaching Equipment & Instruments	
小计 Subtotal	其中:平板电脑 of Which: Tablet PC				小计 Subtotal	当年新增 New Added in Current Year
93243	**4312**	**44163**	**14034**	**1535418.97**	**188690.54**	**28118.91**
284	26	406	204	3420.89	793.63	144.90
1890	708	371	127	26763.73	2312.76	352.64
5916	315	2404	430	88649.98	12000.03	862.77
1750		1049	259	71574.31	5099.11	477.82
685		678	197	25250.00	734.70	9.80
1055	92	1478	360	156908.15	2418.30	220.60
2666	40	629	90	19303.02	2762.06	232.00
1992	260	1297	213	26951.88	4990.40	263.20
162	7	385	207	10994.00	1247.00	3.00
4485	30	1646	697	68769.35	12686.33	2129.87
2163	16	1333	734	30045.52	2747.60	207.80
1456	214	2018	138	34114.60	9149.80	1348.70
2047		540	290	61973.75	12415.54	1686.46
4078	160	805	290	94999.02	5218.76	493.38
3020		1525	533	128508.66	11720.14	1862.00
12204	195	5366	2885	91600.83	14580.73	1467.20
1740	10	2426	1361	45864.33	7204.51	181.30
10271	375	1095	375	74835.72	10814.81	953.60
9049	474	1488	421	58164.00	20226.00	1986.00
4002	576	1360	218	84801.64	12808.42	603.20
605		891	91	12514.54	328.37	104.20
1060		398	152	42035.83	4104.66	2347.98
9313	25	5609	1604	103110.44	15483.69	7307.67
2768	480	794	177	38650.06	4246.45	578.31
1608		1258	594	36865.04	2187.00	1114.60
5633	243	5815	1263	55710.43	6867.74	795.38
1140	36	815	111	34415.36	3089.79	59.42
120		12	1	96.00	35.00	
		34	6	437.50	14.50	9.00
81	30	238	6	8090.39	402.71	316.11

普通中专学校

Condition of Fixed Assets and Teaching

地 区 Region	学校占地面积(平方米) Area of School Sites (m^2) 合计 Total	其中:绿化用地面积 of Which: Green Areas	其中:运动场地面积 of Which: Sports Areas	图书(册) Books (volume) 合计 Total	当年新增 New Added in Current Year	合计 Total
总 计 Total	**251185698**	**63039786**	**37431439**	**189341020**	**8530154**	**1564040**
北 京 Beijing	1513980	409969	333969	1678518	16750	18740
天 津 Tianjin	3027602	581945	421545	2464989	59647	20547
河 北 Hebei	7829967	1387597	1646860	8353061	223122	61908
山 西 Shanxi	6525671	1171549	853885	5147765	178516	32938
内蒙古 Inner Mongolia	3895307	1092320	683219	2429672	346730	18903
辽 宁 Liaoning	5062882	1003165	1224391	5338667	71478	50377
吉 林 Jilin	2536673	533416	478954	1760405	75291	14168
黑龙江 Heilongjiang	2938636	569497	476772	2318457	46760	19389
上 海 Shanghai	2401754	782367	483129	4308642	195593	50984
江 苏 Jiangsu	23170195	7567485	3518288	17703221	617745	164245
浙 江 Zhejiang	3883593	1108980	643475	2793962	224005	28765
安 徽 Anhui	13725846	3053394	1694077	10544878	701641	57658
福 建 Fujian	13143703	3711914	2309127	10675003	627551	96249
江 西 Jiangxi	7568047	2355466	791583	3595699	90743	34430
山 东 Shandong	22622290	5439454	3320193	15118220	1206316	108140
河 南 Henan	12632634	2351613	1769699	11617432	310951	75873
湖 北 Hubei	14355564	3885545	2052693	10399286	263628	83883
湖 南 Hunan	4043403	1030225	609651	3460991	110350	22008
广 东 Guangdong	23799201	7200885	4078144	22161979	952818	216809
广 西 Guangxi	23916053	5520509	2556278	14067498	520355	108843
海 南 Hainan	1270718	313801	250797	1230448	80400	11172
重 庆 Chongqing	2241611	715558	242837	1715638	59985	13642
四 川 Sichuan	12161008	2845780	2244671	10009871	975456	83527
贵 州 Guizhou	4433155	1161433	588056	2619096	197097	27010
云 南 Yunnan	7469688	1389476	773221	5022720	41916	38099
西 藏 Tibet	873883	113511	81925	241628	38383	1990
陕 西 Shaanxi	3771540	686827	451041	2410718	20908	19940
甘 肃 Gansu	7298121	1552371	1135025	4841179	49163	38805
青 海 Qinghai	2229769	570114	346185	1039535	27564	11085
宁 夏 Ningxia	2867037	663172	231222	787769	107079	7555
新 疆 Xinjiang	7976167	2270448	1140527	3484073	92213	26358

资产情况(学校产权)

Resources in Regular SSSs (Owned by Regular SSSs)

计算机数(台) No. of Computers(set)		教室(间) Classroom(room)		固定资产值(万元) Fixed Assets (10,000 yuan)		
其中:教学用计算机 of Which:No. of Computers Used for Instruction		合计 Total	其中:网络多媒体教室 of Which: Network Multimedia Classroom	合计 Total	其中:教学、科研仪器设备资产值 of Which: Teaching Equipment & Instruments	
小计 Subtotal	其中:平板电脑 of Which: Tablet PC				小计 Subtotal	当年新增 New Added in Current Year
1309610	**58607**	**200809**	**78598**	**14506467.98**	**3077153.97**	**371827.72**
16055	168	1414	863	245164.21	72325.42	6978.66
17141	1194	2302	858	167902.54	49560.49	4053.14
51857	4702	6188	1659	383945.68	96173.25	7764.05
27558	257	4707	965	301610.42	65180.86	5917.10
15776		2093	672	243032.09	41067.51	7197.98
40350	1894	4128	1918	360536.09	86389.23	11628.21
10185	191	2054	305	121240.90	18925.03	1992.37
16282	796	2311	803	171407.98	35400.10	3211.89
40855	290	3870	2043	553824.10	156959.47	20467.14
138610	3912	16659	9419	2074659.88	363568.28	38796.96
23751	162	2839	1927	279898.21	64048.81	7269.79
48355	2693	10556	1922	650438.04	120891.41	14322.18
81245	3125	9189	4070	658482.13	175823.30	24801.63
28623	665	4255	1506	325457.64	67446.10	8102.30
88774	5129	20241	5484	1388820.51	221838.97	19334.79
65182	1261	14588	4068	548696.30	124779.15	12790.87
72921	2952	9032	2024	720214.99	131243.50	15466.58
18374	176	1651	544	228727.08	41639.80	3430.15
190637	12197	34666	22295	1674746.00	420795.00	53455.00
91247	6737	10754	3177	806004.68	227212.81	26830.46
9068	1043	1114	592	96534.84	22914.70	4714.76
10683	58	1596	735	123710.44	23699.79	3316.60
66196	1871	12775	2774	693741.65	135865.29	24382.51
23194	1493	3193	1240	159917.26	40376.68	8131.16
31358	3	4205	1078	442602.22	50457.51	7709.64
1385		215	71	32204.59	7458.16	3281.08
16396	1200	3488	2265	179440.37	41769.84	4356.23
32798	1734	4221	1759	336521.49	66123.02	7275.94
8437	676	1649	324	188948.69	24900.83	2743.58
5761	714	986	190	90331.92	17191.11	2704.73
20556	1314	3870	1048	257705.04	65128.55	9400.24

普通中专学校资产

Condition of Fixed Assets and Teaching

地 区 Region	学校占地面积(平方米) Area of School Sites (m^2)			图书(册) Books (volume)		
	合计 Total	其中:绿化用地面积 of Which: Green Areas	其中:运动场地面积 of Which: Sports Areas	合计 Total	当年新增 New Added in Current Year	合计 Total
总 计 Total	**20827035**	**3980307**	**3233645**	**6009170**	**601512**	**49570**
北 京 Beijing	49295	2850	8550			
天 津 Tianjin	155488	8100	34400	97422	21	898
河 北 Hebei	2238135	379119	256543	712869	21249	5775
山 西 Shanxi	670126	65980	64987	500	500	67
内蒙古 Inner Mongolia	425161	60525	94800	37700	650	1554
辽 宁 Liaoning	603976	73812	88888	89040	150	284
吉 林 Jilin	23000	5500	7000	4200	1000	18
黑龙江 Heilongjiang	445467	46756	82066	135070	200	1020
上 海 Shanghai	229470	38494	22084	10000		20
江 苏 Jiangsu	585099	112740	48987	415300	8500	3684
浙 江 Zhejiang	152153	48200	59049	55000	3840	142
安 徽 Anhui	512845	106800	60100	100000		163
福 建 Fujian	1172221	316679	202571	239817	1656	3304
江 西 Jiangxi	360635	88793	71010	21186	1121	1121
山 东 Shandong	962514	322499	149824	257724	11250	2452
河 南 Henan	519174	49231	50986	6500	90	1435
湖 北 Hubei	853774	118571	149691	275220	7390	1866
湖 南 Hunan	184950	115682	14710	40200	1500	701
广 东 Guangdong	2544467	557204	552439	480857	35862	9152
广 西 Guangxi	2902647	486097	267868	2181163	173737	4216
海 南 Hainan	288191	24132	22944	8000		350
重 庆 Chongqing	74167	20439	25568	10680	500	135
四 川 Sichuan	3503418	723464	654805	654092	327000	9727
贵 州 Guizhou	158240	43840	30121			70
云 南 Yunnan	323140	19308	57321	18296	3296	497
西 藏 Tibet						
陕 西 Shaanxi	267703	46458	48322	8000		40
甘 肃 Gansu	420464	74600	88175	135168	2000	720
青 海 Qinghai	126520	860	5000	1126		135
宁 夏 Ningxia	35645	8515	10458			
新 疆 Xinjiang	38950	15059	4378	14040		24

情况(非学校产权中独立使用)

Resources in Regular SSSs (Not Owned by Regular SSSs)

计算机数(台) No. of Computers(set)		教室(间) Classroom(room)		固定资产值(万元) Fixed Assets (10,000 yuan)		
其中:教学用计算机 of Which:No. of Computers Used for Instruction		合计 Total	其中:网络多媒体教室 of Which: Network Multimedia Classroom	合计 Total	其中:教学、科研仪器设备资产值 of Which: Teaching Equipment & Instruments	
小计 Subtotal	其中:平板电脑 of Which: Tablet PC				小计 Subtotal	当年新增 New Added in Current Year
38649	**2248**	**18619**	**5886**	**817744.99**	**103231.71**	**13228.99**
		76	10			
708	708	63	31	20510.00	928.00	28.00
4230	235	1486	222	55000.47	8347.92	708.00
67		157	18	17958.21	1153.40	207.10
573		320	45	11030.00	298.00	3.00
177		695	205	110802.40	951.00	100.00
14		110	11	2359.00	67.00	10.00
966	160	773	90	11904.00	2495.00	1.00
17	7	332	164	8714.00	183.00	3.00
2232		1015	448	33286.81	4910.57	203.91
99		145	76	325.00	58.00	
163	163	66		4932.00	950.50	60.00
2047		540	290	61973.75	12415.54	1686.46
950		208	14	15729.34	583.51	71.65
1554		640	286	59321.93	8143.11	1200.00
1002		457	106	19310.60	3511.30	296.20
1495		2261	1345	42970.73	6446.51	156.30
628		233	21	34475.60	3154.00	174.00
7982	374	1285	339	55344.00	19408.00	1951.00
4002	576	1360	218	84801.64	12808.42	603.20
240		751	62	11650.34	40.00	40.00
116		128	13	13820.00	279.16	89.38
8042	25	3935	1136	76043.64	13320.64	5575.39
70		129	86	3538.90	272.00	42.00
497		724	555	25595.56	67.00	
25		58	16	579.46	18.56	
620		528	70	30591.65	2328.87	
120		12	1	70.00	35.00	
		34	6	437.50	14.50	9.00
13		98	2	4668.46	43.20	10.40

地　区 Region	学校占地面积(平方米) Area of School Sites (m²)			图书(册) Books (volume)		
	合计 Total	其中:绿化用地面积 of Which: Green Areas	其中:运动场地面积 of Which: Sports Areas	合计 Total	当年新增 New Added in Current Year	合计 Total
总　计 Total	**25636397**	**4982588**	**3490715**	**23149171**	**1224456**	**170004**
北　京 Beijing	254306	56880	23576	141592	1380	2329
天　津 Tianjin	75308	4210	20876	120244	160	1984
河　北 Hebei	1312670	127063	233047	2020141	139474	15113
山　西 Shanxi	400336	47176	45875	536761	6855	4985
内蒙古 Inner Mongolia	678735	92628	120015	786151	1200	4267
辽　宁 Liaoning	42668	3008	14407	178810	20940	932
吉　林 Jilin	676990	103345	145178	1604687	49872	6773
黑龙江 Heilongjiang	2340584	663083	313012	846867	15868	6866
上　海 Shanghai	102340	34101	20005	279967	1565	2476
江　苏 Jiangsu	2706924	271430	119578	867719	141190	7406
浙　江 Zhejiang	419995	105255	59444	548304	14107	7041
安　徽 Anhui	1083091	185089	124378	1433197	226671	6391
福　建 Fujian						
江　西 Jiangxi	1090549	192632	94661	936485	13231	4144
山　东 Shandong	2048603	489733	305872	1268312	74163	10020
河　南 Henan	4858856	713986	709767	5099955	270877	30316
湖　北 Hubei	1061994	268943	188499	584191	354	3674
湖　南 Hunan	2078104	662451	312486	1312238	26779	19036
广　东 Guangdong	534343	243771	94405	338727	700	2656
广　西 Guangxi						
海　南 Hainan	62133	15450	6521	23600	495	737
重　庆 Chongqing	732985	151532	125336	864070	20140	9699
四　川 Sichuan	780179	143336	173356	836386	153321	4835
贵　州 Guizhou	447064	72295	32820	645751	5400	3620
云　南 Yunnan	979998	186327	109154	928609	10114	7312
西　藏 Tibet						
陕　西 Shaanxi	112243	7906	11940	259521	500	1804
甘　肃 Gansu	355595	89961	50375	211738	700	2567
青　海 Qinghai	23563	910	1200	111287		427
宁　夏 Ningxia	44770	5435	9390	62786	200	1162
新　疆 Xinjiang	331471	44652	25542	301075	28200	1432

资产情况(学校产权)
Resources in Adult SSSs (Owned by Adult SSSs)

计算机数(台) No. of Computers(set) — 其中:教学用计算机 of Which: No. of Computers Used for Instruction — 小计 Subtotal	计算机数(台) No. of Computers(set) — 其中:教学用计算机 of Which: No. of Computers Used for Instruction — 其中:平板电脑 of Which: Tablet PC	教室(间) Classroom(room) — 合计 Total	教室(间) Classroom(room) — 其中:网络多媒体教室 of Which: Network Multimedia Classroom	固定资产值(万元) Fixed Assets (10,000 yuan) — 合计 Total	固定资产值(万元) Fixed Assets (10,000 yuan) — 其中:教学、科研仪器设备资产值 of Which: Teaching Equipment & Instruments — 小计 Subtotal	固定资产值(万元) Fixed Assets (10,000 yuan) — 其中:教学、科研仪器设备资产值 of Which: Teaching Equipment & Instruments — 当年新增 New Added in Current Year
132938	**4486**	**26304**	**9897**	**1080686.45**	**200169.69**	**21523.23**
1943	56	162	94	14001.20	3793.00	181.00
1744	25	167	51	4157.94	1740.10	102.78
11437	448	2397	345	79858.05	12717.60	1105.05
4284	43	446	84	15330.46	2968.50	409.73
3241		524	135	18444.68	3551.26	230.95
609	138	49	5	7320.00	1328.00	50.00
3925	57	515	84	35109.23	6922.43	368.75
5171	40	793	134	38260.19	5788.02	181.40
1892	365	615	351	15198.86	3552.78	58.25
6218	207	1267	327	80391.80	12099.69	478.55
5394	200	674	333	42273.52	7183.15	496.85
5393	20	1106	161	56100.61	16376.60	3386.20
3023	119	755	473	25575.08	3236.46	328.62
8197	545	2180	621	86175.73	16664.44	2141.13
25076	1131	7921	4442	190760.83	33418.86	4090.05
3205	15	358	91	33856.82	6563.26	149.82
13553	394	624	112	82830.92	12616.80	1009.66
2473	72	337	67	18531.00	7145.00	357.00
478		33	13	2367.75	520.00	88.00
7715	168	1195	376	84512.75	11816.28	1431.52
3940		832	204	24015.76	7294.42	3742.50
2518		672	34	24593.00	7151.27	146.40
5875	2	800	127	36822.26	5573.12	391.18
1389		1292	1097	40839.00	2651.00	113.00
1831	321	216	53	11863.82	3670.77	391.40
80		50	5	2157.00	350.00	42.00
1072		55	15	1341.14	545.36	12.44
1262	120	269	63	7997.05	2931.52	39.00

成人中专学校

Condition of Fixed Assets and Teaching

地 区 Region	学校占地面积(平方米) Area of School Sites (m^2)			图书(册) Books (volume)		
	合计 Total	其中:绿化用地面积 of Which: Green Areas	其中:运动场地面积 of Which: Sports Areas	合计 Total	当年新增 New Added in Current Year	合计 Total
总 计 Total	**2598026**	**412206**	**496670**	**1493118**	**64223**	**14848**
北 京 Beijing	9226			7500	2500	108
天 津 Tianjin	9200	250	780	12276	2000	327
河 北 Hebei	137782	8630	12336	50943	4700	1397
山 西 Shanxi	20001	725	7475	525258		712
内蒙古 Inner Mongolia	18873	4328	8205	3384		72
辽 宁 Liaoning	23524	1600	12000	54000	3000	413
吉 林 Jilin	51867	21773	7402	47080		331
黑龙江 Heilongjiang	48971	9874	7910	24961	100	300
上 海 Shanghai	4581	130	240			160
江 苏 Jiangsu	76391	21650	2280			
浙 江 Zhejiang	11968	1000	500	1000		50
安 徽 Anhui	181116	21020	30700	132000		334
福 建 Fujian						
江 西 Jiangxi	43884	9826	3830	52348	300	264
山 东 Shandong	288466	53376	98327	62866	1600	492
河 南 Henan	874391	148892	144958	297891	27545	6861
湖 北 Hubei	1530	232	218			
湖 南 Hunan	229468	47092	49669	63850	1870	966
广 东 Guangdong	15400	720	11900	500		
广 西 Guangxi						
海 南 Hainan						
重 庆 Chongqing	137006	27858	29340	33119	2978	230
四 川 Sichuan	302587	24870	42300	11500	10000	493
贵 州 Guizhou	51500	1000	19000	30000	2000	450
云 南 Yunnan	14128	2360	1300	31892	5630	281
西 藏 Tibet						
陕 西 Shaanxi	44195	5000	6000	48750		600
甘 肃 Gansu	952					
青 海 Qinghai				2000		7
宁 夏 Ningxia	534					
新 疆 Xinjiang	485					

资产情况(非学校产权中独立使用)
Resources in Adult SSSs (Not Owned by Adult SSSs)

计算机数(台) No. of Computers(set)		教室(间) Classroom(room)		固定资产值(万元) Fixed Assets (10,000 yuan)		
其中:教学用计算机 of Which:No. of Computers Used for Instruction		合计 Total	其中:网络多媒体教室 of Which: Network Multimedia Classroom	合计 Total	其中:教学、科研仪器设备资产值 of Which: Teaching Equipment & Instruments	
小计 Subtotal	其中:平板电脑 of Which: Tablet PC				小计 Subtotal	当年新增 New Added in Current Year
12414	**509**	**5451**	**2877**	**95461.80**	**13309.31**	**2321.58**
78	26	17		90.00	42.00	
260		103	14	693.00	202.00	2.40
1153		338	61	6449.51	1119.61	21.77
166		39	15	2486.04	1365.50	3.00
60		29	15	1226.00	96.70	
245	92	28	4	424.00	192.00	2.00
205		82	29	1479.19	306.00	2.00
192		90	37	2763.70	215.00	30.00
145		35	29	2032.00	884.00	
		85	31	3087.34	225.70	6.90
50		37	36	1633.53	141.00	
314	1	286	13	8173.00	2348.00	1061.00
212		27	10	746.27	76.43	11.43
442		211	28	9241.20	878.20	23.60
6357	90	3542	2375	33583.94	2628.79	502.00
		4				
844		207	107	4198.00	760.00	110.50
				1125.00	326.00	
190		53	21	3881.00	875.60	408.60
413		168	36	3417.38	161.38	11.38
380	300	29	9	5075.00	167.00	125.00
248		13	1	606.70	298.40	
460				3048.00		
		28	6	2.00		

职业高中学校

Condition of Fixed Assets and Teaching Resources

地　区 Region	学校占地面积(平方米) Area of School Sites (m²)			图书(册) Books (volume)		
	合计 Total	其中:绿化用地面积 of Which: Green Areas	其中:运动场地面积 of Which: Sports Areas	合计 Total	当年新增 New Added in Current Year	合计 Total
总　计 Total	**210842926**	**45552188**	**34807846**	**130568470**	**8310044**	**1202739**
北　京 Beijing	2714293	482658	575796	3163940	387298	34987
天　津 Tianjin	714302	117964	124466	1002242	62288	6748
河　北 Hebei	14305037	2360395	2701807	8601474	378542	75491
山　西 Shanxi	7429644	1280258	1080384	3875183	127297	37822
内蒙古 Inner Mongolia	5993070	733068	1280317	2583485	110721	23253
辽　宁 Liaoning	6239173	721212	1371097	3435178	17872	42473
吉　林 Jilin	3411807	613986	803633	2124212	76282	20817
黑龙江 Heilongjiang	5168679	741167	1111284	1597218	60371	25363
上　海 Shanghai	1277985	416818	283465	1979763	50858	28113
江　苏 Jiangsu	7279351	2219461	1137236	6383444	295567	45535
浙　江 Zhejiang	14836209	4564361	2931090	11625930	520397	131865
安　徽 Anhui	20268020	3998131	2719532	16203128	1738725	66353
福　建 Fujian						
江　西 Jiangxi	13859476	2644598	1795845	6407248	276797	44298
山　东 Shandong	12205062	3218341	2271079	7099687	492580	72038
河　南 Henan	17376860	2917992	2414472	10641732	438571	84438
湖　北 Hubei	3934115	1694733	403828	1703403	15518	21307
湖　南 Hunan	13812641	3657556	1986961	8250150	289187	94279
广　东 Guangdong	6024845	1755398	1190092	4771152	416985	57470
广　西 Guangxi						
海　南 Hainan	1839551	504966	362969	712072	29727	9200
重　庆 Chongqing	7960949	1999297	1213826	5004209	350385	48558
四　川 Sichuan	11464649	2380297	2214853	7715934	1060251	76214
贵　州 Guizhou	6749112	1792441	1191247	2427258	331276	31424
云　南 Yunnan	7718096	1557361	975796	3052533	161004	39786
西　藏 Tibet						
陕　西 Shaanxi	10230062	1732559	1687768	7620369	482325	56969
甘　肃 Gansu	2180920	303617	438628	1162089	49181	13873
青　海 Qinghai	117643		15700	5586		55
宁　夏 Ningxia	1797796	432497	134043	509408	21642	5395
新　疆 Xinjiang	3933579	711056	390632	910443	68397	8615

资产情况(学校产权)
in Vocational High Schools (Owned by VHSs)

计算机数(台) No. of Computers(set)		教室(间) Classroom(room)		固定资产值(万元) Fixed Assets (10,000 yuan)		
其中:教学用计算机 of Which:No. of Computers Used for Instruction		合计 Total	其中:网络多媒体教室 of Which: Network Multimedia Classroom	合计 Total	其中:教学、科研仪器设备资产值 of Which: Teaching Equipment & Instruments	
小计 Subtotal	其中:平板电脑 of Which: Tablet PC				小计 Subtotal	当年新增 New Added in Current Year
1010387	**44667**	**177275**	**54235**	**10311025.58**	**2193033.70**	**320800.18**
28277	324	2904	1594	263311.40	95743.00	20531.41
5650	120	676	134	33638.55	14010.55	1057.70
60569	4290	16219	3583	535512.80	131896.17	17684.11
32464	804	6712	1882	312327.06	49678.59	11410.91
19352		3568	1518	261299.28	50055.81	6342.32
34587	1695	4546	1433	360710.51	79328.15	6351.34
16766	1043	4022	1042	178604.39	35969.53	6239.97
20165	683	3781	923	137853.94	36678.64	3979.61
23617	218	1946	1373	234443.93	62028.98	10183.58
38358	1848	4454	2330	481199.82	91581.50	10181.79
111787	1343	13912	8158	1093389.90	259055.19	27272.98
55188	2968	16297	2273	923862.51	177020.47	21374.64
38981	3364	6029	1491	512990.43	79037.95	10886.93
55913	2042	9735	3335	511802.56	127327.75	16313.87
71581	3538	15977	3475	674770.31	131290.89	17201.43
17617	1431	2648	662	139096.07	25662.39	2544.20
82156	4812	10339	2708	663463.55	142264.97	16666.71
49437	1859	5866	3504	348236.00	96966.00	11184.00
7044	663	1590	549	84936.68	20091.91	5624.87
42072	3305	6069	3614	460441.05	100695.65	19623.95
65392	1722	16587	2996	682332.25	132711.82	36499.55
28056	1370	4146	1040	328269.74	54758.95	14338.61
33263	111	4653	1103	286122.64	44392.62	8393.42
47748	4176	9754	2156	527865.67	98779.24	11608.25
12396	570	2502	926	96139.75	21306.76	2363.80
48		72	9	2407.00	65.00	
4816	4	697	218	50852.96	13510.30	1505.59
7087	364	1574	206	125144.83	21124.92	3434.64

职业高中学校资产情况

Condition of Fixed Assets and Teaching Resources

地　区 Region	学校占地面积(平方米) Area of School Sites (m^2)			图书(册) Books (volume)		
	合计 Total	其中:绿化用地面积 of Which: Green Areas	其中:运动场地面积 of Which: Sports Areas	合计 Total	当年新增 New Added in Current Year	合计 Total
总　计 Total	**18304246**	**3290735**	**3074867**	**3740410**	**276861**	**47167**
北　京 Beijing	279886	44428	68933	40599	100	274
天　津 Tianjin	166428	8232	33795	246973		1237
河　北 Hebei	710929	27933	98252	78187	3500	699
山　西 Shanxi	845288	71530	138143	130670	1200	1708
内蒙古 Inner Mongolia	365068	62898	189088	73000		125
辽　宁 Liaoning	575489	114686	178215	61760	794	733
吉　林 Jilin	658840	81532	137109	147812	2900	3342
黑龙江 Heilongjiang	271833	28388	102110	77873	11000	985
上　海 Shanghai	4716	260	947			
江　苏 Jiangsu	474203	109691	55916	267170	22170	1628
浙　江 Zhejiang	622514	88546	91932	138427	11070	1989
安　徽 Anhui	964870	142406	89411	107000	11100	1215
福　建 Fujian						
江　西 Jiangxi	1154233	294579	191933	170803	19890	3326
山　东 Shandong	1380601	276547	240438	59720	6100	1247
河　南 Henan	1329607	209190	220892	363311	7926	5502
湖　北 Hubei	140175	22998	23404	59130		274
湖　南 Hunan	2132858	585892	305606	447340	23956	10432
广　东 Guangdong	337651	52961	89980	5680	5120	269
广　西 Guangxi						
海　南 Hainan	119083	45138	21904	17932	2400	451
重　庆 Chongqing	543477	110786	59413	6180		754
四　川 Sichuan	496088	103721	120821	55475	48075	974
贵　州 Guizhou	1005251	197639	183090	225745	19430	2664
云　南 Yunnan	1566327	200514	91404	86500	7200	745
西　藏 Tibet						
陕　西 Shaanxi	1446950	212323	255302	842623	70330	5960
甘　肃 Gansu	285232	33301	81007	21600	2600	556
青　海 Qinghai						
宁　夏 Ningxia						
新　疆 Xinjiang	426649	164616	5822	8900		78

(非学校产权中独立使用)
in Vocational High Schools (Not Owned by VHSs)

计算机数(台) No. of Computers(set)		教室(间) Classroom(room)		固定资产值(万元) Fixed Assets (10,000 yuan)		
其中:教学用计算机 of Which:No. of Computers Used for Instruction		合计 Total	其中:网络多媒体教室 of Which: Network Multimedia Classroom	合计 Total	其中:教学、科研仪器设备资产值 of Which: Teaching Equipment & Instruments	
小计 Subtotal	其中:平板电脑 of Which: Tablet PC				小计 Subtotal	当年新增 New Added in Current Year
39479	**1525**	**19340**	**4987**	**555829.74**	**65956.99**	**12466.54**
206		313	194	3330.89	751.63	144.90
922		205	82	5560.73	1182.76	322.24
463	80	446	136	22447.70	1482.50	133.00
1447		827	225	21046.06	1570.81	267.72
52		329	137	12994.00	340.00	6.80
633		755	151	45681.75	1275.30	118.60
2447	40	437	50	15464.83	2389.06	220.00
814	100	417	86	11410.18	2258.40	232.20
		18	14	248.00	180.00	0.00
1339		443	150	19506.24	4454.86	1870.86
1747	16	989	556	27207.99	2306.10	158.80
978	50	1646	123	20773.60	5831.30	227.70
2916	160	570	266	78523.41	4558.82	410.30
764		628	185	46545.53	2475.00	638.40
4749	105	1365	404	38209.49	8388.64	669.00
245	10	139	12	2493.20	744.00	25.00
8799	375	655	247	36162.12	6900.81	669.10
237	100	163	42	1695.00	492.00	35.00
365		140	29	864.20	288.37	64.20
754		177	78	23227.83	2640.90	1850.00
858		1506	432	23649.42	2001.67	1720.90
2318	180	636	82	30036.16	3807.45	411.31
690		380	20	9398.80	1667.00	1110.00
5148	243	5757	1247	52082.97	6849.18	795.38
520	36	259	35	3821.71	760.92	59.42
				26.00		
68	30	140	4	3421.93	359.51	305.71

其他机构资产

Condition of Fixed Assets and Teaching Resources in Other

地 区 Region	学校占地面积(平方米) Area of School Sites (m^2)			图书(册) Books (volume)		
	合计 Total	其中:绿化用地面积 of Which: Green Areas	其中:运动场地面积 of Which: Sports Areas	合计 Total	当年新增 New Added in Current Year	合计 Total
总 计 Total	**10991311**	**2803490**	**1647424**	**7237287**	**554392**	**53934**
北 京 Beijing						
天 津 Tianjin						
河 北 Hebei	356999	42575	115279	437684	11000	2020
山 西 Shanxi	170390	3000	33100	14000		180
内蒙古 Inner Mongolia	28456	200	500	1100		40
辽 宁 Liaoning						
吉 林 Jilin	545516	149171	135600	807018	51720	2784
黑龙江 Heilongjiang	8510	5484	1500	7575		376
上 海 Shanghai						
江 苏 Jiangsu	2136081	399874	313035	1282970	79602	9402
浙 江 Zhejiang	706179	188916	115434	267390	37170	5308
安 徽 Anhui	1587593	438159	165407	1082600	227372	6641
福 建 Fujian						
江 西 Jiangxi	743562	623056	75480	154000	21300	812
山 东 Shandong	2096735	348656	167603	622223	19160	5945
河 南 Henan	395747	52398	58715	234687	5030	1678
湖 北 Hubei	139231	35400	33100	186980	5500	2673
湖 南 Hunan	666765	232306	207338	579909	32000	3907
广 东 Guangdong	538793	128182	111241	950893	39393	6327
广 西 Guangxi	93267	400	1885	23303		170
海 南 Hainan	12370		380	1000		68
重 庆 Chongqing	217606	17991	34730	124420	11225	1292
四 川 Sichuan	228456	82856	17977	116687	8070	1955
贵 州 Guizhou	25000	200	15000	12600	100	50
云 南 Yunnan	50821	7485	9687	160722	5400	1699
西 藏 Tibet						
陕 西 Shaanxi	10498	100	920	16200		95
甘 肃 Gansu	43956	1200	8243	45326		260
青 海 Qinghai						
宁 夏 Ningxia	188780	45881	25270	108000	350	252
新 疆 Xinjiang						

情况（学校产权）
Institutions（Owned by SVSs）

计算机数（台） No. of Computers(set)		教室（间） Classroom(room)		固定资产值（万元） Fixed Assets (10,000 yuan)		
其中：教学用计算机 of Which: No. of Computers Used for Instruction		合计 Total	其中：网络多媒体教室 of Which: Network Multimedia Classroom	合计 Total	其中：教学、科研仪器设备资产值 of Which: Teaching Equipment & Instruments	
小计 Subtotal	其中：平板电脑 of Which: Tablet PC				小计 Subtotal	当年新增 New Added in Current Year
44294	**2903**	**6546**	**2962**	**675014.19**	**88424.16**	**6560.86**
1746	136	250	94	31856.20	2714.20	62.00
122		19		30430.00	1020.00	
27		15	2	125.00	60.00	
1972		267	82	35409.10	7084.99	232.81
360		26	20	1297.00	328.00	55.00
7998	484	1326	1058	72594.12	12472.88	1165.68
4562	370	522	374	55239.59	6506.51	214.97
5561	257	1250	344	102247.14	14885.46	945.00
780	25	68	12	6591.77	815.20	111.30
4404	257	807	295	142595.63	10216.37	191.55
1314	88	346	166	23669.39	3130.00	420.00
2266	900	325	38	10365.94	2409.80	433.00
2942	300	340	143	52993.85	8730.78	1153.00
5349	71	476	227	42166.00	8308.00	408.00
147		9	9	10711.00		
40				1765.00	883.00	
1001	12	126	19	24335.15	2667.50	458.00
1685		293	66	12623.73	2604.55	260.70
25		9	1	140.00	67.00	52.00
1521	3	71	11	11799.80	1641.02	139.95
82		1	1	102.78	20.90	17.90
240				2884.00	303.00	
150				3072.00	1555.00	240.00

其他机构资产情况

Condition of Fixed Assets and Teaching Resources

地　区 Region	学校占地面积(平方米) Area of School Sites (m^2)			图书(册) Books (volume)		
	合计 Total	其中:绿化用地面积 of Which: Green Areas	其中:运动场地面积 of Which: Sports Areas	合计 Total	当年新增 New Added in Current Year	合计 Total
总　计 Total	**900767**	**185031**	**142298**	**302669**	**8050**	**3713**
北　京 Beijing						
天　津 Tianjin						
河　北 Hebei	67069	9961	11239	21000		150
山　西 Shanxi	120614	3200	10300	1000		100
内蒙古 Inner Mongolia						
辽　宁 Liaoning						
吉　林 Jilin	1800					
黑龙江 Heilongjiang	27451	920	6480	9988		34
上　海 Shanghai						
江　苏 Jiangsu	101534	14670	17871	122802	2400	1436
浙　江 Zhejiang	74493	5400	30640	16550	550	305
安　徽 Anhui	17500	200	10385			3
福　建 Fujian						
江　西 Jiangxi						
山　东 Shandong	40945	7050	5070	77000		410
河　南 Henan	8700	1400	1600			149
湖　北 Hubei	43500	6000	6850	8000		3
湖　南 Hunan						
广　东 Guangdong	127534	54100	1000	36129	5000	920
广　西 Guangxi						
海　南 Hainan						
重　庆 Chongqing	50363	6080	4100			
四　川 Sichuan						
贵　州 Guizhou						
云　南 Yunnan	219264	76050	36763	10200	100	203
西　藏 Tibet						
陕　西 Shaanxi						
甘　肃 Gansu						
青　海 Qinghai						
宁　夏 Ningxia						
新　疆 Xinjiang						

（非学校产权中独立使用）
in Other Institutions（Not Owned by SVSs）

计算机数（台）No. of Computers（set）		教室（间）Classroom（room）		固定资产值（万元）Fixed Assets（10,000 yuan）		
其中：教学用计算机 of Which：No. of Computers Used for Instruction		合计 Total	其中：网络多媒体教室 of Which：Network Multimedia Classroom	合计 Total	其中：教学、科研仪器设备资产值 of Which：Teaching Equipment & Instruments	
小计 Subtotal	其中：平板电脑 of Which：Tablet PC				小计 Subtotal	当年新增 New Added in Current Year
2701	**30**	**753**	**284**	**66382.44**	**6192.53**	**101.80**
70		134	11	4752.30	1050.00	
70		26	1	30084.00	1009.40	
20		17		874.00	22.00	
914	30	103	68	12888.96	3095.20	48.20
267		162	66	879.00	242.50	49.00
1		20	2	236.00	20.00	
260		46	34	13400.00	223.83	
96		2		496.80	52.00	
		22	4	400.40	14.00	
830		40	40			
		40	40	1107.00	309.00	
173		141	18	1263.98	154.60	4.60

中等职业学校(机构)校舍情况(总计)

Condition of School Buidings in Secondary Vocational Schools (Institutions) (Total)

单位:平方米
unit: m^2

地 区 Region	学校产权建筑面积 Floor Area of School Building Owned by SVSs 合计 Total	其中:危房 of Which: Dilapidated Buildings	其中:当年新增 of Which: New Added in Current Year	其中:被外单位借用 of Which: Floor Space Hired by Other Schools or Units	正在施工校舍建筑面积 Floor Area Under Construction	独立使用非学校产权校舍建筑面积 Floor Area of School Building Not Owned by SVSs
总 计 Total	**214011336**	**2236475**	**8377962**	**564126**	**12097881**	**19670540**
北 京 Beijing	2479300	1974	73618	25133	69549	351207
天 津 Tianjin	1800868		13146	484		277035
河 北 Hebei	10112998	61114	298018	20051	394744	1139724
山 西 Shanxi	6392046	61706	60752	6904	259562	604611
内蒙古 Inner Mongolia	3559090	1947	566266	9620	301129	349421
辽 宁 Liaoning	5344416	10741	55837	8843	198594	1004883
吉 林 Jilin	2854953	13874	106318		133548	458131
黑龙江 Heilongjiang	3198267	40404	36238	3000	73455	485829
上 海 Shanghai	2860727		51616	4997	57661	314495
江 苏 Jiangsu	16537887		281540	29141	850406	311916
浙 江 Zhejiang	10264912		267958	35135	300955	708586
安 徽 Anhui	16274014	61126	711806	55379	916484	804495
福 建 Fujian	5361427	31114	267230	3693	395176	650077
江 西 Jiangxi	7526646	85240	228507	6563	430514	599511
山 东 Shandong	16551371	19268	425356	16878	951304	1081262
河 南 Henan	15908079	144359	346460	34445	695397	1213733
湖 北 Hubei	8578388	52375	131906	8517	160836	588946
湖 南 Hunan	9115504	71209	184776	1130	278891	916433
广 东 Guangdong	15262685	13252	606401	58930	790396	1707577
广 西 Guangxi	7968507	90972	371164	19286	760291	1057188
海 南 Hainan	1722907	53841	80495	23852	112486	290109
重 庆 Chongqing	5880143	13916	348508	46282	274020	460642
四 川 Sichuan	11330950	68371	444517	33434	799024	2082991
贵 州 Guizhou	4194606	768	985816	8633	1058548	621861
云 南 Yunnan	5490588	837050	402085	51132	710285	542569
西 藏 Tibet	297858	5685	24341		40934	
陕 西 Shaanxi	6774618	27425	215774	7960	210129	665345
甘 肃 Gansu	4152405	324564	73826	26934	269628	256438
青 海 Qinghai	951378	11799	34303	6480	136457	28064
宁 夏 Ningxia	1194525	26256	289715		64339	52214
新 疆 Xinjiang	4069273	106125	393669	11290	403139	45247

普通中专学校校舍情况

Condition of School Buidings in Regular Specialized Sec. Schools

单位：平方米

unit：m²

地　区 Region	学校产权建筑面积 Floor Area of School Building Owned by SVSs				正在施工校舍建筑面积 Floor Area Under Construction	独立使用非学校产权校舍建筑面积 Floor Area of School Building Not Owned by SVSs
	合计 Total	其中：危房 of Which：Dilapidated Buildings	其中：当年新增 of Which：New Added in Current Year	其中：被外单位借用 of Which：Floor Space Hired by Other Schools or Units		
总　计 Total	**114488231**	**1194515**	**3975913**	**291165**	**7790520**	**9783560**
北　京 Beijing	889839		900	783	41516	45136
天　津 Tianjin	1430736		8305			113095
河　北 Hebei	4251904	34707	18733	721	89335	831359
山　西 Shanxi	3197442	43858	6068	4722	62687	170110
内蒙古 Inner Mongolia	1586791	1947	465039	6000	63295	195085
辽　宁 Liaoning	2744592	7134	11399	8843	158236	644073
吉　林 Jilin	1008185	3692	66605		78827	32929
黑龙江 Heilongjiang	1339715	15457	12053		49894	341386
上　海 Shanghai	1922488		41848	4997	57661	246748
江　苏 Jiangsu	11663126		204780	23975	662639	118532
浙　江 Zhejiang	2001314		33925	7282	18810	136212
安　徽 Anhui	5765333	37843	358555	39666	804930	36983
福　建 Fujian	5361427	31114	267230	3693	395176	650077
江　西 Jiangxi	3188388	38409	32888	1880	153705	167191
山　东 Shandong	10172222	12408	279841	14687	719226	468118
河　南 Henan	6842077	86081	110791	320	249804	171212
湖　北 Hubei	6751236	52375	103262	7007	153678	445410
湖　南 Hunan	2154154	17708	33902	80	73151	83024
广　东 Guangdong	12054647	13252	516258	58010	683999	1475956
广　西 Guangxi	7916335	90972	371164	19286	760291	1057188
海　南 Hainan	1006753	25140	36801	18641	87093	154978
重　庆 Chongqing	953390	2706	39653		15196	45077
四　川 Sichuan	5586685	13105	168250	30440	487828	1635559
贵　州 Guizhou	1730315	768	164333	8261	467220	81528
云　南 Yunnan	2606687	307176	196604		572082	206732
西　藏 Tibet	297858	5685	24341		40934	
陕　西 Shaanxi	2350531	15516	109962	4000	97170	20511
甘　肃 Gansu	3199218	201829	65599	21391	213426	146932
青　海 Qinghai	911007	11799	34303	6480	136457	6577
宁　夏 Ningxia	648195	26256	77078		46552	51722
新　疆 Xinjiang	2955641	97578	115443		349702	4120

成人中专学校校舍情况

Condition of School Buidings in Adult Specialized Sec. Schools

单位:平方米

unit:m^2

地　区 Region	学校产权建筑面积 Floor Area of School Building Owned by SVSs				正在施工校舍建筑面积 Floor Area Under Construction	独立使用非学校产权校舍建筑面积 Floor Area of School Building Not Owned by SVSs
	合计 Total	其中:危房 of Which: Dilapidated Buildings	其中:当年新增 of Which: New Added in Current Year	其中:被外单位借用 of Which: Floor Space Hired by Other Schools or Units		
总　计 Total	**10243625**	**167923**	**163317**	**62099**	**212791**	**1543844**
北　京 Beijing	142906		7138	11640		12059
天　津 Tianjin	43069		4841	224		11756
河　北 Hebei	580319	953	2799	11030		106439
山　西 Shanxi	166297	6286	120		3049	38323
内蒙古 Inner Mongolia	166735		267		14820	4357
辽　宁 Liaoning	23550					42655
吉　林 Jilin	358163	5000			3600	31056
黑龙江 Heilongjiang	511967	360	3700		1200	26303
上　海 Shanghai	70137					6231
江　苏 Jiangsu	602672		100		35700	34876
浙　江 Zhejiang	267032		520	2860	13137	13057
安　徽 Anhui	781715	1430	27700			163399
福　建 Fujian						
江　西 Jiangxi	267296	6360		1494		9952
山　东 Shandong	798890	5660	27826	1617	5998	146662
河　南 Henan	1944468	2877	44074	4672	88765	564584
湖　北 Hubei	225377					1167
湖　南 Hunan	840935	9797			9152	54396
广　东 Guangdong	203589					2558
广　西 Guangxi						
海　南 Hainan	41227	11349				
重　庆 Chongqing	600747	4802	7824		14286	71298
四　川 Sichuan	369515	4690	4971		1584	97326
贵　州 Guizhou	408733		17700		16500	8100
云　南 Yunnan	355395	97396	1094	25562		13955
西　藏 Tibet						
陕　西 Shaanxi	158480					56247
甘　肃 Gansu	153681	10963	1400		5000	4809
青　海 Qinghai	24348					21302
宁　夏 Ningxia	17390					492
新　疆 Xinjiang	118992		11243	3000		485

职业高中学校校舍情况

Condition of School Buidings in Vocational High Schools

单位:平方米

unit:m^2

地　区 Region	学校产权建筑面积 Floor Area of School Building Owned by SVSs				正在施工 校舍建筑面积 Floor Area Under Construction	独立使用非学校产权校舍建筑面积 Floor Area of School Building Not Owned by SVSs
	合计 Total	其中:危房 of Which: Dilapidated Buildings	其中:当年新增 of Which: New Added in Current Year	其中:被外单位借用 of Which: Floor Space Hired by Other Schools or Units		
总　计 Total	**84535391**	**865157**	**4143449**	**208411**	**3766522**	**7851516**
北　京 Beijing	1446555	1974	65580	12710	28033	294012
天　津 Tianjin	327063			260		152184
河　北 Hebei	5107465	25454	271826	8300	229174	151760
山　西 Shanxi	2986502	11562	44009	2182	187241	395094
内蒙古 Inner Mongolia	1794734		100960	3620	223014	149979
辽　宁 Liaoning	2576274	3607	44438		40358	318155
吉　林 Jilin	1323151	5182	32193		51121	394146
黑龙江 Heilongjiang	1343359	24587	20485	3000	22361	105437
上　海 Shanghai	868102		9768			61516
江　苏 Jiangsu	3421056		72715	4085	150667	38750
浙　江 Zhejiang	7603226		233143	24993	269008	490092
安　徽 Anhui	8898446	21853	308751	15713	88398	600253
福　建 Fujian						
江　西 Jiangxi	4012038	40471	195619	3189	181123	422368
山　东 Shandong	4937314	1200	114689	574	155696	417354
河　南 Henan	6942904	53913	182495	29453	356828	471847
湖　北 Hubei	1488179		28644	1510	7158	95246
湖　南 Hunan	5806129	40819	143929	600	149478	779013
广　东 Guangdong	2552951		79983		106397	218975
广　西 Guangxi						
海　南 Hainan	673451	17352	43694	5211	25393	135131
重　庆 Chongqing	4171906	6408	286376	46282	237046	307859
四　川 Sichuan	5256840	46069	270737	2994	309612	350106
贵　州 Guizhou	2046945		803783	372	574828	532233
云　南 Yunnan	2450414	432478	204387	25570	138203	235895
西　藏 Tibet						
陕　西 Shaanxi	4254233	11909	98798	3960	112959	588587
甘　肃 Gansu	758603	111772	6827	5543	51202	104697
青　海 Qinghai	16023					185
宁　夏 Ningxia	476888		212637		17787	
新　疆 Xinjiang	994640	8547	266983	8290	53437	40642

地　区 Region	学校产权 Floor Area of School 合计 Total	其中:危房 of Which: Dilapidated Buildings
总　计 Total	**4744089**	**8880**
北　京 Beijing		
天　津 Tianjin		
河　北 Hebei	173310	
山　西 Shanxi	41805	
内蒙古 Inner Mongolia	10830	
辽　宁 Liaoning		
吉　林 Jilin	165454	
黑龙江 Heilongjiang	3226	
上　海 Shanghai		
江　苏 Jiangsu	851033	
浙　江 Zhejiang	393340	
安　徽 Anhui	828520	
福　建 Fujian		
江　西 Jiangxi	58924	
山　东 Shandong	642945	
河　南 Henan	178630	1488
湖　北 Hubei	113596	
湖　南 Hunan	314286	2885
广　东 Guangdong	451498	
广　西 Guangxi	52172	
海　南 Hainan	1476	
重　庆 Chongqing	154100	
四　川 Sichuan	117910	4507
贵　州 Guizhou	8613	
云　南 Yunnan	78092	
西　藏 Tibet		
陕　西 Shaanxi	11374	
甘　肃 Gansu	40903	
青　海 Qinghai		
宁　夏 Ningxia	52052	
新　疆 Xinjiang		

校舍情况
in Other Institutions

单位:平方米
unit: m^2

建筑面积 Building Owned by SVSs		正在施工校舍建筑面积 Floor Area Under Construction	独立使用非学校产权校舍建筑面积 Floor Area of School Building Not Owned by SVSs
其中:当年新增 of Which: New Added in Current Year	其中:被外单位借用 of Which: Floor Space Hired by Other Schools or Units		
95283	**2451**	**328048**	**491620**
4660		76235	50166
10555		6585	1084
7520			
			12703
3945	1081	1400	119758
370			69225
16800		23156	3860
		95686	
3000		70384	49128
9100			6090
			47123
6945	450	47110	
10160	920		10088
14655		7492	36408
559			
			85987
7014			

职业技术培训

Basic Statistics of Vocational Technical

地 区 Region	学校数 （所） Schools	教学班（点） （个） External Teaching Sites （class）	结业生数 Graduates	
			合计 Total	其中：女 of Which：Female
总 计 Total	**112293**	**536037**	**47155968**	**22563938**
北 京 Beijing	3595	64954	3201775	1487870
天 津 Tianjin	2708	19339	1121918	531170
河 北 Hebei	5617	17573	1619905	807914
山 西 Shanxi	6045	21111	2071151	809909
内蒙古 Inner Mongolia	1682	3314	389625	161946
辽 宁 Liaoning	6772	38054	1852899	917979
吉 林 Jilin	2607	5309	344711	145055
黑龙江 Heilongjiang	2246	7162	718669	344506
上 海 Shanghai	802	29720	1913296	1047851
江 苏 Jiangsu	7694	71030	7367920	3365600
浙 江 Zhejiang	4452	33445	3039879	1491437
安 徽 Anhui	264	1904	820389	403677
福 建 Fujian	1681	8637	825960	422876
江 西 Jiangxi	658	1469	96670	50366
山 东 Shandong	7069	21743	2045402	1000814
河 南 Henan	10435	20145	2623868	1213959
湖 北 Hubei	1171	4362	339387	156650
湖 南 Hunan	1399	3473	344314	125374
广 东 Guangdong	2287	39602	1930626	973323
广 西 Guangxi	546	2139	318738	138634
海 南 Hainan	243	2002	42730	33036
重 庆 Chongqing	3974	16826	1348800	693365
四 川 Sichuan	5261	22681	2468263	1187161
贵 州 Guizhou	6994	11512	1740821	876147
云 南 Yunnan	10465	26870	5039902	2524729
西 藏 Tibet				
陕 西 Shaanxi	9407	21259	1387479	682987
甘 肃 Gansu	3206	5767	495099	239289
青 海 Qinghai	650	1776	51635	25659
宁 夏 Ningxia	208	1271	36997	18161
新 疆 Xinjiang	2155	11588	1557140	686494

机构基本情况(总计)
Training Institutions (Total)

单位:人次
unit:person

注册学生数 Enrolment		教职工数 Educational Personnel		聘请校外教师 Part-time Teachers
合计 Total	其中:女 of Which: Female	合计 Total	其中:专任教师 of Which: Full-time Teacher	
45159599	**21759819**	**482211**	**274311**	**272832**
2928858	1261914	56304	19032	17869
1213373	582255	15705	7626	10817
1211203	569950	18203	10374	8708
2357672	979012	19440	10234	9895
446540	203328	5763	4176	1790
2242303	1101689	43596	26910	11967
492858	189446	8874	6171	2482
507017	242421	16743	11174	2395
1724000	967277	19136	7762	14942
5976567	2699123	48336	34476	46070
2969009	1465977	20535	14007	27284
507803	272435	2434	1229	3037
798930	407277	11713	5560	7565
105500	53648	2531	1819	778
1882193	914934	30534	23038	11802
2402371	1134619	25464	15838	12885
408187	189969	7624	4791	2074
405473	173340	5472	3376	979
2527852	1523796	26256	15840	11498
322288	140047	2667	642	1693
43708	33539	952	177	746
1437881	679563	6773	3832	5623
2299940	1119233	15600	9071	7438
1755865	878235	16605	5920	8672
4263538	2128143	9163	3940	16153
1460537	734965	29977	17847	16565
534056	257751	8332	5580	3661
55568	27915	470	263	363
62941	30878	2051	1188	727
1815568	797140	4958	2418	6354

职业技术培训

Basic Statistics of Vocational

地 区 Region	学校数 (所) Schools	教学班(点) (个) External Teaching Sites (class)	结业生数 Graduates 合计 Total	其中:女 of Which: Female
总 计 Total	**2982**	**36513**	**2945587**	**1244481**
北 京 Beijing	26	490	55044	23975
天 津 Tianjin	11	174	8717	4553
河 北 Hebei	57	630	57017	30229
山 西 Shanxi	461	6514	749802	174036
内蒙古 Inner Mongolia	51	262	43547	19075
辽 宁 Liaoning	118	819	76322	40873
吉 林 Jilin	75	270	34917	12455
黑龙江 Heilongjiang	97	472	29706	14882
上 海 Shanghai	20	1478	113064	68893
江 苏 Jiangsu	497	8334	399608	190466
浙 江 Zhejiang	177	2518	162347	73186
安 徽 Anhui	34	350	48687	23522
福 建 Fujian	156	1292	179834	101925
江 西 Jiangxi	40	335	23214	10680
山 东 Shandong	58	349	96235	40657
河 南 Henan	254	2028	145571	65974
湖 北 Hubei	67	600	53104	22239
湖 南 Hunan	101	356	43694	24206
广 东 Guangdong	87	854	35399	19020
广 西 Guangxi	14	28	6634	3230
海 南 Hainan	27	183	8960	6965
重 庆 Chongqing	66	671	26090	12092
四 川 Sichuan	115	2862	259204	117266
贵 州 Guizhou	12	134	20512	6261
云 南 Yunnan	22	178	18848	8997
西 藏 Tibet				
陕 西 Shaanxi	221	3294	146807	79332
甘 肃 Gansu	93	616	63039	28851
青 海 Qinghai	1			
宁 夏 Ningxia	1	60	4106	2783
新 疆 Xinjiang	23	362	35558	17858

学校基本情况
Technical Training Schools

单位:人次
unit:person

注册学生数 Enrolment		教职工数 Educational Personnel		聘请校外教师 Part-time Teachers
合计 Total	其中:女 of Which: Female	合计 Total	其中:专任教师 of Which: Full-time Teacher	
3055051	**1315952**	**62083**	**45591**	**17848**
31800	14919	858	505	279
5484	3188	454	345	153
62230	33987	3466	2638	307
774136	185900	3401	2029	1298
42089	19759	1201	990	347
72677	37598	2072	1482	225
61147	22390	922	693	126
32442	13754	2499	1875	233
115521	70898	1311	958	588
406823	192606	12993	9875	5064
160998	79266	2813	2284	2167
51861	25748	824	472	98
156937	91143	2130	1914	862
27163	12152	689	549	279
96129	40873	2228	1842	287
177642	82483	4376	3418	973
51248	22832	2041	1581	353
64552	35776	2624	1685	130
39032	19992	827	547	393
6396	3165	122	98	21
9938	7468	214	162	23
26379	12659	1082	436	502
277141	134081	4841	3185	756
24773	9216	470	395	219
14604	6439	296	161	166
166444	89684	4713	3393	922
67228	29166	2061	1687	813
4106	2783	38	28	14
28131	16027	517	364	250

地 区 Region	学校数 （所） Schools	教学班（点） （个） External Teaching Sites （class）	结业生数 Graduates 合计 Total	结业生数 Graduates 其中：女 of Which：Female
总 计 Total	**89014**	**265130**	**34160351**	**16402966**
北 京 Beijing	2086	8782	902247	520077
天 津 Tianjin	2111	6295	533203	261908
河 北 Hebei	5043	13184	1453319	723287
山 西 Shanxi	4834	9632	1109285	527810
内蒙古 Inner Mongolia	1400	2120	319141	130045
辽 宁 Liaoning	2039	5794	1056474	508984
吉 林 Jilin	1440	1531	234061	95078
黑龙江 Heilongjiang	1217	1845	387474	176421
上 海 Shanghai	117	6078	608070	350440
江 苏 Jiangsu	5613	32785	5367459	2356179
浙 江 Zhejiang	2960	22021	2355779	1144650
安 徽 Anhui	213	1342	762936	374281
福 建 Fujian	1164	4404	451830	211444
江 西 Jiangxi	566	794	54813	30874
山 东 Shandong	5700	14470	1470280	734553
河 南 Henan	9717	17008	2341604	1074440
湖 北 Hubei	929	2029	220810	99625
湖 南 Hunan	1153	2477	268223	85295
广 东 Guangdong	635	17195	1237793	604777
广 西 Guangxi	529	2095	305104	129404
海 南 Hainan	216	1819	33770	26071
重 庆 Chongqing	3700	13266	1228996	628964
四 川 Sichuan	4879	18611	2052145	992720
贵 州 Guizhou	6455	9689	1598087	807200
云 南 Yunnan	10276	26302	4955478	2480628
西 藏 Tibet				
陕 西 Shaanxi	8434	10916	980431	482898
甘 肃 Gansu	2949	4081	394027	192175
青 海 Qinghai	647	1759	49328	24593
宁 夏 Ningxia	7	10	905	266
新 疆 Xinjiang	1985	6796	1427279	627879

培训学校基本情况
Training Schools for Peasants

单位:人次
unit:person

注册学生数 Enrolment		教职工数 Educational Personnel		聘请校外教师 Part-time Teachers
合计 Total	其中:女 of Which: Female	合计 Total	其中:专任教师 of Which: Full-time Teacher	
30430375	**14535051**	**167308**	**90112**	**159048**
453666	257603	1449	807	2846
414251	202550	2424	1240	3450
1014441	488865	9364	4836	7155
1242262	596184	7186	2801	6155
373765	167162	3347	2405	1241
1245673	593484	3993	2389	2369
288833	111605	2608	1310	1703
234944	103017	5967	3555	1477
489647	286671	944	686	2712
4086952	1737466	15038	10980	24689
2193219	1058945	7535	5039	19407
447312	240756	1441	631	2822
453257	211186	4049	602	4889
58979	32118	974	557	380
1310366	643351	13204	10001	7559
2080000	981458	17394	10029	11071
284596	128287	3061	1488	1076
268541	102962	1848	987	715
1253141	611018	6681	3997	3805
308892	130882	2505	530	1662
33770	26071	738	15	723
1198798	606992	3288	1505	4264
1846460	896431	7628	3636	5877
1588544	793803	13283	4001	7387
4179907	2084020	7701	3083	15109
983838	491883	15799	8620	10399
424302	207660	5086	3152	2494
53215	26735	468	261	329
1008	310	36	26	2
1617796	715576	2269	943	5281

地 区 Region	学校数 (所) Schools	教学班(点) (个) External Teaching Sites (class)	结业生数 Graduates	
			合计 Total	其中:女 of Which: Female
总 计 Total	**20297**	**234394**	**10050030**	**4916491**
北 京 Beijing	1483	55682	2244484	943818
天 津 Tianjin	586	12870	579998	264709
河 北 Hebei	517	3759	109569	54398
山 西 Shanxi	750	4965	212064	108063
内蒙古 Inner Mongolia	231	932	26937	12826
辽 宁 Liaoning	4615	31441	720103	368122
吉 林 Jilin	1092	3508	75733	37522
黑龙江 Heilongjiang	932	4845	301489	153203
上 海 Shanghai	665	22164	1192162	628518
江 苏 Jiangsu	1584	29911	1600853	818955
浙 江 Zhejiang	1315	8906	521753	273601
安 徽 Anhui	17	212	8766	5874
福 建 Fujian	361	2941	194296	109507
江 西 Jiangxi	52	340	18643	8812
山 东 Shandong	1311	6924	478887	225604
河 南 Henan	464	1109	136693	73545
湖 北 Hubei	175	1733	65473	34786
湖 南 Hunan	145	640	32397	15873
广 东 Guangdong	1565	21553	657434	349526
广 西 Guangxi	3	16	7000	6000
海 南 Hainan				
重 庆 Chongqing	208	2889	93714	52309
四 川 Sichuan	267	1208	156914	77175
贵 州 Guizhou	527	1689	122222	62686
云 南 Yunnan	167	390	65576	35104
西 藏 Tibet				
陕 西 Shaanxi	752	7049	260241	120757
甘 肃 Gansu	164	1070	38033	18263
青 海 Qinghai	2	17	2307	1066
宁 夏 Ningxia	200	1201	31986	15112
新 疆 Xinjiang	147	4430	94303	40757

基本情况
of Others

单位：人次
unit：person

注册学生数 Enrolment		教职工数 Educational Personnel		聘请校外教师 Part-time Teachers
合计 Total	其中：女 of Which：Female	合计 Total	其中：专任教师 of Which：Full-time Teacher	
11674173	**5908816**	**252820**	**138608**	**95936**
2443392	989392	53997	17720	14744
793638	376517	12827	6041	7214
134532	47098	5373	2900	1246
341274	196928	8853	5404	2442
30686	16407	1215	781	202
923953	470607	37531	23039	9373
142878	55451	5344	4168	653
239631	125650	8277	5744	685
1118832	609708	16881	6118	11642
1482792	769051	20305	13621	16317
614792	327766	10187	6684	5710
8630	5931	169	126	117
188736	104948	5534	3044	1814
19358	9378	868	713	119
475698	230710	15102	11195	3956
144729	70678	3694	2391	841
72343	38850	2522	1722	645
72380	34602	1000	704	134
1235679	892786	18748	11296	7300
7000	6000	40	14	10
212704	59912	2403	1891	857
176339	88721	3131	2250	805
142548	75216	2852	1524	1066
69027	37684	1166	696	878
310255	153398	9465	5834	5244
42526	20925	1185	741	354
2353	1180	2	2	34
57827	27785	1977	1134	711
169641	65537	2172	1111	823

职业技术培训机

Condition of Fixed Assets and Teaching Resources

地　区 Region	占地面积 （平方米） Area of School Sites（m^2）	教学行政用房 建筑面积 （平方米） Administrative （m^2）	图书（册） Books （volume）	合计 Total
总　计 Total	**116835277**	**44814552**	**154785708**	**1020419**
北　京 Beijing	5898810	1819497	31340683	32734
天　津 Tianjin	2308201	880424	23406835	27685
河　北 Hebei	7234690	1613718	4667524	24858
山　西 Shanxi	3283983	1228733	4890930	28230
内蒙古 Inner Mongolia	2706542	909374	1602306	7981
辽　宁 Liaoning	6549102	3007828	4036193	57838
吉　林 Jilin	2693978	578814	758853	5965
黑龙江 Heilongjiang	2422495	783501	1149563	10382
上　海 Shanghai	1417648	1127094	2882132	36355
江　苏 Jiangsu	19309489	10258780	22764612	225898
浙　江 Zhejiang	7457439	3119623	6085102	58669
安　徽 Anhui	1586558	769169	760392	6890
福　建 Fujian	895808	758594	2028301	16006
江　西 Jiangxi	1799944	354886	1141154	8362
山　东 Shandong	6067936	2085347	3181688	33962
河　南 Henan	7049843	2723193	6226792	34710
湖　北 Hubei	9400870	2957870	2318740	22691
湖　南 Hunan	2402381	955380	2983266	18476
广　东 Guangdong	4762688	1897988	13537668	68148
广　西 Guangxi	556539	89173	316442	1118
海　南 Hainan	101789	89086	89410	598
重　庆 Chongqing	831581	555659	916778	10522
四　川 Sichuan	2176246	961888	2744842	18173
贵　州 Guizhou	3399940	721963	2125185	14612
云　南 Yunnan	3364463	1597671	2223592	7406
西　藏 Tibet				
陕　西 Shaanxi	4588787	1655861	4840604	37694
甘　肃 Gansu	3082603	733794	1645224	11565
青　海 Qinghai	353992	57743	144412	634
宁　夏 Ningxia	204526	69697	145928	2371
新　疆 Xinjiang	2926406	452204	3830557	189886

构资产情况
in Vocational Technical Training Institutions

计算机数(台) No. of Computers(set)		教室(间) Classroom(room)		固定资产总值(万元) Fixed Assets (in 10,000 yuan)	
其中:教学用计算机 No. of Computers Used for Instruction		合计 Total	其中:网络多媒体教室 of Which: Network Multimedia Classroom	合计 Total	其中:教学、实习仪器设备资产值 of Which: Teaching Equipment & Instruments
小计 Subtotal	其中:平板电脑 of Which: Tablet PC				
649513	**54152**	**511948**	**283657**	**23873492.53**	**7044833.46**
26995	1706	10083	3819	222595.32	66924.60
16687	4217	4572	967	267634.03	24153.38
22242	598	22319	2088	255589.23	98240.08
27178	110	13180	7836	957479.15	44878.38
6974		7856	514	95665.52	22292.69
53544	15974	34556	5260	454853.83	97556.46
4772	468	6840	1049	73406.97	9995.67
9257	274	4810	1631	68753.46	27754.92
29351	1835	8430	2853	139341.00	57702.00
118840	6596	36139	13765	1287094.15	300238.94
53627	2024	12073	5183	306980.64	73263.82
6209	105	1908	345	2476458.70	9643.20
13812	728	6249	1456	63277.91	17908.29
7425	1076	1804	800	43773.39	8801.71
30460	1722	20203	4240	170085.85	41135.59
31729	2065	31221	7661	182423.90	41162.31
20700	691	3142	562	112923.03	27238.28
16287	208	2274	872	113672.07	22970.01
56814	9220	236892	214453	15073254	5703338
812	106	598	42	7306.10	1666.30
592	10	14	9	2356.14	1468.14
9218	1406	5456	925	40729.74	12931.79
14852	306	6321	902	105520.89	21312.12
13180	992	7592	1863	106780.28	22619.36
6626	441	4224	681	55907.87	8518.31
31147	749	12994	2202	282352.71	114047.64
9994	160	3657	928	841297.57	140699.68
442	318	269	14	5062.05	1721.02
2284	2	912	81	19644.06	12671.97
7463	45	5360	656	41272.97	11978.80

职工技术培训

Condition of Fixed Assets and Teaching

地 区 Region	占地面积 （平方米） Area of School Sites（m^2）	教学行政用房建筑面积 （平方米） Administrative（m^2）	图书（册） Books （volume）	合计 Total
总 计 Total	**27737561**	**9253820**	**20604194**	**171570**
北 京 Beijing	41023	25464	905275	790
天 津 Tianjin	339298	67984	131150	136
河 北 Hebei	1589101	423725	1533725	8369
山 西 Shanxi	1676219	568859	1628129	10599
内蒙古 Inner Mongolia	1325845	433950	843199	3731
辽 宁 Liaoning	947994	296774	547090	4318
吉 林 Jilin	561149	101498	122359	1737
黑龙江 Heilongjiang	680373	186720	329615	3020
上 海 Shanghai	159380	126585	636248	4747
江 苏 Jiangsu	4064196	1595520	2548060	34631
浙 江 Zhejiang	1486591	700072	1167322	11792
安 徽 Anhui	272914	496785	291401	1886
福 建 Fujian	301890	217807	694031	5522
江 西 Jiangxi	585994	187459	285624	3286
山 东 Shandong	701874	194124	301150	4153
河 南 Henan	2962130	986559	1562114	12213
湖 北 Hubei	1707354	306962	1381148	8027
湖 南 Hunan	1538387	566190	1578223	7683
广 东 Guangdong	125028	48984	268424	2189
广 西 Guangxi	95568	22150	37000	467
海 南 Hainan	67519	49336	50610	453
重 庆 Chongqing	39752	49314	49250	2062
四 川 Sichuan	787813	389575	1003394	8183
贵 州 Guizhou	753923	94172	183503	1957
云 南 Yunnan	962062	32111	139260	637
西 藏 Tibet				
陕 西 Shaanxi	1745171	619668	1338079	8570
甘 肃 Gansu	1851298	397420	875741	7027
青 海 Qinghai	126006	42669	65163	523
宁 夏 Ningxia	19900	7240	51420	122
新 疆 Xinjiang	221809	18144	56487	12740

学校资产情况
Resources in Technical Training Schools

计算机数(台) No. of Computers(set)		教室(间) Classroom(room)		固定资产总值(万元) Fixed Assets (in 10,000 yuan)	
其中:教学用计算机 No. of Computers Used for Instruction		合计 Total	其中:网络多媒体教室 of Which: Network Multimedia Classroom	合计 Total	其中:教学、实习仪器设备资产值 of Which: Teaching Equipment & Instruments
小计 Subtotal	其中:平板电脑 of Which: Tablet PC				
139570	**5609**	**54586**	**17005**	**2789902.91**	**815283.82**
611	32	51	28	5901.89	1175.00
136		9	9	7130.70	2201.00
6974	249	1035	172	72852.08	14944.56
9949	25	947	378	922010.93	31233.09
3391		3132	63	43213.46	12347.50
3943	33	1921	207	103518.70	13561.50
1505	102	1151	53	11591.30	1180.90
2609	150	689	89	15491.63	4801.98
3072	50	217	99	43234.00	14628.00
30103	729	7295	2128	316504.47	77025.67
11529	92	1378	846	86451.60	26119.47
1635	40	237	143	23405.00	6079.00
4359	129	1024	146	24305.16	6742.91
2885	460	561	254	22565.85	5948.73
3896	333	917	276	18150.74	4068.37
10748	701	5227	1771	90924.94	21018.05
6924	284	578	173	55791.05	13788.60
7053	143	1013	510	73437.32	14853.63
1916	292	20351	7879	602738.00	487244.00
181		11	1	961.60	358.00
447	10	11	6	2356.14	1468.14
1775	477	271	158	5832.00	2633.00
6989	97	1412	317	61328.64	11097.68
1637	160	252	130	51530.56	9221.50
537	26	181	56	3803.83	1370.15
7366	502	2288	775	64851.68	15717.65
5982	142	1112	253	53164.11	12176.60
339	318	150	14	3570.23	1401.02
121		34	8	188.00	109.00
958	33	1131	63	3097.30	769.12

农村成人文化技术

Condition of Fixed Assets and Teaching Resources

地 区 Region	占地面积 （平方米） Area of School Sites（m^2）	教学行政用房建筑面积 （平方米） Administrative（m^2）	图书（册） Books （volume）	 合计 Total
总　计 Total	**57039966**	**17232948**	**43168190**	**509589**
北　京 Beijing	1523965	351297	1341999	9021
天　津 Tianjin	566610	143573	469529	2918
河　北 Hebei	4989599	921592	2439730	10503
山　西 Shanxi	1124731	345669	1607898	8103
内蒙古 Inner Mongolia	590589	122889	448734	1551
辽　宁 Liaoning	1983798	535544	1019948	6949
吉　林 Jilin	1700083	208768	272160	769
黑龙江 Heilongjiang	1225048	283060	444962	1744
上　海 Shanghai	398509	224304	578216	6821
江　苏 Jiangsu	5717860	1878947	5554347	128031
浙　江 Zhejiang	4973721	1748120	3731006	29158
安　徽 Anhui	1244468	231281	416031	3699
福　建 Fujian	238207	153247	556732	3580
江　西 Jiangxi	158466	48069	208253	2183
山　东 Shandong	3612401	1129868	1932908	13260
河　南 Henan	3604341	1378433	3997594	15603
湖　北 Hubei	7185793	2442333	478735	9279
湖　南 Hunan	580992	277686	1102914	6194
广　东 Guangdong	3176205	789475	4021379	32542
广　西 Guangxi	460171	66223	277942	647
海　南 Hainan	34270	39750	38800	145
重　庆 Chongqing	596796	330581	758383	4918
四　川 Sichuan	912578	289946	1032076	7007
贵　州 Guizhou	2386341	502651	1475513	10401
云　南 Yunnan	2266688	1501303	1948673	5407
西　藏 Tibet				
陕　西 Shaanxi	2217160	651199	2656951	12811
甘　肃 Gansu	1026620	265989	693489	3539
青　海 Qinghai	204486	14268	79249	97
宁　夏 Ningxia	11080	1582	1580	
新　疆 Xinjiang	2328390	355301	3582459	172709

培训学校资产情况
in Technical Training Schools for Peasants

计算机数(台) No. of Computers(set)		教室(间) Classroom(room)		固定资产总值(万元) Fixed Assets (in 10,000 yuan)	
其中:教学用计算机 No. of Computers Used for Instruction		合计 Total	其中:网络多媒体教室 of Which: Network Multimedia Classroom	合计 Total	其中:教学、实习仪器设备资产值 of Which: Teaching Equipment & Instruments
小计 Subtotal	其中:平板电脑 of Which: Tablet PC				
220399	**12857**	**195829**	**78436**	**12615546.01**	**2742193.23**
7967	51	1483	432	24061.71	8326.59
2744	49	1099	127	6857.40	1756.63
9664	48	15918	815	48154.60	10941.06
8029	47	9711	6574	22557.39	6688.67
1355		1248	389	35744.60	4530.10
6359	55	23460	386	43266.23	3924.20
615	67	722	116	17646.40	2653.60
1640	10	875	176	12170.73	1397.74
5784	394	1156	437	21803.00	7418.00
32931	2718	15406	2696	331003.80	46587.31
25912	1484	5001	2258	138087.04	29992.65
3484	39	1565	178	13746.70	2385.20
3125	387	3005	953	13847.42	2492.92
2099	222	422	99	6174.88	577.02
12100	342	7780	2117	82720.21	15915.24
14903	530	21360	4316	59579.20	12658.95
8866	57	1153	213	30503.20	5919.30
5397		857	171	10823.88	2675.00
27699	4374	54992	52345	10573620.00	2335362.00
627	106	587	41	6294.50	1258.30
145		3	3		
4232	378	2845	260	22792.74	6055.89
5742	117	3601	348	21666.79	5429.40
9508	832	6324	1250	43552.54	10152.24
5048	372	3292	472	43823.08	4365.63
8541	156	6731	507	171203.37	75780.63
3160	18	2031	549	785986.16	127774.51
97		111		1361.82	302.00
				38.00	35.00
2626	4	3091	208	26458.62	8837.45

其他培训机构
Condition of Fixed Assets and

地　　区 Region	占地面积 （平方米） Area of School Sites（m^2）	教学行政用房 建筑面积 （平方米） Administrative （m^2）	图书（册） Books （volume）	
				合计 Total
总　计 Total	**32057750**	**18327784**	**91013324**	**339260**
北　京 Beijing	4333822	1442736	29093409	22923
天　津 Tianjin	1402293	668867	22806156	24631
河　北 Hebei	655990	268401	694069	5986
山　西 Shanxi	483033	314205	1654903	9528
内蒙古 Inner Mongolia	790108	352535	310373	2699
辽　宁 Liaoning	3617310	2175510	2469155	46571
吉　林 Jilin	432746	268548	364334	3459
黑龙江 Heilongjiang	517074	313721	374986	5618
上　海 Shanghai	859759	776205	1667668	24787
江　苏 Jiangsu	9527433	6784313	14662205	63236
浙　江 Zhejiang	997127	671431	1186774	17719
安　徽 Anhui	69176	41103	52960	1305
福　建 Fujian	355711	387540	777538	6904
江　西 Jiangxi	1055484	119358	647277	2893
山　东 Shandong	1753661	761355	947630	16549
河　南 Henan	483372	358201	667084	6894
湖　北 Hubei	507723	208575	458857	5385
湖　南 Hunan	283002	111504	302129	4599
广　东 Guangdong	1461455	1059529	9247865	33417
广　西 Guangxi	800	800	1500	4
海　南 Hainan				
重　庆 Chongqing	195033	175764	109145	3542
四　川 Sichuan	475855	282367	709372	2983
贵　州 Guizhou	259676	125140	466169	2254
云　南 Yunnan	135713	64257	135659	1362
西　藏 Tibet				
陕　西 Shaanxi	626456	384994	845574	16313
甘　肃 Gansu	204685	70385	75994	999
青　海 Qinghai	23500	806		14
宁　夏 Ningxia	173546	60875	92928	2249
新　疆 Xinjiang	376207	78759	191611	4437

资产情况
Teaching Resources in Others

计算机数(台) No. of Computers (set)		教室(间) Classroom(room)		固定资产总值(万元) Fixed Assets (in 10,000 yuan)	
其中:教学用计算机 No. of Computers Used for Instruction		合计 Total	其中:网络多媒体教室 of Which: Network Multimedia Classroom	合计 Total	其中:教学、实习仪器设备资产值 of Which: Teaching Equipment & Instruments
小计 Subtotal	其中:平板电脑 of Which: Tablet PC				
289544	**35686**	**261533**	**188216**	**8468043.61**	**3487356.41**
18417	1623	8549	3359	192631.72	57423.01
13807	4168	3464	831	253645.93	20195.75
5604	301	5366	1101	134582.55	72354.46
9200	38	2522	884	12910.83	6956.62
2228		3476	62	16707.46	5415.09
43242	15886	9175	4667	308068.90	80070.76
2652	299	4967	880	44169.27	6161.17
5008	114	3246	1366	41091.10	21555.20
20495	1391	7057	2317	74304.00	35656.00
55806	3149	13438	8941	639585.88	176625.96
16186	448	5694	2079	82442.00	17151.70
1090	26	106	24	2439307.00	1179.00
6328	212	2220	357	25125.33	8672.46
2441	394	821	447	15032.66	2275.96
14464	1047	11506	1847	69214.90	21151.98
6078	834	4634	1574	31919.76	7485.31
4910	350	1411	176	26628.78	7530.38
3837	65	404	191	29410.87	5441.38
27199	4554	161549	154229	3896896.00	2880732.00
4				50.00	50.00
3211	551	2340	507	12105.00	4242.90
2121	92	1308	237	22525.46	4785.04
2035		1016	483	11697.18	3245.62
1041	43	751	153	8280.96	2782.53
15240	91	3975	920	46297.66	22549.36
852		514	126	2147.30	748.57
6		8		130.00	18.00
2163	2	878	73	19418.06	12527.97
3879	8	1138	385	11717.05	2372.23

初中校

Number of Schools, Classes of

地　区 Region	学校数(所)　Schools			
	合计 Total	初级中学 Regular Junior Secondary Schools	九年一贯制学校 9-year Schools	职业初中 Vocational Junior Secondary Schools
总　计 Total	**52804**	**38747**	**14017**	**40**
北　京 Beijing	347	254	93	
天　津 Tianjin	325	287	38	
河　北 Hebei	2381	1979	402	
山　西 Shanxi	1991	1516	475	
内蒙古 Inner Mongolia	749	533	216	
辽　宁 Liaoning	1572	1033	539	
吉　林 Jilin	1200	886	310	4
黑龙江 Heilongjiang	1587	1139	447	1
上　海 Shanghai	519	355	164	
江　苏 Jiangsu	2073	1702	371	
浙　江 Zhejiang	1727	1296	431	
安　徽 Anhui	2902	2221	680	1
福　建 Fujian	1238	1079	159	
江　西 Jiangxi	2101	1545	555	1
山　东 Shandong	2917	2335	582	
河　南 Henan	4550	3918	632	
湖　北 Hubei	2014	1597	416	1
湖　南 Hunan	3301	2200	1101	
广　东 Guangdong	3351	2192	1159	
广　西 Guangxi	1836	1613	223	
海　南 Hainan	387	214	173	
重　庆 Chongqing	939	744	195	
四　川 Sichuan	3895	1873	2019	3
贵　州 Guizhou	2216	1592	607	17
云　南 Yunnan	1685	1469	205	11
西　藏 Tibet	95	92	3	
陕　西 Shaanxi	1741	1317	424	
甘　肃 Gansu	1561	1041	519	1
青　海 Qinghai	260	102	158	
宁　夏 Ningxia	242	177	65	
新　疆 Xinjiang	1102	446	656	

数、班数(总计)
Junior Secondary Schools(Total)

班数(个) Classes				
合计 Total	一年级 Grade 1	二年级 Grade 2	三年级 Grade 3	四年级 Grade 4
909570	**305192**	**300677**	**293544**	**10157**
9521	3204	3221	3070	26
6882	2225	2204	2153	300
40317	14430	13476	12411	
26589	8765	8793	9031	
15274	5090	5089	5049	46
24484	8285	8158	7965	76
15306	5186	5118	4998	4
22240	6552	6590	6589	2509
12455	3239	3208	3093	2915
43252	14419	14451	14373	9
36575	12537	12299	11697	42
43034	14302	14403	14304	25
24926	8604	8383	7939	
32857	11307	10966	10584	
62729	19877	19643	19303	3906
68824	24445	23155	20953	271
31292	10364	10451	10461	16
40268	14020	13476	12772	
82343	26967	27477	27893	6
33243	11684	10973	10586	
6904	2410	2311	2183	
21151	6919	7006	7226	
54987	18068	18438	18481	
38027	13091	12764	12172	
34434	11919	11474	11035	6
2575	872	843	860	
25473	8387	8504	8582	
21937	7181	7331	7425	
4310	1529	1437	1344	
5330	1834	1780	1716	
22031	7480	7255	7296	

初中校数、班数（城区）

Number of Schools, Classes of Junior Secondary Schools (Urban Area)

地 区 Region	学校数（所） Schools				班数（个） Classes				
	合计 Total	初级中学 Regular Junior Secondary Schools	九年一贯制学校 9-year Schools	职业初中 Vocational Junior Secondary Schools	合计 Total	一年级 Grade 1	二年级 Grade 2	三年级 Grade 3	四年级 Grade 4
总 计 Total	**11124**	**7533**	**3587**	**4**	**293969**	**98836**	**96376**	**92716**	**6041**
北 京 Beijing	198	142	56		7563	2556	2556	2425	26
天 津 Tianjin	136	116	20		3943	1292	1287	1268	96
河 北 Hebei	379	295	84		11098	3904	3713	3481	
山 西 Shanxi	344	257	87		8344	2836	2742	2766	
内蒙古 Inner Mongolia	222	171	51		6200	2099	2064	1993	44
辽 宁 Liaoning	649	505	144		12666	4271	4211	4108	76
吉 林 Jilin	287	226	58	3	6510	2222	2169	2115	4
黑龙江 Heilongjiang	431	338	93		9332	2687	2691	2704	1250
上 海 Shanghai	392	280	112		10172	2631	2587	2536	2418
江 苏 Jiangsu	731	586	145		20143	6844	6754	6536	9
浙 江 Zhejiang	600	424	176		15566	5365	5204	4955	42
安 徽 Anhui	369	260	109		9516	3237	3210	3069	
福 建 Fujian	212	160	52		8433	2956	2846	2631	
江 西 Jiangxi	218	114	104		6705	2329	2253	2123	
山 东 Shandong	794	566	228		22089	6944	6718	6525	1902
河 南 Henan	770	608	162		17233	5979	5760	5329	165
湖 北 Hubei	509	376	133		10890	3665	3654	3568	3
湖 南 Hunan	344	211	133		9418	3294	3169	2955	
广 东 Guangdong	1396	698	698		38946	13352	13005	12589	
广 西 Guangxi	279	157	122		6103	2161	2024	1918	
海 南 Hainan	77	25	52		2469	872	820	777	
重 庆 Chongqing	152	109	43		6300	2102	2118	2080	
四 川 Sichuan	407	207	200		12905	4389	4371	4145	
贵 州 Guizhou	338	154	183	1	5928	2089	1977	1862	
云 南 Yunnan	173	96	77		4940	1744	1654	1536	6
西 藏 Tibet	11	11			316	107	102	107	
陕 西 Shaanxi	285	211	74		7472	2548	2472	2452	
甘 肃 Gansu	137	87	50		3904	1319	1296	1289	
青 海 Qinghai	31	13	18		856	294	286	276	
宁 夏 Ningxia	60	56	4		2083	717	699	667	
新 疆 Xinjiang	193	74	119		5926	2031	1964	1931	

初中校数、班数(城乡结合区)
Number of Schools, Classes of Junior Secondary Schools (Urban-rural Transitional Area)

地区 Region	学校数(所) Schools				班数(个) Classes				
	合计 Total	初级中学 Regular Junior Secondary Schools	九年一贯制学校 9-year Schools	职业初中 Vocational Junior Secondary Schools	合计 Total	一年级 Grade 1	二年级 Grade 2	三年级 Grade 3	四年级 Grade 4
总计 Total	**2390**	**1466**	**923**	**1**	**47908**	**16519**	**15809**	**14913**	**667**
北京 Beijing	31	27	4		674	225	228	221	
天津 Tianjin	15	11	4		276	88	99	89	
河北 Hebei	113	85	28		2204	821	725	658	
山西 Shanxi	58	46	12		810	274	268	268	
内蒙古 Inner Mongolia	10	6	4		175	59	60	56	
辽宁 Liaoning	67	48	19		1130	381	379	370	
吉林 Jilin	22	13	9		306	110	103	93	
黑龙江 Heilongjiang	53	38	15		809	222	229	235	123
上海 Shanghai	25	18	7		693	199	183	165	146
江苏 Jiangsu	118	82	36		2293	785	776	732	
浙江 Zhejiang	167	102	65		3256	1149	1100	1007	
安徽 Anhui	74	53	21		1365	471	458	436	
福建 Fujian	47	37	10		1384	487	464	433	
江西 Jiangxi	43	25	18		944	339	315	290	
山东 Shandong	232	160	72		5149	1657	1573	1522	397
河南 Henan	198	153	45		2825	1024	951	849	1
湖北 Hubei	79	50	29		1249	429	419	401	
湖南 Hunan	92	52	40		1994	717	665	612	
广东 Guangdong	516	227	289		12184	4234	4075	3875	
广西 Guangxi	53	29	24		1043	378	342	323	
海南 Hainan	6	2	4		201	73	67	61	
重庆 Chongqing	20	15	5		583	193	193	197	
四川 Sichuan	84	36	48		1806	631	608	567	
贵州 Guizhou	99	42	56	1	1283	450	429	404	
云南 Yunnan	32	24	8		891	322	301	268	
西藏 Tibet									
陕西 Shaanxi	69	53	16		839	276	276	287	
甘肃 Gansu	17	7	10		375	122	126	127	
青海 Qinghai	5	1	4		133	47	46	40	
宁夏 Ningxia	9	8	1		317	107	111	99	
新疆 Xinjiang	36	16	20		717	249	240	228	

初中校数、班数(镇区)
Number of Schools, Classes of Junior Secondary Schools (Counties & Towns Area)

地 区 Region	学校数(所) Schools				班数(个) Classes				
	合计 Total	初级中学 Regular Junior Secondary Schools	九年一贯制学校 9-year Schools	职业初中 Vocational Junior Secondary Schools	合计 Total	一年级 Grade 1	二年级 Grade 2	三年级 Grade 3	四年级 Grade 4
总 计 Total	**23195**	**18437**	**4737**	**21**	**437638**	**146930**	**145089**	**142709**	**2910**
北 京 Beijing	90	67	23		1357	448	462	447	
天 津 Tianjin	108	98	10		2007	638	627	608	134
河 北 Hebei	1138	955	183		21071	7574	7029	6468	
山 西 Shanxi	828	678	150		12832	4203	4246	4383	
内蒙古 Inner Mongolia	387	290	97		8080	2673	2696	2709	2
辽 宁 Liaoning	599	353	246		8829	3003	2939	2887	
吉 林 Jilin	457	364	92	1	5509	1882	1837	1790	
黑龙江 Heilongjiang	624	432	191	1	8893	2693	2699	2701	800
上 海 Shanghai	102	62	40		1970	521	543	481	425
江 苏 Jiangsu	1143	967	176		21051	6913	7018	7120	
浙 江 Zhejiang	823	687	136		17512	5990	5910	5612	
安 徽 Anhui	1124	902	221	1	22181	7422	7399	7355	5
福 建 Fujian	474	452	22		11041	3823	3697	3521	
江 西 Jiangxi	950	746	203	1	17720	6082	5910	5728	
山 东 Shandong	1531	1281	250		31818	10176	10137	10053	1452
河 南 Henan	2016	1710	306		34162	12223	11509	10351	79
湖 北 Hubei	946	814	131	1	14591	4812	4842	4924	13
湖 南 Hunan	1350	1031	319		19734	6899	6589	6246	
广 东 Guangdong	1355	1072	283		34122	10726	11358	12038	
广 西 Guangxi	982	934	48		20556	7242	6783	6531	
海 南 Hainan	262	166	96		4045	1400	1359	1286	
重 庆 Chongqing	558	487	71		12616	4101	4163	4352	
四 川 Sichuan	1708	1104	603	1	30314	9904	10124	10286	
贵 州 Guizhou	817	700	110	7	19454	6646	6519	6289	
云 南 Yunnan	633	589	37	7	16899	5820	5618	5461	
西 藏 Tibet	69	66	3		1771	604	578	589	
陕 西 Shaanxi	1114	853	261		15422	5011	5167	5244	
甘 肃 Gansu	414	330	83	1	9011	2992	3000	3019	
青 海 Qinghai	108	51	57		2434	870	816	748	
宁 夏 Ningxia	89	66	23		2354	801	787	766	
新 疆 Xinjiang	396	130	266		8282	2838	2728	2716	

初中校数、班数(镇乡结合区)
Number of Schools, Classes of Junior Secondary Schools (County-town Transitional Area)

地 区 Region	学校数(所) Schools				班数(个) Classes				
	合计 Total	初级中学 Regular Junior Secondary Schools	九年一贯制学校 9-year Schools	职业初中 Vocational Junior Secondary Schools	合计 Total	一年级 Grade 1	二年级 Grade 2	三年级 Grade 3	四年级 Grade 4
总 计 Total	**6047**	**4777**	**1264**	**6**	**110648**	**37677**	**36719**	**35565**	**687**
北 京 Beijing	26	21	5		376	124	130	122	
天 津 Tianjin	41	39	2		716	230	217	213	56
河 北 Hebei	487	416	71		9324	3412	3128	2784	
山 西 Shanxi	201	151	50		3335	1102	1106	1127	
内蒙古 Inner Mongolia	36	26	10		633	212	208	213	
辽 宁 Liaoning	86	49	37		1253	418	429	406	
吉 林 Jilin	50	35	15		511	172	169	170	
黑龙江 Heilongjiang	58	44	14		797	241	250	254	52
上 海 Shanghai	28	17	11		492	131	131	114	116
江 苏 Jiangsu	308	261	47		5060	1653	1689	1718	
浙 江 Zhejiang	279	227	52		5839	2012	1984	1843	
安 徽 Anhui	281	215	66		5197	1746	1729	1722	
福 建 Fujian	117	111	6		2809	983	947	879	
江 西 Jiangxi	221	162	58	1	3198	1104	1071	1023	
山 东 Shandong	568	465	103		12201	3937	3917	3892	455
河 南 Henan	753	619	134		11116	4061	3762	3285	8
湖 北 Hubei	227	185	41	1	3413	1118	1146	1149	
湖 南 Hunan	522	406	116		6907	2431	2294	2182	
广 东 Guangdong	399	307	92		10379	3308	3460	3611	
广 西 Guangxi	179	170	9		3647	1289	1205	1153	
海 南 Hainan	26	12	14		591	206	196	189	
重 庆 Chongqing	93	85	8		2437	830	800	807	
四 川 Sichuan	329	193	136		4836	1583	1624	1629	
贵 州 Guizhou	184	138	43	3	4182	1497	1375	1310	
云 南 Yunnan	140	127	12	1	4113	1411	1374	1328	
西 藏 Tibet	6	5	1		167	57	52	58	
陕 西 Shaanxi	219	177	42		3247	1064	1060	1123	
甘 肃 Gansu	92	68	24		1786	616	582	588	
青 海 Qinghai	28	9	19		448	161	150	137	
宁 夏 Ningxia	17	12	5		438	142	144	152	
新 疆 Xinjiang	46	25	21		1200	426	390	384	

初中校数、班数(乡村)
Number of Schools, Classes of Junior Secondary Schools (Rural Area)

	学校数(所) Schools				班数(个) Classes				
	合计 Total	初级中学 Regular Junior Secondary Schools	九年一贯制学校 9-year Schools	职业初中 Vocational Junior Secondary Schools	合计 Total	一年级 Grade 1	二年级 Grade 2	三年级 Grade 3	四年级 Grade 4
总　计 Total	**18485**	**12777**	**5693**	**15**	**177963**	**59426**	**59212**	**58119**	**1206**
北　京 Beijing	59	45	14		601	200	203	198	
天　津 Tianjin	81	73	8		932	295	290	277	70
河　北 Hebei	864	729	135		8148	2952	2734	2462	
山　西 Shanxi	819	581	238		5413	1726	1805	1882	
内蒙古 Inner Mongolia	140	72	68		994	318	329	347	
辽　宁 Liaoning	324	175	149		2989	1011	1008	970	
吉　林 Jilin	456	296	160		3287	1082	1112	1093	
黑龙江 Heilongjiang	532	369	163		4015	1172	1200	1184	459
上　海 Shanghai	25	13	12		313	87	78	76	72
江　苏 Jiangsu	199	149	50		2058	662	679	717	
浙　江 Zhejiang	304	185	119		3497	1182	1185	1130	
安　徽 Anhui	1409	1059	350		11337	3643	3794	3880	20
福　建 Fujian	552	467	85		5452	1825	1840	1787	
江　西 Jiangxi	933	685	248		8432	2896	2803	2733	
山　东 Shandong	592	488	104		8822	2757	2788	2725	552
河　南 Henan	1764	1600	164		17429	6243	5886	5273	27
湖　北 Hubei	559	407	152		5811	1887	1955	1969	
湖　南 Hunan	1607	958	649		11116	3827	3718	3571	
广　东 Guangdong	600	422	178		9275	2889	3114	3266	6
广　西 Guangxi	575	522	53		6584	2281	2166	2137	
海　南 Hainan	48	23	25		390	138	132	120	
重　庆 Chongqing	229	148	81		2235	716	725	794	
四　川 Sichuan	1780	562	1216	2	11768	3775	3943	4050	
贵　州 Guizhou	1061	738	314	9	12645	4356	4268	4021	
云　南 Yunnan	879	784	91	4	12595	4355	4202	4038	
西　藏 Tibet	15	15			488	161	163	164	
陕　西 Shaanxi	342	253	89		2579	828	865	886	
甘　肃 Gansu	1010	624	386		9022	2870	3035	3117	
青　海 Qinghai	121	38	83		1020	365	335	320	
宁　夏 Ningxia	93	55	38		893	316	294	283	
新　疆 Xinjiang	513	242	271		7823	2611	2563	2649	

初中学生数(总计)
Number of Students in Junior Secondary Schools(Total)

单位:人
unit:person

地　区 Region	毕业生数 Graduates	招生数 Entrants	在校生数 Enrolment 合计 Total	其中:女 of Which: Female	一年级 Grade 1	二年级 Grade 2	三年级 Grade 3	四年级 Grade 4	预计毕业生数 Estimated Graduates for Next Year
总　计 Total	**15615452**	**14960867**	**44401248**	**20836306**	**14972216**	**14771466**	**14237562**	**420004**	**14225162**
北　京 Beijing	92373	106726	310568	145590	106936	107904	94862	866	94581
天　津 Tianjin	79660	85815	260710	122936	85818	83577	81070	10245	80957
河　北 Hebei	667759	783551	2088470	1001693	783551	702538	602381		602381
山　西 Shanxi	541457	412993	1291442	623502	413040	428225	450177		450177
内蒙古 Inner Mongolia	249435	227562	688464	332964	227562	230867	228145	1890	228143
辽　宁 Liaoning	386556	358177	1057488	502982	358190	354153	341593	3552	341340
吉　林 Jilin	240310	218370	644993	310192	218434	215537	210843	179	210610
黑龙江 Heilongjiang	373316	279083	932839	454696	279083	279570	274885	99301	270157
上　海 Shanghai	94135	120266	436696	206000	120475	115298	107429	93494	93494
江　苏 Jiangsu	675206	618597	1857469	856170	618597	619809	618738	325	618664
浙　江 Zhejiang	485774	512401	1482649	693049	512457	502260	466438	1494	466219
安　徽 Anhui	723950	652595	1997091	911072	652797	667753	675303	1238	675479
福　建 Fujian	371373	386067	1108226	507742	386160	372951	349115		349115
江　西 Jiangxi	626094	610764	1754361	800298	611360	590511	552490		552490
山　东 Shandong	1050979	996384	3179800	1500075	996389	1001958	989436	192017	998973
河　南 Henan	1403358	1377091	3850493	1801658	1377143	1306902	1152105	14343	1149900
湖　北 Hubei	533709	487841	1483710	672211	487919	498585	496461	745	496432
湖　南 Hunan	666508	766477	2142847	984527	766477	723179	653191		653191
广　东 Guangdong	1516552	1299856	4047906	1823617	1300543	1359072	1388291		1388291
广　西 Guangxi	640168	688598	1950761	928572	688645	637739	624377		624377
海　南 Hainan	120500	116957	346790	156089	121788	116999	108003		108003
重　庆 Chongqing	377479	330158	1017592	481929	330590	336859	350143		350143
四　川 Sichuan	1026649	878586	2717198	1301537	878847	918554	919797		919797
贵　州 Guizhou	658485	716233	2103033	1005856	716233	712690	674110		674110
云　南 Yunnan	625128	682003	1874418	904469	682178	623603	568322	315	568281
西　藏 Tibet	43729	42446	126117	61719	42446	41793	41878		41878
陕　西 Shaanxi	455934	383740	1201851	558484	386757	406933	408161		408161
甘　肃 Gansu	419502	334288	1035940	497357	334352	345971	355617		355617
青　海 Qinghai	65029	76729	208095	100798	76776	69101	62218		62218
宁　夏 Ningxia	92913	96920	284758	140199	97023	95994	91741		91741
新　疆 Xinjiang	311432	313593	918473	448323	313650	304581	300242		300242

初中学生数(城区)

Number of Students in Junior Secondary Schools (Urban Area)

单位:人

unit:person

地　区 Region	毕业生数 Graduates	招生数 Entrants	在校生数 Enrolment 合计 Total	其中:女 of Which: Female	一年级 Grade 1	二年级 Grade 2	三年级 Grade 3	四年级 Grade 4	预计毕业生数 Estimated Graduates for Next Year
总　计 Total	**4590441**	**4814726**	**14300203**	**6623498**	**4817167**	**4740435**	**4487427**	**255174**	**4470557**
北　京 Beijing	73580	86946	252472	118267	87062	87919	76625	866	76344
天　津 Tianjin	45319	49272	149429	71451	49273	48658	47921	3577	47617
河　北 Hebei	189451	224538	620786	297390	224538	210549	185699		185699
山　西 Shanxi	169428	142248	432145	210507	142255	143375	146515		146515
内蒙古 Inner Mongolia	105260	102163	306444	147868	102163	102886	99531	1864	99531
辽　宁 Liaoning	187790	186248	554196	262841	186257	186503	177884	3552	177631
吉　林 Jilin	110728	105264	310024	147320	105272	103416	101157	179	100924
黑龙江 Heilongjiang	152862	125954	433788	209475	125954	126336	125501	55997	122657
上　海 Shanghai	78457	96923	356942	168904	97084	93151	88603	78104	78104
江　苏 Jiangsu	289300	300154	875593	404713	300154	293857	281257	325	281183
浙　江 Zhejiang	204912	224022	644640	299864	224039	216321	202786	1494	202567
安　徽 Anhui	157035	155799	463274	207672	155808	155003	152463		152463
福　建 Fujian	120812	143853	401672	181019	143872	136346	121454		121454
江　西 Jiangxi	117481	127613	368756	160999	127656	125875	115225		115225
山　东 Shandong	352778	356217	1142434	534201	356217	348400	338610	99207	337977
河　南 Henan	301506	337745	977758	449559	337784	331134	299242	9598	297733
湖　北 Hubei	176905	177436	529708	237079	177458	178859	173295	96	173315
湖　南 Hunan	153123	186694	520728	235425	186694	176368	157666		157666
广　东 Guangdong	624087	639568	1898900	829625	640247	640851	617802		617802
广　西 Guangxi	96861	119270	332501	152491	119271	111185	102045		102045
海　南 Hainan	43458	45725	133971	57179	46927	45081	41963		41963
重　庆 Chongqing	100662	100972	306289	146188	100996	103306	101987		101987
四　川 Sichuan	219287	217790	656350	314422	217803	224972	213575		213575
贵　州 Guizhou	97715	113123	328382	154830	113123	110997	104262		104262
云　南 Yunnan	82602	99436	269926	132026	99449	90857	79305	315	79264
西　藏 Tibet	4990	5000	14768	7233	5000	4975	4793		4793
陕　西 Shaanxi	127438	126228	379392	175269	126259	128393	124740		124740
甘　肃 Gansu	69648	68379	203509	95621	68379	67765	67365		67365
青　海 Qinghai	13383	15798	44767	21600	15798	15205	13764		13764
宁　夏 Ningxia	36213	39919	116771	56818	39933	39651	37187		37187
新　疆 Xinjiang	87370	94429	273888	135642	94442	92241	87205		87205

初中学生数(城乡结合区)
Number of Students in Junior Secondary Schools (Urban-rural Transitional Area)

单位:人
unit:person

地 区 Region	毕业生数 Graduates	招生数 Entrants	在校生数 Enrolment						预计毕业生数 Estimated Graduates for Next Year
			合计 Total	其中:女 of Which: Female	一年级 Grade 1	二年级 Grade 2	三年级 Grade 3	四年级 Grade 4	
总 计 Total	**733117**	**799024**	**2312158**	**1043894**	**799456**	**769442**	**712445**	**30815**	**711945**
北 京 Beijing	6098	7494	21693	9747	7498	7399	6796		6796
天 津 Tianjin	3390	3344	10140	4768	3344	3677	3119		3119
河 北 Hebei	37504	47036	123768	58854	47036	41215	35517		35517
山 西 Shanxi	14920	12557	37485	18203	12557	12092	12836		12836
内蒙古 Inner Mongolia	2913	2457	7489	3281	2457	2540	2492		2492
辽 宁 Liaoning	16740	16751	48148	22609	16751	16036	15361		15361
吉 林 Jilin	4648	4486	12234	5911	4487	4042	3705		3705
黑龙江 Heilongjiang	15823	9875	35792	17391	9875	10022	10219	5676	10137
上 海 Shanghai	4694	7940	25435	11488	7950	6886	5846	4753	4753
江 苏 Jiangsu	30608	33091	95396	43034	33091	32357	29948		29948
浙 江 Zhejiang	39181	47672	131169	59199	47675	45068	38426		38136
安 徽 Anhui	21144	21734	63742	28265	21734	21486	20522		20522
福 建 Fujian	19235	22861	63875	28988	22862	21685	19328		19328
江 西 Jiangxi	15698	19073	52956	22202	19081	17925	15950		15950
山 东 Shandong	82196	82422	257929	119747	82422	78057	77096	20354	78082
河 南 Henan	42899	53384	145713	65769	53384	49080	43217	32	43196
湖 北 Hubei	19062	19577	58036	24697	19577	19722	18737		18737
湖 南 Hunan	32190	40463	109399	47490	40463	36693	32243		32243
广 东 Guangdong	193286	203484	597362	256925	203795	202874	190693		190693
广 西 Guangxi	16806	21485	58947	27132	21485	19662	17800		17800
海 南 Hainan	3390	4285	11565	5022	4345	3843	3377		3377
重 庆 Chongqing	10229	9017	27867	12652	9017	9453	9397		9397
四 川 Sichuan	27483	29369	86210	40589	29373	29547	27290		27290
贵 州 Guizhou	19496	23509	68751	32280	23509	23522	21720		21720
云 南 Yunnan	15825	18285	48833	23935	18285	16546	14002		14002
西 藏 Tibet									
陕 西 Shaanxi	13683	11098	35821	16012	11125	12082	12614		12614
甘 肃 Gansu	6683	6350	19258	9622	6350	6587	6321		6321
青 海 Qinghai	1630	2407	6491	3236	2407	2271	1813		1813
宁 夏 Ningxia	5794	6117	18479	8811	6117	6252	6110		6110
新 疆 Xinjiang	9869	11401	32175	16035	11404	10821	9950		9950

初中学生数(镇区)

Number of Students in Junior Secondary Schools (Counties & Towns Area)

单位:人
unit:person

地 区 Region	毕业生数 Graduates	招生数 Entrants	在校生数 Enrolment						预计毕业生数 Estimated Graduates for Next Year
			合计 Total	其中:女 of Which: Female	一年级 Grade 1	二年级 Grade 2	三年级 Grade 3	四年级 Grade 4	
总 计 Total	**7885935**	**7400752**	**21955710**	**10344810**	**7408877**	**7311812**	**7115884**	**119137**	**7118296**
北 京 Beijing	13141	13798	41297	19531	13862	14357	13078		13078
天 津 Tianjin	24515	25489	77628	36367	25491	24502	23265	4370	23523
河 北 Hebei	350390	422360	1109647	532667	422360	371601	315686		315686
山 西 Shanxi	265103	202315	635797	307585	202351	209954	223492		223492
内蒙古 Inner Mongolia	128492	114811	349283	169577	114811	117063	117383	26	117381
辽 宁 Liaoning	152344	132877	388474	185551	132877	129534	126063		126063
吉 林 Jilin	84453	76321	223156	109011	76369	74660	72127		72127
黑龙江 Heilongjiang	153832	113956	367363	180099	113956	113117	110684	29606	108786
上 海 Shanghai	13597	20050	69340	32286	20088	19397	16478	13377	13377
江 苏 Jiangsu	348940	293061	901539	413806	293061	299739	308739		308739
浙 江 Zhejiang	239009	244571	710153	334436	244606	241957	223590		223590
安 徽 Anhui	378370	348767	1058799	477330	348902	352426	357253	218	357301
福 建 Fujian	170842	170826	494339	227584	170882	165337	158120		158120
江 西 Jiangxi	347282	338681	970679	442357	339155	325668	305856		305856
山 东 Shandong	552774	511955	1616022	766591	511960	519080	517649	67333	525476
河 南 Henan	713172	712443	1981445	922210	712447	672788	592652	3558	591981
湖 北 Hubei	257033	225227	689455	315774	225272	230529	233005	649	232956
湖 南 Hunan	337536	390439	1087291	499554	390439	366708	330144		330144
广 东 Guangdong	708133	525110	1703759	786750	525115	569114	609530		609530
广 西 Guangxi	412916	445109	1255970	605006	445123	409882	400965		400965
海 南 Hainan	71215	65684	196478	91583	69151	66378	60949		60949
重 庆 Chongqing	234783	197030	610813	288601	197433	201078	212302		212302
四 川 Sichuan	589044	494650	1537993	739101	494880	516744	526369		526369
贵 州 Guizhou	346536	373315	1105933	527518	373315	374217	358401		358401
云 南 Yunnan	313028	339480	941281	458852	339523	312620	289138		289138
西 藏 Tibet	30583	29337	86698	42649	29337	28358	29003		29003
陕 西 Shaanxi	285287	226123	720462	337007	228949	244115	247398		247398
甘 肃 Gansu	170968	143272	440355	209275	143312	146527	150516		150516
青 海 Qinghai	36629	44339	118314	57942	44376	38986	34952		34952
宁 夏 Ningxia	41930	42260	125219	61946	42346	42023	40850		40850
新 疆 Xinjiang	114058	117096	340728	166264	117128	113353	110247		110247

初中学生数(镇乡结合区)
Number of Students in Junior Secondary Schools (County-town Transitional Area)

单位:人
unit:person

地 区 Region	毕业生数 Graduates	招生数 Entrants	在校生数 Enrolment 合计 Total	其中:女 of Which: Female	一年级 Grade 1	二年级 Grade 2	三年级 Grade 3	四年级 Grade 4	预计毕业生数 Estimated Graduates for Next Year
总 计 Total	**1953974**	**1914145**	**5586443**	**2609804**	**1915515**	**1863051**	**1779085**	**28792**	**1781005**
北 京 Beijing	3404	3269	9816	4691	3306	3463	3047		3047
天 津 Tianjin	8176	9169	27714	13060	9169	8566	8116	1863	8167
河 北 Hebei	154752	194779	504097	241556	194779	168925	140393		140393
山 西 Shanxi	65896	52655	163969	78980	52663	53678	57628		57628
内蒙古 Inner Mongolia	11070	9528	28147	13735	9528	9325	9294		9294
辽 宁 Liaoning	20032	17873	53426	25106	17873	18206	17347		17347
吉 林 Jilin	7192	6833	20666	10222	6838	7030	6798		6798
黑龙江 Heilongjiang	14168	10215	32575	15864	10215	10201	10276	1883	10033
上 海 Shanghai	3545	4764	16613	7892	4771	4505	3874	3463	3463
江 苏 Jiangsu	79037	68047	209764	94474	68047	70541	71176		71176
浙 江 Zhejiang	77467	82928	238561	111280	82952	82053	73556		73556
安 徽 Anhui	87527	81541	249015	108169	81546	83154	84315		84315
福 建 Fujian	44109	44798	128442	58245	44816	43288	40338		40338
江 西 Jiangxi	67155	59057	169275	77127	59134	57170	52971		52971
山 东 Shandong	216431	200919	625057	292059	200919	201249	201664	21225	204174
河 南 Henan	218561	228049	624321	289271	228049	213252	182662	358	182675
湖 北 Hubei	59215	52121	160650	74370	52125	54410	54115		54115
湖 南 Hunan	117211	135455	374544	170513	135455	126051	113038		113038
广 东 Guangdong	207589	162972	521067	240849	162972	174461	183634		183634
广 西 Guangxi	77619	80706	228490	110818	80706	74569	73215		73215
海 南 Hainan	10271	10219	30367	13741	10678	10161	9528		9528
重 庆 Chongqing	42634	40519	118895	55807	40520	39101	39274		39274
四 川 Sichuan	86416	75221	232949	111978	75224	78282	79443		79443
贵 州 Guizhou	71103	83697	238226	112558	83697	79132	75397		75397
云 南 Yunnan	78145	84885	236576	116060	84894	79021	72661		72661
西 藏 Tibet	3057	2951	8835	4301	2951	2783	3101		3101
陕 西 Shaanxi	60660	48910	153640	69805	49551	51141	52948		52948
甘 肃 Gansu	31973	28993	86831	41338	29017	28609	29205		29205
青 海 Qinghai	7047	7795	20318	9993	7804	6509	6005		6005
宁 夏 Ningxia	8602	7626	24047	11898	7663	8006	8378		8378
新 疆 Xinjiang	13910	17651	49550	24044	17653	16209	15688		15688

初中学生数(乡村)
Number of Students in Junior Secondary Schools (Rural Area)

单位:人
unit:person

地 区 Region	毕业生数 Graduates	招生数 Entrants	在校生数 Enrolment						预计毕业生数 Estimated Graduates for Next Year
			合计 Total	其中:女 of Which: Female	一年级 Grade 1	二年级 Grade 2	三年级 Grade 3	四年级 Grade 4	
总 计 Total	**3139076**	**2745389**	**8145335**	**3867998**	**2746172**	**2719219**	**2634251**	**45693**	**2636309**
北 京 Beijing	5652	5982	16799	7792	6012	5628	5159		5159
天 津 Tianjin	9826	11054	33653	15118	11054	10417	9884	2298	9817
河 北 Hebei	127918	136653	358037	171636	136653	120388	100996		100996
山 西 Shanxi	106926	68430	223500	105410	68434	74896	80170		80170
内蒙古 Inner Mongolia	15683	10588	32737	15519	10588	10918	11231		11231
辽 宁 Liaoning	46422	39052	114818	54590	39056	38116	37646		37646
吉 林 Jilin	45129	36785	111813	53861	36793	37461	37559		37559
黑龙江 Heilongjiang	66622	39173	131688	65122	39173	40117	38700	13698	38714
上 海 Shanghai	2081	3293	10414	4810	3303	2750	2348	2013	2013
江 苏 Jiangsu	36966	25382	80337	37651	25382	26213	28742		28742
浙 江 Zhejiang	41853	43808	127856	58749	43812	43982	40062		40062
安 徽 Anhui	188545	148029	475018	226070	148087	160324	165587	1020	165715
福 建 Fujian	79719	71388	212215	99139	71406	71268	69541		69541
江 西 Jiangxi	161331	144470	414926	196942	144549	138968	131409		131409
山 东 Shandong	145427	128212	421344	199283	128212	134478	133177	25477	135520
河 南 Henan	388680	326903	891290	429889	326912	302980	260211	1187	260186
湖 北 Hubei	99771	85178	264547	119358	85189	89197	90161		90161
湖 南 Hunan	175849	189344	534828	249548	189344	180103	165381		165381
广 东 Guangdong	184332	135178	445247	207242	135181	149107	160959		160959
广 西 Guangxi	130391	124219	362290	171075	124251	116672	121367		121367
海 南 Hainan	5827	5548	16341	7327	5710	5540	5091		5091
重 庆 Chongqing	42034	32156	100490	47140	32161	32475	35854		35854
四 川 Sichuan	218318	166146	522855	248014	166164	176838	179853		179853
贵 州 Guizhou	214234	229795	668718	323508	229795	227476	211447		211447
云 南 Yunnan	229498	243087	663211	313591	243206	220126	199879		199879
西 藏 Tibet	8156	8109	24651	11837	8109	8460	8082		8082
陕 西 Shaanxi	43209	31389	101997	46208	31549	34425	36023		36023
甘 肃 Gansu	178886	122637	392076	192461	122661	131679	137736		137736
青 海 Qinghai	15017	16592	45014	21256	16602	14910	13502		13502
宁 夏 Ningxia	14770	14741	42768	21435	14744	14320	13704		13704
新 疆 Xinjiang	110004	102068	303857	146417	102080	98987	102790		102790

初中女学生数

Number of Female Students in Junior Secondary Schools

单位:人

unit:person

地　区 Region	毕业生数 Graduates	招生数 Entrants	在校生数 Enrolment 合计 Total	一年级 Grade 1	二年级 Grade 2	三年级 Grade 3	四年级 Grade 4	预计毕业生数 Estimated Graduates for Next Year
总　计 Total	**7427221**	**6958625**	**20836306**	**6962278**	**6921858**	**6750100**	**202070**	**6737781**
北　京 Beijing	43881	49436	145590	49504	50657	45025	404	44913
天　津 Tianjin	38231	40137	122936	40137	39386	38649	4764	38628
河　北 Hebei	326766	368285	1001693	368285	337092	296316		296316
山　西 Shanxi	265240	198145	623502	198157	205785	219560		219560
内蒙古 Inner Mongolia	121725	109326	332964	109326	111266	111492	880	111453
辽　宁 Liaoning	184587	169519	502982	169522	168163	163618	1679	163402
吉　林 Jilin	116381	105343	310192	105350	103710	101054	78	100958
黑龙江 Heilongjiang	182397	135677	454696	135677	135519	134662	48838	132500
上　海 Shanghai	45807	56152	206000	56208	53927	50849	45016	45016
江　苏 Jiangsu	310587	285984	856170	285984	285062	284989	135	284931
浙　江 Zhejiang	228460	238532	693049	238552	235101	218636	760	218537
安　徽 Anhui	337658	296493	911072	296568	303405	310492	607	310602
福　建 Fujian	169709	176395	507742	176417	171696	159629		159629
江　西 Jiangxi	286057	276893	800298	277064	268684	254550		254550
山　东 Shandong	499671	468948	1500075	468950	472605	466799	91721	470842
河　南 Henan	671667	636099	1801658	636107	609809	549056	6686	548166
湖　北 Hubei	243315	221921	672211	221948	225237	224667	359	224640
湖　南 Hunan	314331	346315	984527	346315	332173	306039		306039
广　东 Guangdong	705171	576009	1823617	576252	610485	636880		630005
广　西 Guangxi	304950	324408	928572	324418	305162	298992		298989
海　南 Hainan	55989	52644	156089	53789	51941	50359		50359
重　庆 Chongqing	181927	155160	481929	155215	159542	167172		167172
四　川 Sichuan	498248	416520	1301537	416625	438361	446551		446551
贵　州 Guizhou	322074	339331	1005856	339331	340001	326524		326524
云　南 Yunnan	300850	322810	904469	322850	301329	280147	143	280106
西　藏 Tibet	20908	20542	61719	20542	20645	20532		20532
陕　西 Shaanxi	213894	177900	558484	179390	188856	190238		190238
甘　肃 Gansu	203309	157969	497357	157994	166982	172381		172381
青　海 Qinghai	32066	37105	100798	37123	33191	30484		30484
宁　夏 Ningxia	47119	46737	140199	46772	47114	46313		46313
新　疆 Xinjiang	154246	151890	448323	151906	148972	147445		147445

初中专任教师学历、

Number of Full-time Teachers in Junior Secondary Schools by

地　区 Region	合计 Total	其中:女 of Which: Female	按学历分 By Academic Qualifications			
			研究生毕业 Graduate	本科毕业 Under-graduate	专科毕业 Associate Bachelor	高中阶段毕业 High School Graduate
总　计 Total	**3480979**	**1799565**	**45138**	**2561050**	**849842**	**24180**
北　京 Beijing	31868	23872	3228	27781	825	33
天　津 Tianjin	25967	17326	1274	22427	2069	189
河　北 Hebei	164869	109079	1573	125400	36988	901
山　西 Shanxi	117434	74620	1026	79867	35715	817
内蒙古 Inner Mongolia	61934	38998	1189	46929	13434	344
辽　宁 Liaoning	99362	65420	1619	77459	19735	492
吉　林 Jilin	66821	43016	1048	53396	12076	298
黑龙江 Heilongjiang	97218	60876	692	72985	22740	776
上　海 Shanghai	36049	26031	2151	32933	953	10
江　苏 Jiangsu	176986	87605	4080	154629	17777	498
浙　江 Zhejiang	117879	66361	1765	107181	8694	228
安　徽 Anhui	158168	58335	1307	113228	42744	881
福　建 Fujian	96962	43060	967	79217	16280	493
江　西 Jiangxi	121483	46471	1053	77371	41762	1242
山　东 Shandong	263329	131995	4532	207325	49751	1683
河　南 Henan	279942	155010	2368	178895	96016	2660
湖　北 Hubei	135580	55214	1538	88216	44666	1130
湖　南 Hunan	169041	77378	1747	113609	50598	2969
广　东 Guangdong	276777	149406	4587	193002	77380	1762
广　西 Guangxi	116957	57085	808	84390	30686	1016
海　南 Hainan	25267	11410	174	18139	6778	171
重　庆 Chongqing	76182	35852	805	62526	12443	396
四　川 Sichuan	202665	91351	1092	137963	62911	687
贵　州 Guizhou	115345	44864	372	77118	36882	924
云　南 Yunnan	121875	57525	657	92437	27663	1060
西　藏 Tibet	9060	4353	104	7404	1462	76
陕　西 Shaanxi	110505	60216	2039	83012	24391	1019
甘　肃 Gansu	84348	34485	512	61829	21028	946
青　海 Qinghai	15602	7998	228	11312	3950	109
宁　夏 Ningxia	19395	9972	193	16369	2746	85
新　疆 Xinjiang	86109	54381	410	56701	28699	285

职称情况(总计)
Academic Qualifications and Professional Rank (Total)

单位:人
unit:person

	按职称分 By Professional Rank				
高中阶段毕业以下 Below High School Graduate	中学高级 Senior Secondary	中学一级 1st Grade	中学二级 2nd Grade	中学三级 3rd Grade	未定职级 No-ranking
769	**556896**	**1502837**	**1126940**	**57287**	**237019**
1	6249	12465	10548	101	2505
8	8273	13047	3971	69	607
7	25588	77274	50708	1717	9582
9	9698	38936	52689	3638	12473
38	19225	24222	13858	521	4108
57	41354	36906	16352	1117	3633
3	8732	31837	21866	631	3755
25	22074	47748	24081	684	2631
2	4263	18986	11038	58	1704
2	39559	87153	43763	110	6401
11	24356	56910	31133	354	5126
8	25757	60864	53345	4390	13812
5	17726	42430	32474	941	3391
55	30726	45757	35452	2588	6960
38	38212	121515	88461	2100	13041
3	45543	110486	95913	7178	20822
30	24357	73959	29633	1990	5641
118	17684	89627	47351	1599	12780
46	25398	137862	70441	7268	35808
57	11336	62821	34892	2076	5832
5	3899	9371	10224	255	1518
12	8596	28289	34077	844	4376
12	28348	82442	78575	1344	11956
49	10178	38649	46971	3659	15888
58	20192	46861	43725	3443	7654
14	365	3252	4464	202	777
44	11806	38044	51618	2405	6632
33	6268	26964	42850	2556	5710
3	3776	6308	4350	138	1030
2	3327	6187	6726	216	2939
14	14031	25665	35391	3095	7927

初中专任教师学历、

Number of Full-time Teachers in Junior Secondary Schools by

地 区 Region	合计 Total	其中:女 of Which: Female	按学历分 By Academic Qualifications			
			研究生毕业 Graduate	本科毕业 Under- graduate	专科毕业 Associate Bachelor	高中阶段毕业 High School Graduate
总 计 Total	**1046324**	**659999**	**32940**	**868782**	**141756**	**2744**
北 京 Beijing	24312	18868	2961	20774	550	26
天 津 Tianjin	14573	11173	1128	12544	845	53
河 北 Hebei	44214	32748	937	37415	5789	73
山 西 Shanxi	33794	23769	641	27184	5900	68
内蒙古 Inner Mongolia	23042	16160	867	18526	3608	41
辽 宁 Liaoning	49913	36972	1430	42405	5949	114
吉 林 Jilin	26419	19405	835	22611	2890	83
黑龙江 Heilongjiang	39370	28086	598	32163	6502	106
上 海 Shanghai	28997	21623	1826	26505	663	3
江 苏 Jiangsu	75893	44080	3248	67413	5055	175
浙 江 Zhejiang	49653	30840	1111	45431	3057	46
安 徽 Anhui	31889	15555	628	24943	6211	106
福 建 Fujian	28232	16858	756	24256	3164	55
江 西 Jiangxi	22917	12029	546	17088	5187	91
山 东 Shandong	86222	51794	2783	74391	8822	225
河 南 Henan	64431	41024	1551	50467	12232	180
湖 北 Hubei	44122	22207	1273	33035	9592	219
湖 南 Hunan	32872	19466	1115	26392	5199	160
广 东 Guangdong	123861	74327	4149	98702	20676	326
广 西 Guangxi	19708	12250	552	15692	3357	79
海 南 Hainan	8032	4615	81	6746	1173	27
重 庆 Chongqing	22200	12672	645	19667	1839	48
四 川 Sichuan	43938	25136	727	35786	7330	93
贵 州 Guizhou	17926	10382	185	13755	3868	114
云 南 Yunnan	16507	10219	397	14225	1840	44
西 藏 Tibet	1192	627	26	966	192	8
陕 西 Shaanxi	26251	17279	1139	21868	3157	87
甘 肃 Gansu	14062	7921	292	11370	2355	43
青 海 Qinghai	3044	1975	65	2456	514	8
宁 夏 Ningxia	6865	4154	123	6110	626	6
新 疆 Xinjiang	21873	15785	325	17896	3614	37

职称情况(城区)

Academic Qualifications and Professional Rank (Urban Area)

单位:人
unit:person

高中阶段毕业以下 Below High School Graduate	按职称分 By Professional Rank				
	中学高级 Senior Secondary	中学一级 1st Grade	中学二级 2nd Grade	中学三级 3rd Grade	未定职级 No-ranking
102	**227778**	**456060**	**282043**	**9107**	**71336**
1	5039	9503	7707	57	2006
3	4795	6801	2494	49	434
	9420	21130	10864	317	2483
1	4895	12509	12368	647	3375
	7861	8098	4814	184	2085
15	20714	19656	7231	323	1989
	4774	12652	7536	199	1258
1	11829	18340	7956	175	1070
	3627	15590	8377	35	1368
2	20847	35822	16444	42	2738
8	12490	23061	11617	126	2359
1	6174	11787	9982	1013	2933
1	6313	11275	8858	281	1505
5	7139	8725	5693	241	1119
1	14758	39572	27184	435	4273
1	14419	25663	19697	846	3806
3	12492	21472	8353	417	1388
6	5834	16993	7162	235	2648
8	17001	56875	30352	1679	17954
28	3695	10043	4461	234	1275
5	1575	2799	2770	32	856
1	3480	8808	8805	65	1042
2	8011	18591	14864	137	2335
4	2834	6051	5473	336	3232
1	3536	6985	4776	129	1081
	133	609	376	25	49
	4148	9692	10457	340	1614
2	2363	5788	5211	183	517
1	924	1223	705	65	127
	1620	2553	1916	46	730
1	5038	7394	7540	214	1687

初中专任教师学历、

Number of Full-time Teachers in Junior Secondary Schools by Academic

地 区 Region	合计 Total	其中:女 of Which: Female	按学历分 By Academic Qualifications			
			研究生毕业 Graduate	本科毕业 Under-graduate	专科毕业 Associate Bachelor	高中阶段毕业 High School Graduate
总 计 Total	**174350**	**99941**	**3415**	**137564**	**32585**	**767**
北 京 Beijing	2149	1556	161	1893	95	
天 津 Tianjin	1045	760	58	925	56	6
河 北 Hebei	9342	6843	106	7349	1872	15
山 西 Shanxi	3714	2486	46	2855	799	14
内蒙古 Inner Mongolia	698	457	18	593	86	1
辽 宁 Liaoning	4627	3268	89	3790	719	26
吉 林 Jilin	1535	1065	68	1261	199	7
黑龙江 Heilongjiang	4227	2937	27	3195	964	41
上 海 Shanghai	1949	1367	144	1776	29	
江 苏 Jiangsu	8964	4556	181	8048	705	30
浙 江 Zhejiang	9902	5733	165	8773	944	20
安 徽 Anhui	4480	1748	50	3170	1235	24
福 建 Fujian	4905	2501	48	4132	714	10
江 西 Jiangxi	3236	1412	36	2366	806	25
山 东 Shandong	21669	11859	504	18336	2742	87
河 南 Henan	11604	7092	252	8555	2735	62
湖 北 Hubei	5520	2454	66	3904	1511	39
湖 南 Hunan	7356	4037	182	5817	1313	43
广 东 Guangdong	38397	21258	881	28523	8826	161
广 西 Guangxi	3576	2123	38	2795	716	26
海 南 Hainan	692	345	4	592	96	
重 庆 Chongqing	1878	925	35	1597	236	10
四 川 Sichuan	6427	3556	95	4962	1352	18
贵 州 Guizhou	3548	1859	14	2279	1194	59
云 南 Yunnan	2971	1767	40	2448	468	15
西 藏 Tibet						
陕 西 Shaanxi	3848	2281	53	3160	619	16
甘 肃 Gansu	1602	846	18	1109	470	4
青 海 Qinghai	407	255	10	324	73	
宁 夏 Ningxia	1122	589	4	958	157	3
新 疆 Xinjiang	2960	2006	22	2079	854	5

职称情况(城乡结合区)

Qualifications and Professional Rank (Urban-rural Transitional Area)

单位:人

unit:person

高中阶段毕业以下 Below High School Graduate	按职称分 By Professional Rank				
	中学高级 Senior Secondary	中学一级 1st Grade	中学二级 2nd Grade	中学三级 3rd Grade	未定职级 No-ranking
19	**27981**	**77321**	**49441**	**2044**	**17563**
	340	819	731	12	247
	307	478	204		56
	1522	4716	2478	53	573
	343	1355	1605	42	369
	170	262	206	1	59
3	2167	1715	589	33	123
	276	641	488	5	125
	1269	2039	830	19	70
	211	902	683	4	149
	2104	4229	2233	3	395
	1748	4813	2478	46	817
1	751	1782	1361	129	457
1	1196	1984	1406	38	281
3	824	1278	868	48	218
	2972	10144	7190	129	1234
	2044	4462	3999	154	945
	1101	2877	1150	86	306
1	1032	3886	1570	55	813
6	3171	17838	8994	743	7651
1	597	1990	724	35	230
	102	245	220		125
	159	562	1035	16	106
	956	2484	2413	34	540
2	363	1095	1090	121	879
	649	1286	816	16	204
	504	1418	1626	92	208
1	170	534	830	51	17
	130	158	95	11	13
	268	410	348		96
	535	919	1181	68	257

初中专任教师学历、

Number of Full-time Teachers in Junior Secondary Schools by

地　区 Region	合计 Total	其中:女 of Which: Female	按学历分 By Academic Qualifications			
			研究生毕业 Graduate	本科毕业 Under- graduate	专科毕业 Associate Bachelor	高中阶段毕业 High School Graduate
总　计 Total	**1703507**	**825693**	**9201**	**1212269**	**468557**	**13037**
北　京 Beijing	5047	3404	187	4690	165	5
天　津 Tianjin	7770	4381	117	6754	806	91
河　北 Hebei	84920	55763	479	62803	21124	510
山　西 Shanxi	56385	35595	280	36273	19346	484
内蒙古 Inner Mongolia	33865	20251	274	25081	8293	182
辽　宁 Liaoning	36834	21551	121	26278	10139	268
吉　林 Jilin	24992	15184	173	18985	5711	121
黑龙江 Heilongjiang	38632	23260	64	28066	10187	310
上　海 Shanghai	6090	3815	288	5539	255	7
江　苏 Jiangsu	91194	39393	758	78999	11135	302
浙　江 Zhejiang	56701	29602	522	51379	4654	144
安　徽 Anhui	78979	28744	461	55675	22453	385
福　建 Fujian	44371	18110	165	35642	8305	257
江　西 Jiangxi	65718	24189	337	41165	23536	653
山　东 Shandong	139207	64093	1377	104890	31780	1123
河　南 Henan	135773	75544	507	82339	51665	1261
湖　北 Hubei	65457	24084	114	39178	25445	695
湖　南 Hunan	84213	37653	481	56103	26034	1523
广　东 Guangdong	120913	59179	289	75542	44010	1040
广　西 Guangxi	73134	34782	208	52496	19740	671
海　南 Hainan	15587	6165	91	10397	4976	123
重　庆 Chongqing	45605	19722	151	36467	8714	264
四　川 Sichuan	112318	48642	304	75978	35637	390
贵　州 Guizhou	59518	22008	146	39262	19651	429
云　南 Yunnan	60041	27779	185	45308	13964	556
西　藏 Tibet	6290	2982	67	5109	1042	59
陕　西 Shaanxi	70684	36705	691	51943	17299	714
甘　肃 Gansu	34318	14453	141	25209	8648	308
青　海 Qinghai	8477	4352	124	6094	2196	62
宁　夏 Ningxia	8636	4160	53	7195	1362	25
新　疆 Xinjiang	31838	20148	46	21430	10285	75

职称情况(镇区)
Academic Qualifications and Professional Rank (Counties & Towns Area)

单位:人
unit: person

高中阶段毕业以下 Below High School Graduate	按职称分 By Professional Rank 中学高级 Senior Secondary	中学一级 1st Grade	中学二级 2nd Grade	中学三级 3rd Grade	未定职级 No-ranking
443	**245738**	**750499**	**572729**	**29391**	**105150**
	803	1987	1871	22	364
2	2478	4164	997	13	118
4	12045	39223	27465	1064	5123
2	3833	18491	26732	1860	5469
35	10126	13992	7808	279	1660
28	15699	13092	6322	538	1183
2	2740	12049	8537	258	1408
5	7434	19774	10096	326	1002
1	544	2932	2304	19	291
	17301	46287	24381	57	3168
2	10382	28138	15850	196	2135
5	12898	29947	26015	2292	7827
2	7603	20070	14989	358	1351
27	16619	25785	19030	1315	2969
37	18636	64298	47958	1364	6951
1	20243	53068	47956	4021	10485
25	8611	38119	14868	1067	2792
72	8031	45558	24581	799	5244
32	7060	65344	31531	4305	12673
19	6046	39459	22990	1296	3343
	2109	6008	6701	200	569
9	4543	17013	21274	570	2205
9	15535	46546	43813	754	5670
30	5732	21240	24484	1632	6430
28	10995	24215	20825	1306	2700
13	199	2043	3250	155	643
37	6660	23908	34271	1618	4227
12	2285	11173	17998	796	2066
1	2016	3340	2411	47	663
1	1309	2773	3129	94	1331
2	5223	10463	12292	770	3090

初中专任教师学历、

Number of Full-time Teachers in Junior Secondary Schools by Academic

地 区 Region	合计 Total	其中:女 of Which: Female	按学历分 By Academic Qualifications			
			研究生毕业 Graduate	本科毕业 Under- graduate	专科毕业 Associate Bachelor	高中阶段毕业 High School Graduate
总 计 Total	**430033**	**214820**	**2540**	**305547**	**118352**	**3502**
北 京 Beijing	1470	960	54	1354	60	2
天 津 Tianjin	2750	1546	24	2381	302	41
河 北 Hebei	37396	24780	248	27400	9521	224
山 西 Shanxi	14249	9570	66	9124	4950	109
内蒙古 Inner Mongolia	2844	1758	6	2064	762	12
辽 宁 Liaoning	5131	3048	15	3674	1396	45
吉 林 Jilin	2595	1437	15	1815	737	28
黑龙江 Heilongjiang	3706	2157	3	2567	1064	72
上 海 Shanghai	1658	1027	30	1546	82	
江 苏 Jiangsu	21423	9531	175	18676	2494	78
浙 江 Zhejiang	18833	9768	149	16997	1641	46
安 徽 Anhui	18390	6646	109	13132	5056	92
福 建 Fujian	10795	4368	23	8857	1857	58
江 西 Jiangxi	12473	4460	99	7485	4744	144
山 东 Shandong	53178	25082	580	40512	11672	397
河 南 Henan	44501	25067	109	26196	17845	350
湖 北 Hubei	14496	5328	20	8852	5470	154
湖 南 Hunan	29672	12961	164	19667	9255	547
广 东 Guangdong	35729	18480	118	22363	12932	307
广 西 Guangxi	13426	6496	49	9636	3595	143
海 南 Hainan	2018	873	58	1488	468	4
重 庆 Chongqing	8516	3783	25	6710	1731	50
四 川 Sichuan	18293	8427	118	12900	5210	65
贵 州 Guizhou	12629	5006	25	8254	4228	121
云 南 Yunnan	14325	7066	40	11009	3143	130
西 藏 Tibet	563	262	4	493	62	3
陕 西 Shaanxi	14420	7702	161	10202	3857	191
甘 肃 Gansu	6726	2843	24	4874	1779	48
青 海 Qinghai	1726	826	16	1190	499	21
宁 夏 Ningxia	1652	801	4	1372	274	2
新 疆 Xinjiang	4450	2761	9	2757	1666	18

职称情况（镇乡结合区）

Qualifications and Professional Rank (County-town Transitional Area)

单位：人
unit：person

高中阶段毕业以下 Below High School Graduate	按职称分 By Professional Rank				
	中学高级 Senior Secondary	中学一级 1st Grade	中学二级 2nd Grade	中学三级 3rd Grade	未定职级 No-ranking
92	**58072**	**191137**	**143525**	**7360**	**29939**
	251	588	566	5	60
2	866	1482	356	1	45
3	5098	16867	12536	445	2450
	1001	4678	6426	536	1608
	920	1124	635	34	131
1	2036	1951	933	66	145
	244	1287	841	30	193
	699	1846	1079	24	58
	205	841	571	3	38
	4195	10612	5701	25	890
	3244	9212	5514	93	770
1	2838	6589	5762	618	2583
	1882	4554	3792	108	459
1	2977	4853	3570	260	813
17	7032	24138	18519	462	3027
1	6280	17444	15777	1382	3618
	1801	8522	3331	205	637
39	2568	16291	8478	319	2016
9	2097	19186	8891	940	4615
3	1064	7153	4519	198	492
	263	713	924	27	91
	812	3016	4116	115	457
	2557	7678	7009	101	948
1	1250	4537	4926	417	1499
3	2762	6145	4736	239	443
1	12	171	330	3	47
9	1320	4901	7080	317	802
1	468	2125	3440	261	432
	394	771	443	11	107
	238	534	675	20	185
	698	1328	2049	95	280

初中专任教师学历、

Number of Full-time Teachers in Junior Secondary Schools by

地　区 Region	合计 Total	其中:女 of Which: Female	按学历分 By Academic Qualifications			
			研究生毕业 Graduate	本科毕业 Under- graduate	专科毕业 Associate Bachelor	高中阶段毕业 High School Graduate
总　计 Total	**731148**	**313873**	**2997**	**479999**	**239529**	**8399**
北　京 Beijing	2509	1600	80	2317	110	2
天　津 Tianjin	3624	1772	29	3129	418	45
河　北 Hebei	35735	20568	157	25182	10075	318
山　西 Shanxi	27255	15256	105	16410	10469	265
内蒙古 Inner Mongolia	5027	2587	48	3322	1533	121
辽　宁 Liaoning	12615	6897	68	8776	3647	110
吉　林 Jilin	15410	8427	40	11800	3475	94
黑龙江 Heilongjiang	19216	9530	30	12756	6051	360
上　海 Shanghai	962	593	37	889	35	
江　苏 Jiangsu	9899	4132	74	8217	1587	21
浙　江 Zhejiang	11525	5919	132	10371	983	38
安　徽 Anhui	47300	14036	218	32610	14080	390
福　建 Fujian	24359	8092	46	19319	4811	181
江　西 Jiangxi	32848	10253	170	19118	13039	498
山　东 Shandong	37900	16108	372	28044	9149	335
河　南 Henan	79738	38442	310	46089	32119	1219
湖　北 Hubei	26001	8923	151	16003	9629	216
湖　南 Hunan	51956	20259	151	31114	19365	1286
广　东 Guangdong	32003	15900	149	18758	12694	396
广　西 Guangxi	24115	10053	48	16202	7589	266
海　南 Hainan	1648	630	2	996	629	21
重　庆 Chongqing	8377	3458	9	6392	1890	84
四　川 Sichuan	46409	17573	61	26199	19944	204
贵　州 Guizhou	37901	12474	41	24101	13363	381
云　南 Yunnan	45327	19527	75	32904	11859	460
西　藏 Tibet	1578	744	11	1329	228	9
陕　西 Shaanxi	13570	6232	209	9201	3935	218
甘　肃 Gansu	35968	12111	79	25250	10025	595
青　海 Qinghai	4081	1671	39	2762	1240	39
宁　夏 Ningxia	3894	1658	17	3064	758	54
新　疆 Xinjiang	32398	18448	39	17375	14800	173

职称情况(乡村)

Academic Qualifications and Professional Rank (Rural Area)

单位:人
unit:person

高中阶段毕业以下 Below High School Graduate	按职称分 By Professional Rank				
	中学高级 Senior Secondary	中学一级 1st Grade	中学二级 2nd Grade	中学三级 3rd Grade	未定职级 No-ranking
224	**83380**	**296278**	**272168**	**18789**	**60533**
	407	975	970	22	135
3	1000	2082	480	7	55
3	4123	16921	12379	336	1976
6	970	7936	13589	1131	3629
3	1238	2132	1236	58	363
14	4941	4158	2799	256	461
1	1218	7136	5793	174	1089
19	2811	9634	6029	183	559
1	92	464	357	4	45
	1411	5044	2938	11	495
1	1484	5711	3666	32	632
2	6685	19130	17348	1085	3052
2	3810	11085	8627	302	535
23	6968	11247	10729	1032	2872
	4818	17645	13319	301	1817
1	10881	31755	28260	2311	6531
2	3254	14368	6412	506	1461
40	3819	27076	15608	565	4888
6	1337	15643	8558	1284	5181
10	1595	13319	7441	546	1214
	215	564	753	23	93
2	573	2468	3998	209	1129
1	4802	17305	19898	453	3951
15	1612	11358	17014	1691	6226
29	5661	15661	18124	2008	3873
1	33	600	838	22	85
7	998	4444	6890	447	791
19	1620	10003	19641	1577	3127
1	836	1745	1234	26	240
1	398	861	1681	76	878
11	3770	7808	15559	2111	3150

初中办

Condition of School Buildings in

地　区 Region	校舍建筑面积 Floor Space	教学及辅助用房 Teaching & Assistant Buildings						
		合计 Total	其中 of Which					
			教室 Classroom	实验室 Laboratory	图书室 Library	微机室 PC-room	语音室 Linguistic	体育馆 Gymnasium
总　计 Total	**500794117**	**210620608**	**150532914**	**29816473**	**10784947**	**9288544**	**3119487**	**7078243**
北　京 Beijing	3656232	1419062	912438	258096	90368	68123	9036	81001
天　津 Tianjin	2417928	1205129	824440	179678	68025	49034	20233	63719
河　北 Hebei	22083442	9724012	6715932	1760948	536434	410917	187723	112058
山　西 Shanxi	14584639	5664516	4127724	713129	322445	269733	110507	120978
内蒙古 Inner Mongolia	8599641	3669820	2518532	477997	214508	151719	77571	229493
辽　宁 Liaoning	12852769	5910103	4030926	854869	297369	313410	120890	292639
吉　林 Jilin	7187547	3393964	2391838	470459	147684	186439	92328	105216
黑龙江 Heilongjiang	10000548	5077565	3723209	645934	191373	216542	118721	181786
上　海 Shanghai	6489747	3304970	1943895	577065	215613	142277	47422	378698
江　苏 Jiangsu	31154721	14723994	9633238	2367149	1043539	718191	177222	784655
浙　江 Zhejiang	24541707	10175651	6319321	1536642	631676	425536	136977	1125499
安　徽 Anhui	21249747	9462315	6959715	1246266	463727	504902	112115	175590
福　建 Fujian	11200976	4530202	2933701	853755	314759	191272	49938	186777
江　西 Jiangxi	17154687	6948340	5363248	762914	312526	281433	110380	117839
山　东 Shandong	37308156	15947251	10632352	2842163	899965	704512	250534	617725
河　南 Henan	39160254	14916020	11321960	1951928	692694	639511	178049	131878
湖　北 Hubei	23735630	8389773	6103107	1157880	429309	398021	158847	142609
湖　南 Hunan	28283665	11376480	8627182	1328697	507199	409690	176556	327156
广　东 Guangdong	44712931	20241280	14498462	2618537	983874	697191	329178	1114038
广　西 Guangxi	18539336	6153465	4734447	751828	243434	259869	58129	105758
海　南 Hainan	3674385	1311615	1011001	144445	66775	54574	17283	17537
重　庆 Chongqing	10565762	4044623	3198269	460816	149294	141509	32760	61975
四　川 Sichuan	29639580	12712903	9755772	1475112	564116	585958	155327	176618
贵　州 Guizhou	15663628	6164907	4707478	802398	277674	271333	53649	52375
云　南 Yunnan	15943683	6084203	4568105	871687	249677	273103	70782	50849
西　藏 Tibet	1922144	553537	429093	60686	16635	19662	8797	18664
陕　西 Shaanxi	13706604	5927193	4152650	989156	297959	301663	128483	57282
甘　肃 Gansu	9318169	4306447	3300831	520367	196032	207238	33944	48035
青　海 Qinghai	2422260	1127661	851417	146534	45841	49064	17713	17092
宁　夏 Ningxia	2752276	1353944	897785	260567	69104	75088	19300	32100
新　疆 Xinjiang	10271323	4799663	3344846	728771	245319	271030	59093	150604

学条件(一)(总计)

Junior Secondary Schools (1) (Total)

单位:平方米

unit:m²

行政办公用房 Administrative		生活用房 Residential and Welfare							其他用房 Rooms for Other Purposes	校舍面积中 of the Floor Space	
			教工宿舍 Apartments for Single								
合计 Total	其中:教师办公室 of Which: for Teachers	合计 Total	小计 Subtotal	其中:教师周转宿舍 of Which: Accommodation for Circulation of Teachers	学生宿舍 Students' Dormitories	食堂 Dining Halls	厕所 Toilet	其他 Others		危房面积 Floor Space of Dilapidated Buildings	当年新增校舍 New Floor Space Added in Current Year
46145315	**29534737**	**207285242**	**52078883**	**8924370**	**92564615**	**35898012**	**14173001**	**12570731**	**36742952**	**16751734**	**20621688**
508100	241611	854215	128345	6566	195193	209258	140087	181332	874855	1550	252056
382193	243220	468028	46178	5797	69066	87164	100832	164788	362578		79238
2131842	1524058	8615970	1209597	212596	4607760	1631081	610278	557254	1611618	6207	939191
1614349	1162888	5982669	938154	79540	3123085	1128637	423465	369328	1323105	99357	511069
1045789	698312	3155004	165842	30638	1742644	665254	267562	313702	729028	96337	359630
1771144	1077604	3257400	142617	33162	1180343	895402	464185	574853	1914122	128109	351419
1018388	666017	2048135	56563	15917	929010	486517	256036	320009	727060	42329	273166
1422296	990961	2540330	87380	27840	1254087	536081	329511	333271	960357	348677	312627
813264	414872	1289287	41206	2984	140743	461853	259341	386144	1082226		250897
3215175	1893105	10853998	1756762	227048	4629051	2809012	798429	860744	2361554		908956
2297155	1342112	9332757	1509616	215216	3957639	2395863	735830	733809	2736144		885619
1958711	1282551	8819077	2601696	292552	3850664	1453259	601825	311633	1009644	311722	746648
1000526	471772	4662585	1695713	226430	1707112	724490	271795	263475	1007663	65705	462356
1269818	753851	8101658	2436414	245869	3642171	1289620	397304	336149	834871	1828207	710350
4121620	2450599	13904094	2920178	586980	5847906	2887158	1325565	923287	3335191	317163	2092770
4188837	3054648	18152792	3720691	433357	9067348	3347274	1279122	738357	1902605	1057368	1245067
1823485	1134997	12055060	5069175	741332	4201015	1648427	515158	621285	1467312	584188	662988
2000800	1398932	13173666	4605657	624180	4939381	2138270	727088	763270	1732719	1125578	505067
3264958	1959387	16578869	6157596	399875	6174683	2012513	1104715	1129362	4627824	79581	1098692
930536	639838	10830175	3338182	619476	5519345	1257021	349713	365914	625160	2174282	702556
190246	109003	1939912	812122	188220	776434	219436	83656	48264	232612	96698	112415
740060	437010	5157004	1347852	286522	2612902	801908	218584	175758	624075	451380	391798
2052329	1304812	13764815	3996339	1108194	6335788	2027665	892754	512269	1109533	1141218	1361161
1008218	614268	7793146	1572673	734226	4601303	1010458	393460	215252	697357	15938	1848222
784283	498885	8617204	2352894	594302	4370973	1249084	372085	272168	457993	4083205	1063302
112830	91464	1128909	455496	329075	487562	119787	30066	35998	126868	655	67910
1760998	1277230	5367048	1579955	222063	2244165	849484	399199	294245	651365	140200	407177
1008909	786086	3546532	708671	123015	1705624	525755	338747	267735	456281	2508254	647924
183512	128935	957146	166070	70921	482013	163674	74755	70634	153941	797	298262
321594	206673	927030	108661	36671	487061	164465	94859	71984	149708	8261	157707
1203350	679036	3410727	350588	203806	1682544	702142	316995	358458	857583	38768	915448

初中办

Condition of School Buildings in Junior Secondary

地区 Region	校舍建筑面积 Floor Space	教学及辅助用房 Teaching & Assistant Buildings						
		合计 Total	其中 of Which					
			教室 Classroom	实验室 Laboratory	图书室 Library	微机室 PC-room	语音室 Linguistic	体育馆 Gymnasium
总　计 Total	**140951367**	**67111017**	**45091099**	**9748348**	**3891290**	**2761007**	**985288**	**4633985**
北　京 Beijing	2140483	864662	576443	134747	53948	39353	4676	55495
天　津 Tianjin	1242366	590894	381124	88196	40825	25001	8357	47391
河　北 Hebei	4627239	2288320	1610881	383920	128859	86891	35792	41977
山　西 Shanxi	3313243	1423784	974026	199283	99112	63964	31083	56316
内蒙古 Inner Mongolia	2935198	1470649	964572	199309	92892	57046	27475	129355
辽　宁 Liaoning	5963006	2803308	1828448	395750	149602	135766	46492	247250
吉　林 Jilin	2804118	1375689	976201	160488	52801	68252	30625	87322
黑龙江 Heilongjiang	3613827	1910987	1345662	244809	69779	73382	42900	134455
上　海 Shanghai	5035472	2555567	1494147	433009	166432	107284	41061	313634
江　苏 Jiangsu	13690234	6878368	4274100	1132312	546988	307946	59689	557333
浙　江 Zhejiang	10606438	4734802	2807676	680548	314196	184869	63434	684079
安　徽 Anhui	4333765	2327309	1629223	339172	111818	102889	31067	113140
福　建 Fujian	2754465	1283622	793417	219003	97859	46366	15597	111380
江　西 Jiangxi	2602390	1253436	897133	151416	61615	48120	25172	69980
山　东 Shandong	12675072	5903836	3712606	1026695	377069	259495	92992	434979
河　南 Henan	8486959	3813814	2738116	594976	190899	147199	52182	90442
湖　北 Hubei	6227227	2811202	2006596	415268	142466	115869	46790	84213
湖　南 Hunan	4409959	2014166	1441849	243666	94703	62337	29899	141712
广　东 Guangdong	21678011	10308491	7100634	1312349	546029	358832	167580	823067
广　西 Guangxi	2539060	1192396	865289	141803	52171	46246	11878	75009
海　南 Hainan	750424	296626	239068	21874	12969	10703	2189	9823
重　庆 Chongqing	2122795	1000030	763067	110636	45158	37467	6237	37465
四　川 Sichuan	4964583	2445054	1803997	294322	125820	97035	36050	87830
贵　州 Guizhou	2023198	939851	687100	123621	51457	43018	8659	25996
云　南 Yunnan	1871226	880399	611854	128014	58358	43354	15749	23070
西　藏 Tibet	168779	56929	40860	8600	3165	3727	577	
陕　西 Shaanxi	2629197	1233245	843783	207563	64918	64625	23790	28566
甘　肃 Gansu	1269306	711553	521133	85185	42823	30029	8804	23579
青　海 Qinghai	311191	169040	120346	24649	7658	9839	3756	2792
宁　夏 Ningxia	852354	472982	291509	102137	27306	23357	5666	23007
新　疆 Xinjiang	2309782	1100006	750239	145028	61595	60746	9070	73328

条件(一)(城区)
Schools (1) (Urban Area)

单位:平方米
unit: m^2

行政办公用房 Administrative		生活用房 Residential and Welfare							其他用房 Rooms for Other Purposes	校舍面积中 of the Floor Space	
合计 Total	其中:教师办公室 of Which: for Teachers	合计 Total	教工宿舍 Apartments for Single 小计 Subtotal	其中:教师周转宿舍 of Which: Accommodation for Circulation of Teachers	学生宿舍 Students' Dormitories	食堂 Dining Halls	厕所 Toilet	其他 Others		危房面积 Floor Space of Dilapidated Buildings	当年新增校舍 New Floor Space Added in Current Year
16173309	**9730833**	**40599826**	**7243161**	**901361**	**15794300**	**8451548**	**4454249**	**4656568**	**17067215**	**1659626**	**5129216**
315417	145145	426761	46397	3559	86727	111577	77009	105051	533643	1550	113290
199630	123975	230118	15796	2024	27073	54172	52801	80276	221724		45719
560500	391310	1263118	110211	6665	667169	221199	122539	142000	515301	3780	77832
433795	308906	874378	129361	9849	406075	155833	98156	84953	581286	21588	161219
430045	261090	704928	59832	2669	304288	127422	93937	119449	329576	2303	101476
868430	479491	1148362	59102	4620	228211	332185	226907	301957	1142906	34082	190759
415077	255254	647303	18151	2826	224278	157070	104900	142904	366049	11135	104993
599350	385209	594989	18612	2744	204516	101373	129505	140983	508501	110365	68769
627555	320614	997727	23311	838	108261	332194	202085	331876	854623		167454
1614530	920166	3849567	334067	35043	1506086	1177777	376114	455523	1347769		463479
1104136	647803	3408001	382431	54352	1366732	1001143	331931	325764	1359499		445139
535530	340607	1048062	173239	12594	455606	186454	137450	95313	422864	15260	205444
299735	137797	769325	211584	54373	263857	133227	78919	81738	401783	13108	186711
253726	149814	801953	188718	24964	298641	168764	79504	66326	293275	66948	89845
1600821	899095	3523610	536994	97001	1334986	839284	457895	354451	1646805	29618	615845
1081504	748553	2888358	481723	65683	1397746	549791	268640	190458	703283	184516	289837
696346	426153	2089892	737199	79953	685972	316565	157487	192669	629787	142342	229896
356196	240457	1684657	420863	80902	679233	329544	133163	121854	354940	75878	69993
1764201	1033399	6699616	2009444	128487	2420652	978899	624303	666318	2905703	25579	413718
217667	144725	953472	228949	42565	465899	133518	61217	63889	175525	81283	152458
48530	27868	347248	130047	30316	144027	32750	24890	15534	58020	10257	5670
219354	132995	650675	98131	10313	317366	133438	55026	46714	252736	28845	29705
456305	277609	1760927	275192	30707	849824	345436	182412	108063	302297	65035	337588
261396	166663	634521	98605	15198	333487	96572	69201	36656	187430	3671	161269
159309	95561	665183	145192	42063	281591	124656	52979	60765	166335	379417	92379
12895	10506	86223	44992	18874	29290	5366	3275	3300	12732		9759
357796	249624	776977	197731	27469	268048	116943	83300	110955	261179	32284	51165
173201	124837	265989	22049	4654	98648	32989	48756	63547	118563	313252	79516
41540	28418	55732	7851	2509	10608	5240	15189	16844	44879		23852
120580	68314	193665	15323	3341	96203	39047	28476	14616	65127	4080	38354
348212	188875	558489	22064	4206	233200	111120	76283	115822	303075	3450	106083

初中办

Condition of School Buildings in

地　区 Region	校舍建筑面积 Floor Space	教学及辅助用房 Teaching & Assistant Buildings						
		合计 Total	其中 of Which					
			教室 Classroom	实验室 Laboratory	图书室 Library	微机室 PC-room	语音室 Linguistic	体育馆 Gymnasium
总　计 Total	**28357296**	**12840138**	**8877349**	**1800803**	**664143**	**517266**	**196269**	**784308**
北　京 Beijing	317231	115245	80474	19112	7622	5301	732	2004
天　津 Tianjin	143257	63044	45545	7733	2182	1821	1084	4679
河　北 Hebei	1235139	584652	421473	94768	27801	23504	9020	8086
山　西 Shanxi	350805	166107	126069	19935	8304	7017	2487	2295
内蒙古 Inner Mongolia	140056	61757	33633	13733	2869	2710	2022	6790
辽　宁 Liaoning	590385	275196	178158	42758	13102	13034	5121	23023
吉　林 Jilin	162303	64342	43169	9257	2474	3774	1712	3956
黑龙江 Heilongjiang	386323	196171	135471	26699	8523	7289	4646	13543
上　海 Shanghai	423539	181463	101006	33916	11761	7721	3869	23190
江　苏 Jiangsu	1685404	825390	530818	134350	52922	41625	9374	56301
浙　江 Zhejiang	2396629	1047320	643120	144128	68993	44395	16819	129865
安　徽 Anhui	774283	389615	264471	53787	23818	18986	4342	24211
福　建 Fujian	548530	214189	135024	32937	16502	8119	3773	17834
江　西 Jiangxi	498023	222600	173474	22844	7924	7477	4574	6307
山　东 Shandong	3573453	1560997	1001315	275968	90038	73726	30588	89362
河　南 Henan	1956770	768849	569750	105274	36738	30199	7369	19519
湖　北 Hubei	852046	345943	265396	38473	13198	13856	5060	9960
湖　南 Hunan	1097260	462638	335498	47244	21808	13212	8868	36008
广　东 Guangdong	7650033	3642492	2588690	453610	170993	118231	53855	257113
广　西 Guangxi	397235	166294	131407	15934	5620	6712	1051	5570
海　南 Hainan	60559	22675	17120	2333	1804	429		989
重　庆 Chongqing	193017	86189	71163	8544	3674	2202	453	153
四　川 Sichuan	929811	437694	329350	47012	24348	17408	8433	11143
贵　州 Guizhou	537335	245144	183372	32251	9701	9389	1820	8611
云　南 Yunnan	330978	152121	103745	25387	8849	9929	2503	1708
西　藏 Tibet								
陕　西 Shaanxi	478429	222320	148872	41602	10149	11584	3786	6327
甘　肃 Gansu	149803	76118	57372	8727	3185	3277	670	2887
青　海 Qinghai	63504	32098	24736	3899	1014	1709	674	66
宁　夏 Ningxia	118393	61160	36651	15399	2137	3019	818	3136
新　疆 Xinjiang	316763	150315	101007	23189	6090	9611	746	9672

学条件(一)(城乡结合区)
Junior Secondary Schools (1) (Urban-rural Transitional Area)

单位:平方米
unit:m^2

行政办公用房 Administrative		生活用房 Residential and Welfare							其他用房 Rooms for Other Purposes	校舍面积中 of the Floor Space	
			教工宿舍 Apartments for Single								
合计 Total	其中:教师办公室 of Which: for Teachers	合计 Total	小计 Subtotal	其中:教师周转宿舍 of Which: Accommodation for Circulation of Teachers	学生宿舍 Students' Dormitories	食堂 Dining Halls	厕所 Toilet	其他 Others		危房面积 Floor Space of Dilapidated Buildings	当年新增校舍 New Floor Space Added in Current Year
2771400	**1648452**	**9864647**	**2005833**	**242712**	**4148207**	**2006715**	**858071**	**845821**	**2881111**	**296241**	**1095283**
45472	20206	75843	9483	1224	15482	15190	10076	25612	80671		11684
19536	9961	21573	2892	831	1831	8285	4114	4451	39104		
124179	94753	427718	40081	3229	234838	88231	33674	30894	98590	3780	26205
47923	36242	107246	13179	193	52740	24263	10256	6808	29529		7670
16545	10747	41735	2165	180	20575	9425	4365	5205	20019		
94649	52777	149624	4462		37313	41426	22625	43798	70916	17039	24727
20283	12489	46774	149		16430	12642	6157	11396	30904		630
48197	34272	89652	1211		40089	19636	10407	18309	52303	4218	17273
53312	23059	109111	1974		22684	40788	19019	24646	79653		19095
182739	105458	541054	80360	11640	225004	155681	42075	37934	136221		130132
224477	121477	848027	107219	13257	345364	248108	69842	77494	276805		51304
68708	54501	260207	51476	3505	114725	63132	20313	10561	55753	5237	42543
60085	30779	186686	55307	12849	70036	30072	14555	16716	87570		9176
46724	24469	196753	51591	4151	79664	32719	14287	18492	31946	5676	21327
420738	228247	1189748	145880	46324	524668	293280	128285	97635	401970	15799	172925
205675	142536	847899	119893	16678	454930	182083	58583	32410	134347	8595	43032
71010	39405	396750	129907	16047	159929	63893	22417	20604	38343	17452	61414
79073	55905	467154	115719	20168	192842	98215	29184	31194	88395	39163	10994
573520	331959	2523386	823583	46822	888092	354172	219222	238317	910635	2500	127157
21140	14387	199368	37123	10146	121599	26933	7309	6404	10433	14248	26674
4995	2722	32369	8066	280	15682	4638	3953	30	520		1500
16209	9364	82355	15333	150	44974	13668	4835	3545	8264	1353	1589
75185	45625	373548	69492	12445	180161	76035	36012	11848	43384	25954	96188
67706	29100	191348	31660	5213	103620	27253	15476	13339	33137	3671	111849
25541	14606	125316	32098	10723	51205	19587	9621	12805	28000	87269	21548
76831	49516	158217	49160	6507	51111	21654	13822	22470	21061	9963	26432
21324	17890	38204	2472		17888	4107	6699	7038	14157	34299	5296
6900	3905	13580	494		5115	3067	3231	1673	10926		5258
16967	9285	26911	240		14614	5992	3276	2789	13355		2488
35757	22810	96491	3164	150	45002	22540	14381	11404	34200	25	19173

初中办
Condition of School Buildings in

地　区 Region	校舍建筑面积 Floor Space	教学及辅助用房 Teaching & Assistant Buildings						
		合计 Total	其中 of Which					
			教室 Classroom	实验室 Laboratory	图书室 Library	微机室 PC-room	语音室 Linguistic	体育馆 Gymnasium
总　计 Total	**244555274**	**97294142**	**71026532**	**13812520**	**4727852**	**4288893**	**1510513**	**1927832**
北　京 Beijing	921975	334532	194572	78813	24859	18654	2477	15157
天　津 Tianjin	757189	401064	293330	59057	18026	15533	7396	7722
河　北 Hebei	12151332	5045245	3524464	882686	279892	209382	100490	48331
山　西 Shanxi	7352679	2829648	2125187	340762	143711	130357	53422	36209
内蒙古 Inner Mongolia	4855263	1884090	1314557	244103	106243	79976	43332	95879
辽　宁 Liaoning	5059438	2277689	1636554	327436	107470	127215	50210	28804
吉　林 Jilin	2611561	1173862	835206	171918	52589	67433	35538	11178
黑龙江 Heilongjiang	4371831	2116244	1583234	278547	80279	87730	53750	32704
上　海 Shanghai	1197181	625299	381566	121208	41236	29637	4977	46675
江　苏 Jiangsu	15489704	6999913	4789241	1092055	445174	363376	106674	203393
浙　江 Zhejiang	11447924	4488907	2867671	711717	265173	195737	61899	386710
安　徽 Anhui	9596992	4041554	2996508	536448	200907	216811	47052	43828
福　建 Fujian	4582162	1830560	1202208	358883	125888	77013	20941	45627
江　西 Jiangxi	8997753	3626740	2846377	383378	163682	143296	56021	33986
山　东 Shandong	19395374	7889061	5444714	1418427	401977	344403	125136	154404
河　南 Henan	19355303	6948323	5406286	830394	306644	287976	80136	36887
湖　北 Hubei	12104890	3811326	2813009	502438	183269	192728	80873	39009
湖　南 Hunan	13810470	5357542	4044136	642544	245858	193203	88681	143120
广　东 Guangdong	17790865	7518607	5566630	1019331	335094	253553	123270	220729
广　西 Guangxi	11608581	3580562	2816215	424545	134383	145837	35341	24241
海　南 Hainan	2595692	906889	689322	111655	45041	39142	14237	7492
重　庆 Chongqing	6686510	2399931	1899056	294637	84609	81846	22622	17161
四　川 Sichuan	15397144	6368056	4836007	796451	281955	300888	78506	74249
贵　州 Guizhou	7467944	2795236	2140932	375744	118628	118747	26683	14502
云　南 Yunnan	7559032	2847543	2180204	395857	102939	119073	32726	16744
西　藏 Tibet	1412809	400293	310693	44079	10857	12856	7216	14592
陕　西 Shaanxi	9132278	3878477	2727169	647679	195781	191331	88887	27630
甘　肃 Gansu	3563550	1605430	1234159	203615	64764	73235	14219	15438
青　海 Qinghai	1324659	583525	437017	77469	24774	22543	8615	13107
宁　夏 Ningxia	1272759	588351	399621	108613	28145	34388	9808	7776
新　疆 Xinjiang	4684430	2139643	1490687	332031	108005	114994	29378	64548

学条件(一)(镇区)

Junior Secondary Schools (1) (Counties & Towns Area)

单位:平方米
unit: m²

行政办公用房 Administrative		生活用房 Residential and Welfare							其他用房 Rooms for Other Purposes	校舍面积中 of the Floor Space	
			教工宿舍 Apartments for Single								
合计 Total	其中:教师办公室 of Which: for Teachers	合计 Total	小计 Subtotal	其中:教师周转宿舍 of Which: Accommodation for Circulation of Teachers	学生宿舍 Students' Dormitories	食堂 Dining Halls	厕所 Toilet	其他 Others		危房面积 Floor Space of Dilapidated Buildings	当年新增 New Floor Space Added in Current Year
20798580	**13517610**	**112743807**	**29116951**	**5098019**	**52964392**	**18887298**	**6444357**	**5330809**	**13718745**	**8298010**	**10300592**
110545	52559	245817	45499	446	60448	54211	42594	43065	231081		75596
122598	76735	146604	17780	2533	29224	24701	31060	43839	86923		7200
1050867	752235	5297127	714978	133282	2909911	1047251	328465	296522	758093		594027
767194	554464	3268041	459517	38212	1808482	619470	204246	176326	487796	50582	292810
527347	371395	2112084	83538	23746	1254353	459722	144495	169976	331742	59322	215238
669339	441139	1600795	62345	23072	758955	415772	173512	190211	511615	71369	137197
352180	238469	845653	20336	8146	447233	188815	87951	101318	239866	14181	88010
569340	403574	1332316	41575	16187	744270	290672	129812	125987	353931	169338	191862
155293	80521	228717	13093	1646	14259	107783	48254	45328	187872		69743
1428335	867293	6182749	1232199	163492	2777811	1462719	369033	340987	878707		410799
986414	577565	4872043	890670	137585	2155178	1163500	333764	328931	1100560		355239
812573	529069	4380430	1217763	146159	2069651	731087	254012	107917	362435	140823	338504
397755	191721	2036453	737809	99580	775304	302541	109295	111504	317394	34883	153370
686803	402456	4347744	1284264	132963	2059168	677232	189113	137967	336466	869316	378891
2022071	1235711	8199678	1915209	435636	3568516	1617373	671250	427330	1284564	253763	1218898
1979895	1424069	9629621	1943432	235024	4971472	1745377	616482	352858	797464	411092	641222
776645	478801	6996517	3110511	431065	2425012	927713	237636	295645	520402	328014	262754
964671	667667	6707140	2409192	318305	2572356	1045518	324902	355172	781117	523542	222637
1129142	683132	7816770	3275431	212063	3008409	807607	352908	372415	1326346	38541	485187
534159	373101	7181775	2220328	375078	3725812	819161	206565	209909	312085	1523242	400627
124955	72781	1420768	612994	133019	556298	169475	53211	28790	143080	69627	96158
411773	244233	3592742	974765	226315	1849087	537009	127812	104069	282064	316285	298694
1059654	680007	7406245	1983165	590649	3623635	1111532	431688	256225	563189	591153	646713
457868	259451	3901789	738684	299357	2390057	494540	176453	102055	313051	5728	876675
357873	233333	4176083	1098912	275162	2167763	614716	171220	123472	177533	1854837	546314
75206	58691	834851	342180	255676	353192	92316	23112	24051	102459	655	44051
1139997	839867	3795182	1124146	158374	1657326	602534	254593	156583	318622	79997	312726
384401	286511	1409548	249711	63876	721427	217663	124598	96149	164171	867536	256447
89540	62367	572842	95187	50670	304691	103900	34387	34677	78752	797	151179
144807	94548	489183	41954	15454	278324	84738	45940	38227	50418	2481	69461
509340	284145	1716500	159784	95247	926768	350650	145994	133304	318947	20906	462363

初中办
Condition of School Buildings in

地 区 Region	校舍建筑面积 Floor Space	教学及辅助用房 Teaching & Assistant Buildings						
		合计 Total	其中 of Which					
			教室 Classroom	实验室 Laboratory	图书室 Library	微机室 PC-room	语音室 Linguistic	体育馆 Gymnasium
总 计 Total	**64405048**	**25657223**	**18682102**	**3662626**	**1276814**	**1101714**	**395480**	**538487**
北 京 Beijing	284539	93027	48457	23701	10257	5751	939	3922
天 津 Tianjin	256250	147000	114028	18816	5921	5451	2362	422
河 北 Hebei	5440443	2215235	1552930	386715	125609	89964	42885	17132
山 西 Shanxi	1908992	751384	562315	90778	38129	32310	14734	13118
内蒙古 Inner Mongolia	461265	195398	133008	22711	17315	6198	4143	12023
辽 宁 Liaoning	760477	344756	249753	51614	13929	16848	5780	6832
吉 林 Jilin	274958	127070	93528	16414	4130	7043	3391	2564
黑龙江 Heilongjiang	390473	189490	143423	24548	6334	6966	3879	4340
上 海 Shanghai	299182	153852	95260	32495	8568	7588	1865	8076
江 苏 Jiangsu	3789944	1694818	1138104	283100	108194	90779	23284	51357
浙 江 Zhejiang	3813186	1501017	981046	248708	93964	65309	22599	89391
安 徽 Anhui	2372934	963867	721093	131949	45844	44772	11337	8872
福 建 Fujian	1182296	456702	291434	86107	35593	16884	5367	21317
江 西 Jiangxi	2086989	852401	674713	79026	38431	35567	11847	12817
山 东 Shandong	7180410	2967780	2005294	557401	154143	129283	50515	71144
河 南 Henan	7176366	2495728	1937924	286814	108524	109144	33373	19949
湖 北 Hubei	2915152	913713	699384	103628	42593	44773	19522	3813
湖 南 Hunan	5021069	1913794	1459693	228559	84621	66429	29886	44606
广 东 Guangdong	5041949	2273199	1681193	279884	109887	80717	35488	86030
广 西 Guangxi	1952507	613728	479661	72805	23102	26851	6393	4916
海 南 Hainan	304377	97683	73834	9463	5370	4631	1429	2956
重 庆 Chongqing	1244649	448648	345720	67499	14223	15724	3608	1874
四 川 Sichuan	2868716	1237027	930857	148771	53932	57550	15245	30672
贵 州 Guizhou	1690325	621476	474112	83259	25534	27517	8693	2361
云 南 Yunnan	1871683	741371	586073	84669	24072	26983	7850	11724
西 藏 Tibet	137711	42618	36410	4111	827	785	420	65
陕 西 Shaanxi	1912026	806057	580406	123451	38091	43438	19093	1578
甘 肃 Gansu	750132	341561	259727	44536	14628	14517	4343	3810
青 海 Qinghai	257999	125639	96450	17417	4154	5313	1722	583
宁 夏 Ningxia	207408	94415	66126	16241	5086	5268	1694	
新 疆 Xinjiang	550641	236769	170146	37436	15809	11361	1794	223

学条件(一)(镇乡结合区)

Junior Secondary Schools (1) (County - town Transitional Area)

单位:平方米

unit:m^2

行政办公用房 Administrative		生活用房 Residential and Welfare							其他用房 Rooms for Other Purposes	校舍面积中 of the Floor Space	
合计 Total	其中:教师办公室 of Which: for Teachers	合计 Total	教工宿舍 Apartments for Single: 小计 Subtotal	教工宿舍 Apartments for Single: 其中:教师周转宿舍 of Which: Accommodation for Circulation of Teachers	学生宿舍 Students' Dormitories	食堂 Dining Halls	厕所 Toilet	其他 Others		危房面积 Floor Space of Dilapidated Buildings	当年新增校舍 New Floor Space Added in Current Year
5563536	**3579472**	**29323573**	**7062003**	**1144243**	**13879823**	**5208450**	**1783111**	**1390186**	**3860716**	**1839125**	**3013059**
31727	15472	90935	12784		26612	21391	11488	18660	68850		7066
45641	26879	46542	7337	1547	6533	5627	10668	16377	17067		1046
463071	332136	2463520	345063	53659	1353269	485221	142874	137093	298617		355548
192492	135989	840933	108404	12708	484912	165974	49148	32495	124183	12748	165249
44411	32363	198253	13138	3490	116010	42464	15213	11428	23203	1194	7126
86926	54437	232031	5557	1600	112937	66735	27382	19420	96764	9523	46660
36814	21413	83444	2026	168	41099	17999	9628	12692	27630	3827	872
54827	38127	119829	3967	2716	62778	26437	13386	13261	26327	43573	16964
41956	21374	54045	2883	457	1421	27463	10454	11824	49329		9091
372499	212300	1482499	313924	40697	603125	368872	90559	106019	240128		62888
337547	201525	1601860	280201	50865	734368	383968	107610	95713	372762		160283
188787	121257	1137509	301629	46558	537637	197065	67417	33761	82771	27047	110179
100980	46209	525155	184136	26835	207824	74877	31506	26812	99459	3770	60214
133258	79333	1028292	244681	25015	537263	164143	47786	34419	73038	165488	82724
716221	428676	3011361	652151	140438	1351052	608699	250584	148875	485048	103424	434261
737900	522777	3606135	659830	98622	1906199	671330	239815	128961	336603	179878	318442
189635	114412	1690221	691054	115384	640764	234749	61661	61993	121583	59937	72011
349779	242239	2444022	818267	99748	1010644	382925	115841	116345	313474	195430	65987
361198	218340	1946404	792520	37797	698659	234798	120125	100302	461148	4460	151760
90700	65048	1201870	337145	36284	649692	145672	35858	33503	46209	268456	67079
11295	7023	169560	56205	10723	78612	19200	7542	8001	25839		850
77397	51369	662239	159487	39369	358742	109240	21586	13184	56365	51392	60524
205350	129859	1318741	330835	108055	636335	220331	84367	46873	107598	104721	163360
120792	63175	867774	136707	57323	542534	119764	42290	26479	80283		248940
106443	72824	969750	238031	52101	491356	158020	48666	33677	54119	425881	105875
3922	2935	81228	42280	11210	26980	8373	1221	2374	9943		3292
264587	191776	761506	222757	33957	320411	129391	52554	36393	79876	15129	61668
91179	66141	282126	46437	6876	135748	45454	33551	20936	35266	162157	77526
21212	16030	107667	14243	8537	54857	15331	8360	14876	3481		30309
24474	15998	81428	6603	3723	48327	15522	5681	5295	7091	140	11590
60516	32036	216694	31721	17781	103123	41415	18290	22145	36662	950	53675

初中办

Condition of School Buildings in

地 区 Region	校舍建筑面积 Floor Space	教学及辅助用房 Teaching & Assistant Buildings						
		合计 Total	其中 of Which					
			教室 Classroom	实验室 Laboratory	图书室 Library	微机室 PC-room	语音室 Linguistic	体育馆 Gymnasium
总 计 Total	**115287476**	**46215449**	**34415283**	**6255605**	**2165805**	**2238644**	**623686**	**516426**
北 京 Beijing	593774	219868	141423	44536	11561	10116	1883	10349
天 津 Tianjin	418373	213171	149986	32425	9174	8500	4480	8606
河 北 Hebei	5304871	2390447	1580587	494342	127683	114644	51441	21750
山 西 Shanxi	3918717	1411084	1028511	173084	79622	75412	26002	28453
内蒙古 Inner Mongolia	809180	315081	239403	34585	15373	14697	6764	4259
辽 宁 Liaoning	1830325	829106	565924	131683	40297	50429	24188	16585
吉 林 Jilin	1771868	844413	580431	138053	42294	50754	26165	6716
黑龙江 Heilongjiang	2014890	1050334	794313	122578	41315	55430	22071	14627
上 海 Shanghai	257094	124104	68182	22848	7945	5356	1384	18389
江 苏 Jiangsu	1974783	845713	569897	142782	51377	46869	10859	23929
浙 江 Zhejiang	2487345	951942	643974	144377	52307	44930	11644	54710
安 徽 Anhui	7318990	3093452	2333984	370646	151002	185202	33996	18622
福 建 Fujian	3864349	1416020	938076	275869	91012	67893	13400	29770
江 西 Jiangxi	5554544	2068164	1619738	228120	87229	90017	29187	13873
山 东 Shandong	5237710	2154354	1475032	397041	120919	100614	32406	28342
河 南 Henan	11317992	4153883	3177558	526558	195151	204336	45731	4549
湖 北 Hubei	5403513	1767245	1283502	240174	103574	89424	31184	19387
湖 南 Hunan	10063236	4004772	3141197	442487	166638	154150	57976	42324
广 东 Guangdong	5244055	2414182	1831198	286857	102751	84806	38328	70242
广 西 Guangxi	4391695	1380507	1052943	185480	56880	67786	10910	6508
海 南 Hainan	328269	108100	82611	10916	8765	4729	857	222
重 庆 Chongqing	1756457	644662	536146	55543	19527	22196	3901	7349
四 川 Sichuan	9277853	3899793	3115768	384339	156341	188035	40771	14539
贵 州 Guizhou	6172486	2429820	1879446	303033	107589	109568	18307	11877
云 南 Yunnan	6513425	2356261	1776047	347816	88380	110676	22307	11035
西 藏 Tibet	340556	96315	77540	8007	2613	3079	1004	4072
陕 西 Shaanxi	1945129	815471	581698	133914	37260	45707	15806	1086
甘 肃 Gansu	4485313	1989464	1545539	231567	88445	103974	10921	9018
青 海 Qinghai	786410	375096	294054	44416	13409	16682	5342	1193
宁 夏 Ningxia	627163	292611	206655	49817	13653	17343	3826	1317
新 疆 Xinjiang	3277111	1560014	1103920	251712	75719	95290	20645	12728

学条件(一)(乡村)
Junior Secondary Schools (1) (Rural Area)

单位:平方米
unit:m²

行政办公用房 Administrative		生活用房 Residential and Welfare							其他用房 Rooms for Other Purposes	校舍面积中 of the Floor Space	
合计 Total	其中:教师办公室 of Which: for Teachers	合计 Total	教工宿舍 Apartments for Single 小计 Subtotal	教工宿舍 Apartments for Single 其中:教师周转宿舍 of Which: Accommodation for Circulation of Teachers	学生宿舍 Students' Dormitories	食堂 Dining Halls	厕所 Toilet	其他 Others		危房面积 Floor Space of Dilapidated Buildings	当年新增 New Floor Space Added in Current Year
9173426	**6286294**	**53941609**	**15718771**	**2924990**	**23805923**	**8559166**	**3274395**	**2583354**	**5956992**	**6794098**	**5191880**
82138	43907	181637	36449	2561	48018	43470	20484	33216	110131		63170
59965	42510	91306	12602	1240	12769	8291	16971	40673	53931		26319
520475	380513	2055725	384408	72649	1030680	362631	159274	118732	338224	2427	267332
413360	299518	1840250	349276	31479	908528	353334	121063	108049	254023	27187	57040
88397	65827	337992	22472	4223	184003	78110	29130	24277	67710	34712	42916
233375	156974	508243	21170	5470	193177	147445	63766	82685	259601	22658	23463
251131	172294	555179	18076	4945	257499	140632	63185	75787	121145	17013	80163
253606	202178	613025	27193	8909	305301	144036	70194	66301	97925	68974	51996
30416	13737	62843	4802	500	18223	21876	9002	8940	39731		13700
172310	105646	821682	190496	28513	345154	168516	53282	64234	135078		34678
206605	116744	1052713	236515	23279	435729	231220	70135	79114	276085		85241
610608	412875	3390585	1210694	133799	1325407	535718	210363	108403	224345	155639	202700
303036	142254	1856807	746320	72477	667951	288722	83581	70233	288486	17714	122275
329289	201581	2951961	963432	87942	1284362	443624	128687	131856	205130	891943	241614
498728	315793	2180806	467975	54343	944404	430501	196420	141506	403822	33782	258027
1127438	882026	5634813	1295536	132650	2698130	1052106	394000	195041	401858	461760	314008
350494	230043	2968651	1221465	230314	1090031	404149	120035	132971	317123	113832	170338
679933	490808	4781869	1775602	224973	1687792	763208	269023	286244	596662	526158	212437
371615	242856	2062483	872721	59325	745622	226007	127504	90629	395775	15461	199787
178710	122012	2694928	888905	201833	1327634	304342	81931	92116	137550	569757	149471
16761	8354	171896	69081	24885	76109	17211	5555	3940	31512	16814	10587
108933	59782	913587	274956	49894	446449	131461	35746	24975	89275	106250	63399
536370	347196	4597643	1737982	486838	1862329	570697	278654	147981	244047	485030	376860
288954	188154	3256836	735384	419671	1877759	419346	147806	76541	196876	6539	810278
267101	169991	3775938	1108790	277077	1921619	509712	147886	87931	114125	1848951	424609
24729	22267	207835	68324	54525	105080	22105	3679	8647	11677		14100
263205	187739	794889	258078	36220	318791	130007	61306	26707	71564	27919	43286
451307	374738	1870995	436911	54485	885549	275103	165393	108039	173547	1327466	311961
52432	38150	328572	63032	17742	166714	54534	25179	19113	30310		123231
56207	43811	244182	51384	17876	112534	40680	20443	19141	34163	1700	49892
345798	206016	1135738	168740	104353	522576	240372	94718	109332	235561	14412	347002

初中办

Condition of School Buildings in

地 区 Region	占地面积(平方米) Areas of School Sites (m^2) 合计 Total	其中 of Which 绿化用地面积 Green Areas	运动场地面积 Sports Areas	图书(册) Books & Magazines in Libraries (volume)	计算机数 No. of Computers 合计 Total	其中:教学 of Which: No. of Used for 小计 Subtotal
总 计 Total	**1516915508**	**294026542**	**404381041**	**1253642999**	**5444028**	**4403086**
北 京 Beijing	9833993	1817438	3386118	9369952	80089	65539
天 津 Tianjin	8554496	934512	3086674	9107917	40747	31972
河 北 Hebei	72519051	8068023	22372895	71495725	237725	196452
山 西 Shanxi	41366205	4233762	11278378	32276471	133230	110437
内蒙古 Inner Mongolia	34871122	4652235	10067773	16956526	68914	52245
辽 宁 Liaoning	45674104	6198152	18678161	39458943	223244	168203
吉 林 Jilin	33018212	5993564	11256560	16520386	85713	62223
黑龙江 Heilongjiang	46282342	6213510	16620406	19166712	123929	98170
上 海 Shanghai	11970690	3626023	3610432	22722717	145279	122973
江 苏 Jiangsu	87471440	24959141	24709503	75243103	444375	338249
浙 江 Zhejiang	55134504	14790404	16570020	61253305	368211	316860
安 徽 Anhui	79527758	11525106	16867638	52757568	210663	168221
福 建 Fujian	31550169	8093465	8636831	27098808	117056	93469
江 西 Jiangxi	56990361	10185952	12610676	35765586	128901	101980
山 东 Shandong	128926974	28668629	38839815	109798695	551795	436808
河 南 Henan	114343680	13570430	25874312	95032550	290868	246798
湖 北 Hubei	63113991	20075854	14382366	57276600	198017	172227
湖 南 Hunan	88118475	15822060	17407693	65972679	205451	170219
广 东 Guangdong	114101442	30474202	31259049	110296831	494311	405884
广 西 Guangxi	51867131	9655653	9712926	36571139	133564	101738
海 南 Hainan	16977784	3879888	3317073	7531621	31421	25880
重 庆 Chongqing	22134565	4476327	5766593	14644119	88686	67753
四 川 Sichuan	67731414	12000923	20003046	76441838	284715	225030
贵 州 Guizhou	44669317	9341158	12463519	46870554	137743	115968
云 南 Yunnan	50637106	10596545	8888950	35031639	144585	119140
西 藏 Tibet	6149991	691737	822196	2628335	11823	8833
陕 西 Shaanxi	36427833	5040877	9806617	44016045	155353	130672
甘 肃 Gansu	29846419	3965910	8406915	25530405	112682	92264
青 海 Qinghai	7775286	784739	2138067	6924423	32196	26587
宁 夏 Ningxia	10091983	1843518	2941317	6187691	39873	30165
新 疆 Xinjiang	49237670	11846805	12598522	23694116	122869	100127

学条件(二)(总计)

Junior Secondary Schools (2) (Total)

(台) (set) 用计算机 Computers Instruction	教室(间): Classroom(room)		教室中:普通教室(间) of Which: General Classroom		固定资产总值(万元) Total Volue of Fixed Asset (10,000 yuan)		
						其中:教学仪器设备资产值 of Which: Total Volue of Equip & Instru.	
其中:平板电脑 of Which: Tablet PC	合计 Total	其中:网络多媒体教室 of Which: Network Multimedia Classroom	合计 Total	其中:网络多媒体教室 of Which: Network Multimedia Classroom	合计 Total	小计 Subtotal	其中:实验设备 of Which: for Profession
179595	**1494000**	**621389**	**1170499**	**531718**	**51235003.07**	**5778797.33**	**2127300.15**
717	12123	9209	7531	6452	609871.63	166356.22	17452.16
1461	9086	4180	6181	3488	349049.41	52589.21	17752.53
8853	90870	30856	62351	27193	2009557.58	215826.05	101940.52
1631	43948	15134	33575	13304	1401340.23	123936.16	58113.40
2	23102	7686	19118	7169	1087721.59	83381.30	32855.54
11604	49918	19977	38518	17026	1375781.86	229782.09	79809.65
1480	26131	7160	20928	5860	668236.92	85724.64	41517.33
1964	41123	12113	31707	10637	1010803.74	137159.28	54560.18
2719	21900	18133	15476	13730	1240675.26	226856.60	56883.47
12739	80158	51428	55333	40805	4475723.38	493825.63	150436.77
8565	59701	49010	44296	41152	3072866.37	334902.33	92165.09
11897	75257	25010	60735	22551	2189172.46	179301.89	76079.34
107	27466	12441	19722	9833	1041420.65	122124.50	44306.09
7062	43883	12520	37756	11672	1194762.56	121671.23	51788.09
13076	110470	70893	83249	58994	4169658.19	434378.43	114721.33
7742	137834	41766	112352	36631	2978123.03	248307.11	116172.41
11178	51162	27928	39303	25036	2085413.42	256629.85	107193.34
11658	57086	15977	54074	14246	2126885.09	224566.14	108849.24
32753	117421	62745	96148	52252	5024986.00	671441.00	264966.00
1968	39677	18523	35411	18195	1261066.81	138269.77	66667.43
2838	8970	2029	7102	1878	450009.11	41414.55	18745.69
3191	21433	11966	17656	10781	871784.34	92232.65	29409.18
1576	106260	24049	88070	21052	3134493.96	356107.40	121049.62
6731	53182	11768	43387	11176	1387286.85	127460.49	56510.48
2848	39861	13710	34978	12349	1518837.40	120426.96	47384.95
344	2853	401	2503	285	267504.57	13246.05	3853.51
4385	46910	12206	36063	9762	1312459.00	154728.33	83040.35
6165	43207	10070	25932	8593	1011172.94	102419.97	41960.40
1312	8185	2600	6558	2120	387353.62	27268.83	9644.38
793	8180	3025	6315	2394	384232.53	49719.71	16774.52
236	36643	16876	28171	15102	1136752.57	146742.96	44697.15

初中办

Condition of School Buildings in

地 区 Region	占地面积(平方米) Areas of School Sites (m^2)			图书(册) Books & Magazines in Libraries (volume)	计算机数 No. of Computer	
	合计 Total	其中 of Which			合计 Total	其中:教学 of Which: No. of Used for
		绿化用地面积 Green Areas	运动场地面积 Sports Areas			小计 Subtotal
总 计 Total	**321018052**	**69729025**	**98425400**	**366287680**	**2002450**	**1597213**
北 京 Beijing	4640421	692489	1806705	5689495	50212	41150
天 津 Tianjin	3162831	334626	1111462	4552187	22737	16977
河 北 Hebei	10947688	1386407	3622661	15571646	64638	53040
山 西 Shanxi	7408632	823010	2236387	8039423	36461	29222
内蒙古 Inner Mongolia	7660586	1022575	2589166	6141204	27596	21082
辽 宁 Liaoning	15767183	2093798	7162415	20196759	119401	87350
吉 林 Jilin	6559429	1013451	2732126	6480972	35044	24393
黑龙江 Heilongjiang	10583081	1375851	4086872	6410357	53748	41153
上 海 Shanghai	7852668	2229150	2401887	17046660	113507	96472
江 苏 Jiangsu	31079615	9342234	9472102	32294981	203666	155751
浙 江 Zhejiang	20280638	5931153	5867443	24288700	157230	135941
安 徽 Anhui	10778499	1890921	2684257	10086091	54184	41973
福 建 Fujian	6002984	1400227	1789946	7876800	37881	30172
江 西 Jiangxi	6535968	1198184	1555238	5470133	28469	22415
山 东 Shandong	34470112	7839744	11136459	41279041	221154	174799
河 南 Henan	20037499	2962865	5176535	18986166	86672	70950
湖 北 Hubei	13408984	4119282	3729049	18504573	68038	58466
湖 南 Hunan	11094904	1982823	2445854	8946709	41428	32354
广 东 Guangdong	43603115	11915117	12050801	52772556	293208	237157
广 西 Guangxi	6179263	1367909	1563140	5198867	29009	20844
海 南 Hainan	1607128	344406	388019	1697063	7592	6124
重 庆 Chongqing	3975757	903271	1124089	3805203	25109	20063
四 川 Sichuan	9540946	1948809	3380345	11940954	61680	51119
贵 州 Guizhou	4058204	673647	1209823	6697396	25835	20974
云 南 Yunnan	4438206	1175528	1262660	4692803	23996	19028
西 藏 Tibet	562142	115559	90534	226200	1442	904
陕 西 Shaanxi	5493020	860802	1662137	8791170	35760	28924
甘 肃 Gansu	2819830	455096	1020841	3712368	20549	15848
青 海 Qinghai	965156	160960	315811	1048772	7661	5600
宁 夏 Ningxia	2793514	597541	851185	2109964	14897	10814
新 疆 Xinjiang	6710049	1571590	1899451	5732467	33646	26154

学条件(二)(城区)
Junior Secondary Schools (2) (Urban Area)

(台)(set) 用计算机 Computers Instruction	教室(间): Classroom(room)		教室中:普通教室(间) of Which: General Classroom(room)		固定资产总值(万元) Total Value of Fixed Asset (10,000 yuan)		
其中:平板电脑 of Which: Tablet PC	合计 Total	其中:网络多媒体教室 of Which: Network Multimedia Classroom	合计 Total	其中:网络多媒体教室 of Which: Network Multimedia Classroom	合计 Total	其中:教学仪器设备资产值 of Which: Total Volue of Equip & Instru. 小计 Subtotal	其中:实验设备 of Which: for Profession
64884	**427307**	**253588**	**329812**	**213341**	**18464113.51**	**2459937.56**	**731025.40**
530	7432	5755	4771	4096	373048.82	103498.31	9736.78
1022	3987	2538	2870	2201	205533.48	32290.53	9423.23
1454	14369	7941	11775	7171	452294.03	60446.25	21525.91
336	9421	4590	7477	4070	406131.04	40999.23	15633.83
2	7818	3531	6548	3367	356744.63	34336.21	11858.15
5733	21603	12343	16833	10595	707240.59	141493.67	40313.34
771	9464	4165	7756	3568	312753.68	41771.39	15970.96
620	13810	5706	10765	5114	369298.93	54604.90	18998.52
2024	16996	14116	11952	10626	969025.78	179864.30	40412.21
4734	36005	26384	24208	20312	2480025.93	269078.35	72402.73
5597	25956	21276	19360	17508	1429113.23	157527.58	38882.97
2982	15855	6089	12614	5399	589045.92	56201.21	21582.77
22	7882	5124	5918	4168	325983.72	47610.28	12438.16
1886	7799	3608	6504	3286	276563.75	30795.76	10155.84
5080	39084	29332	28342	23960	1763848.05	195051.61	38150.82
3311	27600	13027	23194	11628	786299.57	80651.85	32851.23
3655	16911	9471	12897	8407	700314.07	99557.34	37562.56
2188	11693	5286	8741	4323	495003.45	50178.61	20455.60
17698	62199	41620	49458	35013	2815957.00	445633.00	155648.00
449	7952	3205	6950	3285	222389.01	28830.14	12291.96
546	1882	490	1740	494	90884.69	10284.11	3601.50
387	5039	3763	4007	3298	245630.53	27065.90	6646.86
550	17514	6925	13695	6200	663607.50	98294.46	26230.82
559	8771	2367	7238	2117	232978.33	24439.79	8763.28
724	5532	2783	4714	2495	216847.23	23554.15	6758.85
	300	102	254	36	21571.07	3328.48	379.27
962	8660	3072	6626	2525	296877.88	35814.67	15974.45
1006	4160	2010	3450	1992	161249.23	20186.63	5582.52
	1073	725	849	652	54665.30	4182.34	2097.88
13	2506	1278	2035	1100	142026.19	20942.90	6531.73
43	8034	4966	6271	4335	301160.88	41423.62	12162.67

初中办

Condition of School Buildings in

地 区 Region	占地面积(平方米) Areas of School Sites (m²) 合计 Total	其中 of Which 绿化用地面积 Green Areas	其中 of Which 运动场地面积 Sports Areas	图书(册) Books & Magazines in Libraries (volume)	计算机数 No. of Computer 合计 Total	其中:教学 of Which: No. of Used for 小计 Subtotal
总 计 Total	**75618767**	**17248138**	**21424111**	**69371395**	**348631**	**281785**
北 京 Beijing	1004523	167828	378098	835017	6507	5592
天 津 Tianjin	356262	35279	118340	414047	2375	1478
河 北 Hebei	3301695	407017	1133207	4453022	15655	13052
山 西 Shanxi	1045576	109785	331452	992835	4097	3373
内蒙古 Inner Mongolia	428636	43735	131585	166008	927	763
辽 宁 Liaoning	1992115	280551	850135	1899754	10711	8168
吉 林 Jilin	553000	112807	199170	274483	2055	1076
黑龙江 Heilongjiang	1556264	204648	557542	728398	4964	3401
上 海 Shanghai	806953	234314	226136	1107996	6845	5643
江 苏 Jiangsu	4754811	1458864	1391456	4004587	24427	18852
浙 江 Zhejiang	4940439	1338237	1395963	5284751	32266	27305
安 徽 Anhui	2279524	449569	488647	1487793	6664	5070
福 建 Fujian	1492387	384518	447747	1381824	6222	5047
江 西 Jiangxi	1576717	231160	328496	809009	3607	2820
山 东 Shandong	12087730	2975968	3534764	10240246	52320	41252
河 南 Henan	5569646	838158	1428407	3707309	15043	12016
湖 北 Hubei	2375237	732451	558464	2032342	6900	5748
湖 南 Hunan	3074900	468540	619293	2290834	8336	6805
广 东 Guangdong	17237667	4859561	4691537	18365967	97404	81174
广 西 Guangxi	1113392	203694	295169	853417	3494	2721
海 南 Hainan	279020	43705	46931	110291	784	728
重 庆 Chongqing	514060	87550	115493	305342	1853	1416
四 川 Sichuan	2164514	600439	650836	1934887	10462	8143
贵 州 Guizhou	1033109	185037	297429	1479567	5296	4545
云 南 Yunnan	757867	165986	237631	881984	3972	3158
西 藏 Tibet						
陕 西 Shaanxi	1200498	170931	383427	1644306	5499	4729
甘 肃 Gansu	300329	41315	117494	485230	1795	1420
青 海 Qinghai	156839	40822	66393	172873	1659	1389
宁 夏 Ningxia	405983	126516	140274	284061	2247	1693
新 疆 Xinjiang	1259074	249153	262595	743215	4245	3208

学条件(二)(城乡结合区)

Junior Secondary Schools (2) (Urban-rural Transitional Area)

(台) (set) 用计算机 Computers Instruction	教室(间): Classroom(room)		教室中:普通教室(间) of Which: General Classroom(room)		固定资产总值(万元) Total Value of Fixed Asset (10,000 yuan)		
其中:平板电脑 of Which: Tablet PC	合计 Total	其中:网络多媒体教室 of Which: Network Multimedia Classroom	合计 Total	其中:网络多媒体教室 of Which: Network Multimedia Classroom	合计 Total	其中:教学仪器设备资产值 of Which: Total Value of Equip & Instru. 小计 Subtotal	其中:实验设备 of Which: for Profession
14319	85419	47073	66200	40241	3625060.84	424538.45	147417.45
115	1049	700	589	513	44381.06	12894.11	1630.50
147	370	284	269	233	21506.14	3302.71	1032.31
501	4282	2197	3555	1999	129259.98	13721.21	5219.10
171	1041	409	790	328	38190.54	3502.20	1900.94
	301	107	257	86	17354.22	764.17	280.00
946	2345	1011	1649	770	77442.07	11023.53	4943.56
57	486	200	379	170	24603.95	1600.89	519.37
126	1246	499	1013	454	34237.21	5566.67	2584.70
	1239	962	823	772	78982.91	12257.34	3510.54
645	4773	3234	3199	2525	316433.83	30393.88	10255.21
971	5944	4564	4657	3898	362146.72	30996.74	9597.66
417	2639	879	1992	756	94744.91	7429.88	2849.24
3	1425	737	1023	594	62510.53	7753.24	2523.65
347	1305	396	1083	360	64302.19	5592.39	1354.85
835	10637	7359	7560	5891	515406.06	43626.59	10588.66
207	6275	2192	5070	1905	180509.96	13186.92	5994.20
338	2321	1186	1730	992	87181.21	10587.57	4173.47
274	2371	853	2229	831	92702.26	10916.49	4910.60
7295	23356	14618	18582	12892	960927.00	150202.00	56586.00
6	1220	588	1125	536	34880.20	5163.28	2067.42
37	156	73	134	62	16335.50	1099.00	401.00
56	454	235	382	268	14367.36	2027.66	557.11
66	3149	1182	2366	1057	129638.36	15059.37	3848.06
279	2213	497	1869	467	54011.25	4869.31	2105.05
282	978	533	862	511	40454.64	4328.78	1958.05
168	1554	399	1067	260	43065.02	5310.09	2644.24
30	383	239	454	309	21955.64	2325.84	872.47
	250	144	191	124	11919.10	877.80	403.60
	449	128	356	113	17750.88	2578.47	540.49
	1208	668	945	565	37860.14	5580.32	1565.40

初中办

Condition of School Buildings in

地 区 Region	占地面积(平方米) Areas of School Sites (m^2) 合计 Total	其中 of Which 绿化用地面积 Green Areas	运动场地面积 Sports Areas	图书(册) Books & Magazines in Libraries (volume)	计算机数 No. of Computer 合计 Total	其中:教学 of Which: No. of Used for 小计 Subtotal
总 计 Total	**765260389**	**148704065**	**198506931**	**593967687**	**2365703**	**1925934**
北 京 Beijing	2972079	661216	983537	2368377	19568	15960
天 津 Tianjin	3090115	358409	1204018	2932705	11189	9562
河 北 Hebei	38997843	4193957	11498538	37508425	119311	98969
山 西 Shanxi	19781562	1992800	5300403	15566737	61008	50897
内蒙古 Inner Mongolia	20926648	2658018	5751156	9181281	35643	26819
辽 宁 Liaoning	20722099	2620528	7959105	13869220	74522	58171
吉 林 Jilin	13607442	2692882	4541731	5625549	28923	21700
黑龙江 Heilongjiang	21384140	3115358	7347804	8781710	47452	37628
上 海 Shanghai	3367375	1126835	1020340	4825828	26920	22304
江 苏 Jiangsu	49097902	13635063	13288358	38086157	213271	161936
浙 江 Zhejiang	27896899	7219335	8560849	30297974	172902	149267
安 徽 Anhui	35313477	5102337	7609089	23595874	88673	70577
福 建 Fujian	13199762	3404100	3507745	10815019	43137	34429
江 西 Jiangxi	29455737	5495260	6365040	18873105	62869	50499
山 东 Shandong	71158850	15499097	20939810	53921110	257045	206761
河 南 Henan	54825836	6352197	12271697	45545910	128478	109878
湖 北 Hubei	33886857	10970181	7252854	26938854	86896	75866
湖 南 Hunan	42618027	8327627	8320055	31443044	91695	75894
广 东 Guangdong	51991116	13850573	14386833	43666451	151983	127370
广 西 Guangxi	32311856	5864047	5921230	22708744	74706	57211
海 南 Hainan	13230421	3013501	2570790	5154332	21173	17662
重 庆 Chongqing	14191347	2870091	3618396	8441188	50045	37615
四 川 Sichuan	35848560	6956007	10537266	38910713	143499	112186
贵 州 Guizhou	22705823	4920147	6073973	22579143	61594	52256
云 南 Yunnan	23699735	4805310	4096741	15911027	64077	53282
西 藏 Tibet	4569209	532633	580303	1960702	8467	6525
陕 西 Shaanxi	24424439	3346527	6406523	29367611	99470	85158
甘 肃 Gansu	10095717	1310780	2897052	9157672	38653	31952
青 海 Qinghai	4132090	366788	1090451	3398961	14833	12703
宁 夏 Ningxia	4425181	719001	1246059	2563741	16438	12642
新 疆 Xinjiang	21332245	4723460	5359185	9970523	51263	42255

学条件(二)(镇区)

Junior Secondary Schools (2) (Counties & Towns Area)

(台) (set) 用计算机 Computers Instruction 其中:平板电脑 of Which: Tablet PC	教室(间): Classroom(room) 合计 Total	其中:网络多媒体教室 of Which: Network Multimedia Classroom	教室中:普通教室(间) of Which: General Classroom(room) 合计 Total	其中:网络多媒体教室 of Which: Network Multimedia Classroom	固定资产总值(万元) Total Value of Fixed Asset (10,000 yuan) 合计 Total	其中:教学仪器设备资产值 of Which: Total Value of Equip & Instru. 小计 Subtotal	其中:实验设备 of Which: for Profession
79277	**699302**	**269062**	**539863**	**233344**	**23489628.51**	**2336719.33**	**963601.37**
57	3055	2371	1875	1641	158688.91	41244.78	5115.52
311	3044	1063	2023	856	92930.64	12586.53	4350.94
4655	52691	17111	33256	15098	1130207.30	107269.29	53247.38
618	21269	7558	16842	6791	676524.69	57197.82	27719.19
	12549	3758	10280	3400	648327.08	43585.43	17977.63
3431	20376	5496	15600	4621	482094.48	63575.40	27657.90
381	8872	1874	6921	1472	211269.21	26922.41	15328.78
855	17055	5069	12950	4455	469881.74	65812.37	26853.97
690	4072	3340	2963	2615	232186.02	37941.38	13944.29
7087	38644	22356	27483	18353	1787790.52	200724.65	68833.71
2553	27117	22469	20038	19155	1394324.50	148100.47	44214.17
5066	32934	11167	26713	10231	996121.68	72340.03	32116.39
55	10674	4166	7768	3359	403807.05	41496.51	18155.26
3645	22058	6406	19224	6287	609070.96	59027.17	26612.41
5953	54917	33349	42316	28108	1937987.56	190353.90	60330.37
2932	67248	19256	55386	16836	1496400.35	109649.38	53258.38
5682	23041	12862	17775	11663	944553.03	102824.41	47208.23
5275	25001	7040	21256	6287	1035910.96	109099.29	54003.23
11878	41156	16581	34721	13371	1709794.00	167143.00	82443.00
1095	22714	11637	20488	11413	751562.86	76110.37	40026.19
2042	5686	1377	4682	1265	317018.74	27587.03	13418.52
2414	12825	6551	10664	6065	504808.26	52015.02	18781.85
835	51068	12562	41732	10961	1717585.12	178824.40	62900.42
3089	23312	6124	19264	6064	706381.09	58594.49	25501.85
1204	17619	6198	15557	5652	710540.15	50064.69	19960.75
344	2173	233	1925	195	201761.20	8429.66	2970.77
3028	31634	8029	24385	6399	862737.69	102895.25	58006.96
3141	24448	4518	8725	3447	370137.09	30679.69	13897.98
647	3826	1268	3139	1009	236188.84	16111.12	5174.14
235	3556	1215	2734	902	171579.77	21323.66	7017.56
79	14668	6058	11178	5373	521457.02	57189.73	16573.62

初中办

Condition of School Buildings in

地 区 Region	占地面积(平方米) Areas of School Sites (m^2)			图书(册) Books & Magazines in Libraries (volume)	计算机数 No. of Computer	
	合计 Total	其中 of Which			合计 Total	其中:教学 of Which: No. of Used for
		绿化用地面积 Green Areas	运动场地面积 Sports Areas			小计 Subtotal
总 计 Total	**197622498**	**38178189**	**50673898**	**156449794**	**615614**	**504062**
北 京 Beijing	868357	178685	293734	638450	4957	3949
天 津 Tianjin	1100315	132945	435813	1100442	4060	3439
河 北 Hebei	17316135	1855941	4790157	15915765	50554	41834
山 西 Shanxi	5034863	437878	1339710	4053357	15050	12629
内蒙古 Inner Mongolia	1928313	348323	532857	850059	3036	2365
辽 宁 Liaoning	2813210	334596	1076177	2249070	10943	8256
吉 林 Jilin	1404420	330860	530296	597281	3353	2604
黑龙江 Heilongjiang	1890499	240792	706689	697165	3993	3154
上 海 Shanghai	901141	287193	310352	1278081	7468	6366
江 苏 Jiangsu	11678635	3293066	3261303	9149277	51029	37953
浙 江 Zhejiang	9651097	2457563	2864366	9924164	55417	49121
安 徽 Anhui	8744018	1137070	1906760	5697283	21642	16551
福 建 Fujian	3469238	810039	1033050	2737754	11476	9115
江 西 Jiangxi	6638988	1241448	1432543	3541246	13162	10281
山 东 Shandong	26059250	5780662	7463115	20013090	96713	76703
河 南 Henan	20414688	2427852	4474870	15375458	44707	38501
湖 北 Hubei	7913989	2522853	1789270	6378322	20115	17140
湖 南 Hunan	15993223	3130666	2946323	11889789	32677	27301
广 东 Guangdong	14432412	3784570	3829846	12172893	43796	38461
广 西 Guangxi	6497982	1180213	1128990	4101850	13027	10317
海 南 Hainan	1269967	289467	241368	576617	2490	1833
重 庆 Chongqing	2468242	412347	677081	1416154	8469	6096
四 川 Sichuan	6916486	1386321	1989262	6776094	28148	21820
贵 州 Guizhou	5585976	1147726	1541620	5055528	14567	12282
云 南 Yunnan	5422035	1176909	1068951	4028680	15235	12633
西 藏 Tibet	377995	77460	51939	237092	1157	711
陕 西 Shaanxi	5188902	817617	1410227	5799202	19348	16813
甘 肃 Gansu	2086275	255877	621373	1924189	7786	6531
青 海 Qinghai	631683	43669	142596	746676	2625	2327
宁 夏 Ningxia	761884	114704	215013	463187	3151	2593
新 疆 Xinjiang	2162280	542877	568247	1065579	5463	4383

学条件(二)(镇乡结合区)
Junior Secondary Schools (2) (County-town Transitional Area)

(台) (set)	教室中(间): Classroom(room)		教室中:普通教室(间) of Which: General Classroom		固定资产总值(万元) Total Volue of Fixed Asset (10,000 yuan)		
用计算机 Computers Instruction 其中:平板电脑 of Which: Tablet PC	合计 Total	其中:网络多媒体教室 of Which: Network Multimedia Classroom	合计 Total	其中:网络多媒体教室 of Which: Network Multimedia Classroom	合计 Total	其中:教学仪器设备资产值 of Which: Total Value of Equip & Instru. 小计 Subtotal	其中:实验设备 of Which: for Profession
22766	**200700**	**73167**	**142299**	**62888**	**6503892.86**	**609499.99**	**258683.45**
15	859	689	511	467	48280.14	10682.58	1196.48
118	1083	377	739	298	31669.84	4365.88	1810.34
1474	27543	6623	14602	5926	513326.17	47410.16	22903.82
217	5077	1923	3842	1656	173377.27	14553.14	8067.13
	1026	268	812	249	98111.99	3944.61	1471.82
993	3051	906	2332	784	82576.90	9835.00	5023.00
	836	153	698	118	18823.92	2425.64	1415.76
159	1520	319	1183	264	32134.08	2961.59	1718.80
4	1122	929	768	712	70094.27	11778.13	4305.02
1209	9086	5511	6252	4339	464009.33	49282.45	16851.79
1224	9167	7568	6694	6411	503243.89	49261.26	14032.46
1217	8259	2141	6701	1926	249997.91	20296.13	9990.79
22	2664	1096	2063	939	110932.40	11547.94	5666.43
1010	4924	1233	4190	1201	174698.51	15134.86	8304.13
1998	20300	12777	15773	10865	746536.12	76069.16	23236.85
931	24019	7190	19815	6207	591025.55	36548.87	18831.17
1254	5632	3049	4479	2803	267897.56	24165.90	11413.61
2363	8887	2234	7754	2132	376051.41	38729.03	20581.61
4158	12983	4927	10691	4110	483076.00	47350.00	25541.00
267	4080	2150	3718	2063	131876.73	15661.03	8968.43
5	628	163	559	142	50622.62	3536.30	1770.80
522	2052	1059	2082	1125	101601.43	7889.81	3264.20
258	9570	2614	7857	2284	391509.53	38474.31	12919.61
987	5132	1349	4142	1379	203425.01	14814.53	6187.38
303	4385	1627	3843	1512	201477.45	13622.96	4420.11
90	232	64	197	80	22983.85	1532.29	553.52
893	6717	1100	5332	920	172084.34	19361.27	11647.67
824	16542	1789	2033	784	80282.64	5798.72	2744.09
181	813	112	661	90	39828.60	3592.43	659.83
45	655	285	507	237	27699.41	3059.72	1374.11
25	1856	942	1469	865	44637.99	5814.29	1811.68

初中办

Condition of School Buildings in

地　区 Region	占地面积(平方米) Areas of School Sites (m^2)			图书(册) Books & Magazines in Libraries (volume)	计算机数 No. of Computer	
	合计 Total	其中 of Which			合计 Total	其中:教学 of Which: No. of Used for
		绿化用地面积 Green Areas	运动场地面积 Sports Areas			小计 Subtotal
总　计 Total	**430637067**	**75593452**	**107448710**	**293387632**	**1075875**	**879939**
北　京 Beijing	2221493	463733	595876	1312080	10309	8429
天　津 Tianjin	2301550	241477	771194	1623025	6821	5433
河　北 Hebei	22573520	2487659	7251696	18415654	53776	44443
山　西 Shanxi	14176011	1417952	3741588	8670311	35761	30318
内蒙古 Inner Mongolia	6283888	971642	1727451	1634041	5675	4344
辽　宁 Liaoning	9184822	1483826	3556641	5392964	29321	22682
吉　林 Jilin	12851341	2287231	3982703	4413865	21746	16130
黑龙江 Heilongjiang	14315121	1722301	5185730	3974645	22729	19389
上　海 Shanghai	750647	270038	188205	850229	4852	4197
江　苏 Jiangsu	7293923	1981844	1949043	4861965	27438	20562
浙　江 Zhejiang	6956967	1639916	2141728	6666631	38079	31652
安　徽 Anhui	33435782	4531848	6574292	19075603	67806	55671
福　建 Fujian	12347423	3289138	3339140	8406989	36038	28868
江　西 Jiangxi	20998656	3492508	4690398	11422348	37563	29066
山　东 Shandong	23298012	5329788	6763546	14598544	73596	55248
河　南 Henan	39480345	4255368	8426080	30500474	75718	65970
湖　北 Hubei	15818150	4986391	3400463	11833173	43083	37895
湖　南 Hunan	34405544	5511610	6641784	25582926	72328	61971
广　东 Guangdong	18507211	4708512	4821415	13857824	49120	41357
广　西 Guangxi	13376012	2423697	2228556	8663528	29849	23683
海　南 Hainan	2140235	521981	358264	680226	2656	2094
重　庆 Chongqing	3967461	702965	1024108	2397728	13532	10075
四　川 Sichuan	22341908	3096107	6085435	25590171	79536	61725
贵　州 Guizhou	17905290	3747364	5179723	17594015	50314	42738
云　南 Yunnan	22499165	4615707	3529549	14427809	56512	46830
西　藏 Tibet	1018640	43545	151359	441433	1914	1404
陕　西 Shaanxi	6510374	833548	1737957	5857264	20123	16590
甘　肃 Gansu	16930872	2200034	4489022	12660365	53480	44464
青　海 Qinghai	2678040	256991	731805	2476690	9702	8284
宁　夏 Ningxia	2873288	526976	844073	1513986	8538	6709
新　疆 Xinjiang	21195376	5551755	5339886	7991126	37960	31718

学条件(二)(乡村)

Junior Secondary Schools (2) (Rural Area)

(台) (set)	教室(间): Classroom(room)		教室中:普通教室(间) of Which: General Classroom		固定资产总值(万元) Total Volue of Fixed Asset (10,000 yuan)		
用计算机 Computers Instruction	合计 Total	其中:网络多媒体教室 of Which: Network Multimedia Classroom	合计 Total	其中:网络多媒体教室 of Which: Network Multimedia Classroom	合计 Total	其中:教学仪器设备资产值 of Which: Total Volue of Equip & Instru.	
其中:平板电脑 of Which: Tablet PC						小计 Subtotal	其中:实验设备 of Which: for Profession
35434	**367391**	**98739**	**300824**	**85033**	**9281261.05**	**982140.43**	**432673.38**
130	1636	1083	885	715	78133.90	21613.13	2599.86
128	2055	579	1288	431	50585.29	7712.15	3978.36
2744	23810	5804	17320	4924	427056.25	48110.51	27167.23
677	13258	2986	9256	2443	318684.50	25739.11	14760.38
	2735	397	2290	402	82649.88	5459.66	3019.76
2440	7939	2138	6085	1810	186446.79	24713.02	11838.41
328	7795	1121	6251	820	144214.03	17030.84	10217.59
489	10258	1338	7992	1068	171623.07	16742.01	8707.69
5	832	677	561	489	39463.46	9050.92	2526.97
918	5509	2688	3642	2140	207906.93	24022.63	9200.33
415	6628	5265	4898	4489	249428.64	29274.28	9067.95
3849	26468	7754	21408	6921	604004.86	50760.65	22380.18
30	8910	3151	6036	2306	311629.88	33017.71	13712.67
1531	14026	2506	12028	2099	309127.85	31848.30	15019.84
2043	16469	8212	12591	6926	467822.58	48972.92	16240.14
1499	42986	9483	33772	8167	695423.11	58005.89	30062.80
1841	11210	5595	8631	4966	440546.32	54248.10	22422.55
4195	20392	3651	24077	3636	595970.68	65288.24	34390.41
3177	14066	4544	11969	3868	499235.00	58665.00	26875.00
424	9011	3681	7973	3497	287114.94	33329.26	14349.28
250	1402	162	680	119	42105.68	3543.41	1725.67
390	3569	1652	2985	1418	121345.55	13151.73	3980.47
191	37678	4562	32643	3891	753301.34	78988.54	31918.38
3083	21099	3277	16885	2995	447927.43	44426.21	22245.35
920	16710	4729	14707	4202	591450.02	46808.12	20665.35
	380	66	324	54	44172.30	1487.91	503.47
395	6616	1105	5052	838	152843.43	16018.41	9058.94
2018	14599	3542	13757	3154	479786.62	51553.65	22479.90
665	3286	607	2570	459	96499.48	6975.37	2372.36
545	2118	532	1546	392	70626.57	7453.15	3225.23
114	13941	5852	10722	5394	314134.67	48129.61	15960.86

小学校数、
Number of Schools, External Teaching Sites &

地 区 Region	学校数(所) Schools	教学点数(个) External Teaching Sites	班数(个)	
			合计 Total	一年级 Grade 1
总 计 Total	**213529**	**82768**	**2499098**	**475667**
北 京 Beijing	1093		23455	4552
天 津 Tianjin	838		15701	3028
河 北 Hebei	12538	5987	144980	28211
山 西 Shanxi	8946	1555	72424	12752
内蒙古 Inner Mongolia	2308	406	34456	6370
辽 宁 Liaoning	4631	275	58106	10008
吉 林 Jilin	5103	100	43753	7540
黑龙江 Heilongjiang	3261	1361	44673	8234
上 海 Shanghai	759		20491	4443
江 苏 Jiangsu	4020	952	101290	19757
浙 江 Zhejiang	3400	593	86059	15581
安 徽 Anhui	11507	4695	119377	23238
福 建 Fujian	5228	2608	69595	13700
江 西 Jiangxi	10650	6250	108232	23206
山 东 Shandong	11151	1961	148704	28240
河 南 Henan	26086	7837	242040	47885
湖 北 Hubei	5746	3356	83910	16471
湖 南 Hunan	9270	7010	113327	22838
广 东 Guangdong	11824	4882	204482	38945
广 西 Guangxi	13499	7952	121549	23390
海 南 Hainan	1739	798	21375	4155
重 庆 Chongqing	4728	652	49608	9510
四 川 Sichuan	7257	9186	131915	25113
贵 州 Guizhou	10632	3406	99014	16659
云 南 Yunnan	12845	3931	111155	19477
西 藏 Tibet	841	496	8714	1756
陕 西 Shaanxi	7356	1258	64955	11598
甘 肃 Gansu	9640	3451	71869	13310
青 海 Qinghai	1250	631	13068	2600
宁 夏 Ningxia	1850	238	15733	2979
新 疆 Xinjiang	3533	941	55088	10121

教学点数及班数(总计)

Classes in Primary Schools(Total)

Classes

二年级 Grade 2	三年级 Grade 3	四年级 Grade 4	五年级 Grade 5	六年级 Grade 6	复式班 Multiple-grade Classes
452855	**423580**	**398959**	**376069**	**359006**	**12962**
4217	4043	3660	3422	3561	
2909	2806	2438	2397	2123	
27644	24874	22555	20380	20519	797
12492	11728	11533	10976	11389	1554
6131	5809	5374	5312	5431	29
9860	9870	9477	9147	9742	2
7641	7534	7312	6682	7044	
8348	8109	7885	7412	4683	2
4310	4171	3815	3647	105	
18417	17353	16262	14874	14623	4
15135	14860	14027	13226	13193	37
21102	20007	18768	17955	17090	1217
12622	11649	10996	10375	10075	178
20639	18255	16537	14669	13354	1572
26674	26613	24770	23184	19220	3
45195	41297	38721	36137	32447	358
15625	14287	13338	12138	11595	456
21400	18569	17638	16362	15691	829
36869	35006	32482	30712	30343	125
22001	20183	18961	17713	17376	1925
3970	3629	3268	3177	3173	3
8876	8231	7835	7535	7602	19
24136	22073	20968	19679	19669	277
17126	16244	15981	16125	16414	465
19050	18678	18160	17767	17624	399
1686	1553	1247	1256	1216	
11293	10660	10433	9965	10015	991
12687	11621	11281	10787	10587	1596
2419	2092	1999	1969	1944	45
2854	2672	2509	2376	2287	56
9527	9104	8729	8713	8871	23

小学校数、

Number of Schools, External Teaching Sites &

地　区 Region	学校数(所) Schools	教学点数(个) External Teaching Sites	班数(个) 合计 Total	一年级 Grade 1
总　计 Total	**26049**	**1151**	**595913**	**112504**
北　京 Beijing	696		18321	3616
天　津 Tianjin	363		8881	1720
河　北 Hebei	1344	84	23023	4116
山　西 Shanxi	936	5	16429	2996
内蒙古 Inner Mongolia	489		11300	2092
辽　宁 Liaoning	1215	3	24751	4473
吉　林 Jilin	547	3	12255	2201
黑龙江 Heilongjiang	669	28	13747	2644
上　海 Shanghai	578		15845	3492
江　苏 Jiangsu	1222	55	41385	7805
浙　江 Zhejiang	992	72	34505	6384
安　徽 Anhui	850	48	17706	3385
福　建 Fujian	968	45	20350	3950
江　西 Jiangxi	684	57	14261	2722
山　东 Shandong	1853	56	40612	8042
河　南 Henan	2054	109	35610	6540
湖　北 Hubei	997	57	22577	4107
湖　南 Hunan	984	112	19751	3656
广　东 Guangdong	3298	109	91140	17565
广　西 Guangxi	699	56	14001	2677
海　南 Hainan	197	11	4889	924
重　庆 Chongqing	496	14	11922	2340
四　川 Sichuan	751	122	22558	4277
贵　州 Guizhou	673	29	11233	1966
云　南 Yunnan	598	50	11080	1992
西　藏 Tibet	22		566	105
陕　西 Shaanxi	933	15	14275	2624
甘　肃 Gansu	371	5	7308	1269
青　海 Qinghai	69		1663	274
宁　夏 Ningxia	161		3514	641
新　疆 Xinjiang	340	6	10455	1909

教学点数及班数(城区)
Classes in Primary Schools (Urban Area)

Classes

二年级 Grade 2	三年级 Grade 3	四年级 Grade 4	五年级 Grade 5	六年级 Grade 6	复式班 Multiple-grade Classes
105245	**101986**	**97240**	**91809**	**87074**	**55**
3303	3156	2848	2644	2754	
1616	1568	1360	1334	1283	
4042	3960	3758	3429	3717	1
2833	2689	2669	2525	2717	
1932	1920	1773	1778	1805	
4193	4171	4048	3748	4118	
2133	2035	2014	1822	2050	
2541	2502	2485	2288	1287	
3313	3231	2953	2830	26	
7244	7101	6722	6280	6231	2
6077	5981	5588	5279	5196	
2983	2988	2875	2750	2721	4
3638	3478	3274	3051	2959	
2551	2392	2307	2126	2143	20
7344	7415	6832	6359	4619	1
6288	5999	5787	5592	5402	2
3959	3840	3724	3479	3462	6
3482	3282	3238	3043	3044	6
16251	15413	14602	13744	13558	7
2467	2356	2252	2141	2106	2
854	817	772	754	768	
2082	1975	1885	1803	1837	
3919	3735	3688	3418	3520	1
1900	1836	1828	1827	1876	
1887	1876	1800	1769	1754	2
98	93	92	91	87	
2444	2372	2335	2238	2261	1
1215	1211	1200	1169	1244	
268	279	282	279	281	
614	591	572	548	548	
1774	1724	1677	1671	1700	

小学校数、

Number of Schools, External Teaching Sites &

地　区 Region	学校数(所) Schools	教学点数(个) External Teaching Sites	班数(个) 合计 Total	一年级 Grade 1
总　计 Total	**8134**	**881**	**123431**	**23466**
北　京 Beijing	110		1865	380
天　津 Tianjin	59		930	167
河　北 Hebei	600	79	6518	1165
山　西 Shanxi	310	3	2769	486
内蒙古 Inner Mongolia	45		398	72
辽　宁 Liaoning	239	2	2816	475
吉　林 Jilin	112	3	975	164
黑龙江 Heilongjiang	95	21	1279	233
上　海 Shanghai	70		1738	368
江　苏 Jiangsu	191	36	4540	918
浙　江 Zhejiang	305	50	9214	1726
安　徽 Anhui	261	30	3097	579
福　建 Fujian	350	26	4236	829
江　西 Jiangxi	286	44	3103	631
山　东 Shandong	756	46	11523	2245
河　南 Henan	844	81	8541	1589
湖　北 Hubei	241	40	3192	601
湖　南 Hunan	296	95	4186	793
广　东 Guangdong	1460	92	32501	6298
广　西 Guangxi	223	49	2839	563
海　南 Hainan	40	9	481	85
重　庆 Chongqing	99	12	1323	270
四　川 Sichuan	127	94	3456	669
贵　州 Guizhou	241	27	3003	525
云　南 Yunnan	219	23	2642	483
西　藏 Tibet				
陕　西 Shaanxi	349	11	3167	577
甘　肃 Gansu	73	3	896	162
青　海 Qinghai	14		226	39
宁　夏 Ningxia	33		509	97
新　疆 Xinjiang	86	5	1468	277

教学点数及班数(城乡结合区)
Classes in Primary Schools (Urban-rural Transitional Area)

Classes

二年级 Grade 2	三年级 Grade 3	四年级 Grade 4	五年级 Grade 5	六年级 Grade 6	复式班 Multiple-grade Classes
22057	**21074**	**20015**	**18924**	**17864**	**31**
346	310	290	267	272	
165	172	144	144	138	
1146	1110	1040	1003	1053	1
478	457	458	443	447	
71	71	65	64	55	
471	477	470	447	476	
170	159	163	151	168	
228	237	240	226	115	
379	358	319	292	22	
838	783	720	652	627	2
1678	1589	1501	1378	1342	
510	513	515	500	479	1
750	710	682	638	627	
573	527	485	454	420	13
2081	2084	1893	1813	1406	1
1526	1460	1403	1323	1240	
565	549	523	481	469	4
744	693	670	635	645	6
5880	5517	5208	4875	4723	
505	466	448	431	425	1
83	79	81	78	75	
233	215	198	198	209	
607	575	562	520	522	1
507	479	491	496	505	
450	444	426	425	414	
546	532	516	499	496	1
153	149	147	142	143	
36	37	37	39	38	
90	83	84	78	77	
248	239	236	232	236	

小学校数、

Number of Schools, External Teaching Sites &

地　区 Region	学校数(所) Schools	教学点数(个) External Teaching Sites	班数(个) 合计 Total	一年级 Grade 1
总　计 Total	**47152**	**8062**	**764511**	**137520**
北　京 Beijing	148		2780	511
天　津 Tianjin	174		3250	610
河　北 Hebei	3411	674	46610	8497
山　西 Shanxi	1766	73	22689	3933
内蒙古 Inner Mongolia	713	13	14653	2534
辽　宁 Liaoning	733	15	14601	2382
吉　林 Jilin	634	12	11141	1879
黑龙江 Heilongjiang	705	64	14632	2563
上　海 Shanghai	118		3456	716
江　苏 Jiangsu	1634	162	44067	8512
浙　江 Zhejiang	1228	104	33915	6093
安　徽 Anhui	2454	570	36690	6890
福　建 Fujian	1428	99	22041	4063
江　西 Jiangxi	2377	692	36952	7046
山　东 Shandong	2962	346	48477	8891
河　南 Henan	5968	929	70859	12705
湖　北 Hubei	1536	313	27654	5097
湖　南 Hunan	2406	615	38512	6874
广　东 Guangdong	2737	463	51329	9129
广　西 Guangxi	2289	1066	31162	5642
海　南 Hainan	477	85	7857	1415
重　庆 Chongqing	1177	64	21278	3934
四　川 Sichuan	2130	839	48192	8871
贵　州 Guizhou	1750	186	24399	3873
云　南 Yunnan	1700	278	22804	3743
西　藏 Tibet	145	5	2115	345
陕　西 Shaanxi	2472	194	27493	4717
甘　肃 Gansu	954	97	12744	2222
青　海 Qinghai	216	24	4141	676
宁　夏 Ningxia	232	20	3795	650
新　疆 Xinjiang	478	60	14223	2507

教学点数及班数(镇区)
Classes in Primary Schools（Counties & Towns Area）

Classes

二年级 Grade 2	三年级 Grade 3	四年级 Grade 4	五年级 Grade 5	六年级 Grade 6	复式班 Multiple-grade Classes
132248	**127691**	**124438**	**120876**	**120940**	**798**
495	483	434	417	440	
608	585	514	509	424	
8423	8046	7542	6936	7132	34
3922	3758	3750	3547	3740	39
2537	2511	2346	2310	2411	4
2434	2458	2373	2382	2572	
1926	1914	1895	1718	1809	
2637	2632	2581	2443	1776	
746	698	637	611	48	
7943	7482	7131	6535	6463	1
5953	5856	5561	5225	5225	2
6130	6057	5885	5827	5814	87
3861	3684	3566	3423	3441	3
6517	6043	5851	5569	5781	145
8377	8564	8157	7759	6729	
12227	11682	11427	11428	11371	19
4981	4661	4508	4252	4127	28
6640	6357	6279	6124	6176	62
8673	8316	8358	8183	8665	5
5242	5052	4990	4977	5150	109
1373	1303	1234	1241	1291	
3697	3520	3416	3322	3389	
8468	7933	7772	7493	7639	16
3972	3962	4001	4213	4365	13
3625	3668	3746	3910	4093	19
350	328	351	379	362	
4681	4505	4484	4406	4518	182
2088	2041	2065	2090	2211	27
685	653	678	712	737	
640	612	606	625	659	3
2397	2327	2300	2310	2382	

小学校数、

Number of Schools, External Teaching Sites &

地　区 Region	学校数(所) Schools	教学点数(个) External Teaching Sites	班数(个)	
			合计 Total	一年级 Grade 1
总　计 Total	**22102**	**6035**	**260611**	**48176**
北　京 Beijing	41		647	117
天　津 Tianjin	89		1332	255
河　北 Hebei	2312	594	26840	5031
山　西 Shanxi	791	46	7649	1349
内蒙古 Inner Mongolia	75	5	1293	220
辽　宁 Liaoning	246	8	2903	462
吉　林 Jilin	171	10	1525	269
黑龙江 Heilongjiang	112	31	1803	305
上　海 Shanghai	33		898	187
江　苏 Jiangsu	636	125	12620	2410
浙　江 Zhejiang	493	82	12436	2279
安　徽 Anhui	998	358	10113	1953
福　建 Fujian	599	65	6691	1236
江　西 Jiangxi	1207	516	11547	2401
山　东 Shandong	1630	248	22292	4059
河　南 Henan	3749	780	34138	6427
湖　北 Hubei	585	221	7845	1508
湖　南 Hunan	1323	494	15386	2863
广　东 Guangdong	1591	368	22619	4100
广　西 Guangxi	1194	807	11759	2218
海　南 Hainan	143	36	1592	281
重　庆 Chongqing	371	49	4122	762
四　川 Sichuan	489	694	9903	1920
贵　州 Guizhou	755	116	7598	1219
云　南 Yunnan	814	162	8543	1425
西　藏 Tibet	10	2	234	38
陕　西 Shaanxi	969	109	8531	1513
甘　肃 Gansu	389	59	3723	657
青　海 Qinghai	78	20	1039	177
宁　夏 Ningxia	86	5	929	156
新　疆 Xinjiang	123	25	2061	379

教学点数及班数(镇乡结合区)

Classes in Primary Schools (County-town Transitional Area)

Classes

二年级 Grade 2	三年级 Grade 3	四年级 Grade 4	五年级 Grade 5	六年级 Grade 6	复式班 Multiple-grade Classes
46305	**43977**	**42141**	**40084**	**39419**	**509**
117	111	105	96	101	
251	238	207	216	165	
4972	4618	4296	3929	3969	25
1345	1261	1253	1185	1232	24
230	218	203	204	218	
473	486	478	485	519	
256	259	265	229	247	
327	327	310	297	237	
193	185	162	154	17	
2289	2148	2042	1890	1840	1
2233	2149	2019	1880	1874	2
1726	1685	1603	1577	1528	41
1184	1128	1086	1037	1017	3
2144	1938	1804	1611	1547	102
3889	3932	3742	3503	3167	
6167	5784	5490	5275	4978	17
1456	1319	1268	1168	1115	11
2761	2526	2479	2353	2356	48
3923	3761	3656	3507	3669	3
2085	1961	1875	1749	1790	81
285	256	257	256	257	
739	678	649	653	641	
1788	1662	1594	1456	1469	14
1257	1248	1256	1296	1315	7
1390	1412	1405	1441	1466	4
40	35	36	45	40	
1479	1406	1369	1327	1334	103
629	598	594	595	629	21
171	170	173	182	166	
151	145	145	156	174	2
355	333	320	332	342	

小学校数、

Number of Schools, External Teaching Sites &

地 区 Region	学校数(所) Schools	教学点数(个) External Teaching Sites	班数(个) 合计 Total	一年级 Grade 1
总 计 Total	**140328**	**73555**	**1138674**	**225643**
北 京 Beijing	249		2354	425
天 津 Tianjin	301		3570	698
河 北 Hebei	7783	5229	75347	15598
山 西 Shanxi	6244	1477	33306	5823
内蒙古 Inner Mongolia	1106	393	8503	1744
辽 宁 Liaoning	2683	257	18754	3153
吉 林 Jilin	3922	85	20357	3460
黑龙江 Heilongjiang	1887	1269	16294	3027
上 海 Shanghai	63		1190	235
江 苏 Jiangsu	1164	735	15838	3440
浙 江 Zhejiang	1180	417	17639	3104
安 徽 Anhui	8203	4077	64981	12963
福 建 Fujian	2832	2464	27204	5687
江 西 Jiangxi	7589	5501	57019	13438
山 东 Shandong	6336	1559	59615	11307
河 南 Henan	18064	6799	135571	28640
湖 北 Hubei	3213	2986	33679	7267
湖 南 Hunan	5880	6283	55064	12308
广 东 Guangdong	5789	4310	62013	12251
广 西 Guangxi	10511	6830	76386	15071
海 南 Hainan	1065	702	8629	1816
重 庆 Chongqing	3055	574	16408	3236
四 川 Sichuan	4376	8225	61165	11965
贵 州 Guizhou	8209	3191	63382	10820
云 南 Yunnan	10547	3603	77271	13742
西 藏 Tibet	674	491	6033	1306
陕 西 Shaanxi	3951	1049	23187	4257
甘 肃 Gansu	8315	3349	51817	9819
青 海 Qinghai	965	607	7264	1650
宁 夏 Ningxia	1457	218	8424	1688
新 疆 Xinjiang	2715	875	30410	5705

教学点数及班数(农村)

Classes in Primary Schools (Rural Area)

Classes

二年级 Grade 2	三年级 Grade 3	四年级 Grade 4	五年级 Grade 5	六年级 Grade 6	复式班 Multiple-grade Classes
215362	**193903**	**177281**	**163384**	**150992**	**12109**
419	404	378	361	367	
685	653	564	554	416	
15179	12868	11255	10015	9670	762
5737	5281	5114	4904	4932	1515
1662	1378	1255	1224	1215	25
3233	3241	3056	3017	3052	2
3582	3585	3403	3142	3185	
3170	2975	2819	2681	1620	2
251	242	225	206	31	
3230	2770	2409	2059	1929	1
3105	3023	2878	2722	2772	35
11989	10962	10008	9378	8555	1126
5123	4487	4156	3901	3675	175
11571	9820	8379	6974	5430	1407
10953	10634	9781	9066	7872	2
26680	23616	21507	19117	15674	337
6685	5786	5106	4407	4006	422
11278	8930	8121	7195	6471	761
11945	11277	9522	8785	8120	113
14292	12775	11719	10595	10120	1814
1743	1509	1262	1182	1114	3
3097	2736	2534	2410	2376	19
11749	10405	9508	8768	8510	260
11254	10446	10152	10085	10173	452
13538	13134	12614	12088	11777	378
1238	1132	804	786	767	
4168	3783	3614	3321	3236	808
9384	8369	8016	7528	7132	1569
1466	1160	1039	978	926	45
1600	1469	1331	1203	1080	53
5356	5053	4752	4732	4789	23

小学学生

Number of Students in Primary

地 区 Region	毕业生数 Graduates	招生数 Entrants		在校学生数	
		合计 Total	其中:受过学前教育 of Which: Those Received the Pre-school Education	合计 Total	其中:女 of Which: Female
总 计 Total	**15810583**	**16953556**	**16417268**	**93605487**	**43312688**
北 京 Beijing	111839	165807	165447	789276	364118
天 津 Tianjin	86133	107372	107085	552116	255520
河 北 Hebei	840140	996124	992916	5462135	2552641
山 西 Shanxi	477274	394203	389473	2296383	1100164
内蒙古 Inner Mongolia	232846	230674	228635	1310595	625303
辽 宁 Liaoning	365054	350633	350128	2044058	966325
吉 林 Jilin	235930	217645	213943	1361868	647975
黑龙江 Heilongjiang	330069	274454	270675	1540035	740522
上 海 Shanghai	134504	181037	180306	792476	362578
江 苏 Jiangsu	639404	851334	850833	4353694	1985323
浙 江 Zhejiang	540378	607545	603788	3495846	1608765
安 徽 Anhui	654897	753090	734770	4091967	1857945
福 建 Fujian	398464	495734	492096	2598375	1189673
江 西 Jiangxi	655898	789067	758227	4081086	1836812
山 东 Shandong	1033007	1156903	1152489	6259820	2901229
河 南 Henan	1644760	1810567	1809601	9399771	4301146
湖 北 Hubei	489395	607979	587401	3282579	1498807
湖 南 Hunan	770482	847605	843674	4678102	2138777
广 东 Guangdong	1370411	1500473	1454155	8079381	3614965
广 西 Guangxi	700641	752867	723793	4262624	1987856
海 南 Hainan	124664	124284	116525	740193	325142
重 庆 Chongqing	326451	375725	367759	1989128	937562
四 川 Sichuan	886816	950346	877498	5259536	2504884
贵 州 Guizhou	723478	510554	452582	3555333	1654132
云 南 Yunnan	713770	613507	540104	3920782	1846844
西 藏 Tibet	46118	51567	28840	294799	143550
陕 西 Shaanxi	400469	388081	384383	2273275	1054698
甘 肃 Gansu	370601	320908	259555	1867268	879660
青 海 Qinghai	83487	78634	68476	474638	228456
宁 夏 Ningxia	101909	100194	91284	603947	288109
新 疆 Xinjiang	321294	348643	320827	1894401	913207

数(总计)

Schools (Total)

单位:人

unit:person

Enrolment						预计毕业生数 Estimated Graduates for Next Year
一年级 Grade 1	二年级 Grade 2	三年级 Grade 3	四年级 Grade 4	五年级 Grade 5	六年级 Grade 6	
17014194	**16452428**	**15968628**	**15277067**	**14523683**	**14369487**	**14798022**
166108	145359	139127	118647	107160	112875	113770
107408	102757	100203	83318	82278	76152	86821
996125	1020143	972557	870400	781395	821515	821515
394370	404772	379644	384356	346587	386654	386821
230674	222335	230175	202241	204506	220664	222108
350928	338410	349377	329469	315280	360594	363812
217823	235270	237621	232709	205832	232613	232885
274451	283013	286112	275576	248604	172279	267639
181210	168965	163597	142492	131424	4788	130650
851334	789696	754184	704838	633413	620229	620603
607618	602773	619191	590099	538999	537166	538748
753377	675854	698878	674818	654231	634809	635790
496485	465123	445193	420888	391111	379575	379575
819315	736429	685153	647002	597603	595584	595584
1156907	1099498	1142465	1062243	976327	822380	994629
1814359	1691320	1565645	1495850	1442441	1390156	1403786
608425	600002	566360	536631	493839	477322	478514
847605	824235	773980	763754	728017	740511	740511
1497546	1429766	1365672	1304540	1235577	1246280	1246461
755708	733313	715499	702775	678534	676795	676795
132334	132720	126708	116731	114671	117029	117029
376050	346187	327554	315557	306394	317386	317386
952660	933629	875383	849136	810582	838146	838146
510594	586647	576400	592197	624443	665052	665052
613613	623151	653430	659159	678436	692993	693452
51570	51235	48373	47986	49336	46299	46299
393729	389352	378533	374298	362109	375254	375254
322133	312352	302739	305745	305056	319243	319243
80880	80953	78333	77126	78858	78488	78488
101311	103589	101690	98565	98357	100435	100435
351544	323580	308852	297921	302283	310221	310221

小学学生

Number of Students in Primary

地 区 Region	毕业生数 Graduates	招生数 Entrants 合计 Total	其中:受过学前教育 of Which: Those Received the Pre-school Education	在校学生数 合计 Total	其中:女 of Which: Female
总 计 Total	**4439115**	**5184555**	**5124551**	**27729719**	**12658832**
北 京 Beijing	89724	135934	135601	635294	292756
天 津 Tianjin	49544	63394	63107	321383	150167
河 北 Hebei	184450	202587	202565	1145508	532837
山 西 Shanxi	142483	137454	135938	764918	365239
内蒙古 Inner Mongolia	93546	95142	94281	523641	250018
辽 宁 Liaoning	177860	191658	191379	1035336	490514
吉 林 Jilin	95152	92184	90734	538414	255441
黑龙江 Heilongjiang	123054	116106	114832	608454	290113
上 海 Shanghai	102724	140534	140091	597993	275515
江 苏 Jiangsu	268774	345534	345406	1823602	829291
浙 江 Zhejiang	218902	261677	259139	1460478	666754
安 徽 Anhui	133675	154976	151480	833475	374526
福 建 Fujian	137774	188660	187556	972594	437268
江 西 Jiangxi	114571	132755	131616	723939	316714
山 东 Shandong	314671	386902	386195	1944625	900083
河 南 Henan	299411	343979	343658	1886622	849276
湖 北 Hubei	162408	188925	185512	1050497	472779
湖 南 Hunan	161760	187331	186992	1028847	462012
广 东 Guangdong	646636	814084	792282	4275373	1864217
广 西 Guangxi	105852	133893	129988	708973	319036
海 南 Hainan	40586	43185	42168	246582	101840
重 庆 Chongqing	86482	105990	102900	539812	257227
四 川 Sichuan	185103	196515	195134	1077315	512727
贵 州 Guizhou	102449	92118	90731	570743	260549
云 南 Yunnan	92530	97003	96131	559453	264159
西 藏 Tibet	4125	5220	4643	28338	13782
陕 西 Shaanxi	112788	129737	129254	698378	321852
甘 肃 Gansu	64551	66038	64887	376327	174794
青 海 Qinghai	15347	15082	15017	91502	43603
宁 夏 Ningxia	31719	33693	33090	189128	89048
新 疆 Xinjiang	80464	86265	82244	472175	224695

数(城区)
Schools (Urban Area)

单位:人
unit: person

Enrolment						预计毕业生数 Estimated Graduates for Next Year
一年级 Grade 1	二年级 Grade 2	三年级 Grade 3	四年级 Grade 4	五年级 Grade 5	六年级 Grade 6	
5187427	**4866502**	**4791725**	**4548640**	**4220127**	**4115298**	**4368939**
136080	116721	111954	95121	85508	89910	90805
63417	59199	57735	48205	46967	45860	49584
202587	204177	202544	187231	162585	186384	186384
137457	135856	127917	126628	110419	126641	126641
95142	87637	92329	78704	80858	88971	90382
191667	172457	175494	167621	149233	178864	182082
92184	91324	89726	89852	79456	95872	96144
116106	111514	111365	109965	97681	61823	108682
140607	126316	123871	106978	99112	1109	98850
345534	316301	318726	298779	273581	270681	271055
261695	251736	259199	244417	223157	220274	221856
154993	133476	139472	139074	132520	133940	133940
188768	176240	169041	158035	143221	137289	137289
134386	126532	122598	118409	108862	113152	113152
386902	347535	363048	328656	298157	220327	308791
344095	333322	317192	307057	295375	289581	297973
188965	185150	177791	175294	161379	161918	162076
187331	179156	169892	170858	159785	161825	161825
812627	769467	733939	690810	640733	627797	627889
133900	123983	120684	115274	108774	106358	106358
44672	42830	41599	40048	38237	39196	39196
106004	93176	88720	85775	81233	84904	84904
196521	182161	177655	177968	167313	175697	175697
92118	95354	92960	94692	95281	100338	100338
97006	93833	96554	90865	89649	91546	92005
5220	5071	4657	4756	4426	4208	4208
129747	118371	116428	114664	107310	111858	111858
66500	61837	62877	62063	58643	64407	64407
15082	14726	15490	15240	15295	15669	15669
33729	32284	31784	30626	29659	31046	31046
86385	78760	78484	74975	75718	77853	77853

小学学生

Number of Students in Primary

地 区 Region	毕业生数 Graduates	招生数 Entrants 合计 Total	其中:受过学前教育 of Which: Those Received the Pre-school Education	在校学生数 合计 Total	其中:女 of Which: Female
总 计 Total	**801391**	**984018**	**967014**	**5198647**	**2329474**
北 京 Beijing	8243	13760	13651	65062	29236
天 津 Tianjin	4820	6141	6093	32772	15194
河 北 Hebei	43101	44971	44971	259416	120305
山 西 Shanxi	19015	16737	16587	92591	44733
内蒙古 Inner Mongolia	2457	2071	2071	11805	5529
辽 宁 Liaoning	17444	16835	16782	98264	46199
吉 林 Jilin	5427	4686	4376	26808	12818
黑龙江 Heilongjiang	12422	8508	8278	47042	22557
上 海 Shanghai	12996	16695	16693	76968	33700
江 苏 Jiangsu	24957	38703	38668	187916	84166
浙 江 Zhejiang	53743	71868	70802	390372	173256
安 徽 Anhui	20069	21832	21781	118146	53984
福 建 Fujian	24844	35521	35170	177065	80399
江 西 Jiangxi	20378	26505	26191	135244	58812
山 东 Shandong	79443	98744	98527	503619	231638
河 南 Henan	52631	65601	65572	343966	154129
湖 北 Hubei	18871	23240	22163	124943	55764
湖 南 Hunan	27431	31956	31928	176257	77236
广 东 Guangdong	214213	284515	275407	1478481	634219
广 西 Guangxi	18294	24301	23616	126341	56639
海 南 Hainan	2924	3001	2621	17781	7607
重 庆 Chongqing	8344	11104	10984	52364	24491
四 川 Sichuan	23543	26784	26687	142749	66894
贵 州 Guizhou	25031	21581	20737	136945	63331
云 南 Yunnan	19869	21372	20963	123121	58651
西 藏 Tibet					
陕 西 Shaanxi	18956	22192	22161	118556	54116
甘 肃 Gansu	6385	7358	7147	40616	19107
青 海 Qinghai	1904	1978	1960	11927	5635
宁 夏 Ningxia	4474	4617	4602	26252	12584
新 疆 Xinjiang	9162	10841	9825	55258	26545

数(城乡结合区)

Schools (Urban-rural Transitional Area)

单位:人

unit: person

Enrolment						预计毕业生数 Estimated Graduates for Next Year
一年级 Grade 1	二年级 Grade 2	三年级 Grade 3	四年级 Grade 4	五年级 Grade 5	六年级 Grade 6	
982350	**933953**	**898972**	**847193**	**786197**	**749982**	**785292**
13825	12797	11351	9772	8634	8683	8683
6152	5964	6110	5029	4870	4647	4839
44971	46369	44989	41660	38289	43138	43138
16738	16650	15376	14910	13857	15060	15060
2071	2053	2133	1738	1952	1858	2198
16840	16212	16692	16085	15245	17190	17190
4686	4469	4374	4397	4285	4597	4597
8508	8419	8842	9021	8037	4215	8888
16708	16665	16007	13906	12732	950	12539
38703	35242	33510	29625	25712	25124	25124
71871	71358	68874	65433	57928	54908	54908
21835	18533	19721	19773	19235	19049	19049
35543	32025	30380	28543	25726	24848	24848
27231	24293	22851	21281	19785	19803	19803
98744	90438	93080	82980	77206	61171	78986
65714	61522	58164	55871	52364	50331	51032
23244	22498	21264	20648	18759	18530	18530
31956	30528	29122	29141	27419	28091	28091
281526	271909	255713	239428	219227	210678	210678
24306	22296	21020	20362	19298	19059	19059
3201	3450	2828	2900	2687	2715	2715
11105	9301	8341	7777	7683	8157	8157
26786	24758	23784	23299	21671	22451	22451
21581	22763	21803	22734	23734	24330	24330
21373	20695	21031	19797	20154	20071	20071
22201	20096	19618	19449	18235	18957	18957
7419	6853	6848	6744	6268	6484	6484
1978	1883	1976	2001	2076	2013	2013
4623	4534	4314	4276	4297	4208	4208
10911	9380	8856	8613	8832	8666	8666

小学学生

Number of Students in Primary

地 区 Region	毕业生数 Graduates	招生数 Entrants 合计 Total	其中:受过学前教育 of Which: Those Received the Pre-school Education	在校学生数 合计 Total	其中:女 of Which: Female
总 计 Total	**5768325**	**5850940**	**5740292**	**33705362**	**15474206**
北 京 Beijing	12924	17525	17514	89910	41721
天 津 Tianjin	18578	22167	22167	119431	54431
河 北 Hebei	306988	352856	351722	2025395	932379
山 西 Shanxi	181865	155639	153617	929131	441097
内蒙古 Inner Mongolia	103743	100986	100171	594694	284603
辽 宁 Liaoning	105045	90982	90943	575979	270556
吉 林 Jilin	73533	68376	66939	446930	212077
黑龙江 Heilongjiang	119106	104592	102731	614638	295021
上 海 Shanghai	23027	30650	30383	144895	65119
江 苏 Jiangsu	295542	383661	383600	1974360	895875
浙 江 Zhejiang	223599	242002	241282	1426294	657894
安 徽 Anhui	256646	275886	272484	1539532	681616
福 建 Fujian	151439	175219	173258	948290	431139
江 西 Jiangxi	309772	319763	308383	1783164	787507
山 东 Shandong	359229	389651	388094	2195410	1006880
河 南 Henan	593697	557132	556808	3234895	1446805
湖 北 Hubei	180709	211576	205694	1187536	546442
湖 南 Hunan	333774	336785	335678	1956493	886228
广 东 Guangdong	396383	373425	362347	2125196	960287
广 西 Guangxi	233337	238866	233813	1372025	628090
海 南 Hainan	56586	51102	48812	325160	143365
重 庆 Chongqing	160435	181630	178863	982202	459958
四 川 Sichuan	386382	414970	401686	2326518	1110097
贵 州 Guizhou	225833	164502	155885	1144890	521045
云 南 Yunnan	184588	150054	143348	975995	462575
西 藏 Tibet	14098	14607	8724	90541	44170
陕 西 Shaanxi	198698	178340	176188	1105293	512452
甘 肃 Gansu	99298	91875	84514	543832	250486
青 海 Qinghai	34936	29625	24386	191718	92850
宁 夏 Ningxia	31673	30617	29274	187974	88594
新 疆 Xinjiang	96862	95879	90984	547041	262847

数(镇区)

Schools (Counties & Towns Area)

单位:人
unit:person

Enrolment						预计毕业生数 Estimated Graduates for Next Year
一年级 Grade 1	二年级 Grade 2	三年级 Grade 3	四年级 Grade 4	五年级 Grade 5	六年级 Grade 6	
5873081	**5754084**	**5651059**	**5551434**	**5386020**	**5489684**	**5597511**
17578	16571	15922	13721	12564	13554	13554
22170	22299	21685	18241	18317	16719	19411
352856	362602	358904	332747	300549	317737	317737
155690	162899	153783	157355	141719	157685	157842
100986	100182	104856	93599	94013	101058	101091
91065	93747	98322	92709	94046	106090	106090
68376	77394	79545	78071	68238	75306	75306
104590	111345	113419	110110	98773	76401	105155
30718	31945	29526	26281	24160	2265	23692
383661	359521	337327	320642	289115	284094	284094
242038	243781	252949	242776	222678	222072	222072
275954	245654	256656	254766	252801	253701	253790
175552	166248	161150	154607	146124	144609	144609
329247	309767	291907	287453	273336	291454	291454
389651	374309	391002	375806	351344	313298	363138
558212	540808	521350	522138	534869	557518	561280
211673	212567	202858	195932	184934	179572	180556
336785	331202	321622	323202	316663	327019	327019
371935	354889	339310	348622	342239	368201	368290
239417	226377	223836	224936	225356	232103	232103
55759	56981	55328	51846	51903	53343	53343
181792	168784	162271	157330	153770	158255	158255
415279	405760	383290	376990	365834	379365	379365
164522	183267	183035	191254	205402	217410	217410
150074	149192	156306	162262	174569	183592	183592
14608	14924	13760	14850	16810	15589	15589
182324	187590	183697	183007	180867	187808	187808
92093	89149	87409	89518	90750	94913	94913
30797	31146	30331	31552	33510	34382	34382
30852	31668	30970	30466	31219	32799	32799
96827	91516	88733	88645	89548	91772	91772

小学学生

Number of Students in Primary

地 区 Region	毕业生数 Graduates	招生数 Entrants		在校学生数	
		合计 Total	其中:受过学前教育 of Which: Those Received the Pre-school Education	合计 Total	其中:女 of Which: Female
总 计 Total	**1726225**	**1791826**	**1761412**	**10119773**	**4648285**
北 京 Beijing	2984	3877	3877	20027	9329
天 津 Tianjin	7272	9115	9115	46523	21237
河 北 Hebei	158337	186516	185607	1054165	486860
山 西 Shanxi	52143	46032	45379	265108	126712
内蒙古 Inner Mongolia	8480	7944	7926	47672	22164
辽 宁 Liaoning	17887	14907	14894	97255	45072
吉 林 Jilin	8301	7916	7818	49299	23112
黑龙江 Heilongjiang	14762	11559	11520	69074	33115
上 海 Shanghai	5886	8046	7977	38157	17405
江 苏 Jiangsu	80190	101452	101440	532265	242284
浙 江 Zhejiang	78608	90766	90708	522403	237317
安 徽 Anhui	56611	62727	61423	343375	154365
福 建 Fujian	39465	48381	48162	251870	115933
江 西 Jiangxi	74843	80742	77535	434074	196012
山 东 Shandong	156313	167914	166953	953499	435846
河 南 Henan	235088	235267	235173	1287501	580427
湖 北 Hubei	45839	56418	54675	305270	140629
湖 南 Hunan	114614	119449	119019	676694	308758
广 东 Guangdong	163146	158464	153982	882712	402761
广 西 Guangxi	70534	71365	70212	406039	190980
海 南 Hainan	10162	8742	8559	55929	23869
重 庆 Chongqing	28480	31502	30634	171709	79974
四 川 Sichuan	65292	70398	68716	378674	180066
贵 州 Guizhou	62224	41904	39004	301919	139251
云 南 Yunnan	61431	49791	47588	328170	154172
西 藏 Tibet	1531	1556	960	9731	4557
陕 西 Shaanxi	54533	50276	49420	305845	140814
甘 肃 Gansu	24770	22466	19270	129906	60820
青 海 Qinghai	7677	6569	5939	43798	21153
宁 夏 Ningxia	6417	6349	5734	39142	18595
新 疆 Xinjiang	12405	13416	12193	71968	34696

数(镇乡结合区)
Schools (County-town Transitional Area)

单位:人
unit:person

Enrolment						预计毕业生数 Estimated Graduates for Next Year
一年级 Grade 1	二年级 Grade 2	三年级 Grade 3	四年级 Grade 4	五年级 Grade 5	六年级 Grade 6	
1799079	**1760821**	**1707320**	**1658341**	**1587451**	**1606761**	**1632031**
3887	3657	3635	3176	2746	2926	2926
9115	8896	8433	6935	7102	6042	7389
186516	191742	186767	172496	154921	161723	161723
46065	46828	42897	44036	40677	44605	44605
7944	8328	8409	7500	7347	8144	8144
14916	15729	16618	15500	16078	18414	18414
7916	8720	8663	8615	7362	8023	8023
11557	12248	12465	12083	11104	9617	11817
8067	8396	7940	6795	6206	753	6059
101452	97785	91219	86950	78957	75902	75902
90786	92901	92991	87900	79564	78261	78261
62740	54860	57748	56092	56332	55603	55604
48464	44480	42832	40612	38335	37147	37147
84953	77409	71726	69113	63291	67582	67582
167914	163919	169641	163953	150298	137774	153859
236176	224726	211300	205522	203226	206551	206793
56460	55998	51768	50270	46532	44242	44242
119449	116880	111386	110213	107984	110782	110782
157545	150397	143840	143060	139217	148653	148742
71804	69071	67718	67442	64235	65769	65769
9323	9811	9223	9121	9001	9450	9450
31535	30049	28159	27150	27274	27542	27542
70428	66818	62325	60850	57912	60341	60341
41907	48426	48013	50596	54793	58184	58184
49796	51236	53821	54628	58367	60322	60322
1556	1665	1519	1538	1819	1634	1634
51747	52962	50560	50591	49319	50666	50666
22490	21371	20524	21004	21361	23156	23156
6616	6830	7315	7348	7997	7692	7692
6415	6282	6332	6123	6614	7376	7376
13540	12401	11533	11129	11480	11885	11885

小学学生

Number of Students in Primary

地　区 Region	毕业生数 Graduates	招生数 Entrants 合计 Total	其中:受过学前教育 of Which: Those Received the Pre-school Education	在校学生数 合计 Total	其中:女 of Which: Female
总　计 Total	**5603143**	**5918061**	**5552425**	**32170406**	**15179650**
北　京 Beijing	9191	12348	12332	64072	29641
天　津 Tianjin	18011	21811	21811	111302	50922
河　北 Hebei	348702	440681	438629	2291232	1087425
山　西 Shanxi	152926	101110	99918	602334	293828
内蒙古 Inner Mongolia	35557	34546	34183	192260	90682
辽　宁 Liaoning	82149	67993	67806	432743	205255
吉　林 Jilin	67245	57085	56270	376524	180457
黑龙江 Heilongjiang	87909	53756	53112	316943	155388
上　海 Shanghai	8753	9853	9832	49588	21944
江　苏 Jiangsu	75088	122139	121827	555732	260157
浙　江 Zhejiang	97877	103866	103367	609074	284117
安　徽 Anhui	264576	322228	310806	1718960	801803
福　建 Fujian	109251	131855	131282	677491	321266
江　西 Jiangxi	231555	336549	318228	1573983	732591
山　东 Shandong	359107	380350	378200	2119785	994266
河　南 Henan	751652	909456	909135	4278254	2005065
湖　北 Hubei	146278	207478	196195	1044546	479586
湖　南 Hunan	274948	323489	321004	1692762	790537
广　东 Guangdong	327392	312964	299526	1678812	790461
广　西 Guangxi	361452	380108	359992	2181626	1040730
海　南 Hainan	27492	29997	25545	168451	79937
重　庆 Chongqing	79534	88105	85996	467114	220377
四　川 Sichuan	315331	338861	280678	1855703	882060
贵　州 Guizhou	395196	253934	205966	1839700	872538
云　南 Yunnan	436652	366450	300625	2385334	1120110
西　藏 Tibet	27895	31740	15473	175920	85598
陕　西 Shaanxi	88983	80004	78941	469604	220394
甘　肃 Gansu	206752	162995	110154	947109	454380
青　海 Qinghai	33204	33927	29073	191418	92003
宁　夏 Ningxia	38517	35884	28920	226845	110467
新　疆 Xinjiang	143968	166499	147599	875185	425665

数(乡村)

Schools (Rural Area)

单位:人
unit: person

Enrolment						
一年级 Grade 1	二年级 Grade 2	三年级 Grade 3	四年级 Grade 4	五年级 Grade 5	六年级 Grade 6	预计毕业生数 Estimated Graduates for Next Year
5953686	**5831842**	**5525844**	**5176993**	**4917536**	**4764505**	**4831572**
12450	12067	11251	9805	9088	9411	9411
21821	21259	20783	16872	16994	13573	17826
440682	453364	411109	350422	318261	317394	317394
101223	106017	97944	100373	94449	102328	102338
34546	34516	32990	29938	29635	30635	30635
68196	72206	75561	69139	72001	75640	75640
57263	66552	68350	64786	58138	61435	61435
53755	60154	61328	55501	52150	34055	53802
9885	10704	10200	9233	8152	1414	8108
122139	113874	98131	85417	70717	65454	65454
103885	107256	107043	102906	93164	94820	94820
322430	296724	302750	280978	268910	247168	248060
132165	122635	115002	108246	101766	97677	97677
355682	300130	270648	241140	215405	190978	190978
380354	377654	388415	357781	326826	288755	322700
912052	817190	727103	666655	612197	543057	544533
207787	202285	185711	165405	147526	135832	135882
323489	313877	282466	269694	251569	251667	251667
312984	305410	292423	265108	252605	250282	250282
382391	382953	370979	362565	344404	338334	338334
31903	32909	29781	24837	24531	24490	24490
88254	84227	76563	72452	71391	74227	74227
340860	345708	314438	294178	277435	283084	283084
253954	308026	300405	306251	323760	347304	347304
366533	380126	400570	406032	414218	417855	417855
31742	31240	29956	28380	28100	26502	26502
81658	83391	78408	76627	73932	75588	75588
163540	161366	152453	154164	155663	159923	159923
35001	35081	32512	30334	30053	28437	28437
36730	39637	38936	37473	37479	36590	36590
168332	153304	141635	134301	137017	140596	140596

五年制小

Number of Students in

	招生数 Entrants		在校生数	
	合计 Total	其中:受过学前教育 of Which:Those Received the Pre-school Education	合计 Total	其中:女 of Which: Female
总　计 Total	**505017**	**502063**	**2371040**	**1112465**
北　京 Beijing	1499	1499	6031	2874
天　津 Tianjin	13452	13452	62045	28707
河　北 Hebei				
山　西 Shanxi	73	73	480	241
内蒙古 Inner Mongolia	1449	1449	8129	3822
辽　宁 Liaoning	3965	3960	18495	8779
吉　林 Jilin	339	339	1515	713
黑龙江 Heilongjiang	110118	107940	525047	250819
上　海 Shanghai	173637	172935	753492	345665
江　苏 Jiangsu	249	249	1640	773
浙　江 Zhejiang	1958	1958	8957	4102
安　徽 Anhui	864	843	5004	2345
福　建 Fujian				
江　西 Jiangxi	5	5	13	7
山　东 Shandong	180610	180590	899157	427617
河　南 Henan	15083	15055	72235	31830
湖　北 Hubei	1106	1106	5709	2760
湖　南 Hunan				
广　东 Guangdong	73	73	507	201
广　西 Guangxi				
海　南 Hainan				
重　庆 Chongqing				
四　川 Sichuan				
贵　州 Guizhou				
云　南 Yunnan	533	533	2580	1208
西　藏 Tibet				
陕　西 Shaanxi				
甘　肃 Gansu	4	4	4	2
青　海 Qinghai				
宁　夏 Ningxia				
新　疆 Xinjiang				

学学生数
5-year Primary Schools

单位:人

unit：person

Enrolment

一年级 Grade 1	二年级 Grade 2	三年级 Grade 3	四年级 Grade 4	五年级 Grade 5
505179	**484762**	**500991**	**451573**	**428535**
1499	1279	1292	1066	895
13457	13618	13228	11073	10669
73	74	74	92	167
1449	1759	1728	1749	1444
3965	3754	3842	3716	3218
339	263	353	288	272
110118	107462	108912	103195	95360
173794	160850	156736	136250	125862
249	259	380	378	374
1958	1767	1924	1726	1582
864	1015	1080	1064	981
5	8			
180610	175765	195328	175205	172249
15083	15130	14265	14127	13630
1106	1059	1208	1144	1192
73	88	83	82	181
533	612	558	418	459
4				

小学女

Number of Female Students

地 区 Region	毕业生数 Graduates	招生数 Entrants 合计 Total	其中:受过学前教育 of Which: Those Received the Pre-school Education	在校学生数 合 计 Total
总 计 Total	**7330087**	**7876592**	**7628092**	**43312688**
北 京 Beijing	51737	77267	77144	364118
天 津 Tianjin	40103	49934	49815	255520
河 北 Hebei	394150	463906	462508	2552641
山 西 Shanxi	228076	189089	187093	1100164
内蒙古 Inner Mongolia	111185	109864	108936	625303
辽 宁 Liaoning	172064	167567	167387	966325
吉 林 Jilin	112610	104020	102343	647975
黑龙江 Heilongjiang	158668	131497	129703	740522
上 海 Shanghai	62100	83268	82919	362578
江 苏 Jiangsu	293821	389851	389660	1985323
浙 江 Zhejiang	249684	279155	277473	1608765
安 徽 Anhui	297225	347757	339209	1857945
福 建 Fujian	181701	226542	224922	1189673
江 西 Jiangxi	297073	357867	344235	1836812
山 东 Shandong	485994	533401	531639	2901229
河 南 Henan	754667	833793	833605	4301146
湖 北 Hubei	221976	278121	269439	1498807
湖 南 Hunan	349930	391422	389822	2138777
广 东 Guangdong	606200	680810	660570	3614965
广 西 Guangxi	326241	352065	338511	1987856
海 南 Hainan	54322	56680	53050	325142
重 庆 Chongqing	153801	178563	174952	937562
四 川 Sichuan	420680	453802	419685	2504884
贵 州 Guizhou	342845	237113	209660	1654132
云 南 Yunnan	336480	290614	255798	1846844
西 藏 Tibet	22157	25203	13932	143550
陕 西 Shaanxi	183736	182340	180945	1054698
甘 肃 Gansu	176417	151059	121570	879660
青 海 Qinghai	40443	38095	33123	228456
宁 夏 Ningxia	48935	47726	43377	288109
新 疆 Xinjiang	155066	168201	155067	913207

学生数
in Primary Schools

单位:人
unit:person

Enrolment						预计毕业生数 Estimated Graduates for Next Year
一年级 Grade 1	二年级 Grade 2	三年级 Grade 3	四年级 Grade 4	五年级 Grade 5	六年级 Grade 6	
7901631	**7640390**	**7382127**	**7077514**	**6677216**	**6633810**	**6830425**
77373	66614	64225	54814	48784	52308	52707
49949	47668	46157	38933	37542	35271	40222
463906	479040	455287	409811	360329	384268	384268
189147	194796	181544	184775	164133	185769	185862
109864	106475	109089	97924	96425	105526	106199
167677	160397	163783	157772	145671	171025	172529
104105	112042	112853	111003	97200	110772	110851
131488	136113	137177	133751	118763	83230	128321
83299	77108	74910	65159	60018	2084	59662
389851	360352	339956	321575	289864	283725	283908
279176	275987	284790	272240	247900	248672	249370
347861	305551	316284	304674	295145	288430	288906
226807	213493	204349	193272	178842	172910	172910
370508	334624	308893	289164	266345	267278	267278
533401	508771	528442	496572	452408	381635	462891
835456	779429	717027	682548	654290	632396	638322
278299	273639	259513	245868	225648	215840	216394
391422	382549	355491	347451	328399	333465	333465
679596	647698	612403	582104	544399	548765	545717
353346	343457	333375	327741	315678	314259	314259
59483	58953	56105	51067	49098	50436	50436
178681	164120	154555	148365	142818	149023	149023
454920	447331	416641	404601	384077	397314	397314
237129	272453	265873	275370	291357	311950	311950
290652	293719	306237	311015	318183	327038	327239
25203	24922	23746	23417	23818	22444	22445
184798	181902	176008	173200	166098	172692	172692
151655	147631	142323	144388	143339	150324	150324
39042	38977	37623	37325	38032	37457	37457
48250	49245	48501	47206	46864	48043	48043
169287	155334	148967	144409	145749	149461	149461

小学教职工
Number of Educational Personnel

地 区 Region	教职工数 合计 Total	专任教师 Full-time Teachers	行政人员 Adm. Personnel
总 计 Total	**5494877**	**5096634**	**176119**
北 京 Beijing	57832	48726	4426
天 津 Tianjin	41939	36668	3460
河 北 Hebei	327187	303727	11588
山 西 Shanxi	180491	166887	4219
内蒙古 Inner Mongolia	124735	100752	5713
辽 宁 Liaoning	137661	118083	15453
吉 林 Jilin	121183	102984	8939
黑龙江 Heilongjiang	136461	120214	7335
上 海 Shanghai	49732	41366	3498
江 苏 Jiangsu	254395	234767	5438
浙 江 Zhejiang	176164	165263	4093
安 徽 Anhui	228704	220050	3984
福 建 Fujian	157126	148222	4466
江 西 Jiangxi	195737	191392	1705
山 东 Shandong	383692	361245	6583
河 南 Henan	499445	474208	8892
湖 北 Hubei	198262	183293	3920
湖 南 Hunan	226630	216179	4423
广 东 Guangdong	417189	380146	24938
广 西 Guangxi	229534	209529	12092
海 南 Hainan	47759	44423	775
重 庆 Chongqing	116804	109032	4558
四 川 Sichuan	261493	247103	5589
贵 州 Guizhou	194500	181598	5730
云 南 Yunnan	233400	223329	3500
西 藏 Tibet	18998	18679	40
陕 西 Shaanxi	163908	151744	6048
甘 肃 Gansu	134468	130375	1739
青 海 Qinghai	23044	22016	142
宁 夏 Ningxia	33244	32524	146
新 疆 Xinjiang	123160	112110	2687

数(总数)
in Primary Schools (Total)

单位：人
unit: person

Educational Personnel			代课教师 Substitute Teachers	兼任教师 Part-time Teachers
教辅人员 Supporting Staff	工勤人员 Workers	校办企业职工 Employees in School-run Factories & Farms		
96889	**124430**	**805**	**167253**	**25854**
2847	1825	8		1058
1042	765	4	429	84
5740	6112	20	20202	489
4228	5088	69	16383	679
8950	9287	33	3031	92
2622	1487	16	737	10
6909	2308	43	1087	115
4905	3981	26	778	340
2303	2530	35	521	159
8678	5395	117	5073	548
2850	3939	19		1362
1718	2952		6563	469
2546	1888	4	6256	179
601	2013	26	9570	470
9745	6110	9	3812	561
4135	12196	14	19011	740
5455	5545	49	9532	504
2382	3617	29	6986	596
3424	8604	77	3646	626
3354	4558	1	11963	2461
476	2058	27	476	511
859	2258	97	2840	389
1214	7584	3	15792	538
1108	6028	36	420	5443
1780	4778	13	1760	6069
47	232		594	15
2506	3591	19	5009	202
973	1374	7	8420	468
171	713	2	3004	125
104	470		1395	271
3217	5144	2	1963	281

小学教职工
Number of Educational Personnel

地　区 Region	教职工数		
	合计 Total	专任教师 Full-time Teachers	行政人员 Adm. Personnel
总　计 Total	**1413266**	**1293251**	**55850**
北　京 Beijing	43723	37767	3107
天　津 Tianjin	26331	22534	2313
河　北 Hebei	61237	56884	2030
山　西 Shanxi	44506	40585	1456
内蒙古 Inner Mongolia	31931	28691	1630
辽　宁 Liaoning	66757	56850	7797
吉　林 Jilin	36614	31041	2598
黑龙江 Heilongjiang	43872	37872	3009
上　海 Shanghai	38429	32409	2614
江　苏 Jiangsu	101404	95289	2122
浙　江 Zhejiang	69845	65424	1483
安　徽 Anhui	38304	36851	624
福　建 Fujian	44333	41972	1059
江　西 Jiangxi	29668	28870	350
山　东 Shandong	104684	97787	2137
河　南 Henan	88788	82610	2148
湖　北 Hubei	55015	50822	1659
湖　南 Hunan	45167	42820	1074
广　东 Guangdong	178601	161711	8623
广　西 Guangxi	29597	27128	1127
海　南 Hainan	11132	9862	174
重　庆 Chongqing	29632	27727	900
四　川 Sichuan	51230	47290	1077
贵　州 Guizhou	22955	21528	746
云　南 Yunnan	25457	23827	547
西　藏 Tibet	1803	1731	16
陕　西 Shaanxi	37271	33093	2407
甘　肃 Gansu	19238	18453	410
青　海 Qinghai	3566	3522	11
宁　夏 Ningxia	9365	9235	33
新　疆 Xinjiang	22811	21066	569

数(城区)

in Primary Schools (Urban Area)

单位 :人

unit: person

Educational Personnel			代课教师 Substitute Teachers	兼任教师 Part-time Teachers
教辅人员 Supporting Staff	工勤人员 Workers	校办企业职工 Employees in School-run Factories & Farms		
27252	**36667**	**246**	**32788**	**4923**
1782	1059	8		1020
842	640	2	98	84
980	1343		2002	47
981	1476	8	3006	126
911	692	7	1094	55
1389	710	11	145	
2247	728		267	8
1599	1384	8	170	166
1740	1641	25	412	150
2209	1742	42	1966	34
1037	1893	8		404
358	471		2373	177
381	917	4	2905	31
86	360	2	558	19
2643	2110	7	800	211
1253	2771	6	3318	89
1191	1335	8	2336	188
483	769	21	1940	354
2175	6036	56	3074	371
414	928		1104	556
192	895	9	250	267
376	618	11	459	117
399	2464		2118	58
196	483	2	45	214
259	824		31	37
8	48			
473	1298		823	42
92	283		94	33
6	27		218	
13	84		229	1
537	638	1	953	64

小学教职工

Number of Educational Personnel

地　区 Region	教职工数 合计 Total	专任教师 Full-time Teachers	行政人员 Adm. Personnel
总　计 Total	**263432**	**241211**	**10176**
北　京 Beijing	4336	3613	367
天　津 Tianjin	2681	2278	254
河　北 Hebei	15497	14532	547
山　西 Shanxi	7132	6606	228
内蒙古 Inner Mongolia	1316	1183	0
辽　宁 Liaoning	7143	6242	774
吉　林 Jilin	3184	2754	233
黑龙江 Heilongjiang	5339	4453	389
上　海 Shanghai	4030	3233	292
江　苏 Jiangsu	10353	9444	269
浙　江 Zhejiang	16400	15297	360
安　徽 Anhui	6568	6182	116
福　建 Fujian	8583	8127	240
江　西 Jiangxi	5939	5850	46
山　东 Shandong	29941	27899	605
河　南 Henan	18715	17679	342
湖　北 Hubei	7279	6714	140
湖　南 Hunan	7912	7428	172
广　东 Guangdong	57426	51352	3275
广　西 Guangxi	5524	5097	205
海　南 Hainan	1175	1059	16
重　庆 Chongqing	2970	2735	123
四　川 Sichuan	6715	6120	162
贵　州 Guizhou	5344	5024	177
云　南 Yunnan	6191	5871	125
西　藏 Tibet			
陕　西 Shaanxi	8476	7569	556
甘　肃 Gansu	2469	2368	33
青　海 Qinghai	387	382	2
宁　夏 Ningxia	1200	1187	5
新　疆 Xinjiang	3207	2933	64

数(城乡结合区)
in Primary Schools (Urban-rural Transitional Area)

单位:人
unit: person

Educational Personnel			代课教师 Substitute Teachers	兼任教师 Part-time Teachers
教辅人员 Supporting Staff	工勤人员 Workers	校办企业职工 Employees in School-run Factories & Farms		
4160	**7858**	**27**	**5213**	**921**
155	201			52
107	41	1	5	16
146	272		398	15
131	167		620	8
21	53		35	18
88	37	2	62	
121	76		9	
261	234	2	18	
101	404		36	2
337	296	7	261	7
251	492			288
179	91		237	25
59	157		446	2
10	33		138	2
860	577		289	77
153	536	5	532	14
197	228		156	4
116	196		406	58
488	2301	10	665	108
51	171		206	76
7	93		35	
19	93		13	24
85	348		361	12
35	108		33	59
44	151		5	4
73	278		156	10
27	41		1	1
2	1		15	
2	6		71	
34	176		4	39

小学教职工

Number of Educational Personnel

地　区 Region	教职工数 合计 Total	专任教师 Full-time Teachers	行政人员 Adm. Personnel
总　计 Total	**1892651**	**1742138**	**59059**
北　京 Beijing	7508	5667	742
天　津 Tianjin	7625	6909	533
河　北 Hebei	111759	102445	3912
山　西 Shanxi	62813	58031	1257
内蒙古 Inner Mongolia	59129	46676	2628
辽　宁 Liaoning	33942	28781	4119
吉　林 Jilin	37243	29929	3161
黑龙江 Heilongjiang	45912	39973	2238
上　海 Shanghai	8394	6684	643
江　苏 Jiangsu	116346	105435	2699
浙　江 Zhejiang	72444	67900	1826
安　徽 Anhui	77712	73919	1688
福　建 Fujian	58101	54141	2198
江　西 Jiangxi	77167	75094	760
山　东 Shandong	133783	124785	2580
河　南 Henan	156353	145737	3164
湖　北 Hubei	69933	64366	1022
湖　南 Hunan	90804	86090	1740
广　东 Guangdong	119773	109745	7432
广　西 Guangxi	74826	67525	3436
海　南 Hainan	19550	18101	344
重　庆 Chongqing	53426	49619	2305
四　川 Sichuan	112847	107203	2333
贵　州 Guizhou	59201	55134	1797
云　南 Yunnan	60231	57020	1039
西　藏 Tibet	6264	6120	13
陕　西 Shaanxi	76831	71435	2201
甘　肃 Gansu	34603	33132	540
青　海 Qinghai	8677	8303	90
宁　夏 Ningxia	9619	9359	56
新　疆 Xinjiang	29835	26880	563

数(镇区)

in Primary Schools (Counties & Towns Area)

单位:人
unit: person

Educational Personnel				
教辅人员 Supporting Staff	工勤人员 Workers	校办企业职工 Employees in School-run Factories & Farms	代课教师 Substitute Teachers	兼任教师 Part-time Teachers
41773	**49259**	**422**	**44573**	**4828**
637	462			1
118	65		184	
2553	2849		5824	200
1674	1797	54	5248	238
4972	4852	1	1135	24
536	501	5	106	4
3087	1025	41	305	32
1844	1849	8	203	67
459	602	6	67	2
5126	3021	65	1578	103
1180	1529	9		462
563	1542		1322	84
1214	548		1107	84
330	973	10	2944	249
3993	2423	2	1488	135
1772	5680		7854	156
2202	2305	38	1986	140
1219	1751	4	1451	149
898	1678	20	190	57
1900	1964	1	1792	391
243	844	18	57	125
373	1047	82	1179	200
496	2812	3	3766	126
494	1742	34	56	1002
770	1392	10	181	376
15	116		46	
1535	1659	1	2285	69
401	523	7	824	89
69	213	2	779	58
58	146		406	144
1042	1349	1	210	61

小学教职工

Number of Educational Personnel

地区 Region	教职工数		
	合计 Total	专任教师 Full-time Teachers	行政人员 Adm. Personnel
总计 Total	**594567**	**555470**	**16824**
北京 Beijing	1654	1261	187
天津 Tianjin	2957	2671	234
河北 Hebei	61492	57134	1887
山西 Shanxi	18880	17621	428
内蒙古 Inner Mongolia	4961	3919	195
辽宁 Liaoning	6285	5355	746
吉林 Jilin	5228	4433	380
黑龙江 Heilongjiang	5941	5428	266
上海 Shanghai	2049	1652	123
江苏 Jiangsu	33198	30139	743
浙江 Zhejiang	25640	23966	632
安徽 Anhui	19641	18911	376
福建 Fujian	14577	13805	468
江西 Jiangxi	21505	21089	124
山东 Shandong	58635	54979	944
河南 Henan	70010	66440	1161
湖北 Hubei	18911	17478	246
湖南 Hunan	33402	31893	549
广东 Guangdong	52474	47992	3605
广西 Guangxi	23967	21925	1163
海南 Hainan	3664	3419	54
重庆 Chongqing	10174	9439	447
四川 Sichuan	20994	19970	401
贵州 Guizhou	16397	15487	400
云南 Yunnan	20273	19480	291
西藏 Tibet	641	622	
陕西 Shaanxi	22293	21131	568
甘肃 Gansu	9520	9187	103
青海 Qinghai	1928	1889	10
宁夏 Ningxia	2300	2249	8
新疆 Xinjiang	4976	4506	85

数(镇乡结合区)
in Primary Schools (County-town Transitional Area)

单位 :人
unit: person

Educational Personnel			代课教师 Substitute Teachers	兼任教师 Part-time Teachers
教辅人员 Supporting Staff	工勤人员 Workers	校办企业职工 Employees in School-run Factories & Farms		
9449	**12723**	**101**	**16962**	**1657**
116	90			
28	24		110	
1019	1452		3067	133
403	420	8	1886	31
553	294		86	22
114	69	1	38	
279	136		11	8
131	115	1	23	
95	176	3	10	2
1465	807	44	629	101
318	723	1		360
118	236		303	36
199	105		611	39
97	193	2	938	17
1562	1149	1	1172	63
497	1912		2939	97
568	619		702	48
336	624		578	122
321	549	7	87	33
357	521	1	1106	120
36	145	10	34	19
67	221		386	8
54	569		973	26
79	413	18	4	185
148	354		53	130
	19		2	
213	380	1	599	3
116	114		418	32
5	22	2	121	1
8	35		42	3
147	237	1	34	18

小学教职工

Number of Educational Personnel

地区 Region	教职工数		
	合计 Total	专任教师 Full-time Teachers	行政人员 Adm. Personnel
总计 Total	**2188960**	**2061245**	**61210**
北京 Beijing	6601	5292	577
天津 Tianjin	7983	7225	614
河北 Hebei	154191	144398	5646
山西 Shanxi	73172	68271	1506
内蒙古 Inner Mongolia	33675	25385	1455
辽宁 Liaoning	36962	32452	3537
吉林 Jilin	47326	42014	3180
黑龙江 Heilongjiang	46677	42369	2088
上海 Shanghai	2909	2273	241
江苏 Jiangsu	36645	34043	617
浙江 Zhejiang	33875	31939	784
安徽 Anhui	112688	109280	1672
福建 Fujian	54692	52109	1209
江西 Jiangxi	88902	87428	595
山东 Shandong	145225	138673	1866
河南 Henan	254304	245861	3580
湖北 Hubei	73314	68105	1239
湖南 Hunan	90659	87269	1609
广东 Guangdong	118815	108690	8883
广西 Guangxi	125111	114876	7529
海南 Hainan	17077	16460	257
重庆 Chongqing	33746	31686	1353
四川 Sichuan	97416	92610	2179
贵州 Guizhou	112344	104936	3187
云南 Yunnan	147712	142482	1914
西藏 Tibet	10931	10828	11
陕西 Shaanxi	49806	47216	1440
甘肃 Gansu	80627	78790	789
青海 Qinghai	10801	10191	41
宁夏 Ningxia	14260	13930	57
新疆 Xinjiang	70514	64164	1555

(乡村)

in Primary Schools (Rural Area)

单位：人
unit: person

Educational Personnel				
教辅人员 Supporting Staff	工勤人员 Workers	校办企业职工 Employees in School-run Factories & Farms	代课教师 Substitute Teachers	兼任教师 Part-time Teachers
27864	**38504**	**137**	**89892**	**16103**
428	304			37
82	60	2	147	
2207	1920	20	12376	242
1573	1815	7	8129	315
3067	3743	25	802	13
697	276		486	6
1575	555	2	515	75
1462	748	10	405	107
104	287	4	42	7
1343	632	10	1529	411
633	517	2		496
797	939		2868	208
951	423		2244	64
185	680	14	6068	202
3109	1577		1524	215
1110	3745	8	7839	495
2062	1905	3	5210	176
680	1097	4	3595	93
351	890	1	382	198
1040	1666		9067	1514
41	319		169	119
110	593	4	1202	72
319	2308		9908	354
418	3803		319	4227
751	2562	3	1548	5656
24	68		548	15
498	634	18	1901	91
480	568		7502	346
96	473		2007	67
33	240		760	126
1638	3157		800	156

小学教职工总数

Number of Primary Schools Educational

地　区 Region	教职工数 合计 Total	专任教师 Full-time Teachers	行政人员 Adm. Personnel
总　计 Total	**204861**	**151800**	**11371**
北　京 Beijing	3046	2245	291
天　津 Tianjin	296	218	32
河　北 Hebei	15137	10715	868
山　西 Shanxi	8392	5579	400
内蒙古 Inner Mongolia	958	670	91
辽　宁 Liaoning	1022	885	70
吉　林 Jilin	1556	1221	105
黑龙江 Heilongjiang	335	266	27
上　海 Shanghai	8913	6735	660
江　苏 Jiangsu	4670	3856	125
浙　江 Zhejiang	11001	8674	465
安　徽 Anhui	6345	4596	304
福　建 Fujian	3596	2656	195
江　西 Jiangxi	2305	1541	153
山　东 Shandong	12616	9516	652
河　南 Henan	42869	30720	2282
湖　北 Hubei	3111	2039	155
湖　南 Hunan	5498	4124	250
广　东 Guangdong	39265	31080	2228
广　西 Guangxi	5046	3522	365
海　南 Hainan	2916	1814	140
重　庆 Chongqing	2658	1995	191
四　川 Sichuan	8458	5863	327
贵　州 Guizhou	4454	3631	279
云　南 Yunnan	2562	2017	198
西　藏 Tibet	50	32	6
陕　西 Shaanxi	6747	4885	437
甘　肃 Gansu	169	123	15
青　海 Qinghai	37	18	1
宁　夏 Ningxia	365	224	15
新　疆 Xinjiang	468	340	44

中民办教职工数
Personnel Maintained by Communities

单位：人
unit: person

Educational Personnel			代课教师 Substitute Teachers	兼任教师 Part-time Teachers
教辅人员 Supporting Staff	工勤人员 Workers	校办企业职工 Employees in School-run Factories & Farms		
7406	**33986**	**298**	**12800**	**2294**
133	376	1		11
15	31		80	34
783	2751	20	1760	34
459	1900	54	897	88
21	176		19	4
25	42			
65	163	2		
7	35			
290	1224	4	134	120
137	542	10	32	
315	1539	8		1168
150	1295		365	31
103	639	3	86	30
108	493	10	17	6
516	1932		284	14
1711	8143	13	7990	204
139	778		376	35
287	816	21	33	194
997	4908	52	177	171
209	950		36	2
60	889	13		12
136	303	33	161	5
236	2032			62
107	402	35	35	20
61	286			46
3	9			
252	1154	19	209	3
12	19			
	18		47	
38	88		18	
31	53		44	

小学女教
Number of Female Educational

地　区 Region	教职工数		
	合计 Total	专任教师 Full-time Teachers	行政人员 Adm. Personnel
总　计 Total	**3209818**	**3066446**	**49568**
北　京 Beijing	43502	38706	2468
天　津 Tianjin	28972	26416	1695
河　北 Hebei	226299	218034	2987
山　西 Shanxi	129559	123412	1312
内蒙古 Inner Mongolia	73099	65979	1861
辽　宁 Liaoning	94477	85013	7453
吉　林 Jilin	77918	70571	3329
黑龙江 Heilongjiang	84215	77581	3263
上　海 Shanghai	38285	33538	2073
江　苏 Jiangsu	150761	145260	1303
浙　江 Zhejiang	120040	115621	953
安　徽 Anhui	103452	101088	518
福　建 Fujian	93346	90990	745
江　西 Jiangxi	103366	101905	362
山　东 Shandong	199262	192826	1404
河　南 Henan	297540	286694	2493
湖　北 Hubei	98318	93480	1063
湖　南 Hunan	127274	123826	1012
广　东 Guangdong	271792	260236	4909
广　西 Guangxi	130469	124994	1952
海　南 Hainan	23460	21973	116
重　庆 Chongqing	62282	60411	811
四　川 Sichuan	139951	135476	1052
贵　州 Guizhou	91253	86390	882
云　南 Yunnan	115946	112416	622
西　藏 Tibet	9839	9720	13
陕　西 Shaanxi	97493	93190	1669
甘　肃 Gansu	62404	61379	260
青　海 Qinghai	12105	11646	35
宁　夏 Ningxia	19164	18821	32
新　疆 Xinjiang	83975	78854	921

职工数

Personnel in Primary Schools

单位：人
unit: person

Educational Personnel			代课教师 Substitute Teachers	兼任教师 Part-time Teachers
教辅人员 Supporting Staff	工勤人员 Workers	校办企业职工 Employees in School-run Factories & Farms		
41525	**51903**	**376**	**122013**	**15201**
1686	641	1		842
639	222		372	66
2473	2787	18	17405	315
2184	2625	26	14040	411
2960	2296	3	2412	69
1652	357	2	694	10
3439	569	10	798	79
2239	1122	10	496	227
1580	1080	14	374	128
2402	1760	36	4300	55
1364	2094	8		884
536	1310		4446	266
884	724	3	5257	127
244	843	12	6992	223
3045	1982	5	2872	248
2359	5986	8	15176	431
1814	1929	32	5487	248
1022	1394	20	5408	449
2279	4338	30	2366	397
1219	2303	1	8688	1427
213	1142	16	274	239
447	547	66	2178	258
516	2905	2	9608	336
399	3549	33	147	3400
511	2397		924	3276
9	97		247	8
1167	1451	16	3224	94
255	508	2	3673	263
58	365	1	1575	55
61	250		1017	178
1869	2330	1	1563	192

小学专任教师学历、
Number of Full-time Teacher in Primary Schools by

地 区 Region	合 计 Total	其中:女 of Which: Female	按学历分 By Educational Attainment			
			研究生毕业 Graduate	本科毕业 Under-graduate	专科毕业 Associate Bachelor	高中阶段毕业 High School Graduate
总 计 Total	**5584644**	**3388375**	**20228**	**2059660**	**2797184**	**697973**
北 京 Beijing	54981	43801	1286	45562	7065	1035
天 津 Tianjin	38275	27676	497	24487	10317	2929
河 北 Hebei	318856	229875	573	115654	171251	31199
山 西 Shanxi	180548	134012	362	65984	95663	18451
内蒙古 Inner Mongolia	110576	72456	424	50500	50524	9025
辽 宁 Liaoning	142656	101590	840	55521	71426	14616
吉 林 Jilin	115116	78954	582	54688	49710	9995
黑龙江 Heilongjiang	136481	88680	202	49125	71877	15114
上 海 Shanghai	49772	40130	1114	33909	13555	1181
江 苏 Jiangsu	258173	159957	1960	158452	79601	18157
浙 江 Zhejiang	183479	128611	1058	117544	55065	9733
安 徽 Anhui	238131	111296	345	73727	123617	40418
福 建 Fujian	154490	95199	391	50233	78281	25452
江 西 Jiangxi	207153	112249	308	62512	100456	43161
山 东 Shandong	387312	210394	2810	178522	150735	55043
河 南 Henan	494515	302810	939	151722	273564	68281
湖 北 Hubei	196556	101312	680	62405	100292	32923
湖 南 Hunan	246273	140716	702	74379	131583	38588
广 东 Guangdong	437532	302062	1965	148240	243835	42907
广 西 Guangxi	215570	129538	446	56138	124550	34025
海 南 Hainan	50466	25946	28	8067	33956	8350
重 庆 Chongqing	115204	63780	469	39387	64639	10567
四 川 Sichuan	305619	166311	546	78386	186438	40167
贵 州 Guizhou	192953	92794	103	43841	119751	27307
云 南 Yunnan	230220	116816	405	66520	127937	33547
西 藏 Tibet	18834	9826	17	5293	12066	1339
陕 西 Shaanxi	162841	100514	617	67814	77479	16781
甘 肃 Gansu	140414	66544	296	53613	61096	24915
青 海 Qinghai	26974	14498	106	11246	13248	2336
宁 夏 Ningxia	34113	19722	58	12920	16653	4414
新 疆 Xinjiang	140561	100306	99	43269	80954	16017

职称情况(总计)
Educational Attainment and Professional Rank (Total)

单位:人
unit: person

	按职称分 By Professional Rank					
高中阶段毕业以下 Below High School Graduate	中学高级 Senior Secondary	小学高级 Senior Primary	小学一级 1st Grade Primary	小学二级 2nd Grade Primary	小学三级 3rd Grade Primary	未定职级 No-ranking
9599	**114805**	**2919927**	**1880106**	**177237**	**12469**	**480100**
33	579	29128	17621	663	157	6833
45	1120	29309	6233	114	20	1479
179	4340	159458	123976	5865	246	24971
88	989	67965	86342	8298	872	16082
103	24560	53828	21526	1881		8781
253	8372	104679	22394	1425	181	5605
141	2011	58535	43728	4390	233	6219
163	8096	78893	44967	1255	74	3196
13	942	24569	17036	564	58	6603
3	11351	163503	65522	3385	10	14402
79	4925	99020	58337	2002	171	19024
24	2047	133342	77206	7245	308	17983
133	1381	92674	44245	5392	110	10688
716	3402	105126	64400	12363	368	21494
202	9067	190774	149834	10162	279	27196
9	7347	231007	185255	18124	1424	51358
256	4375	129732	46852	4100	515	10982
1021	2697	150155	64308	3950	629	24534
585	1807	273720	76648	12367	3305	69685
411	1586	129446	64097	7065	684	12692
65	285	23834	20135	3684	49	2479
142	983	48355	55509	3452	263	6642
82	5205	137921	135865	3609	181	22838
1951	555	83842	69341	14883	1219	23113
1811	733	118703	80799	15167	221	14597
119	325	6063	8866	1258	173	2149
150	1316	60448	82913	7651		10513
494	1197	52454	67012	7911	260	11580
38	1018	16307	6855	436	59	2299
68	467	14702	11939	1096	112	5797
222	1727	52435	60345	7480	288	18286

小学专任教师学历、

Number of Full-time Teacher in Primary Schools by

地 区 Region	合 计 Total	其中:女 of Which: Female	按学历分 By Educational Attainment			
			研究生毕业 Graduate	本科毕业 Under-graduate	专科毕业 Associate Bachelor	高中阶段毕业 High School Graduate
总 计 Total	**1466646**	**1137891**	**14927**	**836580**	**548220**	**66381**
北 京 Beijing	42312	35143	1077	35553	5115	551
天 津 Tianjin	23671	19296	446	16198	5882	1121
河 北 Hebei	61497	52255	314	33619	25133	2416
山 西 Shanxi	44565	38049	235	23411	19085	1827
内蒙古 Inner Mongolia	31225	25049	295	20080	9937	909
辽 宁 Liaoning	62806	51379	736	32970	26171	2887
吉 林 Jilin	33927	28489	449	22040	9977	1444
黑龙江 Heilongjiang	41229	33430	167	22044	16927	2079
上 海 Shanghai	38294	32341	886	27248	9397	756
江 苏 Jiangsu	106012	78294	1598	75848	23874	4689
浙 江 Zhejiang	75357	58287	787	53175	19041	2344
安 徽 Anhui	41489	28267	171	19340	18864	3110
福 建 Fujian	44975	35419	340	24771	17051	2801
江 西 Jiangxi	33178	24805	154	17963	12934	2097
山 东 Shandong	108973	78548	1784	73559	28594	5022
河 南 Henan	89488	71226	622	45769	39358	3735
湖 北 Hubei	56547	40867	547	27650	24316	4017
湖 南 Hunan	48380	37857	470	25261	20565	2048
广 东 Guangdong	202230	155460	1860	102456	90043	7788
广 西 Guangxi	30691	24612	239	13809	14846	1784
海 南 Hainan	11808	8385	21	3534	7443	809
重 庆 Chongqing	29594	21134	306	16843	11425	1010
四 川 Sichuan	56834	41672	435	26385	27341	2652
贵 州 Guizhou	24954	18844	49	9148	13548	2133
云 南 Yunnan	26655	19732	300	13749	10747	1840
西 藏 Tibet	1801	1233	7	608	1001	182
陕 西 Shaanxi	36428	28822	385	21414	13281	1338
甘 肃 Gansu	20228	15081	115	10115	8847	1148
青 海 Qinghai	4449	3427	34	2563	1590	260
宁 夏 Ningxia	9356	7305	35	5187	3758	376
新 疆 Xinjiang	27693	23183	63	14270	12129	1208

职称情况（城区）

Educational Attainment and Professional Rank (Urban Area)

单位：人
unit: person

	按职称分 By Professional Rank					
高中阶段毕业以下 Below High School Graduate	中学高级 Senior Secondary	小学高级 Senior Primary	小学一级 1st Grade Primary	小学二级 2nd Grade Primary	小学三级 3rd Grade Primary	未定职级 No-ranking
538	**40476**	**807477**	**442339**	**32626**	**3942**	**139786**
16	486	22683	13627	525	121	4870
24	500	17682	4449	97	19	924
15	905	34129	20061	1545	94	4763
7	320	18985	19584	1812	116	3748
4	6966	14422	6146	580		3111
42	3227	47825	9087	393	54	2220
17	1061	18463	12114	1031	37	1221
12	3510	24848	11471	364	18	1018
7	778	19865	13228	307	13	4103
3	6135	66141	26919	974	7	5836
10	2914	40246	22727	852	78	8540
4	442	23839	13333	1140	49	2686
12	582	24316	13533	1470	29	5045
30	918	17521	11483	1104	61	2091
14	2962	51470	44569	2285	101	7586
4	1643	44845	31515	3327	344	7814
17	1931	37695	13227	991	157	2546
36	757	30159	12330	556	115	4463
83	992	113293	37146	5983	1962	42854
13	330	19063	6855	978	230	3235
1	130	5559	4022	907		1190
10	409	13656	13799	352	19	1359
21	1130	28291	23983	559	59	2812
76	75	10653	7514	1081	87	5544
19	83	14646	8524	735	84	2583
3	76	897	677	36		115
10	292	15287	16993	1359		2497
3	313	10259	8376	477	15	788
2	104	2436	1238	62	11	598
	137	4759	3108	296	24	1032
23	368	13544	10701	448	38	2594

小学专任教师学历、

Number of Full-time Teacher in Primary Schools by Educational

地　区 Region	合　计 Total	其中：女 of Which: Female	按学历分 By Educational Attainment			
			研究生毕业 Graduate	本科毕业 Under-graduate	专科毕业 Associate Bachelor	高中阶段毕业 High School Graduate
总　计 Total	**285249**	**202908**	**1844**	**135344**	**127352**	**20531**
北　京 Beijing	4108	3241	78	3023	840	164
天　津 Tianjin	2393	1714	39	1724	488	142
河　北 Hebei	16566	13472	83	7565	7930	975
山　西 Shanxi	6932	5685	104	3144	3270	414
内蒙古 Inner Mongolia	1277	899	7	728	483	59
辽　宁 Liaoning	7183	5463	41	3193	3325	611
吉　林 Jilin	3021	2252	17	1738	1072	193
黑龙江 Heilongjiang	4957	3883	54	2056	2415	432
上　海 Shanghai	3820	2895	56	1925	1632	203
江　苏 Jiangsu	11324	7099	100	7010	3436	778
浙　江 Zhejiang	18485	13555	127	11703	5878	775
安　徽 Anhui	6897	3850	9	2454	3516	917
福　建 Fujian	8632	6193	23	4322	3327	955
江　西 Jiangxi	6528	4366	24	2927	2872	697
山　东 Shandong	30841	19476	336	18365	9689	2446
河　南 Henan	19636	14234	72	8296	9794	1473
湖　北 Hubei	7844	4611	29	2873	4076	859
湖　南 Hunan	9089	6527	53	3904	4386	724
广　东 Guangdong	68643	50487	400	29876	34847	3474
广　西 Guangxi	5731	4173	23	2077	3137	490
海　南 Hainan	1198	751		237	776	185
重　庆 Chongqing	2841	1728	3	1011	1619	207
四　川 Sichuan	8303	5665	77	3564	4027	634
贵　州 Guizhou	6014	4062	9	1609	3557	821
云　南 Yunnan	6302	4373	9	2585	3004	690
西　藏 Tibet						
陕　西 Shaanxi	8185	5869	50	4164	3537	426
甘　肃 Gansu	2747	1990	6	1085	1404	252
青　海 Qinghai	581	400	5	307	213	56
宁　夏 Ningxia	1214	846	5	520	600	89
新　疆 Xinjiang	3957	3149	5	1359	2202	390

职称情况(城乡结合区)

Attainment and Professional Rank (Urban-rural Transitional Area)

单位:人
unit: person

高中阶段毕业以下 Below High School Graduate	按职称分 By Professional Rank					
	中学高级 Senior Secondary	小学高级 Senior Primary	小学一级 1st Grade Primary	小学二级 2nd Grade Primary	小学三级 3rd Grade Primary	未定职级 No-ranking
178	**4558**	**143375**	**86109**	**7964**	**1475**	**41768**
3	28	1856	1212	126	37	849
	20	1725	537		1	110
13	225	8483	5856	392	49	1561
	38	2822	3445	223	1	403
	265	541	291	25		155
13	433	5500	960	52	2	236
1	62	1610	1163	79		107
	479	3001	1322	41	2	112
4	23	1000	1006	61	5	1725
	471	6978	2965	133		777
2	340	8392	5963	197	43	3550
1	43	3835	2272	215	21	511
5	43	4711	2732	389	7	750
8	103	3413	2309	276	1	426
5	761	14785	12414	771	32	2078
1	340	9203	7035	911	60	2087
7	192	4976	1727	258	35	656
22	84	5287	2337	116	42	1223
46	252	33044	12555	2342	1021	19429
4	33	3446	1453	146	31	622
	27	687	317	77		90
1	11	1359	1327	27	1	116
1	122	3851	3502	69	11	748
18	13	2552	1542	311	23	1573
14	15	3652	2047	168	9	411
8	51	3066	4139	395		534
	22	1153	1356	69	1	146
	13	318	177	9	7	57
	19	628	352	25	6	184
1	30	1501	1796	61	27	542

小学专任教师学历、

Number of Full-time Teacher in Primary Schools by

地 区 Region	合 计 Total	其中:女 of Which: Female	按学历分 By Educational Attainment			
			研究生毕业 Graduate	本科毕业 Under-graduate	专科毕业 Associate Bachelor	高中阶段毕业 High School Graduate
总 计 Total	**1919217**	**1246278**	**3015**	**676260**	**1034648**	**203410**
北 京 Beijing	6958	5039	156	5648	977	174
天 津 Tianjin	7191	4783	37	4183	2216	753
河 北 Hebei	109659	85654	132	40537	60446	8497
山 西 Shanxi	63194	51234	58	23365	34813	4951
内蒙古 Inner Mongolia	51088	33971	84	21659	25386	3914
辽 宁 Liaoning	41275	28265	54	12800	23298	5028
吉 林 Jilin	33725	24256	57	15722	15160	2765
黑龙江 Heilongjiang	47777	32495	20	16093	27048	4563
上 海 Shanghai	8713	5953	188	5147	3091	281
江 苏 Jiangsu	115960	67211	280	67679	39516	8485
浙 江 Zhejiang	73239	49666	195	44848	23835	4316
安 徽 Anhui	81040	44138	72	25539	44823	10600
福 建 Fujian	55145	35544	32	14570	32488	8036
江 西 Jiangxi	81364	51715	60	26558	42718	11890
山 东 Shandong	136427	78844	547	60842	57513	17451
河 南 Henan	155949	111414	116	47285	92729	15819
湖 北 Hubei	68204	37086	51	19710	37936	10426
湖 南 Hunan	96391	60432	138	27625	55833	12510
广 东 Guangdong	120639	83345	63	27093	79263	13987
广 西 Guangxi	68837	48781	72	19575	41684	7416
海 南 Hainan	21430	11722	4	3216	14952	3233
重 庆 Chongqing	51732	29123	139	14688	32392	4469
四 川 Sichuan	128557	74362	87	30445	82746	15253
贵 州 Guizhou	57547	34289	18	12777	37756	6788
云 南 Yunnan	58275	36789	34	17944	33344	6782
西 藏 Tibet	6205	3624	5	1846	3862	453
陕 西 Shaanxi	77596	50715	159	32150	38708	6534
甘 肃 Gansu	35310	22366	94	14970	16516	3686
青 海 Qinghai	10357	6535	38	4349	5379	588
宁 夏 Ningxia	9993	6617	7	3845	5246	886
新 疆 Xinjiang	39440	30310	18	13552	22974	2876

职称情况(镇区)

Educational Attainment and Professional Rank (Counties & Towns Area)

单位:人

unit: person

高中阶段毕业以下 Below High School Graduate	按职称分 By Professional Rank 中学高级 Senior Secondary	小学高级 Senior Primary	小学一级 1st Grade Primary	小学二级 2nd Grade Primary	小学三级 3rd Grade Primary	未定职级 No-ranking
1884	**44834**	**1025927**	**645937**	**54256**	**3967**	**144296**
3	82	3430	2204	91	22	1129
2	389	5691	867	1		243
47	1494	53554	42604	2158	103	9746
7	233	22775	31474	2549	396	5767
45	11851	25401	9691	670		3475
95	2894	29464	6782	468	81	1586
21	499	16408	13252	1414	69	2083
53	2801	27568	15608	478	38	1284
6	111	3858	3059	184	15	1486
	4667	73963	29214	1873	1	6242
45	1699	40970	23166	725	53	6626
6	633	45826	25202	2238	184	6957
19	509	35031	15263	1661	51	2630
138	1399	41401	26418	4634	120	7392
74	3581	64795	52744	4398	118	10791
	2288	68860	59118	6528	779	18376
81	1450	45138	16098	1518	200	3800
285	858	58863	26754	1448	258	8210
233	330	86508	17384	2655	637	13125
90	638	46145	16871	1725	183	3275
25	94	10793	8313	1331	17	882
44	439	22582	24657	1292	102	2660
26	2808	60545	57057	1006	29	7112
208	199	29592	20160	3300	208	4088
171	258	36038	18548	1996	9	1426
39	199	2440	2627	395	75	469
45	705	27446	40286	3976		5183
44	334	13220	18159	1572	42	1983
3	496	6440	2574	174	23	650
9	144	4159	3622	386	44	1638
20	752	17023	16161	1412	110	3982

小学专任教师学历、

Number of Full-time Teacher in Primary Schools by Educational

地 区 Region	合 计 Total	其中:女 of Which: Female	按学历分 By Educational Attainment			
			研究生毕业 Graduate	本科毕业 Under-graduate	专科毕业 Associate Bachelor	高中阶段毕业 High School Graduate
总 计 Total	**599466**	**379900**	**850**	**199016**	**323466**	**75488**
北 京 Beijing	1579	1093	41	1217	263	55
天 津 Tianjin	2744	1726	20	1499	882	343
河 北 Hebei	59928	46256	46	19761	34976	5135
山 西 Shanxi	19518	15870	5	7116	10662	1730
内蒙古 Inner Mongolia	4360	2991	3	1952	2070	324
辽 宁 Liaoning	7228	4899	11	2404	3945	857
吉 林 Jilin	4910	3359	8	2204	2260	435
黑龙江 Heilongjiang	6048	3782	7	1820	3371	828
上 海 Shanghai	2201	1469	33	1183	919	66
江 苏 Jiangsu	32927	18898	88	18579	11642	2618
浙 江 Zhejiang	25743	17360	53	15479	8589	1600
安 徽 Anhui	20967	10009	20	6106	11318	3521
福 建 Fujian	14163	8772	14	3805	7837	2498
江 西 Jiangxi	22767	12841	12	5949	11806	4937
山 东 Shandong	59132	32564	205	24997	24945	8954
河 南 Henan	71133	46535	35	20105	41953	9040
湖 北 Hubei	18559	8783	8	4484	10646	3407
湖 南 Hunan	35135	20734	58	9450	19887	5633
广 东 Guangdong	51449	36047	43	11296	33744	6273
广 西 Guangxi	22099	15009	7	5524	13479	3069
海 南 Hainan	3821	2006	2	674	2508	632
重 庆 Chongqing	9651	5283	29	2409	6238	961
四 川 Sichuan	24174	13633	34	5707	15068	3359
贵 州 Guizhou	16454	9071	3	3363	10705	2286
云 南 Yunnan	19862	12560	10	5921	11290	2583
西 藏 Tibet	696	435		234	395	53
陕 西 Shaanxi	22038	14648	44	8700	11423	1865
甘 肃 Gansu	9716	5881	1	3808	4578	1316
青 海 Qinghai	2496	1561	5	1007	1292	192
宁 夏 Ningxia	2380	1527	2	768	1295	309
新 疆 Xinjiang	5588	4298	3	1495	3480	609

职称情况（镇乡结合区）

Attainment and Professional Rank（County-town Transitional Area）

单位：人

unit：person

高中阶段毕业以下 Below High School Graduate	按职称分 By Professional Rank					
	中学高级 Senior Secondary	小学高级 Senior Primary	小学一级 1st Grade Primary	小学二级 2nd Grade Primary	小学三级 3rd Grade Primary	未定职级 No-ranking
646	**9385**	**316598**	**205444**	**17330**	**1320**	**49389**
3	17	725	517	26	17	277
	79	2160	391	1		113
10	732	28557	24091	1135	31	5382
5	64	6995	9987	853	71	1548
11	1004	2213	798	70		275
11	536	5071	1098	58	38	427
3	54	2431	1913	128	5	379
22	276	3398	2215	40	10	109
	36	961	618	40	10	536
	1073	20602	8859	508		1885
22	444	13403	8583	221	27	3065
2	179	11869	6603	516	54	1746
9	124	8722	4109	449	17	742
63	323	11759	7027	1402	31	2225
31	1449	28430	22963	1911	40	4339
	1039	31805	27432	2982	314	7561
14	344	12209	4513	355	41	1097
107	324	21699	9097	585	94	3336
93	115	35501	7808	1204	250	6571
20	124	14622	6062	509	50	732
5	14	1695	1724	272	5	111
14	81	3920	4643	266	26	715
6	412	11608	10290	241	22	1601
97	29	7772	6134	1050	77	1392
58	71	12252	6826	394	1	318
14	20	247	299	44	58	28
6	209	7291	11883	1291		1364
13	57	3720	4933	394	7	605
	86	1678	586	38	3	105
6	30	1071	886	65	11	317
1	40	2212	2556	282	10	488

小学专任教师学历、
Number of Full-time Teacher in Primary Schools by

地 区 Region	合 计 Total	其中:女 of Which: Female	按学历分 By Educational Attainment			
			研究生毕业 Graduate	本科毕业 Under-graduate	专科毕业 Associate Bachelor	高中阶段毕业 High School Graduate
总 计 Total	**2198781**	**1004206**	**2286**	**546820**	**1214316**	**428182**
北 京 Beijing	5711	3619	53	4361	973	310
天 津 Tianjin	7413	3597	14	4106	2219	1055
河 北 Hebei	147700	91966	127	41498	85672	20286
山 西 Shanxi	72789	44729	69	19208	41765	11673
内蒙古 Inner Mongolia	28263	13436	45	8761	15201	4202
辽 宁 Liaoning	38575	21946	50	9751	21957	6701
吉 林 Jilin	47464	26209	76	16926	24573	5786
黑龙江 Heilongjiang	47475	22755	15	10988	27902	8472
上 海 Shanghai	2765	1836	40	1514	1067	144
江 苏 Jiangsu	36201	14452	82	14925	16211	4983
浙 江 Zhejiang	34883	20658	76	19521	12189	3073
安 徽 Anhui	115602	38891	102	28848	59930	26708
福 建 Fujian	54370	24236	19	10892	28742	14615
江 西 Jiangxi	92611	35729	94	17991	44804	29174
山 东 Shandong	141912	53002	479	44121	64628	32570
河 南 Henan	249078	120170	201	58668	141477	48727
湖 北 Hubei	71805	23359	82	15045	38040	18480
湖 南 Hunan	101502	42427	94	21493	55185	24030
广 东 Guangdong	114663	63257	42	18691	74529	21132
广 西 Guangxi	116042	56145	135	22754	68020	24825
海 南 Hainan	17228	5839	3	1317	11561	4308
重 庆 Chongqing	33878	13523	24	7856	20822	5088
四 川 Sichuan	120228	50277	24	21556	76351	22262
贵 州 Guizhou	110452	39661	36	21916	68447	18386
云 南 Yunnan	145290	60295	71	34827	83846	24925
西 藏 Tibet	10828	4969	5	2839	7203	704
陕 西 Shaanxi	48817	20977	73	14250	25490	8909
甘 肃 Gansu	84876	29097	87	28528	35733	20081
青 海 Qinghai	12168	4536	34	4334	6279	1488
宁 夏 Ningxia	14764	5800	16	3888	7649	3152
新 疆 Xinjiang	73428	46813	18	15447	45851	11933

职称情况(乡村)

Educational Attainment and Professional Rank (Rural Area)

单位:人
unit: person

	按职称分 By Professional Rank					
高中阶段毕业以下 Below High School Graduate	中学高级 Senior Secondary	小学高级 Senior Primary	小学一级 1st Grade Primary	小学二级 2nd Grade Primary	小学三级 3rd Grade Primary	未定职级 No-ranking
7177	**29495**	**1086523**	**791830**	**90355**	**4560**	**196018**
14	11	3015	1790	47	14	834
19	231	5936	917	16	1	312
117	1941	71775	61311	2162	49	10462
74	436	26205	35284	3937	360	6567
54	5743	14005	5689	631		2195
116	2251	27390	6525	564	46	1799
103	451	23664	18362	1945	127	2915
98	1785	26477	17888	413	18	894
	53	846	749	73	30	1014
	549	23399	9389	538	2	2324
24	312	17804	12444	425	40	3858
14	972	63677	38671	3867	75	8340
102	290	33327	15449	2261	30	3013
548	1085	46204	26499	6625	187	12011
114	2524	74509	52521	3479	60	8819
5	3416	117302	94622	8269	301	25168
158	994	46899	17527	1591	158	4636
700	1082	61133	25224	1946	256	11861
269	485	73919	22118	3729	706	13706
308	618	64238	40371	4362	271	6182
39	61	7482	7800	1446	32	407
88	135	12117	17053	1808	142	2623
35	1267	49085	54825	2044	93	12914
1667	281	43597	41667	10502	924	13481
1621	392	68019	53727	12436	128	10588
77	50	2726	5562	827	98	1565
95	319	17715	25634	2316		2833
447	550	28975	40477	5862	203	8809
33	418	7431	3043	200	25	1051
59	186	5784	5209	414	44	3127
179	607	21868	33483	5620	140	11710

小学办

Condition of School Buildings in Primary

地区 Region	校舍建筑面积 Floor Space	教学及辅助用房 Teaching & Assistant Buildings						
		合计 Total	其中 of Which					
			教室 Classroom	实验室 Laboratory	图书室 Library	微机室 PC-room	语音室 Linguistic	体育馆 Gymnasium
总计 Total	**620648517**	**349119945**	**294287815**	**17652404**	**15125683**	**12127654**	**3462403**	**6463986**
北京 Beijing	6536187	3009179	2338580	220862	150293	137260	17578	144606
天津 Tianjin	4074725	2244218	1827712	96521	99903	91153	39651	89278
河北 Hebei	33078029	19757083	16127555	1349605	1035242	874594	288243	81844
山西 Shanxi	17666147	9002631	7539605	457244	430117	366413	113599	95653
内蒙古 Inner Mongolia	10794159	5101422	4079811	288103	235087	190925	91075	216421
辽宁 Liaoning	11448029	6442067	5122276	396030	318548	312315	97011	195887
吉林 Jilin	8562501	5093427	4222832	292075	211009	219076	76468	71967
黑龙江 Heilongjiang	9431377	5824008	4823893	329757	217984	215381	90623	146370
上海 Shanghai	5022320	2783283	2021480	221200	157575	111816	35411	235801
江苏 Jiangsu	31836729	19242355	15243132	1091974	953078	858171	176081	919919
浙江 Zhejiang	26255765	12909893	9911059	770152	623378	532247	159138	913919
安徽 Anhui	24604030	16063159	13857651	726373	684258	564464	112115	118298
福建 Fujian	20555893	10939240	8962390	595487	586450	430854	95927	268132
江西 Jiangxi	22896521	14313846	12885783	460169	454793	297781	112854	102466
山东 Shandong	35152909	20573592	16436174	1575207	1079882	936897	262970	282462
河南 Henan	52353372	31379273	27310523	1295501	1452333	1044678	202828	73410
湖北 Hubei	27499858	13962592	11516898	880250	676634	579366	174879	134565
湖南 Hunan	31302151	16997185	14693941	854484	597634	390640	160260	300226
广东 Guangdong	61852906	34061906	28638317	1349158	1423763	926218	440239	1284211
广西 Guangxi	28838453	16688923	15200048	527148	541032	275172	51037	94486
海南 Hainan	5638706	2856729	2576699	87785	104961	60510	18137	8637
重庆 Chongqing	17430947	9598734	8561498	359859	256881	230977	56703	132816
四川 Sichuan	30660946	17099994	14781791	757080	631367	596880	156736	176140
贵州 Guizhou	20122996	11674439	10145775	596726	501290	339114	49975	41559
云南 Yunnan	26347062	14023544	12394687	638166	474811	382707	80915	52258
西藏 Tibet	3079921	956155	823209	29968	38750	39323	9303	15602
陕西 Shaanxi	17193499	9370525	7757004	549549	428168	413869	164838	57097
甘肃 Gansu	13453815	7889875	6970951	297659	297248	257899	30460	35658
青海 Qinghai	3299285	1640021	1404818	60262	62570	70298	22685	19388
宁夏 Ningxia	3813579	2181781	1799305	112165	103203	114245	21772	31091
新疆 Xinjiang	9845700	5438866	4312418	385885	297441	266411	52892	123819

学条件(一)(总计)
Schools (1) (Total)

单位:平方米
unit:m^2

行政办公用房 Administrative		生活用房 Residential and Welfare							其他用房 Rooms for Other Purposes	校舍面积中 of the Floor Space	
			教工宿舍 Apartments for Single								
合计 Total	其中:教师办公室 of Which: for Teachers	合计 Total	小计 Subtotal	其中:教师周转宿舍 of Which: Accommodation for Circulation of Teachers	学生宿舍 Students' Dormitories	食堂 Dining Halls	厕所 Toilet	其他 Others		危房面积 Floor Space of Dilapidated Buildings	当年新增 New Added in Current Year
60730192	**42720733**	**152410495**	**50586522**	**7860712**	**33645001**	**26165162**	**25437191**	**16576619**	**58387885**	**29504829**	**29095493**
790558	425384	1105083	117855	9909	116097	262188	286296	322647	1631367	569	425780
533901	362506	615160	26484	2485	14906	100974	201442	271354	681446		80502
3396615	2673235	6283638	1002432	149974	1859727	897132	1490142	1034205	3640693	8928	1686954
2345289	1796285	4354968	876261	72427	1412836	778093	738592	549186	1963259	199681	540096
1381517	1029141	3282754	167704	37602	1513339	668948	454162	478601	1028466	163919	549721
1418555	925562	1676710	76874	13877	220229	388320	522194	469093	1910697	220098	322394
1190164	805189	1302601	47094	6245	201444	270839	420973	362251	976309	91063	243615
1253063	914376	1397068	42345	9214	401319	224743	395326	333335	957238	384955	210693
643172	359048	851260	17160	1671	12267	337857	220108	263868	744605		94217
3455471	1989998	5933957	818575	128932	853635	2177858	1109433	974456	3204946		1741300
2552094	1534379	6607065	1599549	193367	963544	2209739	980389	853844	4186713	728	1459721
2588588	1947443	4423210	1653013	146397	541346	700287	1127774	400790	1529073	322130	854815
1599434	948039	4947522	2292963	254452	794821	564584	794257	500897	3069697	173585	972832
1820706	1266072	5538418	2297413	217412	944757	940358	920720	435170	1223551	3251914	1477961
4174059	2674208	5915513	1233860	196196	748443	1115398	1899014	918798	4489745	232437	2351316
6904021	5508224	10938033	2756847	270576	2769103	1510727	2904791	996565	3132045	1892812	1511752
2064255	1409609	9593407	4180184	519158	2137343	1632924	879323	763633	1879604	866027	885329
2629524	2000164	9082396	3167814	338440	1986504	1859709	1171323	897046	2593046	1628660	847212
4852441	3258902	14188780	7490484	426960	1715963	1298842	1893050	1790441	8749779	158780	1168034
1756155	1411020	8436718	3833124	639881	1987499	1045614	909357	661124	1956657	3497550	1375661
480234	301254	1849876	1236548	224073	320475	117766	114922	60165	451867	168892	195732
1454781	894241	5016573	2327442	393343	942928	787311	567154	391738	1360859	667626	650055
2308933	1561663	9738060	3691324	1100335	2493570	1520093	1347336	685737	1513959	1308234	1947120
1467249	1030237	5844127	1926286	794328	1782358	997349	839827	298307	1137181	23422	2013471
1311816	893419	10095336	3593740	615237	3629302	1539623	930899	401772	916366	8690595	2167041
211378	158280	1802119	806538	569367	569096	293180	68910	64395	110269	7031	333620
2417504	1893022	4309502	1397000	129595	1085362	691117	753898	382125	1095968	259211	406144
1776462	1528451	3125588	1072561	70363	524020	419562	760904	348541	661890	5072026	735462
234641	174359	1233789	328095	127142	452739	175585	113208	164162	190834	18318	334770
482011	325538	769277	240830	55365	87395	138194	207874	94984	380510	58131	392362
1235601	721485	2151987	268123	146389	562634	500248	413593	407389	1019246	137507	1119811

小学办

Condition of School Buildings in Primary

地 区 Region	校舍建筑面积 Floor Space	教学及辅助用房 Teaching & Assistant Buildings						
		合计 Total	其中 of Which					
			教室 Classroom	实验室 Laboratory	图书室 Library	微机室 PC-room	语音室 Linguistic	体育馆 Gymnasium
总 计 Total	**158066383**	**88145120**	**70883164**	**4647815**	**3866696**	**3378494**	**1131049**	**4237902**
北 京 Beijing	4914139	2266928	1801485	135270	108971	97426	11844	111932
天 津 Tianjin	2333937	1213191	971600	46082	53706	45992	17757	78054
河 北 Hebei	5809673	3385592	2805708	189330	159947	137911	52755	39941
山 西 Shanxi	3986500	2129963	1778834	89021	92289	87516	36506	45797
内蒙古 Inner Mongolia	3154756	1681686	1331397	88833	67845	61605	27261	104745
辽 宁 Liaoning	5772301	3128757	2462908	149835	150814	145131	54006	166063
吉 林 Jilin	2798317	1588681	1298536	64746	59939	78008	31174	56278
黑龙江 Heilongjiang	3255375	1926839	1558625	79042	62580	73676	40141	112775
上 海 Shanghai	4047112	2230785	1607787	178331	126640	87536	29921	200570
江 苏 Jiangsu	14386354	8494679	6538543	465787	422443	329466	64713	673727
浙 江 Zhejiang	10446826	5242343	3859105	300024	261586	197572	72006	552050
安 徽 Anhui	4368325	2806366	2340323	129838	108717	120269	34903	72316
福 建 Fujian	5289107	2802560	2201265	168509	162239	116283	30161	124103
江 西 Jiangxi	3051013	1808523	1539486	60570	69862	62195	30185	46225
山 东 Shandong	10851268	6100767	4802097	478014	295484	247893	88287	188992
河 南 Henan	8816039	4929387	4254161	211430	189467	169342	50748	54239
湖 北 Hubei	6202008	3686570	3056601	204242	149517	139789	45428	90993
湖 南 Hunan	5317283	2866059	2330922	155026	109701	86087	39680	144643
广 东 Guangdong	25778633	13762255	10971517	681963	575935	467378	185818	879644
广 西 Guangxi	3145613	1742063	1474223	75059	66270	59786	14255	52470
海 南 Hainan	1055531	579129	514818	15970	20250	16599	6777	4715
重 庆 Chongqing	4321690	2529794	2136300	115738	82250	75609	19848	100049
四 川 Sichuan	5616422	3481859	2842407	184673	153174	138972	49387	113246
贵 州 Guizhou	1908470	1141034	940644	56952	51434	47704	12640	31660
云 南 Yunnan	2569114	1556061	1306838	74791	58168	61034	18532	36698
西 藏 Tibet	189312	101556	83369	2194	1904	2542	1597	9950
陕 西 Shaanxi	3506043	1946833	1622613	109235	76646	83300	30142	24897
甘 肃 Gansu	1599817	955861	828593	26815	34319	39447	8264	18423
青 海 Qinghai	396519	208728	166170	11157	8927	13137	6487	2850
宁 夏 Ningxia	1040119	600599	483900	31962	27945	30756	9014	17022
新 疆 Xinjiang	2138767	1249672	972389	67376	57727	58533	10812	82835

学条件(一)(城区)

Schools (1) (Urban Area)

单位:平方米
unit:m^2

行政办公用房 Administrative		生活用房 Residential and Welfare							其他用房 Rooms for Other Purposes	校舍面积中 of the Floor Space	
合计 Total	其中:教师办公室 of Which: for Teachers	合计 Total	教工宿舍 Apartments for Single 小计 Subtotal	其中:教师周转宿舍 of Which: Accommodation for Circulation of Teachers	学生宿舍 Students' Dormitories	食堂 Dining Halls	厕所 Toilet	其他 Others		危房面积 Floor Space of Dilapidated Buildings	当年新增 New Added in Current Year
17763554	**11086720**	**27332642**	**5947865**	**653544**	**3988895**	**5704024**	**6123364**	**5568494**	**24825067**	**2407818**	**6896918**
589584	327209	779764	56823	3784	75316	184522	208499	254604	1277863	569	230096
318214	216134	335906	5222	449	13424	69555	114029	133676	466626		56685
695125	500801	785985	63012	5823	188068	85917	219444	229544	942971	1888	199752
589657	403304	577889	86594	9127	111824	61225	167078	151168	688991	37377	154593
464493	313971	515528	32085	10240	136678	69383	129864	147518	493049	2866	148095
736898	437886	761620	13268	1805	68856	184772	243679	251045	1145026	31899	239112
407879	252432	373217	1108	260	24850	89030	115268	142961	428540	30713	52003
523176	333706	338992	5479	720	41737	42737	116003	133036	466368	76658	34971
514135	291637	689710	9093	507	12267	256060	178343	233947	612482		69502
1712650	909741	2430518	140052	19840	240385	1040448	515721	493912	1748507		816075
1071746	631018	2183859	274967	35660	298744	846586	399687	363875	1948878		669848
533754	364624	473084	116039	9309	51378	54066	165540	86061	555121	26269	142162
467543	252281	730162	231181	31319	37151	98793	217797	145240	1288842	26080	330228
308116	203429	531154	164618	24483	46885	85681	121402	112568	403220	106277	316059
1357405	754202	1551626	174588	31789	214663	362836	489085	310454	1841470	15417	743704
1218701	861569	1628707	381381	58147	413404	210165	374871	248886	1039244	115561	328184
630205	413736	1263136	487372	35096	163858	233161	190404	188341	622097	105323	181357
462498	328382	1165523	305845	40812	281936	234060	192526	151156	823203	111826	184666
1931955	1203991	5186726	2106535	162241	712227	678111	859090	830763	4897697	71127	451751
278908	209161	735164	293710	28168	146511	91948	118438	84557	389478	160469	278271
115985	79301	281059	169514	31824	50894	21139	30844	8668	79358	11921	32782
482350	286087	777549	153186	15432	146296	202949	145284	129834	531997	38075	171157
566254	371817	1160427	221577	31351	222793	263093	254364	198600	407882	53619	372959
214466	135277	307775	65757	4850	53410	54116	82384	52108	245195	1234	87702
251811	159359	473736	160605	23147	73314	57249	95785	86783	287506	772263	186056
25938	20403	45696	30134	22346	5613	4434	4744	771	16122		3529
490129	335449	624648	159507	11934	121323	82597	144562	116659	444433	60151	104795
227370	160092	191647	17732	1102	13385	10839	75906	73785	224939	498665	88688
45911	29719	93730	2471	120	6391	4146	18968	61754	48150		49263
174433	106071	96045	7778	536	1443	3649	53190	29985	169042	45215	79728
356265	193931	242060	10632	1323	13871	20757	80565	116235	290770	6356	93145

小学办
Condition of School Buildings in Primary

地 区 Region	校舍建筑面积 Floor Space	教学及辅助用房 Teaching & Assistant Buildings						
		合计 Total	其中 of Which					
			教室 Classroom	实验室 Laboratory	图书室 Library	微机室 PC-room	语音室 Linguistic	体育馆 Gymnasium
总 计 Total	**32615007**	**18136929**	**14724798**	**995151**	**819655**	**690999**	**222259**	**684067**
北 京 Beijing	443092	243611	182152	18205	11963	11732	1067	18492
天 津 Tianjin	267206	135132	110293	6006	6944	5529	1859	4501
河 北 Hebei	1527686	881782	709793	62733	48565	44178	14765	1748
山 西 Shanxi	746049	399983	335790	18160	17582	19017	5475	3959
内蒙古 Inner Mongolia	158610	81400	64774	3369	3965	2910	999	5383
辽 宁 Liaoning	663536	345213	278161	19185	17381	16778	5547	8161
吉 林 Jilin	264240	142387	112196	8471	6915	7387	3123	4295
黑龙江 Heilongjiang	389362	242339	193270	11263	8140	9907	4970	14789
上 海 Shanghai	312316	180493	138679	11310	9608	7049	2404	11443
江 苏 Jiangsu	1494449	879703	681136	57130	47639	38283	7834	47681
浙 江 Zhejiang	2546976	1324934	1018421	68774	58395	48013	16289	115042
安 徽 Anhui	753952	443572	370285	23922	21446	17645	4202	6072
福 建 Fujian	1146310	624100	490007	32822	41462	29082	7320	23407
江 西 Jiangxi	616775	408338	361771	12471	14755	11017	3923	4401
山 东 Shandong	3217263	1825178	1456715	146106	91998	81165	27308	21886
河 南 Henan	2111011	1200129	1021562	60234	56143	45752	9471	6967
湖 北 Hubei	940722	527985	436457	30331	23856	20925	8515	7901
湖 南 Hunan	1062997	568202	465057	29986	19861	16037	8467	28794
广 东 Guangdong	9216679	4841399	3864565	240999	201594	159470	63272	311499
广 西 Guangxi	636717	373420	334081	12983	13182	8272	1440	3462
海 南 Hainan	122955	64005	57147	1346	2335	1077	500	1600
重 庆 Chongqing	458068	262669	232443	11802	8089	7124	1541	1670
四 川 Sichuan	861348	535948	445730	26223	23792	21455	4863	13885
贵 州 Guizhou	516220	329525	272852	17953	16315	14039	4082	4284
云 南 Yunnan	671244	408149	350390	16422	15761	13571	3513	8492
西 藏 Tibet								
陕 西 Shaanxi	874512	509723	435439	29201	16739	19315	6326	2703
甘 肃 Gansu	209105	126417	113449	3435	4265	4205	869	194
青 海 Qinghai	40695	21361	16951	1445	1091	1038	756	80
宁 夏 Ningxia	134841	77228	64855	4325	3195	4013	577	263
新 疆 Xinjiang	210071	132604	110377	8539	6679	5014	982	1013

学条件(一)(城乡结合区)
Schools (1)(Urban-rural Transitional Area)

单位:平方米
unit:m^2

行政办公用房 Administrative		生活用房 Residential and Welfare							其他用房 Rooms for Other Purposes	校舍面积中 of the Floor Space	
			教工宿舍 Apartments for Single								
合计 Total	其中:教师办公室 of Which: for Teachers	合计 Total	小计 Subtotal	其中:教师周转宿舍 of Which: Accommodation for Circulation of Teachers	学生宿舍 Students' Dormitories	食堂 Dining Halls	厕所 Toilet	其他 Others		危房面积 Floor Space of Dilapidated Buildings	当年新增 New Added in Current Year
3300421	**2106552**	**6528773**	**1872661**	**181794**	**1043753**	**1254825**	**1323831**	**1033703**	**4648884**	**569345**	**1565893**
55844	27560	66796	10655	550	1947	13641	19170	21383	76841	110	18701
33979	23232	42610	581	64		13931	11983	16115	55485		835
170594	133275	237992	31207	2360	56226	22614	71813	56132	237318	1888	76332
116150	83870	108916	22642	2624	20545	16425	30114	19190	121000	9366	18239
21514	13947	42329	2478	116	11686	8829	6344	12992	13367	2101	3500
72172	45317	93536	1682	130	3590	23775	33830	30659	152615	5500	40743
36969	22998	47287	105	20	6982	9166	10695	20339	37597		926
60572	41601	47990	858	250	5510	6133	14012	21477	38461	10848	5899
42291	23803	54583	3652	186		24597	14076	12258	34949		951
181361	98433	290623	20024	2160	45286	118066	58713	48534	142762		97193
243679	129665	596778	103421	12989	81366	241725	89830	80436	381585		221941
76800	52919	130540	29386	2925	30353	17260	34085	19456	103040	5609	33638
88217	53235	208042	77168	12365	10779	21937	51504	46654	225951	1891	83257
57935	36263	94097	23068	1529	8912	17808	29867	14442	56405	37195	45187
407341	229890	534757	67045	11384	94671	108082	166844	98115	449987	9371	285633
279347	209493	412308	78149	11697	120653	58961	105724	48821	219227	38379	79843
83679	57193	253241	84760	6728	67261	47717	31283	22220	75817	27687	24237
94655	64619	269423	72640	14313	67273	60351	43252	25907	130717	43072	31733
677587	416794	2004458	958655	68464	203827	244147	302170	295659	1693235	10832	208313
43783	36083	164994	49697	6445	49051	22231	25358	18657	54520	56683	30921
13365	8886	38557	24906	5569	6841	2813	3331	666	7028	3833	1013
43194	26842	93492	26418	3743	20212	24550	15103	7209	58713	3602	18836
78569	48110	202077	43111	5891	50587	55706	36289	16384	44754	10336	82006
50620	33314	90102	21352	1012	14626	18742	23109	12273	45973	322	33274
64314	43197	146845	57431	6684	26592	22239	26952	13631	51936	178284	70834
126747	94240	171039	50970	1268	30983	23090	39915	26081	67003	34479	13602
25387	17879	34122	6159	278	5656	2904	11320	8083	23179	71661	16168
4375	2604	10959	502		1999	574	1244	6640	4000		1835
20666	12634	16586	1299	50		1256	6293	7738	20361	3825	5218
28715	18656	23694	2640		339	5555	9608	5552	25058	2471	15085

小学办

Condition of School Buildings in Primary

地　区 Region	校舍建筑面积 Floor Space	教学及辅助用房 Teaching & Assistant Buildings						
		合计 Total	其中 of Which					
			教室 Classroom	实验室 Laboratory	图书室 Library	微机室 PC-room	语音室 Linguistic	体育馆 Gymnasium
总　计 Total	**198103692**	**108699448**	**92016373**	**5466119**	**4429209**	**3924688**	**1313888**	**1549171**
北　京 Beijing	869578	383596	280387	33701	20541	18964	4053	25950
天　津 Tianjin	771540	461650	389864	19082	18692	18505	8722	6785
河　北 Hebei	10661928	6126731	4997430	421655	310624	266274	102189	28559
山　西 Shanxi	5615832	2803416	2353582	151190	122673	111002	39377	25592
内蒙古 Inner Mongolia	4979045	2222263	1773033	120836	103616	89005	51481	84292
辽　宁 Liaoning	2485744	1362690	1122067	90032	57532	62374	21416	9269
吉　林 Jilin	2322548	1282032	1077543	62570	50184	55151	27162	9422
黑龙江 Heilongjiang	2932718	1745818	1480562	84966	56849	62625	32994	27822
上　海 Shanghai	728959	420982	318772	30304	24053	17540	3930	26383
江　苏 Jiangsu	13209531	7952513	6461912	452030	365798	360849	81787	230137
浙　江 Zhejiang	10351170	5085943	3951140	318432	232185	217119	62406	304661
安　徽 Anhui	7692143	4887628	4212794	227489	192399	174414	45804	34728
福　建 Fujian	6494855	3532787	2926701	171671	174902	132796	33063	93654
江　西 Jiangxi	8068105	4942179	4402344	171832	147744	121310	55754	43195
山　东 Shandong	11336917	6449472	5211367	474702	325726	283357	90432	63888
河　南 Henan	15499536	8916320	7795476	359996	379525	299431	66349	15543
湖　北 Hubei	9337678	4535917	3781714	288574	194775	180950	65605	24299
湖　南 Hunan	10786332	5734659	4907165	305020	200786	154024	69798	97866
广　东 Guangdong	16312346	8969835	7698289	318616	345823	244864	148058	214185
广　西 Guangxi	7992196	4378960	3973497	148388	132865	89497	16765	17948
海　南 Hainan	2196470	1059154	949103	36889	36004	27278	7825	2055
重　庆 Chongqing	7442411	4018524	3634773	134782	100475	95114	27832	25548
四　川 Sichuan	11815154	6499497	5615916	292158	232363	244627	67744	46689
贵　州 Guizhou	5580245	3042103	2652894	149192	115990	98739	19846	5442
云　南 Yunnan	6007507	3225680	2834835	140829	109958	104066	28471	7521
西　藏 Tibet	934607	291208	254864	7675	9166	13082	2737	3684
陕　西 Shaanxi	7569360	3993137	3271582	236812	191309	184700	88503	20231
甘　肃 Gansu	3126716	1772486	1545610	78071	65035	66834	9607	7329
青　海 Qinghai	1260452	595004	494456	26350	23017	25568	11012	14601
宁　夏 Ningxia	1042465	600742	502938	30844	23751	29970	6592	6647
新　疆 Xinjiang	2679604	1406522	1143763	81431	64849	74659	16574	25246

学条件(一)(镇区)

Schools (1) (Counties & Towns Area)

单位:平方米

unit: m^2

行政办公用房 Administrative		生活用房 Residential and Welfare							其他用房 Rooms for Other Purposes	校舍面积中 of the Floor Space	
			教工宿舍 Apartments for Single								
合计 Total	其中:教师办公室 of Which: for Teachers	合计 Total	小计 Subtotal	其中:教师周转宿舍 of Which: Accommodation for Circulation of Teachers	学生宿舍 Students' Dormitories	食堂 Dining Halls	厕所 Toilet	其他 Others		危房面积 Floor Space of Dilapidated Buildings	当年新增 New Added in Current Year
19541085	**13512583**	**53812282**	**17861886**	**2953232**	**14179572**	**9486869**	**7269017**	**5014938**	**16050877**	**7188366**	**10565762**
98072	49581	178494	28765	1671	22634	46318	42240	38537	209416		155000
98615	68613	110042	7495	1152	1320	20516	37252	43459	101233		9281
1084436	850625	2262453	330057	48775	805456	358030	446578	322332	1188308	1341	672146
755014	563636	1467752	244384	20867	564326	275341	216024	167677	589650	46403	178280
599306	448188	1798179	69483	19867	951288	387645	184510	205253	359297	42278	296116
320903	216956	449406	20260	6779	100348	118651	99129	111018	352745	69761	39555
318076	210791	452583	14918	2785	141104	114737	90044	91780	269857	19812	116251
361993	271918	572002	10140	2598	235235	107953	112261	106413	252905	93061	120244
99853	51483	116713	5405	444		60178	30410	20720	91411		11528
1351490	806510	2789893	511217	81161	526952	957939	417892	375893	1115635		664731
1018143	608208	2732156	717123	88143	403582	900752	391177	319522	1514928	728	619533
820713	566545	1567840	627062	66676	266591	261013	295787	117387	415962	95204	380966
547826	314885	1690445	715852	87068	402720	188744	235826	147303	723797	61018	298719
739897	474563	1986861	783854	89943	473612	325061	272146	132188	399168	871406	614785
1355916	885428	2300084	594895	89437	384006	431946	585601	303636	1231445	99436	871178
1935899	1534239	3831787	874322	81513	1323267	610477	753393	270328	815530	495566	490704
661411	447246	3701863	1791467	214734	835373	587412	254532	233079	438487	276818	330575
894266	671330	3433338	1201612	129233	828241	722948	366709	313828	724069	539023	312179
1291456	866400	4245735	2312515	125686	715357	333848	437417	446598	1805320	32411	448925
516631	392947	2592850	1221587	213535	649342	311730	234670	175521	503755	998634	377120
175342	103631	806785	492173	97426	180877	59310	44207	30218	155189	57493	87333
608064	369890	2306486	1153553	208289	441850	327246	220918	162919	509337	256467	347914
952279	620745	3790646	1469725	446881	1039305	574235	466867	240514	572732	433383	783121
457875	296533	1709845	565085	246012	599758	255720	200709	88573	370422	4492	677532
422225	279685	2111231	784894	190489	721126	315563	187765	101883	248371	1662227	524857
65098	45572	552893	268013	189771	161884	83940	15215	23841	25408	3267	100421
1027548	811713	2127579	674791	76730	644512	361927	297894	148455	421096	67182	204583
409441	334413	748940	178184	20779	201553	129283	141718	98202	195849	939959	261093
88521	61196	505190	91844	49688	240139	83780	36470	52957	71737	3255	131257
145708	103237	200767	39992	16920	44332	43426	52661	20356	95248	926	158752
319068	185876	671444	61219	38180	273482	131200	100995	104548	282570	16815	281083

小学办

Condition of School Buildings in Primary

地　区 Region	校舍建筑面积 Floor Space	教学及辅助用房 Teaching & Assistant Buildings						
		合计 Total	其中 of Which					
			教室 Classroom	实验室 Laboratory	图书室 Library	微机室 PC-room	语音室 Linguistic	体育馆 Gymnasium
总　计 Total	**66227971**	**37857532**	**32028048**	**1941028**	**1646863**	**1349410**	**403921**	**488262**
北　京 Beijing	171354	79714	57886	11426	5877	4166	204	155
天　津 Tianjin	325228	199935	166332	9522	8437	8124	4170	3350
河　北 Hebei	6013944	3493836	2830951	241828	187009	158434	54747	20867
山　西 Shanxi	1807501	961286	808439	46064	44286	40801	11957	9739
内蒙古 Inner Mongolia	440761	196339	159428	9766	8022	6411	5070	7642
辽　宁 Liaoning	518852	288459	231924	20716	15282	14498	4176	1863
吉　林 Jilin	363987	189158	155617	10805	7577	8671	4434	2054
黑龙江 Heilongjiang	397038	226345	187802	12134	8253	9294	4166	4696
上　海 Shanghai	157570	95057	71896	6682	5435	3959	868	6217
江　苏 Jiangsu	3719433	2265728	1830923	130023	110668	111143	21935	61036
浙　江 Zhejiang	3678042	1850410	1454664	119286	83814	78759	21792	92095
安　徽 Anhui	2094896	1348382	1169276	61359	57355	44279	11587	4526
福　建 Fujian	1895625	1086008	889194	63298	54577	40861	11241	26837
江　西 Jiangxi	2516296	1578193	1417660	58737	51731	32608	10686	6771
山　东 Shandong	5160325	3010888	2425283	226288	153009	131607	38856	35845
河　南 Henan	7495300	4485332	3877384	191575	214818	157600	29290	14665
湖　北 Hubei	2789584	1353920	1110450	95314	68281	58433	17848	3594
湖　南 Hunan	4454465	2419548	2100079	117687	84973	61422	22197	33190
广　东 Guangdong	7395395	4147754	3559099	137567	166284	111337	58071	115396
广　西 Guangxi	2722490	1686578	1545558	52720	52198	27096	4766	4240
海　南 Hainan	473523	228952	208259	6264	8717	4693	902	117
重　庆 Chongqing	1483779	800704	724558	25091	20288	17787	4839	8141
四　川 Sichuan	2384914	1380678	1197574	64688	50119	49851	11917	6529
贵　州 Guizhou	1590058	954513	832921	48078	39963	28438	4575	538
云　南 Yunnan	2079544	1221108	1085256	49816	40538	35373	8507	1618
西　藏 Tibet	86636	29581	25188	476	639	1113	551	1614
陕　西 Shaanxi	2291868	1290233	1064781	75913	57341	58924	25903	7371
甘　肃 Gansu	865472	496274	430508	22717	19554	19268	2684	1543
青　海 Qinghai	267869	145580	128800	4692	4095	5389	2316	288
宁　夏 Ningxia	219194	132466	110192	6468	6506	7830	894	576
新　疆 Xinjiang	367028	214573	170166	14028	11217	11241	2772	5149

学条件(一)(镇乡结合区)

Schools (1) (County-town Transitional Area)

单位:平方米

unit: m^2

行政办公用房 Administrative		生活用房 Residential and Welfare							其他用房 Rooms for Other Purposes	校舍面积中 of the Floor Space	
合计 Total	其中:教师办公室 of Which: for Teachers	合计 Total	教工宿舍 Apartments for Single: 小计 Subtotal	教工宿舍 Apartments for Single: 其中:教师周转宿舍 of Which: Accommodation for Circulation of Teachers	学生宿舍 Students' Dormitories	食堂 Dining Halls	厕所 Toilet	其他 Others		危房面积 Floor Space of Dilapidated Buildings	当年新增 New Added in Current Year
6556798	**4676437**	**16242151**	**5317952**	**698048**	**3593902**	**2892117**	**2722162**	**1716018**	**5571490**	**2720233**	**3217069**
21217	9957	36085	4418	120	6234	7556	9310	8567	34338		16780
42315	29325	45977	4513	660		8226	15409	17829	37001		585
596426	469416	1229554	183542	23351	409965	179695	269928	186424	694128	1341	383482
253091	187762	395126	73651	4325	123181	71063	73482	53749	197998	14602	29935
51348	40316	157289	6413	629	83396	32582	17695	17203	35785	3146	25807
62236	41313	99764	5316	1782	26253	19158	22081	26956	68393	10297	12770
44952	31486	93983	6497	199	38165	24116	14237	10968	35894	6350	10304
48666	33924	75925	1071	604	32765	13727	15430	12932	46102	11546	12122
23524	11122	26540	2108			11827	6471	6134	12449		475
377485	230438	759704	168509	27486	78519	275647	124994	112035	316516		153148
358689	214584	951496	271545	29482	108978	321070	138698	111205	517447		263394
224625	165122	414477	160421	19738	50555	63748	98028	41725	107412	48805	64101
152780	87557	418651	191980	22655	64469	45249	75253	41700	238186	7128	106564
219409	140184	608703	219069	15277	128517	114600	101384	45133	109991	326000	163420
596646	390224	970866	248064	47035	138047	171719	280057	132979	581925	31047	396468
966333	781964	1670441	345322	33627	522990	254240	410595	137294	373194	293668	218695
196503	134158	1111266	491025	60687	262452	183087	85878	88824	127895	93313	89387
372042	278057	1351294	457579	48120	314051	301617	157822	120225	311581	278953	101957
622115	437132	1741192	929866	40844	211437	145711	221671	232507	884334	13506	206860
177482	142512	683871	307267	59775	130187	86844	92401	67172	174559	469861	114954
46331	27668	158442	108920	21771	27795	8867	8766	4094	39798	12534	7006
114905	71971	473342	234045	35712	83952	71464	50684	33197	94828	55334	83322
188494	126271	708815	230642	56988	204733	122870	108868	41702	106927	88698	164946
127363	82374	407404	123917	48390	115124	77893	63724	26746	100778	3137	187753
135979	98557	642245	258817	47773	167679	106530	71846	37373	80212	672444	160512
8266	3377	47543	20127	15188	13196	5926	2022	6272	1246		7152
315681	249653	569249	186988	21733	142271	96078	103859	40053	116705	22303	55829
114242	94688	200375	47146	4745	46062	33734	44908	28525	54581	252919	57967
20901	14114	89305	17111	7312	40724	13662	10338	7470	12083	833	35859
31830	24772	39923	9150	1680	6902	7082	11479	5310	14975	656	26466
44922	26439	63304	2913	360	15303	16529	14844	13715	44229	1812	59049

小学办

Condition of School Buildings in Primary

地 区 Region	校舍建筑面积 Floor Space	教学及辅助用房 Teaching & Assistant Buildings						
		合计 Total	其中 of Which					
			教室 Classroom	实验室 Laboratory	图书室 Library	微机室 PC-room	语音室 Linguistic	体育馆 Gymnasium
总 计 Total	**264478442**	**152275377**	**131388278**	**7538470**	**6829778**	**4824472**	**1017466**	**676913**
北 京 Beijing	752470	358655	256708	51891	20781	20870	1681	6724
天 津 Tianjin	969248	569377	466248	31357	27505	26656	13172	4439
河 北 Hebei	16606428	10244760	8324417	738620	564671	470409	133299	13344
山 西 Shanxi	8063815	4069252	3407189	217033	215155	167895	37716	24264
内蒙古 Inner Mongolia	2660358	1197473	975381	78434	63626	40315	12333	27384
辽 宁 Liaoning	3189984	1950620	1537301	156163	110202	104810	21589	20555
吉 林 Jilin	3441636	2222714	1846753	164759	100886	85917	18132	6267
黑龙江 Heilongjiang	3243284	2151351	1784706	165749	98555	79080	17488	5773
上 海 Shanghai	246249	131516	94921	12565	6882	6740	1560	8848
江 苏 Jiangsu	4240844	2795163	2242677	174157	164837	167856	29581	16055
浙 江 Zhejiang	5457769	2581607	2100814	151696	129607	117556	24726	57208
安 徽 Anhui	12543562	8369165	7304534	369046	383142	269781	31408	11254
福 建 Fujian	8771931	4603893	3834424	255307	249309	181775	32703	50375
江 西 Jiangxi	11777403	7563144	6943953	227767	237187	114276	26915	13046
山 东 Shandong	12964724	8023353	6422710	622491	458672	405647	84251	29582
河 南 Henan	28037797	17533566	15260886	724075	883341	575905	85731	3628
湖 北 Hubei	11960172	5740105	4678583	387434	332342	258627	63846	19273
湖 南 Hunan	15198536	8396467	7455854	394438	287147	150529	50782	57717
广 东 Guangdong	19761927	11329816	9968511	348579	502005	213976	106363	190382
广 西 Guangxi	17700644	10567900	9752328	303701	341897	125889	20017	24068
海 南 Hainan	2386705	1218446	1112778	34926	48707	16633	3535	1867
重 庆 Chongqing	5666846	3050416	2790425	109339	74156	60254	9023	7219
四 川 Sichuan	13229370	7118638	6323468	280249	245830	213281	39605	16205
贵 州 Guizhou	12634281	7491302	6552237	390582	333866	192671	17489	4457
云 南 Yunnan	17770441	9241803	8253014	422546	306685	217607	33912	8039
西 藏 Tibet	1956002	563391	484976	20099	27680	23699	4969	1968
陕 西 Shaanxi	6118096	3430555	2862809	203502	160213	145869	46193	11969
甘 肃 Gansu	8727282	5161528	4596748	192773	197894	151618	12589	9906
青 海 Qinghai	1642314	836289	744192	22755	30626	31593	5186	1937
宁 夏 Ningxia	1730995	980440	812467	49359	51507	53519	6166	7422
新 疆 Xinjiang	5027329	2782672	2196266	237078	174865	133219	25506	15738

学条件(一)(乡村)

Schools (1) (Rural Area)

单位:平方米
unit: m^2

行政办公用房 Administrative		生活用房 Residential and Welfare							其他用房 Rooms for Other Purposes	校舍面积中 of the Floor Space	
合计 Total	其中:教师办公室 of Which: for Teachers	合计 Total	教工宿舍 Apartments for Single: 小计 Subtotal	教工宿舍 Apartments for Single: 其中:教师周转宿舍 of Which: Accommodation for Circulation of Teachers	学生宿舍 Students' Dormitories	食堂 Dining Halls	厕所 Toilet	其他 Others		危房面积 Floor Space of Dilapidated Buildings	当年新增 New Added in Current Year
23425553	**18121430**	**71265571**	**26776771**	**4253936**	**15476534**	**10974269**	**12044810**	**5993187**	**17511941**	**19908645**	**11632813**
102902	48594	146825	32267	4454	18147	31348	35557	29506	144088		40684
117072	77759	169212	13767	884	162	10903	50161	94219	113587		14536
1617054	1321809	3235200	609363	95376	866203	453185	824120	482329	1509414	5699	815056
1000618	829345	2309327	545283	42433	736686	441527	355490	230341	684618	115901	207223
317718	266982	969047	66136	7495	425373	211920	139788	125830	176120	118775	105510
360754	270720	465684	43346	5293	51025	84897	179386	107030	412926	118438	43727
464209	341966	476801	31068	3200	35490	67072	215661	127510	277912	40538	75361
367894	308752	486074	26726	5896	124347	74053	167062	93886	237965	215236	55478
29184	15928	44837	2662	720		21619	11355	9201	40712		13187
391331	273747	713546	167306	27931	86298	179471	175820	104651	340804		260494
462205	295153	1691050	607459	69564	261218	462401	189525	170447	722907		170340
1234121	1016274	2382286	909912	70412	223377	385208	666447	197342	557990	200657	331687
584065	380873	2526915	1345930	136065	354950	277047	340634	208354	1057058	86487	343885
772693	588080	3020403	1348941	102986	424260	529616	527172	190414	421163	2274231	547117
1460738	1034578	2063803	464377	74970	149774	320616	824328	304708	1416830	117584	736434
3749421	3112416	5477539	1501144	130916	1032432	690085	1776527	477351	1277271	1281685	692864
772639	548627	4628408	1901345	269328	1138112	812351	434387	342213	819020	483886	373397
1272760	1000452	4483535	1660357	168395	876327	902701	612088	432062	1045774	977811	350367
1629030	1188511	4756319	3071434	139033	288379	286883	596543	513080	2046762	55242	267358
960616	808912	5108704	2317827	398178	1191646	641936	556249	401046	1063424	2338447	720270
188907	118322	762032	574861	94823	88704	37317	39871	21279	217320	99478	75617
364367	238264	1932538	1020703	169622	354782	257116	200952	98985	319525	373084	130984
790400	569101	4786987	2000022	622103	1231472	682765	626105	246623	533345	821232	791040
794908	598427	3826507	1295444	543466	1129190	687513	556734	157626	521564	17696	1248237
637780	454375	7510369	2648241	401601	2834862	1166811	647349	213106	380489	6256105	1456128
120342	92305	1203530	508391	357250	401599	204806	48951	39783	68739	3764	229670
899827	745860	1557275	562702	40931	319527	246593	311442	117011	230439	131878	96766
1139651	1033946	2185001	876645	48482	309082	279440	543280	176554	241102	3633402	385681
100209	83444	634869	233780	77334	206209	87659	57770	49451	70947	15063	154250
161870	116230	472465	193060	37909	41620	91119	102023	44643	116220	11990	153882
560268	341678	1238483	196272	106886	275281	348291	232033	186606	445906	114336	745583

Condition of School Buildings in Primary

地　区 Region	占地面积(平方米) Areas of School Sites (m^2)			图书(册) Books & Magazines in Libraries (volume)	计算机数 PC	
	合计 Total	其中 of Which			合计 Total	其中:教学 of Which: No. of Used for
		绿化用地面积 Green Areas	运动场地面积 Sports Areas			小计 Subtotal
总　计 Total	**2274275122**	**375972161**	**676434475**	**1770876638**	**7317496**	**5930713**
北　京 Beijing	14179335	2195782	5545043	26562318	203772	170839
天　津 Tianjin	12371301	1288120	4712636	17177735	81318	67495
河　北 Hebei	146695635	14285014	50051753	122321540	449036	376691
山　西 Shanxi	60366962	5625581	18864086	44413303	165777	138201
内蒙古 Inner Mongolia	58551640	7610525	17144897	23378145	94513	71554
辽　宁 Liaoning	52380592	5490421	25158229	44130015	236264	176393
吉　林 Jilin	61432402	11102665	23373894	24690245	95141	68171
黑龙江 Heilongjiang	58951075	6785737	25815732	20275768	115044	90552
上　海 Shanghai	9118028	2469761	2966527	22664606	146555	119573
江　苏 Jiangsu	101529674	25648425	31814829	97926847	613192	501915
浙　江 Zhejiang	61683286	13776904	20458756	89313973	543900	488096
安　徽 Anhui	114361825	14620966	28490908	72654457	253217	202151
福　建 Fujian	52090535	9908326	19212191	62743518	277912	230954
江　西 Jiangxi	76836057	10184004	23141621	47860347	143336	108033
山　东 Shandong	159139286	31295651	59645777	134049861	712486	571277
河　南 Henan	200368232	24349316	48251094	143788223	306681	253711
湖　北 Hubei	92177748	27243340	22593587	82211235	312229	276385
湖　南 Hunan	96677343	13800812	22336539	80827610	220243	179881
广　东 Guangdong	179898298	41837099	56673930	175067314	745399	588234
广　西 Guangxi	102642764	16108008	22306255	56272283	134296	85573
海　南 Hainan	35599648	7769892	7021338	11448722	42775	33634
重　庆 Chongqing	43372871	6792109	12562792	27094187	154314	119470
四　川 Sichuan	77507551	10755412	24126891	82803675	305047	240790
贵　州 Guizhou	63681263	11387991	20164637	54236367	147846	116611
云　南 Yunnan	88483977	14254119	16010612	62475854	195987	148376
西　藏 Tibet	15124856	1794614	1875245	4594197	33017	26169
陕　西 Shaanxi	59045084	7236960	17294408	60737220	211739	177199
甘　肃 Gansu	67823282	8025000	19749857	35410687	133276	106283
青　海 Qinghai	15550691	1431530	3229220	8989552	43415	35503
宁　夏 Ningxia	20613051	3395237	6543007	10568707	61336	47912
新　疆 Xinjiang	76020830	17502840	19298184	24188127	138433	113087

学条件(二)(总计)
Schools (2) (Total)

(台) (set)	教室中: Classroom		教室中:普通教室(间) of Which: General Classroom		固定资产总值(万元) Total Value of Fixed Asset (10,000 yuan)		
用计算机 Computers Instruction	合计 Total	其中:网络多媒体教室 of Which: Network Multimedia Classroom	合计 Total	其中:网络多媒体教室 of Which: Network Multimedia Classroom	合计 Total	其中:教学仪器设备资产值 of Which: Total Value of Equip & Instru.	
其中:平板电脑 of Which:tablet PC						小计 Subtotal	其中:实验设备 for Profession
227025	**3471445**	**939436**	**2879225**	**809045**	**60201121.29**	**7171039.00**	**1886206.23**
5339	31915	26895	22620	20348	1310916.73	439952.07	17246.18
2599	21999	9846	16489	8684	579808.53	79121.57	13472.42
16894	276896	52178	217975	48528	2836860.61	308260.39	121557.46
3068	104114	25164	83656	22578	1524225.62	142142.02	55922.51
490	47704	13030	40435	12109	1279770.51	94576.43	26762.18
12449	71650	22353	56500	18884	1073383.07	222935.36	54595.82
2108	63732	8527	52849	7336	785586.84	98634.58	34305.58
1412	64265	11968	51164	10267	843372.51	113632.45	38841.96
1784	24041	20373	18151	16076	1016080.08	211687.95	41139.97
13806	139381	80421	103869	65486	4648624.69	595291.16	125836.13
6934	103611	89353	79602	76196	3212360.03	439659.55	84858.57
12908	173253	39540	152029	36371	2345977.39	201487.64	55191.11
558	99789	36113	73033	30224	2041850.98	272674.87	65263.41
9182	129587	17212	116970	16160	1425617.31	117128.29	36117.41
15095	217222	96445	168668	78610	3917236.23	451844.71	93818.05
10642	414846	56599	345569	48909	3539026.72	299526.88	119846.43
13543	112762	44315	90388	40470	2144877.06	303376.64	106707.81
10335	110051	19695	106672	18137	2205707.44	225801.60	85662.67
42909	255709	94763	207031	77502	6975810.00	901676.00	264234.00
2707	160680	17178	147627	16524	1887499.22	167602.37	57986.94
3601	23898	2926	21107	2917	605728.29	52238.73	13892.59
7972	57715	26927	55769	25818	1369735.35	153818.77	31701.16
1720	180096	27978	157718	24277	3337451.56	379670.41	96103.65
5879	136106	17621	111705	16234	1561424.75	143275.70	49486.88
4849	141407	18266	126322	16141	2444924.14	175801.67	50126.86
1020	9386	676	9488	543	541037.48	23454.04	5201.81
7470	108960	17504	86461	14315	1637397.84	184491.69	63728.74
6862	85407	10839	75391	9465	1165054.07	115471.76	34837.71
1548	20504	3454	17293	2700	459995.15	32031.98	6146.31
1142	25447	6627	19589	4900	499130.17	69276.52	12630.79
200	59312	24650	47085	22336	984650.92	154495.20	22983.10

地区 Region	占地面积(平方米) Areas of School Sites (m²) 合计 Total	其中 of Which 绿化用地面积 Green Areas	运动场地面积 Sports Areas	图书(册) Books & Magazines in Libraries (volume)	计算机数 PC 合计 Total	其中:教学 of Which: No. of Used for 小计 Subtotal
总 计 Total	**352991477**	**68220128**	**124592219**	**549450846**	**2917061**	**2376205**
北 京 Beijing	8494772	1150511	3332138	20219934	160322	133625
天 津 Tianjin	5033012	500666	1823257	10119668	48502	39742
河 北 Hebei	15555558	1694519	5421199	25993712	115240	97447
山 西 Shanxi	9231516	976334	3097215	13435798	57526	48079
内蒙古 Inner Mongolia	8505047	1106488	3116344	9045352	38692	30404
辽 宁 Liaoning	15506587	1779344	7966372	26068620	149673	112462
吉 林 Jilin	7047945	965313	3141891	9740523	44774	31079
黑龙江 Heilongjiang	8965622	980505	4288361	8031723	59711	46004
上 海 Shanghai	6656951	1770191	2177278	17994463	122390	100539
江 苏 Jiangsu	31801133	8143972	10865365	41405589	269827	219956
浙 江 Zhejiang	20370357	5080801	6567092	34042986	214155	193210
安 徽 Anhui	10357679	1643925	3148210	13807322	75635	61624
福 建 Fujian	9734008	1986052	3749456	22403518	101352	86670
江 西 Jiangxi	7267868	1078437	2038532	9035809	43203	32900
山 东 Shandong	31024725	6003243	12697712	46814433	252240	199726
河 南 Henan	20391844	2577474	6055912	27894379	97322	77807
湖 北 Hubei	13795571	4023614	4230550	24699772	100826	89027
湖 南 Hunan	11582869	2248660	3078483	18099709	70063	58071
广 东 Guangdong	52138041	13586321	17794037	83567433	433921	347025
广 西 Guangxi	7136995	1321696	1930484	9254690	38889	27483
海 南 Hainan	2703773	504165	681622	3121715	14033	11201
重 庆 Chongqing	7897520	1537595	2335383	7878788	59580	48756
四 川 Sichuan	9922477	1803116	3958676	15422749	96561	80215
贵 州 Guizhou	4191746	619251	1596900	8047535	31139	25627
云 南 Yunnan	5721783	1356072	1698918	9493609	46818	36686
西 藏 Tibet	489752	57652	95475	509033	2579	1747
陕 西 Shaanxi	8176395	1213040	2835592	15704521	64958	53323
甘 肃 Gansu	3359329	475407	1319735	5708943	32028	26444
青 海 Qinghai	897161	151349	339197	1892902	12858	10222
宁 夏 Ningxia	3250164	676692	1183779	3202758	21251	15660
新 疆 Xinjiang	5783277	1207723	2027054	6792860	40993	33444

学条件(二)(城区)
Schools (2) (Urban Area)

(台) (set)	教室中: Classroom		教室中:普通教室(间) of Which: General Classroom		固定资产总值(万元) Total Value of Fixed Asset (10,000 yuan)		
用计算机 Computers Instruction / 其中:平板电脑 of Which:tablet PC	合计 Total	其中:网络多媒体教室 of Which: Network Multimedia Classroom	合计 Total	其中:网络多媒体教室 of Which: Network Multimedia Classroom	合计 Total	其中:教学仪器设备资产值 of Which: Total Value of Equip & Instru. 小计 Subtotal	其中:实验设备 for Profession
92236	**726896**	**420053**	**572990**	**353673**	**21037378.31**	**3386930.99**	**681385.76**
4897	23765	20826	17330	15921	1067172.90	353312.25	12954.57
1683	11316	6639	9014	6151	339237.14	51936.20	5345.24
5147	33707	17035	26756	15559	546761.25	86241.43	26277.93
1030	19107	9269	15771	8482	392978.83	50996.89	15911.90
490	13413	6376	11055	5791	356662.71	39951.23	8457.90
7909	30937	16992	24281	14531	617830.34	161339.67	32054.15
1429	14207	4894	11907	4378	329204.70	50781.44	13713.22
722	18066	7328	14463	6486	327901.92	63440.11	16173.98
1653	19246	16627	14318	12966	841656.32	177415.19	32576.35
6907	55294	42415	40292	33812	2490048.53	326712.49	57524.35
3026	40181	35524	30725	29203	1480843.63	196342.00	34202.58
2217	23856	8149	19863	7402	586221.83	56376.12	13256.47
103	25327	16322	19627	13942	673954.13	119521.49	20370.28
3875	14998	6275	12870	6048	300581.79	37149.11	8573.14
5206	54523	37558	40397	31036	1627066.29	211318.52	32349.30
4559	49760	18068	41649	16184	769625.64	86599.40	31268.99
4212	26930	15444	21688	14222	703209.42	114671.90	32230.73
3237	19257	9482	16306	8823	579667.72	81074.90	24512.22
21980	100710	63735	75941	51228	3595954.00	606566.00	165673.00
953	15100	4794	13303	4774	292977.73	37391.04	9517.08
977	4553	1288	4196	1333	164144.43	22360.00	4106.52
1942	14523	13202	11610	8938	556186.80	66920.27	10331.94
827	27743	12590	22304	10929	759967.68	133122.34	23811.45
1106	12757	3486	10674	3169	221892.71	28079.24	6845.48
1749	12849	5250	10975	4755	287460.87	44654.03	8159.38
	670	57	625	54	27052.36	3563.55	1094.78
2812	19070	6366	15224	5346	426709.27	67513.51	18148.49
1468	7589	3294	6344	3026	171863.95	25738.41	5360.33
91	1898	1319	1358	1053	58050.26	7364.38	1147.68
24	4770	2566	3804	2246	165407.68	26975.35	3963.85
5	10774	6883	8320	5885	279085.47	51502.51	5472.48

小学办

Condition of School Buildings in Primary

地　区 Region	占地面积(平方米) Areas of School Sites (m^2) 合计 Total	其中 of Which 绿化用地面积 Green Areas	其中 of Which 运动场地面积 Sports Areas	图书(册) Books & Magazines in Libraries (volume)	计算机数 PC 合计 Total	其中:教学 of Which: No. of Used for 小计 Subtotal
总　计 Total	**101483728**	**20871626**	**33855146**	**98772353**	**504470**	**414255**
北　京 Beijing	1428031	208763	628803	2016043	13286	11039
天　津 Tianjin	919501	83802	345425	1156919	5412	4207
河　北 Hebei	6100030	681202	2253128	5987726	27819	23519
山　西 Shanxi	2432500	265651	753427	2246380	9101	7804
内蒙古 Inner Mongolia	647178	96698	229334	317350	1476	1259
辽　宁 Liaoning	2872134	367913	1515287	2254093	13874	10320
吉　林 Jilin	1413690	255636	611612	617083	3659	2133
黑龙江 Heilongjiang	1720027	225165	766483	719375	5870	4687
上　海 Shanghai	609510	128391	228472	1839147	7954	6631
江　苏 Jiangsu	4696472	1214303	1438997	4128572	25897	20512
浙　江 Zhejiang	6054463	1372588	2040974	8128928	50319	45664
安　徽 Anhui	2892125	477626	754684	1960434	8782	7475
福　建 Fujian	3164157	574134	1133936	4079107	19968	17281
江　西 Jiangxi	1899016	242702	619844	1608304	5371	4140
山　东 Shandong	12564376	2564624	4930770	11939475	66602	52756
河　南 Henan	6907170	950274	1979897	5451805	16698	14208
湖　北 Hubei	3300092	1010727	875450	2834805	11958	10448
湖　南 Hunan	3176602	618590	700237	2895057	10971	9024
广　东 Guangdong	23974735	6774385	7658947	26120922	137980	112054
广　西 Guangxi	2125754	364578	462253	1301628	4680	3324
海　南 Hainan	728337	122307	135304	228652	1013	618
重　庆 Chongqing	1268905	225151	350600	773651	5049	4090
四　川 Sichuan	2052365	445086	744881	2015853	12691	10262
贵　州 Guizhou	1355880	235525	489625	1693552	7192	6090
云　南 Yunnan	1947533	466991	514182	1922633	8980	6979
西　藏 Tibet						
陕　西 Shaanxi	2783219	427305	957230	2953636	11557	9854
甘　肃 Gansu	515076	79694	195530	561461	3055	2476
青　海 Qinghai	131316	19977	44413	146645	1369	951
宁　夏 Ningxia	556926	99549	196156	310692	2953	2264
新　疆 Xinjiang	1246608	272289	299265	562425	2934	2186

学条件(二)(城乡结合区)
Schools (2) (Urban-rural Transitional Area)

(台) (set) 用计算机 Computers Instruction 其中:平板电脑 of Which:tablet PC	教室中: Classroom 合计 Total	其中:网络多媒体教室 of Which: Network Multimedia Classroom	教室中:普通教室(间) of Which: General Classroom 合计 Total	其中:网络多媒体教室 of Which: Network Multimedia Classroom	固定资产总值(万元) Total Value of Fixed Asset (10,000 yuan) 合计 Total	其中:教学仪器设备资产值 of Which: Total Value of Equip & Instru. 小计 Subtotal	其中:实验设备 for Profession
15682	**158371**	**70278**	**121514**	**58616**	**3973362.43**	**522996.48**	**132898.61**
152	2459	1809	1801	1400	81837.91	29798.86	1654.26
182	1273	734	971	605	51410.86	7076.70	867.58
945	11263	3713	8718	3382	139417.30	18843.13	7200.63
120	3564	1032	2857	942	79575.60	8466.83	3125.86
	519	126	421	132	16890.64	1366.49	303.09
1117	3709	1319	2774	1088	78227.12	16013.41	4465.53
31	1329	192	1033	149	23065.76	2200.53	651.18
77	2136	614	1560	495	36376.81	4720.41	1879.99
37	1899	1370	1543	1117	38617.03	9446.67	1533.98
433	6030	3534	4288	2849	234007.56	25932.05	4482.22
391	10080	8644	7872	7327	361170.79	40457.31	7838.41
371	4638	1062	4177	968	97566.24	7036.91	1612.77
9	6025	2558	4408	2186	115674.16	18110.42	3866.03
138	3568	654	2969	669	57683.50	4849.58	1099.43
1657	16772	9736	12151	7836	463361.64	44702.67	9667.53
466	13575	3401	10891	2976	165840.08	14645.66	5446.80
374	4256	1617	3339	1449	88944.00	11625.90	4598.36
623	3885	1300	3307	1120	101525.17	11270.75	3770.78
7134	36630	19873	26207	15859	1225059.00	182215.00	54103.00
138	3216	607	2861	583	63048.58	6120.84	1804.59
72	521	17	468	17	10257.65	887.37	459.75
97	1549	882	1272	777	37126.19	6451.19	1834.47
81	4291	1360	3426	1200	139316.50	16992.78	3129.62
231	3572	850	2910	755	43801.11	5846.33	1457.41
556	3351	948	2872	856	77469.01	7578.97	1305.09
203	4925	822	3786	532	85986.52	10410.33	2947.65
44	1067	379	867	357	18452.83	2546.78	555.09
	189	109	135	75	4123.94	1082.70	112.30
3	629	246	480	203	17741.50	2529.38	314.37
	1451	770	1150	712	19787.40	3770.53	810.82

小学办

Condition of School Buildings in Primary

地　区 Region	占地面积(平方米) Areas of School Sites (m^2) 合计 Total	其中 of Which 绿化用地面积 Green Areas	运动场地面积 Sports Areas	图书(册) Books & Magazines in Libraries (volume)	计算机数 PC 合计 Total	其中:教学 of Which: No. of Used for 小计 Subtotal
总　计 Total	**652119160**	**109951629**	**196560102**	**600533487**	**2353456**	**1926288**
北　京 Beijing	2309353	493773	859470	2755339	22178	18948
天　津 Tianjin	2783823	287246	1147390	3553643	15089	12684
河　北 Hebei	42285153	4184055	14287581	39997789	141959	118041
山　西 Shanxi	16109935	1554459	5024673	15197248	54180	45224
内蒙古 Inner Mongolia	21839052	2493434	6747681	9915449	41854	31792
辽　宁 Liaoning	11786876	1172662	5379309	9580031	46046	35122
吉　林 Jilin	10883349	1909782	4243110	6976468	27369	20195
黑龙江 Heilongjiang	13439682	1527263	5568049	6596789	33721	27886
上　海 Shanghai	1754658	504357	554269	3405020	17896	14335
江　苏 Jiangsu	45448266	11783327	13991723	42884800	259907	212834
浙　江 Zhejiang	25572918	5666231	8356456	37910300	222539	199808
安　徽 Anhui	30772480	3951523	8098879	26276750	89580	70645
福　建 Fujian	15495691	2986566	5840783	21807445	89207	71519
江　西 Jiangxi	24764882	3672882	6874908	20558079	64469	48991
山　东 Shandong	50140059	9775855	18633430	43495009	212330	169618
河　南 Henan	52390814	6007873	12673164	43902543	100902	84671
湖　北 Hubei	29284764	8942416	7456191	30046495	99071	86516
湖　南 Hunan	31949322	4664325	7492454	31123777	80666	66964
广　东 Guangdong	49003192	10924398	16670507	47511863	159744	133425
广　西 Guangxi	24831624	3533635	5559252	18355083	46579	31724
海　南 Hainan	10905099	2042893	2280892	4740075	18477	14340
重　庆 Chongqing	18002489	2795268	5158516	11622230	63014	47983
四　川 Sichuan	27410922	4161538	8746166	36124534	126026	99102
贵　州 Guizhou	16327276	2748785	5207528	17495576	50167	40964
云　南 Yunnan	17781560	3294584	3442842	16279353	52658	40983
西　藏 Tibet	4025976	483757	486565	1357499	10043	8271
陕　西 Shaanxi	22300171	2699594	6733253	28297577	100148	86885
甘　肃 Gansu	10507249	1463358	3307797	9437004	37206	29959
青　海 Qinghai	4670754	455101	986331	3477546	16225	13457
宁　夏 Ningxia	4615214	785528	1503804	2529908	16596	13229
新　疆 Xinjiang	12726557	2985161	3247129	7322265	37610	30173

学条件(二)(镇区)

Schools (2) (Counties & Towns Area)

(台) (set)	教室中: Classroom		教室中:普通教室(间) of Which: General Classroom		固定资产总值(万元) Total Value of Fixed Asset (10,000 yuan)		
用计算机 Computers Instruction	合计 Total	其中:网络多媒体教室 of Which: Network Multimedia Classroom	合计 Total	其中:网络多媒体教室 of Which: Network Multimedia Classroom	合计 Total	其中:教学仪器设备资产值 of Which: Total Value of Equip & Instru.	
其中:平板电脑 of Which:tablet PC						小计 Subtotal	其中:实验设备 for Profession
77225	**998650**	**309230**	**839245**	**276524**	**19562091.76**	**2049322.30**	**610374.31**
192	3795	3051	2619	2253	122304.07	42564.52	1811.66
546	4572	1694	3355	1385	115992.98	11899.31	3221.58
5141	83862	17701	65023	15485	984720.07	103034.38	40367.40
1065	31192	9058	24945	8285	519784.65	46283.10	19280.08
	18812	5901	16055	5658	684908.40	40884.60	12772.34
2992	15279	3185	12048	2648	236230.58	33306.65	10991.41
383	14109	2408	11661	2103	233620.55	27432.90	9825.86
420	17721	3561	14455	3011	293689.37	32543.68	14424.15
85	3467	2740	2766	2311	128258.08	25955.38	6579.18
5127	58774	30251	44862	25403	1735698.68	211698.15	50718.36
2915	41049	35772	32290	31249	1222923.42	167197.04	34815.67
4930	49568	15973	43929	14805	770625.43	69685.99	19421.19
352	28837	11392	21937	9777	672579.35	81489.25	22431.22
3541	40422	8688	36541	8139	556827.94	48629.99	16194.76
5165	67589	29958	54366	25350	1181936.28	123718.40	28556.48
2875	109104	18668	93378	16532	1181173.32	93304.90	37510.87
5334	34635	16195	28814	15143	687379.95	96534.17	39280.12
4574	35785	7350	35914	6761	804025.19	78030.15	31635.31
11888	63006	18933	53939	16649	1699491.00	161138.00	55422.00
794	38929	8433	35434	8276	575359.32	55595.91	19710.11
1709	8099	1225	7077	1245	241694.44	18850.36	6186.20
4822	22730	10084	23461	12925	528985.49	57186.63	12928.77
680	62908	11553	54363	10216	1362833.24	149444.18	39289.57
2168	31297	6739	26007	6348	494617.45	47133.73	15270.24
1731	27958	6476	24678	5853	606122.75	40602.90	12005.24
239	2156	240	1968	237	174436.69	7213.82	1461.77
3588	44593	8559	35311	7074	796402.52	80452.73	29746.26
2553	14782	3604	13339	3281	331599.83	29211.83	7779.98
949	5749	1376	4565	1042	200634.24	13436.69	2472.61
437	4952	2453	3920	1611	150297.38	20189.73	3356.51
30	12919	6009	10225	5469	266939.10	34673.24	4907.42

小学办

Condition of School Buildings in Primary

地 区 Region	占地面积(平方米) Areas of School Sites (m^2) 合计 Total	其中 of Which 绿化用地面积 Green Areas	运动场地面积 Sports Areas	图书(册) Books & Magazines in Libraries (volume)	计算机数 PC 合计 Total	其中:教学 of Which: No. of Used for 小计 Subtotal
总 计 Total	**242374743**	**40528406**	**73311155**	**190930876**	**726296**	**599846**
北 京 Beijing	598246	134210	210956	649135	5177	4457
天 津 Tianjin	1342637	142764	549075	1391927	6229	5127
河 北 Hebei	25730348	2508673	8783763	21786231	75603	63285
山 西 Shanxi	5564115	575674	1841603	4802826	17434	14724
内蒙古 Inner Mongolia	2029966	247590	572771	663773	2984	2322
辽 宁 Liaoning	2826402	276311	1389491	1606619	8412	6532
吉 林 Jilin	2267996	369914	959409	924881	3214	2367
黑龙江 Heilongjiang	2051484	207793	918503	727933	4156	3413
上 海 Shanghai	381013	99172	127942	793859	4090	3392
江 苏 Jiangsu	14541970	3780976	4370713	12390542	74523	61315
浙 江 Zhejiang	9473028	2097135	3098751	13415730	78416	71567
安 徽 Anhui	10119578	1366666	2560174	5860664	20940	15073
福 建 Fujian	5464422	1040965	2075619	5386518	23868	19568
江 西 Jiangxi	8673695	1223788	2644225	4929103	11474	8483
山 东 Shandong	24118956	4677850	9127361	18989606	97575	77016
河 南 Henan	28941335	3452455	6993363	19524042	39141	32503
湖 北 Hubei	9900246	2993259	2415120	7881241	28388	25341
湖 南 Hunan	14332841	1990530	3330723	11889337	29068	24486
广 东 Guangdong	23168962	5260050	7480867	20864668	70177	59072
广 西 Guangxi	10292824	1516646	2235934	4971832	10174	6243
海 南 Hainan	2867710	585978	568796	886623	2967	2470
重 庆 Chongqing	3770739	575946	1105060	2020328	10959	8212
四 川 Sichuan	6775355	1056262	2166007	6091147	23518	18916
贵 州 Guizhou	5136453	958679	1743839	4549451	12897	10653
云 南 Yunnan	6483245	1186881	1338911	5168658	16755	12843
西 藏 Tibet	295510	41513	50760	130390	1003	882
陕 西 Shaanxi	7534639	939174	2392954	7995766	25748	22087
甘 肃 Gansu	3301687	432521	1029082	2344393	9703	7827
青 海 Qinghai	945471	55130	215753	800752	2962	2540
宁 夏 Ningxia	1116650	182778	367711	517156	3593	2907
新 疆 Xinjiang	2327220	551123	645919	975745	5148	4223

学条件(二)(镇乡结合区)

Schools (2) (County-town Transitional Area)

(台) (set)	教室中: Classroom		教室中:普通教室(间) of Which: General Classroom		固定资产总值(万元) Total Value of Fixed Asset (10,000 yuan)		
用计算机 Computers Instruction / 其中:平板电脑 of Which:tablet PC	合计 Total	其中:网络多媒体教室 of Which: Network Multimedia Classroom	合计 Total	其中:网络多媒体教室 of Which: Network Multimedia Classroom	合计 Total	其中:教学仪器设备资产值 of Which: Total Value of Equip & Instru. 小计 Subtotal	其中:实验设备 for Profession
24296	**371666**	**91071**	**313319**	**80698**	**6015437.92**	**598978.09**	**192130.13**
	933	623	623	434	28929.67	8880.77	397.80
246	2086	669	1418	511	45812.34	5246.07	1369.34
3232	49970	8170	38679	6992	526012.49	51620.50	22608.80
309	10914	2813	8378	2525	157596.80	13112.44	5951.19
	1595	422	1348	405	49281.41	2432.78	598.89
186	3099	461	2490	369	44180.29	5951.85	1695.58
3	2171	331	1746	304	50140.24	6862.38	13.00
54	2457	299	2013	246	41418.36	3966.69	1595.25
45	808	692	677	596	28159.19	5864.44	1400.17
1334	17557	8411	12921	6824	450486.50	57191.12	14239.99
1144	15187	12954	11870	11298	418027.57	55253.76	11950.01
1337	14508	3325	12548	3062	205942.97	15107.44	4316.29
32	8942	2684	6502	2184	187755.96	21410.39	6031.44
774	13409	873	12178	828	143955.32	8678.92	3198.51
1811	31695	13006	25331	10802	540656.20	54874.63	12560.35
1072	56248	6955	47798	5928	521850.69	39744.61	17615.88
1386	10624	3889	8567	3564	187732.01	26006.96	11466.20
1637	16153	2356	18120	2092	305478.52	26487.54	11834.80
4349	30092	8878	24501	6543	735219.00	66547.00	23538.00
211	15875	1255	14680	1228	176891.48	13434.41	5146.43
255	1836	183	1539	204	40287.75	3283.93	1057.27
897	4723	1516	7805	4759	102923.54	10245.66	2618.60
228	14188	2220	12347	1971	265076.84	29837.17	7662.30
505	10202	1937	8283	1787	134900.24	12653.69	4418.70
844	10747	1723	9413	1536	190146.66	13742.82	4289.41
	256	32	223	27	17321.19	793.88	195.86
1135	14961	2032	12017	1676	220923.89	20307.31	8117.09
813	4979	839	4815	663	95647.56	8706.29	2503.39
276	1826	189	1654	167	40477.92	2151.20	405.11
172	1328	356	1026	286	29425.21	3307.04	997.16
9	2297	978	1809	887	32780.10	5274.40	1038.32

小学办

Condition of School Buildings in Primary

地　区 Region	占地面积(平方米) Areas of School Sites (m²) 合计 Total	其中 of Which 绿化用地面积 Green Areas	运动场地面积 Sports Areas	图书(册) Books & Magazines in Libraries (volume)	计算机数 PC 合计 Total	其中:教学 of Which: No. of Used for 小计 Subtotal
总　计 Total	**1269164485**	**197800404**	**355282154**	**620892305**	**2046979**	**1628220**
北　京 Beijing	3375210	551498	1353435	3587045	21272	18266
天　津 Tianjin	4554466	500208	1741989	3504424	17727	15069
河　北 Hebei	88854924	8406440	30342973	56330039	191837	161203
山　西 Shanxi	35025511	3094788	10742198	15780257	54071	44898
内蒙古 Inner Mongolia	28207541	4010603	7280872	4417344	13967	9358
辽　宁 Liaoning	25087129	2538415	11812548	8481364	40545	28809
吉　林 Jilin	43501108	8227570	15988893	7973254	22998	16897
黑龙江 Heilongjiang	36545771	4277969	15959322	5647256	21612	16662
上　海 Shanghai	706419	195213	234980	1265123	6269	4699
江　苏 Jiangsu	24280275	5721126	6957741	13636458	83458	69125
浙　江 Zhejiang	15740011	3029872	5535208	17360687	107206	95078
安　徽 Anhui	73231666	9025518	17243819	32570385	88002	69882
福　建 Fujian	26860836	4935708	9621952	18532555	87353	72765
江　西 Jiangxi	44803307	5432685	14228181	18266459	35664	26142
山　东 Shandong	77974502	15516553	28314635	43740419	247916	201933
河　南 Henan	127585574	15763969	29522018	71991301	108457	91233
湖　北 Hubei	49097413	14277310	10906846	27464968	112332	100842
湖　南 Hunan	53145152	6887827	11765602	31604124	69514	54846
广　东 Guangdong	78757065	17326380	22209386	43988018	151734	107784
广　西 Guangxi	70674145	11252677	14816519	28662510	48828	26366
海　南 Hainan	21990776	5222834	4058824	3586932	10265	8093
重　庆 Chongqing	17472862	2459246	5068893	7593169	31720	22731
四　川 Sichuan	40174152	4790758	11422049	31256392	82460	61473
贵　州 Guizhou	43162241	8019955	13360209	28693256	66540	50020
云　南 Yunnan	64980634	9603463	10868852	36702892	96511	70707
西　藏 Tibet	10609128	1253205	1293205	2727665	20395	16151
陕　西 Shaanxi	28568518	3324326	7725563	16735122	46633	36991
甘　肃 Gansu	53956704	6086235	15122325	20264740	64042	49880
青　海 Qinghai	9982776	825080	1903692	3619104	14332	11824
宁　夏 Ningxia	12747673	1933017	3855424	4836041	23489	19023
新　疆 Xinjiang	57510996	13309956	14024001	10073002	59830	49470

学条件(二)(乡村)
Schools (2) (Rural Area)

(台) (set) 用计算机 Computers Instruction	教室中: Classroom		教室中:普通教室(间) of Which: General Classroom		固定资产总值(万元) Total Value of Fixed Asset (10,000 yuan)		
其中:平板电脑 of Which:tablet PC	合计 Total	其中:网络多媒体教室 of Which: Network Multimedia Classroom	合计 Total	其中:网络多媒体教室 of Which: Network Multimedia Classroom	合计 Total	其中:教学仪器设备资产值 of Which: Total Value of Equip & Instru. 小计 Subtotal	其中:实验设备 for Profession
57564	**1745899**	**210153**	**1466990**	**178848**	**19601651.22**	**1734785.71**	**594446.16**
250	4355	3018	2671	2174	121439.76	44075.30	2479.96
370	6111	1513	4120	1148	124578.41	15286.06	4905.60
6606	159327	17442	126196	17484	1305379.29	118984.58	54912.13
973	53815	6837	42940	5811	611462.14	44862.03	20730.52
	15479	753	13325	660	238199.40	13740.60	5531.94
1548	25434	2176	20171	1705	219322.15	28289.04	11550.26
296	35416	1225	29281	855	222761.59	20420.24	10766.50
270	28478	1079	22246	770	221781.22	17648.66	8243.83
46	1328	1006	1067	799	46165.67	8317.38	1984.44
1772	25313	7755	18715	6271	422877.48	56880.53	17593.42
993	22381	18057	16587	15744	508592.98	76120.51	15840.33
5761	99829	15418	88237	14164	989130.13	75425.53	22513.46
103	45625	8399	31469	6505	695317.50	71664.13	22461.91
1766	74167	2249	67559	1973	568207.58	31349.20	11349.50
4724	95110	28929	73905	22224	1108233.66	116807.79	32912.26
3208	255982	19863	210542	16193	1588227.76	119622.58	51066.58
3997	51197	12676	39886	11105	754287.69	92170.57	35196.96
2524	55009	2863	54452	2553	822014.53	66696.55	29515.14
9041	91993	12095	77151	9625	1680365.00	133972.00	43139.00
960	106651	3951	98890	3474	1019162.17	74615.42	28759.75
915	11246	413	9834	339	199889.42	11028.37	3599.87
1208	20462	3641	20698	3955	284563.06	29711.86	8440.45
213	89445	3835	81051	3132	1214650.64	97103.89	33002.63
2605	92052	7396	75024	6717	844914.59	68062.73	27371.16
1369	100600	6540	90669	5533	1551340.52	90544.73	29962.25
781	6560	379	6895	252	339548.43	12676.67	2645.26
1070	45297	2579	35926	1895	414286.05	36525.45	15833.99
2841	63036	3941	55708	3158	661590.29	60521.52	21697.40
508	12857	759	11370	605	201310.65	11230.91	2526.02
681	15725	1608	11865	1043	183425.11	22111.44	5310.43
165	35619	11758	28540	10982	438626.35	68319.45	12603.20

工读学校

Basic Statistics of Correctional

地 区 Region	学校数(所) Schools	班数(个) Classes	离校人数 Sclools Leavers
总 计 Total	**78**	**373**	**3596**
北 京 Beijing	6	45	346
天 津 Tianjin	3		
河 北 Hebei			
山 西 Shanxi	1	10	100
内蒙古 Inner Mongolia			
辽 宁 Liaoning	10	56	503
吉 林 Jilin	4	6	154
黑龙江 Heilongjiang	1	2	3
上 海 Shanghai	13	88	621
江 苏 Jiangsu			
浙 江 Zhejiang	2	16	67
安 徽 Anhui	3	3	16
福 建 Fujian			
江 西 Jiangxi	1		
山 东 Shandong			
河 南 Henan	3	12	15
湖 北 Hubei	2	6	71
湖 南 Hunan	1	6	210
广 东 Guangdong	2	12	124
广 西 Guangxi	3	4	4
海 南 Hainan			
重 庆 Chongqing	3	4	8
四 川 Sichuan	7	36	150
贵 州 Guizhou	6	22	588
云 南 Yunnan	1	6	110
西 藏 Tibet			
陕 西 Shaanxi	1	4	10
甘 肃 Gansu			
青 海 Qinghai			
宁 夏 Ningxia			
新 疆 Xinjiang	5	35	496

基本情况
Work-study Schools

单位:人
unit: person

入校人数 No. of Persons Enrolled	在校生数 Enrolment	教职工数 Educational Personnel 合计 Total	 其中:专任教师 of Which: Full-time Teachers
3891	**9307**	**2687**	**1851**
351	748	294	196
		110	80
111	296	84	67
504	1321	319	226
41	284	115	96
	2	23	20
553	1462	521	406
218	291	106	63
16	20	67	37
59	217	75	57
83	87	48	38
50	70	46	41
123	203	85	55
15	25	36	26
13	35	33	23
271	1074	183	134
538	623	99	88
71	85	49	40
13	42	40	20
861	2422	354	138

特殊教育

Basic Statistics of

地 区 Region	学校数(所) Schools	班数(个) Classes	毕业生数 Graduates	招生数 Entrants	在校生数 合计 Total	其中:女 of Which: Female	小学阶段 一年级 Grade 1	二年级 Grade 2	三年级 Grade 3
总 计 Total	**1933**	**18915**	**50739**	**65977**	**368103**	**132523**	**45138**	**45848**	**43204**
北 京 Beijing	22	352	1706	1156	8348	3015	590	723	720
天 津 Tianjin	20	210	340	418	2980	1000	346	328	317
河 北 Hebei	155	1116	1279	2570	13109	4929	1857	1826	1667
山 西 Shanxi	56	604	1023	1069	7146	3116	999	954	824
内蒙古 Inner Mongolia	42	376	353	701	4328	1513	788	640	526
辽 宁 Liaoning	74	746	1079	852	7977	2845	905	972	872
吉 林 Jilin	47	468	805	740	5610	2085	693	708	633
黑龙江 Heilongjiang	74	852	1002	1205	9317	3605	1109	1050	1034
上 海 Shanghai	29	469	1549	1147	8105	2880	356	458	655
江 苏 Jiangsu	107	1278	3394	3491	23055	8056	2261	2533	2758
浙 江 Zhejiang	82	966	1777	2812	16327	5820	1471	2186	1937
安 徽 Anhui	65	662	1132	2072	10344	3732	1659	1418	1287
福 建 Fujian	73	845	3441	4203	25142	8577	2574	2927	3189
江 西 Jiangxi	85	644	2197	3337	17111	5529	2720	2374	2300
山 东 Shandong	144	1608	2887	3340	20946	7429	2631	2563	2361
河 南 Henan	137	1083	1735	3312	16697	6174	2772	2425	2037
湖 北 Hubei	80	711	1227	1788	10576	3700	1216	1349	1451
湖 南 Hunan	69	528	1286	2240	10097	3958	1824	1313	1061
广 东 Guangdong	99	1297	2527	3862	21799	6995	2490	2688	2378
广 西 Guangxi	65	672	1193	2132	12913	4483	1736	2050	1943
海 南 Hainan	7	78	178	425	1708	501	281	221	174
重 庆 Chongqing	36	349	2101	3316	15622	6072	1967	1666	1592
四 川 Sichuan	119	907	9191	8230	43731	15656	4512	5456	5037
贵 州 Guizhou	60	460	1378	2684	12712	4541	1705	1974	1587
云 南 Yunnan	53	509	2825	3829	17421	6622	2169	2046	1953
西 藏 Tibet	5	45	37	213	835	352	163	155	123
陕 西 Shaanxi	50	400	1109	1278	6494	2455	910	869	767
甘 肃 Gansu	32	260	831	1409	8396	3126	844	967	1033
青 海 Qinghai	12	82	289	368	2120	814	278	271	261
宁 夏 Ningxia	8	83	188	305	1908	775	266	214	277
新 疆 Xinjiang	26	255	680	1473	5229	2168	1046	524	450

基本情况
Special Education

单位:人
unit:person

Enrolment

Primary Education			初中阶段 Junior Secondary Education				高中阶段 Senior Secondary Education		
四年级 Grade 4	五年级 Grade 5	六年级 Grade 6	一年级 Grade 1	二年级 Grade 2	三年级 Grade 3	四年级 Grade 4	一年级 Grade 1	二年级 Grade 2	三年级及以上 Over Grade 3
42693	**42086**	**40098**	**32948**	**32625**	**31574**	**1894**	**3803**	**3232**	**2960**
838	907	1162	810	1021	1187	59	110	117	104
379	332	388	211	228	178	36	95	77	65
1461	1370	1171	1299	1011	1076	10	123	131	107
762	759	713	599	604	578		138	143	73
434	445	441	277	247	285	40	87	76	42
822	847	843	742	755	628	12	241	186	152
657	670	639	521	440	395	66	97	44	47
1201	1214	923	862	718	809	187	90	60	60
815	978	2	1074	1056	1092	967	258	191	203
2898	2802	2762	1987	2022	1834		437	383	378
1928	1766	1918	1460	1598	1424	2	223	206	208
1148	1066	976	724	760	745	5	189	175	192
3174	3370	3376	2087	1988	1968	10	174	130	175
2077	1832	1637	1382	1302	1287		47	58	95
2421	2238	1946	1874	1782	1919	315	304	283	309
1853	1706	1410	1641	1432	1154	65	101	57	44
1168	1271	1070	1014	791	860	47	130	122	87
1157	1057	1005	984	904	758		19	15	
2257	2429	2436	1922	2222	2124	20	326	304	203
1861	1564	1468	674	779	623	53	61	51	50
216	180	179	126	117	134		32	31	17
1628	1533	1693	1773	1821	1759		66	76	48
5301	5381	5634	3989	4142	4025		133	82	39
1605	1508	1452	1011	875	704		137	74	80
1881	2020	2186	1787	1694	1685				
85	71	66	29	35	63		8	15	22
641	737	679	551	620	638		26	44	12
1083	1053	1067	689	795	738		54	51	22
261	275	198	217	186	145		12	11	5
209	283	167	137	143	143		39	14	16
472	422	491	495	537	616		46	25	105

特殊教育基本

Basic Statistics of Special Education

地 区 Region	学校数（所）Schools	班数（个）Classes	毕业生数 Graduates	招生数 Entrants	在校生数				
					合计 Total	其中:女 of Which: Female	小学阶段		
							一年级 Grade 1	二年级 Grade 2	三年级 Grade 3
总 计 Total	**942**	**11263**	**22003**	**26340**	**155918**	**57984**	**18552**	**17325**	**17164**
北 京 Beijing	17	300	1348	951	6650	2361	477	537	565
天 津 Tianjin	17	181	294	309	2418	837	292	239	214
河 北 Hebei	47	513	578	1495	6760	2583	743	695	619
山 西 Shanxi	28	305	573	535	3693	1675	420	424	426
内蒙古 Inner Mongolia	19	251	229	378	2396	862	432	352	311
辽 宁 Liaoning	54	574	950	659	6179	2192	707	688	640
吉 林 Jilin	37	388	620	468	3988	1522	486	467	445
黑龙江 Heilongjiang	38	428	587	464	4163	1548	584	451	468
上 海 Shanghai	26	413	1285	950	6821	2443	328	396	550
江 苏 Jiangsu	80	925	1793	1768	11897	4285	1221	1081	1335
浙 江 Zhejiang	51	614	836	1413	8773	3199	924	1130	1055
安 徽 Anhui	21	287	441	821	3755	1395	595	504	362
福 建 Fujian	36	473	1103	1287	7607	2641	808	890	945
江 西 Jiangxi	24	235	582	654	3768	1218	582	452	443
山 东 Shandong	79	933	1848	1770	10905	4067	1211	1139	1102
河 南 Henan	56	498	870	1332	6623	2460	885	759	699
湖 北 Hubei	43	433	760	983	5841	2027	651	735	784
湖 南 Hunan	27	307	455	815	4223	1595	870	627	485
广 东 Guangdong	62	1052	1776	2400	13505	4502	1544	1619	1422
广 西 Guangxi	21	345	508	703	4466	1715	589	607	641
海 南 Hainan	3	68	130	257	841	304	153	83	66
重 庆 Chongqing	17	183	674	1299	6418	2749	916	674	685
四 川 Sichuan	45	387	1379	1413	7876	2973	870	941	1001
贵 州 Guizhou	17	160	372	571	2441	948	298	305	277
云 南 Yunnan	19	335	848	1127	5183	2141	646	492	610
西 藏 Tibet	1	13	3	23	222	102	23	72	57
陕 西 Shaanxi	18	184	290	352	2160	866	303	325	262
甘 肃 Gansu	14	190	366	393	2629	1143	288	259	335
青 海 Qinghai	3	37	61	86	585	221	67	63	61
宁 夏 Ningxia	5	64	137	143	871	389	129	79	120
新 疆 Xinjiang	17	187	307	521	2261	1021	510	240	179

情况(城区)
(Urban Area)

单位:人
unit:person

Enrolment									
Primary Education			初中阶段 Junior Secondary Education				高中阶段 Senior Secondary Education		
四年级 Grade 4	五年级 Grade 5	六年级 Grade 6	一年级 Grade 1	二年级 Grade 2	三年级 Grade 3	四年级 Grade 4	一年级 Grade 1	二年级 Grade 2	三年级及以上 Over Grade 3
16672	**16884**	**15593**	**14623**	**14331**	**14158**	**1563**	**3446**	**2876**	**2731**
643	708	900	649	825	956	59	110	117	104
286	244	316	204	207	160	36	87	77	56
537	595	543	1033	757	867	10	123	131	107
337	391	386	347	332	353		123	81	73
201	239	161	168	141	181	40	75	60	35
560	676	668	595	601	492	12	227	161	152
461	448	395	401	346	331	39	89	44	36
502	487	296	327	297	391	150	90	60	60
626	793	1	886	888	919	826	245	176	187
1377	1331	1342	1029	1074	982		422	358	345
983	874	915	755	869	803	2	165	136	162
366	313	349	229	232	263	5	180	170	187
886	918	961	652	584	575	10	124	102	152
460	423	338	283	295	292		47	58	95
1184	1188	926	967	934	1185	216	288	269	296
650	692	535	905	787	507	39	82	43	40
673	757	590	549	364	390	46	113	113	76
482	472	470	296	265	222		19	15	
1320	1366	1472	1229	1411	1284	20	320	295	203
661	504	530	247	263	209	53	61	51	50
81	76	85	83	57	77		32	31	17
720	755	763	515	588	626		52	76	48
931	957	897	704	727	684		78	61	25
284	205	199	252	174	184		124	74	65
522	549	563	649	575	577				
37	11	18		2	2				
239	263	274	145	163	139		19	16	12
295	319	359	209	240	198		54	51	22
67	60	70	71	63	35		12	11	5
82	116	62	72	76	66		39	14	16
219	154	209	172	194	208		46	25	105

特殊教育基本

Basic Statistics of Special Education

地 区 Region	学校数（所）Schools	班数（个）Classes	毕业生数 Graduates	招生数 Entrants	在校生数				
					合计 Total	其中:女 of Which: Female	小学阶段		
							一年级 Grade 1	二年级 Grade 2	三年级 Grade 3
总 计 Total	**135**	**1685**	**3254**	**4705**	**25213**	**9346**	**3154**	**2992**	**2743**
北 京 Beijing	1	7	84	82	547	188	40	57	52
天 津 Tianjin			31	19	152	48	4	7	12
河 北 Hebei	13	126	59	166	1158	461	202	207	165
山 西 Shanxi	2	9	2	18	133	44	12	27	25
内蒙古 Inner Mongolia			1	1	9	3	1	1	3
辽 宁 Liaoning	3	57	119	45	690	231	42	117	56
吉 林 Jilin	5	68	92	71	634	254	70	67	48
黑龙江 Heilongjiang	4	48	44	29	457	202	89	40	77
上 海 Shanghai			36	32	151	62	3	3	16
江 苏 Jiangsu	5	63	116	114	970	325	82	96	90
浙 江 Zhejiang	9	119	145	314	1868	676	153	187	156
安 徽 Anhui	6	72	69	225	885	339	224	122	90
福 建 Fujian	8	99	224	306	1597	520	164	174	202
江 西 Jiangxi	3	16	42	90	383	96	63	84	60
山 东 Shandong	20	279	568	531	3283	1202	367	363	391
河 南 Henan	5	52	238	481	1644	607	101	93	88
湖 北 Hubei	8	65	60	94	750	266	119	131	138
湖 南 Hunan	6	48	95	186	654	234	179	96	65
广 东 Guangdong	10	214	377	642	3201	1167	469	446	287
广 西 Guangxi	3	34	25	118	546	171	91	76	100
海 南 Hainan	1	53	120	160	620	236	77	69	54
重 庆 Chongqing	4	51	97	173	861	367	167	73	88
四 川 Sichuan	7	56	218	260	1308	488	134	210	173
贵 州 Guizhou	2	11	30	69	280	110	51	41	49
云 南 Yunnan	3	59	209	301	1296	562	109	95	141
西 藏 Tibet									
陕 西 Shaanxi	3	22	49	57	298	138	41	30	42
甘 肃 Gansu	1	6	43	27	201	93	17	25	31
青 海 Qinghai			1	6	20	4	3	1	3
宁 夏 Ningxia	1	17	20	12	207	100	33	9	19
新 疆 Xinjiang	2	34	40	76	410	152	47	45	22

情况(城乡结合区)
(Urban-rural Transitional Area)

单位:人
unit:person

Enrolment									
Primary Education			初中阶段 Junior Secondary Education				高中阶段 Senior Secondary Education		
四年级 Grade 4	五年级 Grade 5	六年级 Grade 6	一年级 Grade 1	二年级 Grade 2	三年级 Grade 3	四年级 Grade 4	一年级 Grade 1	二年级 Grade 2	三年级及以上 Over Grade 3
2726	**2574**	**2486**	**2625**	**2604**	**2380**	**75**	**377**	**281**	**196**
79	61	82	53	69	54				
21	27	35	15	22	9				
147	112	139	77	48	46		15		
21	17	16	6	4	5				
2	1			1					
55	62	55	62	113	51		48	14	15
62	66	60	62	71	76		27	14	11
58	33	39	32	31	24	17	9	8	
17	21	1	29	24	12	25			
119	129	113	83	92	87		21	30	28
204	172	196	238	256	183		41	34	48
92	65	94	36	51	57	5	17	15	17
233	203	215	124	112	124	10	20	14	2
77	38	19	22	14	6				
391	400	283	265	294	405	18	56	29	21
75	92	85	464	377	244		13	12	
76	75	54	96	45	16				
88	52	94	32	25	23				
275	320	327	294	366	355		39	12	11
76	63	67	24	26	23				
66	53	69	51	48	58		32	26	17
81	90	57	72	68	69		22	52	22
163	143	99	138	125	116			7	
33	31	23	18	21	13				
101	120	105	218	192	215				
39	37	28	28	30	17			6	
19	31	36	17	7	18				
3	2	2	3	2	1				
18	36	26	13	20	11		12	6	4
35	22	67	53	50	62		5	2	

地 区 Region	学校数（所）Schools	班数（个）Classes	毕业生数 Graduates	招生数 Entrants	在校生数 合计 Total	其中:女 of Which: Female	小学阶段 一年级 Grade 1	二年级 Grade 2	三年级 Grade 3
总 计 Total	**872**	**6677**	**20164**	**26694**	**139421**	**50618**	**17468**	**18179**	**16141**
北 京 Beijing	2	16	236	115	934	347	40	138	73
天 津 Tianjin	3	29	33	97	443	125	44	74	82
河 北 Hebei	94	517	587	738	4526	1688	809	809	741
山 西 Shanxi	23	224	331	385	2348	1016	398	368	262
内蒙古 Inner Mongolia	21	108	115	267	1566	542	293	219	175
辽 宁 Liaoning	18	156	118	172	1539	553	166	242	210
吉 林 Jilin	9	68	166	195	1202	429	162	169	143
黑龙江 Heilongjiang	33	403	334	555	4140	1664	421	481	471
上 海 Shanghai	3	55	223	169	1133	396	24	55	92
江 苏 Jiangsu	26	349	1474	1465	9489	3317	824	1111	1147
浙 江 Zhejiang	20	246	770	1076	5553	1936	375	755	607
安 徽 Anhui	38	321	484	924	4492	1605	861	606	625
福 建 Fujian	31	304	1393	1693	10124	3475	1006	1167	1286
江 西 Jiangxi	58	380	978	1599	7680	2646	1240	1008	992
山 东 Shandong	62	654	868	1333	8531	2945	1234	1168	1048
河 南 Henan	79	574	772	1335	7587	2978	1385	1192	990
湖 北 Hubei	31	235	373	583	3547	1282	451	461	516
湖 南 Hunan	38	202	735	1213	4870	2089	775	534	441
广 东 Guangdong	26	124	497	971	4960	1517	528	583	499
广 西 Guangxi	42	306	462	922	4995	1704	678	871	713
海 南 Hainan	2	7	39	96	531	130	56	72	68
重 庆 Chongqing	18	158	1203	1599	6969	2618	774	761	568
四 川 Sichuan	61	447	5191	4267	22265	8113	2041	2687	2346
贵 州 Guizhou	41	291	509	1127	5121	1897	681	870	603
云 南 Yunnan	29	142	988	1464	5475	2076	784	706	429
西 藏 Tibet	2	12	1	92	279	101	46	54	34
陕 西 Shaanxi	27	172	694	736	3378	1271	476	399	339
甘 肃 Gansu	15	54	218	550	2659	926	270	301	289
青 海 Qinghai	9	43	146	191	1039	416	132	125	127
宁 夏 Ningxia	3	19	27	118	648	246	106	68	102
新 疆 Xinjiang	8	61	199	647	1398	570	388	125	123

情况(镇区)
(Counties & Towns Area)

单位:人
unit:person

Enrolment									
Primary Education			初中阶段 Junior Secondary Education				高中阶段 Senior Secondary Education		
四年级 Grade 4	五年级 Grade 5	六年级 Grade 6	一年级 Grade 1	二年级 Grade 2	三年级 Grade 3	四年级 Grade 4	一年级 Grade 1	二年级 Grade 2	三年级及以上 Over Grade 3
16117	**15181**	**14848**	**13738**	**13782**	**12930**	**260**	**309**	**266**	**202**
83	108	131	104	122	135				
69	68	51	5	16	17		8		9
677	528	419	196	188	159				
275	242	200	152	199	175		15	62	
179	166	239	97	92	89		6	4	7
236	135	139	139	136	118		14	4	
127	158	184	79	84	50	27	8		11
570	589	534	431	321	304	18			
164	163		164	148	156	123	13	15	16
1277	1211	1196	910	923	817		15	25	33
664	581	708	569	612	508		58	70	46
513	468	371	354	359	335				
1304	1360	1275	912	894	831		38	28	23
841	753	751	743	665	687				
1020	858	858	830	756	651	65	16	14	13
866	757	679	589	527	539	26	19	14	4
346	355	338	327	349	366	1	17	9	11
542	483	405	640	581	469				
510	522	513	529	629	647				
596	547	474	371	419	326				
72	64	47	39	57	56				
615	496	627	1073	1050	991		14		
2575	2511	2777	2332	2474	2432		55	21	14
591	583	536	476	425	328		13		15
455	494	549	674	716	668				
21	27	24	17	19	37				
303	334	297	370	408	452				
326	293	310	287	307	276				
129	141	65	127	102	91				
61	88	56	49	56	62				
110	98	95	153	148	158				

特殊教育基本

Basic Statistics of Special Education

地区 Region	学校数(所) Schools	班数(个) Classes	毕业生数 Graduates	招生数 Entrants	在校生数		小学阶段		
					合计 Total	其中:女 of Which: Female	一年级 Grade 1	二年级 Grade 2	三年级 Grade 3
总计 Total	**293**	**2141**	**4723**	**7431**	**38335**	**13667**	**5357**	**5749**	**4881**
北京 Beijing			41	18	113	32	5	4	10
天津 Tianjin	1	8	6	68	129	43	16	11	22
河北 Hebei	56	298	307	398	2376	889	434	432	347
山西 Shanxi	7	76	61	116	616	240	122	132	46
内蒙古 Inner Mongolia	2	11	10	36	155	49	25	54	12
辽宁 Liaoning	2	12	27	29	106	35	27	12	10
吉林 Jilin		1	3	4	66	16	3	12	8
黑龙江 Heilongjiang	3	34	78	109	701	329	43	51	58
上海 Shanghai	1	24	45	57	405	143	11	25	39
江苏 Jiangsu	8	116	420	378	2737	947	225	333	342
浙江 Zhejiang	9	143	414	572	2795	949	180	395	294
安徽 Anhui	11	86	64	234	1115	425	217	174	160
福建 Fujian	10	104	327	405	2621	894	288	310	348
江西 Jiangxi	14	74	250	412	1837	592	377	323	243
山东 Shandong	22	263	328	590	3386	1097	504	520	470
河南 Henan	32	202	232	545	2839	1112	625	492	434
湖北 Hubei	9	62	75	82	922	356	99	122	192
湖南 Hunan	9	39	156	261	923	331	233	103	106
广东 Guangdong	9	48	161	296	1630	495	170	225	188
广西 Guangxi	9	82	89	207	1316	474	179	286	175
海南 Hainan	2	7	11	27	144	45	24	35	15
重庆 Chongqing	8	64	212	410	1594	569	219	195	139
四川 Sichuan	11	72	705	708	3765	1363	386	507	489
贵州 Guizhou	17	117	166	394	1731	618	242	349	217
云南 Yunnan	14	75	291	541	2054	774	344	307	221
西藏 Tibet	1	7		3	94	35	3	43	18
陕西 Shaanxi	12	59	138	188	924	350	153	126	112
甘肃 Gansu	7	26	53	154	590	209	105	88	57
青海 Qinghai	3	8	19	37	170	67	32	24	19
宁夏 Ningxia	2	11	3	25	230	92	38	26	56
新疆 Xinjiang	2	12	31	127	251	97	28	33	34

情况（镇乡结合区）
（County-town Transitional Area）

单位：人
unit：person

Enrolment									
Primary Education			初中阶段 Junior Secondary Education				高中阶段 Senior Secondary Education		
四年级 Grade 4	五年级 Grade 5	六年级 Grade 6	一年级 Grade 1	二年级 Grade 2	三年级 Grade 3	四年级 Grade 4	一年级 Grade 1	二年级 Grade 2	三年级及以上 Over Grade 3
4697	**4226**	**4025**	**3153**	**3008**	**2879**	**75**	**109**	**84**	**92**
2	7	15	13	24	33				
20	19	22	3	5	2				9
383	321	208	102	82	67				
72	41	59	50	52	42				
5	21	17	11	6	4				
11	9	18	9	8	2				
10	12	14	1	3	3				
89	55	99	100	105	101				
77	52		62	39	50	50			
378	357	351	243	229	238		9	14	18
314	270	365	264	289	250		58	70	46
150	111	86	81	65	71				
359	355	387	190	173	198				13
222	150	159	128	130	105				
438	377	296	278	241	215	25	16		6
348	292	256	166	107	119				
106	120	116	84	47	36				
96	82	75	69	72	87				
198	191	172	136	177	173				
165	146	131	61	108	65				
30	10	10	6		14				
145	125	159	245	189	178				
455	431	410	347	377	350		13		
187	214	165	149	98	97		13		
193	201	233	180	197	178				
13	17								
116	111	93	67	74	72				
70	75	57	38	36	64				
19	14	17	19	15	11				
5	29	8	22	18	28				
21	11	27	29	42	26				

特殊教育基本
Basic Statistics of Special Education

地　区 Region	学校数 （所） Schools	班数 （个） Classes	毕业生数 Graduates	招生数 Entrants	在校生数				
					合计 Total	其中：女 of Which： Female	小学阶段		
							一年级 Grade 1	二年级 Grade 2	三年级 Grade 3
总　计 Total	**119**	**975**	**8572**	**12943**	**72764**	**23921**	**9118**	**10344**	**9899**
北　京 Beijing	3	36	122	90	764	307	73	48	82
天　津 Tianjin			13	12	119	38	10	15	21
河　北 Hebei	14	86	114	337	1823	658	305	322	307
山　西 Shanxi	5	75	119	149	1105	425	181	162	136
内蒙古 Inner Mongolia	2	17	9	56	366	109	63	69	40
辽　宁 Liaoning	2	16	11	21	259	100	32	42	22
吉　林 Jilin	1	12	19	77	420	134	45	72	45
黑龙江 Heilongjiang	3	21	81	186	1014	393	104	118	95
上　海 Shanghai		1	41	28	151	41	4	7	13
江　苏 Jiangsu	1	4	127	258	1669	454	216	341	276
浙　江 Zhejiang	11	106	171	323	2001	685	172	301	275
安　徽 Anhui	6	54	207	327	2097	732	203	308	300
福　建 Fujian	6	68	945	1223	7411	2461	760	870	958
江　西 Jiangxi	3	29	637	1084	5663	1665	898	914	865
山　东 Shandong	3	21	171	237	1510	417	186	256	211
河　南 Henan	2	11	93	645	2487	736	502	474	348
湖　北 Hubei	6	43	94	222	1188	391	114	153	151
湖　南 Hunan	4	19	96	212	1004	274	179	152	135
广　东 Guangdong	11	121	254	491	3334	976	418	486	457
广　西 Guangxi	2	21	223	507	3452	1064	469	572	589
海　南 Hainan	2	3	9	72	336	67	72	66	40
重　庆 Chongqing	1	8	224	418	2235	705	277	231	339
四　川 Sichuan	13	73	2621	2550	13590	4570	1601	1828	1690
贵　州 Guizhou	2	9	497	986	5150	1696	726	799	707
云　南 Yunnan	5	32	989	1238	6763	2405	739	848	914
西　藏 Tibet	2	20	33	98	334	149	94	29	32
陕　西 Shaanxi	5	44	125	190	956	318	131	145	166
甘　肃 Gansu	3	16	247	466	3108	1057	286	407	409
青　海 Qinghai		2	82	91	496	177	79	83	73
宁　夏 Ningxia			24	44	389	140	31	67	55
新　疆 Xinjiang	1	7	174	305	1570	577	148	159	148

情况(乡村)
(Rural Area)

单位:人
unit:person

Enrolment									
Primary Education			初中阶段 Junior Secondary Education				高中阶段 Senior Secondary Education		
四年级 Grade 4	五年级 Grade 5	六年级 Grade 6	一年级 Grade 1	二年级 Grade 2	三年级 Grade 3	四年级 Grade 4	一年级 Grade 1	二年级 Grade 2	三年级及以上 Over Grade 3
9904	**10021**	**9657**	**4587**	**4512**	**4486**	**71**	**48**	**90**	**27**
112	91	131	57	74	96				
24	20	21	2	5	1				
247	247	209	70	66	50				
150	126	127	100	73	50				
54	40	41	12	14	15		6	12	
26	36	36	8	18	18			21	
69	64	60	41	10	14				
129	138	93	104	100	114	19			
25	22	1	24	20	17	18			
244	260	224	48	25	35				
281	311	295	136	117	113				
269	285	256	141	169	147		9	5	5
984	1092	1140	523	510	562		12		
776	656	548	356	342	308				
217	192	162	77	92	83	34			
337	257	196	147	118	108				
149	159	142	138	78	104				
133	102	130	48	58	67				
427	541	451	164	182	193		6	9	
604	513	464	56	97	88				
63	40	47	4	3	1				
293	282	303	185	183	142				
1795	1913	1960	953	941	909				
730	720	717	283	276	192				
904	977	1074	464	403	440				
27	33	24	12	14	24		8	15	22
99	140	108	36	49	47		7	28	
462	441	398	193	248	264				
65	74	63	19	21	19				
66	79	49	16	11	15				
143	170	187	170	195	250				

地 区 Region	毕业生数 Graduates	招生数 Entrants	在校生数 合 计 Total	小学阶段 Primary Education 一年级 Grade 1	二年级 Grade 2	三年级 Grade 3	四年级 Grade 4
总 计 Total	**17409**	**24163**	**132523**	**16539**	**16444**	**15402**	**15072**
北 京 Beijing	575	406	3015	215	269	260	294
天 津 Tianjin	110	140	1000	112	110	101	136
河 北 Hebei	438	929	4929	719	681	612	558
山 西 Shanxi	428	472	3116	430	383	338	335
内蒙古 Inner Mongolia	117	243	1513	262	219	199	136
辽 宁 Liaoning	438	292	2845	305	324	304	300
吉 林 Jilin	317	278	2085	275	238	238	243
黑龙江 Heilongjiang	443	457	3605	396	397	399	456
上 海 Shanghai	589	402	2880	124	178	229	271
江 苏 Jiangsu	1098	1143	8056	779	901	995	985
浙 江 Zhejiang	555	1022	5820	530	751	696	702
安 徽 Anhui	385	756	3732	585	488	450	385
福 建 Fujian	1024	1464	8577	873	1017	1098	1100
江 西 Jiangxi	654	1146	5529	971	806	759	636
山 东 Shandong	1022	1209	7429	970	877	831	827
河 南 Henan	665	1237	6174	1056	869	793	650
湖 北 Hubei	417	617	3700	423	450	499	440
湖 南 Hunan	546	913	3958	673	482	359	444
广 东 Guangdong	791	1224	6995	811	842	761	678
广 西 Guangxi	394	754	4483	587	766	632	649
海 南 Hainan	66	132	501	79	68	46	68
重 庆 Chongqing	730	1424	6072	838	635	597	552
四 川 Sichuan	3086	3067	15656	1659	1981	1822	1915
贵 州 Guizhou	441	914	4541	580	715	585	574
云 南 Yunnan	970	1459	6622	834	782	730	691
西 藏 Tibet	15	86	352	70	55	56	35
陕 西 Shaanxi	322	532	2455	380	349	267	240
甘 肃 Gansu	319	520	3126	317	408	379	390
青 海 Qinghai	98	152	814	110	106	84	87
宁 夏 Ningxia	83	125	775	110	81	117	84
新 疆 Xinjiang	273	648	2168	466	216	166	211

女学生数
in Special Education

单位：人

unit：person

Enrolment

		初中阶段 Junior Secondary Education				高中阶段 Senior Secondary Education		
五年级 Grade 5	六年级 Grade 6	一年级 Grade 1	二年级 Grade 2	三年级 Grade 3	四年级 Grade 4	一年级 Grade 1	二年级 Grade 2	三年级及以上 Over Grade 3
14707	**13888**	**12242**	**11908**	**11480**	**698**	**1525**	**1371**	**1247**
343	441	281	350	403	28	48	42	41
108	114	79	84	56	17	34	29	20
489	422	455	399	463	4	38	53	36
344	299	267	267	256		77	89	31
150	166	103	88	104	8	39	23	16
301	301	271	288	231	1	76	76	67
233	239	187	168	151	18	46	27	22
475	367	323	309	316	72	41	32	22
349	1	366	380	362	359	102	79	80
920	913	687	722	676		176	150	152
611	664	534	581	494	1	76	89	91
415	348	268	291	274	3	78	58	89
1165	1145	745	619	629	1	68	47	70
538	522	453	390	386		18	18	32
758	688	686	642	678	139	109	104	120
616	536	590	537	415	17	49	29	17
413	355	374	259	311	20	51	65	40
387	324	478	421	374		8	8	
738	727	634	780	691	6	129	113	85
522	504	252	266	206	4	32	36	27
48	53	44	32	36		12	12	3
566	606	735	714	746		25	38	20
1889	1876	1511	1462	1418		63	39	21
520	534	366	287	249		46	40	45
751	790	691	690	663				
29	31	12	17	25		3	2	17
253	216	235	249	236		10	16	4
387	381	274	278	251		23	32	6
112	83	80	71	69		6	5	1
111	64	61	51	59		20	7	10
166	178	200	216	252		22	13	62

特殊教育学校教职工数(总数)

Number of Educational Personnel in Special Education Schools (Total)

单位:人
unit: person

地 区 Region	教职工数 Educational Personnel					代课教师 Substitute Teachers	兼任教师 Part-time Teachers
	合计 Total	专任教师 Full-time Teachers	行政人员 Adm. Personnel	教辅人员 Supporting Staff	工勤人员 Workers		
总 计 Total	**55096**	**45653**	**3561**	**2325**	**3557**	**1171**	**201**
北 京 Beijing	1253	935	135	93	90		
天 津 Tianjin	779	598	89	49	43	6	
河 北 Hebei	3582	2956	266	141	219	91	
山 西 Shanxi	1613	1385	66	43	119	43	17
内蒙古 Inner Mongolia	1317	1121	85	48	63	20	3
辽 宁 Liaoning	2657	2020	437	83	117		
吉 林 Jilin	1717	1388	161	82	86	12	
黑龙江 Heilongjiang	2253	1850	191	79	133	15	5
上 海 Shanghai	1588	1207	169	93	119	10	5
江 苏 Jiangsu	3901	3170	188	215	328	43	
浙 江 Zhejiang	2331	2038	80	71	142		
安 徽 Anhui	1500	1297	68	41	94	124	15
福 建 Fujian	1946	1729	80	43	94	111	3
江 西 Jiangxi	1158	1042	42	14	60	74	6
山 东 Shandong	5684	4692	287	324	381	150	23
河 南 Henan	3799	3264	176	141	218	32	20
湖 北 Hubei	1921	1647	98	54	122	61	5
湖 南 Hunan	1733	1403	166	77	87	22	3
广 东 Guangdong	3405	2714	217	272	202	122	21
广 西 Guangxi	1600	1141	103	182	174	13	1
海 南 Hainan	247	184	15	19	29	14	
重 庆 Chongqing	971	852	62	16	41	14	31
四 川 Sichuan	2315	2055	73	32	155	66	13
贵 州 Guizhou	1267	1093	83	33	58	3	6
云 南 Yunnan	1361	1156	38	30	137		10
西 藏 Tibet	161	136	12	1	12		
陕 西 Shaanxi	1173	956	97	23	97	22	4
甘 肃 Gansu	784	692	24	4	64	2	
青 海 Qinghai	161	139	6	6	10	15	3
宁 夏 Ningxia	259	246	7	1	5	7	
新 疆 Xinjiang	660	547	40	15	58	79	7

特殊教育学校女教职工数
Number of Female Educational Personnel in Special Education Schools

单位:人
unit: person

地 区 Region	教职工数 Educational Personnel					代课教师 Substitute Teachers	兼任教师 Part-time Teachers
	合计 Total	专任教师 Full-time Teachers	行政人员 Adm. Personnel	教辅人员 Supporting Staff	工勤人员 Workers		
总 计 Total	**37685**	**33079**	**1676**	**1490**	**1440**	**872**	**90**
北 京 Beijing	873	723	68	58	24		
天 津 Tianjin	548	454	51	32	11	3	
河 北 Hebei	2678	2356	128	93	101	61	
山 西 Shanxi	1192	1070	35	33	54	33	9
内蒙古 Inner Mongolia	857	796	25	25	11	12	1
辽 宁 Liaoning	1949	1579	293	47	30		
吉 林 Jilin	1198	1057	79	41	21	9	
黑龙江 Heilongjiang	1439	1275	97	37	30	12	5
上 海 Shanghai	1219	992	116	67	44	6	2
江 苏 Jiangsu	2535	2226	69	127	113	36	
浙 江 Zhejiang	1694	1530	27	50	87		
安 徽 Anhui	931	843	27	20	41	95	3
福 建 Fujian	1456	1334	33	33	56	70	2
江 西 Jiangxi	817	753	21	9	34	58	3
山 东 Shandong	3374	2999	101	174	100	109	5
河 南 Henan	2645	2424	57	78	86	27	8
湖 北 Hubei	1188	1067	38	31	52	49	3
湖 南 Hunan	1094	954	63	46	31	21	1
广 东 Guangdong	2482	2036	117	209	120	99	17
广 西 Guangxi	1239	915	56	158	110	11	1
海 南 Hainan	176	138	8	14	16		
重 庆 Chongqing	654	608	26	6	14	11	2
四 川 Sichuan	1536	1423	28	24	61	49	8
贵 州 Guizhou	885	805	35	20	25	1	4
云 南 Yunnan	921	802	15	25	79		5
西 藏 Tibet	86	80	3	1	2		
陕 西 Shaanxi	762	686	33	14	29	17	1
甘 肃 Gansu	507	467	4	4	32	1	
青 海 Qinghai	100	91	1	4	4	11	3
宁 夏 Ningxia	193	191	1	1		7	
新 疆 Xinjiang	457	405	21	9	22	64	7

特殊教育学校专任教师
Number of Full-time Teachers in Special Education Schools

地 区 Region	合计 Total	其中:女 of Which: Female	按学历分 By Educational Attainment			
			研究生毕业 Graduate	本科毕业 Under-graduate	专科毕业 Associate Bachelor	高中阶段毕业 High School Graduate
总 计 Total	**45653**	**33079**	**703**	**25068**	**17569**	**2257**
北 京 Beijing	935	723	60	755	103	17
天 津 Tianjin	598	454	21	395	156	23
河 北 Hebei	2956	2356	13	1539	1286	118
山 西 Shanxi	1385	1070	5	783	499	96
内蒙古 Inner Mongolia	1121	796	13	618	437	50
辽 宁 Liaoning	2020	1579	19	1233	699	63
吉 林 Jilin	1388	1057	10	881	391	106
黑龙江 Heilongjiang	1850	1275	2	842	872	129
上 海 Shanghai	1207	992	74	942	180	11
江 苏 Jiangsu	3170	2226	44	2026	953	145
浙 江 Zhejiang	2038	1530	62	1175	686	106
安 徽 Anhui	1297	843	13	704	508	70
福 建 Fujian	1729	1334	13	850	754	112
江 西 Jiangxi	1042	753	5	506	484	44
山 东 Shandong	4692	2999	94	3010	1389	198
河 南 Henan	3264	2424	17	1428	1631	188
湖 北 Hubei	1647	1067	15	798	716	115
湖 南 Hunan	1403	954	12	599	694	97
广 东 Guangdong	2714	2036	136	1552	858	167
广 西 Guangxi	1141	915	14	483	584	60
海 南 Hainan	184	138		77	98	9
重 庆 Chongqing	852	608	4	451	368	28
四 川 Sichuan	2055	1423	19	800	1131	102
贵 州 Guizhou	1093	805	4	478	563	43
云 南 Yunnan	1156	802	11	712	397	33
西 藏 Tibet	136	80	2	72	58	4
陕 西 Shaanxi	956	686	11	433	444	67
甘 肃 Gansu	692	467	2	424	233	33
青 海 Qinghai	139	91	3	70	57	9
宁 夏 Ningxia	246	191	3	130	103	10
新 疆 Xinjiang	547	405	2	302	237	4

学历、职称情况
by Educational Attainment and Professional Rank

单位：人
unit: person

	按职称分 By Professional Rank					
高中阶段以下毕业 Below High School Graduate	中学高级 Senior Secondary	小学高级 Senior Primary	小学一级 1st Grade Primary	小学二级 2nd Grade Primary	小学三级 3rd Grade Primary	未定职级 No-ranking
56	**4013**	**22891**	**13415**	**1447**	**118**	**3769**
	57	462	325	1		90
3	56	398	95	2		47
	290	1649	798	36	3	180
2	36	493	601	89	1	165
3	259	464	243	30		125
6	187	1334	370	58	6	65
	144	771	415	23		35
5	309	1040	458	8		35
	43	647	452	18	2	45
2	293	1829	747	87	11	203
9	164	886	627	73	3	285
2	109	616	414	79	12	67
	33	936	508	111	16	125
3	111	408	316	58	5	144
1	592	2235	1427	162	9	267
	398	1563	998	167		138
3	176	1027	355	33	2	54
1	114	769	346	40	21	113
1	103	1348	646	54	10	553
	15	659	279	25	2	161
	10	57	49	11		57
1	40	355	360	23	2	72
3	138	910	825	40	1	141
5	34	492	387	57	5	118
3	116	503	382	74	1	80
	3	60	57	5		11
1	48	347	334	26	3	198
	43	273	299	21		56
	31	79	26			3
	7	117	89	12	2	19
2	54	164	187	24	1	117

特殊教育学校

Condition of School Buildings

地 区 Region	校舍建筑面积 Floor Space	教学及辅助用房 Teaching & Assistant Buildings				
		合计 Total	其中 of Which			
			普通教室 General Classroom	专用教室 Special Classroom	实验室 Laboratory	微机室 PC-room
总 计 Total	**7418850**	**3381342**	**1979042**	**999427**	**137448**	**128719**
北 京 Beijing	143562	57679	28443	22221	1322	3452
天 津 Tianjin	96759	44386	23966	15298	711	1459
河 北 Hebei	424977	208062	104205	73434	11174	9296
山 西 Shanxi	185345	66072	40763	17425	1480	3088
内蒙古 Inner Mongolia	177001	84910	49079	26957	3035	3152
辽 宁 Liaoning	217038	97041	43671	40878	3114	4682
吉 林 Jilin	180739	83328	46900	26155	3782	3139
黑龙江 Heilongjiang	213151	96587	48523	36463	3932	4248
上 海 Shanghai	162840	75164	27415	38591	2795	2566
江 苏 Jiangsu	530423	247915	130695	82977	14233	9241
浙 江 Zhejiang	351773	135592	80302	39584	5563	5133
安 徽 Anhui	298541	145548	92553	39345	3622	4569
福 建 Fujian	320510	137224	73387	48414	5126	4365
江 西 Jiangxi	263933	134136	76265	42911	5280	4952
山 东 Shandong	631075	259931	131807	87458	16788	11622
河 南 Henan	397435	184052	114945	44892	7384	8314
湖 北 Hubei	307878	143556	100286	29795	3602	4426
湖 南 Hunan	289612	128875	87152	27516	4067	5192
广 东 Guangdong	397312	185635	120672	45601	5051	7112
广 西 Guangxi	208866	99338	61675	29630	2519	2680
海 南 Hainan	42461	14575	7557	5521	548	552
重 庆 Chongqing	160482	74069	51280	12653	4539	2957
四 川 Sichuan	387089	181224	119104	44166	5524	6243
贵 州 Guizhou	210505	96951	62471	24707	3455	3231
云 南 Yunnan	270314	139892	93170	32233	5324	4697
西 藏 Tibet	37271	12057	10073	1335	167	223
陕 西 Shaanxi	155016	78744	47470	21211	3515	3081
甘 肃 Gansu	144058	76299	50975	16037	4884	2200
青 海 Qinghai	30636	13515	8816	979	2273	441
宁 夏 Ningxia	39779	22518	14605	6181	577	771
新 疆 Xinjiang	142469	56467	30817	18859	2062	1635

办学条件(一)
in Special Education Schools (1)

单位：平方米
unit：m^2

	行政办公用房 Administrative				校舍面积中 of the Floor Space	
图书室 Library	合计 Total	其中:教师办公室 of Which: for Teachers	生活用房 Residential and Welfare	其他用房 Rooms for Other Purposes	危房面积 Floor Space of Dilapidated Buildings	当年新增 New Added in Current Year
136706	**784388**	**457414**	**2168672**	**1084448**	**96641**	**709026**
2241	14649	7031	28222	43012		3505
2952	9795	5841	18673	23905		
9953	50015	29088	110079	56821	2452	31189
3316	23844	14842	64754	30675	5396	22116
2687	18892	14000	58068	15131		11398
4696	26002	16051	51059	42936	7230	11511
3352	23386	12177	49975	24050	2400	18910
3421	29580	18988	54954	32030	5474	41882
3797	21044	10239	29880	36752		3920
10769	54522	29650	132601	95385		4179
5010	36517	21125	107306	72358		14750
5459	27196	17047	95867	29930	550	32020
5932	35918	17893	96406	50962	540	25608
4728	24197	13145	78932	26668	6775	54814
12256	87432	42749	187736	95976	6925	90513
8517	50082	33846	116568	46733	8105	25866
5447	30870	16830	93484	39968	12993	25178
4948	25711	15370	88997	46029	4426	29186
7199	35089	20337	107039	69549	660	26118
2834	13628	9928	69114	26786	300	19857
397	2791	2022	17962	7133		
2640	15643	9884	54020	16750	1046	1670
6187	32481	18656	136672	36712	1039	58760
3087	16093	9452	75508	21953		38797
4468	19360	10969	87391	23671	22023	34181
259	5821	5462	16757	2636		1724
3467	20823	12395	41608	13841		8476
2203	13925	9421	43675	10159	8123	13213
1006	4700	3202	7046	5375	32	1341
384	3902	3024	10540	2819		10980
3094	10480	6750	37779	37743	152	47364

特殊教育学校办学条件(二)

Condition of School Buildings in Special Education Schools (2)

地 区 Region	占地面积(平方米) Areas of School Sites (m^2)			图书(册) Books & Magazines in Libraries (volume)	数字资源 (GB) Digital Resources
	合计 Total	其中 of Which			
		绿化用地面积 Green Areas	运动场地面积 Sports Areas		
总 计 Total	**16677524**	**3451599**	**3850577**	**7368327**	**372981.00**
北 京 Beijing	229177	37492	53039	262509	7212.00
天 津 Tianjin	172566	15427	52248	92427	42494.10
河 北 Hebei	1072012	162918	261215	450481	8503.20
山 西 Shanxi	377562	42095	57674	255152	2326.00
内蒙古 Inner Mongolia	438904	72267	130232	93610	3646.00
辽 宁 Liaoning	533326	65965	152235	403878	25669.90
吉 林 Jilin	472415	88523	149084	151480	2598.00
黑龙江 Heilongjiang	567795	85265	171329	166815	5928.50
上 海 Shanghai	249320	73643	59995	265960	42229.86
江 苏 Jiangsu	1116706	319199	275925	826579	26879.37
浙 江 Zhejiang	701332	174617	172700	284020	5249.15
安 徽 Anhui	709657	186136	140069	221671	4460.00
福 建 Fujian	637363	170369	154751	255503	4877.00
江 西 Jiangxi	557078	127253	141654	135074	8885.00
山 东 Shandong	1752973	388555	415606	714137	13651.84
河 南 Henan	894185	138619	187512	380237	14400.58
湖 北 Hubei	620703	135420	146635	211757	6587.00
湖 南 Hunan	877364	270653	135783	354557	2173.00
广 东 Guangdong	813399	192745	192958	406039	105196.00
广 西 Guangxi	413447	73697	65567	202463	5106.00
海 南 Hainan	93513	14743	22707	20950	100.00
重 庆 Chongqing	294474	60086	55394	70743	8999.10
四 川 Sichuan	659340	119188	152414	392646	4017.80
贵 州 Guizhou	524383	112476	117546	131399	2691.60
云 南 Yunnan	640070	130306	105197	198309	1698.00
西 藏 Tibet	108680	14920	24439	5600	
陕 西 Shaanxi	298725	37763	75399	186594	2779.00
甘 肃 Gansu	274906	46428	71488	118155	11472.00
青 海 Qinghai	80955	11720	23979	16578	1238.00
宁 夏 Ningxia	142003	10680	23550	28926	692.00
新 疆 Xinjiang	353191	72431	62253	64078	1221.00

幼儿园基本情况(总计)
Basic Statistics of Kindergartens (Total)

地 区 Region	园数(所) Kindergartens 合计 Total	其中:少数民族幼儿园 of Which: Minorities	班数(个) Classes	入园(班)人数(人) Entrants	在园(班)人数(人) Enrolment	离园(班)人数(人) Leavers
总 计 Total	**198553**	**4339**	**1343042**	**19700271**	**38946903**	**14917314**
北 京 Beijing	1384	10	12580	128106	348681	88322
天 津 Tianjin	1702	9	8617	93921	233227	80647
河 北 Hebei	10813	73	73930	1063184	2129439	794693
山 西 Shanxi	5882	1	38608	442876	951431	342270
内蒙古 Inner Mongolia	2740	203	19985	225963	515543	199034
辽 宁 Liaoning	9261	49	38363	342110	856147	290291
吉 林 Jilin	3808	89	20328	251058	441934	185611
黑龙江 Heilongjiang	5571	48	23611	304677	540777	260821
上 海 Shanghai	1446	2	16468	166124	501030	157650
江 苏 Jiangsu	4722	1	66132	842565	2318102	789435
浙 江 Zhejiang	9209	1	64058	564073	1868754	606969
安 徽 Anhui	6075	8	56316	950067	1679511	646059
福 建 Fujian	7419	18	47083	594754	1432901	499109
江 西 Jiangxi	11485	21	59863	944893	1563241	661272
山 东 Shandong	18528	42	94260	1161003	2624305	964663
河 南 Henan	14485	47	112330	2026017	3469546	1397486
湖 北 Hubei	6011	6	44653	825253	1473371	572085
湖 南 Hunan	12236	194	68490	974510	1912269	799187
广 东 Guangdong	13793	5	139809	1709973	3545757	1082455
广 西 Guangxi	8886	28	63868	1171140	1817105	786590
海 南 Hainan	1596	24	10649	141149	298772	105499
重 庆 Chongqing	4547		28607	445590	893338	390541
四 川 Sichuan	11759	479	68463	1301954	2314907	991574
贵 州 Guizhou	4016	40	30320	694176	1077687	491678
云 南 Yunnan	5326	24	36395	728977	1190192	583260
西 藏 Tibet	613	219	2790	46229	73405	31386
陕 西 Shaanxi	6356	4	43571	705001	1271034	429786
甘 肃 Gansu	3141	88	20309	307644	549800	225828
青 海 Qinghai	1245	467	5827	92257	166659	69609
宁 夏 Ningxia	634	22	5467	81684	169080	81597
新 疆 Xinjiang	3864	2117	21292	373343	718958	311907

幼儿园基本情况(城区)
Basic Statistics of Kindergartens (Urban Area)

地 区 Region	园数(所) Kindergartens		班数(个) Classes	入园(班)人数(人) Entrants	在园(班)人数(人) Enrolment	离园(班)人数(人) Leavers
	合计 Total	其中:少数民族幼儿园 of Which: Minorities				
总 计 Total	**61239**	**339**	**471208**	**5284877**	**13175629**	**4308058**
北 京 Beijing	970	8	10260	101660	287577	70713
天 津 Tianjin	770	7	4710	51369	129073	38183
河 北 Hebei	1857	44	14226	188130	427216	147004
山 西 Shanxi	1375		10426	125590	293811	102294
内蒙古 Inner Mongolia	1038	24	7579	70559	196303	69570
辽 宁 Liaoning	4741	27	22590	162296	477400	141618
吉 林 Jilin	1911	72	10116	100862	210298	78600
黑龙江 Heilongjiang	2161	7	10363	100502	221395	102289
上 海 Shanghai	1156	2	13270	129667	398801	123701
江 苏 Jiangsu	2340	1	27672	344636	935600	307527
浙 江 Zhejiang	3405		29364	258930	848028	264219
安 徽 Anhui	1538	3	13866	176361	408474	136162
福 建 Fujian	2502	1	17648	208865	542157	176934
江 西 Jiangxi	1956	2	13051	154223	323628	109871
山 东 Shandong	5229	18	33726	362805	961686	331905
河 南 Henan	3431	19	28031	348655	816243	253778
湖 北 Hubei	2175	1	16665	252993	537699	188652
湖 南 Hunan	3028	5	17438	206250	480174	168678
广 东 Guangdong	7646		83684	749554	1968960	560303
广 西 Guangxi	1709	2	12955	157799	361080	118452
海 南 Hainan	640		4467	54735	122716	40189
重 庆 Chongqing	1639		10014	148552	304381	111373
四 川 Sichuan	2544		18163	254020	586907	199751
贵 州 Guizhou	1013	1	6431	108023	212538	77893
云 南 Yunnan	1003	7	7949	116302	270182	98232
西 藏 Tibet	36	1	265	5342	12309	4035
陕 西 Shaanxi	1548	3	12544	168354	391577	122764
甘 肃 Gansu	686	11	5080	62777	159315	57235
青 海 Qinghai	186	4	1196	16907	42538	15279
宁 夏 Ningxia	289	8	2204	26625	71907	26184
新 疆 Xinjiang	717	61	5255	71534	175656	64670

幼儿园基本情况(城乡结合区)

Basic Statistics of Kindergartens (Urban-rural Transitional Area)

地 区 Region	园数(所) Kindergartens 合计 Total	 其中:少数民族幼儿园 of Which: Minorities	班数(个) Classes	入园(班)人数(人) Entrants	在园(班)人数(人) Enrolment	离园(班)人数(人) Leavers
总 计 Total	**12067**	**63**	**80927**	**955612**	**2289332**	**756518**
北 京 Beijing	100		820	8980	20158	5283
天 津 Tianjin	170	1	569	5107	11901	3567
河 北 Hebei	510	2	3307	48352	96108	33954
山 西 Shanxi	275		1702	20024	46703	16136
内蒙古 Inner Mongolia	68		408	3709	9224	2837
辽 宁 Liaoning	571	1	2053	17587	42384	12955
吉 林 Jilin	124	2	596	5944	11668	4116
黑龙江 Heilongjiang	141		754	6520	12563	6530
上 海 Shanghai	95		1084	12356	35795	11521
江 苏 Jiangsu	265		2647	34849	90467	29444
浙 江 Zhejiang	1041		7328	58515	210507	66721
安 徽 Anhui	256		1901	25393	54229	18931
福 建 Fujian	550		3497	39930	102405	35510
江 西 Jiangxi	411	1	2389	29723	57974	18920
山 东 Shandong	1813	5	9296	93817	245742	84842
河 南 Henan	684		4890	67555	140202	45167
湖 北 Hubei	340		2205	35032	69029	23583
湖 南 Hunan	522	2	2855	36561	81055	27730
广 东 Guangdong	2361		21044	241611	607260	182075
广 西 Guangxi	305	1	2311	24812	55367	18347
海 南 Hainan	47		331	4195	8581	3114
重 庆 Chongqing	188		912	13166	27971	10563
四 川 Sichuan	407		2375	31570	71667	24112
贵 州 Guizhou	140		807	16488	27852	12405
云 南 Yunnan	169	1	1235	23325	42764	18449
西 藏 Tibet	1		7	212	212	82
陕 西 Shaanxi	297		2252	30804	64763	21152
甘 肃 Gansu	45		369	4696	12135	4227
青 海 Qinghai	32		144	1790	4573	2108
宁 夏 Ningxia	45	2	321	3881	10843	4593
新 疆 Xinjiang	94	45	518	9108	17230	7544

幼儿园基本情况(镇区)

Basic Statistics of Kindergartens (Counties & Towns Area)

地　区 Region	园数(所) Kindergartens		班数(个) Classes	入园(班)人数(人) Entrants	在园(班)人数(人) Enrolment	离园(班)人数(人) Leavers
	合计 Total	其中:少数民族幼儿园 of Which: Minorities				
总　计 Total	**67436**	**836**	**463356**	**7791227**	**14978832**	**5728075**
北　京 Beijing	208	2	1487	16454	40986	12353
天　津 Tianjin	434		2036	21953	54257	21685
河　北 Hebei	3435	15	24093	374490	741137	277490
山　西 Shanxi	1835	1	12950	179634	385031	138691
内蒙古 Inner Mongolia	1195	121	8380	114723	240687	96909
辽　宁 Liaoning	2288	15	9207	105024	231196	89146
吉　林 Jilin	1276	16	6166	95296	152207	63232
黑龙江 Heilongjiang	1956	8	8620	138999	216969	104981
上　海 Shanghai	231		2674	30539	85499	28498
江　苏 Jiangsu	1789		30966	405926	1121585	386862
浙　江 Zhejiang	3170	1	23475	211590	717424	239091
安　徽 Anhui	2506	2	20546	376011	683164	252057
福　建 Fujian	2674	2	16191	218992	533984	180479
江　西 Jiangxi	4569	4	25974	458731	755736	320218
山　东 Shandong	4798	11	28485	417831	883754	326143
河　南 Henan	4780	19	36243	699503	1181688	464244
湖　北 Hubei	2115	3	15602	331441	562518	224050
湖　南 Hunan	4710	125	27137	437534	855284	354569
广　东 Guangdong	3947		33224	563998	1002825	310536
广　西 Guangxi	3692	5	24063	492880	768254	307898
海　南 Hainan	774	16	4700	65710	139564	49329
重　庆 Chongqing	1886		12615	211299	432008	195001
四　川 Sichuan	4446	58	29771	634997	1126770	466343
贵　州 Guizhou	1713	26	12028	280594	463772	192050
云　南 Yunnan	1708	1	11394	230228	412985	175386
西　藏 Tibet	123	52	702	13859	23531	9007
陕　西 Shaanxi	3004	1	19959	376647	634014	219868
甘　肃 Gansu	892	14	5855	114965	207977	78491
青　海 Qinghai	264	81	1591	34394	56936	23265
宁　夏 Ningxia	188	4	1509	27427	57171	28596
新　疆 Xinjiang	830	233	5713	109558	209919	91607

幼儿园基本情况(镇乡结合区)

Basic Statistics of Kindergartens (County-town Transitional Area)

地 区 Region	园数(所) Kindergartens 合计 Total	其中:少数民族幼儿园 of Which: Minorities	班数(个) Classes	入园(班)人数(人) Entrants	在园(班)人数(人) Enrolment	离园(班)人数(人) Leavers
总 计 Total	**21248**	**194**	**136362**	**2209254**	**4163989**	**1609659**
北 京 Beijing	51		336	3748	8832	2615
天 津 Tianjin	193		865	9769	24902	10168
河 北 Hebei	1916	5	12989	192403	386501	143502
山 西 Shanxi	672		4223	51664	115224	40835
内蒙古 Inner Mongolia	129	14	763	10018	20490	7723
辽 宁 Liaoning	480		1488	14038	33287	12706
吉 林 Jilin	140	6	694	10942	17252	7517
黑龙江 Heilongjiang	238	2	848	13857	21053	12299
上 海 Shanghai	63		633	7362	20346	6698
江 苏 Jiangsu	510		7198	87048	256774	90103
浙 江 Zhejiang	1365	1	8618	76322	260764	87179
安 徽 Anhui	474	1	4363	82375	138840	53567
福 建 Fujian	826	2	4375	57467	137199	47361
江 西 Jiangxi	1195		6032	105076	163381	74815
山 东 Shandong	2575	8	13376	186691	397379	147417
河 南 Henan	1968	7	14404	271089	440183	177679
湖 北 Hubei	566		3918	81169	134731	54246
湖 南 Hunan	1688	26	9473	158894	277876	117779
广 东 Guangdong	1522		12522	214960	374628	114918
广 西 Guangxi	743		5576	119357	162068	79164
海 南 Hainan	124		701	10276	21236	7747
重 庆 Chongqing	508		2837	42423	88657	38688
四 川 Sichuan	1067	11	5810	104682	190337	79397
贵 州 Guizhou	356	4	2499	66470	98009	45139
云 南 Yunnan	589		3733	73075	124655	56913
西 藏 Tibet	12	5	65	1417	2914	1080
陕 西 Shaanxi	833		5492	104103	158840	54333
甘 肃 Gansu	205	5	1088	23770	36627	13800
青 海 Qinghai	56	15	306	5739	9902	4641
宁 夏 Ningxia	38	1	253	5073	9143	5769
新 疆 Xinjiang	146	81	884	17977	31959	13861

幼儿园基本情况(乡村)
Basic Statistics of Kindergartens (Rural Area)

地 区 Region	园数(所) Kindergartens		班数(个) Classes	入园(班)人数(人) Entrants	在园(班)人数(人) Enrolment	离园(班)人数(人) Leavers
	合计 Total	其中:少数民族幼儿园 of Which:Minorities				
总 计 Total	**69878**	**3164**	**408478**	**6624167**	**10792442**	**4881181**
北 京 Beijing	206		833	9992	20118	5256
天 津 Tianjin	498	2	1871	20599	49897	20779
河 北 Hebei	5521	14	35611	500564	961086	370199
山 西 Shanxi	2672		15232	137652	272589	101285
内蒙古 Inner Mongolia	507	58	4026	40681	78553	32555
辽 宁 Liaoning	2232	7	6566	74790	147551	59527
吉 林 Jilin	621	1	4046	54900	79429	43779
黑龙江 Heilongjiang	1454	33	4628	65176	102413	53551
上 海 Shanghai	59		524	5918	16730	5451
江 苏 Jiangsu	593		7494	92003	260917	95046
浙 江 Zhejiang	2634		11219	93553	303302	103659
安 徽 Anhui	2031	3	21904	397695	587873	257840
福 建 Fujian	2243	15	13244	166897	356760	141696
江 西 Jiangxi	4960	15	20838	331939	483877	231183
山 东 Shandong	8501	13	32049	380367	778865	306615
河 南 Henan	6274	9	48056	977859	1471615	679464
湖 北 Hubei	1721	2	12386	240819	373154	159383
湖 南 Hunan	4498	64	23915	330726	576811	275940
广 东 Guangdong	2200	5	22901	396421	573972	211616
广 西 Guangxi	3485	21	26850	520461	687771	360240
海 南 Hainan	182	8	1482	20704	36492	15981
重 庆 Chongqing	1022		5978	85739	156949	84167
四 川 Sichuan	4769	421	20529	412937	601230	325480
贵 州 Guizhou	1290	13	11861	305559	401377	221735
云 南 Yunnan	2615	16	17052	382447	507025	309642
西 藏 Tibet	454	166	1823	27028	37565	18344
陕 西 Shaanxi	1804		11068	160000	245443	87154
甘 肃 Gansu	1563	63	9374	129902	182508	90102
青 海 Qinghai	795	382	3040	40956	67185	31065
宁 夏 Ningxia	157	10	1754	27632	40002	26817
新 疆 Xinjiang	2317	1823	10324	192251	333383	155630

幼儿教育中女儿童数
Number of Female Children in Kindergartens

地　区 Region	入园(班)人数(人) Entrants	在园(班)人数(人) Enrolment	离园(班)人数(人) Leavers
总　计 Total	**9139790**	**17982284**	**7092734**
北　京 Beijing	60714	165226	42821
天　津 Tianjin	43950	108744	39261
河　北 Hebei	498435	997059	386139
山　西 Shanxi	212903	457414	168028
内蒙古 Inner Mongolia	107145	242829	94166
辽　宁 Liaoning	159824	396431	137731
吉　林 Jilin	115409	203600	88824
黑龙江 Heilongjiang	144261	255655	125913
上　海 Shanghai	78174	234949	73646
江　苏 Jiangsu	391051	1072522	369382
浙　江 Zhejiang	259930	856031	287515
安　徽 Anhui	439271	773636	311851
福　建 Fujian	271152	651143	234436
江　西 Jiangxi	430159	704505	309287
山　东 Shandong	529359	1204555	464541
河　南 Henan	950898	1614262	664002
湖　北 Hubei	377095	674455	271851
湖　南 Hunan	456130	885650	385687
广　东 Guangdong	771658	1584165	464776
广　西 Guangxi	534012	820624	375341
海　南 Hainan	62799	129320	47884
重　庆 Chongqing	208663	419031	194224
四　川 Sichuan	619065	1100201	474569
贵　州 Guizhou	317026	488180	237629
云　南 Yunnan	342501	558219	282714
西　藏 Tibet	22903	35890	15727
陕　西 Shaanxi	330490	592645	207615
甘　肃 Gansu	142836	253373	110036
青　海 Qinghai	43675	78807	34991
宁　夏 Ningxia	38439	78275	40325
新　疆 Xinjiang	179863	344888	151822

幼儿园教职工数(总计)

Number of Educational Personnel in Kindergarten (Total)

单位:人

unit: person

地 区 Region	教职工数 Educational Personnel						代课教师 Substitute Teachers	兼任教师 Part-time Teachers
	合计 Total	园长 Kindergarten Heads	专任教师 Full-time Teachers	保健医 Health Physician	保育员 Caretaker	其他 Other		
总 计 Total	**2826753**	**221606**	**1663487**	**72633**	**484534**	**384493**	**163689**	**24025**
北 京 Beijing	53049	2079	28806	1958	8756	11450		459
天 津 Tianjin	20536	1566	12289	666	2945	3070	2201	199
河 北 Hebei	117427	10941	76091	2532	15821	12042	13269	702
山 西 Shanxi	63684	5707	41317	1519	7665	7476	12313	1580
内蒙古 Inner Mongolia	46246	3486	28666	1163	6259	6672	2758	352
辽 宁 Liaoning	77888	8055	48866	1376	8754	10837	1179	1870
吉 林 Jilin	43080	4366	24904	1589	6549	5672	806	456
黑龙江 Heilongjiang	51578	5907	28747	2390	7759	6775	1492	718
上 海 Shanghai	51022	1862	32921	1726	7119	7394	1495	102
江 苏 Jiangsu	175634	7426	106840	4662	36972	19734	20663	1096
浙 江 Zhejiang	190186	9497	110251	5401	34521	30516		633
安 徽 Anhui	83663	7145	51120	2414	14219	8765	6183	710
福 建 Fujian	112862	8276	65227	2671	21075	15613	7737	351
江 西 Jiangxi	102917	12357	61588	2442	15701	10829	2905	854
山 东 Shandong	202288	19908	132518	3624	21978	24260	20506	2086
河 南 Henan	215391	17504	129422	6569	36185	25711	19358	1606
湖 北 Hubei	110376	8458	57736	3079	24324	16779	9040	631
湖 南 Hunan	143726	12743	71160	4208	34716	20899	5671	684
广 东 Guangdong	336666	19772	188182	8434	66026	54252	2007	1326
广 西 Guangxi	94190	9756	52108	1990	17309	13027	2455	1711
海 南 Hainan	25380	2175	13081	935	5285	3904	146	182
重 庆 Chongqing	59744	5168	30199	1491	14360	8526	2655	783
四 川 Sichuan	132832	12913	77336	2820	22574	17189	6824	583
贵 州 Guizhou	54996	4286	34188	992	9115	6415	705	551
云 南 Yunnan	66948	5694	40123	1651	9935	9545	958	1696
西 藏 Tibet	2822	214	2091	19	258	240	224	14
陕 西 Shaanxi	100518	7363	57583	2837	17683	15052	9117	376
甘 肃 Gansu	30370	2741	20621	521	3161	3326	3314	1244
青 海 Qinghai	8047	819	4668	100	981	1479	2365	157
宁 夏 Ningxia	11233	752	6624	271	1544	2042	1851	76
新 疆 Xinjiang	41454	2670	28214	583	4985	5002	3492	237

幼儿园教职工数(城区)

Number of Educational Personnel in Kindergarten (Urban Area)

单位:人

unit: person

地 区 Region	教职工数 Educational Personnel						代课教师 Substitute Teachers	兼任教师 Part-time Teachers
	合计 Total	园长 Kindergarten Heads	专任教师 Full-time Teachers	保健医 Health Physician	保育员 Caretaker	其他 Other		
总 计 Total	**1423614**	**86600**	**802174**	**41299**	**266927**	**226614**	**41473**	**8639**
北 京 Beijing	45642	1647	24443	1725	7804	10023		357
天 津 Tianjin	15488	1079	9138	521	2271	2479	355	193
河 北 Hebei	42313	2760	25322	1139	6870	6222	2161	127
山 西 Shanxi	31107	1954	18917	889	4499	4848	3378	754
内蒙古 Inner Mongolia	22725	1532	13441	701	3252	3799	1259	260
辽 宁 Liaoning	57050	5100	33862	1153	7828	9107	304	767
吉 林 Jilin	26595	2399	14929	962	4419	3886	316	298
黑龙江 Heilongjiang	27328	2541	14632	1391	4349	4415	796	359
上 海 Shanghai	41611	1478	26764	1467	5768	6134	1172	88
江 苏 Jiangsu	96128	4107	54786	2811	21339	13085	4258	252
浙 江 Zhejiang	95312	3826	54757	2912	18897	14920		209
安 徽 Anhui	34622	2325	20028	1096	6823	4350	2183	212
福 建 Fujian	55152	3455	30888	1568	11505	7736	2730	159
江 西 Jiangxi	32100	2780	18190	933	6162	4035	470	285
山 东 Shandong	103274	7302	64020	2377	13355	16220	5810	927
河 南 Henan	86290	5120	50424	2538	16040	12168	4537	622
湖 北 Hubei	55799	3815	28535	1625	12575	9249	2647	203
湖 南 Hunan	54368	3743	26248	1682	13322	9373	712	329
广 东 Guangdong	236553	12210	128322	6373	48755	40893	854	354
广 西 Guangxi	32772	2423	18041	864	6773	4671	396	237
海 南 Hainan	12672	969	6619	532	2624	1928	80	100
重 庆 Chongqing	31206	2300	15667	994	7410	4835	895	337
四 川 Sichuan	57751	3898	31024	1549	11722	9558	1307	71
贵 州 Guizhou	20096	1360	10585	423	4484	3244	99	95
云 南 Yunnan	26200	1454	15056	788	4451	4451	168	96
西 藏 Tibet	780	64	437	12	130	137	34	
陕 西 Shaanxi	42655	2327	23399	1309	7706	7914	1677	117
甘 肃 Gansu	13797	966	8574	329	1870	2058	1120	696
青 海 Qinghai	3477	270	2032	42	373	760	222	13
宁 夏 Ningxia	6802	403	4041	176	850	1332	941	26
新 疆 Xinjiang	15949	993	9053	418	2701	2784	592	96

幼儿园教职工数(城乡结合区)
Number of Educational Personnel in Kindergarten (Urban-rural Transitional Area)

单位:人
unit: person

地　区 Region	教职工数 Educational Personnel						代课教师 Substitute Teachers	兼任教师 Part-time Teachers
	合计 Total	园长 Kindergarten Heads	专任教师 Full-time Teachers	保健医 Health Physician	保育员 Caretaker	其他 Other		
总　计 Total	**218244**	**15155**	**122268**	**6018**	**40650**	**34153**	**6992**	**1234**
北　京 Beijing	2734	168	1526	105	417	518		15
天　津 Tianjin	1288	170	638	64	251	165	39	10
河　北 Hebei	6678	569	4131	161	1037	780	550	30
山　西 Shanxi	3409	292	2174	92	400	451	918	63
内蒙古 Inner Mongolia	863	87	489	29	120	138	63	7
辽　宁 Liaoning	3986	506	2398	59	457	566	35	33
吉　林 Jilin	1428	151	777	51	217	232	12	7
黑龙江 Heilongjiang	1540	152	800	58	229	301	6	33
上　海 Shanghai	3414	113	2022	115	649	515	86	5
江　苏 Jiangsu	8184	382	4710	232	1814	1046	470	1
浙　江 Zhejiang	21451	1140	12007	708	3949	3647		74
安　徽 Anhui	3457	326	1947	124	647	413	383	23
福　建 Fujian	9176	663	5032	231	1900	1350	385	19
江　西 Jiangxi	4931	522	2865	131	796	617	22	40
山　东 Shandong	22980	2175	14799	467	2508	3031	1863	302
河　南 Henan	12363	895	6952	403	2428	1685	471	79
湖　北 Hubei	6225	512	3052	172	1490	999	258	27
湖　南 Hunan	7948	576	3812	260	1985	1315	255	42
广　东 Guangdong	67487	3534	36880	1731	13762	11580	126	72
广　西 Guangxi	4282	404	2421	122	810	525	31	55
海　南 Hainan	802	68	389	42	178	125	10	3
重　庆 Chongqing	2364	221	1110	69	573	391	144	44
四　川 Sichuan	7078	564	3519	230	1569	1196	177	5
贵　州 Guizhou	2102	171	1043	51	486	351	8	13
云　南 Yunnan	3119	206	1732	89	544	548	50	20
西　藏 Tibet	2		2					
陕　西 Shaanxi	6039	398	3174	163	1134	1170	379	19
甘　肃 Gansu	512	37	374	11	33	57	23	163
青　海 Qinghai	367	34	206	3	41	83		1
宁　夏 Ningxia	792	49	441	25	113	164	206	3
新　疆 Xinjiang	1243	70	846	20	113	194	22	26

幼儿园教职工数(镇区)
Number of Educational Personnel in Kindergarten (Counties & Towns Area)

单位:人
unit: person

地区 Region	教职工数 Educational Personnel						代课教师 Substitute Teachers	兼任教师 Part-time Teachers
	合计 Total	园长 Kindergarten Heads	专任教师 Full-time Teachers	保健医 Health Physician	保育员 Caretaker	其他 Other		
总计 Total	**958790**	**76070**	**592986**	**21414**	**157142**	**111178**	**81513**	**9501**
北京 Beijing	5328	262	3083	167	716	1100		69
天津 Tianjin	3123	299	1816	97	462	449	1118	5
河北 Hebei	45585	3871	30052	986	6454	4222	4607	244
山西 Shanxi	22749	1859	15916	443	2452	2079	5715	666
内蒙古 Inner Mongolia	19652	1458	12853	397	2515	2429	1243	50
辽宁 Liaoning	13848	1851	9961	152	646	1238	479	636
吉林 Jilin	12188	1371	7405	456	1676	1280	307	133
黑龙江 Heilongjiang	17652	2046	10172	769	2703	1962	449	260
上海 Shanghai	7890	319	5253	209	1079	1030	280	14
江苏 Jiangsu	67833	2703	44483	1545	13506	5596	14691	813
浙江 Zhejiang	67699	3456	39987	1735	11510	11011		328
安徽 Anhui	33979	2920	22224	861	5038	2936	2668	279
福建 Fujian	40658	2996	24435	796	7030	5401	3327	128
江西 Jiangxi	48827	5288	30596	1086	7234	4623	1572	332
山东 Shandong	55476	5205	39078	770	5402	5021	8254	845
河南 Henan	70619	5753	44238	2023	11150	7455	9408	519
湖北 Hubei	35931	2770	19678	887	7667	4929	3724	290
湖南 Hunan	59224	4925	29993	1590	14946	7770	3342	227
广东 Guangdong	75356	5328	45150	1553	13209	10116	964	612
广西 Guangxi	40791	4127	22968	768	7301	5627	1404	1014
海南 Hainan	10800	1007	5490	345	2312	1646	66	74
重庆 Chongqing	23214	2027	12113	421	5639	3014	1356	351
四川 Sichuan	55429	5059	34791	989	8624	5966	4658	121
贵州 Guizhou	25555	1911	17059	448	3682	2455	412	186
云南 Yunnan	26099	1848	16816	528	3482	3425	480	682
西藏 Tibet	1154	91	974	2	55	32	70	2
陕西 Shaanxi	42605	3249	25974	1026	7262	5094	6429	179
甘肃 Gansu	10940	883	8340	128	817	772	1256	238
青海 Qinghai	2784	253	1709	42	378	402	916	113
宁夏 Ningxia	3493	234	2060	78	537	584	729	43
新疆 Xinjiang	12309	701	8319	117	1658	1514	1589	48

幼儿园教职工数(镇乡结合区)

Number of Educational Personnel in Kindergarten (County-town Transitional Area)

单位:人
unit: person

地 区 Region	教职工数 Educational Personnel						代课教师 Substitute Teachers	兼任教师 Part-time Teachers
	合计 Total	园长 Kindergarten Heads	专任教师 Full-time Teachers	保健医 Health Physician	保育员 Caretaker	其他 Other		
总 计 Total	**255254**	**22612**	**154313**	**5993**	**42152**	**30184**	**23098**	**2128**
北 京 Beijing	942	57	592	28	109	156		6
天 津 Tianjin	824	97	531	23	85	88	496	2
河 北 Hebei	21237	1994	13931	451	3086	1775	2777	138
山 西 Shanxi	6456	619	4378	118	738	603	1796	135
内蒙古 Inner Mongolia	1768	151	1096	42	264	215	158	8
辽 宁 Liaoning	2073	350	1415	28	97	183	37	88
吉 林 Jilin	1315	150	784	51	192	138	15	11
黑龙江 Heilongjiang	1568	230	954	77	183	124	66	20
上 海 Shanghai	2012	88	1150	61	419	294	85	8
江 苏 Jiangsu	16070	702	10272	417	3248	1431	3112	92
浙 江 Zhejiang	24083	1459	13944	648	3931	4101		126
安 徽 Anhui	5882	535	3759	177	913	498	469	62
福 建 Fujian	9766	849	5656	179	1714	1368	824	30
江 西 Jiangxi	8922	1230	5487	204	1133	868	331	64
山 东 Shandong	24446	2582	17146	344	2230	2144	4074	225
河 南 Henan	23938	2250	14337	739	3859	2753	3000	214
湖 北 Hubei	8001	683	4260	172	1790	1096	888	47
湖 南 Hunan	18652	1724	9175	532	4799	2422	1207	88
广 东 Guangdong	26493	1982	15944	574	4557	3436	192	268
广 西 Guangxi	6248	744	3427	128	1092	857	92	153
海 南 Hainan	1692	162	812	63	404	251	9	8
重 庆 Chongqing	5083	515	2447	93	1285	743	222	74
四 川 Sichuan	11298	1168	6223	287	2043	1577	745	29
贵 州 Guizhou	4383	368	2801	91	703	420	93	35
云 南 Yunnan	7484	624	4429	171	1225	1035	99	109
西 藏 Tibet	121	9	101		8	3	32	2
陕 西 Shaanxi	10261	904	6249	252	1591	1265	1685	30
甘 肃 Gansu	1798	183	1365	15	147	88	124	27
青 海 Qinghai	423	50	229	9	66	69	111	1
宁 夏 Ningxia	453	42	290	12	54	55	109	7
新 疆 Xinjiang	1562	111	1129	7	187	128	250	21

幼儿园教职工数(乡村)

Number of Educational Personnel in Kindergarten (Rural Area)

单位:人

unit: person

地 区 Region	教职工数 Educational Personnel						代课教师 Substitute Teachers	兼任教师 Part-time Teachers
	合计 Total	园长 Kindergarten Heads	专任教师 Full-time Teachers	保健医 Health Physician	保育员 Caretaker	其他 Other		
总 计 Total	**444349**	**58936**	**268327**	**9920**	**60465**	**46701**	**40703**	**5885**
北 京 Beijing	2079	170	1280	66	236	327		33
天 津 Tianjin	1925	188	1335	48	212	142	728	1
河 北 Hebei	29529	4310	20717	407	2497	1598	6501	331
山 西 Shanxi	9828	1894	6484	187	714	549	3220	160
内蒙古 Inner Mongolia	3869	496	2372	65	492	444	256	42
辽 宁 Liaoning	6990	1104	5043	71	280	492	396	467
吉 林 Jilin	4297	596	2570	171	454	506	183	25
黑龙江 Heilongjiang	6598	1320	3943	230	707	398	247	99
上 海 Shanghai	1521	65	904	50	272	230	43	
江 苏 Jiangsu	11673	616	7571	306	2127	1053	1714	31
浙 江 Zhejiang	27175	2215	15507	754	4114	4585		96
安 徽 Anhui	15062	1900	8868	457	2358	1479	1332	219
福 建 Fujian	17052	1825	9904	307	2540	2476	1680	64
江 西 Jiangxi	21990	4289	12802	423	2305	2171	863	237
山 东 Shandong	43538	7401	29420	477	3221	3019	6442	314
河 南 Henan	58482	6631	34760	2008	8995	6088	5413	465
湖 北 Hubei	18646	1873	9523	567	4082	2601	2669	138
湖 南 Hunan	30134	4075	14919	936	6448	3756	1617	128
广 东 Guangdong	24757	2234	14710	508	4062	3243	189	360
广 西 Guangxi	20627	3206	11099	358	3235	2729	655	460
海 南 Hainan	1908	199	972	58	349	330		8
重 庆 Chongqing	5324	841	2419	76	1311	677	404	95
四 川 Sichuan	19652	3956	11521	282	2228	1665	859	391
贵 州 Guizhou	9345	1015	6544	121	949	716	194	270
云 南 Yunnan	14649	2392	8251	335	2002	1669	310	918
西 藏 Tibet	888	59	680	5	73	71	120	12
陕 西 Shaanxi	15258	1787	8210	502	2715	2044	1011	80
甘 肃 Gansu	5633	892	3707	64	474	496	938	310
青 海 Qinghai	1786	296	927	16	230	317	1227	31
宁 夏 Ningxia	938	115	523	17	157	126	181	7
新 疆 Xinjiang	13196	976	10842	48	626	704	1311	93

幼儿园女

Number of Female Educational

地区 Region	教职工数 Educational Personnel		
	合计 Total	园长 Kindergarten Heads	专任教师 Full-time Teachers
总　计 Total	**2591701**	**200861**	**1630288**
北　京 Beijing	48803	1999	28212
天　津 Tianjin	18657	1429	11717
河　北 Hebei	105619	8582	72545
山　西 Shanxi	59462	5029	40878
内蒙古 Inner Mongolia	41434	3136	27445
辽　宁 Liaoning	72705	7521	48153
吉　林 Jilin	39120	4082	24294
黑龙江 Heilongjiang	47094	5367	27953
上　海 Shanghai	48497	1834	32588
江　苏 Jiangsu	166107	7168	105818
浙　江 Zhejiang	176519	9145	109331
安　徽 Anhui	76969	6432	50172
福　建 Fujian	104544	8150	64770
江　西 Jiangxi	95584	11496	60838
山　东 Shandong	183462	17015	129682
河　南 Henan	195718	15069	127356
湖　北 Hubei	99260	7532	56452
湖　南 Hunan	128710	11669	70273
广　东 Guangdong	310045	18958	185299
广　西 Guangxi	87226	9207	51553
海　南 Hainan	23216	2089	12892
重　庆 Chongqing	54938	4773	29823
四　川 Sichuan	122278	12025	75966
贵　州 Guizhou	50714	3862	32750
云　南 Yunnan	60726	4906	38675
西　藏 Tibet	2363	165	1810
陕　西 Shaanxi	89522	6257	55883
甘　肃 Gansu	27533	2312	19627
青　海 Qinghai	6907	635	4391
宁　夏 Ningxia	10127	612	6384
新　疆 Xinjiang	37842	2405	26758

教职工数

Personnel in Kindergarten

单位：人
unit: person

保健医 Health Physician	保育员 Caretaker	其他 Other	代课教师 Substitute Teachers	兼任教师 Part-time Teachers
64002	**472132**	**224418**	**153340**	**19952**
1928	8703	7961		398
625	2804	2082	2092	165
2156	15080	7256	12514	572
1322	7525	4708	11670	1291
1015	5840	3998	2408	284
1283	8661	7087	1164	1637
1374	6270	3100	726	292
2145	7398	4231	1324	584
1701	7080	5294	1406	78
4553	36557	12011	19870	1053
5097	34200	18746		542
1982	13716	4667	5716	549
2402	20836	8386	7261	298
1947	15147	6156	2708	671
3176	21040	12549	19494	1734
5288	34796	13209	18083	1224
2670	23677	8929	8340	422
3280	33507	9981	5277	444
7796	65435	32557	1829	1130
1693	16670	8103	2302	1547
837	5142	2256	139	131
1318	14034	4990	2522	666
2508	22044	9735	6396	442
877	8883	4342	652	479
1452	9584	6109	795	1470
15	250	123	190	9
2213	16862	8307	8303	293
466	3050	2078	3112	1144
80	918	883	2071	130
244	1523	1364	1752	55
559	4900	3220	3224	218

幼儿园园长、专任教师

Number of Kindergarten Heads, Full-time Teachers by Educational

地 区 Region	合计 Total	按学历分 By Educational Attainment			
		研究生毕业 Graduate	本科毕业 Under-graduate	专科毕业 Associate Bachelor	高中阶段毕业 High School Graduate
总 计 Total	**1885093**	**4291**	**313650**	**989945**	**526263**
北 京 Beijing	30885	337	10509	15161	4657
天 津 Tianjin	13855	156	6010	5313	2067
河 北 Hebei	87032	152	15123	47803	21472
山 西 Shanxi	47024	112	9130	24304	12554
内蒙古 Inner Mongolia	32152	97	8813	17326	5536
辽 宁 Liaoning	56921	227	8566	30902	15124
吉 林 Jilin	29270	260	7539	14929	5813
黑龙江 Heilongjiang	34654	65	7105	19521	6903
上 海 Shanghai	34783	206	21439	11323	1718
江 苏 Jiangsu	114266	264	37108	61258	14853
浙 江 Zhejiang	119748	153	24807	62989	30980
安 徽 Anhui	58265	93	8107	37062	12124
福 建 Fujian	73503	37	9657	32486	29060
江 西 Jiangxi	73945	78	5859	31115	30998
山 东 Shandong	152426	389	23113	75024	48648
河 南 Henan	146926	199	16783	81416	43224
湖 北 Hubei	66194	137	8591	32377	22939
湖 南 Hunan	83903	120	7120	47743	26736
广 东 Guangdong	207954	400	17332	107185	76040
广 西 Guangxi	61864	92	6179	33795	18629
海 南 Hainan	15256	19	1494	8929	4299
重 庆 Chongqing	35367	70	4536	19385	10689
四 川 Sichuan	90249	135	9419	51518	28675
贵 州 Guizhou	38474	20	4969	20680	11758
云 南 Yunnan	45817	97	8869	22511	12507
西 藏 Tibet	2305	6	415	1455	337
陕 西 Shaanxi	64946	219	11125	38252	14010
甘 肃 Gansu	23362	52	5974	12378	4569
青 海 Qinghai	5487	17	940	2740	1609
宁 夏 Ningxia	7376	22	1299	4658	1278
新 疆 Xinjiang	30884	60	5720	18407	6457

学历、职称情况(总计)
Attainment and Professional Rank (Total)

单位:人
unit:person

高中阶段以下毕业 Below High School Graduate	按职称分 By Professional Rank					
	中学高级 Senior Secondary	小学高级 Senior Primary	小学一级 1st Grade Primary	小学二级 2nd Grade Primary	小学三级 3rd Grade Primary	未定职级 No-ranking
50944	**13574**	**210850**	**242836**	**75699**	**14742**	**1327392**
221	247	5208	6159	2224	343	16704
309	282	4825	2134	117	156	6341
2482	788	20039	16742	2147	289	47027
924	139	5911	8104	2517	549	29804
380	1750	4438	3773	928	100	21163
2102	944	6948	3995	1018	811	43205
729	346	4789	3843	912	386	18994
1060	812	5326	4262	893	325	23036
97	536	9308	12951	1820	117	10051
783	1600	19162	23975	5935	336	63258
819	662	10075	25760	7331	751	75169
879	189	7217	6233	2684	353	41589
2263	257	8215	5630	3875	320	55206
5895	387	3653	4231	2166	543	62965
5252	963	12083	15139	5928	703	117610
5304	823	11324	15122	5902	1320	112435
2150	504	8696	8897	3510	840	43747
2184	410	4421	6523	2696	803	69050
6997	379	15630	15574	6604	2171	167596
3169	198	5093	4764	3095	1184	47530
515	42	793	933	729	204	12555
687	132	2337	3060	807	199	28832
502	337	7536	11617	2085	367	68307
1047	70	4568	4940	1902	401	26593
1833	151	8354	6051	2092	323	28846
92	29	407	750	171	19	929
1340	244	5274	9225	2357	271	47575
389	85	4077	5727	1149	122	12202
181	76	805	418	154	73	3961
119	43	1149	902	202	91	4989
240	149	3189	5402	1749	272	20123

幼儿园园长、专任教师

Number of Kindergarten Heads, Full-time Teachers by Educational

地 区 Region	合计 Total	按学历分 By Educational Attainment			
		研究生毕业 Graduate	本科毕业 Under-graduate	专科毕业 Associate Bachelor	高中阶段毕业 High School Graduate
总 计 Total	**888774**	**3589**	**188166**	**491664**	**193836**
北 京 Beijing	26090	309	8697	13056	3869
天 津 Tianjin	10217	150	5016	3933	1004
河 北 Hebei	28082	121	6050	16427	5214
山 西 Shanxi	20871	64	5030	11374	4165
内蒙古 Inner Mongolia	14973	73	4348	8377	2071
辽 宁 Liaoning	38962	201	6845	23140	8200
吉 林 Jilin	17328	216	4888	8905	3018
黑龙江 Heilongjiang	17173	57	4258	10015	2615
上 海 Shanghai	28242	183	17227	9539	1234
江 苏 Jiangsu	58893	225	24114	30999	3496
浙 江 Zhejiang	58583	133	15037	30750	12425
安 徽 Anhui	22353	80	4006	15054	3045
福 建 Fujian	34343	31	5535	15909	12297
江 西 Jiangxi	20970	44	2838	11124	6338
山 东 Shandong	71322	338	14027	39290	16313
河 南 Henan	55544	170	8772	33145	12711
湖 北 Hubei	32350	119	5735	17094	8863
湖 南 Hunan	29991	100	3855	19537	6222
广 东 Guangdong	140532	376	14299	74902	47695
广 西 Guangxi	20464	71	2980	12618	4464
海 南 Hainan	7588	13	824	4959	1667
重 庆 Chongqing	17967	59	3061	10595	4138
四 川 Sichuan	34922	94	4925	22601	7209
贵 州 Guizhou	11945	11	1772	6508	3406
云 南 Yunnan	16510	83	4161	8932	3150
西 藏 Tibet	501		113	223	113
陕 西 Shaanxi	25726	157	4394	16667	4266
甘 肃 Gansu	9540	43	2179	5449	1761
青 海 Qinghai	2302	8	372	1238	664
宁 夏 Ningxia	4444	21	801	2847	714
新 疆 Xinjiang	10046	39	2007	6457	1489

学历、职称情况(城区)
Attainment and Professional Rank (Urban Area)

单位:人
unit:person

高中阶段以下毕业 Below High School Graduate	按职称分 By Professional Rank					
	中学高级 Senior Secondary	小学高级 Senior Primary	小学一级 1st Grade Primary	小学二级 2nd Grade Primary	小学三级 3rd Grade Primary	未定职级 No-ranking
11519	**7736**	**103443**	**119074**	**38968**	**8179**	**611374**
159	217	4337	5120	2010	338	14068
114	182	3648	1928	114	152	4193
270	289	5155	4237	950	192	17259
238	95	2815	3489	1276	214	12982
104	689	1712	1714	431	77	10350
576	598	4480	2848	592	546	29898
301	234	2263	1600	362	327	12542
228	436	2602	1664	553	236	11682
59	442	8102	10163	1460	95	7980
59	1074	11366	14599	3085	261	28508
238	470	6374	13977	3418	309	34035
168	109	2776	2462	1178	167	15661
571	149	3371	2702	1886	219	26016
626	198	1484	2055	962	164	16107
1354	546	5543	6379	3025	386	55443
746	449	5249	6016	3261	702	39867
539	327	4513	4074	1752	553	21131
277	236	1744	2820	1189	241	23761
3260	291	9316	12053	5035	1370	112467
331	90	1933	2089	1321	420	14611
125	28	423	487	300	186	6164
114	91	1263	1409	462	109	14633
93	126	3085	5252	865	269	25325
248	20	1150	1062	458	61	9194
184	83	3061	2271	1014	199	9882
52	3	97	93	6		302
242	103	1813	2631	876	121	20182
108	45	1524	1677	489	64	5741
20	18	184	187	102	59	1752
61	26	551	451	129	42	3245
54	72	1509	1565	407	100	6393

幼儿园园长、专任教师

Number of Kindergarten Heads, Full-time Teachers by Educational

地区 Region	合计 Total	按学历分 By Educational Attainment			
		研究生毕业 Graduate	本科毕业 Under-graduate	专科毕业 Associate Bachelor	高中阶段毕业 High School Graduate
总计 Total	**137423**	**220**	**17040**	**72985**	**43831**
北京 Beijing	1694	16	389	955	301
天津 Tianjin	808	1	76	335	353
河北 Hebei	4700	6	971	2574	1067
山西 Shanxi	2466	5	412	1349	650
内蒙古 Inner Mongolia	576	3	100	313	152
辽宁 Liaoning	2904	8	348	1469	992
吉林 Jilin	928	8	294	421	187
黑龙江 Heilongjiang	952	1	258	485	188
上海 Shanghai	2135	2	1000	830	282
江苏 Jiangsu	5092	5	1528	3095	450
浙江 Zhejiang	13147	10	1880	6846	4335
安徽 Anhui	2273	2	278	1446	507
福建 Fujian	5695	2	570	2356	2559
江西 Jiangxi	3387	6	215	1544	1430
山东 Shandong	16974	44	2494	8827	5090
河南 Henan	7847	20	802	4551	2282
湖北 Hubei	3564	3	439	1889	1158
湖南 Hunan	4388	10	369	2964	989
广东 Guangdong	40414	37	2608	20283	16161
广西 Guangxi	2825	5	290	1685	775
海南 Hainan	457	1	53	276	125
重庆 Chongqing	1331	1	153	774	374
四川 Sichuan	4083	2	409	2599	1058
贵州 Guizhou	1214		91	609	462
云南 Yunnan	1938	5	324	992	562
西藏 Tibet	2		1	1	
陕西 Shaanxi	3572	11	378	2324	821
甘肃 Gansu	411	2	78	240	80
青海 Qinghai	240		26	117	93
宁夏 Ningxia	490	3	71	275	134
新疆 Xinjiang	916	1	135	561	214

学历、职称情况(城乡结合区)
Attainment and Professional Rank (Urban-rural Transitional Area)

单位:人
unit:person

高中阶段以下毕业 Below High School Graduate	按职称分 By Professional Rank					
	中学高级 Senior Secondary	小学高级 Senior Primary	小学一级 1st Grade Primary	小学二级 2nd Grade Primary	小学三级 3rd Grade Primary	未定职级 No-ranking
3347	**465**	**7542**	**11892**	**4434**	**1018**	**112072**
33	4	96	162	68	1	1363
43	3	26	21		27	731
82	29	865	799	64	8	2935
50	11	259	342	97	36	1721
8	6	20	23			527
87	20	199	126	30	79	2450
18	7	108	95	8	16	694
20	31	188	131	64	22	516
21	26	328	562	72	2	1145
14	35	649	1059	337	16	2996
76	38	503	1989	525	34	10058
40	6	165	179	66	1	1856
208	8	292	290	185	12	4908
192	12	54	133	60	11	3117
519	80	992	1225	560	62	14055
192	46	290	514	321	68	6608
75	19	199	236	192	69	2849
56	9	173	276	183	22	3725
1325	34	1229	2315	1146	347	35343
70	9	141	200	108	42	2325
2		5	13	9	6	424
29	10	79	121	16	4	1101
15	4	100	240	48	22	3669
52		55	67	10	1	1081
55	10	215	229	92	46	1346
			1			1
38	6	134	223	76	23	3110
11		69	126	17		199
4	1		3	16	8	212
7		50	38	8	1	393
5	1	59	154	56	32	614

幼儿园园长、专任教师

Number of Kindergarten Heads, Full-time Teachers by Educational

地　区 Region	合计 Total	按学历分 By Educational Attainment			
		研究生毕业 Graduate	本科毕业 Under-graduate	专科毕业 Associate Bachelor	高中阶段毕业 High School Graduate
总　计 Total	**669056**	**558**	**97888**	**349284**	**201116**
北　京 Beijing	3345	21	1328	1471	493
天　津 Tianjin	2115	4	660	875	474
河　北 Hebei	33923	19	5916	18551	8365
山　西 Shanxi	17775	46	3394	9133	4892
内蒙古 Inner Mongolia	14311	22	3982	7552	2596
辽　宁 Liaoning	11812	17	1284	5280	4355
吉　林 Jilin	8776	29	1910	4444	2091
黑龙江 Heilongjiang	12218	6	2235	6842	2675
上　海 Shanghai	5572	22	3675	1461	377
江　苏 Jiangsu	47186	38	11595	25668	9376
浙　江 Zhejiang	43443	18	7646	23596	11885
安　徽 Anhui	25144	9	3138	15988	5646
福　建 Fujian	27431	6	3430	12065	11005
江　西 Jiangxi	35884	24	2508	14954	15837
山　东 Shandong	44283	31	6596	21152	15022
河　南 Henan	49991	23	5730	28224	14268
湖　北 Hubei	22448	13	2103	10337	8968
湖　南 Hunan	34918	18	2483	19352	12053
广　东 Guangdong	50478	18	2375	24672	20830
广　西 Guangxi	27095	18	2605	14156	8812
海　南 Hainan	6497	6	588	3387	2229
重　庆 Chongqing	14140	10	1318	7370	5079
四　川 Sichuan	39850	38	3906	22842	12863
贵　州 Guizhou	18970	8	2459	10245	5691
云　南 Yunnan	18664	12	3833	9229	4997
西　藏 Tibet	1065	1	184	742	125
陕　西 Shaanxi	29223	56	5634	16682	6246
甘　肃 Gansu	9223	6	2822	4753	1562
青　海 Qinghai	1962	6	423	1032	469
宁　夏 Ningxia	2294	1	419	1496	339
新　疆 Xinjiang	9020	12	1709	5733	1496

学历、职称情况（镇区）

Attainment and Professional Rank（Counties & Towns Area）

单位：人
unit：person

高中阶段以下毕业 Below High School Graduate	按职称分 By Professional Rank 中学高级 Senior Secondary	小学高级 Senior Primary	小学一级 1st Grade Primary	小学二级 2nd Grade Primary	小学三级 3rd Grade Primary	未定职级 No-ranking
20210	**4557**	**79555**	**89201**	**25712**	**4600**	**465431**
32	23	587	788	158		1789
102	49	493	134	3	1	1435
1072	296	7142	6207	743	71	19464
310	30	2460	3581	866	190	10648
159	902	2355	1842	436	22	8754
876	242	1714	701	269	179	8707
302	107	1777	1582	467	43	4800
460	261	1846	1760	232	66	8053
37	77	1057	2454	314	20	1650
509	498	6944	8296	2407	52	28989
298	166	3031	9033	2948	343	27922
363	55	3503	2643	1034	98	17811
925	93	3885	2310	1471	77	19595
2561	137	1754	1760	993	317	30923
1482	296	3927	4936	1399	186	33539
1746	281	4450	5953	1622	321	37364
1027	133	3163	3399	1195	192	14366
1012	138	1991	2751	1086	388	28564
2583	42	5055	2697	1218	653	40813
1504	78	2660	1983	1158	598	20618
287	14	329	392	374	13	5375
363	35	929	1347	314	78	11437
201	190	4078	5365	887	74	29256
567	48	2720	2799	908	223	12272
593	60	4267	2889	712	88	10648
13	25	223	417	108	13	279
605	128	3006	5639	1258	115	19077
80	33	1854	3066	456	49	3765
32	51	537	205	48	12	1109
39	15	460	339	63	46	1371
70	54	1358	1933	565	72	5038

幼儿园园长、专任教师

Number of Kindergarten Heads, Full-time Teachers by Educational

地区 Region	合计 Total	按学历分 By Educational Attainment			
		研究生毕业 Graduate	本科毕业 Under-graduate	专科毕业 Associate Bachelor	高中阶段毕业 High School Graduate
总计 Total	**176925**	**157**	**20805**	**88274**	**60752**
北京 Beijing	649	4	256	270	109
天津 Tianjin	628	1	127	189	244
河北 Hebei	15925	6	2245	8570	4418
山西 Shanxi	4997	31	855	2546	1427
内蒙古 Inner Mongolia	1247	1	319	646	256
辽宁 Liaoning	1765	4	136	709	777
吉林 Jilin	934	2	272	403	200
黑龙江 Heilongjiang	1184	1	171	623	327
上海 Shanghai	1238	9	624	438	136
江苏 Jiangsu	10974	13	2721	6008	2124
浙江 Zhejiang	15403	3	1836	8152	5260
安徽 Anhui	4294	3	442	2541	1218
福建 Fujian	6505	4	749	2704	2745
江西 Jiangxi	6717	3	290	2545	3266
山东 Shandong	19728	15	2262	8910	7753
河南 Henan	16587	4	1442	8962	5383
湖北 Hubei	4943	2	369	2232	2050
湖南 Hunan	10899	3	741	5985	3867
广东 Guangdong	17926	8	665	7796	8144
广西 Guangxi	4171	1	292	2052	1488
海南 Hainan	974	1	120	483	321
重庆 Chongqing	2962	3	195	1549	1139
四川 Sichuan	7391	23	586	3904	2834
贵州 Guizhou	3169	1	372	1681	1051
云南 Yunnan	5053	2	768	2489	1610
西藏 Tibet	110		15	64	28
陕西 Shaanxi	7153	7	1155	3975	1849
甘肃 Gansu	1548	1	456	795	290
青海 Qinghai	279	1	14	131	123
宁夏 Ningxia	332		56	192	64
新疆 Xinjiang	1240		254	730	251

学历、职称情况(镇乡结合区)
Attainment and Professional Rank (County-town Transitional Area)

单位:人
unit: person

高中阶段以下毕业 Below High School Graduate	按职称分 By Professional Rank					
	中学高级 Senior Secondary	小学高级 Senior Primary	小学一级 1st Grade Primary	小学二级 2nd Grade Primary	小学三级 3rd Grade Primary	未定职级 No-ranking
6937	**915**	**15681**	**19743**	**5959**	**1123**	**133504**
10	8	102	152	37		350
67	9	136	17			466
686	124	3290	2928	428	47	9108
138	5	600	1011	186	39	3156
25	95	196	117	29	1	809
139	33	148	103	36	59	1386
57	25	236	200	13	2	458
62	22	152	142	8	4	856
31	15	159	402	67	6	589
108	111	1459	2108	761	15	6520
152	25	605	2303	881	117	11472
90	10	417	353	150	36	3328
303	13	761	340	248	9	5134
613	9	151	141	96	58	6262
788	96	1391	1974	597	95	15575
796	98	918	1333	384	109	13745
290	32	530	640	277	52	3412
303	43	510	892	362	165	8927
1313	14	1088	810	444	155	15415
338	34	189	214	177	47	3510
49		15	41	48	1	869
76	3	115	207	54	17	2566
44	11	384	515	84	5	6392
64	2	334	363	103	28	2339
184	18	764	567	113	17	3574
3		14	33	9		54
167	32	524	1034	209	28	5326
6	7	266	485	64	3	723
10	8	10	8	1	1	251
20	7	77	31	4		213
5	6	140	279	89	7	719

幼儿园园长、专任教师

Number of Kindergarten Heads, Full-time Teachers by Educational

地 区 Region	合计 Total	按学历分 By Educational Attainment			
		研究生毕业 Graduate	本科毕业 Under-graduate	专科毕业 Associate Bachelor	高中阶段毕业 High School Graduate
总 计 Total	**327263**	**144**	**27596**	**148997**	**131311**
北 京 Beijing	1450	7	484	634	295
天 津 Tianjin	1523	2	334	505	589
河 北 Hebei	25027	12	3157	12825	7893
山 西 Shanxi	8378	2	706	3797	3497
内蒙古 Inner Mongolia	2868	2	483	1397	869
辽 宁 Liaoning	6147	9	437	2482	2569
吉 林 Jilin	3166	15	741	1580	704
黑龙江 Heilongjiang	5263	2	612	2664	1613
上 海 Shanghai	969	1	537	323	107
江 苏 Jiangsu	8187	1	1399	4591	1981
浙 江 Zhejiang	17722	2	2124	8643	6670
安 徽 Anhui	10768	4	963	6020	3433
福 建 Fujian	11729		692	4512	5758
江 西 Jiangxi	17091	10	513	5037	8823
山 东 Shandong	36821	20	2490	14582	17313
河 南 Henan	41391	6	2281	20047	16245
湖 北 Hubei	11396	5	753	4946	5108
湖 南 Hunan	18994	2	782	8854	8461
广 东 Guangdong	16944	6	658	7611	7515
广 西 Guangxi	14305	3	594	7021	5353
海 南 Hainan	1171		82	583	403
重 庆 Chongqing	3260	1	157	1420	1472
四 川 Sichuan	15477	3	588	6075	8603
贵 州 Guizhou	7559	1	738	3927	2661
云 南 Yunnan	10643	2	875	4350	4360
西 藏 Tibet	739	5	118	490	99
陕 西 Shaanxi	9997	6	1097	4903	3498
甘 肃 Gansu	4599	3	973	2176	1246
青 海 Qinghai	1223	3	145	470	476
宁 夏 Ningxia	638		79	315	225
新 疆 Xinjiang	11818	9	2004	6217	3472

学历、职称情况（乡村）
Attainment and Professional Rank（Rural Area）

单位：人
unit：person

高中阶段以下毕业 Below High School Graduate	按职称分 By Professional Rank 中学高级 Senior Secondary	小学高级 Senior Primary	小学一级 1st Grade Primary	小学二级 2nd Grade Primary	小学三级 3rd Grade Primary	未定职级 No-ranking
19215	**1281**	**27852**	**34561**	**11019**	**1963**	**250587**
30	7	284	251	56	5	847
93	51	684	72		3	713
1140	203	7742	6298	454	26	10304
376	14	636	1034	375	145	6174
117	159	371	217	61	1	2059
650	104	754	446	157	86	4600
126	5	749	661	83	16	1652
372	115	878	838	108	23	3301
1	17	149	334	46	2	421
215	28	852	1080	443	23	5761
283	26	670	2750	965	99	13212
348	25	938	1128	472	88	8117
767	15	959	618	518	24	9595
2708	52	415	416	211	62	15935
2416	121	2613	3824	1504	131	28628
2812	93	1625	3153	1019	297	35204
584	44	1020	1424	563	95	8250
895	36	686	952	421	174	16725
1154	46	1259	824	351	148	14316
1334	30	500	692	616	166	12301
103		41	54	55	5	1016
210	6	145	304	31	12	2762
208	21	373	1000	333	24	13726
232	2	698	1079	536	117	5127
1056	8	1026	891	366	36	8316
27	1	87	240	57	6	348
493	13	455	955	223	35	8316
201	7	699	984	204	9	2696
129	7	84	26	4	2	1100
19	2	138	112	10	3	373
116	23	322	1904	777	100	8692

幼儿园校舍及其他
Statistics of Kindergarten Buildings

地区 Region	校舍建筑面积 Floor Space	教学及辅助用房 Teaching & Assistant Buildings				
		合计 Total	其中 of Which			
			活动室 Recreational	洗手间 Toilet	睡眠室 Bed Room	保健室 Health Care
总　计 Total	**201842763**	**139832114**	**82156769**	**12213689**	**35699014**	**4377890**
北　京 Beijing	3287354	1965349	1009124	215555	634473	46523
天　津 Tianjin	1435269	957369	576188	102509	225581	26704
河　北 Hebei	8321004	5850889	3625651	443340	1316942	217666
山　西 Shanxi	4595752	3076890	1950956	260336	628609	102374
内蒙古 Inner Mongolia	3254463	2126629	1226836	193297	576714	54396
辽　宁 Liaoning	5227166	3663556	2114389	337902	926804	133682
吉　林 Jilin	2246270	1565370	879638	138302	436938	51972
黑龙江 Heilongjiang	3284035	2201639	1208791	193543	602206	97924
上　海 Shanghai	5093618	3144394	2065936	293483	648742	67929
江　苏 Jiangsu	16909489	11843088	7182247	1076096	2908211	273457
浙　江 Zhejiang	13385658	8945004	5136356	835281	2496908	205834
安　徽 Anhui	5736840	4176806	2613634	357654	877001	143795
福　建 Fujian	7496058	5114864	3168009	487303	1201898	120161
江　西 Jiangxi	7327642	5402804	3054285	444702	1485599	192027
山　东 Shandong	15577077	10880071	6815121	989643	2273991	338239
河 南 Henan	13611529	9968087	5938454	874934	2355719	350148
湖　北 Hubei	7809430	5559648	3051437	521271	1543993	206418
湖　南 Hunan	10629511	7612452	3978158	719928	2193382	362028
广　东 Guangdong	22525039	14659391	8877214	1156237	3674679	352981
广　西 Guangxi	6209336	4559792	2495144	371138	1387567	143208
海　南 Hainan	1438376	1005338	542037	93861	290413	35691
重　庆 Chongqing	3663770	2718650	1608438	221946	698357	86213
四　川 Sichuan	8922818	6514049	3815576	584862	1666771	200810
贵　州 Guizhou	3676268	2626795	1419285	231569	777463	102577
云　南 Yunnan	4999148	3462228	1958251	217575	1047079	115242
西　藏 Tibet	442012	263814	150797	23231	68350	12631
陕　西 Shaanxi	6207000	4251688	2422700	383565	1113088	147449
甘　肃 Gansu	2374775	1608676	1045830	116177	334690	51681
青　海 Qinghai	770873	513800	314009	38679	129656	16139
宁　夏 Ningxia	868650	585724	336667	60414	155943	16628
新　疆 Xinjiang	4516533	3007260	1575611	229356	1021247	105363

情况(总计)(一)
and Others (Total) (1)

单位：平方米
unit：m^2

	行政办公用房 Administrative		生活用房 Residential and Welfare		其他用房 for Other Purposes	校舍面积中 of the Floor Space	
图书室 Picture Books	合计 Total	其中：教师办公室 of Which：Office	合计 Total	其中：厨房 of Which：Kitchen		危房面积 Floor Space of Dilapidated Buildings	当年新增 New Added in Current Year
5384752	**14598530**	**8818278**	**21480593**	**10020688**	**25931526**	**1383596**	**10329816**
59674	268904	118308	413923	194246	639178	666	267821
26387	113127	60787	154808	82244	209965		25962
247290	711469	483076	732435	356674	1026211	29896	338827
134615	476582	322815	456408	192725	585872	34175	213659
75386	271618	158467	396699	185375	459517	1180	233982
150779	360734	210244	544255	321119	658621	15178	148675
58520	155870	92006	238209	116748	286821	5253	67794
99175	249605	149354	395734	201102	437057	18994	155480
68304	385283	159428	681552	223629	882389		136946
403077	1090577	580531	1484194	751509	2491630	2200	943795
270625	903320	504220	1400317	697449	2137017		482503
184722	451660	297027	516594	253447	591780	39694	384339
137493	496207	303348	740374	348633	1144613	7522	359646
226191	481532	309774	716309	354343	726997	48280	264405
463077	1232221	786985	1400979	705742	2063806	35245	846405
448832	1148227	741270	1226606	640808	1268609	42247	442935
236529	527621	321360	894872	429187	827289	54668	443152
358956	803173	515270	1148950	533856	1064936	60574	348725
598280	1309416	697286	2992720	1053555	3563512	25613	513445
162735	321936	217574	751637	390546	575971	128838	312151
43336	87800	49988	188483	81321	156755	10672	50000
103696	222880	139570	362618	173359	359622	30758	122284
246030	552809	349550	979804	458583	876156	66305	1144272
95901	259642	164178	392890	196673	396941	3077	528481
124081	343275	203235	655565	263659	538080	503656	346347
8805	42543	29377	81641	26972	54014	1604	122938
184886	654607	422286	633389	322600	667316	33453	348646
60298	251694	181423	233448	106457	280957	141961	296020
15317	57967	37339	101703	40618	97403	6691	114797
16072	85841	47190	85358	51891	111727	10307	56435
75683	280390	165012	478119	265618	750764	24889	268949

幼儿园校舍及其他

Statistics of Kindergarten Buildings

地 区 Region	校舍建筑面积 Floor Space	教学及辅助用房 Teaching & Assistant Buildings				
		合计 Total	其中 of Which			
			活动室 Recreational	洗手间 Toilet	睡眠室 Bed Room	保健室 Health Care
总 计 Total	**91763492**	**62968201**	**36439121**	**5676849**	**17259753**	**1521202**
北 京 Beijing	2696966	1622096	824935	175905	534875	37192
天 津 Tianjin	908314	592126	347703	64382	150282	13371
河 北 Hebei	2500625	1746502	967665	153961	524573	45359
山 西 Shanxi	1877076	1246252	711440	113701	344111	34252
内蒙古 Inner Mongolia	1485043	1007428	578228	92703	279314	23157
辽 宁 Liaoning	3430954	2383584	1355524	233365	629273	77353
吉 林 Jilin	1318927	919813	515006	88304	258966	26758
黑龙江 Heilongjiang	1552068	1036678	554324	94962	297465	42845
上 海 Shanghai	4078043	2551326	1688027	237120	516541	54071
江 苏 Jiangsu	8300667	5649242	3382585	517001	1481934	104752
浙 江 Zhejiang	6456778	4378801	2545608	409280	1221251	83117
安 徽 Anhui	2082468	1500743	865736	134074	412143	37211
福 建 Fujian	3421439	2329971	1427621	214860	588218	45289
江 西 Jiangxi	2082518	1546297	839023	127334	486444	40952
山 东 Shandong	6993515	4875884	2857898	473586	1230606	129616
河 南 Henan	4939824	3631844	2051958	315711	1046843	91666
湖 北 Hubei	3375846	2428328	1348746	223671	701961	68197
湖 南 Hunan	3444860	2531070	1307841	270028	761078	89665
广 东 Guangdong	15231146	9817244	6030922	788445	2448981	198058
广 西 Guangxi	1938140	1429628	796838	121518	429019	36800
海 南 Hainan	690460	483185	261841	43233	142752	14808
重 庆 Chongqing	1736662	1288895	716815	109948	388004	31050
四 川 Sichuan	3411873	2512410	1417292	207635	748209	58264
贵 州 Guizhou	1053646	777835	424925	64471	237569	24974
云 南 Yunnan	1702049	1164246	658058	78931	367831	25785
西 藏 Tibet	78932	46717	24866	4346	15910	614
陕 西 Shaanxi	2205084	1575915	888646	140656	458854	37423
甘 肃 Gansu	859923	610837	353517	46878	173184	15677
青 海 Qinghai	220447	154268	89554	12833	44016	3740
宁 夏 Ningxia	461686	309811	173057	33244	87074	7940
新 疆 Xinjiang	1227513	819225	432922	84763	252472	21246

情况(城区)(一)
and Others (Urban Area)(1)

单位：平方米
unit：m^2

图书室 Picture Books	行政办公用房 Administrative 合计 Total	其中：教师办公室 of Which：Office	生活用房 Residential and Welfare 合计 Total	其中：厨房 of Which：Kitchen	其他用房 for Other Purposes	校舍面积中 of the Floor Space 危房面积 Floor Space of Dilapidated Buildings	当年新增 New Added in Current Year
2071276	**5992106**	**3078830**	**9745877**	**4560133**	**13057308**	**423900**	**3198013**
49189	216757	92394	336774	155964	521339	666	155631
16388	70936	33821	95768	53097	149484		20204
54944	195809	108364	225906	127623	332408	4665	72414
42748	169512	90900	201585	88124	259727	13636	53747
34026	110593	56155	168198	85049	198824	342	92769
88069	214681	112686	366554	217820	466135	5590	87199
30779	83727	45635	142385	72433	173002	2744	31390
47082	108543	56539	178620	93253	228227	4059	31695
55567	303327	127701	554224	177787	669166		76272
162970	520899	247207	760550	376714	1369976		401321
119545	433447	222814	640670	316577	1003860		186069
51579	147679	80091	189535	104048	244511	11029	54606
53983	212405	115399	314579	155465	564484	2992	126383
52544	116926	64511	164243	86211	255052	9558	73506
184178	500233	270422	658739	360677	958659	21572	224604
125666	352692	187248	426870	224494	528418	10616	82880
85753	205944	110513	339153	169178	402421	8008	143051
102458	215696	117008	315910	152947	382184	26584	106284
350838	814523	411924	2041292	720844	2558087	21274	267485
45453	101913	57417	211094	112071	195505	53799	111611
20551	39450	20528	92214	38583	75611	5477	18406
43078	90118	49481	165392	83965	192257	15487	47498
81010	196867	108851	342883	177772	359713	17372	381152
25896	69679	39252	98279	52954	107853	780	35311
33641	110186	56127	218997	86752	208620	137131	114652
981	9755	3855	10779	3709	11681		9425
50336	168196	81482	205084	112544	255889	2848	70385
21581	65150	39504	80617	44782	103319	30404	56658
4125	14608	8495	32370	11739	19201		16484
8496	49526	23324	42516	28563	59833	8448	23532
27822	82329	39182	124097	68394	201862	8819	25389

幼儿园校舍及其他
Statistics of Kindergarten Buildings

地 区 Region	校舍建筑面积 Floor Space	教学及辅助用房 Teaching & Assistant Buildings				
		合计 Total	其中 of Which			
			活动室 Recreational	洗手间 Toilet	睡眠室 Bed Room	保健室 Health Care
总　计 Total	**14994349**	**10145482**	**5934345**	**922078**	**2629322**	**281359**
北　京 Beijing	178341	107217	56323	12505	31964	3114
天　津 Tianjin	60096	44323	25279	4203	11834	1331
河　北 Hebei	426054	293386	169934	24179	77281	10867
山　西 Shanxi	248355	169158	100587	14674	42254	5512
内蒙古 Inner Mongolia	61700	41174	24331	3938	10104	1112
辽　宁 Liaoning	269963	192779	112555	16695	47221	7948
吉　林 Jilin	75335	50255	27250	6293	12957	2011
黑龙江 Heilongjiang	103958	64255	32257	6146	18875	3712
上　海 Shanghai	326247	211904	136824	19527	45362	4962
江　苏 Jiangsu	790707	540061	328254	48249	131892	13048
浙　江 Zhejiang	1424701	994397	583053	94940	263887	23594
安　徽 Anhui	227588	172798	110383	12809	37358	5299
福　建 Fujian	547469	380073	231868	36249	94914	8314
江　西 Jiangxi	327124	234758	127889	19473	71184	6649
山　东 Shandong	1812942	1253154	755486	119643	288484	37654
河 南 Henan	734300	525111	305683	47197	133450	15988
湖　北 Hubei	409829	305566	171710	26530	79049	11409
湖　南 Hunan	554863	406687	195517	68099	109482	16462
广　东 Guangdong	4657374	2891068	1752110	233787	733220	63080
广　西 Guangxi	271229	202906	109265	17348	64466	5429
海　南 Hainan	36578	28252	13906	2401	10162	860
重　庆 Chongqing	134902	98149	53574	8180	28759	3709
四　川 Sichuan	422449	317093	170083	28128	98484	8689
贵　州 Guizhou	111583	82016	44291	6913	24827	2686
云　南 Yunnan	204607	134587	67675	10792	46458	4106
西　藏 Tibet	1018	668	235	45	186	27
陕　西 Shaanxi	340182	236561	130460	20017	69753	7809
甘　肃 Gansu	41441	28252	17843	1873	6621	916
青　海 Qinghai	21249	15851	10432	693	3793	478
宁　夏 Ningxia	57162	39364	22826	4271	9198	1806
新　疆 Xinjiang	115003	83659	46462	6281	25843	2778

情况(城乡结合区)(一)
and Others (Urban-rural Transitional Area) (1)

单位: 平方米
unit: m^2

	行政办公用房 Administritive		生活用房 Residential and Welfare		其他用房 for Other Purposes	校舍面积中 of the Floor Space	
图书室 Picture Books	合计 Total	其中:教师办公室 of Which: Office	合计 Total	其中:厨房 of Which: Kitchen		危房面积 Floor Space of Dilapidated Buildings	当年新增 New Added in Current Year
378378	**958342**	**529388**	**1767836**	**751846**	**2122689**	**39291**	**587818**
3311	14350	6573	20869	11397	35905		34592
1676	4382	2397	6621	5358	4770		90
11125	37882	22845	36405	19553	58381	1160	21012
6131	22394	14593	20298	9963	36505	278	7278
1689	5304	2588	6171	3692	9051		7146
8360	16498	9879	29519	17721	31167		3519
1744	5148	3408	6500	4761	13432	546	
3265	8536	4580	12407	6560	18760		80
5229	23795	8768	41666	14956	48882		9300
18618	52252	24321	78009	36436	120385		32348
28923	90488	47876	144746	76065	195070		34693
6949	14728	9514	19426	11010	20636	2107	16396
8728	30515	18672	53613	25884	83268		13646
9563	18700	13528	30431	14034	43235	2650	11660
51887	129773	76697	173385	88705	256630	6445	88783
22793	58733	34349	67753	34847	82703	1809	19962
16868	25072	14285	39671	21510	39520	285	28858
17127	34237	20100	55270	25958	58669	2696	29900
108871	247287	127863	731748	223347	787271	1775	88243
6398	13527	9119	31243	16746	23553	4341	16268
923	1455	874	3896	1888	2975		1663
3927	7378	4764	18189	7393	11186	3167	2869
11709	23189	13482	44109	26053	38058		64634
3299	7780	5411	11997	6432	9790		5582
5556	15697	8060	24969	10008	29354	8372	27673
175	105	35	245	145			
8522	33064	14749	35900	19109	34657	1030	15482
999	3727	2759	3817	1582	5645	2630	1680
455	1248	738	2617	1238	1533		2717
1263	4927	3036	6011	3843	6860		875
2295	6171	3525	10335	5652	14838		869

幼儿园校舍及其他
Statistics of Kindergarten Buildings

地 区 Region	校舍建筑面积 Floor Space	教学及辅助用房 Teaching & Assistant Buildings				
		合计 Total	其中 of Which			
			活动室 Recreational	洗手间 Toilet	睡眠室 Bed Room	保健室 Health Care
总 计 Total	**72995278**	**51078886**	**30151166**	**4396768**	**12747820**	**1720985**
北 京 Beijing	407837	241815	129196	27227	72402	5965
天 津 Tianjin	314995	212139	123582	23415	52910	6576
河 北 Hebei	3194205	2261065	1379730	181449	527089	79933
山 西 Shanxi	1755641	1185392	787016	97572	209908	38946
内蒙古 Inner Mongolia	1467830	934125	542464	83180	251227	24652
辽 宁 Liaoning	1107430	797857	474533	66728	189399	31869
吉 林 Jilin	666402	467632	260921	36601	132977	17344
黑龙江 Heilongjiang	1231491	818404	454110	70360	221306	37122
上 海 Shanghai	856415	501729	322403	46333	111469	11589
江 苏 Jiangsu	7364063	5303571	3287832	477926	1202249	136691
浙 江 Zhejiang	4977914	3271082	1872503	303049	916712	78629
安 徽 Anhui	2395167	1761740	1151805	146859	315874	63766
福 建 Fujian	2758636	1903469	1186557	182797	432916	47079
江 西 Jiangxi	3463053	2575224	1461680	208623	704152	91866
山 东 Shandong	4934727	3377384	2136216	303950	674907	112221
河 南 Henan	4720726	3461357	2113797	299910	760764	127221
湖 北 Hubei	2872352	2034479	1115362	193530	546233	85532
湖 南 Hunan	4555703	3262128	1709445	285972	952374	161788
广 东 Guangdong	5373733	3578684	2088393	276317	932687	107282
广 西 Guangxi	2751829	2028658	1104809	161309	623047	65491
海 南 Hainan	617866	432967	234633	41196	121051	17013
重 庆 Chongqing	1528740	1150510	718889	88350	256143	41126
四 川 Sichuan	4024925	2927332	1751480	257511	704284	100537
贵 州 Guizhou	1759002	1253022	671980	110368	378143	47776
云 南 Yunnan	1958735	1386211	777592	83877	430379	46045
西 藏 Tibet	125414	78200	44431	4814	21279	5074
陕 西 Shaanxi	2992127	2003215	1142875	183578	505529	76129
甘 肃 Gansu	871707	584231	399381	44073	101890	19173
青 海 Qinghai	281884	183677	107839	14177	51003	4939
宁 夏 Ningxia	290977	198624	119553	18786	50040	5121
新 疆 Xinjiang	1373752	902963	480159	76931	297477	26490

情况（镇区）（一）

and Others（Counties & Towns Area）(1)

单位：平方米

unit：m²

图书室 Picture Books	行政办公用房 Administrative 合计 Total	其中：教师办公室 of Which：Office	生活用房 Residential and Welfare 合计 Total	其中：厨房 of Which：Kitchen	其他用房 for Other Purposes	校舍面积中 of the Floor Space 危房面积 Floor Space of Dilapidated Buildings	当年新增 New Added in Current Year
2062147	**5492840**	**3506142**	**7556583**	**3487739**	**8866969**	**567253**	**4717606**
7025	33130	16680	50661	26135	82231		56337
5656	23440	13785	38798	19916	40618		686
92864	264037	176941	287152	138097	381951	9117	162440
51950	184807	135386	160623	67257	224819	13880	117940
32602	132916	82844	183450	80532	217339	282	120658
35328	82057	53795	104911	60543	122605	6871	37233
19789	50239	31288	71088	31143	77443	1448	21492
35506	98142	59583	150686	74731	164259	13631	80275
9935	69275	27070	112093	38355	173318		41763
198873	487313	282296	604927	312638	968252	2200	460492
100189	329652	193198	524222	259600	852958		207126
83436	194952	137004	204208	92383	234267	23717	196764
54120	184744	117837	273773	128051	396650	4209	161409
108903	228178	147015	332935	162421	326716	15764	139538
150090	397513	268920	445868	209897	713962	7763	416056
159665	414760	280362	414337	210745	430272	17982	191036
93822	208541	133844	360704	166114	268628	39078	171882
152549	350502	230391	503882	225666	439191	19931	175045
174005	355257	198073	682919	239610	756873	3799	185895
74002	138405	97381	329908	162921	254858	51092	141269
19074	40548	23805	78967	34497	65384	4855	24664
46002	100355	65348	149676	67297	128199	13215	63200
113520	254608	165499	440474	194781	402511	44136	536007
44755	120999	76992	191810	93585	193171	2297	302805
48318	137683	79674	238438	95806	196403	185807	123952
2602	12239	9212	22857	7156	12118		14536
95104	357346	247162	312993	149363	318573	26878	210868
19714	97751	71569	81192	34722	108533	47871	132718
5719	21850	11560	29529	12686	46828	4432	68064
5124	25451	16726	29533	16394	37369	1059	15563
21906	96150	54902	143969	74697	230670	5939	139893

幼儿园校舍及其他

Statistics of Kindergarten Buildings

地 区 Region	校舍建筑面积 Floor Space	教学及辅助用房 Teaching & Assistant Buildings				
		合计 Total	其中 of Which			
			活动室 Recreational	洗手间 Toilet	睡眠室 Bed Room	保健室 Health Care
总 计 Total	**19661350**	**13717949**	**8131944**	**1194830**	**3300615**	**493656**
北 京 Beijing	70819	42249	22088	5175	12228	1541
天 津 Tianjin	105877	75078	46546	8003	15921	2747
河 北 Hebei	1554122	1098457	694263	83671	231140	39502
山 西 Shanxi	499837	332542	219740	27092	56053	13853
内蒙古 Inner Mongolia	121824	77894	48415	5942	18805	2381
辽 宁 Liaoning	176089	124948	72871	11019	28708	5878
吉 林 Jilin	75594	49871	27313	4009	15038	1656
黑龙江 Heilongjiang	108582	75855	41476	6245	21160	3745
上 海 Shanghai	162488	101618	65086	8353	23570	2795
江 苏 Jiangsu	1698136	1196496	731478	114086	277045	32118
浙 江 Zhejiang	1711058	1165199	662788	106857	324869	30189
安 徽 Anhui	413006	302462	196088	26567	53188	12254
福 建 Fujian	679980	468940	284019	47454	109809	13442
江 西 Jiangxi	682781	503834	292662	40930	127306	19452
山 东 Shandong	2149220	1479043	944980	134772	281919	50662
河 南 Henan	1693164	1220634	728365	107436	272228	50075
湖 北 Hubei	649380	463051	250593	48599	121504	21251
湖 南 Hunan	1499647	1048041	545498	89529	303038	55866
广 东 Guangdong	1906081	1260311	744673	103593	307444	40110
广 西 Guangxi	444253	324452	172970	26333	100904	11527
海 南 Hainan	85110	62049	33562	5739	16921	2516
重 庆 Chongqing	323622	245879	153509	18543	53985	8759
四 川 Sichuan	770452	564469	327491	54849	142391	19062
贵 州 Guizhou	348304	241391	128172	21864	74039	8778
云 南 Yunnan	572630	405370	227263	23729	119998	15742
西 藏 Tibet	13611	9515	6666	485	1856	282
陕 西 Shaanxi	718196	486141	283773	41944	116615	18682
甘 肃 Gansu	152865	105389	74438	8184	15767	3585
青 海 Qinghai	40449	28572	18386	1630	6352	493
宁 夏 Ningxia	39110	27208	15062	2074	8187	720
新 疆 Xinjiang	195063	130991	71710	10124	42627	3993

情况(镇乡结合区)(一)

and Others (County-town Transitional Area)(1)

单位：平方米

unit：m^2

	行政办公用房 Administrative		生活用房 Residential and Welfare		其他用房 for Other Purposes	校舍面积中 of the Floor Space	
图书室 Picture Books	合计 Total	其中：教师办公室 of Which：Office	合计 Total	其中：厨房 of Which：Kitchen		危房面积 Floor Space of Dilapidated Buildings	当年新增 New Added in Current Year
596904	**1506546**	**982727**	**2046580**	**948758**	**2390275**	**108630**	**1119336**
1217	5674	3258	8880	5425	14016		7263
1861	7423	4981	13117	6150	10259		244
49881	137794	94791	142782	64223	175089	4872	85153
15804	54184	41408	46089	18469	67022	5843	18794
2351	11359	6472	13251	6331	19320		14306
6472	14148	9026	16003	9895	20990	205	3267
1855	5970	3459	9170	4574	10583		5279
3229	8128	5253	13274	6778	11325	180	7389
1814	15256	5403	20730	8512	24884		12047
41769	107053	63762	151060	76668	243527	2200	73410
40496	111466	65890	188883	94688	245510		61277
14365	31824	24006	35927	16571	42793	4028	24267
14216	44755	30054	66018	32927	100267	312	49940
23484	45113	31524	68383	34150	65451	4337	27921
66710	172442	120300	191525	89674	306210	2420	148627
62530	153505	103931	155849	77185	163176	4549	72123
21104	44228	29765	83745	40134	58356	11130	41487
54110	123965	81091	173833	74979	153808	4099	63574
64491	133736	74245	233190	85082	278844	1350	68378
12718	22506	16531	54844	27937	42451	4992	11681
3311	5206	2964	11219	4526	6636	240	1634
11083	20985	14316	30770	16364	25988	1660	13705
20676	48074	31379	84570	42269	73339	1485	105777
8538	21790	13816	43456	18107	41667		62980
18638	42161	24493	66340	28960	58759	42962	38366
226	1798	1282	1594	976	704		1091
25127	80477	55955	77554	37399	74024	1535	44392
3415	16800	11894	15068	6148	15608	7887	31332
1711	2993	2213	4020	1868	4864	2344	2510
1165	2554	1508	4581	2089	4767		497
2537	13179	7757	20855	9700	30038		20625

幼儿园校舍及其他

Statistics of Kindergarten Buildings

地区 Region	校舍建筑面积 Floor Space	教学及辅助用房 Teaching & Assistant Buildings				
		合计 Total	其中 of Which			
			活动室 Recreational	洗手间 Toilet	睡眠室 Bed Room	保健室 Health Care
总　计 Total	**37083993**	**25785027**	**15566482**	**2140072**	**5691441**	**1135703**
北　京 Beijing	182551	101438	54993	12423	27196	3366
天　津 Tianjin	211960	153104	104903	14712	22389	6757
河　北 Hebei	2626174	1843322	1278256	107930	265280	92374
山　西 Shanxi	963035	645246	452500	49063	74590	29176
内蒙古 Inner Mongolia	301590	185076	106144	17414	46173	6587
辽　宁 Liaoning	688782	482115	284332	37809	108132	24460
吉　林 Jilin	260941	177925	103711	13397	44995	7870
黑龙江 Heilongjiang	500476	346557	200357	28221	83435	17957
上　海 Shanghai	159160	91339	55506	10030	20732	2269
江　苏 Jiangsu	1244759	890275	511830	81169	224028	32014
浙　江 Zhejiang	1950966	1295121	718245	122952	358945	44088
安　徽 Anhui	1259205	914323	596093	76721	148984	42818
福　建 Fujian	1315983	881424	553831	89646	180764	27793
江　西 Jiangxi	1782071	1281283	753582	108745	295003	59209
山　东 Shandong	3648835	2626803	1821007	212107	368478	96402
河　南 Henan	3950979	2874886	1772699	259313	548112	131261
湖　北 Hubei	1561232	1096841	587329	104070	295799	52689
湖　南 Hunan	2628948	1819254	960872	163928	479930	110575
广　东 Guangdong	1920160	1263463	757899	91475	293011	47641
广　西 Guangxi	1519367	1101506	593497	88311	335501	40917
海　南 Hainan	130050	89186	45563	9432	26610	3870
重　庆 Chongqing	398368	279245	172734	23648	54210	14037
四　川 Sichuan	1486020	1074307	646804	119716	214278	42009
贵　州 Guizhou	863620	595938	322380	56730	161751	29827
云　南 Yunnan	1338364	911771	522601	54767	248869	43412
西　藏 Tibet	237666	138897	81500	14071	31161	6943
陕　西 Shaanxi	1009789	672558	391179	59331	148705	33897
甘　肃 Gansu	643145	413608	292932	25226	59616	16831
青　海 Qinghai	268542	175855	116616	11669	34637	7460
宁　夏 Ningxia	115987	77289	44057	8384	18829	3567
新　疆 Xinjiang	1915268	1285072	662530	67662	471298	57627

情况(乡村)(一)
and Others (Rural Area) (1)

单位：平方米
unit：m^2

	行政办公用房 Administrative		生活用房 Residential and Welfare		其他用房 for Other Purposes	校舍面积中 of the Floor Space	
图书室 Picture Books	合计 Total	其中：教师办公室 of Which：Office	合计 Total	其中：厨房 of Which：Kitchen		危房面积 Floor Space of Dilapidated Buildings	当年新增 New Added in Current Year
1251329	**3113584**	**2233306**	**4178133**	**1972816**	**4007249**	**392443**	**2414197**
3460	19017	9234	26488	12147	35608		55853
4343	18751	13181	20242	9231	19863		5072
99482	251623	197771	219377	90954	311852	16114	103973
39917	122263	96529	94200	37344	101326	6659	41972
8758	28109	19468	45051	19794	43354	556	20555
27382	63996	43763	72790	42756	69881	2717	24243
7952	21904	15083	24736	13172	36376	1061	14912
16587	42920	33232	66428	33118	44571	1304	43510
2802	12681	4657	15235	7487	39905		18911
41234	82365	51028	118717	62157	153402		81982
50891	140221	88208	235425	121272	280199		89308
49707	109029	79932	122851	57016	113002	4948	132969
29390	99058	70112	152022	65117	183479	321	71854
64744	136428	98248	219131	105711	145229	22958	51361
128809	334475	247643	296372	135168	391185	5910	205745
163501	380775	273660	385399	205569	309919	13649	169019
56954	113136	77003	195015	93895	156240	7582	128219
103949	236975	167871	329158	155243	243561	14059	67396
73437	139636	87289	268509	93101	248552	540	60065
43280	81618	62776	210635	115554	125608	23947	59271
3711	7802	5655	17302	8241	15760	340	6930
14616	32407	24741	47550	22097	39166	2056	11586
51500	101334	75200	196447	86030	113932	4797	227113
25250	68964	47934	102801	50134	95917		190365
42122	95406	67434	198130	81101	133057	180718	107743
5222	20549	16310	48005	16107	30215	1604	98977
39446	129065	93642	115312	60693	92854	3727	67393
19003	88793	70350	71639	26953	69105	63686	106644
5473	21509	17284	39804	16193	31374	2259	30249
2452	10864	7140	13309	6934	14525	800	17340
25955	101911	70928	210053	122527	318232	10131	103667

幼儿园办学条件(总计)(二)
Statistics of Kindergarten Buildings and Others (Total)(2)

地　区 Region	占地面积(平方米) Areas of School Sites (m^2)			图书(册) Books & Magazines in Libraries (volume)	数字资源 (GB) Digital Resources
	合计 Total	其中 of Which			
		绿化用地面积 Green Areas	运动场地面积 Sports Areas		
总　计 Total	**392967185**	**65117166**	**131194736**	**218970675**	**38352308.24**
北　京 Beijing	5378805	903325	1877876	3988534	644469.37
天　津 Tianjin	2811753	390460	1061333	1276632	202095.64
河　北 Hebei	24610879	2829109	8798908	12360385	1029705.18
山　西 Shanxi	9953565	1056209	3642258	4911849	265577.57
内蒙古 Inner Mongolia	7753867	1038288	2593115	2423259	370607.91
辽　宁 Liaoning	11546378	1582202	4667085	5875836	818029.05
吉　林 Jilin	4925038	702727	1889396	2365920	824766.59
黑龙江 Heilongjiang	7997653	1045470	3029803	1914570	156463.62
上　海 Shanghai	7642815	2149783	2055687	2843965	1280938.24
江　苏 Jiangsu	30846497	6876351	11553616	24227326	928133.56
浙　江 Zhejiang	19915307	3871650	6919253	14915856	965581.98
安　徽 Anhui	12464648	1891321	3750660	6944836	927703.55
福　建 Fujian	10915946	1748161	4071025	5088215	444372.73
江　西 Jiangxi	11665166	1636795	3665451	5602171	684609.54
山　东 Shandong	40724568	7276869	15153071	17269770	1101403.94
河 南 Henan	29785412	4229879	9609408	14284493	3432375.24
湖　北 Hubei	14384501	2980502	4292706	7378215	694275.37
湖　南 Hunan	18559559	2708484	5032240	12291023	1170186.27
广　东 Guangdong	33090436	6827802	10276998	24396257	15305235.00
广　西 Guangxi	8716699	1219993	2894346	4785367	798708.21
海　南 Hainan	2422067	477471	742948	1774431	136921.90
重　庆 Chongqing	5970436	877569	2094950	4436589	817046.48
四　川 Sichuan	14633471	1946465	4705440	12472889	846323.20
贵　州 Guizhou	6749446	926063	2267184	3526677	355762.70
云　南 Yunnan	9171924	1495743	2732913	5736317	636531.11
西　藏 Tibet	1289871	189671	196438	161059	8285.00
陕　西 Shaanxi	13245825	1790136	4153441	9362315	1965232.01
甘　肃 Gansu	5883922	723574	1994347	3008804	356999.18
青　海 Qinghai	3180013	318182	760745	460492	89974.85
宁　夏 Ningxia	1992592	280057	679275	740154	74429.00
新　疆 Xinjiang	14738126	3126855	4032820	2146469	1019564.25

幼儿园办学条件(城区)(二)

Statistics of Kindergarten Buildings and Others (Urban Area) (2)

地　区 Region	占地面积(平方米) Areas of School Sites (m^2)			图书(册) Books & Magazines in Libraries (volume)	数字资源 (GB) Digital Resources
	合计 Total	其中 of Which			
		绿化用地面积 Green Areas	运动场地面积 Sports Areas		
总　计 Total	**140052343**	**24816576**	**47692703**	**100194643**	**23472420.88**
北　京 Beijing	4102003	666628	1451041	3382419	561969.67
天　津 Tianjin	1428619	203472	511390	772229	184976.64
河　北 Hebei	4566926	524035	1600375	3397554	417585.94
山　西 Shanxi	3092237	353983	1114742	1908817	153927.86
内蒙古 Inner Mongolia	2486939	342255	864200	1188728	315328.65
辽　宁 Liaoning	6037048	882698	2260372	3805622	608065.29
吉　林 Jilin	2334122	367242	875945	1293331	638614.59
黑龙江 Heilongjiang	2770014	342900	973885	868299	108711.60
上　海 Shanghai	6019965	1667322	1601715	2302541	1082266.85
江　苏 Jiangsu	13278469	3112216	5108639	11389372	618646.65
浙　江 Zhejiang	8691754	1741093	2970383	7149798	580732.09
安　徽 Anhui	3265659	561050	998172	2759315	512096.30
福　建 Fujian	4343560	669069	1588799	2464836	264990.06
江　西 Jiangxi	2727945	422697	878788	1636146	245194.83
山　东 Shandong	13777476	2280790	5006444	8576133	741793.43
河　南 Henan	8047285	1174153	2802122	4891414	2009020.77
湖　北 Hubei	4874074	954138	1567956	3021975	417985.24
湖　南 Hunan	5000309	768368	1398815	4766523	782862.80
广　东 Guangdong	20254615	4237183	6478476	15365364	10491990.00
广　西 Guangxi	2561929	411817	906407	1693649	323045.64
海　南 Hainan	908702	151581	298659	941454	69299.50
重　庆 Chongqing	2520813	368173	825725	2058612	532880.80
四　川 Sichuan	4924619	722675	1542669	4639058	382223.40
贵　州 Guizhou	1445387	159511	491328	1382364	88124.47
云　南 Yunnan	2400759	466939	743185	2278778	411010.70
西　藏 Tibet	114021	21823	21970	50010	979.00
陕　西 Shaanxi	3454548	491437	1195503	3163071	322116.05
甘　肃 Gansu	1358053	173849	505351	1404493	131921.70
青　海 Qinghai	368240	61102	105860	229296	75291.40
宁　夏 Ningxia	770158	105697	288360	376165	56262.80
新　疆 Xinjiang	2126095	410680	715427	1037277	342506.16

幼儿园办学条件(城乡结合区)(二)

Statistics of Kindergarten Buildings and Others (Urban-rural Transitional Area)(2)

地 区 Region	占地面积(平方米) Areas of School Sites (m^2)			图书(册) Books & Magazines in Libraries (volume)	数字资源 (GB) Digital Resources
	合计 Total	其中 of Which			
		绿化用地面积 Green Areas	运动场地面积 Sports Areas		
总 计 Total	**25051029**	**4599247**	**8539896**	**15252436**	**6891437.73**
北 京 Beijing	372839	68694	118331	169777	28581.90
天 津 Tianjin	83921	7753	25894	51723	6031.00
河 北 Hebei	997377	122318	367090	587567	58701.20
山 西 Shanxi	535051	60597	210318	259474	16879.65
内蒙古 Inner Mongolia	117220	20423	45956	36892	4760.00
辽 宁 Liaoning	558280	76055	217538	250667	49737.70
吉 林 Jilin	175417	36482	60475	54954	91501.00
黑龙江 Heilongjiang	212135	24615	78619	39143	9066.00
上 海 Shanghai	538124	139012	141483	173072	58940.30
江 苏 Jiangsu	1401239	327617	529384	1034829	43926.11
浙 江 Zhejiang	1880325	353298	638258	1500419	156157.70
安 徽 Anhui	417422	63440	128429	344635	37629.20
福 建 Fujian	817162	119779	291188	347405	39928.29
江 西 Jiangxi	420794	53133	131633	216768	45104.10
山 东 Shandong	4133631	738483	1585733	1922456	153544.85
河 南 Henan	1497217	227823	510839	716633	223091.35
湖 北 Hubei	665583	131342	212278	352666	65488.60
湖 南 Hunan	725776	113526	209410	789078	60772.50
广 东 Guangdong	6706775	1477093	2107394	4473224	5406397.00
广 西 Guangxi	339509	46741	115879	196730	47382.74
海 南 Hainan	58933	12966	21038	82745	6016.00
重 庆 Chongqing	221242	31104	72709	143556	62182.00
四 川 Sichuan	643380	94587	197351	532124	31442.40
贵 州 Guizhou	167105	13731	70597	123563	7928.30
云 南 Yunnan	315281	66247	104830	301045	100734.00
西 藏 Tibet	3600	200	456	10500	
陕 西 Shaanxi	567936	99904	192630	409379	31775.70
甘 肃 Gansu	79419	8455	33348	34454	3746.00
青 海 Qinghai	32027	3561	10868	17803	8943.00
宁 夏 Ningxia	97414	8999	35691	30072	12585.80
新 疆 Xinjiang	268895	51269	74249	49083	22463.34

幼儿园办学条件(镇区)(二)
Statistics of Kindergarten Buildings and Others (Counties & Towns Area) (2)

地 区 Region	占地面积(平方米) Areas of School Sites (m^2)			图书(册) Books & Magazines in Libraries (volume)	数字资源 (GB) Digital Resources
	合计 Total	其中 of Which			
		绿化用地面积 Green Areas	运动场地面积 Sports Areas		
总 计 Total	**144485657**	**23435359**	**47703678**	**80781764**	**10316227.46**
北 京 Beijing	817724	146546	294468	464810	61636.00
天 津 Tianjin	660863	98235	257891	262987	10742.70
河 北 Hebei	8159969	934114	2866637	4285488	429624.00
山 西 Shanxi	3618729	370139	1310195	1908746	73352.41
内蒙古 Inner Mongolia	3814440	517119	1278459	1066800	44975.30
辽 宁 Liaoning	2872793	359702	1203033	1276423	115322.02
吉 林 Jilin	1657209	195511	626641	826148	150813.00
黑龙江 Heilongjiang	2972602	375204	1130110	742179	33079.92
上 海 Shanghai	1367055	407810	384659	457476	167140.19
江 苏 Jiangsu	14607506	3159983	5393454	10763034	269656.51
浙 江 Zhejiang	7744599	1507357	2671561	5653439	263848.19
安 徽 Anhui	5222530	782783	1639364	2671321	281568.05
福 建 Fujian	4008357	614685	1543600	1849770	137105.87
江 西 Jiangxi	5319492	738456	1626057	2781566	338512.11
山 东 Shandong	13479633	2504502	4805289	5101502	203964.96
河 南 Henan	10529271	1503570	3247994	5044073	794421.82
湖 北 Hubei	5851160	1235773	1678606	2935521	190446.42
湖 南 Hunan	8065080	1132177	2190722	4915147	256727.47
广 东 Guangdong	8832662	1768828	2613726	6882083	3601372.00
广 西 Guangxi	3563383	459286	1183999	2002071	338155.06
海 南 Hainan	1179869	243309	358792	716340	56303.40
重 庆 Chongqing	2585436	388620	933205	1943324	166352.08
四 川 Sichuan	6608614	853856	2111360	5778364	296387.30
贵 州 Guizhou	3244689	439541	1062310	1618903	159953.93
云 南 Yunnan	3303906	505743	999776	2092646	141330.31
西 藏 Tibet	400325	65057	59378	39361	2658.00
陕 西 Shaanxi	6697775	850364	2025925	4504575	1530552.89
甘 肃 Gansu	1947497	222066	688802	1110308	118421.03
青 海 Qinghai	713653	74543	167831	110934	5892.85
宁 夏 Ningxia	698459	94900	237319	309698	16519.50
新 疆 Xinjiang	3940377	885580	1112515	666727	59392.17

幼儿园办学条件(镇乡结合区)(二)

Statistics of Kindergarten Buildings and Others (County-town Transitional Area) (2)

地 区 Region	占地面积(平方米) Areas of School Sites (m^2)			图书(册) Books & Magazines in Libraries (volume)	数字资源(GB) Digital Resources
	合计 Total	其中 of Which			
		绿化用地面积 Green Areas	运动场地面积 Sports Areas		
总 计 Total	**42071204**	**6781857**	**13878453**	**21899073**	**3326228.06**
北 京 Beijing	187302	33477	55903	72326	10735.00
天 津 Tianjin	265500	34736	110649	100771	3529.50
河 北 Hebei	4369369	486688	1517962	2187892	136595.00
山 西 Shanxi	1096502	98357	418399	570149	20834.30
内蒙古 Inner Mongolia	317518	43619	113146	66987	4031.00
辽 宁 Liaoning	484810	66398	186396	250386	19057.00
吉 林 Jilin	226000	26902	81132	139811	1697.00
黑龙江 Heilongjiang	280248	37009	111116	61108	4373.81
上 海 Shanghai	273298	71905	84237	108006	22049.18
江 苏 Jiangsu	3711934	800730	1373676	2488077	92792.50
浙 江 Zhejiang	2724447	468987	894560	2029321	93893.84
安 徽 Anhui	935153	136405	290099	503529	37559.00
福 建 Fujian	1024799	152862	382647	458113	28115.35
江 西 Jiangxi	1100884	143665	357077	472143	36528.00
山 东 Shandong	6315135	1186742	2248001	2151310	89033.34
河 南 Henan	4055457	599156	1279094	1656621	285016.90
湖 北 Hubei	1330327	294071	370545	664578	36294.50
湖 南 Hunan	3052096	393021	801532	1372202	62271.47
广 东 Guangdong	3013496	615102	912486	2433140	1979234.00
广 西 Guangxi	628488	75725	201290	256335	44704.10
海 南 Hainan	157702	40339	48981	109955	8942.00
重 庆 Chongqing	546340	85606	201550	369913	40115.00
四 川 Sichuan	1342611	188594	417860	1083659	92215.00
贵 州 Guizhou	631588	91010	239227	294047	17981.90
云 南 Yunnan	957698	141113	311447	645836	52176.90
西 藏 Tibet	34610	3192	5784	2761	6.00
陕 西 Shaanxi	1748793	223829	512953	1075915	83016.10
甘 肃 Gansu	333314	49532	125547	154420	10234.50
青 海 Qinghai	121219	13121	36127	20392	1402.00
宁 夏 Ningxia	106555	19123	36136	32584	4036.00
新 疆 Xinjiang	698011	160841	152894	66786	7757.87

幼儿园办学条件(乡村)(二)

Statistics of Kindergarten Buildings and Others (Rural Area) (2)

地 区 Region	占地面积(平方米) Areas of School Sites (m^2)			图书(册) Books & Magazines in Libraries (volume)	数字资源 (GB) Digital Resources
	合计 Total	其中 of Which			
		绿化用地面积 Green Areas	运动场地面积 Sports Areas		
总 计 Total	**108429185**	**16865231**	**35798355**	**37994268**	**4563659.90**
北 京 Beijing	459078	90151	132367	141305	20863.70
天 津 Tianjin	722271	88753	292052	241416	6376.30
河 北 Hebei	11883984	1370960	4331896	4677343	182495.24
山 西 Shanxi	3242599	332087	1217321	1094286	38297.30
内蒙古 Inner Mongolia	1452488	178914	450456	167731	10303.96
辽 宁 Liaoning	2636537	339802	1203680	793791	94641.74
吉 林 Jilin	933707	139974	386810	246441	35339
黑龙江 Heilongjiang	2255037	327366	925808	304092	14672.10
上 海 Shanghai	255795	74651	69313	83948	31531.20
江 苏 Jiangsu	2960522	604152	1051523	2074920	39830.40
浙 江 Zhejiang	3478954	623200	1277309	2112619	121001.70
安 徽 Anhui	3976459	547488	1113124	1514200	134039.20
福 建 Fujian	2564029	464407	938626	773609	42276.80
江 西 Jiangxi	3617729	475642	1160606	1184459	100902.60
山 东 Shandong	13467459	2491577	5341338	3592135	155645.55
河 南 Henan	11208856	1552156	3559292	4349006	628932.65
湖 北 Hubei	3659267	790591	1046144	1420719	85843.71
湖 南 Hunan	5494170	807939	1442703	2609353	130596
广 东 Guangdong	4003159	821791	1184796	2148810	1211873
广 西 Guangxi	2591387	348890	803940	1089647	137507.51
海 南 Hainan	333496	82581	85497	116637	11319
重 庆 Chongqing	864187	120776	336020	434653	117813.60
四 川 Sichuan	3100238	369934	1051411	2055467	167712.50
贵 州 Guizhou	2059370	327011	713546	525410	107684.30
云 南 Yunnan	3467259	523061	989952	1364893	84190.10
西 藏 Tibet	775525	102791	115090	71688	4648
陕 西 Shaanxi	3093502	448335	932013	1694669	112563.07
甘 肃 Gansu	2578372	327659	800194	494003	106656.45
青 海 Qinghai	2098120	182537	487054	120262	8790.60
宁 夏 Ningxia	523975	79460	153596	54291	1646.70
新 疆 Xinjiang	8671654	1830595	2204878	442465	617665.92

第二部分
Part Ⅱ

办 学 条 件
PHYSICAL FACILITIES

教育基本建设投资
Capital Construction Investment in the Educational Sector

教育基本建设

Data on the Completion of Capital Construction

学校类别 Type of School	投资合计 Total Investment Completed in the Curent year (10,000 yuan)	本年完成投资按 Investment by Source of			
		国家预算内 Budgetary Allocation			
		合计 Total	中央 Central	省级 Local	合计 Total
总　计 Total	**29894421**	**21239830**	**4485910**	**16753920**	**7972931**
高等教育学校 Higher Education Schools	8420909	2245594	292059	1953535	6009059
中等职业学校 Secondary Vocational Schools	1930228	1552064	263688	1288377	345264
普通中学 Regular Secondary Schools	9361045	8225321	1621561	6603759	878555
职业初中 Vocational Junior Secondary Schools	19506	16568	2604	13963	2938
小学 Primary Schools	6787572	6268548	1506538	4762010	359635
特殊教育学校 Special Education Schools	128363	125534	27294	98240	2147
幼儿园 Kindergartens	2449232	2117450	657196	1460254	273155
其他 Other	797566	688752	114970	573782	102179

投资完成情况(总计)

Investment in the Educational Sector(Regional Aggregates)

资金来源分(万元) Fund (10,000 yuan)			本年竣工建筑面积(平方米) Building Floor Area Completed (m²)			
自筹资金 Self-raised Fund		其他 Other Sources				
其中 of Which						
学校自筹 Raised by School	个人捐资 Individual Donations		合计 Total	教学及辅助用房 Teaching and Administrative	行政办公用房 Adm. Building Rooms for Other Purpose	其他用房 Others
7603228	**369703**	**681660**	**138452396**	**83309854**	**4167346**	**50975196**
5706129	302930	166257	25454292	12892782	717087	11844423
328334	16929	32900	7184297	4339058	311109	2534130
856006	22550	257169	47256954	26445747	1575204	19236003
2938	0	0	37301	28083	500	8718
342348	17287	159389	36642427	23367738	1135049	12139640
2147	0	682	455706	288890	16818	149998
263281	9874	58628	17981761	13765353	336563	3879845
102045	134	6635	3439658	2182203	75016	1182439

教育基本建设

Data on the Completion of Capital Construction

学校类别 Type of School	投资合计（万人）Total Investment Completed in the Curent year (10,000 yuan)	本年完成投资按 Investment by Source of			
		国家预算内 Budgetary Allocation			
		合计 Total	中央 Central	省级 Local	合计 Total
合　计 Total	**29894421**	**21239830**	**4485910**	**16753920**	**7972931**
北　京 Beijing	649296	594289	17255	577034	55008
天　津 Tianjin	398529	183162	12800	170362	214867
河　北 Hebei	556679	480804	125398	355405	60218
山　西 Shanxi	632729	187832	55427	132405	430841
内蒙古 Inner Mongolia	630082	461861	48429	413432	158179
辽　宁 Liaoning	706570	461713	29744	431969	242933
大　连 Dalian	98287	96857	0	96857	1430
吉　林 Jilin	361708	207891	50210	157681	142682
黑龙江 Heilongjiang	438424	331862	58566	273296	100451
上　海 Shanghai	1026080	587522	7142	580380	426724
江　苏 Jiangsu	2360043	1851095	4982	1846113	413529
浙　江 Zhejiang	1565112	1202962	7163	1195799	341173
宁　波 Ningbo	240131	216801	0	216801	23330
安　徽 Anhui	1286524	959774	305868	653906	325539
福　建 Fujian	552920	302602	17993	284609	208542
厦　门 Xiamen	106299	104162	0	104162	2137
江　西 Jiangxi	892787	742736	214171	528565	141537
山　东 Shandong	1671478	1146295	102277	1044018	415215
青　岛 Qingdao	276821	268983	0	268983	5258
河　南 henan	1810401	927804	402484	525319	841219
湖　北 Hubei	1007892	782417	228316	554101	206121
湖　南 Hunan	735260	559663	201200	358463	171772
广　东 Guangdong	1720439	1295264	7067	1288197	358761
深　圳 Shenzhen	325413	318265	600	317665	7148
广　西 Guangxi	1283127	903077	375585	527493	347315
海　南 Hainan	407215	332227	64457	267771	74988
重　庆 Chongqing	702530	418129	149126	269003	258873
四　川 Sichuan	1116070	828221	389322	438899	257347
贵　州 guizhou	2023201	1435053	436290	998763	570738
云　南 Yunnan	357602	159940	73823	86117	186769
西　藏 Tibet	234759	232671	213744	18927	2029
陕　西 Shaanxi	1252945	754681	162412	592269	473847
甘　肃 Gansu	584686	450567	222602	227965	132785
青　海 Qinghai	456599	416641	61251	355390	39958
宁　夏 Ningxia	307743	270619	89650	180969	37124
新　疆 Xinjiang	1035302	687076	290740	396336	292250
新疆生产建设兵团 The Xinjiang Producation and Construction Corps	82738	78314	59817	18497	4297

投资完成情况
Investment in the Educational Sector

资金来源分(万元) Fund (10,000 yuan)			本年竣工建筑面积(平方米) Building Floor Area Completed (m^2)			
自筹资金 Self-raised Fund		其他 Other Sources	合计 Total	教学及辅助用房 Teaching and Administrative	行政办公用房 Adm. Building Rooms for Other Purpose	其他用房 Others
其中 of Which						
学校自筹 Raised by School	个人捐资 Individual Donations					
7603228	**369703**	**681660**	**138452396**	**83309854**	**4167346**	**50975196**
55008	0	0	800814	450260	57269	293285
214867	0	500	761160	445046	72087	244027
56577	3641	15658	3540013	2416712	103361	1019940
421741	9100	14057	1042716	475044	3000	564672
158179	0	10041	1923374	1272325	47965	603084
242933	0	1925	3193409	1896338	99105	1197966
1430	0	0	592408	393746	37446	161216
142682	0	11135	2059823	1389573	74149	596101
100351	100	6112	2066553	1612848	85783	367922
426724	0	11834	1695039	1354129	232440	108470
413476	53	95419	8786215	6703305	397536	1685374
341173	0	20977	4337865	2817656	201611	1318598
22585	745	0	457367	335886	23088	98393
325539	0	1211	7109624	4399903	188622	2521099
208542	0	41776	2506663	1847713	40881	618069
2137	0	0	643794	323472	3620	316702
139414	2123	8514	5871764	3727243	121700	2022821
414055	1160	109968	9533260	6980043	326098	2227119
5258	0	2580	1011704	703139	120439	188126
784459	56760	41379	10528635	5427357	389554	4711724
205668	453	19354	5893414	3793271	147696	1952447
171772	0	3825	4722615	2832712	58575	1831328
327603	31158	66414	6822706	4265784	232225	2324697
7148	0	0	478164	388913	35419	53832
305600	41716	32734	11492598	5845719	127760	5519119
74988	0	0	1541679	948016	45210	548453
251773	7100	25529	2774543	1302708	86504	1385331
257311	36	30503	6496600	3668974	151926	2675700
570716	22	17410	9698715	5202343	135323	4361049
186769	0	10893	2111106	1142087	59896	909123
2029	0	60	838454	382249	4733	451472
370697	103150	24418	6504878	3041008	198914	3264956
106099	26686	1333	2689289	1588494	75915	1024880
39958	0	0	1351192	623418	65728	662046
37124	0	0	1052937	672040	22494	358403
206550	85701	55976	4769620	2141626	78941	2549053
4297	0	127	751686	498754	14333	238599

第三部分
Part Ⅲ

科学研究活动及其他
SCIENTIFIC RESEARCH ACTIVITES & OTHER

一、自然科学与技术
Natural Science and Technology

	教学与科研人员 Personnel Engaged in S&T Activities		研究与发展人员 R & D Personnel	
	合计 Total	其中:科学家和工程师 of Which: Scientists & Engineers	合计 Total	其中:科学家和工程师 of Which: Scientists & Engineers
总　计 Total	**890798**	**855522**	**359884**	**351886**
按学校规格分 Breakdown by Category of HEIs				
"211"及省部共建高等学校 Key HEIs	310860	295391	154073	149278
其他本科院校 Ordinary Degree Level HEIs	502066	484791	195332	192250
高等专科学校 Short – cycle HEIs	77872	75340	10479	10358
按学校隶属分 Breakdown by Control				
部委院校 HEIs under Other Central Ministries	31265	30011	19578	19216
教育部直属院校 HEIs under Ministry of Education	223364	211313	110360	106635
地方院校 HEIs under Local Govermments	636169	614198	229946	226035
按学校类型分 Breakdown by Type of HEIs				
综合大学 Comprehensive Universities	274294	260528	115718	112184
工科院校 Engineering	279218	272380	120224	118692
农林院校 Agriculture	49293	47127	22146	21586
医药院校 Medicine & Pharmacy	212212	201651	69819	67918
师范院校 Teachers Training	59542	58093	25797	25400
其他院校 Others	16239	15743	6180	6106

科技人力情况
in Regular HEIs

单位：人

unit: person

研究与发展全时人员 R & D FTEs (Full-time Equivalents)		R&D 成果应用及科技服务人员 R & D Personnel		R&D 成果应用及科技服务全时人员 R & D FTEs (Full-time Equivalents)	
合计 Total	其中:科学家和工程师 of Which: Scientists & Engineers	合计 Total	其中:科学家和工程师 of Which: Scientists & Engineers	合计 Total	其中:科学家和工程师 of Which: Scientists & Engineers
215908	**211129**	**44187**	**43366**	**26498**	**25998**
92439	89565	24282	23692	14574	14214
117182	115348	18086	17874	10836	10710
6287	6216	1819	1800	1088	1074
11745	11529	2194	2133	1315	1280
66215	63983	18490	18063	11098	10838
137948	135617	23503	23170	14085	13880
69421	67306	16839	16354	10105	9811
72127	71215	20437	20221	12243	12114
13282	12949	3071	3018	1850	1813
41883	40749	1278	1255	764	751
15486	15244	2143	2102	1286	1261
3709	3666	419	416	250	248

	拨　入 Revenues			
	合　计 Total	政府资金 Government Funds	企事业单位委托 Contract Research Fund	其　他 Others
总　计 Total	**122269046**	**72793677**	**42041437**	**7433932**
按学校规格分 Breakdown by Category of HEIs				
"211"及省部共建高等学校 Key HEIs	83661332	50841503	30036310	2783519
其他本科院校 Ordinary Degree Level HEIs	37658270	21442864	11744397	4471009
高等专科学校 Short – cycle HEIs	949444	509310	260730	179404
按学校隶属分 Breakdown by Control				
部委院校 HEIs under Other Central Ministries	14878913	9340747	5274445	263721
教育部直属院校 HEIs under Ministry of Education	61064021	36897308	22106328	2060385
地方院校 HEIs under Local Govermments	46326112	26555622	14660664	5109826
按学校类型分 Breakdown by Type of HEIs				
综合大学 Comprehensive Universities	39724883	25620273	11880559	2224051
工科院校 Engineering	61697611	31351457	27405514	2940640
农林院校 Agriculture	7787924	6042523	1368006	377395
医药院校 Medicine & Pharmacy	6622592	5389257	322825	910510
师范院校 Teachers Training	5503261	3793237	863104	846920
其他院校 Others	932775	596930	201429	134416

科技经费情况
in Regular HEIs

单位:千元
unit: 1,000 yuan

支 出 Expenditures				
合 计 Total	劳务费 Personnel Costs	业务费 Non-Personnel Expenses	转拨外单位经费 Expenses on Extermal Services	其 他 Others
111816319	**2863223**	**3049897**	**9522205**	**93184879**
76027052	2392474	2388617	7693717	61651186
34898466	463043	641486	1793093	30765960
890801	7706	19794	35395	767733
13309789	186106	390799	1223135	10918774
55349271	2026866	1969165	6184864	44038781
43157259	650251	689933	2114206	38227324
36122258	1320516	734091	3215604	30045935
56543111	1064638	2068672	4830326	46428755
7363353	286445	174575	940943	6022657
5912679	129289	36832	379343	5288488
5017035	60088	34487	150090	4603039
857883	2247	1240	5899	796005

普通高等学校研究与

Statistics of R & D Projects and

	科技课题 R & D Projects			出版科技专著(部) No. of Mono-graphs Published
	课题数(项) No. of Projects	投入人数 No. of Input of S&D Manpower	实际支出(千元) Actual Exp. (1,000 yuan)	
总　计 Total	**458307**	**269307**	**79036497**	**11493**
按学校规格分 Breakdown by Category of HEIs				
"211"及省部共建高等学校 Key HEIs	230835	118894	56111626	3155
其他本科院校 Ordinary Degree Level HEIs	215775	142230	22452470	5858
高等专科学校 Short－cycle HEIs	11697	8183	472401	2480
按学校隶属分 Breakdown by Control				
部委院校 HEIs under Other Central Ministries	28178	14512	9719249	469
教育部直属院校 HEIs under Ministry of Education	172578	85892	41046552	2139
地方院校 HEIs under Local Govermments	257551	168904	28270696	8885
按学校类型分 Breakdown by Type of HEIs				
综合大学 Comprehensive Universities	141008	88355	24770552	2456
工科院校 Engineering	188341	93747	42617589	4778
农林院校 Agriculture	34978	16808	5222542	1040
医药院校 Medicine & Pharmacy	51984	47385	3072131	2318
师范院校 Teachers Training	35483	18620	2904820	625
其他院校 Others	6513	4392	448863	276

发展课题、成果情况
Achievements in Regular HEIs

单位:千元
unit: 1,000 yuan

发表学士论文(篇) No. of Papers Published	成果获奖 Achieverment Awards		技术转让 Techonlogical Transfer		知识产权授权数 No. of Awarded	专利出售 Income from License Arrangements	
	合计 Total	其中:国家奖 of Which: National Awards	合同数 No. of Contracts	收入 Actual Revenues		项数 No. of Items	实现金额(千元) Income
808666	**5144**	**274**	**10534**	**2722576**	**79926**	**2310**	**751585**
377788	2619	216	5945	1931761	40447	1126	591226
394484	2466	58	4515	779272	34941	1142	159690
36394	59	0	74	11543	4538	42	669
44368	255	27	384	95215	5421	132	92483
279420	2010	177	4484	1635480	29498	778	453996
484878	2879	70	5666	991881	45007	1400	205106
255497	1458	96	3080	716476	22687	661	214108
309632	2172	131	5460	1628955	43808	1285	431415
51693	456	28	1290	217753	5364	152	49228
120105	767	12	147	80601	2335	21	22155
58487	225	6	434	60336	3890	165	25223
13252	66	1	123	18455	1842	26	9456

二、社会科学
Social Science

普通高等学校人文、
Professional Manpower in Regular HEIs in the

		学校数（所）No. of HEIs	社科活动人员（人）Personnel Engaged in Social Science Research (person)				
			合 计 Total	高 级 Senior	中 级 Middle	初级 Junior	其他人员 Others
总 计 Total		**1147**	**501198**	**192867**	**221987**	**81511**	**4833**
按学校隶属关系分 Breakdown by Control	教育部直属院校 HEIs under Ministry of Education	73	61813	33633	24225	3654	301
	其他部委院校 HEIs under Other Central Ministries	34	16004	7098	7097	1709	100
	地方院校 HEIs under Local Govermments	1040	423381	152136	190665	76148	4432
按学校规格分 Breakdown by Category of HEIs	本科院校 Regular HEIs	784	439405	176340	194075	65203	3787
	专科院校 Short-cycle HEIs	363	61793	16527	27912	16308	1046
按学校类型分 Breakdown by Type of HEIs	综合大学 Comprehensive Universities	232	139962	57473	59720	21399	1370
	理工农医院校 HEIs Science and Technology, Agriculture and Medicine	508	156460	55549	74562	24981	1368
	师范院校 Teachers Training	158	93498	36600	40121	15959	818
	语文院校 Languages	27	14138	5208	6513	2285	132
	财经院校 Finance and Economics	106	52566	20472	22520	8992	582
	政法院校 Political Science & Law	41	13857	6004	5798	1940	115
	体育院校 Physical Culture	18	6309	2529	2647	1036	97
	艺术院校 Art	42	15053	5170	6167	3473	243
	民族院校 Minorities	15	9355	3862	3939	1446	108

社会科学人力情况
Fields of the Humanities and Social Science

研究与发展人员(人) R & D Personnel (person)						研究与发展人员(人年) R & D Personnel (man/year)					
合计 Total	高级 Senior	中级 Middle	初级 Junior	其他人员 Others	研究生 Postgraduates	合计 Total	高级 Senior	中级 Middle	初级 Junior	其他人员 Others	研究生 Postgraduates
355501	**146803**	**123079**	**30518**	**5100**	**50001**	**85071.3**	**39324.1**	**28713.8**	**6401.6**	**919.9**	**9711.9**
75257	31133	15504	1826	1865	24929	19494.6	9891.8	4193.1	446.8	378.4	4584.5
12958	5463	4626	719	150	2000	3491.4	1579.9	1147.8	166.2	29.4	568.1
267286	110207	102949	27973	3085	23072	62085.3	27852.4	23372.9	5788.6	512.1	4559.3
331070	137886	111704	26641	4854	49985	80326.7	37479.8	26559.7	5699.9	877.2	9710.1
24431	8917	11375	3877	246	16	4744.6	1844.3	2154.1	701.7	42.7	1.8
108695	45435	33320	7610	2396	19934	27181.4	13115.6	8192	1637.8	463.6	3772.4
102719	39728	39532	9276	624	13559	24106.7	10083.7	8950.4	1903.8	104.7	3064.1
67574	28831	23738	6399	966	7640	15544.5	7408	5382.8	1332.5	171.3	1249.9
9751	3972	3847	1010	90	832	2249.2	1056.4	838.4	177.7	18.3	158.4
39909	17262	13690	3605	636	4716	9291.9	4443.2	3196.2	726.7	94.9	830.9
10093	4681	3258	788	147	1219	2265.3	1219.9	698.8	147.5	24.8	174.3
4994	1951	1542	497	67	937	1598.4	722.8	514.4	168.8	16.1	176.3
5626	2178	1913	788	51	696	1480.3	638.1	481.4	189.7	8.5	162.6
6140	2765	2239	545	123	468	1353.6	636.4	459.4	117.1	17.7	123

		学校数（所）No. Of HEIs	拨　入 Revenues						
			合计 Total	科研活动经费 Funds for R&D	科技活动人员工资 Personnel Costs	科研基建费 Capital Construction Funds for R&D	企事业单位委托项目经费 Contract Research Funds Provided by Ent. & Inst.	金融机构贷款 Loans Provided by Financial Inst.	自筹经费 Self-raised Fubds
总　计 Total		**1147**	**107831657**	**45997248.23**	**16182906.56**	**521788**	**28852785.59**	**67852.24**	**13822067.03**
按学校隶属关系分 Breakdown by Control	教育部直属院校 HEIs under Ministry of Education	73	44805146.99	21252884.85	3489050.57	22000	14503410.99	0	3917076.a88
	其他部委院校 HEIs under Other Central Ministries	34	4610003.3	1960303.53	689542.91	80000	936445.01	0	908826.92
	地方院校 HEIs under Local Govermments	1040	58416506.67	22784059.85	12004313.08	419788	13412929.59	67852.24	8996163.23
按学校规格分 Breakdown by Category of HEIs	本科院校 Regular HEIs	784	105428434.1	45360256.04	15186961.9	517534	28559697.43	67852.24	13368772.92
	专科院校 Short-cycle HEIs	363	2403222.87	636992.19	995944.66	4254	293088.16	0	453294.11
按学校类型分 Breakdown by Type of HEIs	综合大学 Comprehensive Universities	232	40377578.78	17499707.07	5164387.97	22646	11488631.46	1425	5024631.08
	理工农医院校 HEIs Science and Technology, Agriculture and Medicine	508	26060849.31	9850382.42	4431153.47	7370	8793280.4	800	2419571.8
	师范院校 Teachers Training	158	17405921.74	7196876.47	3010893.01	103800	4007571.61	0	2764460.57
	语文院校 Languages	27	2722933.03	891995.93	442806.81	32000	488749.49	0	757844.97
	财经院校 Finance and Economics	106	11387420.19	5269748.4	1892415.33	54500	2330649.51	65627.24	1698361.91
	政法院校 Political Science & Law	41	3118769.71	1709758.12	458307.91	40158	345718.53	0	479234.51
	体育院校 Physical Culture	18	1637366.29	980181.18	263148.7	120900	121799.8	0	148377.61
	艺术院校 Art	42	3918690.52	1980804.59	271782.76	140414	1211668.78	0	276281.39
	民族院校 Minorities	15	1202127.39	617794.05	248010.6	0	64716.01	0	253303.19

学研究与发展经费情况
Expenditure in Regular HEIs

单位:百元
unit: 100 Yuan

国外资金 Foreign Funds	其他收入 Others Revenues	支出 Expenditures									转拨给外单位经费 Extra-mural Exp.
		合计 Total	内部支出 Intramural Expenditures								
			小计 Subtotal	科研人员费 Personnel Costs	业务费 Non-Personnel Expenses	科研基建费 Capital Constr-uction Funds for R&D	仪器设备费 Instruments and Equipment	图书资料费 Books and Infor-mation	管理费 Manage-ment	其他 Others	
1434220. 92	**952788. 39**	**99890238. 04**	**98783930. 66**	**21250912. 45**	**47306237. 3**	**480775. 19**	**8292758. 37**	**11592915. 43**	**2973683. 38**	**6886648. 54**	**1106307. 38**
1227781. 1	392942. 6	40825796. 08	40352209. 65	5279367. 24	22185786. 38	29056. 12	3383420. 97	4824588. 12	1470019. 55	3179971. 27	473586. 43
28378. 12	6506. 81	4470221. 58	4436021. 27	731027. 72	2509299. 52	80000	323873. 85	450032. 36	109475. 32	232312. 5	34200. 31
178061. 7	553338. 98	54594220. 38	53995699. 74	15240517. 49	22611151. 4	371719. 07	4585463. 55	6318294. 95	1394188. 51	3474364. 77	598520. 64
1433490. 92	933868. 64	97665587. 71	96593260. 22	20128017. 1	46669682. 43	472743. 7	8214341. 76	11440844. 28	2932168. 21	6735462. 74	1072327. 49
730	18919. 75	2224650. 33	2190670. 44	1122895. 35	636554. 87	8031. 49	78416. 61	152071. 15	41515. 17	151185. 8	33979. 89
718941. 12	457209. 08	37444426. 35	37190110. 61	7275577. 31	17508819. 49	48615	3359321. 34	4740176. 45	1137224. 51	3120376. 51	254315. 74
410570. 48	147720. 74	23805885. 18	23233587. 68	5391701. 29	11445060. 59	16719. 69	1351497. 38	7105156. 41	2172637. 49	4748592. 3	572297. 5
144148. 69	178171. 39	16259313. 72	16171912. 66	3721588. 5	7132358. 3	130570	1679204. 61	9410884. 79	2575273. 9	5548418. 76	87401. 06
30855. 83	78680	2818750. 5	2812380. 7	702154. 02	1346721. 5	24530. 7	292336. 59	9670995. 12	2610899. 36	5699320. 86	6369. 8
30503. 38	45614. 42	10436676. 81	10334435. 5	2530353. 98	4907966. 15	52765. 3	713778. 35	10838123. 85	2827990. 15	6444673. 06	102241. 31
80459. 6	5133. 04	3054111. 5	2989658. 67	618752. 72	1694416. 74	41423	197772. 41	11083155. 86	2870880. 36	6594044. 64	64452. 83
1729	1230	1541520. 29	1534319. 15	321057. 14	601630. 75	127800	284341. 65	11234372. 41	2900281. 63	6612916. 43	7201. 14
3800	33939	3336766. 95	3328238. 95	390958. 82	2192486. 33	38351. 5	292038. 48	11403966. 09	2944443. 61	6813564. 59	8528
13212. 82	5090. 72	1192786. 74	1189286. 74	298768. 67	476777. 45	0	122467. 56	11592915. 43	2973683. 38	6886648. 54	3500

普通高等学校人文、社会科学研
Basic Statistics of Humunities and Social Sciences

		课题数（项）No. of Projects	当年投入人数（人年）Input of Man-year (man/year)	其中：研究生 of Which: Graduate Students	当年拨入经费（百元）Revenues (100 yuan)	当年支出经费（百元）Expenditures (100 yuan)
总　计 Total		**313461**	**84623. 6**	**9686. 4**	**67894445. 71**	**57599680. 34**
按学校隶属关系分 Breakdown by Control	教育部直属院校 HEIs under Ministry of Education	82042	19371	4575. 9	33635999. 27	27420735. 29
	其他部委院校 HEIs under Other Central Ministries	10866	3481. 4	568. 1	2994318. 77	2858286. 63
	地方院校 HEIs under Local Govermments	220553	61771. 2	4542. 4	31264127. 67	27320658. 42
按学校规格分 Breakdown by Category of HEIs	本科院校 Regular HEIs	296890	79886	9684. 6	66932615. 45	56799957. 27
	专科院校 Short-cycle HEIs	16571	4737. 6	1. 8	961830. 26	799723. 07
按学校类型分 Breakdown by Type of HEIs	综合大学 Comprehensive Universities	106030	26978. 5	3764. 8	26604106. 81	22169421. 28
	理工农医院校 HEIs Science and Technology, Agriculture and Medicine	87265	23997. 9	3040. 5	19385527. 27	16696131. 22
	师范院校 Teachers Training	56439	15504. 3	1249	9838606. 21	8474418
	语文院校 Languages	8253	2228. 4	158. 4	1268217. 83	1179934. 25
	财经院校 Finance and Economics	31619	9249. 9	830. 7	6295122. 67	5373853. 4
	政法院校 Political Science & Law	10029	2261. 7	174. 3	1311701. 96	1111714. 67
	体育院校 Physical Culture	3983	1573. 8	176. 1	738216. 98	580430. 77
	艺术院校 Art	5223	1478. 8	169. 6	1728164. 53	1374253. 91
	民族院校 Minorities	4620	1350. 3	123	724781. 45	639522. 84

究与发展课题、成果情况
R & D and Achievements in Regular HEIs

出版专著（部）Monographs Published (titles)	发表论文（篇）No. of Papers Published				研究与咨询报告 Research and Consulting Report	
	合计 Total	国内学术刊物 In Domestic Journals	国外学术刊物 In Foreignal Journals	港澳台刊物 In Hong Kong and Macao Journals	合计 Total	其中：被采纳数 of Which: Accepted Number
13149	**318544**	**307464**	**10318**	**762**	**9486**	**5074**
4099	69267	64032	4831	404	3468	2072
640	12057	11500	487	70	351	104
8410	237220	231932	5000	288	5667	2898
12821	290071	279237	10091	743	8668	4752
328	28473	28227	227	19	818	322
4662	101041	96793	3900	348	3485	2070
2664	86557	83356	3124	77	2629	1527
2723	61906	60598	1181	127	1090	569
437	9131	8625	465	41	147	68
1316	32652	31499	1103	50	1377	541
490	10871	10493	290	88	311	138
87	3739	3608	121	10	210	30
348	6247	6212	28	7	115	101
422	6400	6280	106	14	122	30

附　　表

Appendixes

（摘自国家统计局《2013 年中国统计年鉴》）

Data from“2013 China Statisical Yearbook”

国内生产总值
Gross Domestic Product

单位:亿元

unit: 100 million yuan

年份 Year	国民生产总值 Gross National Product	国内生产总值 Gross Domestic Product								人均国内生产总值(元) Per Capita GDP (yuan)
		合计 Total	第一产业 Primary Industry	第二产业 Secondary Industry			第三产业 Tertiary Industry			
				小计 Subtotal	工业 Industry	建筑业 Construction	小计 Subtotal	交通运输、仓储邮政业 Transportation, Storage and Post	批发和零售住宿餐饮业 Wholesale, Retail & Accommodation, Catering	
1952	679.0	679.0	342.9	141.8	119.8	22.0	194.3	29.0	80.3	119
1953	824.0	824.0	378.0	192.5	163.5	29.0	253.5	35.0	115.5	142
1954	859.0	859.0	392.0	211.7	184.7	27.0	255.3	38.0	120.3	144
1955	910.0	910.0	421.0	222.2	191.2	31.0	266.8	39.0	119.8	150
1956	1028.0	1028.0	443.9	280.7	224.7	56.0	303.4	46.0	131.4	165
1957	1068.0	1068.0	430.0	317.0	271.0	46.0	321.0	49.0	133.0	168
1958	1307.0	1307.0	445.9	483.5	414.5	69.0	377.6	71.0	136.6	200
1959	1439.0	1439.0	383.8	615.5	538.5	77.0	439.7	94.0	145.7	216
1960	1457.0	1457.0	340.7	648.2	568.2	80.0	468.1	104.0	133.1	218
1961	1220.0	1220.0	441.1	388.9	362.1	26.8	390.0	69.2	110.8	185
1962	1149.3	1149.3	453.1	359.3	325.4	33.9	336.9	57.4	80.5	173
1963	1233.3	1233.3	497.5	407.6	365.6	42.0	328.2	55.0	76.1	181
1964	1454.0	1454.0	559.0	513.5	161.1	52.4	381.5	58.4	94.0	208
1965	1716.1	1716.1	651.1	602.2	546.5	55.7	462.8	77.4	118.3	240
1966	1868.0	1868.0	702.2	709.5	648.6	60.9	456.3	85.1	148.1	254
1967	1773.9	1773.9	714.2	602.8	544.9	57.9	456.9	72.3	153.5	235
1968	1723.1	1723.1	726.3	537.3	190.3	47.0	459.5	70.5	138.9	222
1969	1937.9	1937.9	736.2	689.1	626.1	63.0	512.6	84.9	163.6	243
1970	2252.7	2252.7	793.3	912.2	828.1	84.1	547.2	100.2	178.1	275
1971	2426.4	2426.4	826.3	1022.8	926.6	96.2	577.3	108.4	178.3	288
1972	2518.1	2518.1	827.4	1084.2	989.9	94.3	606.5	118.0	194.3	292
1973	2720.9	2720.9	907.5	1173.0	1072.5	100.5	640.4	125.5	211.0	309
1974	2789.9	2789.9	945.2	1192.0	1083.6	108.4	652.7	126.1	206.6	310
1975	2997.3	2997.3	971.1	1370.5	1244.9	125.6	655.7	141.6	175.8	327
1976	2943.7	2943.7	967.0	1337.2	1204.6	132.6	639.5	139.6	147.2	316
1977	3201.9	3201.9	942.1	1509.1	1372.4	136.7	750.7	156.9	213.8	339
1978	3645.2	3645.2	1027.5	1745.2	1607.0	138.2	872.5	182.0	242.3	381
1979	4062.6	4062.6	1270.2	1913.5	1769.7	143.8	878.9	193.7	200.9	419
1980	4545.6	4545.6	1371.6	2192.0	1996.5	195.5	982.0	213.4	193.8	463
1981	4889.5	4891.6	1559.5	2255.5	2048.4	207.1	1076.6	220.7	231.1	492
1982	5330.5	5323.4	1777.4	2383.0	2162.3	220.7	1163.0	246.9	171.4	528
1983	5985.6	5962.7	1978.4	2646.2	2375.6	270.6	1338.1	274.9	198.7	583
1984	7243.8	7208.1	2316.1	3105.7	2789.0	316.7	1786.3	338.5	363.5	695
1985	9040.7	9016.0	2564.4	3866.6	3448.7	417.9	2585.0	421.7	802.4	858
1986	10274.4	10275.2	2788.7	4492.7	3967.0	525.7	2993.8	498.8	852.6	963
1987	12050.6	12058.6	3233.0	5251.6	4585.8	665.8	3574.0	568.3	1059.6	1112
1988	15036.8	15042.8	3865.4	6587.2	5777.2	810.0	4590.3	685.7	1483.4	1366
1989	17000.9	16992.3	4265.9	7278.0	6484.0	794.0	5448.4	812.7	1536.2	1519
1990	18718.3	18667.8	5062.0	7717.4	6858.0	859.4	5888.4	1167.0	1268.9	1644
1991	21826.2	21781.5	5342.2	9102.2	8087.1	1015.1	7337.1	1420.3	1834.6	1893
1992	26937.3	26923.5	5866.6	11699.5	10284.5	1415.0	9357.4	1689.0	2405.0	2311
1993	35260.0	35333.9	6963.8	16454.4	14188.0	2266.5	11915.7	2174.0	2816.6	2998
1994	48108.5	48197.9	9572.7	22445.4	19480.7	2964.7	16179.8	2787.9	3773.4	4044
1995	59810.5	60793.7	12135.8	28679.5	24950.6	3728.8	19978.5	3244.3	4778.6	5046
1996	70142.5	71176.6	14015.4	33835.0	29447.6	4387.4	23326.2	3782.2	5599.7	5846
1997	78060.9	78973.0	14441.9	37543.0	32921.4	4621.6	26988.1	4148.6	6327.4	6420
1998	83024.3	84402.3	14817.6	39004.2	34018.4	4985.8	30580.5	4660.9	6913.2	6796
1999	88479.2	89677.1	14770.0	41033.6	35861.5	5172.1	33873.4	5175.2	7491.1	7159
2000	98000.5	99214.6	14944.7	45555.9	40033.6	5522.3	38714.0	6161.0	8158.6	7858
2001	108068.2	109655.2	15781.3	49512.3	43580.6	5931.7	44361.6	6870.3	9119.4	8622
2002	119095.7	120332.7	16537.0	53896.8	47431.3	6465.5	49898.9	7492.9	9995.4	9398
2003	134977.0	135822.8	17381.7	62436.3	54945.5	7490.8	56004.7	7913.2	11169.5	10542
2004	159453.6	159878.3	21412.7	73904.3	65210.0	8694.3	64561.3	9304.4	12453.8	12336
2005	183617.4	184937.4	22420.0	87598.1	77230.8	10367.3	74919.3	10666.2	13966.2	14185
2006	215904.4	216314.4	24040.0	103719.5	91310.9	12408.6	88554.9	12183.0	16530.7	16500
2007	266422.0	265810.3	28627.0	125831.4	110534.9	15296.5	111351.9	14601.0	20937.8	20169
2008	316030.3	314045.4	33702.0	149003.4	130260.2	18743.2	131340.0	16362.5	26182.3	23708
2009	340320.0	340902.8	35226.0	157638.8	135239.9	22398.8	148038.0	16727.1	28984.5	25608
2010	399759.5	401512.8	40533.6	187383.2	160722.2	26661.0	173596.0	19132.2	35746.1	30015
2011	472115.0	472881.6	47486.2	220412.8	188470.2	31942.7	204982.5	21931.9	43445.2	35181
2012	516282.1	518942.1	52373.6	235162.0	199670.7	35491.3	231406.5	24959.8	59858.6	38420

数据来源:摘自国家统计局《2013 中国统计年鉴》。

各地区国内生产总值(2012年)

Gross Domestic Product by Region (2012)

单位:亿元

unit: 100 million yuan

地 区 Region	国内生产总值 Gross Domestic Product						人均国内生产总值(元) Per Capita GDP (yuan)
	合 计 Total	第一产业 Primary Industry	第二产业 Secondary Industry			第三产业 Tertiary Industry	
			小 计 Subtotal	工 业 Industry	建筑业 Construction		
北 京 Beijing	17879.40	150.20	4059.27	3294.32	764.95	13669.93	87475
天 津 Tianjin	12893.88	171.60	6663.82	6123.06	540.76	6058.46	93173
河 北 Hebei	26575.01	3186.66	14003.57	12511.60	1491.97	9384.78	36584
山 西 Shanxi	12112.83	698.32	6731.56	6023.55	708.01	4682.95	33628
内蒙古 Inner Mongolia	15880.58	1448.58	8801.50	7735.78	1065.71	5630.50	63886
辽 宁 Liaoning	24846.43	2155.82	13230.49	11605.07	1625.42	9460.12	56649
吉 林 Jilin	11939.24	1412.11	6376.77	5582.48	794.29	4150.36	43415
黑龙江 Heilongjiang	13691.58	2113.66	6037.61	5240.65	796.96	5540.31	35711
上 海 Shanghai	20181.72	127.80	7854.77	7097.76	757.01	12199.15	85373
江 苏 Jiangsu	54058.22	3418.29	27121.95	23908.47	3213.48	23517.98	68347
浙 江 Zhejiang	34665.33	1667.88	17316.32	15338.02	1978.30	15681.13	63374
安 徽 Anhui	17212.05	2178.73	9404.84	8025.84	1379.00	5628.48	28792
福 建 Fujian	19701.78	1776.71	10187.94	8541.94	1646.00	7737.13	52763
江 西 Jiangxi	12948.88	1520.23	6942.59	5828.20	1114.39	4486.06	28800
山 东 Shandong	50013.24	4281.70	25735.73	22798.33	2937.40	19995.81	51768
河 南 Henan	29599.31	3769.54	16672.20	15017.56	1654.64	9157.57	31499
湖 北 Hubei	22250.45	2848.77	11193.10	9735.15	1457.95	8208.58	38572
湖 南 Hunan	22154.23	3004.21	10506.42	9138.50	1367.92	8643.60	33480
广 东 Guangdong	57067.92	2847.26	27700.97	25810.07	1890.90	26519.69	54095
广 西 Guangxi	13035.10	2172.37	6247.43	5279.26	968.17	4615.30	27952
海 南 Hainan	2855.54	711.54	804.47	521.15	283.32	1339.53	32377
重 庆 Chongqing	11409.60	940.01	5975.18	4981.01	994.17	4494.41	38914
四 川 Sichuan	23872.80	3297.21	12333.28	10550.53	1782.75	8242.31	29608
贵 州 Guizhou	6852.20	891.91	2677.54	2217.06	460.48	3282.75	19710
云 南 Yunnan	10309.47	1654.55	4419.20	3450.72	968.48	4235.72	22195
西 藏 Tibet	701.03	80.38	242.85	55.35	187.50	377.80	22936
陕 西 Shaanxi	14453.68	1370.16	8073.87	6847.41	1226.46	5009.65	38564
甘 肃 Gansu	5650.20	780.50	2600.09	2070.24	529.85	2269.61	21978
青 海 Qinghai	1893.54	176.91	1092.34	895.89	196.45	624.29	33181
宁 夏 Ningxia	2341.29	199.40	1159.37	878.63	280.74	982.52	36394
新 疆 Xinjiang	7505.31	1320.57	3481.56	2850.06	631.50	2703.18	33796

注:本表绝对数按当年价格计算,指数按可比价格计算。

Note: Absolute figures in this table are calculated at current prices while indices are calculated at comparable prices.

国家财政收支总额及增长速度

Total Government Revenue and Expenditures and Their Increase Rate

年　份 Year	财政收入 （亿元） Revenue （100 million yuan）	财政支出 （亿元） Expenditures （100 million yuan）	增长速度 Increase Rate（%） 财政收入 Revenue	财政支出 Expenditures
1978	1132. 26	1122. 09	29. 5	33. 0
1980	1159. 93	1228. 83	1. 2	-4. 1
1985	2004. 82	2004. 25	22. 0	17. 8
1990	2937. 10	3083. 59	10. 2	9. 2
1991	3149. 48	3386. 62	7. 2	9. 8
1992	3483. 37	3742. 20	10. 6	10. 5
1993	4348. 95	4642. 30	24. 8	24. 1
1994	5218. 10	5792. 62	20. 0	24. 8
1995	6242. 20	6823. 72	19. 6	17. 8
1996	7407. 99	7937. 55	18. 7	16. 3
1997	8651. 14	9233. 56	16. 8	16. 3
1998	9875. 95	10798. 18	14. 2	16. 9
1999	11444. 08	13187. 67	15. 9	22. 1
2000	13395. 23	15886. 50	17. 0	20. 5
2001	16386. 04	18902. 58	22. 3	19. 0
2002	18903. 64	22053. 15	15. 4	16. 7
2003	21715. 25	24649. 95	14. 9	11. 8
2004	26396. 47	28486. 89	21. 6	15. 6
2005	31649. 29	33930. 28	19. 9	19. 1
2006	38760. 20	40422. 73	22. 5	19. 1
2007	51321. 78	49781. 35	32. 4	23. 2
2008	61330. 35	62592. 66	19. 5	25. 7
2009	68518. 30	76299. 93	11. 7	21. 9
2010	83101. 51	89874. 16	21. 3	17. 8
2011	103874. 43	109247. 79	25. 0	21. 6
2012	117253. 52	125952. 97	12. 9	15. 3

数据来源：摘自国家统计局《2013 中国统计年鉴》。

中央财政和地方财政收支总额

Total Revenue and Expenditures of Central and Local Governments

单位:亿元

unit: 100 million yuan

年 份 Year	财政收入 Revenue			财政支出 Expenditures		
	合 计 Total	中 央 Central Government	地 方 Local Government	合 计 Total	中 央 Central Government	地 方 Local Government
1978	1132. 26	175. 77	956. 49	1122. 09	532. 12	589. 97
1980	1159. 93	284. 45	875. 48	1228. 83	666. 81	562. 02
1985	2004. 82	769. 63	1235. 19	2004. 25	795. 25	1209. 00
1990	2937. 10	992. 42	1944. 68	3083. 59	1004. 47	2079. 12
1991	3149. 48	938. 25	2211. 23	3386. 62	1090. 81	2295. 81
1992	3483. 37	979. 51	2503. 86	3742. 20	1170. 44	2571. 76
1993	4348. 95	957. 51	3391. 44	4642. 30	1312. 06	3330. 24
1994	5218. 10	2906. 50	2311. 60	5792. 62	1754. 43	4038. 19
1995	6242. 20	3256. 62	2985. 58	6823. 72	1995. 39	4828. 33
1996	7407. 99	3661. 07	3746. 92	7937. 55	2151. 27	5786. 28
1997	8651. 14	4226. 92	4424. 22	9233. 56	2532. 50	6701. 06
1998	9875. 95	4892. 00	4983. 95	10798. 18	3125. 60	7672. 58
1999	11444. 08	5849. 21	5594. 87	13187. 67	4152. 33	9035. 34
2000	13395. 23	6989. 17	6406. 06	15886. 50	5519. 85	10366. 65
2001	16386. 04	8582. 74	7803. 30	18902. 58	5768. 02	13134. 56
2002	18903. 64	10388. 64	8515. 00	22053. 15	6771. 70	15281. 45
2003	21715. 25	11865. 27	9849. 98	24649. 95	7420. 10	17229. 85
2004	26396. 47	14503. 10	11893. 37	28486. 89	7894. 08	20592. 81
2005	31649. 29	16548. 53	15100. 76	33930. 28	8775. 97	25154. 31
2006	38760. 20	20456. 62	18303. 58	40422. 73	9991. 40	30431. 33
2007	51321. 78	27749. 16	23572. 62	49781. 35	11442. 06	38339. 29
2008	61330. 35	32680. 56	28649. 79	62592. 66	13344. 17	49248. 49
2009	68518. 30	35915. 71	32602. 59	76299. 93	15255. 79	61044. 14
2010	83101. 51	42488. 47	40613. 04	89874. 16	15989. 73	73884. 43
2011	103874. 43	51327. 32	52547. 11	109247. 79	16514. 11	92733. 68
2012	117253. 52	56175. 23	61078. 29	125952. 97	18764. 63	107188. 34

数据来源:摘自国家统计局《2013 中国统计年鉴》。

人口数及构成

Population and Its Composition

单位:万人

unit:10 thousand persons

年 份 Year	年底总人口 Population (year-end)	按性别分 By Sex				按城乡分 By Residence			
		男 Male		女 Female		城镇总人口 Urban		农村总人口 Rural	
		人口数 Population	比重(%) Proportion	人口数 Population	比重(%) Proportion	人口数 Population	比重(%) Proportion	人口数 Population	比重(%) Proportion
1978	96259	49567	51.49	46692	48.51	17245	17.92	79014	82.08
1979	97542	50192	51.63	47350	48.37	18495	36.22	79047	63.78
1980	98705	50785	51.45	47920	48.55	19140	19.39	79565	80.61
1981	100072	51519	51.47	48553	48.53	20171	39.09	79901	60.91
1982	101654	52352	51.50	49302	48.50	21480	40.53	80174	59.47
1983	103008	53152	51.52	49856	48.48	22274	41.76	80734	58.24
1984	104357	53848	51.53	50509	48.47	24017	42.99	80340	57.01
1985	105851	54725	51.70	51126	48.30	25094	23.71	80757	76.29
1986	107507	55581	51.50	51926	48.50	26366	45.89	81141	54.11
1987	109300	56290	51.47	53010	48.53	27674	46.99	81626	53.01
1988	111026	57201	45.89	53825	43.91	28661	48.34	82365	51.66
1989	112704	58099	46.09	54605	44.23	29540	49.95	83164	50.05
1990	114333	58904	51.52	55429	48.48	30195	26.41	84138	73.59
1991	115823	59466	51.34	56357	48.66	31203	26.94	84620	73.06
1992	117171	59811	51.05	57360	48.95	32175	27.46	84996	72.54
1993	118517	60472	51.02	58045	48.98	33173	27.99	85344	72.01
1994	119850	61246	51.10	58604	48.90	34169	28.51	85681	71.49
1995	121121	61808	51.03	59313	48.97	35174	29.04	85947	70.96
1996	122389	62200	50.82	60189	49.18	37304	30.48	85085	69.52
1997	123626	63131	51.07	60495	48.93	39449	31.91	84177	68.09
1998	124761	63940	51.25	60821	48.75	41608	33.35	83153	66.65
1999	125786	64692	51.43	61094	48.57	43748	34.78	82038	65.22
2000	126743	65437	51.63	61306	48.37	45906	36.22	80837	63.78
2001	127627	65672	51.46	61955	48.54	48064	37.66	79563	62.34
2002	128453	66115	51.47	62338	48.53	50212	39.09	78241	60.91
2003	129227	66556	51.50	62671	48.50	52376	40.53	76851	59.47
2004	129988	66976	51.52	63012	48.48	54283	41.76	75705	58.24
2005	130756	67375	51.53	63381	48.47	56212	42.99	74544	57.01
2006	131448	67728	51.52	63720	48.48	58288	44.34	73160	55.66
2007	132129	68048	51.50	64081	48.50	60633	45.89	71496	54.11
2008	132802	68357	51.47	64445	48.53	62403	46.99	70399	53.01
2009	133450	68647	51.44	64803	48.56	64512	48.34	68938	51.66
2010	134091	68748	51.27	65343	48.73	66978	49.95	67113	50.05
2011	134735	69068	51.26	65667	48.74	69079	51.27	65656	48.73
2012	135404	69395	51.25	66009	48.75	71182	52.57	64222	47.43

注:总人口和城镇人口中包括中国人民解放军现役军人,按城乡分人口中现役军人计入城镇人口。

Note: Urban Population include the military personnel of Chinese People's Liberation Army.

各地区按性别分的15岁及以上文盲人口

Illterate Population Aged 15 and Over by Sex and Region

本表是2012年全国人口变动情况抽样调查样本数据，抽样比为0.831‰。

单位：人，%
unit：person，%

地　区 Region	15岁及以上人口（人） Population Aged 15 & Over			文盲人口（人） Illiterate			文盲人口占15岁及以上人口比重 Percentage to total Population Aged 15 & Over（%）		
	合计 Total	男 Male	女 Female	合计 Total	男 Male	女 Female	合计 Total	男 Male	女 Female
合　计 Total	**939526**	**476037**	**463489**	**46619**	**12699**	**33920**	**4.96**	**2.67**	**7.32**
北　京 Beijing	15648	7999	7649	229	47	181	1.46	0.59	2.37
天　津 Tianjin	10408	5121	5287	233	55	178	2.24	1.08	3.36
河　北 Hebei	49895	25215	24680	1879	516	1363	3.77	2.05	5.52
山　西 Shanxi	25396	12932	12464	592	213	379	2.33	1.64	3.04
内蒙古 Inner Mongolia	17897	9132	8765	718	223	494	4.01	2.44	5.64
辽　宁 Liaoning	32819	16446	16373	736	217	519	2.24	1.32	3.17
吉　林 Jilin	20139	10194	9945	372	121	251	1.85	1.19	2.53
黑龙江 Heilongjiang	28112	14234	13878	686	232	454	2.44	1.63	3.27
上　海 Shanghai	18181	9443	8738	406	87	319	2.23	0.92	3.65
江　苏 Jiangsu	57383	27979	29403	2742	602	2140	4.78	2.15	7.28
浙　江 Zhejiang	40062	20367	19694	2051	520	1531	5.12	2.55	7.77
安　徽 Anhui	40915	20962	19953	3385	869	2516	8.27	4.15	12.61
福　建 Fujian	26044	12967	13077	1204	215	989	4.62	1.66	7.56
江　西 Jiangxi	29495	14874	14621	1103	256	847	3.74	1.72	5.79
山　东 Shandong	67769	33826	33944	4204	1051	3153	6.20	3.11	9.29
河　南 Henan	62353	30621	31733	3344	949	2395	5.36	3.10	7.55
湖　北 Hubei	41428	20880	20548	2431	610	1821	5.87	2.92	8.86
湖　南 Hunan	45065	22876	22189	1820	523	1297	4.04	2.29	5.85
广　东 Guangdong	73925	38665	35260	2061	368	1693	2.79	0.95	4.80
广　西 Guangxi	30243	15480	14762	1134	268	867	3.75	1.73	5.87
海　南 Hainan	5985	3146	2839	266	64	202	4.45	2.03	7.13
重　庆 Chongqing	20537	10210	10327	1082	326	756	5.27	3.19	7.32
四　川 Sichuan	56449	29551	26898	3866	1163	2703	6.85	3.94	10.05
贵　州 Guizhou	22393	11333	11060	2679	757	1922	11.97	6.68	17.38
云　南 Yunnan	31272	16012	15259	2608	825	1783	8.34	5.15	11.68
西　藏 Tibet	2000	983	1017	696	287	409	34.81	29.24	40.19
陕　西 Shaanxi	26912	13798	13115	1243	384	859	4.62	2.79	6.55
甘　肃 Gansu	17947	9169	8778	1559	489	1070	8.68	5.33	12.19
青　海 Qinghai	3797	1944	1852	465	154	310	12.24	7.93	16.76
宁　夏 Ningxia	4246	2140	2106	318	100	218	7.50	4.69	10.36
新　疆 Xinjiang	14812	7538	7274	507	207	299	3.42	2.75	4.11

注：本表"文盲人口"指15岁及15岁以上不识字及识字很少人口。

Note：Illiterate population in this table refers to the population aged 15 and over，who are unable or very difficult to read.

各地区按性别和受教育程度分的人口

Population by Sex, Educational Level and Region

本表是 2012 年全国人口变动情况抽样调查样本数据,抽样比为 0.831‰。

单位:人

unit: person

地 区 Region	6 岁及 6 岁以上人口 Population Aged 6 and Over			未上过学 Illterate			小学 Primary School		
	合计 Total	男 Male	女 Female	合计 Total	男 Male	女 Female	合计 Total	男 Male	女 Female
全 国 National Total	**1047865**	**534803**	**513062**	**55454**	**16753**	**38701**	**281681**	**133547**	**148134**
北 京 Beijing	16447	8418	8029	271	63	208	1627	766	862
天 津 Tianjin	11175	5529	5646	297	87	210	1885	879	1006
河 北 Hebei	55844	28412	27432	2383	733	1650	13858	6471	7387
山 西 Shanxi	28388	14483	13905	810	326	485	6039	2780	3259
内蒙古 Inner Mongolia	19598	9999	9599	863	298	564	4794	2242	2551
辽 宁 Liaoning	35238	17655	17583	908	295	612	7069	3281	3788
吉 林 Jilin	21799	11059	10740	480	168	312	5340	2502	2838
黑龙江 Heilongjiang	30608	15559	15049	873	324	549	7476	3498	3979
上 海 Shanghai	19034	9918	9117	466	118	348	2403	1073	1330
江 苏 Jiangsu	62230	30700	31530	3492	879	2613	14701	6570	8130
浙 江 Zhejiang	43285	22088	21197	2383	691	1692	11640	5701	5939
安 徽 Anhui	46039	23855	22184	3700	1011	2689	13071	6043	7029
福 建 Fujian	28931	14525	14406	1606	373	1233	9231	4113	5118
江 西 Jiangxi	34348	17654	16694	1350	381	969	10233	4700	5533
山 东 Shandong	75422	37952	37470	4933	1373	3560	19465	8734	10731
河 南 Henan	72042	36109	35933	3958	1228	2731	17865	8566	9299
湖 北 Hubei	45109	22876	22233	2697	764	1933	10585	4966	5618
湖 南 Hunan	51099	26204	24895	2338	772	1566	15225	7470	7755
广 东 Guangdong	82228	43261	38967	2479	561	1918	18921	8717	10205
广 西 Guangxi	35185	18148	17037	1433	429	1004	12085	5732	6353
海 南 Hainan	6773	3589	3185	312	91	221	1518	721	797
重 庆 Chongqing	23049	11562	11487	1240	387	853	7865	3897	3968
四 川 Sichuan	63113	33010	30103	4353	1350	3003	20810	10475	10334
贵 州 Guizhou	26638	13598	13040	3040	916	2124	9841	4955	4886
云 南 Yunnan	36013	18498	17515	3009	1020	1989	14876	7508	7368
西 藏 Tibet	2332	1157	1175	800	344	456	1001	525	476
陕 西 Shaanxi	29505	15229	14276	1576	536	1040	6841	3162	3679
甘 肃 Gansu	20108	10332	9775	1774	588	1187	6796	3298	3498
青 海 Qinghai	4414	2276	2138	639	247	391	1613	816	797
宁 夏 Ningxia	4961	2525	2436	363	121	241	1644	786	858
新 疆 Xinjiang	16910	8624	8286	629	278	351	5362	2599	2763

地 区 Region	初中 Junior Secondary School			高中 Senior Secondary School			大专及以上 College and Higher Level		
	合计 Total	男 Male	女 Female	合计 Total	男 Male	女 Female	合计 Total	男 Male	女 Female
全 国 National Total	**430799**	**230637**	**200162**	**168941**	**94487**	**74454**	**110990**	**59380**	**51610**
北 京 Beijing	4746	2540	2206	3659	1830	1829	6143	3219	2924
天 津 Tianjin	3990	2082	1908	2450	1250	1199	2553	1230	1323
河 北 Hebei	28314	15063	13251	8059	4427	3632	3232	1719	1513
山 西 Shanxi	13065	6795	6270	5766	3159	2607	2707	1423	1283
内蒙古 Inner Mongolia	8209	4429	3780	3369	1843	1526	2364	1186	1178
辽 宁 Liaoning	15616	8110	7506	5127	2668	2460	6519	3301	3217
吉 林 Jilin	9955	5259	4696	4069	2143	1926	1955	987	969
黑龙江 Heilongjiang	14154	7502	6652	5013	2613	2400	3093	1622	1469
上 海 Shanghai	7728	4219	3509	4046	2202	1844	4392	2305	2087
江 苏 Jiangsu	24602	12890	11712	11062	6330	4732	8373	4030	4344
浙 江 Zhejiang	16056	8916	7141	6733	4211	2522	6473	2569	3903
安 徽 Anhui	18814	10139	8675	5733	3352	2381	4721	3311	1410
福 建 Fujian	11267	6375	4892	4565	2524	2041	2262	1139	1121
江 西 Jiangxi	13805	7183	6622	6114	3660	2453	2846	1731	1116
山 东 Shandong	32127	17189	14938	11530	6563	4967	7367	4094	3274
河 南 Henan	34963	17709	17254	10457	6081	4376	4798	2524	2273
湖 北 Hubei	17468	9217	8251	8844	4742	4102	5514	3185	2329
湖 南 Hunan	21041	10893	10147	8746	4960	3785	3749	2108	1641
广 东 Guangdong	35639	19476	16163	17162	9927	7235	8027	4581	3446
广 西 Guangxi	15085	8278	6807	4302	2458	1844	2281	1252	1029
海 南 Hainan	3082	1686	1396	1167	690	477	694	399	294
重 庆 Chongqing	8224	4242	3982	3421	1796	1626	2299	1241	1058
四 川 Sichuan	23404	13263	10141	8289	4543	3746	6258	3378	2879
贵 州 Guizhou	9289	5184	4105	2720	1577	1144	1749	967	781
云 南 Yunnan	11290	6424	4865	4401	2198	2203	2438	1348	1090
西 藏 Tibet	312	177	135	119	58	61	99	51	47
陕 西 Shaanxi	12385	6654	5731	5552	3108	2445	3150	1769	1381
甘 肃 Gansu	6639	3602	3037	3109	1770	1339	1790	1075	715
青 海 Qinghai	1242	697	546	497	278	219	423	238	185
宁 夏 Ningxia	1871	1030	842	631	355	276	452	232	219
新 疆 Xinjiang	6418	3414	3004	2229	1171	1059	2272	1162	1110

注:本表数据摘自《2013 中国统计年鉴》